The *Guardian*

It is difficult, indeed, to conjecture to what lengths the violence of arbitrary power would at that dismal period proceed. Fear is the most cruel of all passions; and infuriated by the fear of exposure, the Colonial Government seemed determined to strike down every man who should dare even to *look* or *think* disapprobation of its deeds. A frightful system of espionage pervaded every circle of society, and rendered perilous even the confidence of the domestic hearth. . . . Informers and false witnesses abounded; and rumours of "plots" and "disloyal combinations against the Governor," were assiduously kept afloat, for purposes as obvious as they were mischievous. . . . The state of society in Cape Town, and indeed throughout the colony, at this period, was truly deplorable. Mutual confidence was shaken; distrust, apprehension, and gloom everywhere prevailed; and men, according to their several characters and circumstances, were perturbed by angry excitement or prostrated by slavish fear.

—*Thomas Pringle, 1834*

The *Guardian*

The History of South Africa's Extraordinary Anti-Apartheid Newspaper

James Zug

Michigan State University Press • *East Lansing*
UNISA Press • *Pretoria*

♾ The paper used in this publication meets the minimum requirements of ANSI/NISO
Z39.48-1992 (R 1997) (Permanence of Paper).

 Michigan State University Press
East Lansing, Michigan 48823-5245

 1947· CELEBRATING 60 YEARS *of* ·2007
SCHOLARLY PUBLISHING

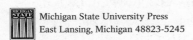 

UNISA Press, Theo van Wijk Building Goldfields Entrance, Office B4-25, Preller Street,
UNISA Muckleneuk Campus, Pretoria, South Africa

Printed and bound in the United States of America.
ISBN 978-0-87013-810-2

13 12 11 10 09 08 07   1 2 3 4 5 6 7 8 9 10

LIBRARY OF CONGRESS CATALOGING-IN-PUBLICATION DATA
Zug, James, 1969–
The Guardian : the history of South Africa's extraordinary anti-apartheid newspaper / James Zug.
p. cm. — (Hidden histories series)
Includes bibliographical references and index.
ISBN 978-0-87013-810-2 (MSU Press pbk. (everywhere but Africa) : alk. paper) —
ISBN 978-1-86888-480-3 (UNISA Press pbk. (Africa only) : alk. paper)
1. Guardian (Cape Town, South Africa) I. Title.
PN5479.C33G839 2007
079.6873'55—dc22
2007022936

Cover and book design by Sharp Des!gns, Inc.
Cover art is used courtesy of UWC-Robben Island Museum Mayibuye Archives and James Zug.

Visit Michigan State University Press on the World Wide Web at *www.msupress.msu.edu*

For Abe Collier

Contents

Abbreviations ix

The *Guardian* Masthead xi

Prologue 1

1 A Very Live Menace: A Cape Town Childhood, 1937–1939 9

2 Forty Thousand No Less: The War Years, 1939–1945 37

3 Brass and Water: Departures, 1945–1950 71

4 The Carry-On: Bannings, 1948–1954 101

5 Fleeting Moments of Happiness: The Democracy Decade, 1950–1959 139

6 The Bloody Pole on the Hill: Sharpeville and Beyond, 1960–1963 185

Epilogue 223

Acknowledgments 231

Notes 237

Index 351

Abbreviations

AMWU	African Mine Workers' Union
ANC	African National Congress
ANCYL	African National Congress Youth League
APO	African Political Organisation
CEC	Central Executive Committee (also known as the PB or Political Bureau)
CID	Criminal Investigation Department
COD	South African Congress of Democrats
CP	Communist Party of South Africa
DIMES	Durban Indian Municipal Employees Barracks
LBC	Left Book Club
NIC	Natal Indian Congress
NIYC	Natal Indian Youth Congress
NLL	National Liberation League
NP	National Party
NRC	Native Representative Council
PAC	Pan-Africanist Congress
PRC	Passive Resistance Campaign
SACP	South African Communist Party

SACPO	South African Coloured People's Organisation
SACTU	South African Congress of Trade Unions
SAT&LC	South African Trades and Labour Council
SCA	Suppression of Communist Act
TIC	Transvaal Indian Congress
TIYC	Transvaal Indian Youth Congress
UCT	University of Cape Town
Wits	University of the Witwatersrand
YCL	Young Communist League

The *Guardian* Masthead

Vera Alberts, *Durban branch manager, 1941–45*
Ray Alexander, *founder, columnist, 1937–63*
Bill Andrews, *columnist, advisor, 1937–50*
Jackie Lax Arenstein, *Durban reporter, 1942–54*
Harold Baldry, *international news columnist, 1937–48*
Brian Bunting, *assistant editor 1946–48; editor-in-chief 1948–63*
Dennis Brutus, *Port Elizabeth sports writer, 1958–63*
Fred Carneson, *Cape Town branch manager, 1948–63; acting editor 1952–53*
Christine Cash, *Cape Town reporter 1942–46; acting editor 1946*
Jack Cope, *Cape Town reporter, 1941–55*
Ebriham Ismail Ebriham, *Durban reporter, 1956–63*
Ruth First, *Johannesburg branch editor, 1947–63*
Norman Flegg, *Cape Town business manager, 1937–51*
Lionel Forman, *acting editor, 1954; international news columnist, 1955–59*
Joe Gqabi, *Johannesburg reporter and photographer, 1958–62*
Michael Harmel, *Johannesburg reporter and columnist, 1940–1963*
Rica Hodgson, *Johannesburg administrator, 1960–63*
Alfred Hutchinson, *Johannesburg reporter, 1955–58*

Sam Kahn, *legal advisor; columnist*
Joe Kaye, *Johannesburg circulation manager, 1941–43*
Willie Kgositile, *Johannesburg reporter, 1960–63*
Wolfie Kodesh, *Cape Town and Johannesburg staffer and seller*
Winnie Kramer, *Johannesburg administrator, 1946–60*
Alex La Guma, *Cape Town reporter and columnist, 1956–62*
Len Lee-Warden, *Cape Town printer, 1951–63*
Beate Lipman, *Johannesburg reporter 1960–63*
Tennyson Makiwane, *Johannesburg reporter, 1956–60*
Nondwe Mankahla, *Port Elizabeth seller and fundraiser, 1955–63*
Douglas Manqina, *Cape Town seller, 1958–63*
Govan Mbeki, *editorial board member; Port Elizabeth branch editor
      1954–62*
Ralph Mgqungwana, *Port Elizabeth administrator, 1955–63*
Premchand Mistrey, *Durban seller; acting branch editor 1957–58*
Wilton Mkwayi, *Port Elizabeth reporter, 1954–60*
Joyce Watson Mohammed, *Johannesburg administrator, 1956–63*
John Morley, *Cape Town circulation manager; Christmas hampers director*
M. P. Naicker, *Durban branch editor, 1956–63*
H. A. Naidoo, *Cape Town editor and columnist, 1943–50*
Henry Nxumalo, *Johannesburg sports columnist, 1947–51*
Carina Pearson, *Cape Town branch manager, 1937–48*
Betty Radford, *editor-in-chief 1937–48*
Robert Resha, *Johannesburg sports columnist, 1956–61*
Albie Sachs, *international news columnist 1959–63*
George Sacks, *columnist 1937–48*
Ivan Schermbrucker, *Johannesburg branch manager, 1947–63*
Dawood Seedat, *Durban branch manager, 1948–56*
Arnold Selby, *Johannesburg Christmas hampers director, 1954–58*
Brian Semana, *Johannesburg reporter, 1960–63*
Naomi Shapiro, *Cape Town reporter, 1946–52*
Jack Simons, *editorial writer, 1937–46*
Harry Snitcher, *legal advisor*
Charlie Stewart, *Cape Town printer, 1937–47*
Amy Thornton, *Cape Town reporter and administrator, 1954–63*
Gladstone Tshume, *Port Elizabeth branch editor, 1953–54*
Mary Butcher Turok, *Cape Town reporter, 1953–58*
Eli Weinberg, *staff photographer, 1952–63*
Rona Worrall, *Johannesburg branch editor, 1941–43*

The newspaper had a continuous twenty-six-year run of publication, initially appearing every Friday, and then every Thursday, from 1937 to 1963. The stretch was only interrupted for five months during the 1960 state of emergency. During its lifetime, it appeared under seven different titles:

- *Cape Guardian*, 19 February 1937–11 June 1937
- *Guardian*, 18 June 1937–22 May 1952
- *Clarion*, 29 May 1952–14 August 1952
- *People's World*, 21 August 1952–30 October 1952
- *Advance*, 6 November 1952–21 October 1954
- *New Age*, 28 October 1954–29 November 1962
- *Spark*, 6 December 1962–28 March 1963

The *Guardian*

Prologue

One autumn morning, two men held a funeral by the sea. They dragged a pair of iron ammunition trunks and shovels into a garden above a Cape Town beach. They slowly dug a five-foot deep, coffin-sized hole. They lowered the trunks into the ground, replaced the soil, and planted flowers to make the grave invisible. After the work was finished, they stood back, wiped their sweaty brows, and looked out at the waves crashing over the boulders that dotted the beach.

They had buried a newspaper.

Each trunk contained years of back issues of the *Guardian* newspaper, wrapped in black plastic sheets. In March 1963 Pretoria, after decades of unrelenting harassment, hounded the legendary twenty-six-year-old newspaper out of existence by house-arresting the entire staff. Reluctantly, the editors declared defeat. They signed final checks, shredded files, sold furniture, typed final letters and closed doors. Telephones rang and were not answered. Sales placards blew listlessly in the streets. Staffers scattered to their fates: jail, exile, a pinched life underground or bathetic inactivity. To pound home their victory, the government decreed it illegal to be in possession of a single issue of the *Guardian*, with instant arrest and three years' imprisonment as punishment. A quarter century of progressive journalism disappeared under the pummeling fist of apartheid. An atmosphere of fear and distrust prevailed.

The final coup de grace occurred in private. A respected Cape Town newspaper printer and former member of parliament, Len Lee-Warden was faced with particularly troubling options. As the *Guardian*'s printer, he owned the only complete set of back issues left inside South Africa. To keep his copies courted arrest; to burn them would destroy a central piece of history.

Without ceremony, Lee-Warden and his gardener laid the *Guardian* to rest in a garden grave.

Before its quiet interment, the *Guardian* led a fascinatingly controversial, brilliant, belittled, hated, and hopeful life. Founded in 1937 by a disparate group of young trade unionists and university professors, the newspaper developed over the next twenty-six years into a central part of the liberation movement. Headquartered in Cape Town, the *Guardian* operated branch offices in Johannesburg, Durban, and Port Elizabeth. Supporters raised the necessary cash—the newspaper never had a corporate owner and proudly lived in genteel but independent poverty—and correspondents posted letters, articles, and photographs from throughout the country. Weekly circulation topped 55,000.

A roll call of *Guardian* contributors reads like a Who's Who of South African politics and literature: Govan Mbeki, the father of future President Thabo, managed the Port Elizabeth branch; Brian Bunting, the son of Communist Party founder S. P. Bunting, edited the newspaper for twenty years; Ruth First, the legendary journalist, ran the Johannesburg office; Alex La Guma and Jack Cope, two of the leading South African novelists of the era, reported from Cape Town; Albie Sachs, a future bestselling author and Constitutional Court judge, wrote the international-affairs column.

Draconian repression came hand-in-hand with the newspaper's importance. The apartheid regime in Pretoria outlawed the newspaper three times (the following week the same newspaper with a new title reappeared). It censored articles. It tapped phones, opened mail, spied on and raided the newspaper's offices. It sealed the *Guardian*'s presses during the 1960 state of emergency and listed the *Guardian* as a co-conspirator—156 people and a *newspaper*—in the epic four-year Treason Trial. Staffers were spared nothing. Special Branch policemen followed, arrested, raided, beat and jailed those working for the *Guardian*. Pretoria deported staffers and banned them from public gatherings; accused ten staffers in the Treason Trial; and jailed fifty-five for four months during the 1960 emergency.

From start to finish, its record inextricably cleaved to the history of South Africa's search for democracy. In the 1930s, the *Guardian* focused on fighting fascism and mobilizing the organized labor movement and the white-only South African Labour Party. Most of the South African stories came from Cape Town and surrounding villages, while international news such as the Spanish Civil War and appeasement of Adolf Hitler dominated the twelve pages of the *Guardian*. Politically, a muddled version of radical liberalism held sway at the editorial offices. None of the original four staff members—white and unpaid—were members of a political party, let alone the Communist Party. Communism, the *Guardian* argued in 1937, was not "practical politics in South Africa to-day."[1]

During the Second World War, the *Guardian*'s allegiances shifted. All four full-time *Guardian* staffers joined the Communist Party, and the editor, Betty Radford, won a seat on the Cape Town city council as a communist. The newspaper still viewed national liberation as secondary to class issues, but working and living conditions for Africans, Indians, and coloureds now merited front-page discussion. No longer a mere Cape Town political broadsheet, the *Guardian* established a nationwide presence. It sold more than 50,000 copies each week, Radford opened branch offices in Durban and Johannesburg, and friends hosted fundraising events across the Union and Southern Rhodesia.

Shattering this sanguinity were postwar milestones like the 1946 mine strike, the 1948 election that brought the apartheid National Party to power, and the 1950 banning of the Communist Party. The newspaper shifted gears. The original *Guardian* quartet departed, and a multiracial cohort of young radicals joined the editorial staff, led by new editor Brian Bunting. As the sole national newspaper allied with the African National Congress, the *Guardian* found itself at the center of the political storm.

After the 1960 Sharpeville massacre and the banning of the ANC came house arrest, solitary confinement, and bitter exile. One of the few still-legal institutions of the liberation movement, the *Guardian* provided a media outlet for the ANC and its emerging armed wing, Umkhonto we Sizwe, and a useful cover for Umkhonto's guerrillas who needed a place to hold meetings. Nelson Mandela, the leader of Umkhonto, regularly issued messages through the weekly, a practice facilitated by the fact that he hid at a staffer's home while on the run from the police. The newspaper, banned twice in the early 1950s, survived a third ban in 1962, but the government did not relent.

In March 1963 Pretoria house-arrested *Guardian* staff members, specifically prohibiting them from being on the premises where a publication was prepared or published. With no one else available—all potential replacements were either in exile or in jail—the newspaper finally folded. Days later, Len Lee-Warden buried the ammunition trunks in his garden.

"**F**uture historians will find our paper invaluable when they settle down to write the real history of South Africa—the people's history," trumpeted the *Guardian* in 1954. "But we not only record the struggle for freedom, we are actively participating in it, week after week, year after year."[2] The *Guardian* had a complicated, nuanced history, which generations of scholars have not appreciated in their zeal to harvest its pages for primary source material on mid-century South Africa. Subjects like Cape Town labor issues in the 1930s, the Communist Party in the 1940s, the African National Congress in the 1950s, and Umkhonto we Sizwe in the early 1960s seemed easily mined from the black agate of the newspaper. The *Guardian* appeared to be merely a conduit for political organizations—a "Communist Party organ" or an "ANC paper."

The *Guardian* did not merely record events but controlled them. It was not merely a weathervane, but a compass that had its own magnetic pull. In the 1930s the *Guardian* noticeably separated itself from the Communist Party and put forth policies inconsistent with the Party line. Throughout the 1950s, the weekly supported the African National Congress with a unique mixture of patronizing advice, hesitancy over the ANC's subversion of class issues, distrust of some of the more conservative Congress leaders, and downright hostility to the strands of anti-communism manifesting themselves in the inchoate Pan Africanist Congress. The newspaper mostly integrated itself into the African National Congress. In 1953, the *Guardian* opened a fourth branch office in Port Elizabeth, the heartland of the ANC, and in 1959 Ruth First instigated the ANC potato boycott after a series of exposures of slave labor and pass-law horrors.

Nonetheless, the weekly still retained its communist underpinnings and steadfastly supported the Soviet Union as the Cold War winds blew. Much of the *Guardian*'s financial support came from Indian and Jewish shopkeepers. Ironically, while the newspaper vociferously denounced capitalism, it was South Africa's small-time capitalists that kept the newspaper afloat.

The *Guardian* stood at the convoluted intersection of South African politics and race. Its masthead defied contemporary standards. Govan Mbeki, an African, ran the Port Elizabeth office, which was almost entirely staffed by Africans; M. P. Naicker, an Indian, directed the Durban branch, populated mostly by Indians and Africans; many of the Johannesburg reporters were African; and Alex La Guma, a coloured writer, was a key figure at the newspaper's headquarters in Cape Town. Yet the *Guardian* was disproportionally white. The editor-in-chief, the Johannesburg branch manager, many reporters and correspondents, the circulation and business managers, the staff photographer and the printer were all white. One fortunate result of having so many whites on board was that the *Guardian* lasted far longer than any black newspaper could have. Whites had access to capital and the byzantine purlieus of newsprint sellers, agents and printers. Whites knew lawyers. Whites needed no passbooks or permission to cross provincial lines. The dissonance between the *Guardian* staffers' skin color and their *sans-culotte* politics seemed strange to white South Africa—so few whites actively sought to end their comfortable lifestyles and privileged positions in society—but it was typical of the complexity of the liberation struggle.

Unlike most political party–affiliated organs, the *Guardian* was an attractive, well-written factory of facts and opinion. It had a far-ranging system of correspondents and informants who enabled the *Guardian* to maintain countrywide coverage. Both its editors-in-chief had worked at daily commercial newspapers before joining the *Guardian*; Jack Cope, an important early staffer, had spent five years in Fleet Street; and one of South Africa's finest investigative journalists, Ruth First, ran the Johannesburg branch office for fifteen years. Access to the leading left-wing political philosophers in the country—men like Jack Simons, Michael Harmel, and Lionel Forman—gave the newspaper an intellectual richness and depth.[3] To tell the stories of urban black South Africans, the *Guardian* hired a cadre of accomplished writers who lived in the townships and knew their subjects well: Tennyson Makiwane in Alexandra, Alex La Guma in Athlone and Robert Resha in Sophiatown. The services of prominent photographers, especially Eli Weinberg, further embedded the newspaper in the African consciousness; for nonliterate readers, Weinberg's pictures told the story in a succinctly artful style.[4]

Contradictions defined the newspaper. The *Guardian* was founded by whites, but served blacks. It was anti-fascist, but until 1941 opposed attacking Hitler. Women served as editors and writers, yet it had a pronounced sexist flavor. The *Guardian* was always in debt, yet it sold across the Union in numbers that the mainstream press envied. It was banned three times, yet except for the state of emergency it never missed a week. It told of scandals and marches and boycotts and beatings, but it also taught that ideas mattered.

Exuding a palpable, ink-stained energy, the *Guardian* powered the Communist Party and the African National Congress. Campaigns needed promotion. Policies needed examination. Leaders needed publicity. Setbacks needed spin. Outrages needed exposure. Both the CP and the ANC spread their messages through the weekly, which was usually the only way they could.

For individual Party and Congress members, the *Guardian* was Holy Writ. Reading the *Guardian* helped clarify ideological issues and informed activists of the national and international battles being fought. But it was a quietly enforced rule that provided the *Guardian*'s most potent attribute. The Communist Party (and to a lesser extent the ANC) demanded that each member hawk the paper each weekend. Abstract theory crystallized into hard-bone reality when one sat in a barren shack in a township, talking about the *Guardian* editorial or discussing the latest strike. For hundreds of activists, selling the *Guardian* was their first class in political education.

The sales system in turn helped the newspaper and the allied political parties. Each Friday young radicals appeared in black neighborhoods, seeing regular customers and meeting new ones, then returning to the office with news that made its way into the *Guardian*. This cycle not only helped sell more copies and solidify the paper, but it got the CP and the ANC members out of the armchairs and meeting rooms and into the streets. They found out what really was going on—which in turn helped propel the liberation struggle into a mass movement.

The *Guardian* also was central to making the improbable possible: the ANC/CP alliance. Considering the groups' mutual distrust in the 1940s, it was remarkable that it happened so quickly—unofficially in the 1950s and publicly in 1960s. The *Guardian* proved the communists' bona fides. It translated Marxism into an African idiom. It stood as a common symbol, adored by the different segments of the black population. It provided a workplace where nonracialism was the norm, and ideology subordinate to political reality. It was the glue that stuck the Congress and the Party together— the anvil, as poet Arthur Nortje wrote in 1962, upon which the struggle was struck.

The newspaper made numerous mistakes. Its early patronizing attitudes towards Africans were plainly racist. It waited too long to support the war against Nazi Germany. Its narrow political views in the 1950s excluded others, like the Liberal Party, the Pan Africanist Congress, or Trotskyist coloured groups, which had legitimate opinions. The weekly shied away from much-needed criticism of the ANC. The fact-checking department was rather slim, for errors of omission and fact, fueled by an obsessive hatred of apartheid, cropped up far too often. The hidebound loyalty to the morally bankrupt, murderous Soviet Union, even after the Khrushchev disclosures and the 1956 Hungarian uprising, cannot be rightly countenanced.

Still, the *Guardian* was the anvil of South Africa, for upon it the stories of the liberation struggle were hammered into ink and newsprint. Each Thursday the sole anti-apartheid newspaper appeared, *vox clamantis in deserto*—a voice crying in the wilderness. When fascism appeared, the *Guardian* spoke up. When wages were kept low, the *Guardian* spoke up. When workers went on strike, the *Guardian* spoke up. When rain poured in through leaky roofs, the *Guardian* spoke up. When apartheid bills passed in Parliament, the *Guardian* spoke up. When the police shipped men to slave farms, the *Guardian* spoke up. When freedom seemed impossible, the *Guardian* spoke up.

It spoke with pennies in the bank, with reporters in jail, with police detectives on the doorstep, with the charge of high treason hanging over its head. It spoke with hope, compassion and courage. For fourteen hundred weeks, it testified to the power of the printed word.

CHAPTER ONE

A Very Live Menace

A Cape Town Childhood, 1937–1939

In January 1936 Victor Gollancz founded the Left Book Club. Each month Gollancz—a committed, if erratic, socialist and London publisher—issued a special, lower-priced Left Book Club edition, bound in his firm's distinctive dark orange boards. George Orwell's *The Road to Wigan Pier*, Edgar Snow's *Red Star over China*, and Arthur Koestler's *Spanish Testament* were some of the best-selling selections in the club's early years. Under its motto "Knowledge, Unity, Responsibility," the club was soon not a sales mechanism but a way of life. A monthly *Left Book News* journal ran over forty pages long. Left Book Club branches organized clubhouses, discussion groups, adult-education schools, film clubs, theatre troupes and writing guilds. Left Book Club choirs sang anthems from the Left Song Book. The Left Book Club travel agency arranged tours of the Soviet Union. The LBC began staging mass rallies against fascism, attended by thousands, and Gollancz established branches in a dozen countries; membership reached 42,000 by April 1937, and 57,000 two years later.[1]

Cape Town boasted a lively affiliate. Packed meeting halls, stirring speeches by trade unionists and the lusty singing of workers' anthems became the norm at LBC meetings.[2] At one Cape Town Left Book Club meeting in November 1936, a long discussion over the right-leaning South

African media ensued. Members noted the paucity of newspaper coverage of trade unions, the South African Labour Party or anti-fascist groups, let alone anything substantive about the latest cause célèbre, the Spanish Civil War. None of the Cape Town newspapers—especially the two mainstream, commercial dailies, the *Cape Times* and *Cape Argus*—satisfied the interests of Cape Town's left-wing community.

The club, in true bureaucratic style, formed an ad hoc subcommittee to look into the matter. Despite their ragtag mandate and almost total lack of professional journalism experience, the committee decided to establish a newspaper.[3]

Cape Town was a natural starting place. Three ethnic groups dominated Cape Town society: Afrikaners, the original Dutch settlers who had inter-mixed with German and French Huguenots; British, who came in waves after Great Britain took over the Cape Colony from Holland during the Napoleonic Wars; and the Cape coloured, a community of brown-skinned people that grew from a mixture of Malaysian slaves, Bushmen, Africans and Afrikaners. Coloured people in Cape Town lived chiefly in two colorful but poor areas, District Six and the Malay Quarter.

Politics found ample and fertile ground in the shadow of Table Mountain. Almost all progressive organizations in South Africa—the Social Democratic Federation (1902), the African Political Organisation (1902), the South African Labour Party (1909), the International Socialists League (1915), and the Communist Party of South Africa (1921)—were founded at conferences held in Cape Town. Political speakers drew hundreds to the Grand Parade in central downtown. Below the bird-dropping-splattered statue of King Edward VI and all along the wide, stone-paved drilling ground, enthusiasts of every political persuasion stood on wooden soapboxes and bent the ears of passersby.

An endemic sense of detachment permeated the conversations. At the metaphorical southern tip of Africa—the actual terminus was a hundred miles east at Cape Aghulas—Cape Town faced seaward. It was the conti-nent's most active port, but it felt cut off from the rest of Africa. Racial ten-sions were notably muted in Cape Town. Very few Africans lived there, so South Africa's fatal question of race relations often went unasked, and seg-regation like that up-country was often absent. Different communities com-monly mixed in Cape Town, as a visitor from Natal wrote in 1911: "Young white men will be seen walking with well-dressed coloured girls, and an older European may often be seen with coloured wife and children of varying shades, taking the air and gazing in shop windows. The doors of a bioscope are open and the crowd waiting admission and jostling each other as they get tickets includes representatives of every colour, . . . and if he enters the overcrowded room, . . . he will find no distinction made, all and any colour occupy the same seats, cheek by jowl, and sometimes on each other's knees."[4] The pace was decidedly sluggish, the atmosphere almost Mediterranean. There was the calm, sweet-smelling public garden at its center, the honey-blue Table Mountain, the local vineyards, the cobblestoned alleys banked by cafés and bookstores, the whitewashed littoral of beaches and the flower stalls in Green Market Square. Parliament met in Cape Town, but it only sat from January to June each year. Tourists invaded in all seasons, giving the city a holiday feeling. The old joke among activists was that in Cape Town the revolution closed down for the weekend.[5]

An unusual sense of urgency, however, suffused the newspaper committee's efforts in the waning weeks of 1936. Pressing the activists from one side was the rise of fascism. Rising to state power in Italy and Germany, fascism first impinged on Africa's consciousness in February 1935 when Mussolini attacked Abyssinia (Ethiopia), the only African country besides Liberia to have avoided colonial rule. In Cape Town, dockworkers responded by refusing to load Italian ships, and for a while, the Communist Party's newspaper, the *South African Worker*, enjoyed a tripling in circulation (to seven thousand).[6]

Fascism, nonetheless, found ample legroom with the poor, rural Afrikaners fighting for survival in the Great Depression, and a half-dozen jingoistic paramilitary organizations sprung up across the country, often identifying themselves according to the color of their shirts. South Africa's open meeting grounds, like the Grand Parade in Cape Town and the steps of the Johannesburg City Hall, became forums for brawls between fascists and progressives. The Communist Party's Sunday-evening rallies at the Johannesburg City Hall usually degenerated from shouting matches to horrific clashes, with sjamboks and knuckle-dusters flashing in the twilight. In response, South African radicals formed the Anti-Fascist League of South Africa and boycotted German goods, but they were unable to stem the tide of violence.[7]

Two incidents in Cape Town particularly stuck out. In March 1936 Louis Weichardt, a vitriolic fascist, announced a Greyshirt meeting for April 2nd at the Grand Parade. The Anti-Fascism League issued a circular denouncing the meeting. On the 2nd, a group of League supporters came to the Grand Parade and heckled Weichardt. Cissie Gool, the daughter of a leading coloured Capetonian, Dr. Abdurahman, stood atop a car and shouted out a competing speech to drown Weichardt out. A melee ensued, and Cape Town experienced one of its first full-blown riots, with running battles in the streets, burning cars and dozens of injured men and women.[8] Six months later, there was more unrest. In October the *Stuttgart*, a ship loaded with Jewish refugees from Nazi Germany, sailed into Table Bay. A crowd of jeering, swastika-waving Greyshirts gave them a South African welcome.[9]

The lack of an adequate response to fascism troubled the radical Left. Both the African National Congress and the Communist Party of South Africa, the two national, radical political institutions, flailed in the mucky throes of organizational lethargy. The ANC, by virtue of its 1912 founding, claimed the title of the oldest liberation movement in Africa. But it was moribund. ANC president Z. R. Mahabane lived in the small Orange Free State village of Winburg and had little money to travel. The Congress's Cape province branch was bitterly divided into two factions, and the Natal branch operated independently of the national organization. The Congress, unlike the short-lived Industrial and Commercial Union, a mass black trade union in the twenties, refrained from direct political action. The results of the annual national convention were usually calls for unity and national days of prayer, or somber deputations to Pretoria or London; the rest of the year, with no national executive committee and only a few hundred members, was silence. In 1936 the government removed Africans from the voter rolls and created a set of separate, segregated structures for Africans—three white Native representatives for Parliament, and a Native Representative Council that supposedly advised the government on African affairs. The ANC barely issued a whisper of protest.[10]

The Communist Party of South Africa's pulse beat as erratically as the ANC's. Founded in 1921, the Party had quickly become a major factor in African politics. By 1930 nineteen of the twenty-three members of the national executive committee were African, as were nine-tenths of the 1,750 rank-and-file members. The Party operated popular African night schools, and the Party newspaper, the *South African Worker*, published articles in African languages. But the tide swiftly turned in the early 1930s when a sectarian group of leaders, using contradictory Comintern directives as weapons, kicked out 90 percent of members and almost all activity ground to a halt. Africans abandoned the Party, and the few remaining activists concentrated on an all-white "People's Front" to face rising fascist sympathizers among working-class whites.[11]

Trade unions served as a substitute arena for political activity for those left standing. Many of the members of the newspaper committee spent their days working with chemical factory employees or tram drivers or stevedores. For these activists, issues needed discussion, the workers needed to be educated and mobilized, meetings and strikes needed publicity, and leaders needed a place to put their views across. They needed a newspaper.

Ray Alexander was the key member of the committee. In November 1929, at age fifteen, Alexander (the name on her passport was Rachile Aleksandrovies Alexander) fled Latvia with the secret police searching for her. Reaching Cape Town, she began to organize factory workers into labor unions; she was fired from her first job for joining a Communist Party march up Adderley Street during her lunch hour.[12] A stocky, imposing woman with a thick Baltic accent and dark hair tied back in a bun, Alexander was a militant force in Cape Town radical circles. She remembered, a half century later, the launch of the *Guardian*: "There was a Garment Workers' Union strike in '36, April, March, and the need for a workers' report, to support workers' struggles was very, very evident. Getting a paper started was the answer. But it took us a long time to get off the ground. We really worked at it, by constantly saying, 'Could we ask this one, could we ask that one? This one for money, this one for circulation?' We felt the need for it. We had many, many meetings about it."

Appointing the newspaper's editor-in-chief was the critical step. The committee held a dinner party in December 1936 at the home of George Sacks and his wife, Betty Radford. During the dinner, it was decided that Radford should be the editor.[13] Radford was an Englishwoman who had come out to South Africa on holiday in 1931 and now was the editor of the *Cape Times*' biweekly women's page.[14] Friendly with Alexander and other Cape Town leftists, Radford had both the necessary journalistic experience and political attitudes.

By bringing Radford into the fold, the committee received a keen political commentator in her husband, George Sacks, a surgeon and a highly regarded writer. With Radford and Sacks, the newspaper now had a substantive core, and Cape Town's sizable intelligentsia began to swirl around them: trade unionists, socialists, coloured leaders, and Labour Party officials. "We were all connected socially," recalled Harry Snitcher, a young Jewish lawyer who joined the group, "and knew each other and saw each other and when we heard about the newspaper idea we knew it was a good one." The few active Communist Party members in Cape Town got involved, though the CP members, including Alexander, were officially not on the editorial board. Alexander explained: "We didn't want to give the impression that it was a communist paper, but really make it a people's front paper. And so that is what it became." Professors and lecturers at the University of Cape Town lent support.[15] Most notable was Harold Baldry, a classics lecturer from England, who learned about the newspaper from his wife's sister, a Party and LBC member.[16] Baldry agreed to write a weekly analysis of foreign news for the newspaper, while his wife, Carina Pearson, assumed the job of managing the circulation and fundraising departments.

As they secured a staff, the committee agonized over who would produce the newspaper, as few presses would print such a left-wing publication. Luckily, Arthur Trommer, a redheaded communist who had recently fled Nazi Germany, knew the right person. Trommer worked as a typesetter and compositor at Stewart Printing and Publishing Company, a local firm run by Charlie Stewart.[17] Stewart, when he was not riding horses on the beach near his home in Camp's Bay, was sympathetic to the Left: he allowed no color bar at his plant, and printed materials for the Friends of the Soviet Union and other radical groups.[18] The timing was also right, as his firm was expanding and wanted new work.[19] At a meeting with the subcommittee, Stewart agreed to supply so much of the necessary start-up capital that he officially became the newspaper's first owner. He also cleaned out a storage room at his printing house at 102 Loop Street that would serve as the *Guardian*'s first home.[20]

For a model of a radical newspaper, the committee turned to the *Daily Worker*. A British communist newspaper founded in 1930, the *Daily Worker* was a penny tabloid that featured volunteer staffs, fundraising groups and house-to-house selling.[21] Emulating the *Daily Worker*, the committee met with shopkeepers and business people in an effort to solicit funding and advertising accounts. Jewish traders on Hanover, Buitenkant and Harrington Streets, an area bordering the large coloured area of District Six, were instrumental in donating money. Norman and Eric Flegg, brothers who ran a successful pharmaceutical firm, gave funds, and Norman agreed to become the newspaper's business manager. The committee also approached shop stewards, union secretaries and common workers, recruiting their support for the newspaper. "From the trade unions, we went to discuss them buying the paper," said Alexander. "You see, it was a question of getting adverts and getting financial support. Betty quite rightly said that she must at least have a feeling that for the first six months there should be funds available. To get adverts we had to show how many people would read the paper. So, the involvement of the trade unions was very, very important in order to get the advertisers and to organize the sales of the *Guardian* before it started."

Naming the newspaper was not easy. According to Alexander, a number of titles were bandied about, and the first official name was *Dawn*. But one volunteer pressed the committee to choose a different title. Thirty years earlier, the volunteer had raised funds to start up an alternative newspaper to be called the Cape Guardian. The newspaper had failed to appear, but to honor that earlier effort, the committee agreed to call the newspaper the Cape Guardian.[22]

In January 1937 the committee hosted a week-long retreat in the Cape Town village of Fish Hoek. There, overlooking the Indian Ocean, they finalized plans and devised a printing schedule.[23]

On Friday, 19 February 1937, a twelve-page, five-column broadsheet called the Cape Guardian appeared on the streets of Cape Town. The newspaper had an address at an obscure printing plant, no masthead and not a hint of support from any political party.

In the style of the day, advertisements blanketed the front page, except for a political cartoon on the top right-hand side. Inside, more advertisements appeared, thirty-seven in all, testifying to the months of advance work—Flag cigarettes, Fairy Headache Powders, Rogalsky's new-laid eggs, Bok antiseptic floor polish, Myrtle Grove cigarettes, Commando brandy, and a 1931 four-cylinder Ford Roadster selling for £50. Two Cape Town cinemas—the New Globe in Woodstock and the Ritz Bio Café on Adderley Street—listed their offerings. Modern Books, the leading progressive bookstore in the Cape, advertised its recent eighteen-shilling arrival, The Letters of Lenin. Tromp van Diggelen took out a full-page advertisement; "The healthiest man in South Africa . . . the man who definitely possesses 'the gift of healing,'" van Diggelen was a British champion wrestler who had bench-pressed 243 pounds with one hand and now sold health manuals by post.

Much of the first edition focused on Cape Town trade unions. "The Obvious Benefits of Trade Unionism" were "Revealed by Ernest Verity," and numerous one-paragraph pieces about Cape unions took up considerable space among the pages. Matthew Barnett, the secretary for the Hotel, Bar and Catering Trades Union Employees Association, placed a meeting announcement and wrote an article concerning his long-titled union. The Cape Guardian's opening editorial, headlined "Racialism Menaces Trades Unions," attacked an exclusively Afrikaner trade union: in an alliterative mood, the weekly proclaimed, "Defeat, destruction and despair have always followed dissension and disunity." A letter to the editor written by Stanley George Raddall, the secretary of the South African Typographical Union, expounded on the Cape Guardian's political stance: "From what I can gather it will be a purely trades union paper, free from all prejudices such as race and colour and will stand for democracy in the true sense of the word. . . . I hope and trust it will do its best to uplift and enlighten not only Trades Unionists, but those outside the ranks so that they might know what they are losing and what a drag they are on others who are trying to improve their positions."

Uplifting and enlightening or not, the *Cape Guardian*'s other obvious interest was politics. Betty Radford wrote a breezy editorial-page column called "Topical" that offered political gossip and opinion. An anonymously written feature called "The Parliamentary Merry-Go-Round by Hurdy-Gurdy" discussed the increasing conservatism in the House of Assembly: "The issue of miscegenation is one of the prize red herrings which the Boys of the Bushveld delight to trail across the political path. . . . The native needs to be treated decently and given some elementary rights, if only for the sake of preserving the white race in South Africa from all becoming poor whites."

Half of the twelve pages concerned international news. Articles examined the Spanish Civil War, attempts at Baltic unity, and the "German Drive to the East." The front-page cartoon depicted Hitler and "his colonial ambitions" in neighboring "South West Africa STIKA." The "Vigilator," Harold Baldry's nom de plume, used an entire page to review overseas events, especially "Roosevelt's Struggle with Big Business" and a "Crisis in British Labour Party."

It was not all somber and serious. The newspaper reviewed a local play and the Left Book Club's choice for January 1937 (Stephen Spender's *Forward From Liberation*), ran a poem, and devoted the back page to sports, mostly the upcoming Springbok rugby tour of New Zealand and Australia.

One thousand copies at a penny each were sold that weekend.[24]

During the next week, a small incident occurred that marked a decisive shift for the fledging newspaper. An unnamed "assistant" on the staff slipped in a headline—"Russians Purge Truth"—above an article concerning the second Moscow show trials. Radford—"the then unwary editor," as she later described herself—did not notice the headline until the issue appeared. She was embarrassed by what she thought was a wrongheaded and potentially controversial gaffe, and vowed never again to put the newspaper to bed without personally examining every caption, photograph, headline and sentence.[25] Radford arranged with Charlie Stewart to assume sole ownership of the weekly, and she registered the *Cape Guardian* with the central post office in her name.[26] As publisher and editor, she had both a legal and professional responsibility for the newspaper, and as the weeks passed, she asserted her control. She wrote a majority of the articles and opinion pieces—the editorial, "Topical," and a feature that ran for the first few years called "What We Think." To fulfill a South African newspaper regulation during election campaigns, the newspaper printed a small notice that read, "All political matter, sub-editing and headlines are by Betty Radford."[27]

Radford was elegant and ambitious. Her family was known in London. Her maternal grandfather, William Willett, directed a prestigious building firm, was a member of the Royal Astronomical Society and earned himself a footnote in history as the inventor of the idea of daylight saving time.[28] Betty grew up in Sloane Square and Surrey, and her father, an army chaplain, sent her to Winchester Girls' School (there was a rumor that Thomas Hardy had also briefly tutored her). Betty Ermyntrude Crachley Radford floated through life with ease. She spoke with a clipped British accent and wore expensive tailored dresses and pearl earrings. In her eleven years as editor of the *Guardian*, she never drew a salary.[29] She told *Guardian* readers of her daily morning routine of reading the *Cape Times* in bed with her breakfast and her Sealyham terriers.[30] Her grand Oranjezicht home on Kensington Crescent on the slopes of Table Mountain was the height of high society. Pauline Podbrey, a white trade unionist whose husband, the Indian leader H. A. Naidoo, worked at the *Guardian* in the 1940s, recalled Radford's presence:

> Now, Betty's place for dinner was a very special occasion. She was aristocracy. . . . And she was intimidating because she didn't approve of me. She warned H.A. not to marry me, "because you can't trust these white, middle-class Jewish girls. They're just out for a bit of fun. She's not serious." She liked H.A. very much and she didn't trust me. She thought I was just playing at across-the-barrier affairs. So that at first she was very haughty as far as that's concerned, when we came here [to Cape Town in 1943]. Afterwards, when we got married and she saw that I was serious, she was prepared to consider me and invite me round. It was at her place that I first came across the whole ceremony of waiters and fingerbowls. She was formidable, I'd say, not tough but formidable.[31]

Radford came to South Africa in 1931 on holiday to visit relatives. She found Cape Town enchanting and decided to stay. This "jack-of-all-trades," as she called herself, found jobs as a secretary, a publishers' agent, and an investigator for the *Cape Times* Fresh Air Fund before latching onto the *Cape Times*' women's page. In August 1936 she married George Sacks. They honeymooned for three and one-half months in Europe and the Soviet Union. "That visit," Radford later wrote of their visit to Moscow and Leningrad, "determined me to work for Socialism with all the energy I have."[32]

It was socialism, not communism, and that was an important distinction for Radford. She was not a member of the Communist Party and did not have a true political home. Peter Abrahams, the coloured novelist, spent a few months in early 1939 in Cape Town and came into contact with Radford while raising funds for a coloured school. After persuading the "finely dressed" editor to give a donation, Abrahams classified Radford "as belonging to the humanist Left" because she "saw an ugly world and wanted to make it better. . . . [She was not] hell-bent on revolution for its own sake." Radford told Abrahams that she was a socialist, though not an "avowed communist" like Ray Alexander.[33] In these early years of the *Guardian*, Radford sometimes struggled to find her feet in the rocky political landscape. When Ralph Bunche, the African American social scientist and future Nobel Peace Prize winner, came to Cape Town in late 1937, he spent many evenings with Radford and Sacks. In his diary, he recorded one particular conversation: "Betty Sacks says she can't see why Cape coloured are so bitter vs. the Labor Party. George explains it on the basis of Labor Party's past of segregation and discrimination vs. coloured worker. I said that coloured tend to identify Labor Party with the poor whites. Betty claimed that Labor Party is not the party of the poor whites—that they supported the Nationalist Party."[34] Radford's inability to comprehend coloured people's anger at the Labour Party for its white-only membership rule revealed her political naïveté.

Her husband was more attuned to the nuances of local politics. Raised in the Karoo village of Outdshoorn and educated at the University of Cape Town and the University of Dublin, Sacks had started a consulting surgery practice in Cape Town in 1927.[35] The tall, balding, bespectacled doctor was a respected Marxist theoretician and the author of *The Jewish Question* and *The Intelligent Man's Guide to Jew Baiting*, the latter published by Victor Gollancz in 1935.[36] Although busy with his well-established surgery practice and his lectures at the University of Cape Town Medical School, Sacks contributed a great deal to the *Guardian* in the early years, writing and editing numerous articles.[37] His interest in journalism developed so strongly that in 1937 Sacks assumed the editorship of a new quarterly called the *Critic*.

Printed and published by Charlie Stewart, the *Critic* was a short-lived but interesting journal. George Findlay, a communist author, was the Pretoria editor; Harold Baldry supplied long pieces about Europe; and Sacks had space to pontificate on subjects like the South African press and the infamous abdication of King Edward VIII.[38]

As Sacks and Radford developed their political and professional lives, they remained devoted to each other. They collected art together, sampled wines and vacationed at the fashionable Cape resorts of Hermanus and Plettenburg Bay for weeks at a time.[39] "George was very protective towards Betty and very much in love," remembered Pauline Podbrey. They were the *Guardian*'s foundation, a two-pronged, closely-knit core. In a telling comment, a Johannesburg colleague, Hilda Bernstein, later said that in the 1930s the *Guardian* "was very much Betty Radford and George Sacks' private hobby-horse. It was Betty's paper, George and Betty's paper."[40]

The hobbyhorse had other riders, and as Radford said, a "little band of enthusiasts" joined them in the *Guardian* office.[41] Carina Pearson, the circulation manager, handled the day-to-day operations of the newspaper. She supervised the growing list of subscribers, the advertising division, the *Guardian*'s fundraising efforts and the distribution network of agents, paid sellers and volunteers.[42] Pearson, under the name "Hannah," wrote a weekly cooking and household advice column. Her métier was helping women avoid "wash-day worries" and supplying them with handy recipes and childcare tips. Three months after starting the column, Radford teased Pearson by writing that "our Hannah is a wretched cook."[43] Pearson and Radford were simpatico members of Cape Town society. Pearson, like Radford, never accepted a salary, and while other activists spent their Saturdays selling the *Guardian* or canvassing for funds, Pearson guiltily admitted to sunbathing on the beach at Muizenburg.[44]

Jack Simons began writing the *Guardian*'s page-four editorials in November 1937. Fresh from earning a doctorate at the London School of Economics, Simons had just returned home to teach African government and law at the University of Cape Town. His incisive weekly *Guardian* commentary, as well as his column called "Law for the Working Man" cemented his reputation within radical circles (so did his marriage to Ray Alexander). Simons, said Amy Thornton, "was always the biggest draw card, up until he was banned. I see this frail old man now, but he was tall and strapping, an enormous voice and easily the most electrifying academic anywhere. He had such a kind of warmth and immediacy . . . not being the least bit condescending, but able to speak in a way that people could understand him. It is a very rare talent, and not many people have it." He taught Marxism to hundreds of colleagues; wrote clear, understandable prose; and arbitrated political conflicts with fairness. And he was quickly becoming one of UCT's most popular professors. He stood astride the political waters as a Communist Party colossus.

Bill Andrews was another Cape Town giant who stamped his mark on the *Guardian*. English-born, Andrews had become politicized while working on the Witwatersrand mines as a railway fitter and turner. In 1909 he founded and chaired the South African Labour Party, and between 1912 and 1915 he was a member of Parliament. Andrews quit Parliament and the Labour Party over their support for the First World War and founded the breakaway International Socialist League, which segued in 1921 into the Communist Party of South Africa. As the first secretary of the Party, he edited its organ the *International* and was elected to the executive of the Comintern, the Soviet Union's committee for international affairs. In 1922 he was jailed for playing a leading role in the famed mine strike, the Rand Revolt. With his three-piece suits, felt hat, and gray eyes, he looked every inch like the elder statesman of the South African Left.[45] Soon after the *Guardian*'s birth, Andrews took an "active and helpful interest in its growth," according to Radford, and began contributing advice and a five-part series on strikes at the turn of the century.[46] In October 1937 Andrews traveled to Moscow for the twentieth anniversary of the Bolshevik Revolution; he sent back to the *Guardian* some of his speeches and reports about life in the Soviet Union, and upon his return wrote a full-page article about his impressions.[47] Andrews's high visibility conferred a legitimacy on the newspaper that was irreplaceable. He also donated a tincture of stability. He personified the idea of taking the long view.

The one person who really enabled the *Guardian* to survive its infancy was Harold Baldry. Carina Pearson's taciturn, dour husband, Baldry was a classics lecturer at the University of Cape Town. Baldry (who not only was unsalaried but also had donated funds to help start the newspaper) soon gained fame as the *Guardian*'s foreign-page writer.[48] Politically congruent with George Sacks, Baldry also wrote from a socialist, non–Communist Party stance. His column, titled "Behind the Overseas News" and written under the name "Vigilator," ran into the thousands of words across a full page each week. Baldry's trenchant, methodical analysis of the week's events became the leading feature of the newspaper. Johnny Kaye, a Johannesburg subscriber, wrote in a letter to the editor in April 1938 that "several of us await the arrival of each issue with great eagerness to get the 'slant' on foreign events."[49] Buttressed by editorials, news articles, cables from Europe, and small photographs, the column received a much-needed shot of humor in an accompanying cartoon by Vic Clapham. A young leftist and son of the founder of the Comrades ultra-marathon, Clapham's bitingly satiric cartoons melded perfectly with Baldry's metronomic prose.

On 30 September 1938 Neville Chamberlain secured "peace in our time" by handing Germany the Sudetenland in the Munich Agreement. When she heard the news, Radford quickly cobbled together recent Vigilator columns and Clapham cartoons into a pamphlet. As early as April 1938 Vigilator had warned about the threat to Czechoslovakia, and before the Agreement he had argued that the goal of Chamberlain and his French counterpart Daladier was not to stop Nazi aggression, but to turn it towards the USSR.[50] Now there was proof. Stewart's rushed out the pamphlet, and "The Munich Swindle" sold 25,000 copies that weekend—when the circulation of the *Guardian* was just 4,000.[51] A buzz about the weekly swarmed through South Africa's political classes. People wrote to the *Guardian* begging for copies.[52] Some of the interest stemmed from the fact that mainstream South African newspapers championed an opposing viewpoint; in fact, the editor of the *Cape Argus*, K. C. McClausland, was fired when he criticized Chamberlain's policy.[53]

International news, after the "Munich Swindle," ascended to the top of the *Guardian*'s list of priorities. Radford placed a slogan below the *Guardian* masthead: "Presenting the Truth to South Africa about Events Within and Without"—and the emphasis was on the "without." Headlines rang out— "Mussolini Menaces Us"—while articles examined Nazi propaganda in Austria.[54] The *Guardian* exhibited a fine sense of humor, with Clapham cartoons depicting a newly discovered species ("Nevilleopterygll—fish without backbone") and a headline about Mussolini reading "Yours with an Axis to Grind."[55]

The Spanish Civil War was perhaps most constantly covered. In her "Topical" column, Radford discussed the Committee for Spanish Relief, a group led by Petronella van Heerden, a local Afrikaner doctor, and later she issued a front-page appeal asking for money for the group.[56] On the two-year anniversary of the beginning of the war, she printed pictures of El Campesino and La Pasionaria, two legendary Republican leaders.[57] When the newspaper's Johannesburg correspondent, Charles Fox, visited a Basque refugee camp in Oxfordshire, England, the weekly published his lengthy report.[58] In March 1938 a French boat, calling in Cape Town on its way to

Spain, agreed to carry food to the struggling Republicans. Radford raised funds and spent them "to the best advantage, on tinned milk, cod-liver oil, sugar, tobacco, cigarettes, and medical supplies."[59]

Anxious to expose international fascism at every step, the *Guardian* sometimes tripped. In a June 1938 "Topical," Radford reported on an overseas news agency, Transocean, that charged suspiciously low prices for its wireless service. Through the help of some friends at the *Cape Argus*, she discovered that Transocean was a Nazi-controlled propaganda machine run from Berlin. Radford then tried to connect the dots to Reuters, the giant conservative British news agency, which supposedly owned Transocean.[60] For the next few months Radford attacked Reuters, carrying bold, two-column headlines like "Watch Reuters: When You See News from Reuters-Transocean, Reach for the Salt Cellar."[61] Having nothing to do with Transocean and tired of the libelous attacks, Reuters sued the *Guardian* for £5,000. Radford quickly settled the matter out of court and printed a withdrawal of her claims.[62]

Inside South Africa, the newspaper chronicled a rising crescendo of racial intolerance. The usual Sunday-night battles with the Blackshirts at the Johannesburg City Hall drew *Guardian* attention.[63] One 1938 article told the story of a Blackshirt (wearing a Nazi uniform) hitting an African bicyclist while driving in Johannesburg. A crowd gathered at the scene and stormed the Blackshirt's car, smashing the windows and ripping the doors off.[64] Other articles informed readers on how a Greyshirt mob failed to disrupt a meeting in Woodstock, and Blackshirt activity in Salt River.[65] In 1938 "Hurdy-Gurdy," at the time written by an Afrikaner named Johannes Ziervogel, reported on a "Tweedledum and Tweedledee" by-election in the conservative Cederberg town of Piketburg, featuring Louis Weichardt of the Greyshirts and a National Party member.[66] Headlines called a cabinet minister, Oswald Pirow, a "dictator," and a series of profiles on members of Parliament began with rough treatment of D. F. Malan, the leader of the right-wing National Party:

MALANITE MATHEMATICS:
1 Capitalist = 1 Jew
1 Jew = 1 Communist
therefore 1 Capitalist = 1 Communist.[67]

Coupled with the fight against fascism, the *Guardian* devoted a large amount of copy to the labor movement. Trade-union officials constantly sent in letters to the editor or submitted articles.[68] Radford discussed the annual conference of the South African Trades and Labour Council (SAT&LC), the committee that oversaw a (largely white) trade-union coalition. The back page, carrying the heading "The Industrial Front," evolved into a smorgasbord of trade-union news and announcements.[69] The *Guardian* occasionally invited a factory worker to write a column: "Dock-workers' Difficulties by Crateshifter," or "Super-Heater on Salt River Workers."[70] Union functions—dances, banquets, and annual general meetings—received publicity in the weekly, and Radford strongly championed any new union.[71] Space fillers read "Join Your Union—Are You a Sponger?"[72] In one issue, the *Guardian* discussed the "plight" of diamond workers in Wynberg, interviewed Jimmy Emmerich about the big wage increases he secured for his bus drivers and conductors and proclaimed the opening of a chemical workers' library.[73] Thirteen Cape Town unions sent 1937 May Day greetings to the newspaper.[74]

A *Guardian* tradition of investigative reporting began with a 1937 exposure of factory conditions for women workers in the Cape. Ray Alexander escorted Betty Radford to meat, fish and chemical factories; they met with thirty-three gut scrapers in a Maitland abattoir who got paid four pennies an hour. The factories astonished and horrified Radford, who told her readers, "I begin to be afraid that I may make your flesh creep too much by telling you true stories of how other people live."[75] Her articles prompted an inquiry by the government's Department of Labour, and some improvements in wages and working conditions.[76] Another early success was a *Guardian*-led campaign to close stores earlier on Friday nights. Shop assistants, who worked until ten o'clock on Friday evenings with no overtime pay, sought the *Guardian*'s help in ending the workingday at seven. After a year of protest, the government instituted earlier closing hours.[77]

The deep connections to the labor movement were something the *Guardian* was happy to develop, as it enabled the newspaper to pay its bills. In 1938 the *Guardian* started a classified-advertising section on the back page—called "What's On"—charging a rate of three shillings and sixpence per inch. With the section's inception Radford wrote, "Organisations are urged to advertise their meetings and functions in the *Guardian* thereby ensuring a good attendance."[78] In a "buy South African" mood, Radford declared: "Support Home Industries: The *Guardian* is a South African weekly newspaper printed in Cape Town by South African workers."[79] Distribution was especially important. The railway and harbor workers were active sellers of the weekly, and in August 1938 the newspaper proudly announced that

Cape Town sweets workers had "doubled their sales of the *Guardian* in the last two weeks."[80]

In some respects, the *Guardian* became an unofficial Cape Town trade-union organ. In April 1937 the Cape district committee of the South African Trades and Labour Council asked its member unions to encourage the flow of news to the weekly, and the ordering of yearly subscriptions.[81] A year later, Eli Weinberg, the secretary of the committee, wrote in his SAT&LC annual report that "This committee wishes to place on record the yeoman services rendered by the *Guardian* to the Trade Union Movement. The *Guardian* is regularly publishing news from the Trade Unions and supports the struggle of the organised workers' movement. We hope that this valuable paper will continue its good work for many years to come. We suggest to Trade Unions to take a keen interest in distributing the *Guardian* amongst their members."[82] As far as the unions were concerned, the weekly had hit the mark.

In a different area, however, the newspaper missed its targets. A political newspaper, the *Guardian* had no political home. In the years to come, when the weekly was closely aligned with the Communist Party, readers assumed that the *Guardian* had always been a Party organ. In the 1930s, however, the newspaper was proudly, almost defiantly independent. Autonomy from the Party occurred partially because of organizational decrepitude. The Communist Party's headquarters, a thousand miles away in Johannesburg, could have been on another continent, with the slow speed of mail and the expense of the telegraph and telephone. The Cape Town branch of the Party was, for all practical purposes, nonexistent. There were no meetings, no reports, no formal structures in place. A few dozen disillusioned communists lived in Cape Town, but all focused their political lives elsewhere—Ray Alexander and Jimmy La Guma in trade unions, Jack Simons in his teaching, Sam Kahn in his law practice, Jimmy Emmerich in the Labour Party, Harry Snitcher in the Socialist Party, Cissie Gool in her new position on the Cape Town city council (the first woman to win a seat).[83] The *Guardian*'s central figures were not Party members in 1937: Radford, Sacks, Pearson, Baldry, Stewart, and Clapham. Even Bill Andrews, having been expelled in 1931, was officially off the rolls.

The *Guardian* was not antagonistic to communism. Radford told readers that "the stupidities of capitalism are surely nowhere more apparent than in South Africa," and "capitalism is unchristian."[84] One headline, over some photographs of Russian factory workers and peasants, read: "Happy Workers in the USSR."[85] The National Liberation League, a Party-inspired group, had a *Guardian* column.[86]

The Left Book Club, allied with the Party, topped the list of *Guardian* causes. The weekly outlined the LBC's new membership scheme; Charles Fox, the *Guardian*'s Johannesburg correspondent, reported upon the "sterile discussions over long-dead controversies" that were damaging the Transvaal LBC branch; and the newspaper recounted a public LBC debate that saw Harold Baldry taking the side for collective security in case of war.[87] "A guinea dance for five bob," the LBC's 1938 Cape Town spring dance at the Hotel Edward became a fundraiser for the *Guardian*, which, according to the LBC, was giving "True Facts on the European Crisis."[88] Each month the *Guardian* reviewed the LBC's book choice; it panned the April 1937 selection, *The Road to Wigan Pier* by George Orwell, for the same reason that Victor Gollancz had hesitated to publish it and had added a disclaiming foreword: Orwell had attacked fellow-traveling "snob-Bolsheviks" in the book's second half.[89]

Nonetheless, the *Guardian* called itself a socialist paper.[90] The difference between socialism and communism was not simply semiotics. The weekly spoke with pride about its lack of political mentors, declaring itself to be "free and independent in views" and "The Independent Democratic Weekly."[91] As late as April 1941 the editorial board of the *Guardian* had just one Party member.[92] Even Leon Trotsky, archenemy of Moscow, made his way into the pages of the newspaper when Modern Books advertised his 1937 book, *The Revolution Betrayed*.[93] In September 1937, with some prescience, Radford answered accusations by *Die Burger*, a conservative Cape Town Afrikaans daily, that South Africa's trade unions were full of communists:

> By implication, *Die Burger* regards the *Guardian* as a mouthpiece of tainted trades unionism. Our position is clear. We have stated it before and we repeat it now. We do not regard Communism as practical politics in South Africa to-day. But we do regard Fascism as a very live menace to the immediate future of this country. We believe a Malanite Government would ... be the ruination of the hopes of all decent-minded people for the evolution of a liberal and democratic-minded South Africa. ... This is the credo of the *Guardian*. The *Guardian* will fight tooth and nail for the preservation of that modicum of democracy which persists in South Africa. It will fight to make political democracy coterminous with economic democracy for we hold that one is incomplete without the other. To that end it pledges its support to all those groups and individuals who share its outlook. The *Guardian* is for the under-dog.[94]

With communism not being practical politics, the *Guardian* turned to more mainstream political parties to help preserve South Africa's modicum of democracy. One movement was the short-lived Socialist Party, led by a former Labour Party MP, Duncan Campbell Burnside. In the *Guardian*'s third issue, Burnside wrote a long article titled "South Africa's Salvation . . . Liberalism or Further Over to the Left?" A month later he answered his own question by giving the *Guardian* the manifesto of his new party, and the newspaper reported from Parliament that a "Great Speech by Socialist MP Burnside Settles Nationalists."[95]

Most of the attention concentrated on the South African Labour Party. Ever since Bill Andrews led the party's radicals away in 1915, the Labour Party had been an awkward farrago of socialists, trade unionists and disillusioned United Party supporters. A whites-only membership rule and an insipid liberalism did not stop the *Guardian* from supporting what it called the "Party" (many radicals, including Party members, worked with the Labour Party). In the very first issue, Betty Radford called Walter Madeley, the Labour Party leader and Minister of Labour, "one of the quickest wits" in Parliament. Each year the newspaper sent staff reporters to the Labour Party's annual conference who filled the weekly's pages with resolutions and statements.[96] Nine months before the May 1938 general election—an unheard of gap in those days—the newspaper began discussing the coming vote: "The *Guardian* will do its utmost to further the campaign for a united Labour effort. . . . We must double our circulation before the elections."[97] In September 1937 Duncan Burnside contributed a full-page "Outspoken Article on the Weakness of the Left" that discussed the election.[98] A fortnight later Will Costello, a Labour Party leader, replied with a front-page piece, while on page five Jimmy Emmerich pondered the labor movement's role in politics. The next Friday, the newspaper printed a long letter to the editor from Wilfred Harrison, a veteran socialist, criticizing Costello's views. In December 1937 the *Guardian* printed the Labour Party's "Native Policy," written by Costello:

> Once having attained their own independent state, they would not be allowed to compete in white South Africa . . . native townships would be situated outside European towns. . . . Our policy of separation is actually a policy of co-operation. Co-operation between the whites and the Natives under present conditions is impossible. Natives living among Europeans can never think as Natives, nor do Natives in such circumstances have confidence in one another. The Natives' feeling of inferiority to the white race makes them an easy prey for the exploiter. If I were a Native I would

agitate for separation, knowing as I would that I could never become a part of the white race.[99]

In discussing this policy—which was frighteningly close to apartheid—Jack Simons editorialized that "we have repeatedly pointed to the undeniable fact that if Labour were really given the opportunity to put its native policy into practice, it would destroy the economy within a week."[100] Despite this misgiving, the *Guardian* continued to support the Labour Party. Indeed, Radford gave Costello almost a full page to ruminate on the elections the week after Simons's editorial.

The 1938 election towered over the newspaper. Radford profiled, pictured, and interviewed each of the five Cape Town Socialist and Labour candidates, called for election-day volunteers, appealed for the trade-union vote, and urged readers to "Vote Labour, Vote Socialist."[101] In the last days before the poll, Radford and other *Guardian* staff members canvassed house-to-house for Labour and Socialist candidates.[102] "The *Guardian* had a very definite, positive effect on my campaign," Snitcher later said. "They were the only ones who covered my meetings, my little rallies."[103] After the May elections, in which all five men were decidedly trounced (Labour and Socialist together received nationally 51,895 out of a possible 829,886, or one-sixteenth the vote; Labour won just three seats and the Socialists none) the weekly analyzed the results. "Greyshirtism," counseled Emmerich. Simons editorialized against the Labour Party, which was "stagnating as the political arm of the craft unions." Radford wrote that the essential problem was that the Labour Party did not recruit enough Afrikaners: "Above all, their language and their cultural sympathies must be respected. There is no room for ridiculous chauvinism in a Labour movement. Every active worker should make himself proficient in both official languages."[104]

Brian Bunting, one of the Communist Party's historians and Radford's successor as editor, wrote that the *Guardian* "started off as a trade union–oriented journal, a liberal journal. It didn't have any specific political colour that you could identify. . . . A reader got good value for his one penny in those days . . . a good strong draught of liberal radicalism."[105] There was a benign, comfortable feel to the weekly, a sort of innocence before the corruption of apartheid and the melee of mass movements.

It was also politically incorrect. Despite its female editor and managerial staff, the *Guardian* was not home to the kind of gender equality that Marxism-Leninism advocated (admittedly, neither was the Soviet Union). Occasionally, women were portrayed in progressive ways. "Can Women

Obtain Emancipation in a Capitalist State?" asked a provocative headline in April 1937.[106] The weekly thrashed out the "politics of lipstick" and, during the 1938 general election, advised working women how to vote and still get to work. (White women were granted suffrage in 1930.[107]) While discussing the mainstream press, George Sacks wrote that "the endless 'Beauty Hints' and 'Woman's Page' which are frequently nothing but a setting for refrigerator advertisements must surely be a source of annoyance to the intelligent woman who resents the implication that the rest of the paper is outside her ken."[108]

Yet that was exactly the kind of cloying gloze that the *Guardian* produced. The weekly portrayed women as supporters of men. The women's page almost entirely concentrated on the conventional realms of fashion, childcare and interior decorating. Carina Pearson gave tips to help make "it less tiring for a busy housewife."[109] Marjorie Willett, Betty Radford's niece, became the women's page "shopping reporter," who was on the lookout for the "best shopping opportunities in Cape Town."[110] The newspaper counseled mothers with varicose veins, and "The *Guardian*'s Health and Beauty Expert" asked women readers, "Are You Too Fat?"[111] The weekly's advertisements entrenched these old-fashioned views. Complexion creams promised to help women "win his admiration."[112] Foschini, a Cape Town store, declared, "Working Girls: Sunny Days are ahead and so we *must* have a new outfit."[113] Radford reinforced these attitudes. She signed her "Topical" column "Journeyman," printed letters to the editor that began "Dear Sir," and during her political career in the 1940s strove to ingratiate herself with conservative voters by calling herself Betty Sacks.[114]

The *Guardian*'s policy towards racial questions also diverged from revolutionary thought. The weekly was written by and for white readers.[115] The *Guardian* differed from the other national commercial newspapers who were not interested in what was happening in African, Indian, and coloured townships; a visit to an abattoir might have actually made a *Cape Times* reader's flesh crawl. However, the *Guardian*'s audience were white, educated readers who inhabited a world far removed from the majority of South Africans—at the time only 13 percent of the African adult population were literate, and even fewer were middle or upper class.[116] Radford ran prolix, meandering essays with laborious language and unwieldy argot. Letters to the editor began with drawing-room phrases: "I should like to say how terribly disappointed I was. . . ."[117] The *Guardian*'s advertisements flogged goods that were beyond the means of most blacks: expensive brandy, imported shirts, tailored suits, fancy furniture, Swiss watches, and British clocks. M. K. Bazaars, a Cape

Town store, regular advertised, in full-page glory, "a Turkish smoke of exceptional quality."[118] An illustrative 1937 headline read "South Africans Should Drink More Wine, No Need For Inferiority Complex—It is a national duty to drink South African wines."[119] One early seller of the *Guardian*, Jean Bernadt, remembered how she would put on "hats and gloves" before going out to sell the newspaper, in order "to create the best impression."[120] A passionate *Guardian* reader wrote to say, "I would rather do without food than without the *Guardian*," but such a statement could not apply to the millions of South Africans who were living in abject poverty.[121] In February 1939 the *Guardian* celebrated its second anniversary by holding a "Hobo Dance" at the Hotel Avalon in Gardens. Radford told guests to "Bring Your Cob and Billycan" and wear "careworn cheesecutters, beat bowlers, tattered trilbys and a happy grin. Patches will predominate. Whiskers will be worn." The sit-down dinner and dancing by orchestra until midnight cost seven shillings and sixpence, a fortnight's wages for many workers.[122]

What few articles there were about people who wore tattered trilbys were apparently a few too many. In May 1937 Radford answered readers' complaints in an editorial: "Readers of the *Guardian* have asked us why so much of our space is given over to the grievances of the Native and Coloured peoples. We have been told that it is tiring to read of the hardships which affect them. We do so of set purpose. Until we can persuade our White readers that their welfare is bound up with that of the Natives and Coloureds we shall not see any social advance in South Africa. . . . We shall continue to write of the Natives and Coloured people, for in that way we shall help ourselves."[123] In the first issue of the *Guardian*, Radford was even blunter: "The native needs to be treated decently and given some elementary rights, if only for the sake of preserving the white race in South Africa from all becoming poor whites."[124] Trade unions, the weekly's bread and butter, did not give the *Guardian* reason to change its views. Almost all of the unions the weekly supported were white-only unions, where racial issues were defined as problems between English and Afrikaans-speaking whites. Intermingling between races was frowned upon, especially the most serious flashpoint, miscegenation. In 1939 Radford wrote that "nobody but a fool is arguing for intermarriage."[125] With an eye to its reputation, Radford delineated the *Guardian*'s racial policy most clearly in a "What We Think" essay published in the newspaper's fifty-first issue:

> History is with us when we assert that continued contact with the European mode of life will force the Native to modify his own tribal and primitive

mode of existence. It is quite impossible to believe that we can continue to work our mines, our farms and our factories with Natives and sell the products to them without destroying their way of living. If this is so—and nobody can deny it—then the only rational thing for us is to anticipate this and make the transition easier. In other words we must *do* what our statesmen *say* they are doing, that is—act as guardians to people who are emerging from one level of civilisation to another. Guardianship does not necessarily mean repression, nor does it necessarily call for "blood and force." It does demand a sense of responsibility on the part of the more advanced European race.[126]

Africans, not surprisingly, felt little allegiance to such a newspaper, and African leaders, even communists like Moses Kotane, brushed away any suggestion that the *Guardian* spoke for the African community. In 1940 Kotane wrote that "Africans have no newspaper which today serves their interests, a newspaper which teaches them the value of organisation, unity, and struggle for the betterment of their political, economic and social conditions."[127] It would be another decade before the heavy coat of paternalism dropped away and Africans took the *Guardian* seriously.

As the newspaper went through its first years of operation, it struggled to find solid footing. The first move for the *Guardian* was from the back storage room at Stewart's printing house on Long Street. Radford and Pearson worked alone there, amid a few stools and two desks and towering gray stacks of newsprint. They had no telephone, no secretary, no typist, no messenger, and no one to fix tea—as was customary at most South African offices.[128] In April 1937 Stewart moved his printing operations to 17–19 Mechau Street, a short alley down by the shipping docks. The *Guardian* moved with Stewart and occupied a ground-floor office. Radford immediately hired secretaries, typists, and an African office "boy."[129]

Still, the newspaper lacked the excellence a national newspaper would take for granted. Typographical errors often crept into its pages. It sometimes printed advertisements upside down. The size of the weekly haphazardly fluctuated between four and sixteen pages; the four issues of July 1939, for example, appeared in three different lengths. Regular columns skipped around from week to week. Articles appeared in Afrikaans.[130] For a while in 1937, the *Guardian* even had a "Stop Press" section on the editorial page that followed the custom of most daily newspapers by running late-breaking news. Radford prided herself on producing an eye-pleasing layout, with sub-headlines; callouts; captions above some paragraphs within articles; alternatively bold, regular, and capitalized type; and the judicious use of photographs, cartoons, and sketches. Once, in "Topical," Radford hinted at her interest in a good-looking broadsheet when she criticized a new Labour Party journal, *Forum*: "It's unattractive to the eye. . . . Its whole effect is tedious. The print is not good and most of the articles look as though they're half-ashamed of themselves. Can't we have bigger, bolder headlines, more sub-heads, bolder type?"[131] Despite her efforts, the weekly sometimes looked like a messy jumble, and *Guardian* readers often saw tiny space fillers—"Advertise in the *Guardian*"—an indication of a poorly designed newspaper.

Readers did not seem to mind. Circulation inched upwards each week. After the initial run of 1,000 for the first issue, circulation rose steadily to 2,000 by the end of the year. Thanks to "The Munich Swindle," circulation doubled to 4,000 by the end of 1938.[132] In 1939 circulation doubled again, to 8,000 copies per week. Not overly impressive, the figures revealed a growing base of readers. "From the first, the *Guardian* was a strong baby," Radford later remembered, "and once it started it didn't mean to stop."[133] Advertising revenue was a requisite part of the *Guardian*'s finances in the 1930s. On average there were twenty-five advertisements in each issue. Articles appeared on the front page, but still much of it was advertisements.[134]

Distribution of the newspaper, under the control of Carina Pearson, depended upon a variety of methods. Open-air bookstalls that lined the railway stations sold the *Guardian*, as did ordinary shops, and a good indication of the *Guardian*'s rate of growth was its developing list of agents or business proprietors who agreed to sell the weekly at their stores. In May 1937 Pearson listed twenty-seven agents in Cape Town.[135] In June there were thirty-five; in August, forty-one; in December, forty-six. In January 1938 the *Guardian* had fifty-two agents in Cape Town and fifteen in the suburbs; by June it had sixty-seven agents in twenty-seven places, including three shops in Johannesburg, two in Springs, and one each in Durban, East London, and Wellington. By October 1938 the *Guardian* had seventy-three agents.

If a reader did not wish to go out and buy a copy each week from their local pharmacist or hairdresser, they could take out a subscription. For five shillings a year—eight pennies more than a year's worth of street-bought *Guardians*—a subscriber had the pleasure of receiving his issue in his mail box. Pearson often asked readers to "get friends to subscribe" and "cure your apathetic or reactionary friends by giving them a year's paid subscription," adding that "a specimen copy will be dispatched" to potential subscribers.[136]

Away from the major South African cities, a *Guardian* subscription was almost a talisman. In the late thirties, Fred Carneson worked in the post office in the tiny Natal coast hamlet of Port Shepstone (he had joined the Communist Party at age sixteen and, because the post office forbade its workers to get involved in politics, he had earned a transfer to Port Shepstone). Not knowing anybody in the village, Carneson lived a lonely life, working alone in the obscure post office and eating his meals and sleeping at a mostly empty boarding house. One day at work, he noticed that the local doctor was a subscriber to the *Guardian*. Carneson introduced himself and soon was eating dinner each night with the doctor and his family. "It was a real pleasure to meet a fellow in spirit," Carneson said. "What I liked about him, what drew me to him was that there weren't that many Afrikaners in those days who were progressive."[137]

There was no organized system of individual sales, but some activists, taking the initiative, began to hawk copies door-to-door or at Grand Parade meetings, or would badger proprietors to become *Guardian* agents. "I assumed responsibility for delivering the *Guardian*," Jean Bernadt recalled. "I had a round which started in Long Street, and we actually sought outlets. . . . I used to go in my husband's car and they gave me a run which used to go up Kloof Street and it was a regular weekly thing. Anyway Cjivsy [Magalivic, a Yugoslav airman] and I used to take a pile of the *Guardian* and walk all over the Gardens, a penny at a time and sell it. Then we used to go down to Sir Lowry Road. If somebody gave us tuppence [two pennies], we used to think: 'Oh, a sympathizer.'"[138] Bernadt was unusual, for a filler in 1938 spoke of the weekly's usual method of circulation: "Pass it on!—When you have finished your *Guardian*, give the other chap a chance! Pass it on to your next-door neighbor or leave it on the bus or train."[139]

Enticing new readers was the purpose of *Guardian* pamphlets. In September 1939 Radford issued a two-penny pamphlet called "Time to Wake Up Mister." Concerned with Nazi encroachments in South-West Africa, it contained twelve Vic Clapham front-page cartoons and the slogan "The *Guardian* will unblinker the public."[140] Three months later she collected more of Clapham's cartoons, added commentary from Vigilator, and produced a sixteen-page pamphlet, "Pins and Needles: A Pictorial Tribute to Justice, Tolerance and Benevolence of the Existing Scheme of Things."[141]

Despite being a political newspaper, the *Guardian* cultivated a relaxed side. A poem or short story appeared almost each week. An interview with Ernest Hemingway ran in 1939.[142] Humorous columns, like "This Week's

Nasty Thoughts" or "Bunk and Debunk—This Week's Worst Nonsense," kept things lively with sarcastic commentary on local and international news.[143] The most tempting aspect of the weekly, for many readers, was its horse-racing tips. In 1937 the *Guardian* hired a shrewd handicapper for the Cape Town races at Kenilworth and Milnerton. Although nameless—"our tipster is one of those shy people who like to benefit humanity anonymously"—people familiar with the *Guardian* guessed that it could be Sam Kahn.[144] Whoever he was, he was considered the best in Cape Town, and many times he correctly picked all the races.[145] A Salt River trade unionist and bookmaker complained that "The *Guardian*'s no good to me. It's too hot on the winners."[146]

Holding back the *Guardian* more than anything else was that it was a Cape Town newspaper. In June 1937, after seventeen issues, Radford dropped the *Cape* from the title—the first and last voluntary name change the weekly would undergo. Despite the change, the *Guardian* focused predominantly on Cape Town news. Its advertisements were for Cape Town stores, its racing tips were for Cape Town tracks, and its film listings were for Cape Town cinemas. Of the seventy-three agents selling the *Guardian* at the end of 1938, only eight were outside Cape Town. "We very much felt it was a Cape Town newspaper," recalled Rusty Bernstein, a Communist Party leader in Johannesburg. "We weren't deeply connected to the paper. It was on the other hand the only English-language paper expressing our point-of-view. I don't think anyone in Johannesburg felt any responsibility for what was going into it or its editorial content. We had no input at all. It was purely a Cape Town affair. We operated back then as separate countries."

At first the weekly passively waited for news, depending on a letter to the editor or a report from a Capetonian who had visited another region of the country.[147] In August 1937 Radford hired the *Guardian*'s first Johannesburg correspondent, a Quaker Englishman named Charles Fox. In his column "News of the Week from Johannesburg," Fox covered Labour Party conferences, the Sunday-night fights at the Johannesburg City Hall steps and local Left Book Club affairs.[148] In December, Simon Bass joined Fox in the Transvaal. Based in the West Rand town of Krugersdorp, Bass filed regular reports on the 1938 elections and trade-union activities.[149] Using the *Guardian*'s trade-union connections, Radford solicited news from Johannesburg union leaders like Garment Workers' Union chief Solly Sachs, SAT&LC member E. J. Burford, and T. C. Robertson, a Labour Party leader and editor of its weekly *Forward*.[150] George Findlay, another trade union leader, began to dispatch articles from Pretoria.[151]

Even with the trickle of news, the provincialism that washed over the early *Guardian* did not flow away so easily. In Johannesburg only three stores carried the weekly: the People's Bookshop in the Trades Hall building on Kerk Street, Salmon's Bookshop on Eloff Street, and Vanguard Books, run by Trotskyist (and well-known nudist) Fanny Klenerman. Habitués of the Commissioner Street cafés and penny drinkshops sometimes left their copies of the *Guardian* on their tables.[152] Issy Diamond, a one-man discussion group, always had a stack of *Guardians* in the corner of his barbershop on Commissioner Street. Diamond's was the informal heart of alternative politics for the city. Posters of Marx, Lenin, and Stalin adorned the wall, and Diamond's mouth flew as fast as his scissors as he talked incessantly about politics.[153]

Some people took steps to lift the newspaper bundles beyond the café tables and hair-speckled floors. Jean Bernadt described how she helped bring the weekly to the Transvaal by encouraging selling at meetings: "I went to Johannesburg in 1938 and nobody there would sell the *Guardian*. It was in the People's Bookshop and it used to lie there and people used to sometimes buy it there. And I said, 'What the hell, we always take the *Guardian* to meetings.' All of a sudden I became a *Guardian* seller, and I used to take the *Guardian* to meetings. And again, if somebody gave me sixpence, I thought what a wonderful supporter."[154] Some Johannesburg sympathizers followed Bernadt's example and began to take the newspaper to the Sunday-evening meetings at the City Hall steps. One person who purchased a copy was Arnold Selby, a young messenger at an automobile workshop and Labour Party member.

> At the time our shop steward, a fellow named Smithy and the Taylor brothers would talk a lot to me and tell me that Hitler was out to destroy the trade unions and that he was either killing trade union members or putting them in jail. My father, a mine worker, was of like mind. Smithy and the Taylor brothers suggested that I should join them in demonstrations in Johannesburg city centre to protest against Hitler, the civil war in Spain, defend the trade unions and to "give the Nazis hell." Often such demonstrations ended with violence in which the Blackshirts and the Greyshirts were particularly violent. If they could succeed in isolating you from your group, then you were in for a tough time and probably a long stay in hospital. At work on Mondays we would tell the others how we gave the Nazis "a real what for." On the quiet, I believe that Smithy and the Taylor brothers enjoyed a good punch up, especially when it came to the Nazis. It was at such a demonstration that I bought the *Guardian*, my first

copy. Stepwise I got involved, in a small way, in the activities of the anti-fascist league. I became a regular buyer of the *Guardian*. At that time my horizons and my knowledge were cramped and burdened with semi-literacy. The *Guardian* was my first serious regular reading matter. From it I learned a lot world-wise and language-wise. For this I will always be indebted to the *Guardian*.

On Friday, 1 September 1939, Hitler's tanks rolled across the border of Poland. On the same day, the *Guardian* made its weekly appearance on the streets of Cape Town. On the front page was a Clapham cartoon about a fish—the "World"—about to eat a fishing hook with "Russian Treachery" as the bait, and "'Firm Stand' Twaddle" and the "War Scare" as the fishing line. As an embarrassed *Guardian* learned that day, it was no twaddle or scare. The Second World War had begun.

Whether to support the Allies or protest against the "imperialist war" became a contentious issue across South Africa. In the House of Assembly, the pro-Germany prime minister, J. W. Hertzog, lost a vote to remain neutral (80 to 67), allowing Boer War and First World War hero Field Marshal Jan Christiaan Smuts to return to power in a pro-Britain, pro-war government. The African National Congress approved the declaration of war at its annual conference in December. The Transvaal and Natal Indian Congresses split, with pro-war conservatives gaining control. The South African Trades & Labour Council voted 30 to 23 to support the war.[155] Under Victor Gollancz's direction, the Left Book Club, the distant mother of the *Guardian*, supported the war; in protest, the South African branch seceded from the LBC and changed its name to the Left Club.

For communists around the world, it was a confusing time. They had been warning everyone for years about Hitler, so they were particularly stunned by the Nazi-Soviet Pact, the non-aggression treaty that ministers Ribbentrop and Molotov signed on 23 August, barely a week before the German invasion of Poland.

The Comintern in Moscow ordered communist parties around the world to fall into the anti-war line. It was not easy. The anti-war posture required a fair amount of ideological gymnastics. To be anti-war meant to be against workers killing each other, against violence, against big business profiting from the whole affair; but it also meant being on the same side as the Nazis and those knuckle-dusting Blackshirts with whom so many battles had been fought. Such an unfortunate coincidence strained many activists' imaginations.

In London, the British Communist Party did not officially come out against the war until 3 October. In South Africa, Transvaalers in the Party especially wanted to support the war, but, on 4 September, after a long weekend of debate, the Communist Party of South Africa declared itself in favor of a policy of neutrality.[156] At least one person, Hyman Basner, publicly dropped out of the Party over the decision.

The *Guardian* vacillated. On 8 September, instead of obediently following the Party's new anti-war line, the newspaper tried to avoid the whole issue. The "Health and Beauty Expert" discussed test-tube babies, and Radford discussed the upcoming *Guardian* film screening. Harold Baldry's Vigilator examined the war issue only at the end of his column: "It must be carefully and patiently explained to the masses who are opposed to participation in the war that an outright adoption of the 'neutrality' standpoint strengthens the capitalist group." The next week, the *Guardian* still had not made up its mind. "Confusion exists," Radford admitted.

A week later, Vigilator rolled out the weekly's tentative war policy: "At present Chamberlain's line of action can be used for progressive ends, and the obvious duty of progressive people is to support the war for as long as that position lasts—that is until Hitlerism is destroyed. The important thing is that their support must be critical. Those who have betrayed us so often must not be blindly trusted, but watched at every stage."[157]

Amazingly, this left-wing newspaper put forth a pro-war position when most South African communists, socialists and Trotskyists had come out against the war. The stance was simply untenable. Johnny Gomas voiced a typical sentiment explaining his anti-war view: "I am satisfied with the statement of the famous English scientist Professor J.B.S. Haldane, that he would rather be a Jew in Hitler's Berlin than a native in Johannesburg. . . . How can we be interested in fighting Nazism thousands of miles away, while in reality we have a similar monster devouring us here daily?"[158] Still, the weekly's readership was staunchly, if awkwardly, anti-war, and the *Guardian* had little choice but to eventually join them.

On 13 October, after seven issues, the *Guardian* finally announced its opposition. The newspaper "stood for a policy of replacing the governments of Britain and France by People's Governments ready to co-operate with the Soviet Union either in forcing peace upon Hitler or by annihilating him on two fronts if he refused."[159] It had been a punishingly difficult interregnum, and the anti-war stance was almost indigestible, but the *Guardian* had placed itself in the right position to prosper in the 1940s.[160]

CHAPTER TWO

Forty Thousand No Less

The War Years, 1939–1945

It was the first day of 1939. Johannesburg's usual summer torpor, accentuated by New Year's Day grogginess, was evident in a dusty, stifling room in the Trades Hall on Kerk Street. The Communist Party was finishing its four-day national conference. Everything was in tatters. The Party newspaper, the *South African Worker* (*Umsebenzi*), had closed nine months before after twenty-three years of publication. Membership numbered under three hundred; only thirteen delegates came to the Trades Hall, making it more of a long dinner party than a national conference.[1] The delegates had spent much of the past three days discussing the recent Voortrekker celebrations (it was the centennial of the Great Trek) that had roused fascism among Afrikaners.

On the final day, a crucial motion lay unresolved. Moses Kotane proposed switching the head office to Cape Town. The Transvaalers angrily opposed the proposition. One Johannesburg official, Edwin Mofutsanyana, the Party's general secretary, offered a different solution: dividing the Party into African and non-African sections, effectively imposing an internal version of segregation. Mofutsanyana's wife, Josie Mpana, spoke against the idea, as did the Capetonians, and Kotane even threatened to walk out of the Party. As a summer-afternoon thunderstorm began to crackle in the sky, Kotane brought his motion to a vote. It could not have been closer. Six voted in favor, five against, and two abstained. The Capetonian coup d'état complete, the delegates elected a new political bureau, the elite committee that directed the Party on a daily basis. Bill Andrews was made chairman. Moses Kotane replaced Mofutsanyana in the highest office of general-secretary, and Cissie Gool, Sam Kahn, Ray Alexander, and Jack Simons formed what was now called the Central Executive Committee. The following week, the Party signed a lease at 73 Plein Street, the same street where it was founded eighteen years earlier.[2]

The decision to shift headquarters had an immediate impact on Cape Town's independent newspaper. In Paris in 1901, a young Vladimir Lenin wrote an essay, "Where to Begin," in which he outlined the role a newspaper can play in building a political party. "A newspaper is not only a collective propagandist and a collective agitator, it is also a collective organiser," Lenin wrote. "This work will train and bring into the foreground not only the most skillful propagandists, but the most capable organisers, the most talented political party leaders capable, at the right moment, of releasing the slogan for the decisive struggle and taking the lead in that struggle."[3] The Party needed a newspaper to make the headquarters shift successful, and the *Guardian*, with its left-leaning sensibilities, morphed into a Party organ.

The Party took over the weekly's distribution network. Selling the *Guardian* became a mandatory duty for Cape Town members. The Central Executive Committee assigned Party members to particular neighborhoods. On Fridays, Saturdays and Sundays, communists met at the newspaper's offices, collected a bundle or two of *Guardians*, and went hawking. The Party was very public in its enthusiasm for selling the *Guardian*. In July 1939 the Cape Town branch issued a cyclostyled leaflet called "The Party Organiser" that read, "The *Guardian* reports that sales are going up, having risen by nearly 3,000 since March. The paper is doing excellent work in counteracting the poisonous propaganda of the fascist and Nationalist press and other capitalist news agencies. Some comrades are engaged in pushing up the sales, and all comrades are urged to help in every way possible those comrades who have made themselves responsible for getting out the *Guardian* regularly every Friday."[4] The Party called for support of the newspaper at its national conference every year, and on the back cover of its bimonthly journal, *Freedom*, proclaimed, "Socialism must come! Read the *Guardian*, a people's paper for the people."[5] In May 1944 the "Cape Party Organiser," after noting that members were "selling the *Guardian* at factories and from door to door (house to house selling means that we talk to our people individually)," sponsored a contest in which readers contributed the last line of a "polimerick":

The Guardian *speaks for the toilers*
Let's guard it in turn from the spoilers
Who're out to smash our press
Forty thousand no less. . . . [6]

Going from door to door, house to house, and factory to factory profoundly influenced the sellers. They got out of the stuffy rooms where doctrine and theory led to interminable discussions. They met people and learned about individual problems and specific issues. They took concepts and translated them into plain English. Denis Goldberg went often with his parents to textile factories in Salt River and Woodstock to sell the *Guardian.* "We used to go every Friday," Goldberg recalled, "and stand at the gates at the end of the day and sell to the workers. One of the owners—it was payday—always put pennies in their pay packets so they could buy a *Guardian.* And you had to explain what was in the paper, why they should buy it. Selling the *Guardian* was my first class of political education. This is where I learned my politics. This is where I understood what I had been living through."

A *Guardian* seller quickly discovered that being a member of an organization meant more than attending a few meetings. "I am sure there were young left-wingers all over the world who sold these kinds of papers," remembered Albie Sachs, a young activist in the 1950s, "papers that relied very much on the enthusiasm and conviction and willingness of its sellers. I can recall every Saturday afternoon from about 1951 selling the *Guardian.* It was actually quite valuable for me and a major part of my education. It took me to areas I never went. I passed through, but didn't know people from those areas, Schotcheskloof, the Bo-Kaap. I would see people like Moses Kotane and H. A. Naidoo, but the paper took me there every week." For many white sellers, the *Guardian* provided the first opportunity to meet and get to know non-whites, ending the segregated isolation that was so characteristic of South Africa.

Fred Carneson, the lonely Port Shepstone postman, learned that speed was often a casualty when selling the weekly. After moving to Cape Town in 1944, he sold the *Guardian* on a regular beat in the poor, working-class neighborhood of Woodstock. "I'd knock," he said,

and they'd open the door. I'd walk through to the kitchen. There would be my money on the mantle-shelf there. I'd take my money and we'd sit down, maybe have a cup of tea or something and talk. And then you'd pick up all kinds of stories from the people themselves. . . . They'd raise personal problems with you and you'd try and sort them out because the next week you know you're going to go back there again. . . . That used to happen a lot to our sellers. We used to take up the personal problems to the people and win their confidence and respect that way.[7]

Communists from all races benefited from selling the newspaper. In 1941 Harry Gwala was a young university student in Pietermaritzburg when he started reading the *Guardian*. "I came into the Communist Party via the *Guardian*," he said. "It was when I read the *Guardian* that I became politically aware. I then started selling the paper. In those days we had to increase sales. It was our duty. We went in teams to factories. Many of the buyers were from the Indian community. It was very popular. I learned how to talk politics and I learned how to be politically active."

Gerson Ginsburg was the top *Guardian* seller in Cape Town in the 1940s. A textile worker, Ginsburg was a keen supporter of the local Garment Workers' Union and sold the newspaper in District Six.[8] By 1944 his weekly turnover reached twenty-three dozen, or almost three hundred copies.[9] An infamous version of Ginsburg was a Jewish man with an unruly mop of hair and a ready laugh named Wolfie Kodesh. Raised in the slums of Woodstock, Kodesh knew first-hand the issues affecting most Capetonians.[10] A member of the Communist Party since Moses Kotane hired his sister as a secretary in 1939, Kodesh was the quintessential rank-and-file man. He rarely held committee positions or spoke at public meetings. Instead, he ran errands, distributed leaflets, turned the handle of the duplicating machine and sold the *Guardian*. He relished his weekly route through the Bo-Kaap, the old Malay quarter huddled below Signal Hill. After seeing the Bo-Kaap's problem with rats, he was able to persuade the city's health department to provide rubbish bins and to fumigate the quarter's houses. "And this opened their eyes, you see, because they could see, 'Now daardie *Guardian* ou, hy kom hier,' you know, we've got a better life," remembered Kodesh. "They knew me as 'The *Guardian*.' That's what they called me: 'Hier kom die *Guardian*.' One Friday evening I was coming into Chiapinni Street, and they had a lot of gangs and there was a hell of a fight going on. . . . As I came round the corner I saw this, and what to do now? And you know, there were shouts and I heard them saying, 'Laat die *Guardian* deur.' They practically stopped fighting until I got through."

While gang fights were unusual for a weekly route, *Guardian* sellers regularly discovered that people bought the newspaper for decidedly apolitical reasons. Some wrapped their fish, especially during snoek season, in the newspaper. Others wanted to check the horse-racing tips. Above all, many noticed that black buyers felt obligated to purchase a copy from a white seller. It was an act of charity, a way to end the embarrassment cheaply—for just a penny, the white person would leave. Amy Thornton started selling the *Guardian* in the late 1940s while a student at the University of Cape Town. "From the days when the Party was legal, it was always important to sell the newspaper," she said.

> We used to meet on Saturday afternoons, up in the Bo-Kaap, up in this part of town [Woodstock], and go door-to-door and sell. Knock on the door, a child would usually open, you know. This was District Six, you see. And a little child would run into the passage and stare at you. You were on your own and you were white. They'd shout, "Ma. Mensa!" And they'd continue standing and staring at you. Then the adult would come and you'd say, "Would you like to buy the *Guardian*?"
>
> Quite often people bought. I suspect some bought because they didn't have the guts to say no to a white woman. The people who always took a few, you know, every corner had what was called the bobby shop. A sort of Muslim or Indian shop, little grocery shop on the corner. Not takeaways. They'd sell little packets of sugar, tea, coffee, groceries, sweets, cool drinks. The days of selling cooked food didn't exist then. They'd always take a few *Guardian*s. One doesn't know whether they'd sell them or thrown them away. But, in their own way, they were fairly supportive.[11]

During the 1940s, especially after the Soviet Union joined the Allies, the Communist Party almost resembled a mass organization. Membership quadrupled in three years, reaching fifteen hundred in early 1944, and many more fellow travelers attended open-air rallies at Cape Town's Grand Parade, on the steps of the Johannesburg City Hall or in Durban's Red Square.[12] But keeping these new members was not that easy. Carneson recalled that "one of the problems which faced us continuously was how to retain membership, how to politicize your members, how to give them theoretical understanding. . . . A big meeting on the Parade, hundreds used to come forward and sign the application form. They'd take the first step and now you had to try and incorporate them in the Party."[13] It was the job of the *Guardian* to turn recruits into bonafide members.[14]

The effect of the Party's move to Cape Town on the weekly was instantaneous. Circulation, which had plateaued after the Munich Swindle spurt, rose unusually briskly in 1939, going from 4,000 at New Year's to 5,500 in April, 6,000 in May, 7,000 in July, and 8,000 by the end of the year.[15]

A nuanced relationship developed. Officially, the Party did not control the *Guardian*, a legal fact that was crucial in the newspaper's survival when the apartheid regime banned the Communist Party in 1950. However, the *Guardian* was a Party newspaper, not in letter, but in spirit. According to Jack Simons, the *Guardian*'s editorial writer, the debate over the weekly's status came up right after the 1939 headquarters shift: "The PB discussed it. Harry Snitcher quite frequently pressed for more tight control, but the general feeling of the membership was that this shouldn't be done, that we wouldn't gain anything by it. As long as the *Guardian* was prepared to publish the Central Committee's resolutions, give publicity to our activities, that was enough, and we were satisfied that on the general line it was in keeping with our policy."[16] Instead of co-opting the newspaper, the Party simply spread like a river delta around the *Guardian* island. "The Central Committee would perhaps discuss from time to time what it would like to see in the paper," said Brian Bunting, Radford's successor as editor of the *Guardian*. "Later on, for instance, when I was elected to the Central Committee, whatever was being discussed and debated would be reflected in the columns of the paper. . . . I suppose that explains quite a lot about the development of the paper, because the connections between the two were very considerable."[17]

Like a fairy godmother, the Party watched over the newspaper and waved a magic wand anytime the weekly got into trouble. This was most apparent in staff issues. The Party operated as the *Guardian*'s human-resources department, shuffling staff from city to city, filling in gaps and hiring new journalists. Almost all the editorial employees in the 1940s and 1950s came to the weekly via the Party. Some later even scoffed at the idea of a formal interview process, of submitting curriculum vitae and letters of reference, or negotiating salary and benefits. Instead, the Party leadership asked Party members to take on the job.

Because of Party discipline, invariably they went; invariably they were accepted on the staff without a murmur. "We didn't regard it as the property of the Communist Party," said Fred Carneson, who joined the newspaper in the late 1940s, "although, as communists working on a progressive paper like that, we felt we were responsible to the Party for what we were doing on a paper of that nature. If at any time there was a crisis at the paper, on the editorial board, and we had to look around for people willing to work on the paper, then the Party would step in and look around for somebody and persuade some Party member to take on the job, leave what he was doing and take it on."[18]

In May 1941 the Party further strengthened its connection to the editorial staff. That month, Betty Radford, George Sacks, Harold Baldry and Carina Pearson filled out an application form, paid monthly dues of one shilling, and received a small, red membership card.[19] The private hobby-horse went public. Rife with ramifications, Communist Party membership for the *Guardian* quartet was the end, according to Ray and Jack Simons, of "a long apprenticeship in radical politics."[20]

Each of them flew eagerly into the world of the Communist Party. Baldry, the *Guardian*'s international-news columnist, spoke at Party meetings, gave lectures at various Party forums, and regularly contributed articles to *Freedom*.[21] Pearson, the circulation manager, joined the CP's Cape Town district committee and was elected chair of the Cape Town branch of the Friends of the Soviet Union, an aid organization unofficially run by the Party.[22] The Baldry's Vredehoek home, high on the slopes of Table Mountain, was an informal meeting place for the Party. One wartime acquaintance from Rhodesia, a young woman named Doris Lessing, thought of the Baldrys as "bastions of the local Communist Party" whose home "was positively the area office for every kind of progressive activity."[23]

George Sacks developed into one of the leading communist intellectuals. He wrote lengthy Party pamphlets, including "Let's Talk about Russia" (1942) and "Communism for South Africa" (1942).[24] He served as secretary for the Cape Town branch of the FSU, and as editor of the Party journal *Freedom*. He frequently penned long pieces in the *Guardian* about communism, edited a column titled "The Communists Answer Your Questions," and for six straight months in 1943 authored a weekly series of articles entitled "What Do You Know about Communism?"[25] Sacks unsuccessfully ran for Parliament in the 1943 general election, seeking the Salt River seat for the Party-linked Independent Labour Party. Polling a paltry 851 votes (11.4 percent of the votes cast), the surgeon was decisively beaten.[26] At the Party's annual national conference in January 1945, Sacks was elected to the Central Committee, a seventeen-person board that oversaw the Party's operations.[27]

Betty Radford became one of the principal political figures in Cape Town. Her stature was subtly evident in the internee issue. In 1940 Smuts herded thousands of anti-war protesters, mostly fascists in the Oxwagon Sentinel, into internment camps. By a twist of political fate, a tiny group of left-wing protesters had the unfortunate fate to join them. Fanny Klenerman, the Vanguard Books owner, tried to bring their situation to the nation's attention. She wrote to Radford in March 1941 to ask for her support. Radford replied five days later after holding a meeting with Donald Molteno, one of the three Native Representatives in the House of Assembly in Parliament, and Party leader

Jack Simons.[28] Calling for and holding a meeting with such major figures on such short notice—probably at UCT where both men were law professors—implied that Radford was a potent force in South African radical politics.

Radford soon was not only involved in informal discussions, but running organizations. Days after joining the Party, Radford was elected to the Party's Cape Town District Committee, and she joined the editorial board of *Inkululeko,* the Party's monthly newspaper.[29] She developed into a respected soapbox orator at the weekly Party gathering on the Grand Parade.[30] One arena for work was the Springbok Legion, a servicemen's group founded by the Party. Radford directed the Cape Town branch of the Legion's Home Front League.[31]

In 1943 the Party asked Radford to stand for the Cape Town city-council election for the eighth-ward seat of Woodstock. She accepted and, along with the young lawyer Sam Kahn, won the election under the Communist Party banner. Radford, calling herself Mrs. Betty Sacks, polled 920 votes, beating D. F. Nelson by 329 votes.[32] She immediately sought and won the chair of the scholarships committee, the first time a new councilor had been elected to chair a committee.[33] Another first was when Radford opened the council's first ward bureau to serve her new constituents. The office at 5 Queen's Road, Woodstock, immediately became a hive of activity. Radford started a vegetable club, and every Friday, members would meet at Queen's Road to collect produce the club bought in bulk at cheaper prices.[34] In a few months, the local Party branch in Woodstock took over the running of the Queen's Road office, but council work still took a good deal of Radford's time, and often an "unavoidable absence" or "pressures on . . . editor's time" caused the omission of "Topical" in the *Guardian.*[35]

The work for the Party inspired Radford. After a 1944 visit to Johannesburg's northern white suburbs and the southwestern African townships, Radford wrote that "my blood still boils at too low a temperature to accept these contrasts."[36] In South Africa's Supreme Court later that year, contesting a libel suit, Radford answered a question concerning her Party membership: "Yes and I am proud to say so." The justice smiled and told her, "The comment is unnecessary."[37]

The *Guardian* quartet expanded into a symphonic orchestra, as substantive political and editorial support came from all levels of the Communist Party hierarchy. Bill Andrews officially rejoined the Party on May Day 1938 and assumed the national chairmanship in January 1939. He took on the *Guardian* as one of his top priorities, and a close and enduring friendship developed between Andrews and Betty Radford. As the former editor of the

Party's first newspaper, the *International*, Andrews brimmed with advice on running a radical newspaper. Most afternoons, Andrews visited the *Guardian* offices, not the least because Radford often had the pleasure of giving the carless Andrews a ride to his small home in Camp's Bay, a fifteen-minute drive south of town. He regularly had Sunday dinner with her and George Sacks.[38] He wrote articles for the *Guardian* at least once a month—some as Party chairman, others as a union leader—and when Jack Simons was away, Andrews often wrote a "guest editorial."[39] In March 1943 Andrews officially inherited the mantle of "industrial editor" at the newspaper, supplying a sober, detailed update each week on trade-union news.[40] Andrews became a *Guardian* institution, the gray-haired father figure whose (as Radford said) "wise and willing counsel contribut[ed] immeasurably" to the success of the newspaper.[41]

Equally valuable were the rest of the Party hierarchy. The Party's general-secretary, Moses Kotane, an African from the western Transvaal who had been a liberation leader since the 1920s, often supplied articles or granted interviews.[42] Jack Simons, now chair of African Law at the University of Cape Town, continued to write the *Guardian*'s editorials and advised Radford on political matters. His wife, Ray Alexander, contributed dozens of trade-union articles and, as she remembered, developed a weekly custom with Radford. On Tuesdays, after Radford put the newspaper to bed, she drove Alexander (who until 1950 did not own a car) out to outlying districts and farms to organize workers.[43] Harry Snitcher, the district chairman for most of the 1940s, and Sam Kahn, by now a leading South African politician, were the *Guardian*'s legal advisors and represented the *Guardian* in court.[44] Rhoda Pepys, a local artist, drew dozens of front-page portraits and lino-cut illustrations for the weekly during the war under the pseudonym "Pep."[45] Cape trade unionists Nancy Dick, Abe Jacobs, and Abe Scholtz all wrote occasional pieces.[46] A devoted *Guardian* supporter was Rex Close. The district secretary for the Party in the Cape, and son of the South African ambassador to the United States, Close contributed over a dozen poems to the *Guardian*, including "Ghost of Lenin."[47]

Jack Cope was a central figure at the *Guardian* during the war. A handsome and erudite man, Cope exuded confidence. He had worked both as a farmer in Natal and as a cub reporter on Fleet Street in London (his brother John was a correspondent for the Manchester *Guardian*). He lived with his wife (and first cousin) Lesley de Villiers in a beautiful bungalow at Clifton's First Beach.[48] Besides serving as the organizing secretary for Medical Aid for Russia and on the editorial board of *Soviet Life*, a monthly magazine published by Stewart, Cope worked full-time as a staff writer at the *Guardian*. Some of his long historical sketches became the rough drafts of his later novels.[49]

Only two *Guardian* staff members in the 1940s were not members of the Communist Party: Norman Flegg, the weekly's business manager, and Christine Cash, a reporter. Flegg, not content with totting up numbers, wrote numerous articles, book reviews and even a few poems for the weekly during the war.[50] His crowning achievement was a twenty-part series in 1941 entitled "What It Means to You," which ranged from analyzing the results of the 1870 Paris Commune to the causes of the Cape bakery wage dispute.[51] Joining the staff as a full-time reporter in September 1944 was Cash, a *Cape Times* veteran and former colleague of Radford's. Despite her name, Cash was not a fundraiser, but an experienced journalist who did a series of investigative reports on wartime food rationing and even wrote an open letter to the minister of justice, Colin Steyn, about illegal profiteering in the abattoir industry.[52]

A large number of supernumeraries joined the *Guardian* team by means of the *Guardian* leagues. Founded in January 1940 by Carina Pearson as a way to raise funds for the newspaper, the Cape Town league, headed by Harry Snitcher's wife Mussie, held functions of limitless variety: "bio vaudeville evenings," picnics, excursions, *Guardian* birthday parties, Christmas and New Year's Eve parties, bridge parties, song parties, dances, concerts, rumble sales, jumble sales, bazaars, fairs, film shows, marionette shows, exhibitions, pageants, auctions, gramophone evenings and even a two-week "*Guardian* camp" during the December holidays.[53] More than four hundred friends came to the *Guardian*'s annual birthday party in February, and its annual black-tie Christmas dance was a major fundraiser.[54] At the parties, "somebody would make an appeal for funds," *Guardian* stalwart Jean Bernadt recalled.

> There was a marvelous old man, Mr. Rabinowitz, from Paarl, he limped and he was the head of a timber company and he used to give money like a hundred pounds. . . . There was another, a shirt maker . . . he was always on an ego trip, he liked to be recognized as a great supporter of the left. He used to come to these parties. We all supported it, we had functions and rummage sales. We used to go out collecting. You see, the political climate was so favorable to the left, especially after the Soviet Union was attacked by the Nazis. There was a feeling of goodwill. We used to go from door-to-door and

we used to say: 'Look, this is the only paper that is anti-Hitler, anti-Nazism and we must fight for it. This is the only voice.'[55]

Physically, the *Guardian* outgrew its offices at Stewart's printing plant on Mechau Street. In late 1940 Radford moved the newspaper's headquarters to the third floor of the Chames Building at 6 Barrack Street. The Chames Building boasted a long history of radical journalism. The offices of the Social Democratic Federation—the first socialist organization in Africa, founded in 1902—had been there. The SDF subletted to a few trade unions, ran a bar, and operated a printing press—all on two busy floors.[56] Now, almost forty years later, the *Guardian* moved into the same building, though sadly both the printing press and the bar were as forgotten as the SDF. Barrack Street at mid-century was in the heart of downtown Cape Town. Just off the corner of Plein Street, the *Guardian* was four buildings down from Sam Kahn's legal chambers, within earshot of Parliament, a few steps from Communist Party headquarters, and a two-minute walk to the Grand Parade. Like most progressive organizations' offices, the *Guardian*'s would never be called well-appointed. After entering through a low doorway, a visitor passed a row of wooden postboxes on the left and then climbed up a rickety wooden staircase to the third floor. It was a warren of eight rooms: four belonged to the *Guardian*, another was the Cape Town chapter of the Friends of the Soviet Union's, and a dressmaker's shop occupied the last.[57] Each cavernous room had twenty-foot-high ceilings, sunny windows, and its own door to the hallway and to neighboring rooms—except the editor's office in the far back corner, which had only one door but a pleasant view of the Parliament buildings.[58] Ancient furniture (mostly supplied by sympathetic wholesalers), castoff typewriters, old strike posters, pockmarked desks, and the inevitable stacks of back issues gave the offices a comfortable, if threadbare, atmosphere.[59]

Ensconced in its new offices, the *Guardian* revamped and divided itself into four branches, like most commercial newspapers. One room was for the administrative staff, which included three typists, a number of young secretaries, and "Alfred, the office boy"; reporters like Cash occupied a second room; the third was for Pearson and her circulation, advertising, and fundraising staff; and Radford worked from the back office.[60] Despite the new offices, increased staff, and hustle and bustle of visitors, Radford and Pearson still dominated the *Guardian*'s headquarters. When Doris Lessing visited Cape Town near the end of the war, she spent a week volunteering at Barrack Street. She found that Radford and Pearson "were the two eminences of the *Guardian* newspaper." One viewed them from afar, especially if you were "a little visitor from that unimportant, little country Rhodesia. No one took the slightest notice of me. Why should they?"[61]

Mistakes, however, occurred in the whirlwind of growth. In 1943 the Party, trying to make the Central Executive Committee more representative, ordered a few black communists to headquarters in Cape Town.[62] One of them was Harry Allimuthu Naidoo. Born in Durban to a fourteen-year-old Hindu woman, H.A., as he was known to everyone, left school early to work at a clothing factory.[63] One afternoon in 1934 Naidoo and a fellow Indian, George Poonen, were walking down West Street in the heart of Durban's Indian quarter. Eddie Roux, a communist organizer, approached them, sold each a copy of the communist paper *Umsebenzi*, and invited them to come to a meeting that night. The two teenagers came and joined the Party that evening, with Naidoo immediately becoming the district secretary. Both began to organize Natal laborers, especially the thousands of poorly paid sugar-cane workers.[64] By the early 1940s Naidoo advised dozens of trade unions and a top political figure in the Indian community. He started dating a Lithuanian-born Jewish woman named Pauline Podbrey.[65]

When the Party asked Naidoo to join the Central Executive Committee, the couple jumped at the chance to live in liberal Cape Town. Naidoo worked full-time as a *Guardian* reporter and editor, served as the Party's national treasurer, and wrote a best-selling pamphlet, "Communist Party Policy on India."[66] The decision, however, to bring Naidoo down to Cape Town was a poor one in hindsight. Naidoo loved his trade-union work in Natal, which was impossible for him to replicate in Cape Town, with its lack of Indians and color barriers still strong. "To remove him from the Durban scene would be like pulling the linchpin from the movement," Podbrey later wrote. "When he left Durban, HA relinquished his public persona and the adulation of the crowd. I realized he was missing not only the activity but also the acclaim that had been his in Natal. His work on the *Guardian* and his place on the Central [Executive] Committee enhanced his standing in the Party, but he'd lost touch with the people, the masses . . . the transformation didn't suit his temperament."[67] The interracial couple's situation in Cape Town, while better than in Durban, was still painful. Naidoo and Podbrey married, settled in Newlands and had children, but they still could not walk the streets or go to the beach together without courting harassment. When the Buntings left for a holiday, they gave Naidoo and Podbrey their bungalow on the rocky slopes above the four beaches of Clifton. "We could not swim together or lie on the beach, but it was marvelous to spend a fortnight within sight and sound of the ocean."[68] A perpetual sadness shadowed the young couple, perched above the sun-drenched beach, forbidden by their country's great weakness to go down to the water.

As the *Guardian* grew, its locus of power inevitably shifted from the languid, lazy Cape to the eye of the South African political hurricane, Johannesburg.

Uninhabited veld until gold was rediscovered there in 1886, Johannesburg was by the 1930s the largest city in sub-Saharan Africa. Factories, sweatshops, the stock exchange, and 40 Main Street, where the Anglo-American conglomerate was headquartered, drew people like a magnet. Cinemas (called bioscopes) sold motion picture stories from abroad, and emporiums sold everything else. Below it all was the Witwatersrand, the richest and deepest gold-bearing reef in the world. Johannesburg was not a pretty city. Nearly six thousand feet above the sea on the African highveld plateau, the city was at heart still a mining camp: brassy, reckless, sweaty and powered by impossible dreams. Gangsters in low-slung convertibles sped past unsightly mountains of mining slag impregnated with arsenic. At night, stamp batteries crushed ore, and yellow dust blanketed the air. Crisscrossed by muddy, unpaved roads, the city had only one appreciable park, one struggling art museum and one public library—but dozens of brothels and hundreds of taverns.

Surrounding the city was a second city, the ring of townships and squatter camps where most black Johannesburgers lived. Coal smoke hovered like a gray cloud over their homes. Rarely was there sanitation, drainage, running water or electricity. Each morning before dawn, thousands of men and women made an exodus, leaving for work in the white city.

Everyone wanted to go to Jo'burg, to Gauteng, to Egoli, to the city of gold. "All roads," wrote Alan Paton in his 1948 novel *Cry, the Beloved Country*, "lead to Johannesburg."[69]

The roads filled up during the Second World War. Famine, drought and lack of land in the African reserves, coupled with a suspension of influx-control laws and the wartime expansion of industry, produced a massive migration of Africans into the cities—between 1936 and 1946, Johannesburg's official African population doubled to 400,000, while in Cape Town the number ballooned from 15,000 to 60,000.[70] These Africans did not passively accept low wages, spiraling transportation expenses, insulting pass laws and abysmal housing situations. Bus boycotts and factory strikes became common, and Africans raided shopkeepers who hoarded food in violation of ration laws.

Against this backdrop, the African National Congress shook off its cautious ways. The Congress, under the more centralized and dynamic rule of A. B. Xuma, moved towards direct action. It formed a Youth League, guided by young militants like Anton Lembede and Nelson Mandela; helped squatter communities negotiate for land tenancy; organized anti-pass conventions; and endorsed the 1943 Atlantic Charter's support for national self-determination.

It was not just a burgeoning African population and an invigorated ANC that attracted the *Guardian* to Johannesburg. Just like Cape Town, a revitalizing local Communist Party harnessed the weekly. The Party before the war was wary of newcomers and bereft of old members. In 1938 when Rowley Arenstein, a budding lawyer and communist, moved to Johannesburg and attempted to join the Party, it took him six months to find it.[71] As soon as he got his membership card, Arenstein started to use the *Guardian* as a tool to activate its members.[72]

At first the most enthusiastic *Guardian* sellers were the teenagers in the Young Communist League. Formed in 1921, the YCL had survived the sectarian 1930s with an active core of members, most of whom were under the minimum eighteen-year-old age requirement for full Party membership. They met every Friday evening in the waiting room of Dr. Max Joffe's general practice and surgery near City Hall to discuss politics and munch on takeaway food. Fully steeled, the youngsters headed out into the streets to sell the *Guardian*.[73] They soon noticed the simple fact that it was easier to persuade ordinary people to buy a copy of a Cape Town newspaper if it contained Johannesburg news.[74]

It was not the only newspaper in town. The Communist Party's *South African Worker* had closed in 1938, and beginning in 1939 a new monthly appeared called *Inkululeko* (Zulu for "freedom"). *Inkululeko* distinguished itself from the *Guardian* by running articles in African languages, coming out much less frequently (it was edited by committee for its first four years), having much less remarkable writing and having a Transvaal-dominated agenda. (*Inkululeko* vanished once the government banned the Party in 1950.)

In November 1939 Betty Radford hosted a conference in Johannesburg to create a *Guardian* bureau. Thirty-five delegates from trade unions, the Friends of the Soviet Union, the Left Book Club and the Communist Party organized editorial and business committees, as well as a Johannesburg *Guardian* league.[75] Setting up a branch office, however, proved to be a complicated affair, and over twenty months passed before the *Guardian* office opened.[76] Situated at 201 Empire Buildings on Commissioner Street at the corner of Kruis Street, the new office was a few blocks from Joubert Park and a ten-minute stroll to either the financial heart of the city or the contested steps of the City Hall. The offices of the Johannesburg district of the Party and its monthly organ, *Inkululeko*, were on the same floor. The first manager of the office was Rona Worrall.[77] A former teacher who was married to a Springbok Legion official, John O'Meara, Worrall was, according to Betty Radford, a "beautiful, precise, and efficient woman."[78] She ran the *Guardian* office for two years.[79]

A variety of communists helped Worrall construct a viable branch office. Joe Kaye ran the office's circulation operations for two years.[80] Maurice Cohen supplied a humorous feature on Johannesburg society called "Pleasure for the People," while his wife Selma covered the local city council.[81] Issy Wolfson, chairman of the Yeoville Party branch and former national treasurer for the Party, wrote numerous articles, as did Danie Du Plessis, the district Party chairman and Hilda Watts, a communist city councilor.[82] "The *Guardian* was inseparable from the Communist Party during the war," said Rusty Bernstein, Hilda Watts's husband and an eminent Party official . "The offices seemed to be one and the same. The distribution of the papers was handled through our office and members used to hawk it door-to-door, on street corners, key points like beer halls where people assembled."[83] Bernstein sold the newspaper each Saturday at the Mai-Mai municipal beer hall on Von Wielligh Street—a lone white man in a noisy corrugated-iron shed filled with drinking black men—and then later moved to selling on Sundays to white railwaymen in Braamfontein.

Michael Harmel superseded everyone else in Johannesburg. He had subscribed to the *Guardian* since its founding. Michael's father, Arthur, had been a secretary for the Dublin Socialist Society in Ireland. Now owning a pharmacy in Doornfontein, the mostly Jewish district of Johannesburg, and raising his son alone (Michael's mother had died when he was an infant), Arthur thought a *Guardian* subscription was fine, but political activity was not. When Michael finished his master's degree at Rhodes University, Arthur deported him to London to cool his political heels.[84] The young Harmel worked as a dishwasher in a West End restaurant, but spent his free time selling the *Daily Worker* on street corners. Returning to Johannesburg in 1939, Harmel joined the Party and quickly violated his father's wishes.[85] A balding, sloppily dressed, prickly man who read all night and slept late into the morning, Harmel held no permanent job except as a Party oracle and theoretician. In effect, he was a competitor with Jack Simons for the role of the Party's intellectual leader.[86] Like Simons, Harmel wrote for the *Guardian*. He was the chief correspondent in the Transvaal, filing stories on everything from mine-workers' conditions to the far-right tabloid *Die Transvaler* to anti-pass conferences.[87]

The Johannesburg *Guardian* league, like its Cape Town counterpart, organized frequent fundraising events. Throughout 1940 and 1941, the league offered a series of *Guardian* concerts on the first Tuesday of every month in which one could hear a BBC radio performance for two shillings and sixpence.[88] In 1942 the *Guardian* league created branches in a dozen Johannesburg neighborhoods.[89] The Hillbrow league was run by a Mrs. Lieberman, who coined the alliterative motto "Many a mickle makes a muckle."[90] The most sustaining league tradition in Johannesburg was the annual birthday party at Bram and Molly Fischer's home on Beaumont Street in Oaklands. Every February the Fischers hosted a notoriously festive gathering. Bram was a transcendant figure. Born into a prominent Afrikaner family, he was a Rhodes Scholar and a leading Johannesburg lawyer, and yet, despite his white establishment bonafides, he wholeheartedly committed himself to the Party and the ANC. The *Guardian* birthday party was for twenty years the most public example of his extraordinary leap of faith.[91]

Beyond the new branch office, dedicated selling by the Communist Party, and increased visibility from the *Guardian* leagues, the hiring of African sellers invigorated the dissemination of the weekly. Working for a commission of four pennies for every dozen sold, Africans stood at popular crossroads, often wearing a sandwich board covered with a *Guardian* poster.[92] Richard Ramaphakela usually moved five hundred copies each Sunday outside Crystals in Doornfontein, and John Sibongani sold a thousand *Guardians* each weekend across the city, earning the moniker "Mr. *Guardian*."[93]

In 1941 Radford split the *Guardian* in two, creating a southern edition for the Cape province and a northern edition for the rest of the country.[94] Usually, the only differences were the front and back page and some different advertising.[95] By the beginning of 1942, the northern edition outsold the southern edition three to two, forever assuming dominance and proving again that the political heart of the country was in Johannesburg.[96]

During the war, the *Guardian* became a national newspaper. Almost every post office had a subscriber; almost every town had an agent selling it; almost every village had a reader. After Johannesburg, the most obvious place for the *Guardian* to gain a foothold was Durban. Nestled in between the green waters of the Indian Ocean and the thousand rolling hills of Zululand, Durban could not be more different from Johannesburg. Instead of the brown slag heaps and the arid highveld, there was the mile-long sandy beach right at the edge of the business district. Durban was dominated by Indians, descendants of the nineteenth-century indentured servants and laborers that were brought from the Indian subcontinent to work the sugar-cane fields.

In November 1941, less than four months after Commissioner Street opened, the *Guardian* officially launched its Durban office.[97] Located at 15 Provident Building at 324 Smith Street, it initially did not have either a telephone or a postal box. Two months later, the *Guardian* moved to 6 Pembroke Chambers at 472 West Street, in the heart of Durban's bustling Indian quarter.[98] The first person in charge of the Durban office was an eighteen-year-old Englishwoman named Vera Alberts, whose appearance in Durban that summer was, as remembered by Pauline Podbrey, a singular event:

> It was a hot, steamy, late afternoon and I was sitting in HA's office, watching [George] Poonen next door as he bent over his desk, humming tunelessly and drawing lines in his ledger. . . . A strange white woman walked in unannounced and flopped unceremoniously into a chair.
>
> "My name's Vera Alberts," she announced as she looked about her. Her black eyes regarded us without surprise, as though she had expected to find everything just so, or—which seemed more likely—as though she had trained herself never to betray curiosity. Her thin, sharp features and sallow skin were clearly not South African; they betrayed a lack of sunshine and air. But what stamped her as even more a stranger was her extraordinary outfit. On this humid Durban day when the rest of us wore our coolest, thinnest outfit, Vera appeared in a tailored tweed suit with a mannish hat to match, a satin, long-sleeved blouse and a pair of thick brown leather gloves. Even more extraordinary were her shoes. These were not where one might expect to see them—on her feet—but in her hands, as casually as her handbag. On her feet were her silk stockings, tattered and shredded. . . .
>
> "I am a comrade from London," she announced.[99]

Naidoo and Podbrey arranged for the Englishwoman to stay in Poonen's house. Alberts and Poonen soon fell in love, got married, and had two daughters; Alberts insisted on making their home in the Indian quarter, in further violation of South African taboos. Volatile and combative, always with a cigarette in hand, Alberts took on the *Guardian* job with her signature verve and ran a furiously active branch.[100]

A number of others helped her. Peter Abrahams, in Durban waiting to go overseas, wrote a few articles and placed an advertisement for *Here Friend*, his book of self-published poems: "No definite price is being charged, but send what you think a little booklet of Verse with a Left Wing punch in it deserves."[101] Harry Bloom, a young advocate who was Yusuf Dadoo's lawyer during his wartime detention, started his writing career at the *Guardian*. He penned articles from Durban and drew cartoons under the nom de plume Walter Storm.[102] With the advice of the Party, Alberts hired Jacqueline Lax as the *Guardian*'s full-time Durban reporter in late 1942.[103] Lax had joined the Party the year before and had just become a member of the district committee. As Durban correspondent, Lax investigated Natal's biggest industry, the sugar-cane fields—"Little Better Than Slavery: Sugar Workers' Conditions"—and conditions at the Durban Indian Municipal Employees Society Magazine Barracks, condemned in 1920 but still crowded with Indian railway workers.[104]

The addition of a Durban office meant a Durban *Guardian* league. Errol Shanley, a Party leader and Durban district secretary for the South African Trades and Labour Council, headed the league's committee. They raised £110 at a mock trial in which the "guilty" all received summonses to the court, "fines" were imposed, and those who were acquitted were fined anyway for "contempt of court."[105] The weekly soon had seven Durban agents selling copies, including the faithful Modern Hairdressers, which received and held "spare jumble" for the *Guardian*.[106] The DIMES barracks were a major area of circulation, with twelve dozen sold there each week (one issue that discussed the barracks sold more than five hundred copies).[107] In part due to *Guardian* selling, the local Communist Party grew by leaps and bounds, with nine branches in 1942 ballooning to twenty in 1945.[108]

Ismail Meer, in the Young Communists' League in Johannesburg, moved back to Durban during the war and sold the *Guardian* each week. "It was the only paper that was read by all the different races," he said. "Durban sales were good sales. But this is a bit of a humorous story. We used to have a big sale where Victoria Street ended up and the buses used to be there and also the Indian market used to be there. And thousands of copies went out one week and we said, 'What the hell is this today?'—such a big rush and all copies gone. And some of us went to investigate. We found that with the fishing season, there'd been thousands of fish in the port and people were spending a penny for the *Guardian* to wrap their fish."

Spread by politics or fish, the *Guardian* could be bought everywhere. In Pretoria, the fourth-largest *Guardian* city, a half-dozen agents sold the weekly, as did the Party at its offices on Church Street.[109] On the weekends, Party sellers, led by George and Jean Findlay, strolled around the non-white townships of Lady Selbourne, Marabastad and Asiatic Bazaar, pushing the newspaper.[110] Even the conservative SAT&LC branch in Pretoria adopted the *Guardian* as its official organ.[111] Party member Ethel Woolf—a "human dynamo," according to Betty Radford—ran Pretoria's *Guardian* league, as well as a *Guardian* reader's league among coloured and Indian communities; three hundred people attended a 1942 reader's league meeting.[112] So strong was the local *Guardian* league that in a 1942 national fundraising drive for the weekly, Pretoria accumulated the most of any *Guardian* league.[113] One event was particularly noteworthy. While one hundred Africans watched a dance performance at a *Guardian* fundraiser in Pretoria, a mob of Afrikaner hooligans tried to crash the party. They roared into the crowd, smashed a duplicating machine, and stole gramophone records; the mob had been incensed by rumors that Africans were dancing with white women, but it turned out there was only one white woman at the fundraiser and she was spinning records on the gramophone.[114]

Port Elizabeth, situated on the Indian Ocean in the eastern Cape, had a less explosive *Guardian* presence. A small Communist Party contingent operated a local *Guardian* league, and near the end of the war secured temporary offices at 84 Russell Road, staffed by volunteers.[115] "It was a sensation for people like ourselves, intellectuals and so forth," Miriam Hepner recalled. "We were rather isolated in PE and were terribly excited and thrilled about the *Guardian*." East London had a sizable community reading the newspaper and a *Guardian* league.[116] Helped by Fred Carneson and Harry Gwala, Pietermaritzburg started a *Guardian* league in May 1942, held socials every Monday evening and sold forty-five dozen newspapers a week.[117] King William's Town, Mossel Bay, and Worcester had regular *Guardian* correspondents; towns like Queenstown, Uitenhage, and George had appreciable readerships; and *Guardian* leagues in Kimberly, Witbank, Springs, Brakpan, Sydenham and Paarl raised money.[118] The *Guardian* was sold at railway bookstalls in Bloemfontein, the Orange Free State city and judicial capital of the country; one resident, Nakie Smith, had the honor, until she died in 1949 at the age of 104, of being the oldest *Guardian* subscriber.[119]

A gauge of the *Guardian*'s popularity in southern Africa was a 1942 list of May Day greetings. Of the eighty-three paid greetings, five came from Pretoria, eleven from Johannesburg, twenty-eight from Durban, and two from Rhodesia.[120] (In Rhodesia, both Bulawayo and Salisbury had dynamic

Guardian leagues.[121]) The newspaper counted *Guardian* subscribers in over a dozen countries, including the United States, Australia, New Zealand, Canada, Great Britain, Ireland, Kenya, Nigeria and Mozambique.[122] The South African army also had *Guardian* readers. "Up North" in Europe or northern Africa, South African soldiers used the *Guardian* as a recruiting tool for the Springbok Legion.[123] Two of the founders of the Legion, John Morley and Vic Clapham, were regular *Guardian* contributors. In part because of the *Guardian*, the Legion's membership reached over 55,000 in 1944.[124] To get the newspaper past the eyes of army censors, *Guardian* supporters privately posted it to friends in the army, while information officers like Cecil Williams and Brian Bunting circulated issues in official educational envelopes.[125]

Read in Cape Town and Cairo and everywhere in between, the *Guardian* experienced a tremendous surge in circulation. In 1940 it was at 12,000; in 1941 it jumped sometimes by a thousand each week; and the week after the Nazi invasion of the USSR, a twelve-page special issue sold 8,500 more copies than the week before, making the circulation top 22,000. By February 1942 the figure was 27,200, and in June 1942 it reached 33,000, giving Radford a tripling in circulation in fourteen months. A year later 42,500 people bought the *Guardian*, and by the end of the war circulation was steady at 50,000.[126] At a time when the foremost South African commercial weekly, the *Sunday Times*, had a circulation of 140,000, the *Guardian*'s figures were astounding.[127]

In March 1943 Pretoria instituted newsprint restrictions, reducing the *Guardian* to eight pages.[128] When faced with a potential cut in circulation from 33,000 to 22,000, the newspaper appealed for exemption by sending a delegation to Colin Steyn, the minister of justice. Surprisingly, the appeal was not only successful, but Steyn granted the *Guardian* an increased allocation, arguing that the weekly was essential "in fostering the home front spirit in the factories."[129] Radford, calling this exemption from paper restrictions a "great tribute" to the *Guardian* and its supporters, raised the weekly's sales figures to 50,000 while other South African newspapers lost circulation.[130]

With space at a premium, Radford shrank the annual May Day pages of greetings, reduced sports coverage—which had occupied much of the back page in the early years—excerpted letters to the editor, sharply edited columns and told correspondents to keep their reports "as short as possible and not more than three hundred words."[131] While in the 1930s a single article might fill a page or more, now dozens of one- and two-paragraph pieces dotted each page. The front page lost all its advertisements and instead gleamed with as many as a dozen complete articles. Advertising, though, did not disappear. As many as fifty advertisements graced the *Guardian* each week, at three shillings per inch, making over one-third of the newspaper advertising.[132] The *Guardian*'s burgeoning circulation figures led to more advertising, as did a wartime tax regulation that allowed businesses to write off the cost of advertising.[133]

Despite the buoyant advertising and circulation figures, the *Guardian*'s bank account was no more flush with cash than in the 1930s. The two branch offices, the separate editions, the expense of shipping thousands of *Guardians* by rail, the cables from London, the photographs and sketches, the rent at Barrack Street, licenses, telegrams, telephones and wages—it all added up to £20,000 a year in expenses.[134]

The *Guardian* attacked the situation with characteristic vigor. Radford suggested readers put the weekly in their wills.[135] She produced a number of new leaflets, including Donald Molteno's 1941 "All Aid to the Soviet Union," and issued a number of four-page keepsake supplements.[136] *Guardian* leagues placed distinctive orange-and-black *Guardian* collection tins at many factories and shops. *Guardian* readers and supporters, urged to individually post money to Barrack Street, saw their offerings printed on the editorial page with a note of praise from Carina Pearson. On average the newspaper received about £300 a month from individual donations and fundraising events. The giving was irregular; some weeks £20 arrived, while other weeks it might be £500.[137] Many readers donated like clockwork; Fred Carneson faithfully remitted £5 every month from Pietermaritzburg.[138] Supporters sent other things besides money. The *Guardian* offered a six-volt, thirteen-plate British battery in "first-class condition," and at the end of one fruitful season, a reader from Elgin posted a case of apples to be sold.[13]

When batteries and apples were not enough, Pearson and Radford launched a national capital campaign to raise £2,500. The appeal, headquartered in Johannesburg with Johnny Kaye as the national organizer, offered a life-size bust of Lenin to the reader with the "best" donation.[140] Charlie Stewart agreed to print one issue without charge, adding £75 to the campaign.[141] The *Guardian* leagues mustered a nationwide house-to-house canvassing day on 16 August 1942.[142] After three months the *Guardian* had raised £2,847, and its circulation not coincidentally rose from 33,000 to over 40,000.[143]

Less than two months later, the *Guardian* reported that it had £25 10s. 2d. in its bank account.[144] Radford simply did not worry about money. Even with newsprint selling at exorbitant rates, Radford printed ten- and twelve-page editions. She toyed with expanding the *Guardian* from a five-column tabloid to a seven-column broadsheet format, oscillating from size to size each week. She often ordered a print run that exceeded the demand, thus leaving Barrack Street with curling stacks of *Guardian*s in the hallways.[145] Since the weekly was in her name, she felt at ease buying expensive overseas cables or printing extra copies. Growth was her watchword. She added two branch offices in just four months. If the advertisements for *Guardian* jobs were any indication, the newspaper's administrative and editorial staffs grew at similar speeds. In July 1941 Radford could claim that the entire Cape Town staff, "except for the office boy," were volunteers, but a year later a dozen staff members drew monthly salaries.[146] Radford appealed for typist-bookkeepers, circulation managers, shorthand typists, clerks for the circulation department, national sales managers, journalists, editorial staff writers, organizing secretaries and a "reporter, cum-jack-of-all-editorial-trades."[147] One help-wanted notice—"Situation Vacant: for intelligent young man or woman" in the Cape Town editorial staff—drew over thirty replies.[148] The political views of the applicants were paramount: "Situation Vacant: energetic, efficient young man or woman with Left political sympathies to manage sales and general office organising."[149]

Politics, as always, came before pounds sterling.

The content of the *Guardian* pages reflected an overwhelming preoccupation with the Second World War. Anti-war after its initial, six-week hesitation, Barrack Street had displayed a vague interest in the goings-on in Europe and North Africa for the first two years of the war, paying attention to the German blitzkrieg and the British desperation at Dunkirk, but not bothering to analyze the news in depth. The largest amount of coverage came in May 1940 when the weekly ran a three-page special report from a Communist Party conference explaining in depth its anti-war position. The newspaper's only preoccupation was the plight of the South Africa anti-war internees.[150]

In one week everything changed. Harold Baldry, writing in his Vigilator column in the 19 June 1941 edition, responded to the hearsay that Germany was about to invade the USSR: "Study the dope put out by Goebbels and his henchmen in the past, and the reason for the present flood of rumours sticks out a mile." What stuck out a mile was Vigilator's embarrassed face when Nazi tanks rumbled across the border into Russia three days later. On 26 June the *Guardian* endured a complete volte-face. After twenty months

· of chafing at the anti-war bit, it galloped out a pro-war, pro-Allies stance in a twelve-page issue that devoted five pages to the USSR (including twenty-two Red Army photographs) and lead with a frothy banner headline: "ALL SUPPORT FOR SOVIET UNION: DEFEND THE CAUSE OF LIBERTY, DEMOCRACY AND HUMAN DECENCY.": "Our loyalty is to Socialism and not necessarily to Russia. If Timbuctoo were Socialist, it would mean the same," Radford wrote, denying any policy flip-flop. "The attitude of the *Guardian* has been consistent. From its inception it has been bitterly anti-Fascist."

Timbuktu it was not, and "The War for Freedom" had begun, as the *Guardian* threw itself wholeheartedly into the effort to save that "great and progressive country. . . . the socialist sixth of the earth."[151] The weekly followed battles in Ethiopia, Egypt, Italy, and above London, but concentrated on the eastern front.[152] Radford followed the nine-hundred-day siege of Leningrad week to week and celebrated the Red Army's "birthday" as if it was May Day. A main feature of the *Guardian* was "This Week's War News," an entire page of maps, charts, descriptions of battles, and biographies of Russian generals. The *Guardian* printed dozens of articles by the renowned Russian writer Ilya Ehrenburg and hundreds of stock photographs of Russian soldiers, all supplied by the Soviet Information Agency in Pretoria and the Soviet Press Agency in Moscow.[153] Editorials and a *Guardian* petition, signed by four thousand people, called for Pretoria to open diplomatic relations with the USSR.[154] The lack of a western front greatly concerned Barrack Street; with a bit of sloganeering, a typical headline read, "Spring Mud Won't Stop Red Army, But Moscow Anxious about Second Front."[155]

The world poured into Barrack Street through the small slips of cabled articles. Reporters with titles like "Imperial Correspondent" sent news from every continent and ocean.[156] Eric Cook was the most prolific. A former New Zealand farmer, Cook ran a news service, blandly called the Democratic and General News Service, that issued left-leaning reports each week from London.[157] Cook was known for solid prose and for his signature emerald green trousers.[158] The most celebrated *Guardian* correspondent, however, was Sergeant John. Born Lance Morley-Turner, Sergeant John was a rail-thin Englishman with a glass eye. He had a mysterious past that included fighting with the Black and Tans in Ireland.[159] Called the "Red Sergeant" because he drove around the battlefront in a jeep sporting a outsized red flag, Sergeant John posted monthly dispatches from Kenya, Egypt, Libya and Italy.[160]

Radford was very loyal to the Soviet Union and raised the country up to mythic proportions. She opined that the Soviet Union proved that "socialism is more efficient than capitalism" by the "torrent of magnificent victories on the Eastern Front," and told readers of her "deep affection" for the Russian people as a result of her 1936 honeymoon.[161] When the South African government banned Russian books, the newspaper splashed a five-inch headline about the incident and provided a form to fill out and post to Prime Minister Smuts.[162] On D-Day, 6 June 1944, when the Allies landed on the beaches of Normandy and established the western front, an ecstatic Betty Radford draped a red flag from the third-floor window of her office on Barrack Street.[163]

Tanks rumbled and bombs exploded thousands of miles away, but there was no doubt that South Africa was at war. Durban slept under a nightly blackout, while the rest of the coast endured dimmed lamps at home, reduced cinema lighting, no lights on secondary streets, and the upper parts of main streetlights were blackened.[164] The *Guardian* zealously examined the war's ramifications for South Africa. Articles exposed the lack of Cape Town bomb shelters and the failures of food rationing—"Butterless People Demand Margarine."[165] For a £50 donation, readers received twelve packets of free "victory seeds" for wartime gardens; Radford explained that "Gardening is a healthy occupation and every row of vegetables—even if they are only grown in a window-box—will help the national effort."[166] The *Guardian* taught readers how to buy war bonds, gave stern warnings about spies, printed Springbok Legion application forms and admonished overactive mattress buyers: "Springs Are Scarce—Our Army Needs Our Steel."[167] When Afrikaner neo-Nazis, led by future minister of justice and *Guardian* nemesis B. J. Vorster, began a sabotage campaign in 1941 and bombed cinemas in Pretoria and buildings in Potchestroom, the weekly avidly covered such incidents in a feature titled "Fifth Column Front."[168] Despite the grim horror of war, the *Guardian*'s humor remained intact. In 1943 Betty Radford printed photographs of the opulent Johannesburg homes of the Shah of Iran and Prince Paul of Yugoslavia, both in exile because of their support of Germany; the caption below read: "We only found one swell motor-car in his large double garage. Perhaps there is a slump in the market for Quislings to-day."[169]

Communism in South Africa was an all-pervading obsession. Accounts of the Party's activities permeated the *Guardian*, with announcements, committee statements and memorandums, and interviews surfacing every week.[170] The Party's annual national conference garnered pages of copy each January, "CP News" was a regular back-page feature, and the newspaper dutifully promulgated the Party's national campaigns—the "Six-Point Programme" in 1941, the "Defend South Africa" and "Awake South Africa" in 1942, and the "Rights and Justice" in 1943.[171] The *Guardian* interviewed

Inkululeko's editor on its first anniversary and often encouraged support for its sister newspaper (in Johannesburg, Party members sold both newspapers simultaneously).[172] In many matters, like the 1941 Nazi invasion, the newspaper deferred to the Party for guidance, letting a Central Committee statement suffice for stated policy. The *Guardian* made no attempt to appear separate and independent from the Party. In court in 1943, Betty Radford testified that "The *Guardian* is a newspaper which at all times material hereto has expressed a policy sympathetic to that of the Communist Party of South Africa."[173]

Columns like Bill Andrews's "Industrial Editor," smaller features like "Trade Union Flashes" and "Trade Union Notebook," and the Barrack Street telegraphic address, "Worker, Cape Town," demonstrated the weekly's continuing interests in organized labor.[174] The minister of labour, Walter Madelay, gave the *Guardian* an exclusive message for workers on the anniversary of the Bolshevik Revolution.[175] May Day still marked a major milestone each year, as Radford printed special editions with four pages of paid greetings: in 1942, eighty-three organizations paid five shillings for two inches of greeting space.[176]

It was more than cheery messages. The newspaper got involved in a contentious strike in Paarl, a town in the wine-growing region outside Cape Town. Led by Ray Alexander, 350 members of the Food and Canning Workers' Union struck in September 1941 at the Jones' Jam factory. The strike lasted for five months. The *Guardian* organized a Paarl Workers' Relief Fund, with Bill Andrews as treasurer, reported on progress and praised its successful conclusion.[177]

Andrews came in for a good dose of hagiography via the *Guardian*. In 1943 Jack Cope, the Cape Town staff writer and future novelist and poet, wrote his first book: *Comrade Bill: The Life and Times of W. H. Andrews, Workers' Leader*. It was no historical masterpiece. Cope did not bother with footnotes or a bibliography, interviewed just a few veteran unionists and was sometimes painfully sycophantic. Published by Stewart and richly applauded by the *Guardian*'s Michael Harmel, its first reviewer, *Comrade Bill* was nonetheless a landmark book, as it was the first devoted to the history of the South African labor movement.[178]

One reason for the publication of the Andrews biography was electoral maneuvering. *Guardian* coverage of the July 1943 general elections was so intense that it supplanted war news, and Vigilator explained a two-week absence from his column to his "being much more concerned with local than overseas events."[179] Radford profiled the nine Communist Party candidates, including her husband George Sacks.[180] She also held a competition in which readers sent a three-hundred-word essay entitled "Experiences of a Canvasser for the Communist Party," the winner receiving a framed print of a Soviet painting.[181] The *Guardian* closed its offices on election day to allow for unfettered canvassing, and five years after advising its readers to vote Labour, the *Guardian* urged, "If you can vote, vote Communist."[182] The newspaper's 1 July 1943 edition, six days before the election, set an all-time circulation record of 55,000 copies.[183]

Inherent in the weekly's election slogan was a recognition that some of the *Guardian* readers and supporters were not white and therefore could not vote. In the early years, almost all Guardian readers were white; by 1945 Barrack Street estimated that Africans bought 15,000 issues a week.[184] With the coloured and Indian populations weighing in as well, perhaps half of the *Guardian*'s circulation by the end of the war was dependent on black South Africans.

This remarkable transition was due in part to the Communist Party's insistence in organizing in black areas. The word *ikomunisi* was whispered in townships throughout the country, as the Party used trade unions, advisory boards, ad hoc committees and city councils as venues for expanded political work.[185] The *Guardian* reflected this new interest in black South Africa. Beginning a *Guardian* tradition, H. A. Naidoo wrote an investigative piece in 1943 on prison conditions for blacks at the main Cape Town prison on Roeland Street.[186] A *Guardian* investigation of illegal evictions in Fordsburg succeeded in getting the tenants' homes returned.[187] When two Africans were shot dead in a police raid in Sophiatown, Radford wrote an indignant telegram of protest to the minister of justice, Colin Steyn.[188] From Durban came a small article on how Clairwood Indians walked ten miles for water, and how "mothers and babies sleep on concrete" at a women's hostel.[189] In 1941 Radford ran two graphic front-page photographs of children stricken with rickets, with the headline "Time to Wake Up Mister."[190]

Hideous housing conditions in particular became a *Guardian* fascination. Selma Cohen, a Johannesburg staff reporter, went to the African location of Pimville to report on eighty-five homes that had collapsed during summer rains. "Damp Houses but No Doctors" read the headline of a story about the African location in Worcester.[191] Winter flooding in the Cape Flats wreaked havoc on makeshift shanties of corrugated iron; cardboard and plastic collapsed. Radford's report on Elsie's River, a coloured township, was one common story; after one visit with Harry Snitcher she said, "the conditions are horrible."[192] She was even more persistent covering Windermere on the Cape Flats, running photographs each time it flooded and joining a Friends of Windermere committee to help change conditions in the shanty town. One graphic photograph bore the sense of exhaustion: "It's Still Wet at Windermere."[193]

The weekly wrestled with South Africa's racial inequities. It thoroughly examined the color-bar clause in the 1941 Factories Bill.[194] An editorial, a Central Committee statement, a "Topical" column and an article discussed the 1944 Native Wages Commission's report.[195] Half a page proclaimed the joint efforts of the ANC and the Party to create the African Mine Workers' Union.[196] The weekly covered the 1944 Alexandra bus boycott, which communists helped direct.[197] A picture of a particularly run-down part of District Six where war veterans lived had the telling caption "Scarcely a home for a hero."[198] Ray Alexander wrote articles about the need for African trade-union recognition.[199] For three years, a common *Guardian* slogan was "Guns Not Passes," a reference to the government's decision not to arm black soldiers.[200]

African National Congress leaders began to communicate with the weekly. Radford interviewed A. B. Xuma, the ANC president, about "Native Crime and Disease," and sometimes wrote *Guardian* articles.[201] Clements Kadalie, founder and leader of the famed 1920s Industrial and Commercial Union, wrote a long letter to Barrack Street from semi-retirement in East London.[202] The *Guardian* did not yet send a reporter to the ANC's annual national conferences, but in 1943 they ran a small report from one of the delegates.[203]

Sometimes the *Guardian* moved beyond mere reporting. When drought and a typhus epidemic threatened thousands in the Eastern Cape, Radford created a *Guardian* Hunger Relief Fund, collecting hundreds of blankets, boxes of clothing, and nearly £2,000.[204] Radford traveled out to the Transkei to personally deliver the blankets, clothing, and money to over four hundred families.[205]

In 1941 Jack Simons wrote on the weekly's fifth anniversary: "Our paper must reflect the views and record the struggles and problems of the worker in the factory and home, the trade unionist, the African in reserves and locations, the people of the slums."[206] South Africa's majority population group—the indigenous, oppressed Africans—finally graced the list of *Guardian* priorities. Importantly, the newspaper called them "Africans," not "Natives," a difference particularly telling when in Parliament some members still referred to them as "kaffirs" and "black niggers."[207]

Still, Simons placed Africans low on the list. An air of paternalism and white liberal guilt pervaded the pages of the *Guardian*. In 1942 Radford printed an open letter to Prime Minister Smuts concerning Africans and the war, urging Smuts to "show them that we do not look upon them as second-class citizens."[208] Often, Barrack Street discussed Africans within the context of the Party, a filter that hid the real causes of African poverty—the lack of political or economic rights. A Johannesburg district-committee statement on the Orlando squatters movement formed the foundation of the newspaper's coverage of that important issue.[209] A series of articles on African *shebeens*, or illegal bars, characteristically bore the headline "Communist Comment on Shebeen and Skolly Menace."[210] The *Guardian* listened intently to black communists. Alpheus W. Maliba, treasurer of *Inkululeko* and leader of a populist rural organization among the Venda people of the Northern Transvaal, wrote pieces that for the first time brought *Guardian* readers to the poverty-stricken rural areas.[211] Yusuf Dadoo regularly submitted articles or gave interviews about Indian affairs.[212] Commissioner Street often interviewed Edwin Mofutsanyana, supported his Native Representative Council election bid, and when one thousand Africans were arrested in Johannesburg one day in 1943, went to him for comment.[213]

The pass-law issue became emblematic of the *Guardian*'s conflicting interests. "One Conviction a Minute," trumpeted the weekly in 1941. Barrack Street sent a reporter to a Party-organized anti-pass conference in November 1943, but when the ANC finally held its own anti-pass conference in May 1944, the *Guardian* put the meeting on page five.[214] Realizing its slighting of a major event, the newspaper later ran three photographs and a long Harmel eyewitness report of the conference.[215] The weekly traced the subsequent million-signature campaign, and when the campaign miserably failed, the *Guardian* did not mince its words: "Indignant speeches are not enough to break these chains."[216]

A few white *Guardian* readers were not happy with the newspaper's new multiracial interests. The issue, as in years past, was that while many whites wanted to improve conditions for blacks, they did not want to lower their own standards of living. Evidence of this continuing tension coursed through the *Guardian*'s pages. "If I had known of your intention to publish the scurrilous type of article which has appeared in recent issues I would certainly not have become a subscriber," wrote Will Costello, the Labour Party leader, angrily canceling his *Guardian* subscription after the weekly had protested the Labour Party's color bar. "Your veiled attacks on the S.A. Labour Party . . . and your lying statements . . . convince me that your paper is plainly Communistic in its outlook and policy."[217] In 1942 Radford wrote about readers' mutterings in "Topical" under the heading "Stand Or Fall":

"I know many European readers of the *Guardian* are critical of our emphasis on the importance of South Africa's racial problems. . . ."[218] In a December 1943 column, she told of a revelatory conversation with Bill Andrews. He "stamped up and down my office this week voicing his views on the colour bar in industry. It's got to go, he said, but not at the expense of the white worker."[219] Radford calmed him by suggesting he write a string of articles explaining his position, and so for the next three weeks, the newspaper ran Andrews's series of "The Problem of the Unskilled Worker."[220] Nonetheless, in the editor's backroom office on Barrack Street, it became clear: the official leader of the most revolutionary organization in the country was still not in favor of a revolution.

Just as there was an intractable split within the *Guardian*, so too were the governing white authorities confused about what the newspaper meant. The *Guardian* was, on one hand, an accepted and appreciated member of the white society. Its contributors, its correspondents and its subscriber list were almost all white; its heavy advertisement share, its staff members' city-council victories, its interviews with parliamentarians, and cabinet-minister messages—all indicated a general level of incorporation into white South Africa. No one seemed threatened by the *Guardian*'s relationship to the Communist Party. The Smuts government granted diplomatic recognition to the USSR in 1942. Both the mayor of Johannesburg and the minister of justice were patrons of the Friends of the Soviet Union. Medical Aid to Russia, another organization founded by communists, received more than £80,000 in its first two months of operation.[221]

Under the surface, troubling matters told a different story. In 1942 *Inkululeko* was banned from the British protectorates of Bechuanaland, Basutoland and Swaziland. A year later, four white men forced their way into *Inkululeko*'s offices on Commissioner Street—down the hall from the *Guardian*'s rooms—threw paraffin on the floor, and set the offices on fire (*Bantu World*'s offices and the Jewish Workers' Clubhouse were also firebombed during the war). In 1944 *Inkululeko*'s editors discovered that a secret postal ban had been preventing subscribers from receiving copies for almost a full year.[222]

In 1942 the South African Broadcasting Company, a conservative, government-owned organization, allowed the South African Trades & Labour Council to give a May Day radio broadcast. The Jewish Workers' Club choir sang "The Internationale," the Minister of Labour Walter Madelay and union leader A. A. Moore spoke for fifteen minutes from Johannesburg, and then Bill Andrews, as chairman of the Communist Party, spoke from Cape Town.[223] Many considered Andrews's speech a transcendent moment of recognition for the Party, but the SABC actually censored his speech. (They forbade him to make references to Anglo-Russian relations and edited a comment about race.)

Such censorship blighted the *Guardian*'s pages as well.[224] In early 1942 the controller of censorship, Brigadier H. J. Lenton, detained cables from the *Guardian*'s London correspondent, the emerald-trousered Eric Cook, forwarding them on to Barrack Street too late for publication.[225] In March the British government announced a decision that cables "likely to create disharmony between ourselves and Allied countries" would be stopped in London.[226] In April, Lenton banned all of Cook's cables.[227] Radford sent a bitter letter to Lenton, Donald Molteno raised the matter in Parliament, and four *Guardian* supporters traveled up to Pretoria to complain to Lenton's boss, the minister of Posts and Telegraphs.[228] Radford chided her newspaper colleagues when no editorials of support for the *Guardian* appeared, concluding that the South African media "for the moment is suffering from the hallucination that it is a free press."[229] The London-based National Union of Journalists and National Council of Civil Liberties, not under the same illusion, investigated the question.[230]

In May, without any explanation, Lenton lifted the ban.[231] But a year later, he again slowed up Cook's cables, detaining them for between twelve and twenty-four hours, enough to disrupt publication.[232] Lenton then switched from delaying to destroying and began to cut out words and phrases from the cables with very little regard for the political content. One week he deleted 272 words, while another week he snipped a mere two words out of an 850-word cable.[233] For months, the random deletions continued. Without any indication of irony, he made deep cuts in a Cook cable discussing censorship in Britain.[234] Finally, in February 1944, when Lenton cut three Cook cables in two weeks, Radford was beyond patience. With a staffer on another telephone to record the conversation, she called Lenton to complain. Lenton replied to Radford's queries about Cook's cables by saying, "You know that sort of muck that fellow sends." Radford told him she had a witness on line and would publish this conversation. Lenton swore, "You damn swine," and hung up the telephone.[235] The next week he cut sixty-two words from a Cook cable.[236]

After another *Guardian* delegation to Pretoria—this time to the minister of the interior—found no relief, Radford asked Donald Molteno to again raise the matter in the House of Assembly.[237] Prime Minister Smuts answered that Lenton had censored material "undesirable in the interests of the Allied war effort," and claimed Cook was using "extracts without context from certain [British] journals known to be extremist."[238] Hitting on the true cause of the harassment, Jack Simons editorialized that Smuts was really trying to stifle criticism of his government. Unperturbed, Lenton continued cutting and delaying cables until the issue disappeared with the storming of the beaches at Normandy.[239]

Hostility came from other parts of the government. In January 1943 Eric Louw, a Nationalist MP, put a motion before the House calling for the government to ban the Communist Party, deport all aliens, stop arming non-Europeans and sever consular relations with the USSR.[240] When the motion was debated two weeks later, reference was made to the *Guardian* and the minister of justice, Colin Steyn, a patron of the FSU and speaker at Medical Aid for Russia meetings:

> Louw: The *Guardian* is a Communistic paper. The Minister of Justice will not deny that this publication is an out and out communistic one.
>
> An Hon. Member: It is his paper.
>
> Louw: Yes, I understand that he had given this paper an interview and I want to draw attention to the fact that while the *Guardian* is making bitter attacks on the Minister of Native Affairs, it has in many of its issues referred in terms of praise to the Minister of Justice. He is a friend of the *Guardian*.[241]

Responding quickly, the *Guardian* published an interview in its next issue with Bill Andrews. Andrews attacked Louw's "slipshod argument" and "un-reliability," while saying Louw was "depending on hearsay." In a paragraph of all capitalized letters, Andrews argued: "What I want strongly to point out is this: We stand beside the Government in this time of national crisis, whereas Mr Louw and his Party and the people for whom he speaks engage in dastardly sabotage and subversive propaganda all over the country. They stand for the victory of a foreign power and the enslavement of their country."[242]

Louw sued the *Guardian*, Andrews, and Stewart, the *Guardian* printer, for defamation over the paragraph, claiming damages of £3,000.[243] Radford wrote letters to Louw's lawyer, trying to head off the prospect of going to court—"We write to ask you to specify to which portions of the article concerned your client took exception"—and saying the weekly was "prepared to publish a statement but we cannot agree that the article in question was defamation."[244] Louw responded by raising the ante to £5,000.[245] Radford formed a *Guardian* defense fund to raise the money, but in September 1943, after their lawyers met, Louw and the *Guardian* settled the matter out of court for £150.[246]

Flirting with defamation became a more serious character flaw for the newspaper only a few months later. In July 1943 the African Mine Workers' Union sent Barrack Street a fifty-page memorandum that was soon to be submitted to the Lansdown Commission (which was investigating conditions in the gold mines). With the entire office focused on the general elections and trying to satisfy the fifty-five thousand people who wanted to buy a *Guardian*, Radford, "very busy at the time," unwittingly made a mistake.[247] She excerpted the memorandum, under the headline "Miners Unmask Slave System," for four pages, accompanying it with an article by Andrews, who called it "impressive" and "great."[248] Radford did not read Andrews's article before it appeared and only glanced at the memorandum.[249] In subsequent issues, other articles on the document and the AMWU's appearance before the commission ran in the weekly. One commented, "In addition to promoting poverty, hunger and misery among their employees, the mines include in their activities victimization, terrorism and espionage, according to the evidence in court last week."[250]

At dawn on New Year's Day 1944, Radford and Sacks came home from a night of dancing. As luck would have it, they also had mail waiting. In the dim morning light, Radford pulled four long white envelopes out of her mailbox. Each envelope contained a letter from a mining company suing the *Guardian* for £40,000 defamation.[251] They argued that the *Guardian*'s evidence and statements about the AMWU's memorandum were false, that the recruitment of black workers would be hindered, and that the *Guardian* should not have published the memorandum until it actually had been submitted to the commission.[252] Radford set up another *Guardian* defense fund and posted 3,500 appeals to subscribers, sympathizers, and leftist organizations.[253] She admitted that a number of the *Guardian*'s allegations about the mines were unfounded, but still denied any defamation.[254] The *Guardian* defense fund meanwhile flourished, with over £1,000 arriving in the first week and rising to £6,000 by the end of 1944.[255]

Again, lawyers reached a compromise. The Building Workers' Industrial Union, led by Danie Du Plessis, officially asked the SAT&LC executive to intervene with the Chamber of Mines, the overseers of all South African mining. After discussions and letter writing, a deal was struck: the four mining companies told the Chamber of Mines, which told the SAT&LC, which told Du Plessis, who told Betty Radford that if the *Guardian* published an unqualified apology and withdrawal of the alleged libelous comments, they would drop the action. Radford rashly rejected the deal, preferring to fight the matter in court.[256]

This was a costly error. After Harry Snitcher argued the case before the South Africa Supreme Court, the *Guardian* lost and was ordered to pay £750 to each company and costs, a total of £6,710.[257] Luckily, the newspaper's defense fund had raised £6,237, so almost all the money was already on hand. The case, *Randfontein Estates Gold Mining Co., Witwatersrand, Ltd. v. Sacks and Others*, set a precedent in libel cases for South African law and scared the *Guardian* half to death.[258]

For South Africa, the Second World War effectively came to a close in May 1945 with the surrender of Nazi Germany. In those first days of May, the *Guardian* mourned the death of U.S. president Franklin Roosevelt, ran thoughtful editorials on the Nazi concentration camps, and cheered as South African prisoners of war returned home.[259]

On V-E Day, the *Guardian* printed a special twelve-page, two-color, one-penny edition. Photographs from the battles in Europe and joyful messages from dozens of friends like Paul Robeson, the African American singer and activist, garlanded the commemorative edition.[260] "They said it would take three years to beat the Nazis. It has taken six. But here we are at last," wrote Harold Baldry in an "End-of-the-War Survey" that spoke realistically about the meaning of peace. "Dunkirk. Moscow. Alamein. Stalingrad. Normandy. Berlin. It was a long road and a hard one—the hardest in world history. A road paved with dead, surrounded by the ruins of cities and the wreckage of human lives. Little wonder that there's rejoicing now that we've reached the end. From 'Frisco to Vladivostok, from Iceland to the Cape, mankind celebrates the victory over Fascism. All except the Malans and Pirows, the surviving fascists and their friends. But not with the blind joy of 1918." Blind joy was something never seen again in the pages of the *Guardian*.

CHAPTER THREE

Brass and Water

Departures, 1945–1950

The war had been a great boon to the *Guardian*. In six years, its circulation had soared from 6,000 to 50,000, its staff had expanded from three to two dozen, and people talked about it both on the floor of Parliament and in the muddy streets of shantytowns.

The rest of the 1940s was a disaster. In a suddenly hostile political environment, communism retreated before a postwar backlash that was highlighted by a two-year sedition trial involving the Party's leadership, including the *Guardian*'s editor, Betty Radford. Circulation plummeted to less than 20,000, advertisers fled in wholesale fashion and donations dropped off in a vertiginous slide. The editorial staff of the newspaper hemorrhaged; by the end of 1950 only three members of the *Guardian*'s V-E Day office team still worked at Barrack Street.

Optimism reigned in the first year after the war. There was, for the last time in the *Guardian*'s history, money in the bank.[1] With the scrapping of newsprint restrictions in June 1945, Radford introduced a new *Guardian* masthead, standardized a seven-column broadsheet format and made permanent the Thursday publication day.[2] She even discussed the possibility of a daily *Guardian*.[3] After considering plans to create a co-operative company, she incorporated the newspaper, so that a financial scare like the mine defamation case would not again threaten the existence of the weekly.[4]

The 1946 mine strike punctured the newspaper's buoyancy. On 15 August 1946, three days after 100,000 African gold miners rose up to protest living and working conditions on the Witwatersrand mines, the *Guardian* came out with an electric, three-inch front-page headline hailing the events as the GREATEST STRIKE IN SOUTH AFRICAN HISTORY. Radford printed a telegram from Communist Party chief Bill Andrews to Prime Minister Smuts (both were veterans of the other landmark strike in South African history, the 1922 Rand Revolt). Filling half of the weekly's eight pages, news of the strike included statements from the mine-workers' union and a tally of the strike fund.

A week later, the newspaper had an entirely different atmosphere. With rifles and clubs, the police had forcibly ended the strike, killing at least nine miners and injuring thousands. In the *Guardian*'s report, Michael Harmel, the newspaper's Johannesburg correspondent, contributed a full-page diary that detailed the marches, the strikes (twelve mines had been brought to a total standstill), and the brutal beatings. Radford produced a list of organizations that had supported or opposed the strike under a banner, "Where They Stand." There, in black and white, was hard evidence that the Left was in tatters, for both the Labour Party and the South African Trades & Labour Council—foundation blocks of the *Guardian* in the 1930s—had come out against the strike.[5]

On Saturday, 21 September, seven weeks after the start of the mine strike, a rattled Smuts administration went on the offensive. In nine cities across the Union, hundreds of members of the Special Branch (known formerly as the Criminal Investigation Department) visited the offices and homes of dozens of radicals.[6] The detectives seized truckloads of papers, pamphlets, letters, ledgers and books from the Communist Party, Springbok Legion, Friends of the Soviet Union, Natal Indian Congress and trade unions.

Smuts specifically targeted the *Guardian*. The Special Branch raided all three offices, as well as the homes of almost every staff member. At Barrack Street, the scene was chaotic. Because it was a Saturday morning, only Radford was working in the office when a posse of detectives marched up the long flights of stairs. They served Radford with search warrants issued against herself; Carina Pearson, the circulation manager; and Norman Flegg, the business manager. Radford immediately protested that the detectives held no search warrant for the *Guardian* itself and had no right to inspect the offices. Dismissing "the editress," according to a report in the Johannesburg *Star*,

the police rummaged through the editorial, business and circulation departments, opening packages, pilfering desks and cabinets and hauling away
piles of documents.[7] Bill Andrews walked into the office during the raid, and
two detectives drove him back to his bungalow in Camps Bay, where they
searched for two hours and left with every scrap of correspondence he had
collected and filed over the past seventy-six years.[8] The thoroughness of the
CID's search reflected the government's ignorance; they did not know what
they were looking for.[9]

Five days later, a new issue of the *Guardian* emerged from Barrack
Street. Page five ran half blank in protest against the raids that had taken the
bulk of the newspaper's articles. Radford sued the government for the return
of all the weekly's documents, since the warrants had been issued to search
individuals' premises, not the *Guardian*. On 15 October the courts agreed
with the *Guardian* and ordered the CID to return all seized documents.[10]

The purpose of the nationwide raids became evident two months later.
Pretoria arrested eight Central Executive Committee members of the Party,
including Radford, Andrews, Jack Simons, Harry Snitcher and H. A. Naidoo,
and charged them with sedition—a serious charge, for sedition was second
only to treason and could result in a life sentence. The Crown released each
Party leader on £200 bail.[11] The trial began with a preparatory examination
in January 1947. Hoping to blame the Party for the mine strike, the government tried to prove that the Party had breached the Official Secrets Act,
maintained a secret army and engineered each move of the strikers. Each
plank of their case proved warped. The violation of the Official Secrets Act
rested on a technicality, that the Party had called for a boycott of boats going
to Indonesia as part of its 1945 "Hands Off Java" campaign; the secret army
turned out to be the Springbok Legion, which was neither secret nor an
army; and the evidence about the mine strike came from vague passages in
correspondence between Johannesburg and Cape Town Party officials. The
next twelve months was an almost comical saga that presaged the Treason
Trial a decade later: the Crown brought the defendants to trial in October
1947; the judge demanded their release due to irregularities in the charges;
the police rearrested the defendants as they walked out of the court; in May
1948 the judge quashed the indictment; and in October 1948 the Crown
withdrew all charges.[12]

The Sedition Trial was the main reason why Betty Radford decided to
quit the *Guardian*. She was exhausted. For over eleven years, she solicited
and edited or wrote each article. She composed a weekly column. She laid out
the newspaper. She managed the staff. She called the *Guardian* editorship "a

grueling and harassing job."[13] Outside Barrack Street, Radford rushed from activity to activity. As a city councilwoman, she answered letters, telegrams, and telephone calls; attended meetings; spoke at rallies; and wrote up reports. As a Party leader, she served on the Central Executive Committee, which met at minimum every Thursday evening and usually more often, and she spent many late evenings talking strategy.

After all the intense work, Radford's health failed. In the summer of 1946, she got pregnant, but soon after, while holidaying at the seaside resort of Plettenberg Bay, she contracted tick-bite fever. An illness marked by dangerously high body temperatures, swelling, and headaches, the fever forced her to return to Cape Town. She gamely went to work for a few days, and then her doctor ordered her to bed for a fortnight.[14] Soon after, she miscarried her baby, and, now forty years old, she gave up trying to bear a child.[15] For much of the next four months, she stayed at home—depressed, ill and unable to get out of bed—leaving Christine Cash in charge of Barrack Street.[16] In September 1946 Radford declined to run again for her seat on the Cape Town city council.[17]

The Sedition Trial battered her enthusiasm for political work. Although she posted bail the same day she was arrested, Radford and her husband were noticeably frightened by the prospect of a long-term jail sentence.[18] Radford spent weeks in Johannesburg when the case shifted there. She discussed strategy with her lawyers and codefendants and spoke at fundraisers for a Party defense fund. But her penchant for courtroom saber rattling, so apparent two years earlier in the mine libel case, disappeared. A photograph of the Sedition Trialists leaving court in November 1946 showed a dapper Bill Andrews, a smiling Fred Carneson and a blanched, frowning Radford.[19]

After the *annus horribilis* of 1946, Radford brightened considerably in 1947. Her health improved and she traveled with Andrews and H. A. Naidoo to Port Elizabeth in April for a week of trade-union meetings.[20] In August, she ran for city council again, but narrowly lost to a Cape Town businessman and was unable to regain her seat.[21] At the same time, the government withdrew all charges against her in the Sedition Trial. Because she was the only accused person released, a storm of rumor swirled around the unexpected discharge, and Radford later suggested that it was Colin Steyn, the former minister of justice and a personal friend of Radford's, who intervened on her behalf.[22]

By then her political acumen had failed her. In her "Topical" column on 12 June 1947, she discussed the sensitive situation of the Native Representative Council boycott. The NRC—an advisory board created in 1936 when the government removed all Africans from the voter rolls, and long considered a "toy telephone" for its inability to get its opinions heard—had become politically untenable. The council adjourned during the mine strike, and most NRC members, with the somewhat tentative support of the ANC and the Party, boycotted the council's meetings thereafter.[23] Radford voiced a natural but provocative opinion, under the heading "Looking Ahead," when she blithely suggested the NRC boycott might end because of electoral pragmatism:

> There is a possibility of an interesting situation arising as a result of the African decision to boycott elections under the NRC Act of 1936. Next year's general election will be a critical one for South Africa, and I can foresee that the African peoples' leaders may be asked to reconsider their decision in the interests of the country. A reduction in the very small number of progressive MP's might greatly strengthen the Nationalists and lead to an openly Fascist Government. It is true that some Europeans may be prepared to stand against the expressed wishes of the majority of Africans, but they would scarcely be of a calibre to exercise much influence in the struggle against Fascism.

The following morning, the *Cape Times* ran a page-two story on Radford's prediction. "The article indicates a complete change of attitude in the Communist 'high command' for on May 26 the party announced its support of the boycott," the *Cape Times* said under the headline NATIVES URGED TO VOTE—CHANGED VIEW OF COMMUNISTS. "There is little doubt that the movement is mainly influenced by the passive resistance campaign of disaffected Indians in the Union." In the same issue, the *Cape Times* led off its editorial page by stating that Radford's comments were "comforting, as showing some glimmer of reality to find the *Guardian*, the local Communist weekly, hinting that perhaps the decision to boycott may be unwise."

Glimmers turned into blasts. The "news flashed up to Johannesburg," as Radford remembered, and activists sprung up to condemn Radford's straying from the Party line.[24] "I was amazed to read your remarks in 'Topical,'" Michael Harmel, the *Guardian* Johannesburg correspondent, wrote to Radford. Yusuf Dadoo issued a message (which Radford published on the front page of the *Guardian*): "No one in his right senses can quarrel with Betty Radford's contention that the Malanazis present a live and real danger to South Africa. . . . But I do object most strongly to Betty Radford's approach to the coming elections, which is not only misleading but which bristles with the very same danger she tries to avoid."[25] Bill Andrews mentioned the incident in a diary entry concerning the regular Thursday evening CEC meeting: "Betty came late and went away unwell after about ten minutes. Probably upset—with the storm her article about the African boycott has aroused in Party circles."[26] Four days after the column, the Central Committee issued a statement refuting Radford.[27]

On 19 June, Radford published both Harmel's and Dadoo's letters and issued a retraction under the heading "Was Not Intended." "Into this rambling paragraph the *Cape Times* read a significance which certainly was not intended and wasn't there," she wrote. "Some supporters of the boycott swallowed the story whole, without bothering to read the *Guardian* and were naturally highly indignant. . . . [Dadoo] apparently thinks I'm in favour of the United Party as the bulwark against Fascism in this country. . . . The necessity is to determine how best to safeguard the democracy we have and how it may be most rapidly extended." In "Topical," Radford further apologized for her remarks: "This column—not that you've ever thought it—is not the voice of the Communist Party's 'high command' whoever they may be. It is a personal column written by me and is good, bad, or indifferent depending on the writer's feeling bright, tired or too busy." Radford also posted a letter to the editor of the *Cape Times*, condemning the daily for attributing "far too much significance to my remarks," for quoting "them incorrectly," for supposing Radford represented the "high command," and for calling the *Guardian* the CP's official organ.[28]

Radford's comments struck a nerve. The Party fought for national liberation, and the boycott of "toy telephone" segregationist structures like the NRC made sense. Yet it participated in white-only structures, like Parliament and city councils. Her comments were not so outlandish in the end: the Party reversed its attitude at the December 1947 annual national conference, and by a vote of 57–7 came out against the NRC boycott.[29] The flurry of recriminations, then, told a deeper story. The crackdown after the mine strike was part of a sea change of attitudes. Gone were the heady days of the war, when anyone could join the Party, and the Party looked like it might bring about the revolution. Gone were the days of rambling paragraphs.

On 8 September 1947, less than a week after her city-council election defeat and twelve days after the Sedition-Trial discharge, Betty Radford and George Sacks sailed to England. Radford was in a state of collapse, and Sacks prescribed an extended rest in England, among family and friends. They planned to stay for ten weeks, but instead five months passed before they steamed back into Table Bay. Although the trip was mostly a curative one, Radford did maintain a political profile. In London she interviewed Harry Politt, the British CP leader, and spoke at the *Daily Worker*'s eighteenth-birthday celebration.[30] She traveled to Paris, Milan and then Prague, where she interviewed the Czechoslovakian foreign secretary and visited a former Nazi death camp. She posted long letters to the *Guardian* describing her travels.[31]

At the end of February 1948, the Cape Town *Guardian* league threw a welcoming cocktail party for Radford (it netted £70), and the editor sat down again at her backroom desk at Barrack Street.[32] She published a long letter, discussing the "many new plans for The *Guardian*."[33] Despite her sabbatical and her high hopes upon returning, Radford could not summon enough passion for her job. Telephone calls went unanswered, correspondence piled up. "In a moment of aberration," as she called it, Radford threw half an article in the wastepaper basket one day.[34] She stopped writing reviews and asked others to help edit. Instead of listing just herself as "responsible for all political matter," as she had done a decade before, she added three other staff members.[35]

At the end of August Betty Radford resigned her position as editor of the *Guardian*. In her valedictory issue of 2 September 1948, she wrote a brief history of the newspaper, and with an eye to future historians said, "Perhaps one day we will get together and write the story of its early days." At a farewell party, the editorial staff gave her a complete bound set of *Guardian* back issues.[36]

Radford took more than half a year to let go completely. She continued to write "Topical." She reviewed Eddie Roux's seminal book *Time Longer Than Rope* and wrote obituaries.[37] She gave her support to the first licensed hotel for non-Europeans in Cape Town and in her explanation hinted at the bitterness enveloping her political persona: "This doesn't mean I am a supporter of apartheid, in case you consider this a plea for it."[38] On 24 March 1949, ending a tradition that had begun six hundred issues before, Radford wrote her last "Topical" column.[39]

Thereafter, a silence. In the 1950s Radford and Sacks completely disassociated themselves from the liberation movement. They retained almost none of the friendships formed while guiding the *Guardian*. Even casual socializing stopped. In turn, the movement ostracized them. The nickname for the Communist Party was "The Family," and when one left, it was seen as a personal betrayal. Among the hundred *Guardian* staff members interviewed for this book, not one could recall a single conversation with Radford and Sacks in the 1950s, except Brian Bunting, who resentfully remembered that

Radford had sold her bound collection of the *Guardian* to an American collector.[40] In 1961, soon after the state of emergency ended, Radford and Sacks emigrated to London.[41] They settled in Kensington. For five years Sacks worked as an assistant editor at the British medical journal, the *Lancet*. In August 1973 Betty Radford died at the age of 67; in December 1981 George Sacks died at the age of 81.[42]

Radford gave the best years of her life to the *Guardian*. Without her, the newspaper certainly would have never survived. She took the idea of a trade-union, anti-fascist journal and, by widening its focus, created a publishing phenomenon. The *Guardian* was influential, respected and financially stable when she resigned, and no subsequently apolitical years could diminish those rather astounding facts. Sacks had contributed as well with his timely, well-structured articles. In 1938 he wrote an article called "In Defense of Parlour Bolsheviks" that addressed the conflict at the heart of the life that he and his wife lived. Agitating for the working class while living in the upper class presented a "Great Dilemma" for the armchair radical: "By virtue of his economic and social background he is cut off from the group of people whom he recognises as the only possible architects of a changing order." The only options, Sacks believed, were to become an ultra-revolutionary Trotskyist and "have nothing to do with the drudgery of meetings or interminable discussions in cold draughty rooms," or to internalize the conflict and try to overcome the differences on a "personal" level.[43] Neither Radford nor Sacks had been able to overcome the contradictions of background and class.

At least once, Radford felt free from it all. On the day the Allies landed on the beaches of Normandy, she proudly unfurled a red banner out the third-story window at Barrack Street. It was her best moment.

The loss of the founding editor triggered an avalanche of exits from the *Guardian*.

Following Betty Radford and George Sacks's pattern, Carina Pearson and Harold Baldry holidayed in Europe after the war, returned to Cape Town, left the newspaper and the Party, endured ostracism and eventually emigrated to London. In July 1947, after a farewell soiree at Ray Alexander and Jack Simons's home, Pearson and Baldry and their one child sailed for England for a six-month holiday.[44] In November 1948, hard on the heels of Radford's resignation two months earlier, Carina Pearson left her position as circulation manager, and Harold Baldry abandoned his "Behind the Overseas News" column.

Six weeks later, Doris Lessing came to Cape Town with her two-year-old son and a suitcase containing a draft of her first novel, *The Grass Is Singing*.[45] The twenty-nine-year-old Rhodesian communist needed a place to stay while she waited for a berth on a ship sailing to England. She went directly to the Baldrys' house in Oranjezicht. Two years earlier, the Baldrys had issued an open invitation to Lessing to stay with them whenever she returned to Cape Town, but times had changed. "I went into their beautiful house, which was on one of the hills overlooking the bay. I was full of comradely emotions," remembered Lessing. "I was greeted with an unmistakable atmosphere of liberal detachment and the words: 'Of course we have left the Party, and we are no longer prepared to be made use of.'" Pearson refused her a bed and harangued her about the folly of coming to Cape Town in the high season with no accommodation secured. All the boarding houses and hotels were full. Lessing murmured about calling for a taxi, and Pearson curtly showed her to a telephone. Luckily, the taxi driver (a National Party supporter) had an aunt who ran a cheap boarding house in Cape Town. Lessing and her son managed to stay in a back room for a month, until they sailed for Plymouth.[46]

In 1954 Carina Pearson and Harold Baldry emigrated to Southampton, England. Baldry became a classics professor at the university there and wrote a number of influential books on Greek literature.[47] Pearson died in December 1985, and Baldry, the last of the founding *Guardian* quartet, died in November 1991.

Three other contributors departed after the war. In 1946 Donald Molteno, who had worked with the newspaper since its founding, resigned from the *Guardian*'s newly created board of directors. Radford had asked him to join the board with the assurance that there would be "a broadening of its basis of policy." Instead, Molteno found "that strong support was being given to the Communist Party," which Radford had apparently told him would not occur.[48] Christine Cash, the weekly's primary staff reporter, left in 1946 and emigrated to England. There she wrote a column for a Scottish newspaper, gave radio broadcasts about women for the BBC and wrote a book for would-be emigrants to South Africa. After moving to Dallas, Texas, to run a cattle ranch, she suddenly died in February 1950.[49] When Baldry resigned, Harry Bloom, a regular Durban correspondent during the war, took over his column. Bloom, under his pseudonym Walter Storm, added a new twist to Vigilator's distant analysis by reporting on European events while actually in Europe. Bloom was too good at his job and soon left the *Guardian* to write for more lucrative overseas newspapers. He also wanted to finish his first novel, *Episode*, which was published to much acclaim in 1956.[50]

A new group of journalists stepped into the breach, considerably changing the direction and shape of the decade-old newspaper. In June 1946 the Communist Party leadership invited Brian Bunting to come down from Johannesburg to assist the ailing Radford.[51] The invitation was not unexpected, for Bunting seemed destined to run a radical newspaper. His pedigree was impeccable. In 1866 his grandfather, Thomas Percival Bunting, founded the *Contemporary Review*, a leading monthly magazine based in Oxford; T.P. was friends with Gladstone and knighted in 1908. Bunting's father, Sidney Percival Bunting, came out to South Africa during the Boer War and, with Bill Andrews, created the International Socialist League in 1915, and its successor, the Communist Party of South Africa, in 1921. S.P. was treasurer and secretary of the Party, and editor for many years of the Party newspaper, the *International*. Throughout the twenties he led the "Negrophilists" faction in the Party, who fought for an emphasis on Africans rather than white workers. Losing that battle, Bunting, along with Bill Andrews, Fanny Klenerman, and Solly Sachs, was purged from the Party in 1931 for "right-wing deviations," which included speaking at a rally from the same platform as ANC leaders.[52]

By then, Brian Percy Bunting was in the midst of a most unusual childhood. In his home, the clipped Oxford accent of his father mingled with the Yiddish of his mother, Rebecca Notlowitz, who had grown up in Lithuania. At age two, Brian traveled to Europe and stayed in London while his father met with Lenin in Moscow.[53] A flood of visitors came to talk politics at the Bunting's Regent Street house in Johannesburg. Often, S.P. took Brian and his older brother Arthur to African townships like Evaton or Prospect, where he addressed street-corner meetings, and the boys played with local children and ate roasted corn. The family made an annual pilgrimage to Rosettenville to see a rock pockmarked by bullets fired by strike-breaking police during the 1922 Rand Revolt.[54] In the winter of 1929 when S.P. ran for the Transkei seat in Parliament, Brian, age nine, joined him on the hustings, traveling to remote villages in a rickety old van.[55] At fifteen, Brian matriculated at the University of the Witwatersrand. While at Wits, he edited the campus newspaper, *Wu's Views*, and a literary magazine, *Umpa*, and was elected president of the student representative council.[56] After graduation in 1939, he worked as a night-shift subeditor at the *Rand Daily Mail* and the *Sunday Times* while finishing his honors thesis on the influence of the Industrial Revolution on the English novel.[57] In 1942 he joined the army and fought as an air mechanic and information officer. After demobilization he returned to Johannesburg to edit the Springbok Legion's monthly newspaper, *Fighting Talk*.

Despite his father's bitter expulsion, Bunting joined the Communist Party at age twenty. "With me the question of membership in the Party was rather academic," he recalled, "because my father and mother were both in the Party. Although he was expelled and so on and so forth, we still considered ourselves to be communists. We had a quarrel with the local leadership, but, as far as the movement as a whole was concerned, we felt a loyalty towards it. Joining the Party wasn't breaking new ground, but rather returning to an old pitch."

In June 1946, on the day he married Sonia Isaacman, Bunting boarded the night train to Cape Town. Their honeymoon would wait.[58] Bunting started work at the *Guardian* as an assistant editor and immediately fell into a enjoyable routine. "It was a lively office," he recalled, "people coming and going, a real centre of activity. And as a journalist, a trained journalist, I found my work quite rewarding."[59] Within the Party hierarchy, Bunting rose quickly. In January 1948 he was elected to the Central Executive Committee, and three months later, a week before his twenty-ninth birthday, he became chairman of the Cape Town branch.[60] With Radford increasingly absent, the assistant editor gradually assumed a good deal of responsibility. He wrote lengthy articles; reported on meetings; reviewed numerous books, plays, and concerts; and took over editorial writing from Jack Simons.[61] When Radford was gone on her five-month holiday in Europe, he served as acting editor.

Bunting was the natural successor to Radford. With his horn-rimmed glasses and jutting, stone-tight Bunting jaw, he stamped his personality on the newspaper. Bunting could be faulted for a vinegary disdain for ideological flexibility. Yet he was a brilliant, agile newspaperman, a political mastermind, and above all, a man unhesitatingly dedicated to the struggle. He became the voice of the *Guardian* and the main reason that voice was heard for so long.

Old Party stalwarts stayed with the weekly during the transition. Ray Alexander contributed trade-union pieces, and although he relinquished the editorial writing task in 1947 to Bunting, Jack Simons offered occasional articles as well as advice.[62] In 1946 H. A. Naidoo, along with Solly Sachs and Hymie Basner, went overseas for seven months, first to the United Nations in New York and then to the Empire conference in London as a delegate from the South African Indian Congress. Naidoo raised over £250 in America for the Party's Sedition Trial fund, posted numerous reports and photographs back to the *Guardian,* and received a standing ovation from seven hundred delegates at the British Communist Party's annual national conference.[63] After his return in March 1947, Naidoo soon took over from Harry Bloom and assumed the international-news analysis column.[64]

With Christine Cash's departure, the weekly needed a new staff reporter. Hired originally in 1946 as a secretary for Radford, Naomi Shapiro took the job. A shy, unassuming woman from Paarl, Shapiro quickly became a key contributor, and so dependable that Bunting transferred her in 1948 to fill a three-month gap at the Johannesburg office.[65]

Racial diversity finally came to the weekly with Henry Nxumalo. A Zulu from Durban, Nxumalo had worked in a boilermaker's shop before finding a job in Johannesburg as a messenger for the black commercial daily, *Bantu World.* He rose through the ranks and became a sports writer there, before heading off to war to work for a South African Army newspaper in Egypt.[66] Upon returning to South Africa, he did welfare work for the British Empire Service League, the Springbok Legion's rival servicemen's society. In July 1947 Nxumalo joined the *Guardian* with a "World of Sport" column, on the back page next to the horse-racing tips. Covering everything from boxing to rugby to cricket to American baseball, Nxumalo's column became a popular feature.[67]

No addition was more important than Ruth First. Like Bunting, she came from a family steeped in radical politics. Her parents, both émigrés from Lithuania, were Party members in Johannesburg, and her father Julius had been chairman of the Party in the 1920s. At age fourteen, First joined the Junior Left Book Club, and four years later, the Young Communist League. After studying at the University of the Witwatersrand, she found a job in the research division of the social-welfare department of the Johannesburg City Council.[68] When the 1946 mine strike exploded, First joined an emergency strike committee. She drafted, hand-printed and distributed leaflets, tossing them over fences into mining camps, and she even set up a duplicating machine in her boardinghouse room.[69] After the police arrested the entire Johannesburg Party district committee, First became the acting district secretary and abandoned her welfare job to work full-time for the Party. At the end of the year, the Party decided that the *Guardian* needed a Transvaal branch manager (no one had officially replaced Rona Worrall when she left during the war). The former social worker fit the bill.

First was a fascinating woman. Strikingly beautiful, she kept her hair coiffed. She favored Italian shoes, and French handbags and perfume. Four times a year she had a shopping session at Johannesburg's most elite store, Eric Pugen, and every year or two she bought a new Citroën. She even remembered to pack silk underwear when she went off to jail for the Treason Trial.[70] Yet her penchant for fashion melded perfectly with her daily trips into the townships and her regular Monday evening Party district committee meetings. In a political world controlled by men, First cut an intimidating swath. "Fiery in her politics and fashionable in her dress," wrote her daughter, and First knowingly coupled her feminine style with a sharp, abrupt tongue and a sagacious mind. Many colleagues later recalled First with the phrase "Ruth didn't suffer fools gladly." Lionel Forman, a fellow communist and colleague at the weekly, wrote a little limerick about her:

> There was a young liberal called Ruth
> An absolute stranger to truth
> Whose temper was bad
> (I know it—By gad)
> A temper most surely uncouth.[71]

A champion cussing artist joined First at Commissioner Street. Ivan Schermbrucker had spent his childhood in the Transkei. After finishing high school in Umtata, he worked in the mines, fought in the war, returned a committed communist, and with his ability to speak fluent Xhosa, landed a job in the Native Affairs Department. At the same time First came to the *Guardian*, Schermbrucker latched on as the Johannesburg circulation and office manager. He matched First with an equally fiery temper. "Ivan had a reputation for being the biggest swearer in the whole of South Africa," Albie Sachs remembered. "He was a sweet, gentle, super guy, but at work he swore and swore and swore and swore."[72]

First and Schermbrucker formed a close alliance that changed the *Guardian*'s role in the political life of Johannesburg. Both loved jokes and parties, and nothing animated them more than scoring a political point against Pretoria. Moreover, Schermbrucker's ability to speak Xhosa and his engaging personality gave the *Guardian* an essential access to the African scene. Three decades later, First wrote to Schermbrucker's wife Leslie: "I remember all his swear words, and his impatience, but also his loving care and concerns. His passions, and fury, but his gentleness over the persons and problems that matter. . . . I wish I had rushed less in those old newspaper days and taken more time to savour that extraordinary team partnership we had going in the office . . . [with his] salty vitality and disrespect for everything except the real act, the real thing. And I would love to hear him curse in Portuguese."[73]

A quiet Jewish woman named Winnie Kramer teamed up with the two foul-mouthed firebrands. Kramer, another daughter of Baltic émigrés, joined the *Guardian* in late 1946 as the chief administrative officer in charge of all the bookkeeping.[74] Complementing these new additions, Michael Harmel, the weekly's longtime Johannesburg correspondent, remained a book reviewer, and in June 1949 assumed Radford's "Topical" column. Renamed "By the Way," and written under the pseudonym Alan Doyle, the column contained crisp chunks of the quotable and the quotidian.[75]

Mirroring the changing editorial staff was the material the weekly printed. In many respects, the *Guardian* carried on its traditional role for the Party. Although Radford wrote in her 1947 *Cape Times* letter during the NRC crisis that the *Guardian* was "not the official organ of that [Communist] Party," such parsing fooled nobody.[76]

The Central Executive Committee, which included editor Betty Radford, exerted enormous influence on the weekly. It decided editorial policy. It hired new staff members. It publicly raised money for the newspaper.[77] In return, the *Guardian* was the unofficial mouthpiece of the Party. Statements, interviews, photographs, announcements of meetings, reports on campaigns—the gallimaufry of *Guardian* concerns reflected how inseparable it was from the Party. National and district conferences found themselves breathlessly covered in the weekly's pages, with the newspaper's New Year issue always opening with three weeks of front-page articles and photographs from the annual national conference.[78] May Day still dawned with greetings from communist-run trade unions and associations.[79] The *Guardian* publicized the effort to raise money for the legal fees of the Sedition Trial–bound Central Executive Committee, and ran full pages of verbatim testimony from the trial.[80]

The weekly threw its weight behind the Party's next foray into white electoral politics. During the 1948 general election, the *Guardian* vigorously backed the campaigns of communists, and its post-election commentary led with a Party statement.[81] When Sam Kahn became an MP—the Party's first—after a November 1948 by-election, the *Guardian* launched a fusillade of coverage: photographs showed "extraordinary scenes of enthusiasm" at the announcement of his election victory, and the weekly ran his maiden parliamentary speech in full.[82] Nothing defined the relationship more clearly than a back-page comment by Betty Radford in 1947: "The place for all honest and courageous people in South Africa is inside the Communist Party."[83] Above stood the masthead of the *Guardian*, in bright Marxist red.

Internationally, the *Guardian* sailed a communist course. A sense of urgency, now prompted not by the war against Germany but the cold war, breezed through the pages of the weekly. US WAR MANIA FRIGHTENS WORLD rang out the headlines.[84] "Daily the acts of the capitalist classes who rule the western world discredit their claim to leadership of the world." Brian Bunting ended a 1948 editorial: "And daily it becomes clearer that the struggle for socialism is not a mere matter of substituting one ideology for another, but a fight for the very future of humanity. From this struggle no one has the right to stand aside."[85] The weekly greeted the New Year in 1949 with two articles placed side by side, one headlined IN KUOMINTANG CHINA— A SLAVE GIRL COSTS A HUNDRED DOLLARS. . . . , and the other . . . . BUT RUSSIA SPECIALISES IN CHILD WELFARE.[86] A strident tone hammered home the preferred thinking, yet the *Guardian* maintained its usual humorous side. One columnist, the pseudonymous Diogenes, reported the current joke: "The latest definition of a Hollywood Communist is a man who has six telephones but still talks about the party line."[87]

Flexibility within the Party-*Guardian* relationship existed. Bunting later recalled a sense of informality in policymaking: "It worked much more naturally because I was a member of the Central Committee and most of the other people who had contact with the paper were, if not members of the Central Committee, members of the Party. It was just natural that the decisions of the Party about this and that and the general line that would be followed would be reflected in the columns of the paper. You wouldn't have a formal discussion about the *Guardian*, and formal instructions issued by this, that and the other—that didn't happen. It was just something that flowed naturally." Not all the *Guardian* editorial staff carried Party membership cards, most notably Christine Cash and Henry Nxumalo. Hyman Basner, a prominent Jewish lawyer in the Transvaal and an MP representing the African population, wrote the *Guardian*'s parliamentary column in 1947. (Basner had been a member of the Party from 1933 until 1939, when he quit in protest of its anti-war policy.) In preparation for the 1948 general election, the *Guardian* ran a series of meditative articles written by various South Africans under the Lenin-echoing title "What Is To Be Done?" Basner discussed his "feelers" concerning the idea of starting a new political party, and Colin Legum, a Labour Party politician, also offered his views.[88]

Delineating the *Guardian*'s role in South African politics was the February 1947 visit of the British royal family. A decade after 1936, the year of the three kings, the British monarchy had recovered some of its glory, and many South Africans still revered the throne. Communists considered the monarchy an anachronism and a weapon of the oppressors, so the visit of King George VI, his wife, and two daughters drew negative publicity in the weekly. For three months, the *Guardian* printed graphic photographs of shantytowns and slums under the heading "What the King Won't See."[89] Sam Kahn gave a blistering interview to the newspaper, calling the visit "a wicked waste."[90] Editorials rang out in favor of a boycott of the royals, and during the week of their actual visit to Cape Town, the *Guardian* ran a long article on "People's Needs Lost among Royal Glamour."[91]

A special twelve-page edition celebrating the weekly's tenth anniversary bumped right up against the royals. Normally, the *Guardian* used a Thursday-night freight train to send its northern edition to the Transvaal. On this particular week, the train's two cargo compartments were full—one with the royal family's luggage, the other with a corpse— and a railway worker threw the *Guardian* bundles onto a Friday-morning train. Railway officials forgot to inform Commissioner Street about the delay and then lost track of the bundles. Ruth First and Winnie Kramer, still in their first month on the job, spent Friday evening and all of Saturday in the midsummer heat searching frantically for the lost *Guardian*s. After twenty hours, just before abandoning the hunt, they triumphantly located the bundles in a shunted railway siding. There was no sign of the emperor's clothes, or, for that matter, the corpse.[92]

The *Guardian*'s growing commitment to the national liberation struggle shook more foundations than a king's visit. What had been a mild, patronizing interest in the 1930s and a low-end priority during the war developed into the central bailiwick of the weekly. From page-seven doldrums, African issues flew past the trade unions and white politics to the rarefied heights of front-page outrage.[93] The "native question," as they said in South Africa, was for the *Guardian* no longer a question.

Prompting the *Guardian*'s evolution were not any eye-opening epiphanies at Barrack Street, but a variety of subtle changes to the South African political landscape, especially the emerging militancy of the African National Congress. The Congress was moribund during the war—in 1941 Moses Kotane, the Party general-secretary and ANC executive member, called the Congress "a sports club"—and two years later one Congress official esti- mated that membership stood at just 253.[94] However, A. B. Xuma slowly changed the Congress after becoming president in December 1940; he re- vised the ANC's antiquated constitution to make the Congress a year-round organization, and leased their first permanent office space in 1943.[95] More- over, radical young men like Nelson Mandela, Walter Sisulu, and Oliver Tambo breathed new life into the Congress by creating an ANC Youth League. Many of the Youth Leaguers came from Fort Hare, the only univer- sity in South Africa for Africans and other blacks. Fort Hare bred student militancy, with ANC statesman Professor Z. K. Matthews spreading the con- tagion of resistance among eager students.[96] The aftermath of the 1946 mine strike gave renewed impetus to the young Turks. "The mine strike of 1946 was one of those great social events which at one illuminate and accelerate history," Michael Harmel later wrote. "It spelt the end of the compromising, concession-begging tendencies which had hitherto dominated African poli- tics."[97] The Youth Leaguers fought the old ANC guard, forced administrative changes, and propelled the Congress towards mass action. More and more Africans paid the annual dues of two shillings and sixpence and by 1947 membership had risen to 7,000.[98]

For the Communist Party, these transformations meant they finally had a political partner with which to work. In turn, the Party's leadership be- came more intrigued with politics than economics. They moved "national liberation" to the front of its 1950 annual report and relegated a shorter section on the "trade union movement" to the end—a complete reversal of earlier reports.

The relationship between the Congress and the Party was fraught with tension. Though the Youth League's first chairman, William Nkomo, was a Party member, and its first secretary, Lionel Majambozi, was in the Young Communist League, the Youth League opposed any interaction with the communists, and in both 1945 and 1947 attempted to purge Party members from the ANC.[99] Dismissing the Party and the *Guardian* as "Vendors of For- eign Methods," Mandela sneered that "their voice is negligible and in the last analysis counts for nothing."[100] When Ruth First, as secretary of the Pro- gressive Youth Council, asked to affiliate with the Youth League in March 1945, the Youth League flatly refused, referring to a "yawning gulf between your policy or philosophic outlook and ours." If they joined forces, the Youth League contended, it would "result in chaos, ineffective action and mutual jealousies, rivalry and suspicion."[101]

In some ways the Youth League's push for power within the ANC dictated its anti-communist position. The old guard, especially in the Transvaal, had always worked with the Party: Transvaal ANC president C. S. Ramohanoe served on *Inkululeko*'s editorial board from 1944 to 1950; Abner Kunene, a leader of the Alexandra shanty committee, was *Inkululeko*'s business manager; and dozens of ANC leaders carried Party membership cards. Furthermore, in 1945 *Inkululeko* daringly claimed to be the ANC's mouthpiece, and more than half the photographs printed in the newspaper between 1946 and 1950 were of ANC leaders.[102]

The *Guardian* exhibited these strands of attraction and repulsion. On any political issue pertaining to Africans, the weekly went directly to ANC leaders, even militant Youth Leaguers like Anton Lembede, for a quotation.[103] Naomi Shapiro recalled that during her 1947 tenure at Commissioner Street, the routine went as follows: "In Johannesburg you'd start at the beginning of the week and go to the ANC offices and to the trade union offices, J. B. Marks, and the TIC [Transvaal Indian Congress] offices and that's how you got your news."[104] Many African leaders wrote pieces for the *Guardian*. In 1947 J. B. Marks gave a memorable obituary of Lembede to the newspaper that ended, "To his critics I say let us write the late Lembede's virtues in brass and his vices, if any, on water. Farewell, Lembede, farewell."[105] Congress men and women contributed to the steady stream of unsolicited letters to the editor.[106] The weekly printed dozens of photographs of ANC rallies, eyewitness reports from branch conferences, and the traditional annual national convention held each December in Bloemfontein.[107] Unreleased Congress memoranda found their way into *Guardian* offices, and for much of 1947 the weekly ran a column titled "African National Congress News."[108]

Even with the political stakes rising, the *Guardian* smashed occasional volleys of criticism at the callow Congress. With no newspaper of its own, the Congress was appreciative of the weekly's attentions; in a letter to the editor in February 1950, A. P. Mda, president of the ANCYL, wrote, "The *Guardian* is the only paper that reported on the [1949] ANC conference in Bloemfontein with an amount of objectivity."[109] But with contentious issues, objectivity sometimes fell by the wayside. Although the *Guardian* itself was guilty of sowing seeds of confusion on the NRC boycott issue, the weekly harshly condemned any ANC deviation. In a 1948 New Year's message, printed in the black commercial daily *Bantu World*, ANC president Xuma had advocated ending the boycott and returning the present NRC members back to the council. The *Guardian*, with the brazen headline DR XUMA IGNORES ANC DECISION ON ELECTIONS, came down hard on the president (although the Party had just advocated the same thing at its annual conference a month before). Xuma had "thrown the whole electorate into confusion," Barrack Street declared. "It is time Dr. Xuma stopped making individual statements."[110] Two weeks later, the weekly ran an interview with Edwin Mofutsanyana in which he condemned the conservative *Bantu World* editor Selope Thema for his "scurrilous attacks" over the boycott.[111] In 1950 the weekly noted the ANC's new NRC policy of non-collaboration: "If this means nothing more than the resignation of individuals from public bodies, it will in fact be a retreat and a screen for inactivity."[112]

The People's Assembly produced almost as much wrangling as the NRC boycott. During the 1948 elections, the ANC, the Party and other progressive groups organized a shadow parliament. Called the People's Assembly, it aired grievances and issued a People's Charter calling for a democratically elected government.[113] The Youth League opposed the assembly because it involved non-Africans and communists. In July 1948 the *Guardian* ran an article on an eight-hour discussion about the People's Assembly that occurred at the ANC's Transvaal conference, which included C. S. Ramohanoe, the Transvaal ANC president and *Guardian* ally, barely weathering a no-confidence motion put forth by the Youth League. (Ramohanoe, who called the ANCYL leaders "armchair politicians who keep going from place to place preaching Congress and doing nothing," had been under fire since 1945, when during the Alexandra bus boycott, he promised but failed to quit his job as a chief dispatcher for PUTCO, the boycotted firm.)[114] In April 1948 Xuma wrote a long letter to the editor correcting a *Guardian* statement concerning the People's Assembly; Betty Radford replied that "The *Guardian* strongly objects to Dr. Xuma's accusations of distortion and misrepresentation."[115]

Xuma was a quixotic figure for the *Guardian*. Although he was too conservative for their liking, the weekly could ill afford to ignore him. An American-educated medical doctor with an American wife (the former Madie Hall from North Carolina, who headed the ANC Women's League), Xuma lived in a grand house in Sophiatown, with a surgery and small farm attached.[116] Ruth First often quoted him as the representative of African opinion in exclusive interviews and photographs.[117] Barrack Street got a classic quotation from him about the new political term, *apartheid*: "It is a handy election bogey with a new name. It is old wine in new bottles."[118] As with the NRC issue, the weekly attacked him when the King visited for having shamefully "hurried to greet the King at Eshowe," a move that reeked of the submissive Congress deputations in the 1920s.[119] Xuma's astonishing March 1950 resignation played out in the newspaper. He gave a long interview to the weekly explaining his reasons, while Tambo, Mandela and Sisulu, described by Xuma as a "clique," responded three weeks later with their own *Guardian* statement.[120]

Not only did the *Guardian* overtly become involved with the ANC leadership, but it began to earnestly probe the living and working conditions of the people the ANC represented. "What the King Won't See"—but what *Guardian* readers saw—were devastating photographs of emaciated children, dilapidated houses and cramped mine compounds. The *Guardian* exposed life in "tent towns," where thousands of job-seeking Africans lived as squatters. Discussing shantytowns became, in a way, the newspaper's raison d'être, as it explained who lived there and how they managed to survive.[121] Even a jaundiced eye could not help but be outraged at life in Alexandra township in Johannesburg. Alexandra was called "Dark City" because despite the fact that it had been a settled African township since 1912, there was no electricity available for its residents. Two weeks after policemen stormed into an Alexandra squatter camp and arrested four hundred residents, the government tricked hundreds of families into moving to another township and deported a camp leader to a town eighty miles away.[122] The *Guardian* linked the March 1947 Langa riots in Cape Town (one person died and nineteen were arrested) to unrest over housing conditions—especially over the divide-and-rule strategy of keeping separate quarters for bachelors.[123] Barrack Street followed the various bus and tram boycotts and highlighted commuter-train crashes, like the 1949 Orlando disaster in which seventy people were killed.[124] Other articles explored issues such as education—"Nigger Degrees Not Wanted"—the lives of street flower sellers, daycare in the Cape Flats, and health-care issues.[125] Interracial relationships, always a stormy subject for South Africa, graced the front pages. The *Guardian* boldly ran photographs of interracial couples and followed the notorious Seretse Affair in which London had removed the hereditary chief of the Batswana people in the protectorate of Bechuanaland because he had married a white woman.[126]

Spearheading the charge into African life was Ruth First. In her first four weeks at the *Guardian*, the twenty-two-year-old reported on a tin workers' strike, opined on the royal visit, visited a Sophiatown squatter camp, and interviewed Yusuf Dadoo, Michael Scott, H. M. Basner and Anton Lembede.[127] Two months later, she illegally crept into municipal workers' compounds and took photographs at night while holding a flashlight in her free hand.[128] She sent three African employees of the *Guardian* to secretly investigate a price-fixing racket in the sugar industry.[129] She ventured into squatter camps and African townships across the Transvaal and Orange Free State, and datelines as scattered as Pietersburg and Harrismith bore the name of Ruth First.[130] She cultivated close relationships with many political figures, ranging from Youth Leaguers, to the British priest Father Trevor Huddleston, to Walter Sisulu, to Indian leaders like Ismail Meer, whose fourth-floor flat in Market Street was a hotbed of political discussion, dancing, spicy meals and romance.[131]

First landed her first significant scoop after only five months on the job. It was a story about Bethal, a tiny Afrikaner village in the Eastern Transvaal. Bethal's economy, so typical of the South African countryside, was dependent on cheap, seasonal labor. To find workers, Bethal farmers colluded with the police who gave Africans ensnared in the tangled web of the pass laws or caught entering the country illegally the choice of a long jail term or a short contract on Bethal's potato, bean and maize farms. Most chose the farms.[132]

They deeply regretted it. The farmers ill-treated them. Work hours were long—usually dawn to dusk, and until midnight during a full moon. They flogged the workers and demanded they dig out potatoes with their hands instead of spades, to ensure undamaged produce.[133] One farmer hung a laborer from a tree by his feet, pouring boiling water in his mouth when he cried for water and thrashing him to his death. In 1944 a farmer whipped two Bethal workers, Phillip Lebova and Frans Masai, after they tried to escape from his farm. The Catholic diocese in Johannesburg wrote to the Native Affairs Department about the incident. H. M. Basner, the Native Representative in Parliament, heard about the letter but decided not to act, because the farm where it occurred was owned by Jews, and he feared fanning the flames of local anti-Semitism.[134]

In June 1947, while reading at her desk at Commissioner Street, Ruth First came across "a rather cryptic little paragraph" in the 13 June edition of *De Echo*, a weekly Bethal newspaper. The local farmers' union, the Boere Arbeidsvereeniging, had decided to stop supplying laborers to farmers who abused workers. They reached the decision because Balthasar Johannes Brenkman, a foreman in Kalabasfontein, had been fined £75 after beating workers with sjamboks, setting dogs on them, and forcing them to sleep naked and chained with donkey hobbles. Deciding "to do an inspection 'in loco'" First called Michael Scott, an Anglican priest known for his crusading advocacy of African rights.[135] On 25 June First and Scott drove to Bethal, where they met with Gert Sibande, a local ANC official. Sibande took them to two depots for newly arrived recruits, corrugated iron shacks where on Fridays the Boere Arbeidsvereeniging brought men caught crossing the border from Rhodesia. After spending the weekend locked in the shacks, the Africans were forced to sign a six-month contract worth £12.[136] Sibande then escorted First and Scott to three claustrophobic farm compounds where the contracted workers slept.[137] The scenes shocked First, as her lead paragraph in the next edition of the weekly stated: "It is not every day that the Johannesburg reporter for the *Guardian* meets an African farm worker who, when asked to describe conditions on the farm on which he works, silently takes off his shirt to show large weals and scars on his back, shoulders and arms. . . . We saw not a single blanket in any of the compounds. Food consisted of "a clod of mealie meal and a pumpkin wrapped in a piece of sacking, each man taking a handful at a time."[138] After spending the night with Sibande in Bethal, First and Scott visited another farm and then drove back to Johannesburg. Thursday afternoon, the deadline for that week's *Guardian*, had passed.[139] They took the story to a liberal Johannesburg newspaper, the *Rand Daily Mail*. The editor hesitated to print such a scandalous article, but "after a good deal of discussion and after he had made some investigations through his own staff," according to Scott, "he decided to publish."[140]

On Friday, 27 June 1947, Bethal entered the South African lexicon under the growing rubric of towns of shame. Placed on page seven with the small headline NEAR SLAVERY IN BETHAL DISTRICT, the article outlined what they had seen.[141] By the time First was able to publish her *Guardian* article the following Thursday, with a five-column front-page headline—THERE ARE MORE BETHALS—and a Vic Clapham cartoon, the story was the lead front-page feature in every South African daily newspaper. Prime Minister Smuts quickly announced a commission of inquiry and ordered Minister of Justice Harry Lawrence to "remedy the position once and for all with the most drastic means at his disposal."[142] Lawrence sent a battery of policemen, Security Branch detectives and Native Affairs Department officials to ninety-one farms in the Bethal district. Africans living in the Bethal location raised £17 to send six representatives to give evidence in Johannesburg.[143] Lawrence and NAD officials stayed up until two in the morning to finish the report to the prime minister.[144]

Hours of candle burning did not lead to justice. The police arrested just four white foremen, Lawrence's report listed only seven Bethal farms that were involved in cases of extreme abuse (the "majority of Bethal farmers treat their labour properly"), and in November 1947 Lawrence removed his Native Labour Inspectors from Bethal.[145] Election-year politics caused the cover-up. Bethal was a tenuous United Party seat. Worried about platteland Afrikaners, who were considered the swing voters in the upcoming 1948 general election, Smuts backed off. It was too late. Transvaal Afrikaners were furious with the government because of perceived interference over the Bethal case. During the election campaign, J. G. Strijdom, a future prime minister, led a Stryddag (struggle day) in Bethal to rally support for the Nationalists. "A vote for Jan Smuts is a vote for Joe Stalin," the Nationalists sloganeered.[146] The platteland voted solidly for the Nationalists, proving to be the tipping point that brought them to power. It was a scenario First predicted in her final paragraph of her original 3 July 1947 *Guardian* report on Bethal: "Meanwhile the feudal farmer tyrant continues to reign supreme on his own land. Nationalist and United Party caucuses listen to his voice from the platteland and his vote will be eagerly solicited by both parties in the coming election."

Refusing to succumb to the politically-driven apathy, First and Scott returned to Bethal two weeks later. They saw the other side of Bethal this time. In the town hall, they stood in front of 1,500 irate members of the Boere Arbeidsvereeniging. After reading a few paragraphs of his prepared speech, Scott stopped. The roars of anger cascaded down upon him, shouts of "tar and feather him! . . . He's an Uitlander! . . . Deport him!" First and Scott fled the hall.[147] Nonetheless, First stuck to her story. She followed up leads that enabled her to describe how the government and the farming community colluded on labor issues. She found a government notice approving the farm contracts for foreign Africans and reported on special police cars waiting at the Rhodesian border to transport illegals to farms.[148] She interviewed former Bethal laborers, including one Basuto man who after six months' work at a farm in Springs was paid £3.[149] First snapped pictures of lorries carrying pass-law convicts from the main Johannesburg jail, the Fort, to Transvaal farms and reported on Johannesburg's "seven special police sections working by motor-car, motor-cycle and on foot to bring foreign Natives to the book."[150] In February 1950 the *Guardian* ran a large back-page headline above a First article about Bethal: "'THE WORST PLACE GOD HAS MADE'—A STATE OF TERROR IN BETHAL."[151]

Besides throwing the 1948 election to the National Party, the Bethal scandal stimulated the Congress. The ANC wrote to Smuts requesting a seat on the commission of inquiry. Two Bethal laborers attended the 1947 ANC national conference in Bloemfontein, and the executive passed a resolution demanding an inquiry into conditions in the Bethal farming district.[152] Gert Sibande rose to national prominence, became president of the Transvaal ANC, and earned the nickname "The Lion of the East." Five thousand Africans demonstrated in Bethal on the ANC's Day of Protest in June 1950. As Harold Baldry and his "Munich Swindle" pamphlet did a decade earlier, First and Bethal put the newspaper on a new map—an African map.

After years of conservatism, both Indians and coloureds in South Africa revolted against growing persecution. Before the turn of the century, Mahatma Gandhi had founded the first Indian political organization in South Africa, but it was young militants in the Transvaal Indian Congress and the Natal Indian Congress that mounted a necessary revitalization campaign similar to the ANC's Youth League.

The newly invigorated TIC and NIC faced a fresh threat. In the mid-forties Smuts passed the Trading and Occupation of Land Restriction and the Asiatic Land Tenure Acts. Both laws sought to segregate Indians by prohibiting land transfers between Indians and non-Indians. In 1946 the TIC and NIC launched a Passive Resistance Campaign against the two acts and other racist laws, including one outlawing the crossing of provincial borders without a permit. In the PRC, a precursor to the 1952 Defiance Campaign, Indians held mass rallies and picketed land reserved for whites, and over two thousand resisters, many of them women, went to jail.

The *Guardian* followed the resistance campaign assiduously, publishing many articles and photographs of resisters. When the Crown sentenced Yusuf Dadoo, the Indian leader, to three months hard labor, Barrack Street published his statement in court.[153] (The coverage was not enough, and in March 1947 the Transvaal committee in charge of the campaign telegrammed the *Guardian* to ask why there had been a "news blackout" about the latest batch of resisters.[154]) When internal Indian Congress conflicts arose, the *Guardian* wholeheartedly supported the radical elements. A series of articles on the Natal Indian Congress in September 1947 raised the ire of archconservative A. J. Kajee, who threatened to sue the weekly for defamation. Scarred by the Louw affair, the *Guardian* issued an apology.[155]

Indian news became a weekly staple. Jackie Lax reported from all around Natal.[156] Leaders like Dadoo, G. M. Naicker, and Dawood Seedat wrote letters and granted interviews.[157] In November 1949 Naomi Shapiro, after reading the archrival *Die Burger*, informed Dadoo of his government ban against appearing at public meetings.[158] The *Guardian* dissected the 1949 Durban riots, in which Indians and Africans fought running battles in the streets, leaving 142 dead and more than 40,000 in refugee camps.[159] The weekly did not shirk from the true cause of the riots, which was not Indian-Zulu animosity but legislative racism: AFRICANS REVOLT AGAINST REPRESSION rang out the headline.

Coloureds, key supporters of the weekly since the 1930s, also generated more *Guardian* interest after the war. The weekly visited the shantytowns in the Cape Flats and tried to change the stereotype of the "bergie," coloured people who lived in the hills around the Cape: "They are not 'won't works'" read a caption below two photographs.[160] Yet coloureds proved more than a *Guardian* canvas for a telling portrait of life under apartheid. After the war, prices for basic staple items rose, and distribution of the rationed food grew erratic. Coloureds marched on Parliament and, with the help of communists, raided the shops of alleged profiteers.[161]

In stepped John Morley. Sergeant John was back in Cape Town and irrepressible as ever.[162] Morley saw the long queues that coloured women stood in to collect rations as a perfect opportunity to do political work. In March 1946 he organized the waiting women into committees. These committees, at first mandated only to keep order in the queues, expanded in number from twelve in April 1946 to forty by December 1946 and fifty-nine by November 1947, representing more than 45,000 coloured women.[163]. In April 1947 two hundred of the women formed a Women's Food Committee (Morley was elected chair), and dances, rallies in the Grand Parade, and canvassing for elections became part of the WFC's mandate.[164]

Consciousness grew even more when Morley assumed the position of the *Guardian*'s circulation manager after the departure of Carina Pearson in 1947. He recruited dozens of coloured women and their children to sell the *Guardian* as a part-time job.[165] Morley's motto was simple: "Read the *Guardian*, Feed the Mind."

The *Guardian* still floundered in the era's sexist atmosphere. Advertisements had not improved from the 1930s. "Will I Ever Wear a Wedding Veil?" asked a woman with bad breath, and a man told a new Colgate user, "I want to be with you always now—you're so dainty and sweet." Palmolive soap charged women to "keep your skin smooth, youthful, kissable. Keep that lovely schoolgirl complexion to attract a man's attention, arouse his interest in you and tempt his caresses."[166]

The 1948 *Guardian* beauty contest, the brainchild of acting editor Brian Bunting, was perhaps the most egregious example. Bunting restricted contestants to paid-up trade-union members in the Cape, and applicants mailed

Barrack Street sixpence in stamps as an entry fee, a photograph, and their age, weight, and height.[167] In weeks, hundreds of photographs had reached Barrack Street, as Bunting told readers: "It is a pleasure to open our mail these days—it is almost certain to contain pictures of beautiful girls!"[168] For readers' delectation, he printed sample photographs and added captions like "Twenty-two years old, with brown eyes and darker brown hair, tipping the scales at 96 pounds and 5 ft 3 inches in her socks, in brief a beautiful girl! And she lives and works in Cape Town, too!"[169] A panel of judges picked twenty-six semifinalists to participate in a series of evening parades at the Avalon Theatre in District Six and the Palace Theatre in Salt River.[170] At one parade Betty Radford exclaimed to the line of hopefuls, "You are even prettier in real life than in your photographs."[171]

With much fanfare, the judges crowned Tulip Jacobs as Miss *Guardian*. A coloured dressmaker in Hazendaal, Jacobs earned extra money waitressing in Camps Bay, had "a natural bent for painting flowers and was an enthusiastic jazz pianist."[172] As Radford handed her a check for £30, the "vivacious twenty-year-old brunette" gushed, "Oh, how exciting . . . I am so glad, and Mom will be so pleased."[173]

An enormous project involving huge outlays of time, energy, and precious copy space, the *Guardian* beauty contest did have one saving grace. In South Africa even a beauty contest was a political act. The Monday after the parade, Jacob's father came to Barrack Street to thank the weekly for running the contest without a color bar.[174]

Whether managing a women's food committee or parading women on a stage, the newspaper ended the decade in a radically different position than when it started. The *Guardian* was now a black newspaper, and its health as a company slipped from a position of robust strength to a near bankruptcy.

Circulation dropped as dramatically as it had risen. From its wartime high of 50,000, the weekly's figures hovered at 40,000 until 1949, when it slipped inexorably each week down to below 30,000 by the end of the year.[175] Advertising revenue bottomed out. The government closed the wartime tax loophole that enabled advertisers to deduct their expenses. Like circulation, the number of advertisements remained steady until 1949. A 1947 survey revealed that seventy-two companies advertised in the *Guardian*.[176] Dozens of reputable firms used the *Guardian*: Colgate, OK Bazaars ("Africa's Largest Department Store"), Eno's fruit salt, Brylcreem, Coca-Cola, Pyramid brandy, Ottoman cigarettes and Vaseline hair tonic. Yet, the number of advertisements per issue dropped to 35 in 1949 and to 20 in 1950.[177]

Donations also slumped. To stay solvent, the *Guardian* needed £700 a month in donations, but often only half of that arrived at Barrack Street.[178] Running at a loss became a normal operating procedure, with the gap between income and expenditure soaring to £600 a month.[179] Four weeks after the change of editors in 1948, Brian Bunting printed a front-page appeal for money: YOUR *GUARDIAN* IS IN DANGER—BUT YOU CAN SAVE IT. Threatening a "truncated and crippled *Guardian*," Bunting said he would close branch offices and cut staff. Prominent political figures paid tribute to the newspaper in support of the appeal for funds, including Betty Radford, Trevor Huddleston, Eddie Roux, Julius Lewin, Govan Mbeki, Jimmy La Guma and A.W.G. Champion.[180]

Blame lay not at the desk of Brian Bunting. The new political landscape after the May 1948 election led to the weekly's parlous financial situation. Subscribing, let alone donating money, selling or giving advertising, became a frightening prospect for many. After the National Party's ascension to power, Ronald Segal, a radical journalist, wrote, "the timid and the prudent fled from even the most pallid association" with the *Guardian*.[181] "It was very much a poorer paper after the war. A financial battle had to be fought every month . . . commercial outlets for the paper dropped away and we had to build up independent machinery for distribution," Fred Carneson, a *Guardian* staffer, said. "The old people got out when the pressure started building up, they weren't stayers. Once the unifying factors of the war dropped away, the political climate turned chilly, people started to drift away. They were people who weren't able to attune themselves to the new realities of the struggle."[182]

Fighting the hemorrhaging bank account, the *Guardian* used a variety of methods to staunch the bleeding. The weekly placed advertisements in the newspaper trade journal *Selling*, describing its "100% insertion guarantee being given to advertisers in this profitable medium for national reminder advertising." Searching for a marketing niche, the *Guardian* called itself "the ONLY paper which effectively reaches the South African worker of the middle and lower income group, both European and Non-European," the latter of which, "estimated at 85 percent of total sales, read and understand English."[183] Besides the beauty contest, the *Guardian* proffered a number of gimmicks aimed at drawing new readers. In 1950 it held a Toddler Competition in which proud mothers sent Barrack Street photographs of their children in hopes of winning a £10 grand prize.[184] A crossword puzzle appeared in

1947.[185] Barrack Street dispatched *Guardian* "Scouts" to factories to recruit union supporters.[186] In Cape Town, the local African National Congress branch planned *Guardian* bazaars and donated money.[187] The possibilities for fundraising were endless: "Are you feeling shabby and jaded? Then go and buy yourself a new outfit and send your old one to the *Guardian*. We can sell it to swell our funds. We are never too tired to collect."[188] Or this: "Two Claremont women auctioned a French poodle pup (paternity unknown) at a house warming party last week-end."[189]

Stepping up their efforts, the *Guardian* leagues ran nationwide fundraising campaigns.[190] They offered *Guardian* calendars and *Guardian* holiday note cards, jumble sales, gramophone evenings and a People's Ball featuring "Alfredo, the human flame thrower."[191] "It was just another aspect of our political work," remembered Trudy Gelb, a *Guardian*-league leader. "Everything had its role, you see, and the *Guardian* Leagues were a part of that. It wasn't just the money, though the money was rather critical to keeping the paper going. It was the fact we brought people together. We glued them together by having fun."

The two must-do events on the calendar of the South African Left were the newspaper's two annual parties. A highlight of the Cape summer season was the *Guardian*'s black-tie Christmas Eve dance at Hilary and Norman Flegg's estate in Newlands.[192] The Bram and Molly Fischer birthday party was especially famous. To host the hundreds of friends who religiously attended, they pitched a tent on the back lawn and cleared away the dining room. In 1954 they built a swimming pool, a rare accoutrement for a leftist family in Johannesberg, and the party became an opportunity for friends of all races to splash and swim in the midsummer heat. Bram Fischer usually demonstrated his patented head-first flip. As the night wore on, some revelers left sandwiches in the inner recesses of the piano (to be found months later); others disappeared into the far reaches of the garden; and more than a few took off their clothes and skinny-dipped.[193]

Naked swimming aside, people took the fundraising seriously. The Fischers charged each couple a one pound, one shilling entrance fee, usually netting more than £300 for the newspaper each year. Bram was especially diligent. Once, he found that one of his favorite jackets was among the pile of clothes destined for a *Guardian* jumble sale; he paid Molly £5 to keep it.[194]

Despite such altruism, there was no end to the financial problems. Bunting broke with tradition and raised the price of a *Guardian*. After thirteen years at one penny, the *Guardian*, starting in January 1950, cost two pennies, and a year's subscription jumped from £5 to £7 6s.[195]

Death punished the *Guardian* during this time of heightening crisis. In 1946 Charlie Stewart, printer of the *Guardian*, bought a rotary press in Boston in order to increase his printing capacity. While unloading the dismantled press at the Cape Town docks, stevedores (ironically probably readers of the weekly) mistakenly switched containers and sent half of the press to Bombay. Shipping officials forecast a six-month delay before the shipment would return.[196] In despair over what appeared to be a ruinous situation, Stewart committed suicide.[197]

Stewart's partners, faced with the mounting debt incurred by the Bombay-bound press, doubled printing prices. In April 1948, after eleven years of collaboration, the *Guardian* reluctantly left Stewart's. They turned to a political rival, the United Party, which ran a printing house called Unie Volkspers. Despite the weekly's constant attacks on the UP, Unie Volkspers took on the *Guardian* at the old Stewart price.[198] Stewart, however, with his flexibility about bills and his keen interest in the *Guardian*'s success, could never really be replaced.

Another death served as the postscript to the first years of the newspaper. In December 1950, Bill Andrews died of heart failure at Groot Schuur Hospital in Cape Town. He had retired from political life two years earlier, his health failing.[199] In April 1950, Andrews had celebrated his eightieth birthday.[200] On 30 November the *Guardian* ran a final article by Andrews entitled KEEP THE TRADES & LABOUR COUNCIL GOING. A month later he was dead.

Although the *Guardian* celebrated his birthday every year thereafter, the passing of the legendary Andrews represented the dénouement of an era. The mine strike, the Sedition Trial and the introduction of apartheid had forever changed the country.[201] A transformed *Guardian*, with its youthful staff and new policies, was poised to face the future. The past—like the white-haired trade unionist with his pipe and three-piece suits and crackling gray eyes—was gone.

CHAPTER FOUR

The Carry-On

Bannings, 1948–1954

The trouble began on 26 May 1948, the day of the general election. The National Party under D. F. Malan polled 443,700 votes; the United Party got 623,500. But the Nats won the whites-only election because of an electoral bias favoring rural voters. The swing of power was not overly dramatic—the UP went from 89 seats to 65, while the NP went from 43 to 70—but the effect of a new governing party was profound. Jan Smuts was out of power (he even lost his own seat in Parliament). The National Party introduced apartheid, the word which summed up their racial policies. They classified people into one of four racial groups (white, coloured, Indian, and African), instituted more formal segregation, and began to dictate where people could live and work.[1]

For South Africa's communists, the 26th was a terrible watershed. All three Communist Party candidates lost badly in the election (this on top of the landslide defeat of all four Party candidates in the October 1945 Johannesburg city-council elections, a defeat so thorough that one candidate, Michael Harmel, even lost his deposit). Moreover, the National Party represented a victory for policies they had been fighting for decades.

However, one bright spot emerged. In a by-election a few months later for Donald Molteno's seat as one of the three Native Representatives in

Parliament, Sam Kahn became the first Communist Party member to earn a seat in the House of Assembly (the Party had not yet been founded when Bill Andrews served before the First World War). The young lawyer proved to be an earlier version of Helen Suzman, a loud but lonely voice of opposition. Kahn lambasted the Nats for their apartheid legislation. He called the new Mixed Marriages Act, which forbade interracial couples, "the immoral off-spring of an illicit union between racial superstition and biological ignorance" and branded the bill's sponsor, Eben Dönges, a "leading political misanthro-pologist."[2] He mischievously slipped the full text of the *Communist Manifesto* into the Hansard (the official report of Parliamentary proceedings), ensuring that the revered foundation stone of communism would be available to all, courtesy of the government printer.[3] In private, Kahn maintained good friendships with many parliamentary colleagues across the aisle, and he played poker and had drinks regularly with NP members.[4]

Having Kahn in such a commanding position was a boon to the *Guardian*. He often stopped by the weekly's offices on his way to and from the House of Assembly—his legal chambers were at 24 Barrack Street, only a half dozen buildings down from the newspaper—put his feet up on a desk, and told the latest gossip. He assumed the *Guardian*'s parliamentary column. Each week for four years, Kahn reported the mundane and the mirac-ulous in his "In Parliament and Out" column. (Once he and sports writer Henry Nxumalo switched spots, with Kahn writing about cricket and Nxu-malo about the kaffir beer racket.)[5] In 1950 Kahn started a weekly feature called "Barrister," where he discussed apartheid's legal ramifications. "Bar-rister" ran the entire decade and decoded more laws in plainer language than any other public forum in South Africa.[6] Kahn's most ironic contribu-tion came during parliamentary breaks on Fridays, when he walked around the benches, hawking the *Guardian*; he usually sold three dozen copies to various MP's, including cabinet ministers.[7]

The news the parliamentarians read did not please them, and it was not long before they cracked down. Their first step was to ban Kahn and fellow Party leader Yusuf Dadoo from addressing public meetings in specific cities. Kahn and Dadoo responded by going on a nationwide tour. They would speak in a city on the growing intolerance and censorship of the National Party, and then Pretoria would add the city to the list of places in which they were forbidden to address meetings.[8]

This charade of hopscotching from town to town, governmental decrees trailing behind them like an unwanted younger sibling, aroused a sense of outrage among many South Africans. The Transvaal branches of the African

National Congress, the Indian Congress, and the Party organized a "Defend Free Speech" convention. In March 1950, more than 500 delegates and 10,000 onlookers converged in Johannesburg. James Moroka, the new ANC president, traveled from Park Station to City Hall in a flower-bedecked carriage led by a white horse; other ANC leaders, including J. B. Marks, followed on horseback.[9] The convention issued a call for a series of marches and meetings, culminating in a one-day strike on May Day.

Unity was still elusive. The ANC Youth League, having already designated May Day as a strike day as part of the implementation of the 1949 Programme of Action, opposed the strike and disrupted planning sessions. As the May Day weekend approached, the government suddenly banned all public meetings, processions, and demonstrations in the Transvaal. Two thousand policemen streamed into Johannesburg, and on Thursday, 27 April, the *Rand Daily Mail* reported a government official saying that "All agitators will be shot."

The banner headline on the front page of the 27 April edition of the *Guardian*, put to bed on the 25th, originally read "Mass Rallies for Freedom Day—Organisers Warn Against Provocation." With the Youth League disruptions and the threat of governmental violence, Ruth First decided to change the headline. The *Guardian* bundles arrived in Johannesburg by rail on Friday morning. For the next twenty hours, the *Guardian* staff—led by First, Ivan Schermbrucker, and Winnie Kramer—feverishly blacked out announcements of Transvaal meetings, gluing a red strip of paper on top of every front page that read: "Important Notice—Transvaal Political Meetings and Processions for April 29th–30th and May 1st Have Been BANNED by the Government. ALL SUCH MEETINGS HAVE BEEN CANCELED. All Announcements of Such Meetings in This Issue Are CANCELED. The Public Is PROHIBITED from Attending. The *GUARDIAN*."[10]

Gluing and blacking were not enough, and Monday, 1 May 1950 became a day of reckoning for South Africa. In Cape Town the protests went off peacefully. The *Guardian* ran a photograph the next week of a detective slumped in a police car, eyes shut, dozing through the late autumn day. But in the Transvaal, few heeded the *Guardian* stickers. Seven hundred people marched through the town of Bethal. Trying to break up marches, the police killed six people in Alexandria and four in Benoni.[11] In Sophiatown the police baton-charged and fired on a demonstration and the crowd, killing eight men and wounding twenty. Leading the demonstration, Nelson Mandela and Walter Sisulu dove to the ground as mounted police galloped around them, then ducked into a building while hearing the sickening thud of bullets smacking into the walls.[12] Another Youth League member, Bloke Modisane, memorably described the atmosphere: "The shooting, the screaming, the dying continued for what seemed the whole day, and the snap staccato of the guns echoed from all around Sophiatown; and the smell and the decay of death spread over the township, over the burning cinders and the smog."[13] One part-time *Guardian* reporter, Lionel Forman, was in downtown Johannesburg at the Defend Free Speech convention headquarters in Market Street. After arresting Maulvi Cachalia, an Indian youth leader, a riot squad baton-charged the crowd. Forman crouched in a doorway to take photographs of the mayhem. A police sergeant grabbed Forman, hustled him into a squad car, and radioed his headquarters:

> "I have arrested a Jew communist," he reported in Afrikaans.
> "What for?" crackled a voice back over the radio.
> "He's taking pictures here."
> "What?"
> "Pictures."
> "Pictures?"
> "He's taking pictures."
> "No, man," laughed the voice. "You can't arrest a man for taking pictures."

Three of Forman's hard-earned photographs ran in the 11 May 1950 edition of the newspaper.[14]

Mourning for the victims of the startling violence—policemen had not openly fired upon unarmed civilians since the 1921 Bulhoek Massacre—conflated with a protest against a new bill in Parliament. Called the Suppression of Communism Act, the bill gave the government wide-ranging powers to ban organizations, newspapers, and people deemed to promote the spread of "communism." The SCA determined that communism was any "doctrine or scheme which aims at the encouragement of feelings of hostility between the European and Non-European races of the Union." Dubbed "Swart's Gestapo Bill" by the *Guardian* after Minister of Justice Charles Swart, the SCA meant trouble.[15] Brian Bunting devoted the first four pages of the 11 May issue to the SCA, with a Party statement, a piece by Michael Harmel on the history of communism and a long article on the Party's "Proud Record." The weekly noted ruefully on page four: "The entire contents of this page would be unlawful if Swart's Anti-Communism Bill became law." Betty Radford, called out of retirement to give her opinion, wrote that "free expression is in itself something of a social safety valve to those denied direct representation in the bodies governing the country." In Parliament, Sam Kahn placed copies of the *Guardian* on the desks of the twelve cabinet ministers; only four were returned, and after Kahn mentioned the unpaid-for newspapers in a speech, one shilling four pence mysteriously appeared on his desk.[16]

On 14 May, a tense fortnight after the May Day massacres, the ANC and its Youth League, the Communist Party, and the Indian Congresses formed a coordinating committee to lead the fight against the SCA. To protest the May Day massacre and the SCA, the ANC, for the first time in its forty-two-year history, called for a nationwide general strike.

Behind the scenes, the Party scrambled under the Damocles' sword of the SCA. On 5 May the Central Committee, hastily called to Cape Town, considered the two basic choices: going underground or disbanding. Creating a secret Party would be a gargantuan challenge, considering the fact that the Party was not a really revolutionary movement and Pretoria, from its mine-strike raids and back-issues of the *Guardian*, knew who were the Party leaders. Ten years' imprisonment without the possibility of a fine loomed for anyone caught working for "communism." The committee voted 15 to 2 in favor of voluntarily dissolving the Party.[17]

On 15 June, with the Party's offices empty and its papers hidden or destroyed, Sam Kahn rose in the House of Assembly during the second reading of the SCA and poetically announced the dissolution of the Communist Party of South Africa: "You cannot imprison ideas. You cannot impale people's thoughts on bayonets. You cannot crush thought with knobkerries. You cannot concentrate views behind barbed wire, and no amount of suppression, no amount of brutal force to hinder people in the expression of their political views and the attainment of their aspirations will ever succeed. Life will always assert itself."[18]

Eight days later, the Suppression of Communism Act passed in Parliament.[19] The lead story in the 22 June *Guardian* was "Communist Party Dissolves—But Justice Will Triumph." Bunting devoted two pages to Kahn's speech—"perhaps the best speech of his Parliamentary career"—and filled the back page with news of a police baton-charge on a crowd outside Parliament.[20] No one noted that exactly—and only—nine years before, the Nazis had invaded the Soviet Union.

The next week, Bunting delineated the *Guardian*'s policy in a front-page editorial. Despite its now precarious legal position, the weekly would be dedicated "to give publicity to the wrongs and injustices which are daily perpetrated in this country, to fight against the tyranny of the colour bar, to give expression to the grievances and aspirations of the oppressed peoples of this country, to press for social reforms, and to continue the struggle for the achievement of equal rights for all South Africans, irrespective of race, creed or colour."[21] On the back page, Sam Kahn concluded his column on the work of the 1950 House of Assembly by adding, "In all, an appalling Parliament."

For the *Guardian*, dissolution was a disaster. Although its policy of official separation from the Party saved its life, the newspaper was still in intensive care.[22] In a matter of weeks, it had lost its ideological wellspring; its intricate system of correspondents, fundraisers, and sellers; and its core audience. Because the Party informally oversaw the hiring of new staff members, it had also lost its human-resource department.

The *Guardian* needed new policies and new support. It even needed a new language. The reflexive pandering towards the Soviet Union and open use of Marxist nomenclature were no longer possible. Albie Sachs, later a *Guardian* staff writer, said, "I would say the Suppression of Communism Act actually did us a big favor because it meant we couldn't use the jargon and ever-ready phrases and formulations. We were compelled to use more substantive ways of thinking and writing, and I think it saved us from a hell of a lot of nonsense. It made us articulate. It made us think."

The mere mechanics of distributing the newspaper, with the majority of sellers now without the Party's discipline, were daunting. "Some odd individuals might have kept up the selling, but the point was that keeping up the apparatus was a full-time job," said Rusty Bernstein. "You needed constant exhortation and encouragement and Party discipline. It wasn't that people weren't exactly dedicated to newspaper selling that they kept doing it on their own. They needed the Party and the Party was gone. Selling the paper was one of the things that fell by the wayside." The issue was exacerbated one Monday morning in March 1949, less than ten months after the general election. A railway official telephoned Brian Bunting to inform him that the *Guardian* could no longer be sold at railway bookstalls. Apparently, the minister of transport, Paul Sauer, had banned the weekly from all shops on the railway concourses. Bunting called Sauer, who refused to confirm the ban or offer a reason for it. The ban was in place, however, and sales suffered because many commuters bought their newspapers on the platforms as they traveled to and from work.[23]

Psychologically, the railway-station ban put Barrack Street on the defensive, and rumors of a possible banning of the *Guardian* itself quickly surfaced.[24] All heads turned towards Minister of Justice Swart. "Blackie" Swart had spent time as a child in a Boer War concentration camp and was jailed during the abortive Boer Rebellion of 1914. After studying journalism at Columbia University and trying his hand as an extra in cowboy movies in Hollywood (he was six foot seven), he returned to South Africa to help lead the fascist Ossewa Brandwag.[25] The previous three ministers of justice—Jan Smuts from 1937–1939, Colin Steyn during the war, and Harry Lawrence after the war—had handled Barrack Street with kid gloves. Swart, who once wielded a cat-o'-nine-tails in the House of Assembly to stress his allegiance to law and order, itched for a bare-knuckle fight.

In Parliament in May 1949, a Nationalist MP asked Swart to "prevent the printing and circulation of communist papers in South Africa." Swart stood up, called for a ban on the Party's Sunday meetings on the Grand Parade and accused the *Guardian* of the old bugaboo that it "stirred up hatred between Europeans and Non-Europeans." Sam Kahn rose the following day to defend the weekly: "There has been this reference to the question of banning the *Guardian*. The *Guardian* is a newspaper which appears openly, and from all this talk about Communism, it is clear that the Government will not be satisfied until it has driven underground every movement in this country that is opposed to the present Government."[26]

Nothing happened immediately, though, as Swart apparently felt obligated to follow a legalistic approach and wait until the Suppression of Communism Act passed. There was an almost Kafkaesque absurdity to the SCA's banning system. Under Section 7 (1), in order to ban a newspaper, Swart had to appoint an "authorizing officer" who would direct a committee of three persons—one who must have been a magistrate—to investigate materials and make a recommendation to the government, which could in turn ban the newspaper. The unwieldy process nonetheless allowed Pretoria to ban newspapers without having to prove in court that the newspaper had broken any law.

In October 1950 Swart appointed William O'Brien, a Kimberley prosecutor and former Transvaal assistant attorney general, as authorizing officer in an inquiry into the affairs of the *Guardian*. O'Brien's first act was to sign search warrants.

On Friday, 24 November 1950, six plainclothes detectives arrived at Barrack Street at half past three in the afternoon. They served a search warrant on Bunting and told him that no one could leave the office. Bunting asked if he could invite Sam Kahn, the newspaper's lawyer, to the office. At first the detectives refused, but after Kahn, in his persuasive way, talked to them on the telephone, they relented; Kahn walked over from his chambers and remained throughout their search. The *Cape Times* reported the next morning that the detectives and the *Guardian* staff "treated each other with courtesy," and at four o'clock the detectives "were given tea." After six in the evening, the men left with more than two hundred documents: *Guardian* balance sheets, account books, minutes of staff meetings, a year's worth of back issues, bulletins from the U.S. Consul in Cape Town, and clippings from overseas news services. In an ironic reference to the September 1946 raid, the detectives told Bunting that they would try to return the documents before the end of the month.[27]

The scene was similar at the *Guardian*'s branch offices. In Johannesburg, Ruth First called Vernon Berrange when detectives arrived. Berrange came to Commissioner Street and demanded O'Brien's certificate of appointment (which the detectives did not have).[28]

In Durban, Dawood Seedat caused even more problems. Seedat, a trained bookkeeper who always wore a red tie and wrote in green ink, had been jailed during the Second World War for famously declaring, "The British empire is not an empire, it is a vampire."[29] Seedat helped start the Natal Indian Youth Congress, was secretary of the Durban Party branch, and joined the *Guardian* in 1948 to manage the Durban office. When two Security Branch men arrived at lunchtime at West Street, the offices were empty and the door was locked. At half past two, a dapper, red-tied Seedat casually strolled up the steps and encountered the waiting detectives. They served the warrant, which Seedat accepted only under protest. He opened the offices' door and directly went to the telephone. The detectives stopped him. Seedat said he was only calling his wife, Fatima. He made one phone call, then another, talking entirely in Hindi. A frustrated detective slammed his hand on the cradle, cutting Seedat off in mid-sentence. Four more Security Branch men arrived, including one armed detective who paced the room nervously. After two hours, the men wrote out an inventory of seized articles that filled two and one-half foolscap pages, a list that included personal letters, financial statements, collection tins, checks, pamphlets and a framed picture of Joseph Stalin.[30]

Responding to the raids, Bunting gathered reporters at Barrack Street Saturday morning and told them that "while at the United Nations Dr. Donges [the cabinet minister and Kahn's leading 'misanthropologist'] is still talking about the right of recourse to the courts, the Government is using backhand methods. And we have no appeal."[31] Bunting wrote a letter to Swart protesting the raid and threatened "a possible bout of expensive litigation."[32]

Bunting also made sure that the next issue put the matter in historical context. Behind the lead headline reporting the raid, "We Have Nothing to Hide," Jack Cope reminded readers of the last time this sort of thing happened: the 1824 Somerset Affair. Lord Charles Somerset, the governor of the Cape colony, had attempted to censor the *South African Commercial Advertiser* and the *South African Journal*, the first independent publications in the colony, after one had reported on a case before the Supreme Court in which a man ridiculed Lord Somerset. Both newspapers suspended publication in protest of Somerset's censoring. Somerset retaliated by sealing their press, expelling one of the editors, and summoning another, Thomas Pringle, to his office. Pringle recalled ten years later:

> There was a storm on his brow, and it burst forth at once upon me like a long-gathered south-easter from Table Mountain. "So, sir!" he began—"You are the one of those who dare insult me and oppose my government!"— and then he launched forth into a long tirade of abuse; scolding, upbraiding and taunting me,—with all the domineering arrogance of mien and sneering insolence of expression of which he was so great a master—reproaching me above all for my *ingratitude* for his personal favours. . . .
>
> I stood up, however [no small task, as Pringle was lame from a fractured right hip sustained in a childhood accident], and confronted this most arrogant man with a look of disdain under which his haughty face instantly sunk. . . . I told him that I was quite sensible of the position in which I stood—a very humble individual before the representative of my sovereign; but I also knew what was due to myself as a British subject and a gentleman, and that I would not submit to be *rated* in the style he had assumed by any man, whatever were his station or his rank. I repelled his charges of having acted unworthy of my character as a government servant and a loyal subject;—I defended my conduct in regard to the press, and the character of our magazine, which he said was full of "calumny and falsehood;"—I asserted my right to petition the king for the extension of the freedom of the press to the colony.[33]

With Pringle's courageous stance, newspapers resumed publication in 1825, and freedom of the press was finally established in South Africa with an 1829 press ordinance.

For the first time since 1829, the press ordinance was under serious threat. In January 1951 Swart answered a parliamentary question, saying that a SCA investigation of "communist influences in certain English newspapers in the Union" was under way.[34] In March, Bunting wrote a letter to William O'Brien demanding the return of the *Guardian*'s documents seized in the November raid, as their absence was "hampering the efficient functioning" of the weekly.[35] O'Brien replied that a committee of three had been appointed to investigate the *Guardian*, and they "may well desire to examine the documents."[36] Bunting wrote back that surely, after four months' time, the committee of three had had "ample opportunity" to examine them.[37] In June, Margaret Ballinger, a Native Representative, put forth a question in Parliament to Swart as to whether he had actually appointed a committee of three. "Yes, to draw up a factual report," he said, for the first time publicly admitting that he was investigating the *Guardian*.[38]

Working in secret, the committee of three submitted a report to Swart in June 1951.[39] Swart sat on the report for five months. In October the secretary to the Department of Justice, A.J.N. Jansen, gave notice to one of the *Guardian*'s lawyers, Hymie Bernadt: "Gentlemen, enclosed for information and any comments or representations which your client may desire to make [is] a summary of the findings of fact."[40] The four-page report, with its nine clauses and eleven subclauses, revealed why the committee of three spent half a year sifting through the *Guardian*'s papers, and why Swart shelved the report for another five months: there was no proof of lawbreaking. The report said that the Communist Party and "its Supreme Committee" had considered the newspaper "a matter of great importance . . . as a propaganda means of increasing membership . . . and that the Party wholeheartedly supported it and aided its development." The report noted that "throughout the history of the *Guardian*, its financial situation was never on a sound footing," and that "the *Guardian* was a regular subscriber to Communist-controlled periodicals and papers." All this was legal at the time.

Some charges were almost humorously false. "It is abundantly clear," the report declared, "that the policy of the *Guardian* was guided by the Communist Party over the period of 1936 to 1943. It kept a watching brief over the said publication, pointed out deflections from 'Party Line' and guided, directed and reprimanded. . . . The Party began to control the material to be published. . . . The Party assumed a dictatorial attitude towards the *Guardian*." The dates were wrong and arbitrary, and in the 1930s Radford had very little to do with the Party.

Despite the slipshod reasoning, the findings staggered Barrack Street.

By coincidence, when the letter arrived, Brian Bunting was in London. He hastily called a press conference in a Fleet Street pub and denounced Pretoria.[41] At Barrack Street, Naomi Shapiro, the acting editor, issued a press statement: "There are no facts at all, but false inference, untruths and distortions." Ignoring the 1943 Louw affair and the mine libel case, Shapiro said the weekly "has never been prosecuted for any offense, let alone convicted." But she was correct in pointing out a central irony to the whole rigmarole around the findings of fact: "The charge is based entirely on the dangerous principle of victimising the paper retrospectively for something which was never an offense under South African law, and for something which in any event is quite untrue." Shapiro was unsure how to respond to the findings of fact, and four days before the allotted twenty-one days expired, the *Guardian*'s lawyers asked Jansen for an extension because of Bunting's absence. In addition, they asked for Swart to explain "what facts are alleged to support" the findings, and "the nature of the test that has been applied by the Committee in arriving at its conclusions regarding the financial soundness of the newspaper." Jansen replied a week later, saying: "The Minister has been referred and states that he has nothing to add except section six [of the SCA] from which it is clear that your clients have been granted a concession which the law does not require. In any event the various matters referred to in my previous letter, and the annexure thereto are peculiarly within the knowledge of your clients, and it is not understood why they should require any further particulars."[42] Swart did, however, grant an extension until the end of November.

When Bunting returned from London, he hammered out a hostile, seven-page representation to Swart. He outlined the history of the affair, beginning with the November 1950 raid, and ripped apart the findings of fact. He took exception to four clauses and three subclauses, arguing that he and his predecessor, Betty Radford, had "always, in fact, been given full liberty to decide the policy of the *Guardian*." In conclusion, Bunting reiterated Shapiro's statement: "Even conceding that the allegations made by the Committee of three are correct, which we deny, it was legal."[43]

Legality, Bunting knew, was no longer the issue. He needed public pressure to bully Pretoria into not banning the weekly. He roused human-rights organizations in London and was able to have the matter discussed at the United Nations in New York.[44] He formed a Freedom of the Press Committee, which organized a national conference in Johannesburg attended by two dozen delegates who represented seventy-seven organizations.[45] In Cape Town, the committee, chaired by Jack Cope, received permission from the

Cape Town City Council to put tables on Adderley Street, St. George's Street and the Grand Parade where they asked passersby to sign postcards protesting the banning threat; almost three thousand people did.[46] Besides the postcard campaign, the committee distributed leaflets and organized a massive "Save The *Guardian*" rally in the Cape Town City Hall.[47] Sam Kahn pressed the issue in Parliament. During a January 1952 speech about the cost of living in South Africa, Kahn compared Swart to Lord Somerset: "Now we have the Minister of Justice, the modern Lord Charles, who is threatening the integrity and the freedom of the press and has caused, for well-nigh two years, the *Guardian* to live under the shadow of fear."[48]

The shadow of fear extended to other newspapers, and the South African press, whose freedom the weekly was defending, took notice. *Die Burger* called the potential ban "in principle a sickening business."[49] The *Cape Times* wrote in an editorial: "The public will follow closely the long-drawn-out manoeuvers for putting the *Guardian* newspaper out of existence by executive decree. . . . For all the public will know or can do about it, the Minister might use the report for lighting his pipe. A similar fate is as likely to befall any 'representations' which the *Guardian* might make."[50]

Pipes appeared to be lit a lot, as months went by without any government action. In February 1952, Alex Hepple, a Labour Party MP, asked Swart whether the cabinet would accept a deputation from the opposition to discuss the banning issue. Swart replied that the cabinet had just taken a decision at its weekly meeting the previous day.[51] Three days later, during a budget debate, a United Party MP, Hymie Davidoff, again brought up the issue:

> Why is the honourable, the Minister of Justice, not telling them what is going to happen? He is placing the *Guardian* in an almost impossible position; they cannot continue with their business. These people are afraid they may be forced out of circulation any time, they cannot get advertisements, and it's damaging their business to such an extent that they do not know what is going to happen to them. Is that the Minister's intention? . . .From his attitude it appears to me that as far as the *Guardian* is concerned, he would much rather see its death by degrees than its death by decrees.[52]

Death by degrees was working. Since the banning affair started in November 1949, circulation had sunk by a third, and advertisements had suddenly become very scarce.[53] In April 1952 the police arrived at Barrack Street armed not with search warrants, but with boxes of *Guardian* documents.

Apparently the committee of three had finished perusing the weekly's files. In early May, Kahn, hinting at highly placed sources, issued a statement suggesting that the *Guardian* would not be banned.[54] With that assurance, Brian and Sonia Bunting drove to Johannesburg, collected Ruth First and Joe Slovo, and went to Rustenburg in the Western Transvaal for a winter holiday.

On Friday, 23 May 1952, the South African government banned the *Guardian*.[55]

Near noon, Naomi Shapiro, acting editor in Brian Bunting's absence, answered a telephone call. It was a reporter from the South African Press Association, asking if Shapiro had seen that week's *Government Gazette*.[56] There, in an Extraordinary Edition published that morning, was the *Guardian*'s death knell. Signed on 8 April 1952 by Governor-General E. G. Jansen and Minister of Justice Charles Swart, Proclamation Number 103 prohibited the "printing, publication or dissemination of the *Guardian*" on the grounds that it was under the control and guidance of the banned Communist Party, and that it propagated the Party's views.

"We were left holding the baby," Shapiro recalled. Despite years of warning, contingency plans were merely provisional. "The shock wore off and everyone realized that nothing was prepared."[57] Shapiro called Commissioner Street and talked hurriedly with Ivan Schermbrucker, who tried to locate Bunting and First but did not have a telephone number or address for them. When he finally reached them after numerous phone calls, they said they had just heard the news: it was the lead story on Radio South Africa's afternoon bulletin.

All day across the Union, sellers hawked copies of the banned newspaper without interference, and subscribers received their *Guardian* as usual in the post.[58] On Saturday, Bunting chaired an emergency meeting at Commissioner Street and then led the entire *Guardian* bureau over to the City Hall steps to hear Solly Sachs speak. While banning the newspaper, Pretoria had also banned Sachs, the former Party leader, from running his Garment Workers' Union. (The government also banned Michael Harmel from his work with the Transvaal Peace Council and removed Sam Kahn from his seat in Parliament and Fred Carneson from his seat on the Cape Provincial Council, because the men had been Party members.[59]) Fifteen thousand people gathered at City Hall to hear Sachs speak. The police baton-charged the crowd—a few cops wildly wielded chairs—and injured sixty-five people. Pictures of women getting beaten filled the Sunday newspapers.[60]

Despite the diversions of chair-brandishing policemen and dumped parliamentarians, the banning of the *Guardian* remained a front-page story in newspapers around the world. Each offered reasons for the timing of the proscription. The *Times* of London suggested that it was a birthday present for D. F. Malan, who turned seventy-eight on 22 May.[61] Walter Sisulu, commenting in *Spark*, a weekly produced by the Transvaal Indian Youth Congress, assumed that it was pure politics: "We are quite aware that the simultaneous attack of the people's leaders and the *Guardian* is not accidental, but a clever political trick to create imaginary dangers of a Black Revolution and the Communist Bogey, which is designed to capture Afrikaner votes at the next election."[62] The *Star* in Johannesburg and the *Natal Daily News* went a step further, arguing that the banning was specifically attributable to the upcoming Wakkerstroom by-election.[63] The *Rand Daily Mail* and the *Cape Times* believed it was a diversion from the High Court Bill, a recently tabled bill aimed at circumventing the South African Constitution in order to remove coloured voters from the common voting roll.[64]

Anger supplanted detached analysis for many newspapers. "Like a man struggling in a bog" was the metaphor the *Natal Witness* used to describe the government.[65] The *Cape Argus* wrote it was "the essence of dictatorship."[66] The *Cape Times* discussed how the suppression came "without the faintest shadow of a judicial process . . . after an interval of timidity.[67] The *Manchester Guardian* asked, "Why now? What have these people been doing for the past two years? What evidence of illegal activity is brought forth? None and none is needed."[68] The *Times* of London spiced up its account of the ban with a quotation from Kahn calling the committee of three's investigation a "bogus inquiry."[69] The *New York Times* quoted the U.S. State Department as saying it was "disgusted with the banning."[70] Even *Die Burger* did not wholly applaud Swart's move, saying it "would have preferred that, if a newspaper were to be banned, it were to be done by resolution of Parliament."[71]

Supporters gathered to voice their disappointment. Two thousand students at the University of the Witwatersrand passed a resolution at a rally condemning the ban, as did the Student Representative Council at the University of Cape Town.[72] In the Kahn-less Parliament, Arthur Barlow, a United Party MP and the senior member of the House of Assembly, brought up the ban, amid heavy shouting and heckling, during a June 10 debate: "The Minister cannot ban the *Guardian* under the law—the Minister is an accessory; he is right in it up to his neck. It is nothing to laugh about. I have no time for the *Guardian* and its policy. I am not interested in it at all, but to stop a newspaper in these days is to go back to the time of Lord Charles Somerset."[73]

Precedents besides the Somerset affair now presented themselves. One option was simply to wait. During the Anglo-Boer War, military authorities in the Cape banned South Africa's first black political newspaper, *Imvo Zabantsundu*. The monthly waited out the ban and was reinstated after fifteen months.[74]. In the Transvaal during the same war, Paul Kruger sealed the presses of the *Star*. The day after, the *Star* appeared under the name the *Comet*. Kruger, not amused but realizing the legality of the ruse, relented and the *Star* returned the following day.

Either way, something needed to be done. The Buntings left Johannesburg after the City Hall fiasco and drove through the night back to Cape Town. On Sunday afternoon, Brian dusted off the *Guardian* board of directors to plot strategy. They decided not to appeal the ban, although they did issue a searing press statement deriding the "slender reasons for the ban," accusing Pretoria of trying "to cripple the organised working class," and concluding that "only a Government which is desperate and which has no faith in the public or in the future can rule in such a way."[75] Forty people, it was noted, would be unemployed.[76]

On Monday, the *Guardian* editorial staff met and decided that the newspaper would simply change titles. The *Guardian* became the *Clarion*.[77] Tongue in cheek, the *Rand Daily Mail* reported on Tuesday that it was only a "strange coincidence" that this new weekly, the *Clarion*, would have the same staff, editor, offices, agents, and policy.[78] The *Star*, mindful of its own history, called the emergence of a new masthead "a poser for Mr. Swart."[79] Indeed, the minister now looked foolish for all his pipe-lighting ponderings. To outlaw the *Clarion*, he would have to swing through the SCA gymnastics again. *Forward*, the Labour Party journal, outlined the possible results of another ban: "A week later it could start up again as the *Trumpet* or the *Defender*. The staff are not likely to run out of thinking up new names every month or so."[80]

On Thursday, 29 May 1952, six days after the government suppressed the *Guardian*, a four-page *Clarion* published by B. P. Bunting and printed by Stewart Printing Company appeared on the streets of Cape Town. Eight thousand more copies than the previous week's *Guardian* were sold, kicking the circulation figures up to 33,000.[81] Inside was the usual *Guardian* fare—trade-union news, international tidbits, and a healthy draft of radical politics. The newspaper quoted Sam Kahn's farewell speech in Parliament and printed messages of support from friends outraged by the ban. Bunting wrote in a front-page editorial: "I, as editor of the *Guardian*, do not accept that decision [the ban] as either just or lawful, and I intend to carry on a campaign against it until it is reversed. As part of that campaign, may I introduce to you this week the *Clarion*."

That early winter afternoon was a historic day. The weekly proved it could survive a ban and preserve its streak of continuous publication. (All three times the government banned the weekly, it issued the proclamation on a Friday; if they had outlawed the newspaper on a Tuesday, just when the presses were rolling, the streak would certainly have been halted.) Coming out so quickly was plucky, for if Pretoria convinced a court of law that the *Clarion* was in fact really the *Guardian*, the penalty was up to three years' imprisonment without the option of a fine.[82] "We were still a bit afraid," recalled Bunting. "We were really going day by day then. We never thought the paper would last that long after the banning, that it would last another thirteen years."

Barrack Street's sense of humor survived as well. On that Thursday, the entire staff went out selling the newspaper—"to give it the widest possible circulation," as Bunting told the *Rand Daily Mail*.[83] Carrying a bundle of *Clarion*s and a camera, Bunting, Shapiro, and Kahn walked from Barrack Street up Plein Street to the steps of Parliament. Kahn saw Charles Swart walking out of the House and flagged him down on the steps. A small crowd gathered to see the minister's reaction. Offering him a fresh copy of the "banned" newspaper, Kahn pointed to the masthead and roared with glee: "I call it the Carry-On." Glumly pulling two pennies out of his pocket, Swart bought the copy. Kahn grinned, and Shapiro snapped a priceless photograph. The next week the *Clarion* printed a copy on its front page. The *Times* of London reported the incident, and for years afterwards it was often the first matter discussed when the *Guardian* surfaced in conversation.[84] For once, the joke was on the government.

Switching mastheads proved to be a rather complicated affair. The second issue of the *Clarion* came out with eight pages, four advertisements, one brilliant photograph of the Kahn/Swart "Carry-on," and space fillers reading "Down With the Malan Government." Brian Bunting ran an open letter written to Minister Swart: "You have no possible grounds of complaint against the paper other than unreasonable obscurantist nationalist prejudice against the expression of any decent progressive opinion in this country." He signed the letter, "Yours in Disgust."

To distribute the *Clarion*, Bunting rehired many of the agents who sold the *Guardian* and sent a *Clarion* to all *Guardian* subscribers "in hopes that it might interest you."[85] In June he replaced the *Guardian* board of directors by forming the Competent Publishing and Printing Company. The irrepressible Kahn returned to the weekly with his parliamentary column renamed "On Parade." Bunting substituted Michael Harmel's editorial-page column "By the Way" with his own column, "*Clarion* Call." The "Chanticleer," also written by Bunting, analyzed international news. Financially, the new weekly was troubled. Circulation soared up to 35,000, but donations plummeted.[86] In August 1952, Bunting raised the price of the newspaper to three pennies, and a year's subscription from 7s. 6d. to £1 5s.

Made a fool on the front steps of Parliament, Swart struck back at the weekly. On 30 July, he ordered a raid on the *Clarion*'s Durban branch offices. The Security Branch visited West Street using a search warrant issued for Rowley Arenstein, Jackie Lax's husband, who had an office in the same building. This time, Dawood Seedat did not squabble about making telephone calls.[87]

To further pester the newspaper, Swart employed an unusual bureaucratic ploy. In 1948 another newspaper had registered the *Clarion* as a title. Although the newspaper had disappeared in less than a year, the Department of the Interior told Bunting to obtain permission from the old proprietors for use of the name. The proprietors demanded £1,000, then £500. Bunting offered £50, which they rejected. Bunting decided it was easier to change the title.[88] He asked readers for suggestions and chose *People's World*.[89] In the *Clarion*'s farewell issue on 14 August 1952, Bunting wrote in a distinctly tired tone: "We hope we will have no further trouble from any quarter about our name, or about anything else. We have a job to do, and we want to have the chance of doing it in peace, without interference."

Wishful thinking, for the Department of the Interior was equally unhappy with the *People's World*—no doubt Dr. Dönges was getting his revenge. Two weeks after the weekly's appearance, Bunting received notice that a *People's Weekly* had complained that their tabloid was getting confused with the weekly. Barrack Street had to change the name again. Bunting wisely sent the Department of the Interior a new name—*Advance*—and waited for a successful registration before switching logos. Unfortunately this delay was expensive. Posting an unregistered newspaper cost four times the price of a registered one, so Barrack Street took a bath in the interim.[90] In addition, Bunting was taken to court and fined for publishing an unregistered newspaper.[91] Until the new title was legal, *People's World* was in a holding pattern: most issues were just four pages, and below the logo was the phrase "Formerly the *Clarion*." On 6 November 1952, *Advance* appeared, and the title changes, for now, were over.

Flapdoodles over mastheads were not the only bureaucratic roadblock thrown at Barrack Street. In September 1952, Brian Bunting, after four years as editor, announced his candidacy to take Sam Kahn's seat in Parliament. In response, Minister Swart passed an amendment to the Suppression of Communism Act declaring that no person who had been named as a "communist" could stand for Parliament. The day before Swart's amendment became law, Bunting slipped his name onto the ballot. Swart sued Bunting, but lost the case on a technicality.[92] Because he was a "named communist," Bunting could not attend election rallies, yet in November 1952 he won the seat easily, capturing 85 percent of the vote.[93] Three weeks later, Bunting received a banning order from Swart, forbidding him from attending any meeting "except gatherings of bonafide religious, recreational or social matters."[94] Still, Bunting was able to assume his seat in Parliament for the 1953 session. The weekly printed his "hard-hitting" speeches condemning the Nationalist Party and their apartheid policies, and he took over Kahn's parliamentary column in the newspaper.[95]

In June 1953, the government appointed a commission of inquiry to investigate whether Bunting could be removed from Parliament for being a "communist." Over three days in July, the commission interrogated Bunting for a grueling nineteen hours. He stubbornly refused to give an ideological inch to his colleagues:

> —So the ultimate objective of the Communist Party to which you did subscribe was a state in South Africa in which every element of society would form a single party and govern the country?
> —Well, it could be put that way.
> —But is that not the way it is put?
> —It is not put quite like that. But with reservations which might arise from your interpretation of what you say, I would not disagree with that.[96]

The commission offered to cut a deal: if Bunting disassociated himself from the principles of the former Communist Party, they would take his name off the list of "communists," enabling him to retain his seat. Bunting refused: "It has been suggested," he told Parliament, "that I should abjure my past opinions and announce myself to be a reformed character. I am not prepared to do so. If the price I have to pay for being true to my opinions is expulsion from this House, I am prepared to pay it."[97] Within twenty-four hours of the submission of the commission's 222-page report recommending his removal, Swart posted a letter informing Bunting that he had lost his seat.[98]

Ray Alexander stepped up to the wicket. The trade unionist easily won the by-election to succeed Bunting. This time, Swart announced a new amendment that any former "communist" could not serve in Parliament. The day the by-election results were announced, Alexander, together with Fred Carneson, walked to the House of Assembly to assume a seat now forbidden to her. At the Adderley Street entrance to Parliament, Security Branch detectives stopped them. Alexander and Carneson then went along a path leading past the Senate building to the front steps of the House of Assembly. There, two men took Alexander by the arm and dragged her off the premises. She sent a letter demanding her parliamentary salary—her tenure officially started on election day—and received £28 for one week's work. Alexander donated the sum to the weekly.[99]

Throughout this parliamentary saga, a number of core staff members left Barrack Street. Naomi Shapiro departed at the end of 1952, when her husband, Jack Barnett, took a job as an architect in Israel.[100] Shapiro had filled the weekly's feature well with timely, well-sourced articles on a huge range of subjects, and her departure was regretted.[101]

Another top reporter also left to go overseas, but this time involuntarily. In 1950 the police arrested H. A. Naidoo and deported him to Durban for not holding the necessary permits required of Indians to cross provincial boundaries. A few weeks later, Naidoo snuck back into Cape Town. He hid in an old hut on the slopes of Table Mountain, worked odd hours at Barrack Street and grabbed brief moments with his family.

Such conditions were unfit for a newspaper reporter, and the Party gave permission for him and his wife, Pauline Podbrey, to leave the country. A regular departure was impossible, because Naidoo had no passport and the government was unlikely to grant him one, so Podbrey, Nancy Dick (a trade unionist), Dawood Seedat (in town for a holiday), and Wolfie Kodesh decided he would stow away on a ship bound for Europe. With Seedat translating, they took a group of Malay sailors to lunch and struck a deal: in return for £300, six chickens, and a crate of brandy, the sailors agreed to hide Naidoo on their ship. At the appointed hour for transferring Naidoo onto the ship, the tone-deaf Kodesh spent half an hour walking up and down the Cape Town docks whistling the signal—"It's a Long Way from Tipperary"—before the sailors finally appeared and bundled Naidoo aboard. The ship sailed. After spending the night in an empty 55-gallon drum on deck, Naidoo was discovered by an officer the next morning and marched off to see the captain, who, as luck would have it, was still drunk from a farewell party the night before. Naidoo, in halting English, pretended to be illiterate, and the captain let him stay on board until the ship reached England. Podbrey, accompanied by Sonia Bunting, sailed a few weeks later.

Naidoo and Podbrey worked for Radio Budapest in Hungary. In 1955, disillusioned with the communist world, they returned to England. Naidoo died in 1971.[102]

A further loss came with the 1951 death of the last remaining founding staff member, Norman Flegg. The business manager since the newspaper's launch in 1937, Flegg kept all the account books, wrote occasional articles, and hosted the annual Christmas Eve dinner dance at his house in Newlands. Interested in buying a factory in Natal, he asked Ray Alexander and Hymie Bernadt to join him in a tour. Both declined, so Flegg flew alone. His plane crashed in the Drakensburg Mountains, killing him instantly.[103]

Spunky, enthusiastic and sometime incautious replacements came to Barrack Street. Mary Butcher, a Christian Scientist from Natal, took Shapiro's position as a Cape Town reporter. While studying social work at the University of Cape Town, Butcher had joined the Modern Youth Society—a college-age group of mostly white activists that included Herman Toivo Y. Toiva, later a South West African People's Organization leader. After finishing her degree, Butcher worked with Jack Tarshish at his wholesale stocking and furniture firm on Roeland Street. Tarshish was a Polish-born communist who gave his progressive employees flexible hours so they could work part-time on Party projects.[104] In the middle of 1953, Bunting hired Butcher to work as a reporter.

Another Tarshish employee who migrated to the weekly was Fred Carneson. The former Port Shepstone postal worker, Carneson moved to Cape Town after the war with his wife Sarah Rubin, a Party member from Durban.[105] Carneson became district secretary for the Party, edited its monthly journal *Freedom* and sold the *Guardian* on Saturdays in Woodstock. After dissolution, he worked at Tarshish's factory until October 1952, when Bunting offered him the editorship.[106]

> They asked me if I'd take a chance. Now I'd had no journalistic experience whatsoever. I said alright, I'll give it a go provided Brian is around to give advice and guidance. So I stepped in and became the editor of a bloody weekly newspaper. I tell you, what a sweat. I held the fort successfully, but it was just about the hardest thing I could do. I used to agonize trying to get

the layout, the inches and counting the bloody words. Oh, later, of course, I became more experienced and just took it down to the printers. They knew when, they'll tell you where to chop it. I used to do the layout sheet till three in the morning and it was a waste of time. . . . As far as I'm concerned I wasn't a journalist. I stepped in because at that time there was no one else. I was willing to give it a go.[107]

In September 1953, when Pretoria unceremoniously relieved Bunting of his duties in the House of Assembly, he returned to Barrack Street, allowing grateful Carneson, after an exhausting year, to move from the editor's office to the fundraising department. (Carneson also assumed the directorship of Competent, the company that officially owned the weekly.) Sam Kahn, resuming his parliamentary column, wrote that Bunting "has returned to the editorial chair of the *Advance* newspaper in which his message can be raised not merely as a banner over Parliament, but as a gigantic banner over the whole country."[108]

Banner-raising soon took a backseat. With his passport about to expire and no chance of the government renewing it, Bunting wanted to make one final trip overseas to see relatives and visit socialist Europe.[109] He asked Lionel Forman to serve as acting editor. Forman, the harassed photographer during the 1950 May Day violence, had been born Christmas Day 1927 to Lithuanian immigrants and had grown up in a working-class borough in Johannesburg. At age fifteen he joined the Young Communist League, and two years later the Party. (As evidenced by so many Guardian staffers, the Party apparently did not stick to its minimum-age requirement of eighteen.) After earning a bachelor's degree at the University of the Witwatersrand and a master's in social sciences at the University of Cape Town, Forman returned to the Transvaal to study law. In March 1950 he began editing the *Witwatersrand Student*, transforming the campus rag into a highly regarded newspaper, with crossword puzzles, prizes, and cartoons—and a formidable editorial staff, including Lionel Abrahams and Charles Bloomberg.[110] After finishing law school in 1952, Forman represented South Africa in Warsaw at a conference of the International Union of Students. He stayed in Europe for two years, working for the IUS in Prague, where he and his Wits girlfriend Sadie Kreel were married. Finishing his term in Prague, the Formans rented a cottage in Sussex, England, where he wrote his autobiography.

The reason why a twenty-five-year-old man was writing his memoir was that he was dying. A childhood bout with rheumatic fever had permanently damaged his heart. Doctors warned he could die at any minute from heart failure, but with massive daily doses of drugs—at one point he took forty pills a day—and fortitude, Forman cheated death for a while longer. While writing in Sussex, Forman received a telegram from Barrack Street asking him to come edit *Advance*. Forman agreed, and rushed to finish his manuscript by writing 73,000 words in three months.[111]

On New Year's Day 1954, the editor's pen was passed in an unusually synchronized ceremony at the Cape Town docks. The Formans sailed into town from England that morning. Customs officials, agitated because Forman's passport had expired the previous year and was full of stamps from Eastern Bloc countries, searched all his belongings. But they missed the manuscript Sadie had sewn into the baby carriage's mattress. Disembarking, the Formans greeted the Buntings. Brian and Lionel huddled at the end of the quay and went over a few matters about *Advance*. Then Brian and Sonia Bunting, still recovering from their annual New Year's Eve party, boarded the ship and sailed on its return journey to England.[112]

The following morning, Forman started work at Barrack Street. The next four months marked a brief but profound moment in the history of the weekly. The atmosphere shifted. While Bunting ran the newspaper with a professional efficiency, Forman played it loose and easy. His desk was completely hidden by teetering piles of paper. Deadlines passed, letters got lost and articles rambled. While Bunting had all the copy ready for the printer on Monday, Forman waded through his desk and cobbled articles together at the last possible minute on Tuesday evening.[113] Forman loved newspaper layout and spent happy hours dawdling over constructing the pages and dreaming up witty headlines.[114] He continued articles to other parts of the same page, threw in some Afrikaans and abutted half-page-deep headlines with sharply cropped photographs.[115] "Lionel had a great balance," Albie Sachs said. "He was a provocative, challenging kind of writer, immensely popular with our readers. When he was editing the paper, he took the layout very seriously. He had an English book about layout and tried out original forms and designs. And he was very funny. He had a very very lovely, ironical sense of humor. Despite his heart problems, he was happy. He lived for the revolution, for the struggle. His attitude always was, 'Come the revolution,' he used to say, 'I'm going to go make trouble somewhere else.'"

Iconoclastic thinking like Forman's became a flashpoint for the newspaper. The dissolution of the Communist Party of South Africa completely changed the radical Left. The balance of political power, situated in Cape Town since the late 1930s, swung back to Johannesburg. The Transvaalers felt the Capetonians had dissolved the Party without their consent. They also thought dissolution was a farce, that the leadership in Cape Town were developing an underground Party. When no call came, they began meeting in scattered clusters, and in 1953 they formally but secretly reconstituted the Party, renaming it the South African Communist Party.[116] Headquartered in Johannesburg, the new Party had many Cape Town members, and both Brian Bunting and Fred Carneson were at its founding national conference, but Johannesburgers ran the Party: Ruth First, Bram Fischer, Joe Slovo, Michael Harmel, and Hilda and Rusty Bernstein served on its Central Committee, and First hosted two of the SACP's earliest underground conferences at her father's factory.[117]

Unease had always bubbled up between the two cities—after the 1946 mine strike, when the Johannesburg Party leaders pleaded guilty and the government then arrested the Central Executive Committee members (all Capetonians), the Cape Town leaders half suspected the Johannesburgers of disloyalty—and dissolution and reconstitution did nothing to lessen the tension.[118] "There were quite a lot of disagreements between the two groups," Sadie Forman said. "I remember one meeting where Michael Harmel told Fred [Carneson] he was wet behind the ears. The feeling was all the brains were here [in Cape Town] and all the apparatchiks were in Johannesburg. Jo'burg was a poker school. That's what they did there."[119] While the new Party developed closer ties with the African National Congress, the Capetonians stood slightly to the side. There was little Congress activity in Cape Town—in 1947 there were only 376 paid-up ANC members in the city.[120] In general, Capetonians in the Party still felt the ANC lacked political maturity and class understanding. They did not throw their weight into the ANC-allied South African Congress of Democrats; most of the white communists in Cape Town—including Jack Simons, Ray Alexander, Brian Bunting, Fred Carneson, Sam Kahn—did not officially join the COD (though some of them could not because of banning orders).[121] Simons, in fact, did not join the reconstituted Party until after he and Alexander went into exile; his wife, Alexander, did join in 1953 and she was so devoted to Party discipline that other Party members, like Bram Fischer, noticed that Simons did not know about covert work in which Alexander was involved.

Perhaps his ignorance was due to where they lived. Cape Town still embraced its soporific side. "There was a small-town closeness about it, a slow gossiping on pavements in the inert heat that muffled the clashes of colour in the country beyond," Ronald Segal wrote in 1956: "On the Rand or in Durban and Port Elizabeth, the atmosphere was taut. But in Cape Town the complacency seemed to have survived unchanged, and Parliament, then in session, in the Gardens at the top of Adderley Street, might have as well have been mutilating the statute book of some distant state."[122] The main public activity for activists in the city was the *Guardian*. "In Cape Town, when you joined the movement, you joined the *Guardian*," said Ben Turok, a young communist who was active in both cities.[123] In the Transvaal, on the other hand, most communists saw the *Guardian* more as a conduit to and through the struggle, and less an institution in its own right. They joined the COD and sought close assimilation within the Congress movement, and they used rather than worked for the weekly.

Commissioner Street now pulled more weight than Barrack Street. Financially, most of the monies raised for the weekly came from the Transvaal. The Commissioner Street staff ballooned to twelve full-time employees, nearly double the size of Barrack Street.[124] The balance swung so completely that serious discussions occurred over the question of relocating the *Guardian* up in Johannesburg.[125] The content of the newspaper shifted up-country. While in 1938 there were twice as many articles about Cape Town than Johannesburg on the front page, and in 1949 a relative equality, in 1956 even the southern edition had a greater number of articles about the Rand than about the Cape.[126]

For both cities, the newspaper functioned in a subtle but critical way. The new Communist Party, deeply underground, operated a pyramid system of cells with no lateral and limited vertical contact. Each cell contained a half dozen members. To avoid detection, the cell members ditched cars, left dropped messages and read memoranda under the flickering light of street-lamps before burning the documents.[127] "My cell would meet in the most awkward situations," said Brian Bunting. "One week we'd meet on the slopes of Lion's Head and we always seemed to get rained on. The next time in a stuffy car. Or out in the bush."[128] Close friends did not know of each other's affiliation.[129] Amy Thornton recalled attending a youth festival in Bucharest in 1953 and being unable to answer questions from communists from other countries about why there was no official Party in South Africa: "Nearly all of them came from conditions of illegality. I arrived back in Cape Town thinking, 'You know, we really ought to have a communist party in South Africa.' So I arranged a place where we could go and I invited a whole lot of people to come and discuss the communist party. They must have been very amused. And there was this discussion. Nothing was decided. On the way home the person giving me a lift said to me, 'Would you like to join the Communist Party?'"

Under the circumstances, the weekly provided the Party with a number of tools. The newspaper's circulation scheme still functioned as a method of political education, but under different circumstances. Selling the newspaper under the aegis of the Congress of Democrats occurred as it had under the Party in the 1940s.[130] The Party itself did not force members to sell in groups because that would be a security risk, but many individual members continued or developed their own weekly routes.

The weekly also disseminated Party news and views. "From time to time statements in the name of one or another known Party leader were published openly in the press," wrote Bunting, "and it was understood by everybody that these statements represented the 'Party Line' on the issue under discussion."[131] Such messages appeared regularly in the weekly via interviews, letters to the editors, articles and even "guest editorials."[132] Yusuf Dadoo, the key Indian communist in the Transvaal, often issued statements to the newspaper.[133] Moses Kotane, the Party chairman, regularly delivered messages from his home on Mount Street in District Six to his comrades via the weekly. The thinly veiled reports, as Rusty Bernstein later said, "were clearly for us to take and absorb."[134] In 1962 Kotane was quoted as saying, "In the absence of our organisation which has been suppressed, *New Age* was our spokesman."[135] One sizable message was a 1954 pamphlet Kotane authored, "South Africa's Way Forward: An *Advance* Study Document," which was basically the Party's first annual report since dissolution.

Internationally, the newspaper supported the Soviet Union. Locally, the weekly was the only national voice for non-racialism and democracy, and against anti-Semitism and fascism. Yet its reporting and editorializing about overseas matters sided with and flattered a genocidal regime that at the time was finishing a thirty-five year reign of terror on its own citizens.[136] The newspaper saw every international event through Moscow's prism, whether discussing the plight of Julius and Ethel Rosenberg, the Korean War, the rise and fall of Marshall Tito in Yugoslavia or the coming of communism in China.[137] It greeted Sputnik with deafening cheers and the death of Joseph Stalin with tears. "When Stalin died," Sam Kahn wrote in March 1953, "the Russian earth shook with the sobbing of millions and was wet with the tears of mourning for the man etched deep in their hearts. . . . In death he has joined Lenin as he did in life."[138]

Staffers sent back absurdly positive reports datelined in the Soviet Union. "We were satisfied from what we saw that had there been widespread disaffection or opposition to the regime, it could have been ventilated through the ballot box," Bunting wrote after his 1954 visit: "We were assured that there is complete religious freedom in the Soviet Union . . . How many times have we read in the *Rand Daily Mail* or the *Cape Mail* or the *Citizen* that the streets of Moscow are wide but deserted, that the people shuffle about in a dispirited fashion. . . . We were, of course, not victims of capitalist propaganda before we arrived in the Soviet Union."[139] Comments turned out to be false: "There is no 'split' between Russia and China," the newspaper reported in September 1960, just as the Sino-Russo rift was becoming permanent.

Sometimes it was horribly hateful. In 1953 the newspaper supported a anti-Semitic pogrom orchestrated by Stalin. Despite the many Jewish staffers, the weekly equated Zionism with Nazism and approved of the crackdown after the apparent Jewish conspiracy in Czechoslovakia. "The investigation showed that a new channel of treason and espionage had been created. It was Zionism," the newspaper approvingly quoted the Czech president. "Normally, it would have been hard for a former banker, factory owner or even a rich peasant to get into the Communist Party, and he would never be able to hold a leading position. But with people of Jewish origin and Zionist inclinations we did not pay so much attention to their class origins."[140]

The naive fealty to Moscow stemmed in part from Brian Bunting. A committed communist, he remained in the Party and loyal to Marxism throughout the rest of his political career, even after the fall of the Soviet Union. He worked as a TASS correspondent in London and edited the Party's journal, the *African Communist*. Bunting argued it was his duty as editor to present pro-Soviet positions, which, he told colleagues, reflected the thinking of the majority of people in the South African liberation struggle.[141] However, loyalty to the Soviet regime cannot be blamed on Bunting alone. Other staffers maintained robust pro-Moscow stances. Moreover, Bunting ran the weekly by consensus. He held editorial meetings every Friday where discussions were free and passionate.[142] And the other branch offices operated with a fair amount of freedom and influence.

In a way, the movement was to blame. Marxist ideology and Leninist strategy provided radical South Africans with the foundations upon which they could depend during the battles they fought. It gave them an internal, steel-like strength and certainty—extremely rigid but steadfast. It was also apparently second nature; unlike European communist parties, the South African Communist Party did not suffer any mass defections after the various exposures of the Soviet Union's rottenness in the 1950s.[143]

The pace of the South African struggle was another factor. Everyone was too busy and beleaguered by events at home to have serious discussions about countries far away. "It's rather hard to make people understand how inward-looking we were," said Hilda Bernstein, a communist city councilor in Johannesburg and *Guardian* supporter. "You thought what you were doing was the most important and the rest of the world was the fringe. It was extremely concentrated on the problems of apartheid and South Africa." The focus was always on apartheid and the avalanching slide towards a police state. "You never thought about democracy," said Mary Butcher, a Cape Town staffer. "What were you comparing it with? You compare it with the South African regime. That was your point of reference. Compared with that, I mean, the Party was something imaginative and forward-thinking, etc., whereas, these people were just dragging the country into the Dark Ages. I mean, that is what was happening. It was awful. Every, every year, more and more laws were introduced to destroy what was beginning to emerge in this country. I mean, it was a mighty vicious period to be in. I think you can only judge the Party in that context." The moral compass pointed so vigorously in South Africa that few had the time to navigate other countries' issues.

Geography contributed to the myopia. Closer to Antarctica than Europe, South African intellectuals had little way to discern the wheat of truth from the bits of propagandistic chaff and third-hand information that floated past. An enemy of Pretoria was necessarily going to be a friend of South African radicals, and the vitriol that coursed between the First and Second Worlds left them little opportunity to carve out a middle ground. Only a few people had been to the Soviet Union, and none of them had really learned the truth about Stalin's reign of terror (Hilda Bernstein's father was a Bolshevik official living in Moscow, and yet she got it wrong). Even the official line became hard to get, as the Soviet consulate in Pretoria closed in 1956. Albie Sachs, who wrote the weekly's international column, recalled the difficulties of getting truthful information:

> Our sources were very indirect. We had a handful of correspondents, but they were mostly in Africa. We were dependent on newspapers from other countries, the *Daily Worker* from England, *People's World* from San Francisco, papers from New Zealand and Australia, *New Age*, this paper from India, a sophisticated journal in East Berlin edited by an American named John Peet, and the Hsinhua—a news agency in China that sent these little packets of very thin rice paper rolled up, full of news. In terms of the cold war, we had no other way to get news. Maybe just the occasional person

who had been on holiday somewhere. But they came weeks late. If I had to look through it now and cut out what I know now is false and falsely-based, I would have to take out a hell of a lot. I feel considerable pain in that I accepted the veracity of what we got. But what strengthened me then was the knowledge that the same people who were bitterly hostile to the Soviet Union tended to be bitterly hostile to us. I knew we were engaged in an honest fight and they told a lot of lies about us. They made up any old thing. There was a huge anti-Soviet propaganda machine, so they made it much easier for us. . . . It was a very painful period, a very tense period. If it [Stalin's crimes against humanity] was true it was horrible. If it wasn't true, it represented a massive kind of onslaught that was very difficult to overcome, and we had to fight to find out what was true and what was not true. We did have too much tunnel-vision."[144]

Discipline was essential, and the Party punished heretical views, as editor of *Advance*, Lionel Forman discovered.[145] On 1 April 1954, in an editorial entitled "Don't Spread Malan's Lie," Forman argued that ethnicity should be encouraged. The uniting of all the people of South Africa under the banner of the ANC, he argued, could be homogenizing and disempowering. "Our Zulu poets must sing the sagas of liberation in their mother tongue," Forman wrote. "The people must rock with laughter at Sotho satires on the Nats. Let our folk dances exemplify a kick in the pants for Malan and our music the drumbeats of freedom. . . . From this issue *Advance* will make a start by paying particular care to avoid the terminology of the oppressor, using correct terms."[146] Once readers realized that the editorial was no April Fool's joke, a storm of controversy broke. Ethnicity could not be dealt with in such a mature way, and his call to celebrate diversity seemed too close to Pretoria's apartheid policies. In a blistering letter printed three weeks later, Yusuf Dadoo slammed Forman, saying it was "neither duty nor task of editorials" to raise such issues of "theoretical gnat-chasing." Forman replied with a long reflective piece supporting his viewpoint with detailed examinations of race and class. To diffuse the situation, the Party convened a special weekend symposium in Cape Town, where leaders gave papers on the subject.[147]

1956 was the defining year for the weekly's Achilles' heel. In February, Khrushchev gave a four-hour speech to the twentieth congress of the USSR's Communist Party in which he detailed some of Stalin's crimes. Because the session was closed to foreigners, it took awhile before word filtered out to South Africa, and the weekly—confused and shocked like so many other communist groups around the world—initially avoided comment. When it first mentioned the speech, it quickly said that there had been extensive coverage in newspapers around the world; two weeks later, it curtly acknowledged the criticism of Stalin. It was April before Michael Harmel gave the official South Africa Communist Party line: "It is said that Stalin developed an exaggerated and incorrect theory of the intensification of the class struggle after the defeat of capitalism and that this led to an overemphasis on the role of the security services." But, Harmel went on, it was not really Stalin's fault. The gang led by security chief Beria had undermined Soviet democracy, and the current criticism was merely revealing the strength and democratic health of the communist system.[148]

The invasion of Hungary in November, however, was a more public disaster. In the first issue after Soviet tanks rumbled into Budapest, Lionel Forman, the overseas-news writer, told about his years living in Prague and stated the obvious: "The fighting in the streets of Budapest has come as a shock to us and the best way to overcome the shock is to face the facts that underlie the revolt. . . . There have been terrible errors and terrible barbarities."[149] In Cape Town, Fred Carneson hosted a standing-room-only Party meeting where Forman passionately argued against the Soviet invasion. Everyone tried to rationalize their views. "It was quite a time," Albie Sachs said. "I remember Brian going through very deep soul-searching, and I think for forty-eight hours there just wasn't any communication. It was really difficult for all of us. We all went through quite a crisis, quite a tense time. Bunting came back and said, 'This is the line.' But Lionel had lived there in Czechoslovakia, he knew the students."[150]

Three weeks later, the international column reverted to its pro-Soviet line. Under the headline "The Smoke Clears in Hungary," the weekly said, "What the daily press has done its utmost to conceal—the fact the Hungarian revolt underwent a complete change of character from its starting point as a workers' protest at the slowness of the pace of government reform into a completely counter-revolutionary mob frenzy led and exploited by the worst enemies of progress—has emerged clearly."[151] A few days later Forman dropped in on some newspaper colleagues, who kidded him for the about-face: "We pulled his leg about this," recalled one of them, Benjamin Pogrund, "as we knew he was the usual writer of the column: 'That was a great piece you wrote, Lionel,' we said to him, 'but what happened the next time? Why did you switch sides?' I remember Lionel looked very embarrassed and muttered, 'I did not write the second column.'"[152] Brian Bunting, temporarily cutting off Forman, had written it. "Lionel was very distressed," Sachs said.

"It didn't stop him and he felt he had to say what he believed, but he was very upset with people who wouldn't listen to what he was saying based on first-hand experience. He was very upset people wouldn't listen."

Forman pressed ahead, and in November 1958 he produced the inaugural issue of the *South African Socialist Review*. As with Hungary, the Party quashed Forman's journal and no further issues appeared. A year later, when Forman called for a "multi-national socialist party," the Party dispatched Carneson to Forman's house to tell him to stop ruffling the waters.[153]

Since the Party was extremely influential and operated as a sort of think tank for the ANC, such an aversion to differing opinions weakened the liberation movement as a whole. The censuring was unhealthy, and careers of brilliant thinkers like Forman's were stifled by the Party's uncritical, unquestioning stance.

The new political paradigm wreaked havoc on Barrack Street's bank account. Sales figures dropped dramatically over the course of 1950, bottoming out at a paltry 19,000 by year's end. Not since 1941, before the Nazi invasion of the Soviet Union, had so few *Guardians* been sold each week. In 1951 Bunting ran a publicity campaign for 10,000 new *Guardian* readers by offering £1 to each supporter who brought in ten new subscribers.[154] Moderately successful, the campaign boosted sales to 25,000 per week. The banning of the *Guardian* in 1952 raised figures, and the weekly momentarily rode the passion of the Defiance Campaign to top the 40,000 mark in 1952.[155] Throughout 1953 and 1954, *Advance*'s circulation hovered around 35,000.[156] Advertising, however, fell away completely. Only three or four small advertisements appeared each week, and some weeks none at all. Most of the *Guardian* leagues scattered across the Union and Southern Rhodesia ceased to function, and besides occasional private dinner parties, the annual Christmas and birthday parties, and an *Advance* Readers Group, no one held large fundraising events. The days of jumble sales and gramophone evenings had passed.[157]

The Security Branch, under orders from Minister Swart, bore some responsibility. In 1954 Bunting admitted in the weekly that "revenues from functions, dances, lectures, etc., have declined because of police intimidation. Many people who normally support us have been driven away by police raids."[158] The level of harassment was not unbearable, but the increasing number of raids, and tapped telephone lines were a nuisance, and many people abandoned overt support for Barrack Street.

With the breakdown of the *Guardian*'s old distribution system, African sellers became even more important. In Johannesburg, Titus Mamuru sold twenty dozen a week at Park Station, as did Lydia Tshehla at the main railway station; Hosiah Tsehla usually went through forty dozen in Alexandra; and David Dhlamini maintained his spot at the top of the group by selling more than five hundred a week in the Indian market district.[159]

In Cape Town, John Motloheloa directed a team of sellers, including Jack Masiane, Grimaas Qinisile, Looksmart Solwandle, Greenwood Ngotyana, Joseph Sono, Jellico Ntshona, Zollie Malindi, Omar Gallant and Douglas Manqina.[160] All were ANC members (many were also in the new Party), and each one was a master at selling the weekly. Gallant, always with a fat cigar, sold *New Age* in Claremont and Wynberg; Solwandle maintained a weekly route in Camp's Bay, Bantry Bay and Sea Point. Most Fridays, Motloheloa and Masiane boarded the rush-hour Bellville-bound train in separate cars. Meeting in the middle, they acted surprised at seeing each other. In a rich, auctioneer-style patter, they loudly discussed the latest issue of the newspaper until people around them asked for copies. Then they would go to another compartment and do it again, all the way to Elsie's River.[161]

For Douglas Manqina, selling the weekly went from being a job to being a political education. A Transkei native, Manqina came to Cape Town during the Second World War and worked as a quarryman. In 1958 he secured a job selling the newspaper. Initially he had problems. Although a member of the ANC, he was not particularly well versed about politics, and discovered he had to learn who were the political players and what were the issues and then be able to explain it all to his buyers. On Mondays and Tuesdays he went out with the staff of the South African Congress of Trade Unions to sell the weekly to laborers during their lunchtime breaks; on Thursdays and Fridays he walked through African and coloured townships and white working-class districts; on the weekends he attended ANC rallies and sold on the Grand Parade. "See, you talk until your mouth is very pained, until you are tired of talking. Talking from the morning until the sun is set, selling the newspaper," Manqina said. "You see, in our tradition, we are like this—the neighbors are staying together and men, sometimes women, they discuss these political situations. They read the newspaper in conversations."[162]

At the same time that sellers pushed the newspaper, the other side of the balance sheet worsened. In July 1953 *Advance* needed £1,300 a month to publish; fifteen months later it needed £2,000.[163] Sales netted between £500 and £700 a month, but donations, the traditional lifeblood of the weekly, did not make up the difference. Averaging £800 a month, donations flowed into Barrack Street so irregularly that one week only £2 would arrive, and then the next week £1,000.[164] For many issues in 1954, *Advance* was a mere four pages, and at the end of the year Bunting threatened to shut down the Durban office and permanently issue a four-page newspaper unless £5,000 arrived in two months.[165] Carneson added that the weekly could not "operate on a hand-to-mouth basis." Yet that was exactly what transpired.[166] Carneson cut salary checks late, postponed paying bills until the following month and eventually had no choice but to go into permanent debt.[167]

Debt, it turned out, was not such a bad thing. After the *Guardian*'s first ban, Barrack Street learned that a debt-ridden newspaper was an attractive buy because an investor could write off any profits against the debt at time of sale. "Oh, we had a lovely loss," said Fred Carneson about the weekly's second banning in 1954. "We weren't bankrupt because we got donations. We could pay the bills. Neither the Party nor the paper ever welched on any debt, whatsoever. . . . The old company had nothing. It didn't have a paper, that had been closed down. It didn't have offices. What it did have was a nice large loss. There it was. The company stayed in existence. It wasn't banned. . . . the only asset we had was a nice big loss that could be offset. . . . So they'd give us a new big lump sum and that would help us get started, maybe a couple of hundred pounds."[168]

Clearly, though, the weekly could not depend on a ban to get cash. Instead, the financial savior of the newspaper in the 1950s was Johnny Morley, who started a *Guardian* Christmas club. A way of encouraging year-round spending, a Christmas club sold large food parcels after a patron paid a small amount every week during the year. Located in a crowded room in District Six, Johnny's Xmas Club—"Above All Justice, Before All Honesty"—offered its customers seven parcels containing various amounts of food and clothes.[169] In its first year in 1949, the club had agents in fourteen suburbs and over 1,000 families participating; Morley gave the *Guardian* £750 in profits.[170] The bonus was seen in circulation: every parcel included a year's subscription to the *Guardian*. In 1952, 5,000 families bought one of Johnny's Christmas parcels; two years later, that figure had doubled.[171] The parcels were amazingly comprehensive. "Johnny's 1956 Special," which cost £5 6s., consisted of "fish oil, ham, Vienna sausages, beef, corned beef, sardines, baked beans, peas, corn, rice, canned fruit, Nestle cream, tea, coffee, milk, chocolates, cake mix and one subscription."[172]

By accident, Commissioner Street copied Morley. In September 1954 Pretoria banned Bettie du Toit, a trade unionist, just after she launched her own food-parcel scheme. Unable to run it now, she requested that the weekly come to the rescue—her customers had gotten a year's subscription in their hampers. Ivan Schermbrucker asked a friend, Arnold Selby, to take it on.[173] Recently banned from the African Textile Workers' Industrial Union, Selby had taken a job at a dry-cleaning firm. His new salary was £125 a month, nearly a hundred pounds more than what he earned at the union. "It was back to £8 a week," remembered Selby, when he accepted Schermbrucker's invitation.

Called Arnold's Xmas Hampers, Selby's scheme instantly took off—in the first year Arnold's had 450 customers and made a profit of £500—and formed a twin backbone with Morley's in support of the newspaper.[174] Driving a niveous, two-stroke Lambretta scooter, Selby became a familiar figure in the Rand townships (he also lived in Soweto, an unusual situation for a white person).[175]

Although helped by Schermbrucker and Winnie Krämer, Selby eventually hired his own staff at Commissioner Street, including Conrad Dnibe, Joyce Wood Exteen, Joyce Watson Mohammed, Esther Mtshali, Thomas Letlalo, and Agnes Nkosi. Mohammed, the daughter of the well-known coloured Food and Canning trade-unionist Mary Moodley, canvassed homes in East Rand townships for new members.[176] Soon she worked at Commissioner Street, taking weekly payments from customers and filing their small red cards covered in stamps:[177]

> We really did a lot of good work. The hampers really helped a lot, because they paid off one shilling a week and you had something. They were happy, because they really got their money's worth at the end of the year. And they got a newspaper. There were strong bonds between the people and the paper. People come into the office, you know, there was always a cup of tea. You don't just come and pay, 'How are you?' Talking to them about their problems. The conversations were so wonderful. It was really, you know, it was a pleasure working there. . . . We gave people the best for their money. I mean, we were not just there for the sake of making money. Getting to know the people, politicizing—that was the main thing of the hampers.

Printing problems continued to bedevil the newspaper. In 1951 Unie Volkspers, the printing house that took over the *Guardian*'s contract after Charlie Stewart's suicide in 1947, went bankrupt. Barrack Street had to find a new printer immediately, and Fred Carneson approached Len Lee-Warden.[178] An English linotype operator, Lee-Warden had come to South Africa in 1936 after serving a five-year apprenticeship in London, and had manned the press at the *Cape Times* and the *Rand Daily Mail* (as well as for a short time at the *Palestine Post* in Jerusalem while on an extended honeymoon).[179] In 1949 Lee-Warden started his own printing works in a back room of a furniture shop in Keerom Street. A year later he moved his press, called Pioneer, to a church hall in Woodstock.

He was the obvious choice for the *Guardian*. He was married to the sister of Party organizer Ike Horovitch, he had done some printing jobs for the Communist Party before dissolution, and because he had supervised the night shift at Stewart's in 1946, he had printed the newspaper before. Still, Carneson had to practically beg. "Fred came to ask me if I would do it," Lee-Warden recalled. "I said I couldn't. But he said to me, 'If you don't do it, there's no one in Cape Town who will.' He had put it out on tender, and there hadn't been one tender." Lee-Warden said that he could not handle a newspaper, that he only printed small things like flyers, letterheads and stickers. Carneson offered to lend him the money to upgrade his equipment and guaranteed a contract with the *Guardian*.

Lee-Warden declined the assistance but agreed to take on the newspaper. He bought a second-hand flatbed press and a folding machine from Unie Volkspers, a linotype machine from Stewart's, moved a third time to Shelly Road in Salt River, and began printing the *Guardian*.[180] To finance the expansion, Lee-Warden took on a sleeping partner. He was a prominent businessman who was a director of the monthly Catholic newspaper *Southern Cross*. (He gave £3,000 and got a share of Pioneer's profits.) One day the partner came to Pioneer's offices, furious about the fact that Pioneer printed the *Guardian*, a communist newspaper. Lee-Warden calmly took him aside and said that it was not a communist newspaper—that if it were, then they would all be in jail. The partner, not mollified, demanded that either Lee-Warden stop printing the *Guardian* or return his money. The money was already absorbed into the operations, and Lee-Warden refused to abandon the newspaper.

He brilliantly solved the problem. No other printer in Cape Town dared print the *Guardian*, but Lee-Warden remembered a friend who printed the *Worcester Standard*. The friend agreed to take on the *Guardian*, but with the caveat that he did just the printing and folding but not the setting of type. "And so we were, in all truth, able to tell our sleeping partner that we were no longer going to print the *Guardian*," Lee-Warden said. "Using the word 'print' of course in inverted commas."[181]

Setting type in Salt River and printing in Worcester took an enormous amount of deceit. To keep the plan a secret, Lee-Warden and Bunting worked alone at Pioneer Press every Monday evening from six o'clock until after midnight setting the newspaper in type. They locked the pages into metal crates, put the crates into special wooden cases Lee-Warden had built for this maneuver, and piled the cases in the trunk of Lee-Warden's Nash sedan. Lee-Warden drove home, slept until half past four, and then made the two-hour drive to Worcester, where he deposited the crates at the printing plant. On Thursday, bundles of *Guardians* arrived by rail from Worcester bearing the imprint of the Worcester Standard Electric Press. This devious ju-jitsu lasted a year—through the banning of the *Guardian*—with Lee-Warden getting grudging extensions from the partner before Pioneer earned enough money to pay him off.

Fate conspired against Lee-Warden. As soon as he concluded the Worcester scam, Cape Town experienced its worst shortage of newsprint in memory. In desperation, Lee-Warden called the printing manager at *Die Burger* and asked if he would sell his excess scraps of newsprint that remained on *Die Burger*'s industrial-sized reels after use. The manager agreed, not knowing with whom Pioneer had contracts, and Lee-Warden hired a technician who stripped the newsprint off the rolls and threaded them into one useable piece. The resulting newsprint was scuffed and dirty, but in the crisis it was suitable. "If *Die Burger* had known," Bunting remembered, "they would have died on the spot."[182]

These aggravations, unusual for a printing house, did not nonplus Lee-Warden. "Yes, well, it was a commercial proposition," he said years later, "otherwise we wouldn't have done it. Also, as far as I was concerned, the feeling was that the paper had the right to exist. It was not necessarily a political thing. The thing was that this paper had a legitimate right to exist. . . . The freedom of the press was somehow something that was deeply instilled in you automatically."[183]

Freedom of the press was not as strongly instilled in the minister of justice, and before long, rumors of another Swart ban floated over Barrack Street. In anticipation, Bunting, Carneson and Kahn founded a second publishing firm, the Real Publishing and Printing Company.[184] Although Real had no assets and no purpose—it was basically unreal—it was a safety valve in case Swart moved against *Advance*.

On 31 August 1954, the day after Prime Minister Malan cordially received a contingent of Belgium journalists, Pretoria launched its single most comprehensive attack ever on the weekly. The raid concentrated solely on the weekly: in September 1946 the police had visited a dozen organizations and did not even have a search warrant for the *Guardian* and in November 1950 detectives just visited the three *Guardian* offices. Now, fifty Security Branch men raided all four *Advance* offices, including the new Port Elizabeth branch, and the homes of nearly every staff member. They turned Pioneer Press upside down. Detectives checked the hammers in Michael Harmel's piano and scoured Yusuf Dadoo's cake tins. They even visited an Indian journalist named Joe Francis, who told them, truthfully, that he had no connection to the newspaper.

The 31st was a Saturday. In Johannesburg, Ivan Schermbrucker arrived at Commissioner Street at eight in the morning to find six detectives waiting. After a morning of searching, they left with seven boxes of account ledgers, bank deposit books and correspondence.

In Cape Town, it was almost a joke. Bunting had gotten word of the impending raid and had instructed the *Advance* staff not to come into Barrack Street that day. When the police arrived, the offices were locked, and just a telephonist and a typist were standing in the third-floor hallway. The detectives telephoned both Bunting and Carneson. As they waited, they looked through copies of that week's newspaper that lay in bundles in the hall. The *Cape Times* reported that "the detectives read a front-page story of their raid, alleging that it was a preliminary to a Government intention to ban the newspaper."

Six hours later, Bunting and Carneson walked up the stairs and unlocked the doors. The Security Branch men searched all four rooms, going through every desk, cupboard, and filing cabinet. One cabinet, containing the newspaper's financial records, was locked. Carneson tried to track down the bookkeeper who possessed the only key. When the bookkeeper could not be found, the detectives insisted on bringing in a professional locksmith. But the locksmith could not open the cabinet. Eventually, with the streets now dark, the bookkeeper arrived with the key.[185]

From the search warrants, *Advance* knew Swart had appointed another authorizing officer and that a ban was imminent. Following the routine from two years before, the weekly launched a publicity campaign. Bunting sent a letter to all subscribers, supporters, hamper-scheme customers, and fellow newspapers, appealing for donations and asking for messages of protest to be sent to Pretoria. "Even if you disagree with the views expressed in *Advance*," he wrote, "we hope you will agree we have a right to express them provided they are not in conflict with the law."[186] *Advance* ran on its front page an open letter to Swart denouncing his actions.[187]

Swart, however, was less of a fool this time. He did not form a commit-tee of three, he gave no notice of any "findings of fact," and he did not wait a year and a half before taking action. He sent the police back to Barrack Street for another search at the end of September, and in October banned the weekly.[188] On 22 October 1954, the *Government Gazette* printed a let-ter signed by Swart and Jansen that read in its entirety: "Under and by virtue of the powers vested in me by section 6 of the Suppression of Com-munism Act as amended, I do hereby prohibit the printing, publication and dissemination in the Union of South Africa and the territory of South-West Africa of the publication called *Advance*. God Save the Queen."[189]

"Flabbergasted," Bunting told reporters who came to Barrack Street that Thursday to get his reaction, as sales agents hurried down the stairs with final copies of *Advance*. "I am flabbergasted. This time there has been no warning. . . . The news came like a bolt from the blue, with no official warn-ing. From beginning to end we have been left completely in the dark."[190]

A week later, a newspaper came out of Barrack Street: a four-page edi-tion of *New Age*.[191] Published by Real Publishing and Printing, printed by Pioneer, and edited by Jack Cope, *New Age* had the same editorial staff, administration, agents, and printer. "We put Jack Cope in as editor," Bunting recalled, "purely as a formal move, to make it seem as legal as pos-sible. Of course, it was the same paper. It was the *Guardian* with yet another new name. We made some cosmetic changes so Swart could swallow it."[192] As before, Bunting sent subscribers a copy of *New Age*, saying, "We enclose a copy of a new paper which is now being published in Cape Town and we shall be pleased to make arrangements with the publishers to take over the unexpired portion of your subscription."[193]

The latest *Guardian* reincarnation had a surprisingly easy registration, and *New Age* was entered into the General Post Office roll on 18 Novem-ber.[194] Carneson recalled: "There was no loophole that they could say that we hadn't changed. It was rather tricky. Also, you see, we didn't miss an edi-tion. We never missed a week. It was a problem. We'd bring up new directors, all sorts of things like that. They were all lined up in advance—no pun in-tended. Of course, the whole thing, everybody knew we were the same, but nothing was done illegally."[195]

In contrast to 1952, the response to the 1954 ban was muted. Bunting sent two open letters to Swart: "I wish to lodge the strongest possible protest against your high-handed action," one began.[196] The ANC and its allied or-ganizations issued statements of condemnation; Oliver Tambo called for "fearless opposition" to the ban. Even the Liberal Party said that "whatever might have been thought of the editorial policy and ideology of *Advance*, which often attacked the Liberal Party in an irresponsible manner, it is the indubitable right of any newspaper in a democratic society to print its opinions without fear or favour." But the South African media did not respond like they had two years before. Only two daily newspapers and two weeklies commented.[197] In *Forward*, Alex Hepple asked a week after the ban, "Has South Africa strayed so far from the ways of liberty that the suppression of a newspaper is accepted as a normal event? Has the Press nothing to say? Why are our editors and journalists so obviously silent?"[198]

There was no answer, and Bunting wrote to various newspapers asking for editorial comment about the ban. In his letter to Morris Broughton, editor of the *Cape Argus*, Bunting said: "Since *Advance* was banned last week, however, I have looked in vain for any comment in your columns. Yet, I venture to suggest the banning of *Advance* is an even more flagrant example of dictatorship than the banning of the *Guardian*. . . . I write to you, as one of the 'watchdogs of freedom' in this country, whether you do not see any reason to query this wholesale assault on personal liberty and specifically whether you will join with me in protesting against the banning of the newspaper *Advance*." A few weeks later, Broughton replied on the same day the *Cape Argus* ran an editorial about the ban. In the letter and the editorial, Broughton explained that he had waited to see if Swart would modify his decision. He reasoned that *Advance* had not been proscribed because of its anti-apartheid stance: "Many other newspapers have been equally if not more outspokenly critical both of the government and/or apartheid and they still enjoy their full liberty." *Advance* was banned, Broughton wrote, because Bunting had been personally banned, and thus, by the ever-logical eyes of Pretoria, was "counted unfit to conduct" a political newspaper. "Others who have passed over the incident without comment," said Broughton, "doubtless hold that both person and newspaper were instruments of a proscribed ideology." Incensed by the self-serving and groundless analysis, Bunting wrote back to Broughton five days later. He repeated his charge that the fundamental issue was not whether he was fit or unfit, by the judgment of the government, to run a newspaper, but that freedom of the press was being trampled. There was no reply.[199]

The lack of protest was an indication of how far down the slippery slope of repression the country had slid. Into this harsh world, *New Age*, the fifth newspaper in three years to come out of Barrack Street, was born.

CHAPTER FIVE

Fleeting Moments of Happiness

The Democracy Decade, 1950–1959

"**N**ew Age is a battlefield," the weekly told its readers, and nowhere was the battle joined more fiercely than between the African National Congress and the apartheid regime.[1]

In January 1951 the newspaper officially shifted its editorial policy. Brian Bunting issued a new list of priorities. "Non-European affairs" rated number one, while foreign news was third and trade-union news was fifth.[2] The de-emphasis of labor issues and foreign news, the previous decade's staples, meant room for the ANC. With the Communist Party no longer a public movement, the newspaper quickly made itself comfortable in its new political home. It supported a second ANC stay-at-home on May Day 1951. To encourage the ANC-led boycott of the tercentenary celebrations of the beginning of white colonization in South Africa on 6 April 1652, the newspaper ran an eight-part series called "1652 and All That," written by Eddie Roux, the veteran activist and biographer of S. P. Bunting.[3]

Auspiciously, 1952 opened with the *Guardian* praising the ANC's historic decision to start a Campaign for the Defiance of Unjust Laws.[4] A nationwide civil-disobedience operation modeled on Gandhian principles, the Defiance Campaign became the ANC's most important move in its first half century. For the last six months of 1952, men and women of all races purposely courted arrest by violating curfew and pass laws, entering African locations without permits, and using whites-only facilities. The campaign succeeded brilliantly. The publicity was overwhelming, the ANC's membership rolls ballooned from 7,000 to more than 100,000, it forged a national identity with clearly defined ideologies and policies, and it finally became the primary organization in the liberation struggle.[5]

Some observers, pointing to the seven-week delay in implementing the 8 April 1952 banning order, suggested that the minister of justice banned the *Guardian* precisely to diminish support for the upcoming campaign, due to begin five weeks later. (Swart was not that clever, for if he was, he would have then banned it just days before the start.) In any case, during much of the Defiance Campaign, Barrack Street sold 40,000 copies a week, a 40 percent rise in circulation over pre-campaign figures.[6] "The minister's action set alight the fuse which led to the explosion of the Defiance Campaign," Brian Bunting wrote. "The Government's ban on the *Guardian* automatically ensured that the *Clarion* would become the voice and organiser of the resistance campaign."[7] Other South African newspapers, most notably the *Rand Daily Mail*, covered the campaign—it was, after all, the major political news story of the year. But because of the ban, an aura of martyrdom hovered around the *Guardian*. Lines were being drawn, and the newspaper was very clearly on the side of the ANC.

The newspaper, never claiming journalistic objectivity, also had the advantage of throwing its full weight into the campaign. Reporters regularly interviewed Nelson Mandela, the "volunteer-in-chief" of the campaign, and when it seemed to be taking an anti-white turn in October 1952, Mandela issued a statement in the weekly calling on whites to join it.[8] Headlines declared "Government Rattled by Defiance Campaign."[9] Photographs showed volunteers, with their thumbs lifted in the popular Congress pose, heading for arrest. The pictures, which sometimes spread across two pages, were pivotal for many illiterate ANC supporters.[10] Barrack Street printed instructions on how to be a volunteer and asked its readers to pray, fast and attend nightly church services.[11]

The newspaper played an even more critical role in the buildup to the Congress of the People. When ANC paid-up membership sagged in 1953 to a reported 28,900, the ANC and its new affiliates—the South African Congress of Trade Unions, the Congress of Democrats (a whites-only group), the South African Indian Congress, and the South African Coloured People's Organisation—decided to organize a national convention.[12] On the last weekend of June 1955, 3,000 people gathered on a soccer field in

Kliptown, a coloured township a dozen miles outside Johannesburg.[13] They heard speeches, sang songs and approved the Freedom Charter, a policy document.

The two years preparing for the Congress of the People were probably more vital to the ANC than the actual weekend. (Many activists like Walter Sisulu believed the government would ban the Congress of the People before it took place, which made its buildup even more valuable.)[14] Thousands of "Freedom Volunteers" fanned out into every corner of South Africa, publicizing the convention and collecting suggestions for the Freedom Charter.[15] Wearing a khaki uniform, the volunteers carried copies of *New Age* to help make conversation. "We would take out the paper," Wolfie Kodesh said, "and point to a picture and read something from an article and explain what was going on. The paper was a way to break the ice and give us some measure of a bona fide. It proved we were real."[16]

News of the Kliptown convention dominated the pages of the weekly. Bunting printed a *"New Age* Study Document" for readers to "cut out and keep for reference."[17] Reporters covered village elections for delegates, editorials called for mass participation and announcements told of upcoming meetings.[18] "All Roads Lead to Kliptown" trumpeted *New Age* two days before the convention, and during the historic weekend, the newspaper was highly visible, with many supporters selling the latest issue and Sonia Bunting, Brian's wife, addressing the meeting on the second day. The week afterwards, a three-page spread of photographs and a full copy of the Freedom Charter (*New Age* was the first to publish the document) appeared in the newspaper, and throughout the rest of the year, the weekly spearheaded the campaign to collect one million signatures for the Charter.

Another Congress issue in the newspaper was bus boycotts. When the coloured people of Cape Town started a bus boycott in 1956, *New Age* shrewdly headlined the story "Common Struggle Unites People of Cape Town and Montgomery, USA."[19] Evaton's eleven-month bus boycott garnered much copy in 1956, and the famed 1957 three-month Alexandra bus boycott—*Azikhwelwa* ("We will not ride")—drew months of front-page photographs and articles; Arnold Selby publicly fasted for a fortnight in protest of police violence; staff members regularly rose at five in the morning to watch the mass exodus of walkers making the seven-mile journey to Johannesburg; and Tennyson Makiwane, a new staffer, told about how he got arrested in a police blitz against boycotters.[20] *New Age* gave ample coverage when other cities like Port Elizabeth, East London, Bloemfontein and Uitenhage joined in solidarity.

Some news had a yearly rhythm. The 26th of June was an annual strike day, and Barrack Street reprinted Congress telegrams and memoranda about it each year.[21] While in the 1930s the weekly attended the annual national conference of the Labour Party, and in the 1940s that of the Communist Party, in the 1950s the newspaper went to the ANC's yearly gathering in Bloemfontein. Each December at least two reporters and a photographer supplied articles, photographs, memoranda, reactions, and resolutions from the conference.[22] *New Age* even ran photographs of another gaggle of guests in Bloemfontein: Special Branch detectives.[23]

Leaders of the ANC appeared in the newspaper with such a steady regularity that Moses Mabhida, an important ANC and Communist Party member, later said that "it was through the pages of the *Guardian* that our people's leaders—Nelson Mandela, Oliver Tambo and many others—became known throughout the country."[24] One of the many crucial contributions was a 1958 article by Oliver Tambo defending the ANC's alliance with the Congress of Democrats.[25] The ANC also encouraged members to sell the *Guardian*, as the Party did in the 1940s, although they tended to be less devoted. "It was part-time for me and only in Orlando," said Walter Sisulu, secretary of the ANC in the early 1950s. "You would have gotten the impression that the ANC had ordered us to sell because many activists found themselves selling. But we looked at the material and saw how useful it will be when it gets in the hands of the people." Most importantly, the newspaper provided communication when governmental repression would have otherwise prevented it. As a response to the Defiance Campaign, Pretoria banned Congress leaders, forcing them to resign from the ANC, forbidding them from attending political gatherings and often restricting them to local magisterial districts. (Some were even forbidden to talk to more than one person at a time.) To counteract the effects of the proscriptions, the newspaper started a column: "Let the Banned Speak." Almost every week, a banned ANC leader wrote a long essay in *New Age* about the state of South African politics.

A wide range of correspondence from across the Union also performed an indispensable job by writing regular letters to the editor. This gave page four of *New Age* a tremendously varied amount of information from the hinterlands and from obscure townships.[26] Future leaders like Chris Hani, Thabo Mbeki, Gatsha Buthelezi and Hastings Banda wrote to Barrack Street. E. Lulamile Vara, a Youth Leaguer in Cradock, penned two letters a month for years. The datelines came from almost every town in the country, giving the weekly true national representation. South Africa is a large country (one-ninth the size of the United States), and in the 1950s means of communication were antiquated. Long-distance telephone service was spotty. Television would not be introduced until the mid-1970s. Radio was still in its infancy. The South African Broadcasting Service started broadcasting in African languages only in 1952 (and then just to the township of Soweto; it was not until the mid-1960s that rural listeners could listen to African language broadcasts, and FM radio only appeared in 1961). With a hostile government issuing its own propaganda, *New Age* was the only bridge over which the liberation movement could reach rural activists. Some Congress-affiliated organizations leaned heavily on the weekly. The minutes of a Federation of South African Women national executive meeting in 1959 quietly hinted at the role *New Age* played: "Regional report Cape Eastern—Although regular correspondence is not maintained with this Region, news is often obtained from *New Age* reports."[27]

"Let the Banned Speak" and the letters page provided a unique platform through which both leaders and ordinary people could speak and could be heard.[28] When Pretoria was trying to silence opposition, these *New Age* features were an essential tool in the liberation struggle.

Acknowledging the salience of the ANC, Brian Bunting opened a *New Age* office in the Eastern Cape. Many of the militants in the ANC Youth League came from the region. Fort Hare was in the Eastern Cape town of Alice. Events in the Eastern Cape—a raucous 1948 laundry workers' strike, the 1949 Port Elizabeth bus boycott, and the 1952 Defiance Campaign, in which over half of the 8,000 resisters came from the Eastern Cape—produced a remarkable statistic: at the end of 1952, 60 percent of the ANC's 100,000 members were in the Eastern Cape.[29]

In February 1953 *New Age* opened an office at Court Chambers, 27 Adderley Street, in downtown Port Elizabeth. Court Chambers, an imposing two-story sandstone building, housed a number of trade-union offices. The weekly occupied two rooms at the northern end of the second floor, with the editor's office in the corner. Curiously, Port Elizabeth's police headquarters lay directly across the street, and members of each organization warily eyed the comings and goings at the other's building.[30] The police were not the only unfriendly group in town. The conservative city council forbade the selling of the *Guardian* on the streets of Port Elizabeth; the ban lasted until 1957, when two youngsters "Beat the Bay Barrier" by stealthily slipping applications for selling licenses past the council.[31] The council placed many restrictions on Africans in Port Elizabeth, including nightly curfews and a permanent ban on open-air meetings, that further hampered the gathering of news for the weekly.

Gladstone Tshume first ran the Adderley Street office. "Comrade Glad" had worked as a coal dealer in Grahamstown before organizing dock and textile workers in Port Elizabeth for the Communist Party. He led a 1946 dock workers' strike, was a member of the 1949 boycott committee and chaired the Defiance Campaign in the Eastern Cape.[32] Although a lay preacher, he often stuttered so badly when speaking in public that he jumped with frustration.[33]

Tshume was a trade unionist, not a journalist, and in 1954 Bunting decided the office needed more experience. He chose Govan Mbeki. A cerebral writer and passionate politician, Mbeki came from a relatively well-to-do family. His elderly father, a devout Methodist and village headman, lived in the district's first stone house and had a dining-room table that could seat sixteen people. Mbeki attended Healdtown, a Methodist coeducational boarding school, and then the University of Fort Hare. In 1933 he encountered Eddie Roux at an open-air lecture on a hill behind the university, and soon joined the ANC. After five years at Fort Hare, Mbeki remained in the Transkei—except for a stint teaching high school in Durban—and carved out a niche as one of the region's authoritative intellectuals. He authored two books of essays; founded the *Territorial Magazine*, an African fortnightly that in 1940 was renamed *Inkundla ya Bantu*; and helped write "Africans' Claims in South Africa," an influential 1943 ANC policy document.[34] He also served on the governing board of Fort Hare and on a council, the Bunga, that helped govern the Transkei, and he helped his wife Epainette run a trading store in Idutywa, Transkei (she continued to run the shop into the twenty-first century, even after her son Thabo became president of the country).

"Kingpin" of the liberation movement, according to Ruth First, Mbeki had "a sharp mind, intolerant of the foolish and the faint-hearted," and that intolerance led to some unexpected career changes.[35] In 1939, Clarkebury, a teacher-training college, fired him; in 1943 he was forced to resign from *Inkundla*; and in 1954 he was dismissed after twenty-one months from a teaching post in Ladysmith, Natal (he had been organizing local coal workers). Mbeki was pondering a job offer from the *Golden City Post* when Fred Carneson and Ivan Schermbrucker arrived in Ladysmith and persuaded him to take over the Adderley Street office.

Mbeki's arrival at Adderley Street signaled a new step for the weekly. He was very familiar with the newspaper, having written for it and having served on its board, and his years at *Inkundla* had polished his editing and reporting abilities.[36] He broke the news on the 1956 Transkei drought (which prompted an ANC demand for government relief), followed the periodic removals in Korsten township, investigated conditions at Kougapoort Prison, and reported on scandals at his alma mater, Fort Hare.[37]

One of Mbeki's colleagues in Port Elizabeth was a special writer named Christopher Gell. A tall, cadaverous Scot who had retired from the Indian civil service after a case of polio paralyzed him from the neck down, Gell spent all but three hours of each day attached to an iron lung. In those three hours, he filled a day, sending articles to *New Age* and other newspapers around the world, and hosting visitors who sought political advice. "To many Africans he is magic," wrote one visitor to his house. "He talks with tremendous energy, animated, witty, outrageous, caustic, irrepressible, interspersing his diatribes with devastating confidences, pausing sometimes to scribble a name down for you or dash off a letter of introduction, swearing, laughing, quoting Schweitzer, in a most extraordinary flood of stimulation and conviction." When he died in 1958, ANC members carried his coffin.[38]

The greatest influence on Adderley Street, however, was the M-Plan. At the 1953 annual conference of the Transvaal ANC, Nelson Mandela proposed a new, decentralized organizational structure, that would mobilize the masses and preserve an organizational integrity in times of crisis. The ANC would divide black residential areas into cells and zones, down to individual street blocks, with interlocking levels of leaders who would manage the structure and offer a curriculum of history and economic lectures—"The World We Live In," "How We Are Governed," and "The Need for Change."[39] A few ANC branches attempted to implement Mandela's idea—most notably in Langa in Cape Town, and in Cato Manor in Durban—but the only South African city to fully enact what was dubbed M-Plan was Port Elizabeth. Throughout the African townships of New Brighton, Korsten, Schauder and KwaZakele, M-Plan stewards organized the selling of *New Age*. "I would pick up twenty-one bundles of *New Age* each Friday at Adderley Street and distribute them in my zone," Nondwe Mankahla, an M-Plan steward in New Brighton, remembered. "It was hard work. We worked very, very hard selling the paper. I sold them and became the best seller of *New Age*. I won a dinner set from Johannesburg once for selling the most." Mbeki soon hired Mankahla as a part-time seller and fundraiser. Other stewards also joined *New Age*, including James Kati, who sold the newspaper each day in downtown Port Elizabeth, and Ralph Mgqungwana, who handled administrative tasks at Adderley Street.[40]

Like elsewhere, Congress men and women used *New Age* in a familiar fashion.[41] In 1953 Wilton Mkwayi joined the newspaper as a part-time employee at Adderley Street. Mkwayi, the eldest of thirteen children, had left school in sixth grade to work in a dynamite factory in Somerset West and then a tin factory in Port Elizabeth. He joined the African Textile Workers' Union and the ANC.[42] He later spoke about the carry-on readership of the weekly:

> When you read the paper, you will not throw it away afterwards. You give it to someone else. You will find some people, at the end of the next month still reading it as if it came yesterday. I would say that there are so many issues after this one and they would say, 'Well, the news is new to me because I've never read it. . . .' In the rural areas and the townships, people would come together to listen to someone reading *New Age*. You would go to someone's place and people would be waiting there for *New Age* to arrive. He would read it and they would sit and listen and, what I liked, they would not forget as we forget. They would discuss what was in the paper. The whole village would know about it. . . . They were all really supporting the struggle to the extent that the man in the street and villages, even those managers in the factories when you go, they regarded this paper as ANC. You explain and you know, they say, 'No, we hear you saying that, but all the supporters of the paper are ANC.' And some will say, 'It is a trick of you people to say that this is independent. For example it seems that you have a pile of names because the paper is banned on Tuesday and Friday the paper is coming out with another name.' They—the people—they regarded this as their paper.[43]

By 1956 half of *New Age*'s sales in Port Elizabeth came from stewards in the townships. The M-Plan worked.[44]

Commissioner Street formed the heart of left-wing Johannesburg. The offices were spacious and welcoming, if a bit cluttered. More importantly, a host of similarly inclined organizations were in the same building, so the halls, stairwells and front steps teemed with interlocking knots of conversing colleagues. On the other hand, the ANC's office—Walter Sisulu set it up after he became the organization's first full-time paid employee in 1949—consisted of a dilapidated room reached by an alley in the Indian business quarter.[45] "Whenever you wanted to know what was going on or find somebody, you could always find somebody at the *New Age* office," said Rusty Bernstein. "The building was a kind of radical organization headquarters and people were coming and going, so it wasn't a quiet place where people were just working. Arnold coming in and out with the hampers. It wasn't a purely social, club atmosphere, but I always remember going to Commissioner Street, to go see someone."[46] Ruth First's daughter wrote that the offices were "like falling into the center of a whirlwind":

> For a start, the noise was incredible: Telephones rang, duplicators churned, and staples clicked. But it was the occupants who raised the level to an all-time high as they shouted down phones, at each other, to the air. And as for the mess—well, its proportions were mythic: Piles of leaflets teetered precariously on desks, banners jostled with collection boxes, old clothes collected for rummage sales spilled from their boxes. But none of that made the office either unfriendly or difficult to negotiate. For the place was buzzing with a kind of exhilaration. . . . Everybody inside the shabby building moved at double speed, shouting, laughing, heckling, swapping anecdotes with bagels and advice with old pamphlets.[47]

Ruth First was at the center of the storm. Colleagues had a Xhosa phrase for her: "Yimazi ephah neenkati"—a mare that holds its own in a race with stallions.[48] Along with her husband, Joe Slovo, First raised three daughters in the 1950s. Gillian Slovo remembered her hard-working mother always tapping away at the typewriter late into the night.[49] Much of what she was typing were articles for *Fighting Talk*, the monthly journal founded by the Springbok Legion and turned into a Party platform in the 1950s.[50] As editor-in-chief, she harbored a good deal of loyalty towards the journal, despite its tiny circulation, and spent many off-hours persuading colleagues to produce articles, and then editing and laying them out.[51]

A cynosure of the political scene on the Rand, First whirled through her days. She rushed into Commissioner Street, yelled orders, made telephone calls, dashed off telegrams, dictated letters, and then hurtled down the stairs and jumped into her slope-backed Citroën that sped through the streets like a black torpedo.[52] One colleague remembered a time when, "a SB guy came looking for 'Miss First.' The policeman sat in a chair in the office until a smart-looking, glamorous woman with a new hat, dark glasses, high heels, and gloves came hurrying in. He rose and said, 'I am looking for Miss First.' Ruth stopped and said, 'No, she's not here' and walked away."[53]

She often was rushing off to meetings with Congress leaders. Trevor Huddleston said that First frequently visited his Sophiatown parish to keep her finger on the pulse of the townships.[54] "I got used to Ruth First," Walter Sisulu said. "She would be in touch with me through the week. In fact nearly every day she would pop in or ring me. We'd exchange views and discuss what should be highlighted. And that went on for years. . . . We quarreled a lot, and I became very attached to her in all that. And I thought, 'No, she means well even when she is wrong.'" On weekends, she hosted cocktail parties or dinners at her home in Roosevelt Park. According to the quaint phrasing of the *Times* of London, the Slovos had "become an important centre for multi-racial political gatherings."[55] Sometimes she dug a pit in her garden, filled it with burning coals, and spit-roasted a lamb with herbs.[56]

Amidst all this, she still held down her job, reporting for *New Age*.[57] When riots broke out in March 1952 in Newclare, a shantytown near Sophiatown, First scooped the story that a Basuto gang known as the Russians was responsible for the violence; four years later, when the Russians began disrupting the Evaton bus boycott—killing nine people—First discovered the police were busing the gang to Evaton.[58] In 1959 she and Ben Turok drove to the northwest Cape to locate a chief who had been banished to a remote hamlet; every hour, as her car bumped along the sandy back roads, she elegantly wiped the dust from her face.[59]

These were her Camelot years, a time of sheer adrenaline rushes and breathless optimism. She and her husband Joe were rising stars in an ever-expanding firmament. Her oldest daughter, Shawn Slovo, recalled the atmosphere surrounding her family:

> When we were conceived in the early 1950s, it was a very different time in South Africa. No one could envisage the way things were going to develop. It was fun, the political games. And you were all young, you were all in your twenties and thirties. It was subterfuge and plotting and planning and meeting in cars and having parties and turning up the music loud, to drown out the buggings. And the multi-racial socializing. You were one of the few South Africans that could move with ease in different societies and dance and have the benefit of the music and the foods and the curries. It was a very exciting life.[60]

It was true, as Anthony Sampson wrote, that "Ruth First had the aura of *New Age*," and it was a glorious, hopeful aura.[61] It was soon to end, and she was playing host in the mansion where she was not long to be mistress.

An expanding group of diverse writers surrounded the galvanic First. Michael Harmel still occupied an exalted place at Commissioner Street, but he was busy with a smattering of other projects: he helped run the quarterly journal *Liberation: A Journal of Democratic Discussion*; he wrote numerous articles for *Fighting Talk*; he finished a long-awaited novel in 1959 (it never was published); and after Pretoria shut down Indian schools in Fordsburg, he founded and ran an alternative private academy, Central Indian High School.[62] Congress colleagues dominated the staff at Central Indian—Dennis Brutus, Molly Fisher, and Duma Nokwe taught there—and one in particular stood out. Known affectionately as "Tough" for his outwardly scowling manner and very tall frame, Alfred Hutchinson was an emerging ANC theorist, and at age twenty-seven he joined the ANC's national executive committee, the sixteen-person body that ran the Congress on a daily basis.[63] He also joined *New Age* as a reporter.

First could transcend gender, class and race barriers when grooming young writers. She might have been hard on her staff, but beneath her façade of brisk professionalism was a deep appreciation of the craft of journalism. "I'll never forget Ruth's advice about writing," said Willie Kgositile, a *New Age* reporter in the 1960s. "No adjectives, no adverbs, no qualifiers. You had to bring the action. Be precise. You had to write with verbs."[64] After Hutchinson began contemplating switching from teaching to writing, he left a note for First on her desk: "You call it habit, routine—I hope I'm right. Chekhov's definition of talent—work. Endless work and making an increasing effort to be worthy of it. These things were beyond my grasp. Perhaps I'm too ambitious; perhaps I'm just plain lazy. But I'm shaken. . . . I don't seem to be able to keep notebooks, but will try."[65] For months, First pushed Hutchinson to write an article on Gert Sibande and the situation in Bethal. After borrowing some of First's notes on Sibande, Hutchinson described the challenges of the piece:

> What does the farmer think? How do the potatoes, bloodstained, taste in his mouth? . . . What of the jelly-like restlessness that is manifest to even the blindest? . . . I must show the poor squatter not as object and broken but with some fight left in him; with an intimation that things could be otherwise. He is robbed, beaten; insulted, arrested. But he must also know fleeting moments of happiness—just like the rolling veld sweeping upwards to meet the sky. I would like to have him as fully rounded as possible—or should I? Perhaps his circumstance can only produce a jagged character. I gather from Tennyson that the people around Bethal have a character of their own. Perhaps it is as it should be.

> Inspiration Gone,
> Hutch

First published his Bethal article on the back page of the 6 September 1956 edition.

Advising Hutchinson on the article was Tennyson Xola Makiwane, another African reporter for *New Age*. Makiwane, nicknamed T.X., was the grandson of Reverend Elijah Makiwane. This was no ordinary legacy. The reverend went on a 1909 deputation of African leaders to London to protest the color-bar clause in the Act of Union; he founded the African Mission Church in the Cape; and from 1873 to 1881 he was the first African editor of a newspaper in Africa, *Isigidimi*, a Xhosa-language monthly.[66] T.X. studied at Lovedale mission school and Fort Hare—from which he was expelled in 1954—and in the 1950s was considered a rising star in Johannesburg's ANC Youth League circles.[67]

In 1956 he started writing for *New Age*. His articles focused on township culture. Although he (like Hutchinson) lived in Alexandra, Makiwane often threw on an modish hat and went to Sophiatown, the legendary focal point of African culture on the Rand. Built on a 237-acre farm—it was named after the original farmer's wife Sophia, and bore streets with her children's names—Sophiatown was home to over 100,000 people: Africans (it was one of the few urban places in the country where Africans could own land), Chinese, coloureds, Indians and one celebrated white woman, Regina Brooke.[68] Sophiatown was two or three District Sixes thrown together, a sprawling city-within-a-city that boasted the only swimming pool for Africans on the Rand, twenty churches, seventeen schools, and two cinemas—including the largest movie theatre in Africa, the Odin, with seating for a thousand. Kids shot dice on sand sidewalks outside shops and played soccer in the unpaved streets. *Tsotsis*—brigades of petty thieves, pickpockets, marijuana peddlers—roamed the narrow alleys, preying on *moegoes* (greenhorns). Gangs took names from American gangster movies—the Americans, Gestapo, and Berliners—wore fedoras and double-breasted suits, and operated gambling dens, prostitution rings and a prospering black market in stolen goods. At night, residents jammed shebeens and jazz clubs like The Back of the Moon, Cabin in the Sky, and The Thirty-Nine Steps.

Some compared Sophiatown to the Latin Quarter of Paris, and Trevor Huddleston, the Anglican priest who lived there in the 1950s, was reminded of the Umbrian hills of Italy; but for Makiwane, it was a giant canvas upon which he could splash his unromanticizing, roiling words.[69] He wrote about "coffee-carts" that served greasy fat cakes and black coffee for sixpence. He chronicled the anticipatory joy of a Sophiatown Friday afternoon, taught *New Age* readers the freedom songs that filtered from second-story windows, and described *kwela* jazz, the new sound led by a trumpeter named Hugh Masekela and a singer named Miriam Makeba.[70] He wrote so much about Sophiatown's gritty underworld that First dubbed him *New Age*'s "crime reporter."[71] And he reported on the saddest story of all: the Sophiatown removals in the late 1950s that destroyed the township.

Makiwane painted other pictures outside Sophiatown—he covered a 1957 uprising in Zeerust and described the funeral of a cousin who was killed on an Eastern Transvaal farm after a pass arrest—but daily life in the townships interested him most, and he invested much energy in even the simplest of stories, as the lead for an otherwise routine article on a food program for schoolchildren attests: "Broad smiles beamed from the children as they walked away clinging tightly to their purchases—a pint of milk in a container, held closely against the body or balanced on the head by the girls. The slices of bread and peanut butter seemed even thicker in their little hands. Every morning they stand squeezed against one another in the queues of the African children's feeding schemes. One or two of the younger kids look shy, but expectation glitters from their eyes."[72]

Sports, which had taken a back seat when Henry Nxumalo left the *Guardian* in 1951 to join *Drum*, revived under the pen of Robert Resha. A former gold miner—he had lost the index finger of his left hand in an accident—Resha worked as a bus conductor and was one of the foremost Congress leaders in the Transvaal: he was secretary of the Transvaal ANC branch, leader of the Sophiatown-removal resistance campaign and a member of the ANC's national executive.[73] Resha was an electrifying speaker ("to hear Robert speak at a meeting was almost like watching an orchestra being conducted," Helen Joseph said), and his house on Bertha Street was a local headquarters for his so-called "Soft-Town Boys" posse, and for many of the famed 1950s Sophiatown generation of writers like *Drum* journalists Bloke Modisane, Nat Nakasa, Es'kia Mphahlele, Casey Motsisi, and Can Themba, and composer Todd Matshikiza.[74] Resha was a fashion plate who never hesitated to roll up his sleeves and throw punches. His wife Maggie Resha wrote that "Robert was very tidy. He wanted to be smart-looking from Monday to Monday; he could not wear a jacket from the wardrobe without the pockets and sleeves being pressed. . . . [He was] well-known as a 'quick to fight' person, willing to settle with fists what he could not settle with words. Personally, I think he was a man of no nonsense."[75] Resha had dabbled in sports writing for a number of African newspapers before becoming *New Age*'s sports reporter in 1956.[76]

Joe Gqabi was another ANC leader on the staff at Commissioner Street. A muscular amateur boxer, Gqabi started working as a reporter in 1958, but he soon gravitated towards taking photographs for the weekly.[77] Gqabi's mentor and close friend was the liberation movement's chief photographer, Eli Weinberg.[78] Like Ray Alexander, Weinberg was a Jewish socialist who had fled Latvia as a teenager and had become active in South Africa's organized labor movement. In 1952 Pretoria banned Weinberg from trade-union work, and he turned a casual photography hobby into a full-time occupation. Weinberg attended meetings and rallies, ranged across the townships and shantytowns, and took seated portraits. "Our roving photographer," according to the weekly, Weinberg donated hundreds of photographs to *New Age*, and Bunting ran a series called "How People Live" centered around Weinberg photographs.[79]

With its deep integration into the ANC, *New Age*'s Johannesburg office played a key role in the Congress's protests against the pass laws. For decades, the government had tried to extend the system of pass laws to African women. African men had been forced to carry the insidious "dompas" since the early days of the colony, and in the 1950s the police arrested on average a thousand men each day.[80] African women had always managed to keep their exemption, although at times, such as in 1913, they had to lead mass demonstrations to drive the point home. In December 1955 Pretoria sent out mobile units to issue passes to African women in rural Free State and Transvaal towns. Ruth First broke the story in *New Age* and secured an interview with a Native Affairs Department spokesman, who discussed the new "influx control regulations" coming into force.[81] Within days, the ANC issued a statement calling for rallies and regional conferences.[82]

Despite the publicity, 1,500 Free State women paid 3s. 6d. to obtain a passbook. Hearing the news, Ruth First, Robert Resha, and Lilian Ngoyi, an ANC leader, immediately drove to the village of Winburg (the site of a 1913 rally) and watched several hundred women there publicly burn the passbooks in front of the magistrate's court and get arrested.[83] Because of the timely *New Age* reports and subsequent ANC organizing, women in a dozen towns led marches, burned passes, and handed in petitions to local officials about employment and residence permits. Four hundred women marched in Orlando, 104 were arrested in Ermelo, and 360 African domestic workers marched to the Native Commissioner in Johannesburg.[84] *Umteto unzima*, women said to First—"The law is very heavy."[85]

With the raised consciousness caused by the pass-burnings and demonstrations, the ANC-affiliated Federation of South African Women planned a march in Pretoria in August 1956. Over 20,000 women of all races descended on the Union Buildings and handed over a signed petition protesting apartheid laws. An official for the absent prime minister accepted the petition. A clock struck three o'clock, and the entire crowd raised their arms high in the Congress salute and went silent for a full half hour. Lilian Ngoyi then led the crowd in singing the liberation anthem "Nkosi Sikelele Afrika," and Free State women followed with a new song: *Wathint' a bafazi, wa uthint' imbolodo uzo kufa*—"You have struck a rock. You have tampered with the women. You shall be destroyed."[86]

A different kind of rock was struck against the pass laws early one morning in April 1959. An emaciated man wearing a ragged burlap sack walked into Commissioner Street. Ruth First was not surprisingly out of the office, so Wolfie Kodesh, who was working for *New Age* in Johannesburg at the time, received the man. His story was appallingly familiar. After a police raid in Alexandra, he had been arrested for a pass-law offense. The police shackled his hands and legs, took him to a labor depot, and gave him the choice of three months in jail or two weeks of farm work. The man opted for the fortnight of labor. A farmer named Potgieter drove him to a Bethal-district farm. He dug up potatoes with his bare hands for twelve hours a day, slept without a blanket or bedding in a lice-ridden compound, and was forced to wear a potato sack for clothing. When he protested, Potgieter beat him with a sjambok. Some of his fellow workers died from exhaustion and malnutrition, and Potgieter simply buried them in mounds at the edge of his fields. When he caught a worker trying to flee, he mutilated his feet. The man had managed to escape, walking for six days back to Johannesburg. He said he had a message to deliver to the wife and children of a friend, James Sadike, who also worked on Potgieter's farm.

The story horrified Kodesh. When First returned to the offices, he took her and Joe Gqabi in his 1948 black Chevrolet sedan to Bethal. They drove for two hours around the district before finding Potgieter's farm halfway between Bethal and Heidelberg. They saw rows of figures bent over the ground like something out of a Millet painting. Gqabi jumped out. "I'll pretend I'm a cousin of Sadike and just want to leave a message from his wife," he said, and walked across the field with a meek "kaffir" gait. Kodesh steered the Chevy behind some trees where he noticed some mounds in the field. "You know, Ruth," said Kodesh, "during the war, in the Ethiopian campaign, when we landed, we were running along a beach, running over these mounds. Being soldiers, we had heavy boots on. We kicked the mounds, and, of course, there are dead Italians and so on buried there. And those mounds look exactly like these mounds here."

Suddenly Gqabi appeared sprinting across the field, screaming for Kodesh to start the car. Gqabi dove into the car, and they roared off down the road. After he caught his breath, Gqabi told them, "I went along the fields and met Potgieter's son who agreed to let me give the message to Sadike. As I walked to the workers, Potgieter came by and asked his son what was happening. When the son told him, he said, 'Nie, something's wrong here' and ran after me. His son got in a bakkie [pickup truck] and tried to run me down."

"Let's go back," Kodesh suggested, "but Joe, you lie on the back seat out of sight." They coasted back to the farm. Three men on bicycles glimpsed the car and gave chase with sjamboks.

Escaping with the story, they returned to Johannesburg, and First wrote it up for the 30 April 1959 issue of *New Age*. She also went to see a lawyer and secured a writ of habeas corpus for Potgieter to produce Sadike. Potgieter brought Sadike to Johannesburg dressed in a potato sack and sitting in a cage in the back of his bakkie. When Sadike emerged, his wife saw the thin man looking like a windblown scarecrow and shook her head. "No," she said, "this is not my husband." Potgieter smirked in victory. First groaned, thinking she had made a ghastly mistake. Sadike came closer and smiled weakly, and his wife greeted him. It was her husband.[87]

Bethal again made the front pages of newspapers around the country. The prime minister ordered another commission of inquiry. Farmers' unions investigated the charges. Pathologists went to Potgieter's farm and exhumed a dozen bodies from the mounds Kodesh had spotted.

In response, the ANC called for a boycott of potatoes, despite the fact that potatoes were a staple food for most rural Africans. With the help of *New Age* and the slogan *Awadlin Ga De Jeoe*—"We don't eat them"—the boycott stuck.[88] Fish and bread replaced fish and chips for factory workers. Congress households banned potato crisps. Sacks of rotting potatoes piled up at markets, warehouses, and railway sidings. Some, like Robert Resha, were so disgusted by what the potato came to symbolize that they never ate one again.[89]

First provided more reasons for the boycott. She enlisted her husband, Joe Slovo, to sneak into the courts and gather pass-law trial records.[90] She discovered a government "youth camp" that sold teenagers to farmers, and found a thirteen-year-old boy kidnapped in Umtata and forced to work in the Eastern Tranvaal's potato belt.[91] She found out that for the first six months in 1958, the police had contracted out more than 36,000 short-term prisoners to Transvaal farms.[92] After headlines like "A Whipping Was a Daily

Bread" and "Farm Labourer Dies after Savage Beating—Another Victim of the Pass Laws," *New Age* printed a twenty-four-page pamphlet called "The Farm Labour Scandal." Written by First, the pamphlet detailed the history of South Africa's migrant-labor system and its various outrages

After three months, the ANC called off the boycott when the government outlawed the shipping of pass offenders to farms. The ANC realized it had a sizable economic muscle—it was years before the potato industry recovered—and it came to understand the power of ordinary people making decisions about their daily lives.

For years, the Natal *New Age* office had been a minor backwater compared to the mainstream torrents in Cape Town and Johannesburg. The Communist Party was relatively inactive in Durban in the late 1940s and after dissolution. Dawood Seedat, although politically committed, did not run a tightly administered operation.[93] He never hired full-time sellers, antagonized some within the Indian community with his strong opinions, and the office on West Street was in need of a fresh start.

Instant change came in 1956 with the appointment of M. P. Naicker as Durban branch manager. Marimuthu Pragalathan Naicker had joined the Party at age eighteen, led trade unions (especially sugar-cane workers), and revitalized the Natal Indian Congress, serving as NIC vice president from 1945 until he was banned in 1952. Naicker spent four months in jail during the Passive Resistance Campaign and was arrested twice during the Defiance Campaign. After the Congress of the People, which Naicker helped organize, *New Age* approached the jovial, well-admired activist about taking over the Durban office.[94] His lack of journalistic experience was not important; it was his political acumen and energy that made him so attractive.[95]

His first step was to relocate the *New Age* offices from West Street around the corner to Lodgson House on Grey Street.[96] The new sixth-floor office boasted three rooms with views of the mosques that dotted the Indian quarter, and immediately became the chief meeting place for left-wing Durban. The ANC's offices in Lakhani Chambers, four buildings away, were often deserted by comparison.[97] "When people came from rural areas, from Zululand or the Transkei, they knew *New Age* better than the Congress and headed first for Lodgson House," one staffer, Ebrahim Ismail Ebrahim, recalled. "I remember there was a little grousing now and again from some ANC people, saying that people instead of coming to Congress, they'd rather come to the *New Age* offices. Maybe it was because MP always had tea and bread there."

In the traditional style, Naicker raised circulation and improved news-gathering by deepening the weekly's connections to local organizations. He persuaded the Natal Indian Congress to ask its members to sell the newspaper, and he got the NIC's Youth League involved by betting that it could not sell as many issues as their counterparts in the Transvaal Indian Congress.[98] Naicker not only improved the administration and distribution of the weekly, but he wrote a number of important articles, including some on beer-hall riots.[99] In addition, he acted as the conduit to Albert Luthuli. Soon after he had been elected ANC president in 1952, Pretoria had banned Luthuli and confined him to his house in the Natal village of Groutville, thirty miles from Durban. Living in virtual exile, Luthuli communicated to his supporters and colleagues through *New Age*. He had a *New Age* subscription, and every few days called Naicker to discuss some article in the weekly, listen to political gossip, and talk of possible actions. Every few weeks, Naicker went by train to Groutville to meet with Luthuli, and the future Nobel Prize winner would spend the afternoon talking politics before handing over a statement or an article.[100]

When Naicker was too busy to go meet with Luthuli, he often sent Ebrahim Ismail Ebrahim. Born in 1937 to a Transvaal Indian father and a Natal Indian mother, Ebrahim was raised under the shadow of his father being deported to Johannesburg. At fifteen, Ebrahim joined the NIC. He hawked the newspaper on Fridays and Saturday mornings at Durban's main bus terminal; on average he sold three hundred copies of *New Age* a week.[101] When Naicker arrived at the weekly, he hired Ebrahim—nicknamed Ebe—as a salaried seller and a part-time assistant at Grey Street. Each afternoon after school, Ebrahim worked at the offices or walked the streets with his bundles of *New Age*.[102]

In Cape Town, the core team remained the same throughout the fifties: Brian Bunting edited, Carneson managed, Lionel Forman analyzed the international news, and John Morley ran the circulation and hamper-scheme divisions.[103] (Sonia Bunting joined her husband at Barrack Street, working part-time each day doing administrative work.)[104] The usual cadre of supporters contributed articles: Ray Alexander produced long articles under the nom de plume E. R. Braverman, Sam Kahn wrote a seminal piece about the beginnings of military cooperation between the apartheid regime and the new state of Israel, and Jack Simons gave an occasional book review.[105] Following the publication of his first novel, *The Fair House*, in 1955, Jack Cope left the weekly after more than a dozen years of service as editor, reporter, and art reviewer to concentrate on writing fiction.[106] Naomi Shapiro temporarily replaced him and covered Parliament, squatter camps in Nyanga, demolitions in Paarl, and South African Congress of Trade Union's conferences.[107]

It was Alex La Guma who breathed new life into *New Age*. La Guma grew up in the coloured quarter of District Six, which he recalled fondly: "Its life blood is the hawkers bawling their wares above the jazz from the music shops: 'Aartappels, ja. Uiwe, ja,'" wrote La Guma in the weekly: "Ragged youngsters leaping on and off the speeding trackless trams with the agility of monkeys; harassed mothers getting in the groceries; shop assistants; the Durango Kids of 1956 [a local gang]; and knots of loungers under the balconies and in the doorways leading up to the dim and mysterious rooms above the rows of shops and cafes."[108] The smell of frying oil hung in the air. Like Sophiatown, District Six was a ghetto, but a beloved, fructifying ghetto.

At age seventeen, La Guma left school to work in furniture warehouses and metal factories. The son of longtime communist Jimmy La Guma, he joined the Communist Party in 1948, assumed a spot on the Cape Town district committee and helped lead the new South African Coloured People's Organisation. In 1956 he started writing articles for *New Age*. He investigated conditions at Roeland Street jail (things were worse than when H. A. Naidoo visited in 1943), gazed at gangs in District Six and told the story of one African's removal from his home in Windermere.[109] La Guma established a reputation as a precocious writer with his column called "Up My Alley." Styled after Radford's "Topical" and Harmel's "By the Way," "Up My Alley" gave the weekly's editorial-opinion page an ironic anchor. Every week for the next six years, La Guma exposed the absurdities of life under apartheid with his fluid, mordant prose:

> Spring is pouring out all over. Nice weather for ducks, but in many homes there is enough water to float a snoeking fleet. I was having tea and a chat with a friend of mine the other day when the sound of music from another part of the house caused me to ask, "Is your youngster learning to play the xylophone?" "Xylophone, nothing," growled my friend. "That's the rain leaking into the basins we've put on the kitchen floor." A moment later a harder downpour sent a long trickle through the dining room ceiling into my cup. "Drink up," said my friend, cackling. "Your tea'll get cold."

> Do sharks prefer white meat? You'd better ask a shark, but it appears that the folks at Margate, Natal, think so. Because I've just seen a picture of anti-shark nets strung around the European section of the beach. All nice

and fancy like something out of Buck Rogers. With the beauty queen of the South Coast splashing about by way of illustration that the contraption really works.

Anyway, they haven't bothered about safety nets around the Non-European beach yet. That'll come later they say. The same old line. I suppose they're going to wait until Mr Shark finds out he can't get at the white meat and decides to sample the third grade black.

I'm surprised somebody hasn't thought of erecting a similar sort of net to prevent contravention of the Immorality Act.[110]

New Age was the paper of record for the liberation movement. Among Africans, it was often their first substantive taste of a newspaper (adult African literacy had doubled from 12 percent in 1931 to 24 percent in 1951).[111] In 1948 the Guardian claimed that 85 percent of its readership was non-white, and after dissolution and the Defiance Campaign that percentage inched over 90 percent. Among politically active South Africans, the weekly was automatic. In 1957 Edwin Munger, an American academic, came to South Africa to write a book about the political situation. Munger met with New Age reporters and had dinner at Ruth First's home. "When I discuss political developments with politically conscious Africans, Indians or Coloured people in Johannesburg," Munger wrote, "I find it well to assume that I am talking to a reader of New Age, regardless of the political complexion of my conversational partner."[112]

Reading New Age was a political act, and many proudly did so in public.[113] Left-wing lawyers ostentatiously poured through its pages in court, almost daring officialdom to make a disparaging comment.[114] At shebeens, cafes, and barber shops, men and women flipped through the pages and talked about what they saw. In Retsies, a popular restaurant on Pritchard Street in Johannesburg that was run by ANC leader Elias Moretsele, New Age posters hung on the cement walls, and bundles of copies lay by the door.[115]

Anthony Sampson, a British journalist who edited the magazine Drum in the 1950s, said the weekly was "the only paper for Africans which had their confidence."[116] Its foreign policy, Sampson noted, was "as obedient to Moscow as the Daily Worker, but in its home reporting it reflected what all Africans were saying and what many Liberals would have said if they dared." The paper, he added, was so successful at being "an open-sesame into the African world" that after the banning of Advance, "the Government tired of the game: perhaps because it was useful to have information about

Congress activities, or because it was tiresome to have to introduce new laws, the Progressive newspaper was allowed to continue its weekly barracking from the Left."[117]

From a distance, the newspaper looked intimately involved in the Congress movement; yet with its unique history, *New Age* never married the ANC. The Congress knew a national newspaper was critical, and that the Defiance Campaign and the Congress of the People would not have occurred without the weekly.[118] Yet it was perennially anxious about not owning its own organ. Ever since *Abantu-Batho* closed down in July 1931, the Congress endeavored to replace it. The ANC Youth League produced one key political journal that ran from 1943 to 1951, *Inkundla ya Bantu*—Govan Mbeki and Jordan Ngubane gave it incisive political commentary—but it was more of an intraparty debating platform and its top circulation was 7,000. (Still, Mbeki spent much of his time vainly trying to persuade ANC president Xuma to endorse *Inkundla* as the official Congress newspaper.[119]) Newspapers sympathetic to the ANC sprung up through the years, but they disappeared quickly: in a sampling of thirty black newspapers that were allied in some way with the Congress from 1912 to 1960, the average life span was only twenty-seven months.[120] With the resurgence of the ANC in the 1950s, the impetus to create a Congress newspaper gathered force. In 1954 the National Action Council, the group in charge of organizing the Congress of the People, resolved "to consider calling together the editors of *New Age* and other pro-Congress papers with a proposal for pooling resources in a single, national, three-language edition paper."[121] Such a plan never went beyond the discussion stage, but the National Action Council did manage to irregularly produce a tabloid, *The Congress Speaks*, as part of the COP campaign.

Pragmatism played a role. "I think it's largely a question of finance and organization," said Brian Bunting.

> It is not easy to get a paper going, to keep it going and so on. . . . We identified completely with ANC policies, and if they had to issue a statement, the paper was there, the machinery of distribution, everything. . . . There was a ready-made apparatus which they used. I don't think they could have done better with their own organ. . . . If you were going to produce another paper like that, it was going to be in competition with us for one thing. We probably both would have destroyed one another. There was no political need for another vehicle. . . . As the paper became more consolidated as the sort of organ of the movement as a whole, the whole way in which it went, in all sorts of ways, was determined by collective discussion, by suggestions, by

assistance from all sides, by segments of the movement. You'd get reactions from all your offices, and they didn't like this or they didn't like that or they wanted this or they wanted that. The job of editor was more of achieving consensus between a lot of pressures."[122]

Beyond mere utility, there was a sense that the ANC needed the Party's experience in the less glamorous role of organization building. "The organization that did the running around and day-to-day agitation was the Party," Bunting said. "It wasn't the ANC. We had the meetings, we ran around with the paper. We ran around with pamphlets. We held meetings on the Parade. The task of mobilizing, propagandizing, organizing the people was a Party task, much more than the ANC."[123] Rusty Bernstein, a Party leader in Johannesburg in the 1950s, also argued that it was the Party's famous discipline that made the newspaper so helpful to the Congress: "The ANC was a very loose organization. You could join the ANC and pay five shillings and not ever attend a branch meeting. . . . Our people brought into the ANC and, for that matter, the trade unions a very particular style of work which was indigenous to these organizations, and I think that was our biggest contribution. Frankly, a lot of commentators write about the great theoretical contribution we made to these organizations. I think in some ways it's the other way around. They made a great theoretical contribution to us, but we made a really important organizational contribution to them and gave them what they lacked, which was a sort of organized, disciplined core."[124]

Ideologically, Barrack Street gave weekly lessons about class and economics that accelerated the ANC's commitment to socialism and loyalty to the Soviet Union.[125] One image might suffice. In 1961 in Cape Town, Nelson Mandela met with Randolph Vigne, a Liberal Party leader. Mandela was underground at the time, with the South African police desperately searching for him. They met in a hotel lobby. As Vigne approached the bearded black revolutionary, he saw Mandela—who had been anti-communist fifteen years before—triumphantly waving a copy of New Age. On the cover was the story of another successful Soviet space launch.[126]

The newspaper helped create the alliance between the ANC and the Communist Party that coalesced in the 1950s and became official in the 1960s.[127] The weekly offered a tangible space for the two organizations to work together. There were physical places where they came together— offices, bookshops, Ruth First's living room, Bram Fischer's swimming pool—but the newspaper was the only public, national, legal institution that had allowed them to work side by side. Harry Gwala, a leading member of both the ANC and the Party in Natal, judged the situation this way: "The *Guardian* drew the two groups together. Progressive elements within each movement came together via the paper to discuss ideas. What I discovered in the 1950s was that progressive elements within the ANC took the *Guardian* as their own property. It was the only paper in those days that we in African political circles trusted. The paper accelerated the uniting ten-fold."

The ANC used the newspaper in the same way the Party did in the 1940s, as a way to educate new members. In 1952, when membership increased ten-fold in a year, the weekly became essential. Even the fact that the newspaper was for the Congress but not *of* the Congress—or white, not black—was not a stumbling block. Many activists, like Flag Boshielo, an ANC and Party member in the northern Transvaal, used the newspaper. "It was a certain comrade called Flag Boshielo who, more than anybody else, told me that in this movement we have got white people who are very close to us, who agree with us completely," recalled John Nkadimeng, a founding member of SACTU. "One of the reasons why he wanted to read this paper, the *Guardian*, with me was to try to sort of indicate that particular concept to me. That's how I was conscientized politically."[128] Whether it was in the four *New Age* offices or out in the townships and villages, the newspaper granted both communists and Africans the opportunity to discuss and to act.

Although the newspaper maintained its independent status, it rarely offered advice or disapproval to the ANC. Suffering from a sort of political sclerosis, *New Age* relinquished its earlier stance of condemning Congress mistakes. The editors thought the ANC was too fragile in the 1950s, and that any sharp criticism would have damaged rather than instructed.[129] Tactical errors—the poorly planned Western Areas campaign to protest the demolition of Sophiatown, the Bantu Education boycott, and the 1958 general-election stay-away—did not elicit much discussion in *New Age*.[130]

Occasionally, *New Age* gave space to internal ANC debates about possible campaigns. In late 1959, for instance, when the Congress contemplated asking supporters to withdraw savings from government-owned post-office accounts, the weekly had two Congressmen square off in essays for and against the boycott.[131] When there was criticism, the weekly usually had an underlying motive. In January 1956 Ruth First sent an unusual report to Barrack Street from the ANC annual national conference. She assailed the Congress for the "hot-headed speeches," the "skimpy and haphazard" debate on the national executive report, and the "poor conference planning

and . . . inadequate preparation . . . and inept handling of its proceedings."
Her anger came from the ANC's banning of *Bantu World*, a black commercial newspaper, from the conference. First, aware of *New Age*'s own troubled
history with the freedom of the press ideal, called the move "unnecessary
. . . an unreal expectation that the press . . . must support Congress policy.
Congress thus creates dangerous precedents for its future relations with the
press and sets itself up as a censor of the press."[132]

New Age's criticism reached its apogee during the emergence of an anti-
communist, anti-white wing within the ANC that split off to form the Pan
Africanist Congress. From the beginning, Barrack Street scorned and belittled the PAC. When the Africanists first made their presence known, at a
special ANC conference in March 1956 held to ratify the Freedom Charter,
they shouted out "Stalin is dead!" from the back of the hall and scuffled
with officials who tried to remove them. Ruth First reported "the only opposition came from a tiny group of 16 'Africanists' who were discredited
and completely routed by their own disruptive tactics."[133] As the Africanists
grew stronger, the weekly's attacks grew strident. In 1958 an editorial read,
"Now is not the time to emphasize any differences which may exist within
our ranks."[134] Later in the year, when the Africanists officially broke away
from the Congress, *New Age* exclaimed "good riddance."[135] At the PAC's
first press conference in April 1959, Robert Resha, representing the weekly,
pressed its leaders on the matter of cooperation with other organizations.
His insistent questions ruffled the PAC leaders and the meeting collapsed.[136]

Equally clear was *New Age*'s hostility towards other political parties on
the South African Left. The Liberal Party—founded in 1953 by people like
Alan Paton, author of the best-selling novel *Cry, the Beloved Country*, and
Margaret Ballinger, a Native Representative in Parliament—competed with
the Congress of Democrats for support among whites. As with the launching
of the PAC, a hostile Barrack Street greeted the new party with unmistakable scorn. It scoffed at the LP's rejection of the principle of universal suffrage and its anti-communist stance, and when reporting on a 1955 Liberal
Party conference, the weekly told readers not to "take these drawing-room
political adventures too seriously."[137] In 1956 a moment of civility appeared
when *New Age* interviewed Patrick Duncan and Paton: "Liberal Party Leaders Urge Closer Liberal-Congress Unity," read the headline.[138]

Unity was elusive, however, because of a personal rivalry between Brian
Bunting and Patrick Duncan.[139] The son of a former governor-general of
South Africa, Duncan made worldwide news in 1952 when he broke
apartheid laws during the Defiance Campaign.[140] In 1958 Duncan began

editing the Liberal's fortnightly newspaper, *Contact*, from his offices in Cape Town. Bunting and Duncan did not get along, and a rising rhetorical arms race over Duncan's obsessive hatred of communism led to fireworks. In *New Age* in January 1959 Albert Luthuli appealed to the Liberal Party to drop the anti-communist plank from its constitution.[141] Duncan, writing in *Contact*, answered by cataloguing Soviet crimes, calling communists "the worst oppressors of the modern age" and adding: "Far, therefore, from accepting Chief Luthuli's appeal, I appeal to him to use his eyes and to see where he is allowing his Congress to be led. . . . How many times has the ANC followed a line during the last five years which would displease the Kremlin—surely not one."[142] Duncan's article offended Luthuli and angered Bunting, and Duncan's own standing in the Liberal Party plummeted.[143]

Another political battle Barrack Street waged was against the Non-European Unity Movement. Founded in 1943 in the Cape, the Unity Movement emerged from a myriad of radical coloured associations. Its leaders, mostly Trotskyist teachers, opposed unprincipled political action, which meant that they rarely did anything but talk about why they were not doing anything. (The Unity Movement lost considerable ground in opposing the Defiance Campaign.)[144] *New Age* unfailingly reproached the NEUM. In 1956 during the coloured bus boycott in Cape Town, a headline read, "Unity Movement Who Scabbed on Bus Boycott."[145] Brian Bunting supported I. D. Mkize, the principal of Langa High School, who disliked the Unity Movement. When Mkize's cohorts disrupted an NEUM meeting in Langa, Barrack Street reported the incident with the headline "Unity Movement Driven Out of Langa." The subsequent NEUM meeting, attended by *New Age* reporter Mary Butcher, received no coverage in the weekly because Butcher was shouted out of the meeting.[146]

A piquant column that reflected their rivalry appeared in the Unity Movement's newspaper, *Torch*, two weeks after the *Guardian* was banned in 1952:

> I'm sure everyone—except the fascists—must have jeered at the Nats when they read that the editor of the suppressed *Guardian* was bringing out a new paper called the *Clarion*. It was a smart piece of work and really cocked a snook at the Government. So far so good. . . . It will come as a surprise to the disenfranchised millions of Non-Whites to hear that up to now elections have been free, just as it will come as a surprise to them to be told by the *Clarion* that through the victimisation of Kahn and Carneson the African people have lost 'their representatives.' In principle we

certainly herald the appearance of this new paper, but we are certainly
not going to stomach the poison it peddles.[147]

Raids, riots, marches, meetings, rallies, demands, arrests, deportations,
bans, banishments, spies and ever more raids—this was the cold argot of
New Age.

Under such a groaning mass of information, *New Age* suffered from a
case of schizophrenia. On one hand, Barrack Street sought a modicum of
discipline. Brian Bunting, hard-nosed and unflappable, kept a sense of metronomic steadiness in the eight pages. Each week, in the same place, appeared
an editorial, letters to the editor, a small report from Fred Carneson on the
inevitably parlous state of Barrack Street's finances, a page of international
news and analysis, horse-racing tips, and columns like La Guma's "Up My
Alley," Sam Kahn's "The Law and You," and "Art and the People," which
a variety of contributors wrote after Jack Cope left the newspaper.[148] "Brian
was a very steady person, very reliable, well-organized, very mature," said
Albie Sachs. "He ran the Friday editorial meeting with a steady hand. We
would discuss what should go in and what position to adopt, and the priorities for the editorial, what had been successful the week before. It was all
fairly professionally done."[149] Such soothing regularity helped make the
newspaper more digestible.

"The philosophers have only interpreted the world in various ways,"
reads the epitaph on the grave of Karl Marx in Highgate Cemetery in London. "The point, however, is to change it." The conflict between reporting
and exhorting was never greater than at *New Age.* A tsunami of information—new laws, new scandals, new bans—threatened to engulf Barrack
Street. Each week, *New Age* reported a new disgrace and also a new response. "We had no qualms about using the paper as a tool for the struggle,"
said Brian Bunting. "We would be quite open about it." Exclamatory headlines called for action: "Save Elizabeth Mafekeng from Exile!" and "Stop
That A-Bomb Test!" and "We Don't Want Storm-Troops in S.A.!"[150] A report
on the opening of an NIC conference led with "Build Congress!"[151] Often
the weekly trumpeted the word "exclusive" above an interview with a Congress leader, which ignored the fact that no other media outlet was angling
for the same interview.[152] "I can remember Brian saying, 'But where is your
punch-line, at the end?'" said Albie Sachs. "You've got to end on a high
note, so the people are mobilized. Sachs added:

We had conflicts over how political the newspaper should be. I remember one Christmas, it was the Christmas edition and Wolfie was very upset. I had run a photograph of Alfred Nzo dressed up as Father Christmas, giving out funds to the ANC. It was very funny and very light, but Wolfie was cross because he had sent me a scoop from Basutoland about Elizabeth Mafekeng. He'd gotten the first interview with her. I ran it across the bottom of the page and the first thing he saw was Father Christmas.

The newspaper nervously straddled the two kinds of approaches, according to Bunting:

> This was a complication all along the line. We had to appeal to two types of people: intellectuals who wanted insight into things, who wanted arguments and explanations, and all sorts of people without academic qualifications. You had to make it intelligible to everyone. You couldn't afford the sort of formulae which the academics go in for. You have to convey sometimes complex ideas as simply as possible. We tried not to produce a paper full of standard clichés and formulae and phrases or one with sarcasm. I mean, I can remember articles in the *International* written by my father where he took whole chunks of quoted material right out of Virgil. We tried as far as possible to be fresh while at the same time speaking to basic policies and ideas. But the political mill inevitably ground you down to the smallest common denominator.[153]

Ruth First was partially responsible for *New Age*'s hoarse, high-strung voice. Her muckraking in the townships and farms led to the banner headlines, and her prose did not mask her outrage. She also groomed a stable of young men who had little interest in dry theory: Makiwane, Hutchinson, Resha, Gqabi, Nxumalo, and later Willie Kgostitile were freewheeling free spirits, habitués of the shebeen rather than the parlor.

Outsiders could see the excesses of political reporting. "It was taboo for a journalist to be totally political," said Jurgen Schadeburg, a photographer with *Drum* after 1951. "So *New Age* was, for us, not a completely legitimate newspaper. It felt too biased."[154] Benjamin Pogrund, ex–Liberal Party member and a reporter on black politics for the *Rand Daily Mail* in the late 1950s and 1960s, recalled his impressions of *New Age*:

> My memory of it is of great admiration for the briskness and vigour of its writing, and the fact that it reported on issues affecting blacks which until

then no one else had done. But I was, of course, not merely a reader and because of my job I had to check out every story that it carried. . . . I often found that the details were inaccurate. On some occasions I found that the stories themselves were so wide of the mark as to not even rate. . . . The overriding point was that the newspaper, as I had known while living in Cape Town, was dedicated to particular interests and factual reporting was second to this. At that time the paper was backing the ANC leadership and everything was subordinated to this. One instance of this was in the reporting of the emergence of the Africanists: *New Age*'s reporting provided significant and interesting reflections of the ANC leadership's situation but most times hardly gave any reasonable picture of the overall situation.[155]

Despite the concentration on politics, the newspaper continued to run items more for enjoyment than education. Sonia Bunting gave out recipes. *New Age* supporters like playwright Cecil Williams regularly reviewed new novels, plays, films, concerts, and art exhibitions.[156] In 1956 Michael Harmel assessed a collection of stories by a young, unknown Johannesburg writer destined to win the Nobel Prize for Literature: "Miss Gordimer will never rise to her full stature as an artist until she becomes filled with the importance and truth of what she has to say—as opposed to how cleverly, wittily and gracefully she can say it."[157] Bunting handled the bulk of the reviewing chores. He hammered Trevor Huddleston's 1956 book *Naught for Your Comfort*: "He was never an organic part of the liberation movement itself . . . [he] never knew the discipline and the comradeship."[158] He trashed *Dr. Zhivago*, Boris Pasternak's novel: "a good book with a bad philosophy." Harmel corrected him a month later, saying it was "a bad book with a bad philosophy."[159]

Somehow, *New Age* doubled as a literary journal. Bunting published poetry by Pablo Neruda, Christopher Okigbo, Dennis Brutus, and Arthur Norje.[160] Each week for ten months in 1954, Bunting serialized *A Bend in the Road*, a novel written by a little known coloured writer named Katie Hendricks (and illustrated by Leslie Cope).[161] In 1957 Lionel Forman wrote a "fairy tale" with the following preface: "Any resemblance between the chief character and Verwoerd is an absolutely astounding coincidence."[162] *New Age* held three short-story competitions in the late 1950s. These contests—judged by writers like Harry Bloom, Duma Nokwe, Jack Cope, Phyllis Altman, Uys Krige, and Richard van der Ross—awarded a £10 grand prize and publication in *New Age*. As part of the contest, Bunting ran more than forty stories in the weekly, advising, "Let life itself be your raw material."[163] With the successes of the short-story competitions, he held another beauty contest, crowning "Miss *New Age*" in August 1958 at Moslem Hall in Port Elizabeth.[164]

The most cheeky contribution was Alex La Guma's cartoon strip called *Little Libby: The Adventures of Liberation Chabalala*, which ran for thirty-seven straight weeks in 1959. An impish rogue, Little Libby is kidnapped by Kasper Katchum and forced to work on a potato farm. He escapes to Johannesburg, visits shebeens, joins a criminal underworld run by a cleaver-wielding Boss Chopper, matches wits with Sergeant Shark of the Special Branch, and twice visits the *New Age* offices for a bite of political sustenance. Eventually, Libby turns over a new leaf and joins the ANC. *Little Libby*, reminiscent of Depression-era cartoon strips like *Flash Gordon* and *Blondie*, was a crude, yet potent piece of political satire.[165]

Another way *New Age* kept its bearings, if not its sense of humor, was by trying to pretend it was just an ordinary newspaper. In 1950 Brian Bunting tried to join the South African Society of Journalists. The SASJ was an all-white trade union, but Bunting wanted to join it in part to end the anomaly of a trade-union newspaper having an entirely nonunion staff. Bunting persuaded an SASJ member, Stanley Uys, to propose him and Naomi Shapiro for membership. Uys, a South African correspondent who wrote about parliamentary affairs for the Johannesburg *Sunday Times* and occasionally wrote pseudonymous pieces for the *Guardian*, placed their names for membership in the Cape Town branch. In Parliament (perhaps hearing of the applications), Charles Swart, the minister of justice, accused white trade unions, including the SASJ, of harboring communists. The SASJ Cape Town branch, not knowing how to handle the provocative applications in light of Swart's accusations, referred the matter to the SASJ executive council. At an open meeting in Cape Town, the council informed Bunting and Shapiro of its decision to reject them. It gave no reason, but said that they could use their own imaginations. Uys, not willing to drop the matter, put it to a vote of the Cape Town branch, which polled 15 to 7 in favor of reversing the council's decision and accepting the two *Guardian* journalists. Feeling their point made, Bunting and Shapiro withdrew their application.[166]

Later that year, the government appointed a commission of inquiry into the state of the South African press. With magnificent consistency, the commission failed to issue its annually promised report until 1961. Instead, for eleven years behind closed doors, the commission grilled editors and reporters, confronted foreign correspondents with copies of their cables, and pored over account ledgers—all in an attempt to provide Pretoria with a cause for censorship.[167] In 1955 the commission asked Bunting to testify. In consultation with Sam Kahn and Bram Fischer, Bunting told the commission he would not appear before them in private, and that he hoped his refusal would result in a court case "to test the validity of the Commission's proceedings."[168] The commission replied by asking Bunting for a short précis of the *Guardian*'s history. Bunting delivered a pugnacious seven-page report, detailing the years of government repression and the bannings of the *Guardian* and *Advance*.[169] Eventually, Bunting did testify, without noticeable effect.

Bunting frequently attacked his fellow colleagues in the South African media. The Afrikaans press and *New Age* regularly traded insults. *Die Burger* often called for the banning of the weekly and decried articles that, according to Bunting, they thought were "extravagant, untruthful or simply horrifying, especially those which contain the demand for complete political, social and economic equality."[170] The battles with *Die Burger* were as old as the newspaper—in its first month of existence, the *Cape Guardian* accused *Die Burger* of disrupting trade unions—and it was almost automatic that the two newspapers, at opposite ends of the political spectrum, would scrap.[171]

Less obvious to later generations, who were under the well-cultivated but erroneous impression that the English press was anti-apartheid, was the fact that the *Guardian*'s English colleagues were not much closer politically than the Afrikaners. The English press derided the Nationalist Party—Arthur Barlow, a veteran newspaper editor and United Party MP, wrote in 1960, "I have never known the *Cape Times* publish anything good about Verwoerd. It is always a sneer and a jeer"—but with Africans, they generally were patronizing at best and more often racist.[172] They consistently opposed African political and economic aspirations, and more often than not approved of apartheid legislation. "The Native strike has ended just as it was bound to do," gloated the *Rand Daily Mail* after the 1946 mine strike. "Quite a number of strikers have sore heads; a few are dead; and not a single one of the points for which they struck has been gained."[173] "The brutal and bloody clashes between Zulu and Basotho factions in the townships," wrote the Johannesburg *Star* in 1957, "indicate both a residual savagery among many Native people of our urban communities and a failure of the European civilising mission."[174] Ruth First and Michael Scott gained access to the pages of the *Rand Daily Mail* when the Bethal scoop materialized, but four years later, after Scott helped turn the United Nations against the apartheid regime, the *Mail* referred to him as "a hostile foreigner."[175]

Silence infuriated the weekly more than anything else. "Newspaper propaganda might be defined as the art of omission," Betty Radford wrote in 1945, and what the mainstream English press ignored was the weekly's raison d'être.[176] Three weeks after the Treason Trial arrests, only the Port Elizabeth *Evening Post* joined *New Age* at the ANC's annual national conference (a year earlier, a dozen newspapers were in attendance). Brian Bunting asked, "Is there a conspiracy to give the public the impression that since some of its leaders are arrested, the ANC has ceased to be a worthwhile political force?"[177] Three years later, he collected a series of *New Age* articles on the South African media into a pamphlet called "The Story Behind the Non-White Press." Called a "one-man war" by one rival newspaper, the pamphlet bitterly attacked the English press. "It takes a great upheaval among the non-White population before the daily press will take notice of what is going on," Bunting wrote.

> The line of the English-language press, dailies and weeklies, is, as usual, to trade on the white readers' abysmal ignorance of most things African. . . . The basic delusion of this press seems to be that if you ignore a ticklish problem, it will go away. . . . Either these papers print no news at all, or play down the news and hope that if they, ostrich-like, keep their heads buried in the sand long enough, others will take up the same position. Has it struck no one on the big newspapers that withholding a true assessment of a situation from one's readers is an open invitation to panic and hysteria if what you prophesy won't happen does come off after all?[178]

In March 1962 the gap deepened between the weekly and the rest of the South African press when the government passed the Publications and Entertainments Act, and the Newspaper Press Union voted 25 to 7 to adopt a "code of conduct" for NPU-member newspapers in which they agreed to self-censorship in return for exclusion from provisions of the Act.[179] This bargain with the devil affronted *New Age*. "The proprietors of the English dailies have also fastened the gag upon themselves in exchange for their own immunity from censorship," Ruth First wrote. "They have traded their freedom to write as they please and they have retired from the battle before it is half fought, and in doing so they have thrown all other publications to the Nazi wolves—*Fighting Talk*, *New Age*, *Contact* and many more. This is not surrender; it is treachery."[180] Other organizations protested the NPU's action, and the SASJ notably advised its members to refuse to abide by the NPU's code of conduct, but such capitulation was an ominous sign for the weekly.[181]

Much of the weekly's media energies, however, focused on black newspapers. Lack of competition had always been important to the *Guardian*'s success. The ANC never had its own newspaper. Coloured political organizations produced fortnightlies, like *Torch*, and there were some Indian newspapers like *Indian Opinion*—founded by Mahatma Gandhi—but they all were too provincial and conservative (although *Torch* did have some influence in the Transkei). In the African world, there were some notable rivals. Two Johannesburg weeklies with six-figure circulations, *Bantu World* and the *Golden City Post*, dominated the commercial black press. The *Post*, founded in 1955, thrived on a cocktail of crime, scandal, sports and sex. *Bantu World* had a long and interesting history—it was first published in 1932—but it was far too conservative for many readers and focused too much on such items as its "Social and Personal" column on weddings and dances.[182] The *World*'s editor from 1932 to 1952, Selope Thema, had been a kind of éminence grise in the Transvaal ANC's hierarchy (even editing *Abantu-Batho* for a brief period), but he had fallen out of step with the younger militants in the ANC and had opposed the Defiance Campaign.[183] In addition, the *World* was owned by the mining industry's Argus group, a fact that limited its political reach.

Drum, headquartered in Johannesburg, was the largest-selling magazine in Africa and the most famous black publication out of South Africa in the twentieth century. It boasted the work of a former *Guardian* columnist, Henry Nxumalo, who did investigative exposés. Nxumalo, the first African employee at *Drum*, wrote one about Bethal's farm labor in 1952, and another on the conditions inside a Johannesburg prison in which he went undercover, disguising himself as a regular, passbook-violating African. His bold work earned him the nickname "Mr. *Drum*" (the prison article was headlined, "Mr *Drum* Goes to Jail").[184] The magazine serialized Alan Paton's *Cry, the Beloved Country*, and first published important African writers. Still, it thumped out a steady beat of shebeen gossip, fluffy interviews and glossy photographs, and never seriously competed with the *Guardian*.

All of them were fair game for a slightly self-righteous Barrack Street.[185] When the *Golden City Post* ran an editorial on a *New Age* article and then refused to print a reply from Barrack Street, Bunting fulminated at the *Post*'s ethics.[186] *Bantu World* was a "malodorous newspaper," according to Bunting, that "opposes every ANC campaign . . . opposes the unity of the oppressed peoples of South Africa in the Congress movement [and] never criticises the mining industry."[187] In 1956, when the ANC excluded a *World* reporter from its national conference, the *World*'s editor—evidently not noticing Ruth First's reports on the matter—wrote to Barrack Street asking why Bunting, twice a victim of a newspaper banning, did not protest against this blatant act of censorship. Bunting replied by comparing *Bantu World* to Hitler and asked Michael Harmel to explain the weekly's rationalization: "But if it prints lies, then it can't come into the ANC conference. Yes, I can hear some of you saying, but then why not exclude the *Transvaler*, the *Rand Daily Mail* and the *Cape Times*? They also print lies and are even more hostile than the *Bantu World*. No doubt they do and they are, but unlike the latter they do not specialise in attempting to disrupt the ANC. An important difference."[188]

Drum drew *New Age*'s fire as well.[189] In 1955 Ruth First assailed the magazine, because "the careful editorial fence-sitting and the completely neutral air . . . will deceive the simpletons. . . . It seems to us that the time for tolerance has run out. A Congress boycott would not be out of order, unless *Drum* beats a different tune."[190] *New Age* printed a photograph of black tennis star Althea Gibson getting kissed by her white opponent, Darlene Hard, after winning the finals at Wimbledon, a photograph *Drum* balked at printing on its October 1957 South African edition cover because the magazine feared a backlash over a white woman kissing a black woman (*Drum*'s editor, Sylvester Stein, resigned over the issue.)[191] In 1956 *Drum* received a temporary respite from *New Age*'s attacks when Henry Nxumalo was mugged and stabbed to death while doing an investigation in Sophiatown.[192]

Underneath all the hostility lay certain channels of cooperation. Some commercial press reporters, like Stanley Uys, wrote for the weekly; others, like Lillian Isaacson, a *Cape Times* journalist, reviewed books.[193] The *Rand Daily Mail* sometimes sent a bouquet of flowers to Barrack Street in February for the newspaper's birthday.[194] Often, *New Age* borrowed photographs.[195] Other times, as in the Solly Jooma case, the weekly ran stories passed on from other newspapers' reporters. A Transvaal Indian Youth Congress member and well-known soccer player, Jooma had won £9,000 in damages after a Constable Visser had beaten him up.[196] Enraged by the court's decision, Visser had tracked down Jooma and beat him to death. "I hacked his forehead with the heel of my boot," Visser later testified during his trial, in which he was convicted of murder.[197] Two years later Howard Lawrence, a coloured reporter for the *Golden City Post*, saw Visser walking in Adderley Street in downtown Cape Town. Lawrence photographed Visser, but the *Post* would not run the picture, so he passed it along to an eager *New Age*.[198]

Throughout the fifties, the government tried to subdue the surge in African opposition. It banned hundreds of leaders from organizations, began eavesdropping on telephone conversations, and started opening mail. It also became more violent: in 1940, the courts sentenced less than 2,000 people to whippings for criminal offenses; in 1955, 14,379 people were flogged a total of 78,573 strokes.[199] The sjambok supplanted the springbok as the national symbol.

The Special Branch became obsessed with *New Age*. They staked out all four offices with almost continuous surveillance and regularly crossed the street and entered the offices to take away documents. They wiretapped telephones, opened mail, and detained cables from overseas. "The police were always coming in," said one Johannesburg employee, Joyce Watson. "They would ask, 'Is Mr. Scarumbrucker in?' So they say, 'Scarumbrucker,' then you know, ahh, only the Special Branch. They couldn't say 'Schermbrucker.' I would say, 'Ivan, somebody's after you, they ask about Mr. Scarumbrucker.'"[200]

At home, it was no different. They raided staff members' homes so often, remembered Jackie Arenstein, "that they eventually wouldn't even knock on the door. They'd just walk in, as if they were expected, as if they were old friends."[201] Once, upon hearing the tell-tale thumping on the front door at 2 A.M., Margaret Bunting, age nine, quickly collected all her father's papers on his desk, thrust them under her mattress, and then feigned sleep.[202] Very often detectives followed staffers as they traveled to and from work. Hilda Bernstein recalled the rules they followed: "Watch the rear-view mirror of the car when driving away from the house to check who may be following. Never say anything of consequence on the telephone—telephones are always dangerous; unplug them or bury them beneath blankets and cushions when talking politics. They can be used to pick up and transmit conversations even when the receiver is down; so turn up the radio or keep a record playing during a meeting to baffle the tape-recorder."[203] The police hassled readers who sent letters to the editor: six days after the weekly ran a letter from N.P.D. Tshawe, a politically unknown student at a minor agricultural college in the Orange Free State, the police showed up at Tshawe's dormitory door.[204]

Social situations were hazardous. The police camped outside parties, hoping to catch violations of the laws that prohibited whites from serving alcohol to Africans. Detectives inelegantly crashed a 1958 party at the Slovo's house, with a photographer from *Die Vaderland* jumping onto a dining-room table. "Some ugly things were going on in the garden," one detective reported. "Stately-looking Winnie Mandela, Nelson's wife, doing a slow trot around the floor, her partner dancing away in a wide circle around her. And

Ruth Slovo, dressed in a pitch-black, tight-fit, darting forwards and backwards, barefoot."[205] Fred Carneson shoved detectives, and Joe Slovo had to stand on a chair to calm the guests.

Almost every staff member was banned. Pretoria banned them from attending political rallies or meetings, from membership in specific organizations, from talking with another banned person, and from leaving a particular magisterial district. Sometimes they banned an individual from talking to more than one person at a time.[206] The Security Branch was renowned for its almost comical inefficiencies, but every once in a while they enforced the banning orders with emphasis. In July 1954 the Security Branch interrupted a Saturday-evening party at the Buntings to arrest both Sam Kahn and Brian Bunting on charges of violating their banning orders; released on £50 bail, both spent the rest of the year fighting the charges, eventually securing an acquittal.[207] Besides the quotidian hassles and handicaps a ban imposed, there was also a more metaphysical hardship. "Banning not only confines one physically," wrote Nelson Mandela, "it imprisons one's spirit. It induces a kind of psychological claustrophobia that makes one yearn not only for freedom of movement but spiritual escape. Banning was a dangerous game, for one was not shackled or chained behind bars; the bans were laws and regulations that could easily be violated and often were. One could slip away unseen for short periods of time and have the temporary illusion of freedom. The insidious effect of bans was that at a certain point one began to think that the oppressor was not without but within."[208] The strain of political work took its toll. Alan Paton recalled flying home from London in the mid-1950s and sitting next to Ruth First, whom he compared to Vernon Berrangé, a pitiless tough leftist lawyer:

> Of her courage there could be no doubt, but for all that she had to steel herself for the landing in Johannesburg. She nodded to me perfunctorily, but she had more pressing things on her mind. Her face was tight and strained, not so grim as that of Berrangé, because she was younger, not yet thirty, and her face was less lived. She spent several hours on the flight tearing pieces of paper to pieces, each about the size of a fingernail. The plane was half empty, and she occupied a seat on the opposite side of the aisle from myself. She made no attempt to hide what she was doing, probably because she knew it was highly unlikely that I would go to the security police to tell them how Ruth First had occupied herself.
>
> I was occupied also, not in destroying papers, but in watching a young lady doing so. I was fascinated but I watched her obliquely. In any event she

seemed totally intent on her task and totally oblivious to her surroundings. When she accumulated a small pile of paper fragments she would go to the lavatory and get rid of them. . . . Eventually Ruth First's job was done, and she sat taut and motionless, waiting for the arrival at Jan Smuts airport, Johannesburg. I was pretty taut myself, but much less so than she, because I had no secret knowledge of revolutions and revolutionaries. I was, like so many other liberals, useless but decent.[209]

The life of a *New Age* supporter was anything but motionless. Mandela recalled getting into a minor car accident in the Orange Free State town of Kroonstad. When a white policeman on the scene spied a copy of the weekly from under the floor mat, he "held it up in the air like a pirate with his booty: 'Wragtig ons het 'n Kommunis gevang!'—My word, we've caught a Communist!"[210] Four hours passed before the police allowed Mandela to continue on his way.

Detention like that became commonplace, as almost every black staff member saw the inside of a jail cell at one time or another. The Crown accused Govan Mbeki of violating the Group Areas Act in 1957, and Robert Resha of violating the pass laws in 1958. The police twice arrested Alex La Guma for being in an African location without a permit. They arrested Tennyson Makiwane for photographing a women's anti-pass demonstration.[211] The police dragged Joe Gqabi by his lapels and detained him for an afternoon when he tried to take a photograph of Garnet "Hosepipe" Parkin, a Springs policeman convicted of using a rubber tube as his favorite tool for extracting confessions.[212]

Street sellers endured constant harassment. In Cape Town, John Motloheloa found himself continually in trouble. The police charged him with illegally putting up a *New Age* selling poster outside an Elsie's River shop, and with selling at the Mowbray bus terminal.[213] "If you were arrested once for the day," Douglas Manqina recalled, "you were lucky, that was good. Sometimes it was twice or three times."[214]

The government used deportation as a way to remove employees. They sent Jenny Joseph, a British citizen and occasional reporter for *New Age*, back to London. They deported Cape Town seller Nathaniel Molaoa to Bechuanaland, and Greenwood Ngotyana, Jack Masiane and John Motloheloa to Basutoland.[215] The Motloheloa case was particularly farcical. They brought an old, nearly deaf aunt from Basutoland to testify at the *New Age* seller's deportation hearing. The prosecutor asked the aunt if she remembered her nephew. "Oh, yes, that is him, though I've seen him very little since he left Maseru," she said quietly. Motloheloa's lawyers protested, saying the aunt was old, and her testimony, after all these years, was unreliable. The prosecution asked if she had been present at his birth. "Oh, yes, I was there. He was born with a lump on his head." The aunt then rose and shuffled over to Motloheloa who had bowed his head in disappointment at his aunt's memory. "Yes," she concluded after rubbing his scalp, "this is John."[216]

In 1957 the police put a twist on the incessant pass-law arrests by deploying plainclothes policemen in downtown Johannesburg. *New Age* called them the "Ghost Squad," as they would suddenly materialize and swoop down on unsuspecting Africans, demand their passbooks, and sweep them away.[217] A ghost haunted Alex La Guma and Tennyson Makiwane one day after leaving Commissioner Street, as La Guma detailed in "Up My Alley": "An oaf in plain clothes elbowed Mr TM and snarled: 'Pass, man. Pass.' We may be on trial for treason, but I'm sure we don't look like suspicious characters. Tennyson grinned and hummed, 'All day, all night, Marianne,' and showed the cop the Certificate of Merit with which all treason accused have been issued by the Clerk of the Court. The 'ghost' glared at the paper, glared at us and handed it back."[218]

Subterfuge clearly was the order of the day. When Brian Bunting traveled to South-West Africa in 1959 to write a report on deadly riots in Windhoek, Security Branch men took the same flight from Cape Town to Windhoek, hounded him during his meetings and raided his hotel room at five in the morning; Bunting resorted to conducting his interviews at night in the bush outside town.[219] A banned Eli Weinberg was in a conundrum with the Congress of the People. Dozens of policemen swarmed the Kliptown soccer field, and he had already been arrested in July 1954 for taking photographs of an anti-removal rally in Sophiatown.[220] "I had arranged for myself a grandstand view from a nearby roof, where I set up my equipment," Weinberg said.

> I found to my dismay that my vantage point attracted other members of the public who clambered up on the same roof and settled down right in front of where I was working. This also attracted the security police. . . . An angry Colonel Spengler, head of the Special Branch, comes storming up to me: "Weinberg, if you don't bugger off this minute, I will arrest you and charge you with attending a gathering!" I had no alternative but to bugger off, but actually this proved fortunate, as shortly afterwards armed police surrounded the Congress, searched and took names of everybody present and

confiscated documents, papers, leaflets and even film. By that time I was already ensconced in my darkroom, developing the photographs for delivery for the next edition of *New Age*.[221]

These games were often quite serious. Hooligans vandalized Robert Resha's house and stenciled "Death to the Jews" on the Bunting's garage one night.[222] Unknown assailants fired rifle shots at La Guma as he sat working at his desk; one bullet grazed his neck, but he survived. A few days later he received a letter saying, "Sorry we missed you. Will call again. The Patriots." Later, the phone rang in the middle of the night. Blanche La Guma answered it. In a obviously disguised voice, a man said, "Tell your husband to watch his step. We are going to get him. You won't see him alive after tonight. This is the supreme commander of the Ku Klux Klan." Such "patriots" were never found.[223]

The repression made it difficult to operate the newspaper. The bugging of the offices and their telephones made substantive conversations at work impossible: sometimes the Security Branch detectives, listening in, would interrupt conversations to reprimand banned people for talking to each other, and one particularly asthmatic eavesdropper breathed so heavily on Bram Fischer's brother's telephone that callers thought Fisher was ill.[224] Account ledgers, correspondence, upcoming articles, unused letters to the editor, and balance sheets had to be kept away from the offices. People stored them at houses of sympathizers, buried them in back yards—in Johannesburg, *New Age* used an ambassador's home—or built false bottoms and secret compartments in their desks and cupboards.[225] Staffers wasted hours retrieving and re-hiding *New Age* documents. They constantly switched typewriters so that articles could not be traced to banned reporters.[226] Planning for the week's edition was an uncertain affair, as Ruth First pithily said, for "you never knew whether your copy was going to end up at the printer's or the police station."[227] *New Age* reporters were often refused press credentials and found it hard to gain access to certain meetings and conferences.[228] Reporting on rural issues was especially problematic. Beyond the morass of regulations, curfews and permit laws, the government passed Proclamation 110, which instructed headmen and chiefs to report to officials "the activities of persons who disturb or obstruct the peace, order and good government by the holding of unauthorised meetings, the distribution of publications and pamphlets, or in any other matter." The buying and selling of *New Age* caused many Proclamation 110 reports.[229]

The first issue of the *Guardian* appeared in Cape Town in February 1937. It was plump with advertising, yet above the front page fold revealed its true nature with a scathing political cartoon about fascism in Namibia.

Despite the dedicated efforts of many political activists, much of the *Guardian's* robust circulation stemmed from the paid work of African sellers on the streets of South Africa's cities.

Mrs. Betty Sacks (Betty Radford) (left) is relinquishing the post of Editor of the Guardian and will be succeeded by Mr. Brian Bunting (above). See editorial on this page and comment on page 4.

In the *Guardian's* 26-year history, just two people served as editor-in-chief. Betty Radford, an English-born journalist, ran the paper for its first eleven years before Brian Bunting took over. Pictured at left while living in exile in London, Bunting was the courageous public face of the *Guardian* during its most tumultuous years.

Fred Carneson (*top left*), Ivan Schermbrucker (*above*) and Michael Harmel (*left*) were three central figures at the *Guardian* for most of its history. Carneson ran the Cape Town office, raised funds, managed the circulation department and even served as acting editor for eleven harrowing months; Schermbrucker, known equally for his ability to speak fluent Xhosa and to swear in English, managed the Johannesburg office; Harmel, a Johannesburg columnist and correspondent, was one of the liberation movement's chief ideologues.

Ruth First, a glamorous woman with a sharp intellect, took over the Johannesburg branch office in 1946 and within months produced a story that rocked South Africa: pass law violators who were being abused on potato farms in the Bethal district of Mpumalanga.

In 1952 the apartheid regime banned the *Guardian* for the first time, but not before the paper raised a vigorous protest in the name of the freedom of the press. Leaders of the Congress movement converged at a meeting: Yusuf Dadoo is speaking at the podium; seated to his right is Ruth First; to his left are Moses Kotane and James Phillips; and alone in the front row is Joe Slovo.

The *Guardian* was one of the few public institutions in South Africa where men and women of all races worked together on an equal basis. Henry Nxumalo (with the pipe) was a Zulu from Durban, who wrote the *Guardian* sports column for four years before going on to greater fame as an investigative reporter at *Drum* magazine. H.A. Naidoo (pictured with his wife Pauline Podbrey) was an Indian leader, also from Durban, who worked in Cape Town as a reporter and columnist. Both men had tragic ends: Nxumalo was knifed to death in Sophiatown in 1956; Naidoo was one of the first activists to go into exile under apartheid, in 1950, and died young two decades later.

TREASON TRIAL

The ACCUSED

DECEMBER 1956

Ten staff members and the *Guardian*'s printer were among those, pictured here by the paper's staff photographer Eli Weinberg, who were charged with treason at a mass trial in the late 1950s. Among the accused were Govan Mbeki (*below, left*), the paper's Port Elizabeth branch editor and father of South African President Thabo Mbeki; Robert Resha (*center*), a sports columnist from Sophiatown; and Alex La Guma (*right*), a colored columnist from Cape Town who became, in exile, a celebrated novelist.

BOMB ATTACKS OPEN NEW PHASE IN S.A.

NEW AGE

Vol. 8, No. 10. Registered at the G.P.O. as a Newspaper   6d.

SOUTHERN EDITION   Thursday, December 21, 1961   5c.

Secret Organisation Declares Its Aims

African Students Form New Organisation

DURBAN.

THE birth of the African Students' Association in Durban last week-end marked an important step forward in the unity of African students fighting against Bantu Education and for a free and democratic South Africa.

The Association, it is hoped, will co-ordinate the activities of students in various institutions in South

(Continued on page 2)

TEN EXPLOSIONS—FIVE IN JOHANNESBURG AND FIVE IN PORT ELIZABETH—PLUS AN ATTEMPTED EXPLOSION IN DURBAN MARKED THE CLOSE OF THE NATIONALIST-PROCLAIMED DAY OF THE COVENANT ON DECEMBER 16 (WHEN DR. VERWOERD'S SPEECH APPEALED FOR "NATIONAL UNITY BETWEEN THE TWO WHITE RACES").

The explosions coincided with the announcement of a new organisation "Umkhonto we Sizwe" (Zulu for "Spear of the Nation"). Posters carrying the announcement of the formation of the new body appeared on walls in Johannesburg, some near newspaper offices which were telephoned to look out for the announcement.

THE TARGETS

The attacks, made with what appeared to be home-made bombs and one with dynamite, were directed, said the announcement, against Government installations, particularly those connected with the policy of apartheid and race discrimination.

The Johannesburg targets were the Government pass office in Newtown, the Bantu Commissioner's Court in Fordsburg, the office of the Resettlement Board in Meadowlands, the Municipal offices in Dube and the post office in Fordsburg.

In Dube the police found the body of Mr. Petrus Molefe, rubber

(Continued on page 3)

BIRTH OF A NATION

LIEUTENANT ALEXANDER NYIRENDA, OF THE 6th BATTALION, King's African Rifles, planting the Tanganyika flag on the summit of Mount Kilimanjaro and lighting a symbolic torch of unity at midnight on Friday December 8 simultaneously with the hoisting of the same flag at the National Stadium to mark the independence of Tanganyika.

S.A. REPRESENTED AT TANGANYIKA CELEBRATIONS

At the Dar es Salaam airport to meet Dr. Y. M. Dadoo on his arrival to attend the Tanganyika independence celebrations recently were, from the left, Mr. J. J. Hadebe, representative of the banned African National Congress; Mr. Job Lusinde, Minister of Local Government and Housing; Mr. Tennyson Makiwane, official guest, and Dr. Dadoo, official guest representing the S.A. Indian Congress.

New Age Asked 6 Questions

"No Comment" Says U.C.C.A. Chairman

CAPE TOWN.

"WE operate within the framework of Government policy and I am not prepared to say anything that might embarrass the Government and the Council," Mr. Tom Swartz, chairman of the Union Council of Coloured Affairs, told New Age last week when asked to comment on the Prime Minister's 10-year plan for the Coloured people.

Dr. Verwoerd is reported to have told the UCCA at its recent session: "Within five years the framework of a Coloured 'parliament' and 'cabinet' could be created and within 10 years the Coloured community would be in full control of their own affairs if they co-operated with the Government's plans for their development."

The Prime Minister also said that the Council would be a channel between the Coloured states and the central government in the same way as the Department of Foreign

(Continued on page 3)

Umkhonto we Sizwe, the armed wing of the African National Congress, used the paper as its mouthpiece and its offices as meeting places. Both MP Naicker (*far left*), the Durban branch editor, and Joe Gqabi, a reporter and photographer in Johannesburg, were Umkhonto soldiers while on the staff.

The final issue was published in March 1963. After more than twenty-six years, six name changes, and three bannings, the paper closed down just days before the staff was banned from working at a newspaper. Within weeks most were being tortured in jail, were in hiding, or were going into exile. Of the five journalists pictured here, Naicker and First died in exile, Mbeki spent twenty-four years in prison on Robben Island and Bunting and Carneson returned from London to South Africa after the release of Nelson Mandela in 1990.

Informers and undercover spies swarmed around *New Age*. In 1956 Ruth First wrote a long article about "The Facts Behind Verwoerd's Spy System," which was run, apparently, through the Native Affairs Department's information division.[230] Govan Mbeki discovered police spies at a Port Elizabeth rugby tournament.[231] The Special Branch tried to enlist many *New Age* employees and sellers.[232] After one arrest, the police asked Douglas Manqina if he would spy on *New Age*, dangling a high-paying job on the Langa city council and cash for him; Manqina refused.[233] The Special Branch was more successful with a man named Oliver Mti. Passing himself off as an ANC member, Mti persuaded First to hire him as a part-time reporter in 1957. It was two years before she discovered Mti was passing along information to the Special Branch.[234]

The greatest source of trouble was the Treason Trial, a landmark mass show trial. On 27 September 1956, one thousand detectives raided the radical South African Left. They body-searched 500 people and invaded hundreds of homes—they took 369 items from Hilda and Rusty Bernstein's home.[235] They ransacked the four *New Age* offices and took away truckloads of papers. That day, Nelson Mandela walked up the old stairwell at Barrack Street to have a meeting with the editors. As he reached the third floor, he heard an argument between Fred Carneson and detectives, and the dull scrape of furniture being moved, and he quickly slipped back down to the street.[236] The nationwide raid brought in truckloads of booty, and for three months the government sorted and sifted the seized material.

On Wednesday morning, 5 December 1956, the arrests came. As usual, it was well before dawn. Lionel Forman, asleep in his bed with his wife Sadie, awoke to persistent pounding on his door and thought, hopefully, that the maid had just lost her key. But he knew she would not hammer that loudly. Forman went to the door and sleepily greeted the Security Branch sergeant who handed him the arrest warrant. "HOOGVERRAAD—HIGH TREASON," read the reason for the arrest. Forman wiped his eyes, read it again, and let out a laugh. The sergeant quickly said, "You can laugh, but you get hanged for treason."[237]

One hundred and fifty-six men and women experienced that same early-morning jolt.[238] The "Roll of Honour" the newspaper printed the next week read like a *New Age*'s "Who's Who." Pretoria had arrested ten staff members: Sonia Bunting, Fred Carneson, Ruth First, Lionel Forman, Alex La Guma, Alfred Hutchinson, Tennyson Makiwane, Wilton Mkwayi, M. P. Naicker and Robert Resha. *New Age*'s printer, Len Lee-Warden, was there, despite the fact that he was a member of Parliament.[239] Almost all of the rest of the 156 had a direct connection to Barrack Street: sellers like Andries "General China" Chamile and Paul Joseph; senior advisors like Rusty Bernstein, Moses Kotane, Nelson Mandela and Walter Sisulu; racing correspondent Errol Shanley; and fundraisers like Ismail Meer. Even former staff members like Jackie Lax Arenstein and Dawood Seedat, and former board member Douglas Thompson, were included in the group.

Not only were its office managers, reporters, branch chiefs, sellers, correspondents, advisors, fundraisers, and printer charged with a capital offense, but the newspaper itself was on trial for treason. Accused No. 157 was Real Printing and Publishing Company, the firm whose only asset was *New Age*. (Within weeks Pretoria added Competent Printing and Publishing, the firm that had published *Advance*.)[240] The government did not elaborate on how it planned to hang a newspaper.

"The high treason charge set the country agog with wagging tongues and the running of frightened feet," wrote Don Mattera, a Sophiatown gangster at the time.[241] The Trial lasted more than four years, and although the shock wore off after the first weeks—the Crown granted bail after sixteen days—the country remained riveted by the case. The accused stayed in Johannesburg and attended daily sessions in court in alphabetically assigned seats (First, arrested as Mrs. Slovo, successfully battled to sit among the F's).[242] In February 1958 the government dropped the charges against Real and Competent, and eight months later it discharged 120 people, including all the *New Age* staff members.[243] But for the rest, the case moved to Pretoria and dragged on through long-winded examinations and cross-examinations. Oswald Pirow, the former cabinet minister in the *Guardian*'s first years, came out of retirement to lead the prosecution. Nelson Mandela recalled feeling a sense of equilibrium each morning when he came into the courtroom and saw Pirow at his table reading the right-wing *Nuwe Order*, and Bram Fischer, one of the lead attorneys for the defense, at his table reading *New Age*.[244]

Despite the massive disruption caused by the trial, *New Age* still came out every Thursday afternoon. Brian Bunting, along with Govan Mbeki and Ivan Schermbrucker, shouldered the majority of the editorial burden; they had escaped arrest because they had been banned in 1952 from political work, and the Crown's indictment period started that year. With his usual steadfastness, Bunting maintained the newspaper's production schedule, wrote articles and editorials and directed the printing operation at Pioneer.[245]

Still, desperate for assistance, especially in the first months of the Trial, Bunting brought in two young University of Cape Town graduates, Amy

Thornton and Albie Sachs. Thornton, a spunky Party member and longtime volunteer at Barrack Street (she spent her Saturdays cutting and filing each article and photograph into the weekly's copious files), worked as a reporter for the duration of the Trial.[246] Sachs, the son of Solly Sachs, the Garment Workers' Union leader and an emerging Party theoretician, took over Lionel Forman's foreign news column. Sachs was a committed activist—during the Defiance Campaign, he and Mary Butcher and two other Modern Youth Society members had written telegrams to Prime Minister Malan at the non-white counter in Cape Town's main post office—and a busy lawyer who worked in Forman's law practice.[247]

Other loyal *New Age* supporters filled in. With Carneson away, Athol Thorne took over the management of Real Printing and Publishing.[248] Wolfie Kodesh moved to Johannesburg to assist Schermbrucker at Commissioner Street, which was overwhelmed with Congress leaders stopping by during court recesses or having a cup of tea at the end of the day—about twenty Trialists ate lunch there every day.[249] Michael Harmel helped cover the explosive story about the Alexandra bus boycott. Mary Butcher, now writing under her married name of Turok, wrote numerous articles about events in Johannesburg.[250] In Durban, Premchand Mistrey, an NIC member and *New Age* seller, managed the office in M. P. Naicker's absence.[251] Only in Port Elizabeth, with just Wilton Mkwayi under arrest, was the crisis minimized.

Coverage of the case was massive. For months, Bunting printed pages upon pages of verbatim testimony. First, Resha, and Makiwane wrote articles and Lionel Forman, along with Solly Sachs, even wrote a book, *The South African Treason Trial*, that was published in London in 1957.[252] La Guma moved his column up to Johannesburg and gave court cameos of some of his fellow accused, illustrated by Isaac Horovitch's pen-and-ink sketches.[253] Eli Weinberg took both individual photographs of the scenes outside the courtrooms and the famous group portrait of all 156 accused. *New Age* accepted donations for the Treason Trial Defense Fund.[254]

The strangest result of the Trial was the firebombing of Barrack Street. One Tuesday morning in March 1957, a policewoman patrolling Plein Street noticed flames coming out of the Chames Building. She called the fire brigade, which arrived just a few minutes before the fire destroyed the entire building. Three out of the four *New Age* offices on the third floor, as well as most of a dress-shop storeroom down the hall, were gutted. Flames wrecked cabinets, chairs, bookcases, adding machines, typewriters, duplicators and desks. In the heat, windows had shattered and the window frames disintegrated. The weekly's collection of back issues had burnt.

The fire was a clear case of arson—the police found bottles of paraffin in each room and a half-burnt paraffin-soaked rag stuffed under the locked door to the editor's office, the only room not to burn.[255] At first, everyone blamed the Special Branch. However, when Fred Carneson came down from Johannesburg the following week, the true story emerged. Two of Carneson's bookkeeping assistants had been skimming money from *New Age*'s accounts. With Carneson away at the trial, no one noticed any discrepancies. As time wore on, the assistants had panicked and tried to burn the account books. Carneson fired the assistants and had them arrested, but the police, not sympathetic to the newspaper, did not pursue the case, and let them go.[256] Bunting temporarily moved offices to Sam Kahn's chambers, and the next issue appeared as usual two days later.

Embezzling employees were not the only reason the newspaper was in financial trouble. The weekly was simply a losing proposition. Circulation hovered between 25,000 and 30,000.[257] After the banning of *Advance* in 1954, only two or three microscopic advertisements appeared each week; the steady ones were from Eli Weinberg and a Johannesburg optician.[258] No one dared to give business to a newspaper so completely vilified by Pretoria.[259] The only significant advertising came courtesy of a 1957 ANC boycott of Nationalist Party–controlled companies. After three months, Chapman's, one of the firms on the boycott list, approached the ANC and gave written assurances that no Nationalists were on its board of directors. To prove their allegiance, Chapman's placed a quarter-page advertisement in *New Age*.[260]

The already dwindling trickle of donations evaporated.[261] In grave circumstances, money would come in—after the 1957 fire, £1,400 arrived at Barrack Street in the next fortnight—but the day-to-day horror of apartheid meant that few people had money to spare, and most of them were scared to donate to the weekly.[262] Each month was a struggle. In June 1958, for example, newspaper sales netted £1,243 and advertising brought in £32, which meant *New Age* needed almost £1,000 in donations—yet only £433 arrived. Again and again, the bank account shrank to nearly nothing: in May 1955 Carneson reported less than £100 in the Cape Town bank, £47 in Johannesburg, and April's salaries had not yet been paid; four months later, £5 was in the bank in Cape Town and the newspaper was £200 in debt; in September 1956, during the "worst crisis in our history," £20 was in the bank and both rent and wages were unpaid; two months later, salaries and rent were again unpaid and now just £10 was in the bank. At one point in 1957, the weekly was unable to pay its Pioneer printing bill on time, and twice Carneson took out loans.[263] By March 1960 *New Age* had a £3,000 debt.

Inflated salaries for staff members were not a cause. In 1963, after seventeen years of working at Barrack Street, fifteen as editor, Bunting received a monthly paycheck of £75.[264] Mbeki started out earning £30 a month and in 1963 got £50; Ebrahim Ismail Ebrahim earned £15 as a staff writer.[265] To save money during the Treason Trial, Bunting cut the salaries of the accused staff members in half.[266] All columnists, like Forman and Sachs, worked for free. Sellers earned very little. Ebrahim earned one penny for every newspaper he sold, while Douglas Manqina earned threepence for every newspaper after the initial one hundred.[267] Moreover, many staffers regularly donated money back to *New Age*.[268]

Support from the ANC and its allies came in verbal, not paper form. Resolutions calling for donations came at annual national conferences.[269] Carneson often appended an exhortation from a Congress leader in his weekly fundraising column: "Every penny for *New Age* is a penny well-spent for freedom," declared Yusuf Dadoo.[270] But very rarely did the branches or the national executive donate money.[271] An exception was the Congress of Democrats. The national executive of the COD annually donated £15, and individual branches, especially Johannesburg, gave money, advertisements, and even furniture.[272] One notable contributor was Julius First, Ruth's father, who quietly helped bankroll the newspaper while he served as treasurer of the underground Party.

Most branches of the ANC and its allies organized sales of the newspaper, although it was often haphazard compared with the disciplined selling of the Communist Party in the 1940s. No one was more committed than the ebullient twenty-somethings in the Transvaal Indian Youth Congress. They published their own newsletter, *Spark: The Voice of Oppressed Youth*; poked their noses into every rally and protest they could find; and even smeared black-tar slogans on the façades of the Anglo-American building, the Transvaal Supreme Court, the Central Post Office, and the Johannesburg municipal office.[273] Paul Joseph—"our old friend," as *New Age* called him in 1958—was a typical TIYC leader: he wrote numerous articles for the newspaper and maintained a selling route on the weekends.[274] "One house I would pass every Saturday," Joseph said. "There was a man sitting outside in the yard, reading the Bible. His wife would never buy a paper when I asked them until one Saturday she did. I asked her why and she told me her husband had run off with another woman. You got to know the people when you sold *New Age*. It gave us an incredible political education and experience. . . . I remember one woman I sold to, she gave me a letter once for *New Age*, about getting beaten up by her husband."

Fred Carneson and Ivan Schermbrucker tried everything to stave off financial defeat. They assisted Johnny Morley and Arnold Selby with their Christmas hamper schemes. They sold *New Age* Christmas cards and calendars.[275] They planned the annual Christmas Eve dance, now hosted by Sam Kahn, and occasional jumble sales.[276] They offered Ronald Segal's 1961 novel, *The Tokoloshe*, to *New Age* subscribers for 2s. 6d.: "No person who is politically conscious can afford to miss this opportunity of acquiring the best political satire of this century."[277] In May 1957 they doubled the price of the newspaper from threepence to sixpence—the price of the weekly, constant for the first thirteen years, rose 600 percent in the next seven years—and lifted a year's subscription to £21.[278] To make the price hike palatable, they issued a flier with dozens of Congress leaders saying, "Pay 6d for a New South Africa."[279] In March 1956 they launched a £10,000 campaign and collected over half that amount in five months.[280] In June 1958 they asked for two hundred people to each guarantee a monthly donation of £5; one hundred readers responded.[281] They designated August 1958 "*New Age* Month" and offered a dinner service to the person who secured the most donations, and a free year's subscription to *New Age* to anyone who brought in six new subscribers.[282]

Pamphlets provided cash and educational value. Lionel Forman wrote two: "Chapters in the History of the March to Freedom," and "Black and White in South African History" (the later posthumously published in 1960, with an introduction by Ray Alexander). Ruth First wrote "The Farm Labour Scandal Exposure," and "New Life in China"; Michael Harmel wrote one about Olive Schreiner; Moses Kotane wrote "The Great Crisis Ahead: A Call to Unity"; and Bunting wrote "The Story Behind the Non-White Press," and "Apartheid: The Road to Poverty." The most popular pamphlet, however, was the most utilitarian one: "The Law and You," a £1, twenty-six-page booklet written anonymously by Sam Kahn. It was so full of essential analysis of the Kafkaesque tangle of apartheid laws that Kahn updated and reprinted it five times, and once published it in Zulu.[283]

The financial saviors of the newspaper were small-town Indian shopkeepers in Natal and the Transvaal. Once a year, Bunting or Carneson drove up to Natal to raise money.[284] M. P. Naicker or Ismail Meer took them out to meet with Indian businessmen.[285] The key to success was securing a donation from the wealthiest and most respected man in town, as the rest of the Indians in the area gave according to his standards. One such trip to Natal in 1959 raised £1,562.[286]

In the Transvaal, the bait for donations was Yusuf Dadoo. The president of the South African Indian Congress, Dadoo was seen as South Africa's successor to Mahatma Gandhi. "He was a communist and people knew that," recalled Carneson, "but everywhere the Indians loved him. He was like Gandhi. Every house you went into had on the wall in the living room a picture of Gandhi and a picture of Dadoo."[287] He held the respect of Africans as well, and in Orlando in the heart of Soweto, the public meeting ground was called "Dadoo Square." Dadoo had supported the weekly since its early days—issuing interviews, counseling on policy, and serving on its board of directors—and in the 1950s was romantically involved with Commissioner Street administrator Winnie Kramer. "If Dadoo was with us, the traders just gave him a blank check and said, 'Fill in the amount,'" said Wolfie Kodesh. "Without him, they gave us money, but they decided the amount. The love for Dadoo was unbelievable. When Dadoo sneezed, the whole Indian community would get a cold."[288]

Sometimes, though, a little deception was necessary. For years, Bram Fischer went on *New Age* fundraising drives. His Indian escorts spoke privately to the shopkeepers in Gujarati, and as if by magic, bills of money materialized. Fischer attributed the shopkeepers' willingness to donate to the fact that he was a well-known leader and the cause was worthy. After some time, he discovered the truth: his comrades were telling the shopkeepers that Fischer, the son of the judge-president of the Orange Free State, would soon be a judge himself. To ensure his benevolence when they would come before him, the comrades said, they needed to pay now. Fischer was shocked at the dissembling and insisted on talking to the shopkeepers himself. He found that they were often apolitical, but always generous.[289]

For the weekly, the decade began with the death of Bill Andrews, and it ended with the death of Lionel Forman.

After returning the editor's chair to Bunting, Forman finished his law degree at the University of the Witwatersrand and opened his own very active practice in Cape Town.[290] He also enrolled in UCT's history Ph.D. program, writing his dissertation on African politics from 1870 to 1948.[291] *New Age* published long excerpts from his thesis: "Did Dingane Kill Retief?" asked the ever controversial Forman.[292] He continued to deliver his foreign-news column, and when Bunting was away from Barrack Street, he filled in as acting editor.[293]

Still, it was obvious his heart condition was deteriorating. In the last four years of the fifties, he spoke at just two public meetings (in August 1959,

Pretoria nonetheless banned him from attending gatherings for five years).[294] The first thing Wolfie Kodesh thought upon seeing the stairs of Barrack Street after thirty years was an image of Forman leaning against the handrail, panting for breath, sweat beading on his forehead, and his lips turning blue as he tried to walk up to the third floor.

In the winter of 1959 Forman became seriously ill. A university friend named Christiaan Barnard—the doctor who in 1968 would perform the world's first heart transplant—had just come back from America with a new heart-lung surgical technique. For Forman, it was a last chance. On 14 October 1959, Sadie Forman gave birth to a baby girl. Five days later, Forman went into Groot Schuur Hospital. During surgery, his heart failed.[295]

Telephone calls, telegrams, and letters engulfed Barrack Street. The weekly printed tributes to Forman, and also the note he wrote to his wife and children just minutes before he was wheeled into surgery: "Now that I am legally safe as houses, I want it trumpeted from the housetops, Lionel Forman believed in communism till the day he died."[296]

On Sunday, 25 October 1959, more than three hundred friends (and a troop of Security Branch detectives) came to a memorial service at the Banqueting Hall in Cape Town. Sam Kahn, who presided over the service, told the crowd: "And if this is the moment to speak of his faults, he had the persistent obstinacy of sticking to his guns even when he knew he was right."[297] At the end of the service, the mourners rose to their feet and sang a hymn some friends in Langa had written to honor Forman. They concluded the service with the standard benedictory rendition of the African anthem, "Nkosi 'Sikele Afrika."

When silence returned, someone started singing again. It was a song that had not been heard in public in South Africa since 1950. People joined in one by one until the whole hall echoed with the words of "The Internationale": "Then comrades come rally and the last fight let us face . . ." They raised their clenched fists high, their voices soared, and they sang for the memory of Lionel Forman.[298]

CHAPTER SIX

The Bloody Pole on the Hill

Sharpeville and Beyond, 1960–1963

The new decade, the fourth and final one graced by the ink and newsprint of the *Guardian* newspaper, was greeted with shouts of enthusiasm at the annual New Year's Eve party at Brian and Sonia Bunting's hillside cottage above Clifton. One hundred and fifty friends danced to a gramophone, drank champagne and talked about Lionel Forman, who had died just nine weeks before. Johnny Morley told Irish jokes and heartily cackled. Alex La Guma strummed a guitar and sang Cape coloured tunes and clever parodies of political anthems.[1] Ray Alexander sat with a succession of individual friends in the kitchen, one after another, so as to not violate the banning order forbidding her to meet with more than one person at a time. As the evening wore on, some revelers went down to Clifton Beach and swam in the cool Atlantic surf. One couple attempted to walk up Lion's Head for sunrise, but got lost.

As the sun rose, the guests melted away, until the house was empty. Brian and Sonia cleaned up and then drove to Barrack Street. It was a Thursday, and the newspaper would be coming out that afternoon. Work needed to be done.[2]

Three weeks later the worst mining disaster in South African history occurred in Coalbrook in the Orange Free State. Four hundred and thirty-five miners died in the accident.[3] Ruth First sent Joe Gqabi to write and photograph the story. Unable to meet with the white mine authorities, Gqabi struck a deal with *Rand Daily Mail* reporter Benjamin Pogrund: Gqabi interviewed the surviving black miners and Pogrund met with the white owners. As they shared their findings near the pithead, a group of white miners surrounded them, snarling at Pogrund for talking to an African.[4]

For a month Gqabi covered the disaster in depth, pointing out instances of negligence on the part of the owners and reporting on a moving final scene: a group of Basuto miners lowered a microphone five hundred feet down a borehole and called into the darkness, "Come to my voice and speak. If you cannot move, throw coal at my voice." There was no reply.[5]

In the midst of the Coalbrook affair, the pass laws again became a flashpoint. The African National Congress, at its annual national conference in December, had designated 31 March as a day for a nationwide strike in protest of the pass laws. The newly formed Pan Africanist Congress forestalled the ANC with their own day of protest planned for ten days earlier.[6]

On 21 March 1960 the PAC president, Robert Sobukwe, solemnly marched from his home to the Soweto police headquarters in Orlando, where he and fifty other PAC men told the police they had no passes and offered themselves up for arrest.[7]

Thirty miles away in a small town called Sharpeville, ten thousand people pressed against the fence of the local police station. Planes that had swooped down and dispersed a similarly sized PAC group in Evaton instead brought cheers from the Sharpeville crowd. The twelve policemen inside the station, jittery because their telephone was out of order, radioed for support, and by midday three hundred policemen, including the head of the Special Branch, arrived and lined up behind the fence with loaded sten guns. A gate was opened to admit four PAC organizers who wished to be arrested. Dozens of demonstrators surged through the gate amid a hail of stones from the crowd. Someone yelled, "Fire!" and in the next forty seconds the police fired 743 bullets. Sixty-nine dead bodies, including ten children, lay scattered on the ground. Most of them had been shot in the back. Three hours later, as ambulances and reporters descended on the carnage, a thunderclap sounded and rain washed away the blood.[8]

Five hours later, the police fired upon protesters in Langa, killing two people and wounding forty-nine. The township rioted, as people burned the homes of African constables, torched municipal buildings, and overturned a car, killing the driver.[9] The next day Chief Albert Luthuli, the ANC president, publicly burned his pass. The 28th was a national day of mourning, and the entire country was brought to a standstill. That night thousands of bonfires lit up the Johannesburg skyline. In Orlando, teenagers danced through the streets, tearing down telephone poles and singing "thina sululusha"—we are the youth.[10] In Cape Town, the male migrant workers in Langa and neighboring Nyanga went on a general strike. The police responded by closing off the two townships. The Treason Trial—the defense's second witness, Luthuli, had just taken the witness chair—was halted, and the government suspended the pass laws.

As the crisis worsened, the focus shifted to a single man, a twenty-three-year-old economics student named Philip Kgosana. He studied at the University of Cape Town, but lived in a Langa hostel with a canning worker as a roommate. Just before Sharpeville, Kgosana had become the PAC's district chairman, and on 23 and 25 March he led Langa marchers to Caledon Square, Cape Town's police headquarters, to protest the massacres.[11]

For advice, he turned to Patrick Duncan, the editor of *Contact*—Kgosana sold *Contact* to pay his tuition. Every day after the massacre, Kgosana visited *Contact*'s offices, and on the 23rd he attended one of Duncan's formal dinner parties.[12] When Kgosana was arrested during the 25 March protest, Duncan went to Caledon Square and intervened to have him released.[13] An important element of Kgosana and Duncan's friendship was their mutual distrust of communism, and Kgosana told the strikers in Langa to be wary of *New Age*.[14]

With the story of the century brewing, Brian Bunting refused to take a backseat to Duncan. Bunting covered the "Mass Slaughter" in Sharpeville and the Langa violence in depth, but he needed a profile of the new student-turned-leader. and repeatedly sent interview requests to Kgosana.[15] On 24 March the PAC leader relented and rang Barrack Street from Duncan's offices to arrange a time for an interview. When Duncan overheard Kgosana asking for Bunting, he grabbed the telephone and slammed it down.[16] Kgosana left Duncan, walked over to Barrack Street, and gave a long interview to Bunting, who laughed with glee when Kgosana told him about Duncan's reaction. In return for the interview, Bunting and his wife Sonia drove £200 worth of food to Langa.[17]

Before dawn on 30 March 1960, the South African government secretly declared martial law. Policemen swept into homes across the nation to arrest more than two hundred activists. At daybreak they raided Langa, arresting and beating workers, and forcing strikers onto buses to take them to their jobs. Langa residents spontaneously decided to march to Cape Town, and a crowd of 30,000 Africans gathered and started to walk the eight miles to the city. Kgosana, anxious to avoid arrest, had been staying in another township and had to catch a lift from a *Christian Science Monitor* reporter to the front of the column of people as they entered the city from De Waal Drive.[18] Kgosana wore white short pants. Incredibly, at the moment when revolution was most achievable, the man in charge was a young university student wearing shorts.[19]

White South Africa trembled nonetheless. Police helicopters hovered overhead, armored cars cruised the streets, and the army established machine-gun emplacements in front of Parliament. When Colonel I.B.S. Terblanche, the Cape Town commanding police officer, saw the enormous crowd coursing into town, he fell to his knees and prayed. Kgosana averted an obvious confrontation by stopping the marchers at the corner of Roeland and Buitekant streets and walking with a dozen lieutenants, five photographers, and a few journalists to Parliament. Halfway there, a Security Branch detective took Kgosana by the arm and steered him towards a small but boisterous crowd of blacks gathered at Caledon Square. Terblanche, relieved at Kgosana's arrival without the thirty thousand in tow, handed him a microphone connected to a police bullhorn. Kgosana briefly talked to the cluster of Africans and signaled for the Langa marchers to come down Buitekant Street and join him at Caledon Square.

It was a Wednesday, the quietest day of the work week at Barrack Street, but the entire staff was in the office because of the news of the mass arrests. When they heard about the Langa marchers, they hurried out to the street and up to the roof of a building above the square.[20]

On the steps of the police station, Kgosana spoke to the masses: "We came here to ask Colonel Terblanche to protect us from the police." The crowd laughed. Kgosana turned and for twenty minutes negotiated with Terblanche, the same man who had released him from prison five days earlier. Kgosana asked to see the minister of justice, Francois Erasmus. Terblanche told him the minister was at lunch, and promised Kgosana an audience with Erasmus if he sent the crowd home. Kgosana accepted Terblanche's gentleman's agreement. He called for silence and told his followers to return to Langa. "Let us go home in peace, my friends" he said. "Let us be silent, just like people who are going to a graveyard." The crowd dispersed, and a police car led them back to Langa.[21]

At five in the afternoon, after cooling their heels with Patrick Duncan in *Contact*'s office, Kgosana and five other PAC officials returned to Caledon Square.[22] Instead of meeting with the minister, they were arrested and thrown into solitary confinement. That evening, the prime minister went on the radio and publicly declared that the country was under a state of emergency.

South Africa crossed a Rubicon. Martial law went into effect. All meetings were forbidden. The police cordoned off Langa and Nyanga, shutting off electricity, water, and telephone service and imposing a curfew. After four days of house-to-house beatings, the general strike in Cape Town ended. Africans in Durban and Johannesburg tried to emulate the Langa marchers, but the police turned them back before they reached the city centers.[23] The government reinstated the pass laws. Most of all, they banned the ANC (and the PAC). After forty-eight years, the Congress had finally become such a thorn in the side of Pretoria that the apartheid regime tried to eradicate it: it became illegal to be a member of the ANC or to further its aims.

Beginning with the predawn raids on 30 March, the Special Branch arrested almost everyone connected with the liberation movement. They picked up all national and regional executive members of the Congress and its allies, as well as anyone who had been remotely politically active.[24] The day after the Langa march, for instance, the police detained most of the *New Age* staff. Brian Bunting, M. P. Naicker, Govan Mbeki, Ivan Schermbrucker, Amy Thornton, Douglas Manqina, and Alex La Guma led the list of fifty-five *New Age* staff members held in jail.[25]

That same day, the weekly appeared as usual. Bunting's interview with Kgosana and reports on the township violence held center stage. The Security Branch confiscated thousands of copies from street sellers, but it still went through the mail to subscribers.[26]

Chaos descended upon the weekly. The staff not in jail scrambled to go into hiding. There were rumors of a possible shutdown of the newspaper. Barrack Street was nearly empty. Albie Sachs, the young lawyer who wrote the international-news feature for *New Age*, was the only staffer to come in. He telephoned the police to see if *New Age* was still allowed to publish. The police said yes, so he laid the edition out. He carefully wrote an editorial protesting the ANC banning and secured some photographs taken at the march, but without any other reporters, he struggled to fill the eight pages. On Monday afternoon, as scheduled, he took the copy to the Pioneer Press for printing. Sachs was excited about manning the great *New Age* ship, the young reporter ferrying the paper through stormy seas to safety. But there was also a sense of sinking doom that pervaded the ghostly offices.[27]

On 5 April 1960, the minister of justice issued a *Government Gazette Extraordinary* ordering *New Age* and *Torch*, the weekly published by the coloured organization, the Unity Movement, to cease publication for the duration of the emergency.[28] For the first time since February 1937, the newspaper was not going to meet its weekly Thursday publication.

The police went to all four *New Age* offices and ordered them shut, and detectives arrived at Pioneer's plant in Salt River.[29] Len Lee-Warden, Pioneer's director, had just begun churning out the 7 April issue. About one hundred copies had been printed and folded. The policemen stopped the press, seized all the copies, and dismantled the type.[30]

Besides Sachs's careful editorial, the issue included a full page of reporting on the Treason Trial, an Eli Weinberg photograph of mourners at Congress leader Ida Mntwana's funeral, an article on Malawian leader Hastings Banda, and news of ANC leader Oliver Tambo's dramatic escape to Bechuanaland. Sachs ran a three-column front-page photograph of Kgosana under the banner "Go Home in Peace," and filled two pages inside with more photographs of the historic march. He wrote about the Special Branch's confiscations of the 31 March issue and added, "We are assured that provided no 'subversive' matter is published, the paper can continue to come out." He even managed to insert a little levity: the minister of justice had a "guest editorial" on the emergency regulations, and Sachs added a photograph of three PAC members who, while waiting to surrender at Caledon Square, were seen reading *New Age*.

Forcibly removed from the reading public, the 7 April issue of *New Age* symbolized what the next thirty years would mean to the country. Because of the weekly's disappearance, most South Africans did not read about the events following the dismissal of the Langa marchers from Caledon Square. Instead, there was a repressive silence.

For the thousands of men and women held in jail, they knew nothing about *New Age's* banning. They also did not know how long the emergency was going to last, and the indefinite nature of their detention weighed heavily. Conditions were spartan. Most prisoners had no running water, little exercise, bad food and cramped quarters. Still, they passed the time. Govan Mbeki, kept in Rooi Hell, Port Elizabeth's jail, practiced ballroom dancing and freedom songs, played tiddlywinks with grains of maize, and complained about the awful prison food.[31] Douglas Manqina fought off fleas in a crowded cell in Worcester.[32] Alex La Guma was kept at Roeland Street, about which he had reported just a few years before. With time on his hands, he wrote the majority of his first novel, *A Walk in the Night*. He also lost six pounds, gained gray hairs and developed "a very strong dislike for mealie-pap and beans."[33] Cecil Williams, a playwright and longtime supporter of the weekly, created a Shakespeare theatre company, "The Fortress Mummers," and Eli Weinberg founded a choir that sang in Yiddish and Sotho.[34] Bunting played hours of chess.[35] Jack Barnett, the husband of *Guardian* reporter Naomi

Shapiro, set up his architectural drawing boards and designed the Welkom town hall.[36] At the Fort in Johannesburg, Winnie Kramer slept on a straw mattress.[37] The first woman arrested in Cape Town was Amy Thornton. She spent her first week at Roeland Street in solitary confinement. The *New Age* staffer protested by going on a hunger strike and copying the Preamble of the Freedom Charter on her prison wall with a stick of lipstick. Eventually allowed to join the other women prisoners, she learned knitting and practiced ballet.[38] In Pretoria, the white women, still treated with an old-fashioned respect, held French classes, played Scrabble and took hot baths once a day.[39]

Hundreds of activists fled the country. Oliver Tambo, the ANC leader, and Ronald Segal, the editor of the leftist journal *Africa South*, left Cape Town on the day of the Langa march and drove north in Segal's mother's Vauxhall, eventually reaching Bechuanaland. Yusuf Dadoo followed a week later. Ruth First donned a red wig, bundled her three daughters into her car and drove through the night to Mbabane, the capital of Swaziland.[40]

Within the country, a hastily-created network of underground activists sprang up, as the liberation movement tried to reestablish some form of political activity in the wake of the ANC banning and the mass arrests. The ANC leadership coalesced into an ad hoc three-man secretariat—the "emergency committee"—that ostensibly ran the Congress: Michael Harmel, Moses Kotane, and Ben Turok, *New Age* staffer Mary Butcher's husband. These three men held meetings, wrote statements, and organized the distribution of flyers and leaflets. Because the government refused to say publicly who was in jail, they issued a bulletin listing the names of detainees; at the bottom they advised readers: "Read it. Study it. Pass it on. But do not get caught with it, or tell anyone where you got it."[41] In June, after heated discussions, they published a leaflet announcing the existence of the South African Communist Party.

Below the secretariat were a smattering of isolated activists. Fred Carneson, Ray Alexander, and Albie Sachs coordinated the Cape Town underground. Wolfie Kodesh acted as a conduit between the emergency committee and the rest of the underground. He found duplicating machines to print out their leaflets; ferried Kotane, Harmel, or Turok to secret meetings in his dark Volkswagen—disguised as a dry-cleaning van; brought them food, clothing, and bottles of whiskey; and secured new safe houses (they hid in ten different houses over the five months). The police had staked out his own apartment, so he too was on the run and slept on golf courses or in his car.[42]

Other people underground got caught. Sonia Bunting lived in hiding in Somerset West. Sachs then told her to drive to Johannesburg and join a convoy leaving for Mbabane. In Johannesburg, the Special Branch recognized her car and arrested her.[43]

In August 1960 the situation brightened. The government started releasing detainees. Some of those underground returned from hiding, and exiles in Swaziland, like Ruth First, crept back into the country.[44]

Some New Age staff members pushed for the weekly to reappear as a sign of defiance. Bunting, by this time released from jail, refused—he wanted to always follow the letter of the law so the apartheid regime had no legitimate cause for proscription.[45] It turned out to be a wise decision. In October 1960 Pretoria charged Kodesh and Carneson, the two directors of Real Printing and Publishing, with subversion. They alleged that the 31 March 1960 issue contained statements that violated the emergency regulations. Kodesh and Carneson countered by arguing that the edition had already been printed before the emergency was declared. New Age won the case.[46]

Back at Barrack Street, New Age prepared for the lifting of the emergency. There was a good deal of confusion.[47] Carneson and Schermbrucker traveled to Natal and wiped out a £3,000 debt with a major drive among Indian shopkeepers.[48] Sachs, with great pride, returned a briefcase to Bunting. When Sachs was alone in the office at the beginning of the emergency, he had noticed a fancy, locked briefcase in Bunting's office. Imagining that it held top-secret papers, he took it away from Barrack Street and hid it for four months. When Bunting was released from jail, Sachs, with a flourish, presented the briefcase with all its important documents. Bunting opened it. Inside, there were no papers—just a moldy sandwich and one very ripe banana.[49]

On 31 August 1960 Pretoria lifted the state of emergency.

Eight days later, a new issue of New Age appeared. Five months of proscription, fifty-five staffers in jail, and the banning of the ANC was not enough to deter the weekly, and Barrack Street's unique spin on South African politics was back. "Freedom Is Within Our Grasp: Govt. Received Terrific Setback from Emergency" trumpeted the front-page headline next to a photograph of a smiling Nelson Mandela and Duma Nokwe walking home in Soweto after being released. Inside were more photographs of reunited families. Alex La Guma in his "Up My Alley" column rated the prison warders he met while in jail, and two pages detailed other experiences of those detained, including a report on what the Special Branch asked during interrogations. Sachs penned a long article about the circumstances surrounding New Age's banning, and four enormous photographs of the Langa march—"Pictures from Our Banned Issue"—accompanied a memoir of the historic day by activist Alf Wannenburgh. One page looked at the latest court proceedings from the Treason Trial; another examined the "Battle for The Congo." "Liberation is near," readers were told in the editorial. "We must not get used to tyranny. We must not let freedom go by default."[50]

"*New Age* Was Snapped Up in the Townships" read the headline of a Robert Resha article the following week. Resha toured Johannesburg that first Friday and reported brisk sales. *New Age*'s African sellers went through more than double their usual stock. Outside Retsies, the popular African café on Pritchard Street, Resha saw a clamoring mob—of newspaper readers: "It was difficult to see who was selling and who was the buyer of *New Age*, for everyone seemed to have a copy or two. I spoke to three persons who had more than one copy each. They were stocking up for their friends." Resha walked to Market Street, where he bumped into a couple of Treason Trialists selling *New Age*. They also were running short of copies. Resha went to Mofolo township, sold his usual two dozen copies to longtime customers, and ran into Hosiah Tsehla, a veteran Alexandra *New Age* seller. "People were longing for *New Age*," Tsehla told him. "I have not seen the African people so happy for a long time. When they see *New Age*, they seem to feel that freedom is just around the corner."[51]

Quite a corner it was, before freedom came into view. A carapace of stability gave outsiders the illusion that all was well. Every Thursday, bundles of *New Age* appeared. The main editorial staff remained intact. Underneath, however, it was a mess. Swirling currents of exile and departure flooded the newspaper's foundations. Key figures like Arnold Selby, Tennyson Makiwane, and Alfred Hutchinson had left the country before Sharpeville, and during the emergency, the exodus continued.[52] Sam Kahn was gone. He had initially fled to Swaziland and, amid rumors of assassination attempts on his life, flew to Bechuanaland, then Ghana, and eventually London.[53] Winnie Kramer left immediately after her August 1960 release from detention; she joined Yusuf Dadoo in London, and the two married.[54]

The most improbable exit was Wilton Mkwayi's. On 31 March 1960 the police arrested a cadre of Treason Trialists as they left the Pretoria courthouse after a day of testimony. In the hubbub, Mkwayi had gotten separated from his fellow accused as the arrests began, and approached a guard to find out what was happening. The guard ordered him to leave the premises. Mkwayi told him he was one of the accused, but the guard, fiercely obstinate, called him a liar and threatened to arrest him. Mkwayi shrugged his shoulders and walked away.[55] After staying underground for two months, he was smuggled out of the country to Swaziland. In September 1960 *New Age* ran a photograph of him—and Moses Mabhida and Ambrose Makiwane—with a cryptic caption saying the men were "somewhere in Africa."[56]

A final injection of new blood flowed into the weekly. Howard Lawrence, a coloured reporter for *Drum, Golden City Post*, and the *Cape Herald*, joined the staff in Cape Town. In Durban, Jackie Arenstein convinced her young cousin Ronnie Kasrils to sell *New Age* on Friday evenings at the Durban train station: "*New Age*! I' phepha lomzabalazo!" he would shout—*New Age*, the paper of the struggle. He soon started helping around the office.[57] Leonard Mdingi, a former correspondent in Mpondoland and member of Umkhonto, had also moved to Durban, and he worked part-time for the weekly.[58] In Port Elizabeth, Ernest Cole snapped photographs for *New Age*; often Brian Bunting created two-page spreads to highlight Cole's stunning work.[59] Dennis Brutus, a coloured poet and high-school English teacher, contributed many articles from Port Elizabeth, especially on the movement to ban South Africa from international sports.[60]

The most tumultuous transitions occurred in Johannesburg. In August 1961 *New Age* left Commissioner Street after twenty years and took new offices at 6 Mercantile House, 155 President Street.[61] Rica Hodgson, a veteran activist, took over Winnie Kramer's job, as well as helping with fundraising.[62] Ruth First hired three new reporters: Beate Lipman, a young white woman who helped found the Congress of Democrats and the Federation of South African Women; Brian Somana, an ANC Youth Leaguer; and Willie Kgositile, a freelance writer who had written a piece about a Sophiatown demonstration that neither the *Golden City Post* nor *Bantu World* would publish. He took it to Ruth First, she ran it and asked him to join the staff as a part-time reporter.[63]

"**M**uch like the situation ten years earlier when Pretoria banned the Communist Party, the ANC proscription destroyed *New Age*'s intricate system of contacts throughout the country. The weekly's correspondents and collaborators reeled from jail or exile, and few people were willing and able, according to Ruth First, to alert *New Age* "when some new vicious scheme of the police and the administration came to light."[64] Moreover, it had to constantly test the boundaries of what was legal. As in 1950, the weekly scrambled to reinvent itself.

Supporting the ANC remained an essential part of the newspaper's policy. Lift Ban on ANC!" demanded the lead headline in the second issue of

New Age after the end of the emergency. "No Peace Without People's Leaders."[65] The Congress endeavored to reestablish itself outside South Africa, and *New Age* kept its name in front of South Africans, boosted the now heavily discouraged membership and provided a conduit for official statements. The newspaper covered ANC activities abroad, including the opening of Congress offices in Algeria and a June 26 celebration in Dar es Salaam.[66] Yusuf Dadoo detailed the ANC's "Government in Exile" plans, and the weekly printed his postal address in London so birthday messages could reach him.[67] Oliver Tambo, the ANC's leader in exile, wrote bylined articles describing his hopes.[68] In August 1961 *New Age* ran a three-column, three-inch photograph of Tambo and other ANC leaders at a Tanganyika conference.[69] The weekly reprinted ANC leaflets that had been illegally produced and distributed in South Africa.[70] A report from the 1962 ANC conference in Lobatsi, Bechuanaland—the first official ANC conference in three years—appeared in the weekly.[71]

New Age still kept in touch with ANC leaders still inside South Africa. Both Walter Sisulu and Duma Nokwe wrote articles.[72] When A. B. Xuma, the former ANC president, died in 1962, the newspaper ran a lengthy obituary.[73] The current ANC president, Albert Luthuli, was still confined to Groutville, but he kept closely in touch with Lodgson House in Durban. He wrote ANC comments for the weekly, sent letters to the editor, and posted "Africa Day Messages." *New Age* reprinted his 1961 Nobel Prize for Peace acceptance speech in full, filling three pages, and he gave *New Age* a statement of thanks for all those who had sent messages of congratulations.[74] Before and after the crucial 1961 white general election, Luthuli sent "election surveys" giving the ANC point of view. Barrack Street sold a framed picture of Luthuli for five shillings from its offices. In June 1962 *New Age* printed Luthuli's final public statement before it became illegal to print anything written or spoken by him.[75]

The weekly traced the ANC's last-ditch attempts at reconciliation with the apartheid regime. In March 1961 in Pietermaritzburg, the ANC held a national conference where 1,400 delegates—representing 145 organizations—met to discuss the current political deadlock. A surprise appearance by Nelson Mandela highlighted the conference. His banning orders had expired the day before the conference, and so for the first time since 1952—and the last time until 1990—Mandela spoke in public. An Eli Weinberg photograph in *New Age* depicted Mandela "delivering his inspiring opening address."[76]

The Pietermaritzburg conference called for a three-day strike starting on Monday, 29 May 1961 to force the government to agree to a national convention. Mandela went underground to direct the stay-away. Pretoria quickly passed a law in early May enabling the police to detain people for twelve days without charging them with a crime or granting them bail; immediately the Special Branch arrested hundreds of Congress leaders and threw them into solitary confinement.[77] So transfixed was the weekly's audience by the upcoming strike that for the first time ever, not a single penny arrived at Barrack Street for donation.

The general strike passed amid extreme tension. Pretoria banned all gatherings. Armored cars patrolled the township broadcasting warnings that all strikers would be banished to rural areas, and helicopters with flashing searchlights hovered over trouble spots. Two people were killed in police confrontations with strikers. Port Elizabeth had about a 75 percent stay-away; Johannesburg, 60 percent; and Durban, 50 percent—and some African students boycotted school. The government did not accede to the national convention request, and *New Age* admitted that "This was no 100 percent victory" and spoke of "despondency in the people's camp."[78]

Nonviolent protest, many in the liberation movement believed, was now blocked. After bitter discussions, and with sizable misgivings, some activists within the ANC and the Communist Party turned to a campaign of guerrilla warfare and sabotage. On 16 December 1961, six days after ANC president Albert Luthuli accepted the Nobel Prize for Peace in Oslo, the campaign opened. Umkhonto we Sizwe ("the spear of the nation"), the armed wing of the ANC and the Party, dynamited electrical power pylons in Johannesburg, Durban and Port Elizabeth. War had been declared.

New Age specifically supported Umkhonto we Sizwe (MK). Weinberg photographed Umkhonto slogans painted on city walls and notices plastered on telephone poles.[79] Barrack Street ran pictures of the many sabotaged buildings and electricity pylons; the Thursday after the initial 16 December bombings saw a cheeky juxtaposition on the front page: a photograph of a damaged pylon with the headline "A New Phase in South Africa" appeared next to a photograph of a man planting a flag on top of Mount Kilimanjaro to celebrate the independence of Tanzania, with the headline "Birth of a Nation." The weekly published numerous Umkhonto statements, including its original manifesto and its first anniversary message.[80] So helpful was *New Age* that in April 1963, some MK soldiers assumed that the bombing campaign had been suspended; instead it was just that the weekly had gone out of existence and there was no other reliable outlet for reports on attacks.[81]

Brian Bunting carefully explained how materials from an underground army reached Barrack Street. For the initial Umkhonto declaration in

December 1961, *New Age* said it was "telephoned to look out for the announcement" on posters on walls "near newspaper offices." Other times, a proclamation "found its way into newspaper offices"; "a copy of the leaflet was sent to the Johannesburg office of *New Age*"; a letter was "received through the post"; and "the statement was slipped under the door of the Johannesburg office of *New Age*."

Shamelessly dissembling, *New Age* in fact functioned as an indispensable part of the underground ANC, Party and Umkhonto. The newspaper's four offices provided a cover for clandestine work. Daytime political discussions, dropped messages, forwarded documents and covert planning sessions could take place without attracting attention. In Durban a so-called "Daily Committee" that ran the Congress movement in Natal met each morning at eight at Lodgson House.[82]

The weekly served as a sort of membership directory. When one Durban MK cadre, Bruno Mtolo, arrived in Johannesburg for an Umkhonto meeting, Mtolo proved his identity by pulling out an old copy of *New Age* and pointing to a photograph of himself at a SACTU meeting with his name in the captions.[83] Some of the help the weekly supplied was as ethereal as a smoke ring. In early 1963 the police captured its first group of MK soldiers. While they were awaiting trial in Leeukop Prison in Johannesburg, they persuaded their guard to go to the newspaper's offices and borrow money to buy them tobacco. The guard did so—Schermbrucker gave him R5—and tossed two packets of tobacco into their cell. Unfortunately, they forgot to ask him for matches.[84]

The staff at *New Age* broke the law every day. Almost all of them—especially Fred Carneson, Mary Turok, Michael Harmel, M. P. Naicker, Ruth First and Ivan Schermbrucker—worked in the underground ANC. More seriously, Ebrahim Ismail Ebrahim, Robert Resha, Albie Sachs, Ronnie Kasrils, Wolfie Kodesh, Joe Gqabi and Looksmart Solwandle were active Umkhonto saboteurs.[85]

Clandestine lives overlapped with ordinary *New Age* duties. Govan Mbeki, like Slovo, sat on Umkhonto's High Command. He spent only one day a week laboring at Adderley Street, devoting the other six days to underground work. He had a contact on New Brighton's advisory board who secretly funneled him information about government corruption in the townships, material that later appeared in *New Age*. Not knowing this man was Mbeki's contact, some MK comrades asked Mbeki if they could blow up his house for being a collaborator. Mbeki sternly said no. Accusing Mbeki of being arbitrary, they went over his head to Jack Hodgson in Johannesburg, but luckily Hodgson agreed with Mbeki's decision without knowing Mkeki's reasons.[86]

Curious things would happen at a staffer's home. Rica Hodgson, the chief administrator for *New Age*'s Johannesburg office, lived with her husband Jack in a fourth-floor flat that was Umkhonto's Johannesburg bomb factory. Bags of potash dotted the rooms like dead plants, and Joe Slovo and other MK leaders spent hours grinding the potash with mortars and pestles—as if they were pounding corn to make porridge—until purplish grains coated the carpets and curtains. Jack Hodgson also brought home hundreds of ballpoint pens to practice constructing timing devices.[87]

In Durban, neither M. P. Naicker, the branch manager, nor staffer Ebrahim Ismail Ebrahim knew that the other worked for the underground Communist Party and for Umkhonto.[88] In late October 1962, an MK cell—consisting of Ebrahim, Ronnie Kasrils, Billy Nair, Bruno Mtolo, and Coetsie Naicker, M. P. Naicker's brother—dynamited three electrical pylons in Clairwood. The explosions plunged Durban into total darkness for the night. The next morning, a nonchalant Ebrahim walked into Lodgson House. When the news of the sabotage came on Radio South Africa, M. P. Naicker and Ebrahim discussed covering the story, and Ebrahim told him he would go to Clairwood and photograph the pylons. Ebrahim went to the area and asked locals to direct him to the pylons so it would not appear that he knew where they were. On 8 November 1962 Ebrahim's two large photographs of the fallen pylons ran on the front page of *New Age*.[89]

Immediately after the Pietermaritzburg conference in March 1961, Nelson Mandela went underground. Throughout the next seventeen months, he depended upon the assistance of *New Age*. Although Mandela assiduously courted the mainstream white press in South Africa, as well as British media, he used *New Age* to reach black South Africans. *New Age* dubbed him the Black Pimpernel (named after the French Revolution's Scarlet Pimpernel) for his courage and ability to avoid the police.[90] After the 1961 general strike, the weekly ran an interview on its front page in which Mandela admitted the strike "was not the national success I had hoped for" (he kept on telling the other local and foreign media that it was "a tremendous success"), and he hinted at the formation of Umkhonto: "If peaceful protests like these are to be put down by mobilization of the army and the police then the people might be forced to use other methods of struggle." It was the first intimation South Africans got that the ANC might resort to violence, and a month later the ANC national executive committee criticized Mandela for going public with a policy to which it had not yet agreed.[91] Four weeks later, *New Age* scooped the world by being the first publication to print Mandela's famous "Letter from the Underground," in which he announced his intention not to surrender to the authorities.[92] It was a stirring piece of writing. "The struggle is my life," Mandela wrote. "I will continue fighting for freedom until the end of my days."

Beate Lipman then wrote a long story on Mandela's wife, Winnie, and their two children, aged two and five months. "Wife's Brave Acceptance of Nelson's Decision," ran the headline, with a large photograph of Winnie, Zindiswa, and Zenani. Winnie laughed about how unsettled their married life had been, noting that since they were married in 1958 they had never been together on the day of their wedding anniversary.[93]

In August 1961 Mandela used the pages of the weekly to fight regional political battles. In 1954 ANC members in the Orange Free State helped start a political party called the Basutoland Congress Party, which soon became the major African nationalist movement in the British colony.[94] After Sharpeville, the BCP took in many fleeing Congress members, but in 1961, matters soured. The ANC exiles criticized BCP policy. The BCP retaliated by passing a resolution that no BCP member could be a member of another organization and expelling most of the ANC exiles.[95] Then the president of the BCP, Ntsu Mokhehle told BCP Youth Leaguers that the ANC was destroying his party. He alleged that the ANC was forming cells in Basutoland; that John Motloheloa, the *New Age* seller, was organizing a Basutoland Communist Party; that Mandela had scampered to Maseru during the failed May stay-away; and that the ANC exiles were "cowards."[96]

The week after reporting Mokhehle's speech, *New Age* ran an article headlined "Mandela Replies to Mokhehle." Despite being underground and hounded by the largest manhunt ever launched in South Africa, Mandela had penned "a written statement that reached the *New Age* office on Monday morning this week." Defending the ANC, Mandela reminded Mokhehle of a recent meeting in which they had "agreed to work for complete unity and harmony," and he denied having ever left South Africa during the stay-away, calling the allegation "devoid of all truth and most reckless." When Mokhehle further abused the ANC in a Johannesburg daily, Mandela wrote another statement ("sent in to *New Age* over the week-end") that said "Mr. Mokhehle is taking advantage of the illegality of the ANC to make frivolous accusations against it in hope that no voice will be raised in its defense." In reference to his present status underground, he added, "As for my own personal position, I would like to point out that not for one single moment have I left the country since the May strike. South Africans have fed and sheltered me."[97]

New Age kept the topic in the news by printing a dozen letters to the editor. One Basuto in Johannesburg wrote that "Mokhehle is a tried and principled leader. He does not take his orders from Moscow or Kruschov [*sic*] as your paper does."[98] The ANC itself sent Barrack Street a letter, "the latest shot fired in the battle" between the BCP and the Congress.[99] (An interesting coda to the story was that when Mandela was inaugurated as President of South Africa in 1994, one of his well-wishers was the prime minister of Lesotho, Ntsu Mokhehle.)[100]

Defending the ANC through the pages of *New Age* was easy for Mandela, since he was in close contact with staffers. In the first months of hiding, he spent the night at the homes of a number of staffers. In Port Elizabeth he stayed with sports reporter Dennis Brutus for a couple of nights, teaching Brutus's sons how to box.[101] During the May stay-away, Ruth First was his minder. She arranged for a British television reporter to film an interview with Mandela—it was the first time he would appear on television and the last until 1990—at the Zoo Lake home of a University of Witwatersrand professor, and guided a host of print reporters, including Stanley Uys, to various safe houses in Hillbrow and Yeoville to meet with Mandela.[102]

In July 1961 Wolfie Kodesh took over as minder of the Black Pimpernel.[103] After all the cold nights he slept on the Observatory Golf Course during the emergency, Kodesh rented a ground-floor flat at 52 West Street in Berea. By accident, the safe house was needed. At an ANC meeting in Yeoville involving Walter Sisulu, J. B. Marks, and Mandela, Kodesh overheard an elderly white neighbor telephone the police. Because Mandela's driver was due back in three hours, Kodesh spirited him away to Berea.

For two months, Mandela stayed with Kodesh. At dawn, Mandela rose from a cot in the living room—he refused to kick Kodesh out of his own bed—put on sweats, and ran in place for an hour to get exercise.[104] After breakfast, Kodesh drove into town and worked at Commissioner Street until lunchtime, then told First he was off to do a story and doubled back to the flat. Mandela and Kodesh spent the afternoons talking and planning in the flat with the blinds tightly drawn. In the evenings, Kodesh drove Mandela to meetings in his black 1949 Chevrolet.

It was a tense, exhilarating time. One night Kodesh led Mandela to an old brickworks near Kempton Park to test a new bomb constructed by Jack Hodgson. After trying out some improvised Molotov cocktails in one building, Hodgson then exploded his nitroglycerin bomb (using one of his ballpoint pens for the timing device) in a pit, which sent up a mushroom cloud of soil and debris.[105] This was the first Umkhonto explosion, and although it made them proud, it also sent them hurrying out of the brickworks.

Housing an African in a whites-only neighborhood was a security risk. Mandela, like many Africans, enjoyed *amasi*, fermented milk, and placed a pint of milk on Kodesh's windowsill to sour in the highveld sun. One evening, Kodesh overheard two passing Africans talking about the glass and the improbable fact that an African was living in Berea.[106] Another problem was the fact that a Zulu housecleaner, employed by the building's landlords, routinely came to clean the flat. Mandela and Kodesh had tea with him, with Mandela calling himself David Motsamayi and pretending to be a scholar waiting for an overseas scholarship. The cleaner became a friend and even ran errands for Mandela. A few weeks later, though, Kodesh thought they were discovered when he saw the cleaner reading a magazine with pictures of Mandela and headlines reading "Black Pimpernel Still At Large." It was obvious the cleaner knew who Kodesh's roommate was, but Mandela assured Kodesh that he would never give him away.[107]

Mandela was right. The cleaner did not inform on him; but the night after the fermented milk incident, Kodesh drove Mandela to a white doctor's house and deposited him there. After a few weeks there and then in Natal, Mandela moved to a new Umkhonto safe house on a farm in Rivonia outside Johannesburg. There he lived with Michael Harmel. During the 1960 emergency, Harmel had proved to be a difficult companion in hiding, and more than once had violated critical security measures. At Rivonia it was more of the same, and one night Mandela came back to the farm after a meeting to find all the house's lights on, the front door open, the radio loudly playing, and Harmel asleep in his bed.[108]

In January 1962 Mandela slipped over the border into Bechuanaland. For the next half year he toured around Africa and Europe, meeting with presidents and foreign ministers, and holding planning sessions with ANC officials. The weekly broke the story of Mandela's departure from South Africa when Tennyson Makiwane reported on Mandela's arrival in Addis Ababa for a conference. "Will Return on Completion of African Tour," assured the headline.[109] In March, *New Age* ran a photograph of "Tambo and Mandela Reunited," a picture of the two leaders smiling in the Ethiopian sun.

In July 1962 the Black Pimpernel slipped back into the country. On 5 August 1962 the police caught Mandela and Cecil Williams, the *New Age* supporter and playwright, on a highway in Natal.[110]

"Release Nelson Mandela" trumpeted *New Age*, when the police announced the arrest two days later. The weekly ran photographs of Mandela, his wife Winnie, protesters at Durban's city hall, and a slogan spray-painted on a Durban fence: "Free Mandela." Winnie Mandela, the weekly said in reference to the gossip flying through the country about who might have betrayed her husband, "has asked *New Age* to appeal to people to repudiate any person starting wild rumours about the arrest of her husband." *New Age* highlighted his subsequent trial, where he appeared in a Xhosa leopard-skin cloak and quoted his eloquent plea in mitigation, which no other South African newspaper quoted in full.[111]

One of the few legal entities functioning in the country, *New Age* thrust a powerful, public fist into the South African sky. "The paper became after the bannings the standard-bearer, if you like, of the entire liberation movement in South Africa," said Fred Carneson. "There it was, like a bloody pole stuck on top of the hill. A fortress, it was. Everybody saw it. It was an enormous source of encouragement."[112]

Some of the news in the weekly was not particularly dramatic. Brian Bunting still analyzed parliamentary bills, and a 1962 "guest editorial" signed by Bunting, Carneson, and Ray Alexander protested the rise in defense spending in the national budget.[113] Alexander, under her pseudonym E. R. Braverman, continued to cover trade-union news, reviewed a book on the Sharpeville massacre, and wrote an obituary for veteran trade unionist Joey Fourie.[114]

But much of the material was passionate. When the long-expected Treason Trial acquittals were announced in March 1961, Bunting ran photographs of jubilant men and women hugging outside the magistrate's court.[115] Banishment, another insidious tool of the apartheid regime, became a hot-button issue. The newspaper had long worried about banishment camps—makeshift huts in remote, uninhabited regions of the country where Pretoria dumped opponents. In 1956 Ruth First traveled to the Frenchdale detention camp in the Northern Cape, where she interviewed a banished ANC man.[116] In 1959 *New Age* ran a five-photograph spread on a banishment camp and covered the roller-coaster story of Elizabeth Mafekeng, an ANC leader who, threatened with banishment, fled to Basutoland.[117] In 1961 *New Age* spearheaded a pursuit for twenty banished men who could not be found; some had been missing for as long as eight years.[118]

Helen Joseph then took on the story. In 1962, hours after she was freed from a five-year banning order that had restricted her to Johannesburg, the Congress of Democrats leader motored out of town on assignment for *New*

Age. Joseph traveled 8,000 miles in two months, searching for the men and women banished by Pretoria; she found thirty-eight of the official list of forty (a total of 116 people had been banished over the years). One eighty-year-old man, who had fought for South Africa in the First World War, lived alone in a tin shack a thousand miles from his home. Another man had been banished, released, and banished again; Joseph had learned, during her travels, that the man's wife had died, and she had the painful task of informing him of his loss. The banished, she wrote in her *New Age* series "A Journey to the Living Dead," "sit there in the desert sun and the dry hot wind waiting for death or release, whichever comes first."[119]

Black Africa also burst onto the scene. The newspaper had always been interested in life beyond the Limpopo River, but the curiosity had been mostly superficial. In 1939 Betty Radford initiated a feature called "In Darkest Africa," in which readers sent in reports from other newspapers and the best contributors were given original Vic Clapham cartoons.[120] After a few months the column failed, as readers apparently could not find enough clippings. "Pan-African Review," a feature H. A. Naidoo cobbled together from news items, appeared after the Second World War, but it too lasted only a short while.[121]

New Age exhibited a renewed interest after Ghana became the first African colony to gain independence in 1957. Bunting launched another news-clipping column, "Africa Round-Up," and Lionel Forman sometimes devoted some of his international-news summary to Africa. In 1959 Bunting ran two new features, "Know Your Continent" and "Africa on the March," and inaugurated an annual "Africa Day" issue in April. Two years later he started a column called "Africa Forum," in which readers were given space to discuss "problems facing Africa."[122]

Secondhand clippings by then no longer sufficed, and staff writers traveled to neighboring countries to personally report: Bunting made trips to South-West Africa in 1959 and Basutoland in 1961; Ruth First went to SWA and Bechuanaland in 1961; Joe Gqabi visited Swaziland and Basutoland in 1961; and Wolfie Kodesh visited Basutoland in 1960.[123] Victor Zaza wrote insightful letters from Lusaka, and *New Age* renewed its early 1940s contacts in Rhodesia and secured a correspondent in Salisbury.[124] After the ANC went into exile, *New Age* enlisted Congress members to file reports. Oliver Tambo wrote a profile on Jomo Kenyatta in 1961, and Tennyson Makiwane posted articles from a half dozen different datelines.[125] The weekly even received firsthand stories from the seminal 1962 Kampala Conference, at which the greatest African writers of the age met.[126]

The weekly did not fear taking sides in the decolonization process. The war in Algeria received full-page treatment, and many liberation movements, like the Zanzibar Nationalist Party, Frelimo in Mozambique and Swapo in South-West Africa, sent statements to Barrack Street. After the 1960 emergency, one of the first pieces of news in the unbanned *New Age* was a long report on the Meueda Massacre in Mozambique.[127] The newspaper started to profile liberation leaders who would soon run their countries—starting with a 1955 piece on Kwame Nkrumah, the founder of Ghana, and subsequently Kenneth Kaunda (Zambia), Jomo Kenyatta (Kenya), and Julius Nyerere (Tanzania), as well as letters to the editor from Sam Nujoma (Namibia) and Hastings Banda (Malawi).[128] King Sobhuza II offered *New Age* an exclusive statement about business activities in the Kingdom of Swaziland.[129] "We took it quite seriously," said Albie Sachs. "We were the only ones to support the nationalist movements. We sometimes had problems with individual leaders. I recall a dust-up with Brian over Nkrumah, who I thought was reactionary, married to an American woman. But Brian said, 'No, we can't go that sort of route. It's not up to us to decide.'"[130]

A bold example of *New Age*'s attitude was the black-and-white map of Africa it produced and inserted into the 22 June 1961 issue. At the bottom were fifty African nations, listed with their capitals, their populations—total and "Non-African"—and their governing status. Shaded in black on the map were the twenty-nine "Free" countries, and in white, the twenty-one states "still under white or colonial domination." In November 1962, Bunting ran a photograph of Joshua Nkomo in which the Rhodesian leader was pointing to the wall of his hut—he lived under twenty-four-hour house arrest—where the *New Age* map was tacked. "The black ink on the map is running down Africa," he said with a smile.[131]

The rise to premiership, house arrest, torture and murder of Patrice Lumumba in the Congo was a particularly important news story for *New Age*. In June 1960 Lumumba became prime minister of Congo, Africa's largest nation, after leading the independence movement against Belgium. "The tall, rake-thin young man with a small goatee beard and horn-rimmed spectacles," as *New Age* described him, was overthrown in a coup d'état led by Joseph Mobuto, and killed in January 1961.[132] Full-page obituaries, strident editorials, and headlines reading "Patrice Lumumba—Murdered by the Imperialists" dominated the weekly.

Local politics complicated the reporting. After the coup, but before his murder, *New Age* pounced on Patrick Duncan for supporting the Belgian authorities and Mobuto in a *Contact* article. "Evidently believing that any stick, no matter how dirty, is good enough with which to beat his enemy," editorialized Bunting, "Mr Duncan is spitting in the face of all genuine African patriots. . . . [He] always shows a fine disregard for facts. . . . It is obvious that Mr Duncan's anti-communist blinkers let no light through."[133] Letters both for and against the attack, including one from Duncan, arrived at Barrack Street.[134]

Nelson Mandela discovered *New Age*'s impact in Africa on his fourteen-nation tour through the continent in 1962. In Cairo, he met with President Nasser and his officials. They were angry with *New Age* for its attacks on Egyptian rule, including a 1961 article that reported the torture of political prisoners at a Cairo jail.[135] "The officials I saw," Mandela recalled, "expressed criticism of articles appearing in *New Age* which dealt with General Nasser's attacks on communism, but I told them that *New Age* did not necessarily express the policy of our movement, and that I would take up this complaint with *New Age* and try and use my influence to change their line, because it was not our duty to say in what manner any state should achieve its freedom."[136] Nasser even replied to *New Age* after it published an open letter from Cecil Williams about the political situation in Egypt.

Another flag that flew from the *New Age* pole on the hill was in Mpondoland. One of the justifications for the turn to armed struggle was that rural African consciousness had suddenly been radicalized to a new, revolutionary degree. The countryside was in revolt, and Umkhonto we Sizwe, so went the argument, would ride the wave of anger and mobilization. The evidence was the Mpondoland uprising. An isolated, mountainous region in northern Transkei, Mpondoland had remained outside colonial control for most of the nineteenth century; Great Britain took over the Cape in 1805, and yet it exerted no real jurisdiction over Mpondoland until 1894. After 1948 Pretoria tried to take control of the region, and the Mpondos retaliated by not paying taxes, burning huts of government informers and boycotting shops in the Mpondoland capital of Bizana (Oliver Tambo's hometown). In October 1960 five thousand Mpondos marched through Bizana, led by an elderly man carrying a black flag in mourning for comrades who had been killed by the police.[137]

In November 1960, unable to quell the uprising, the government declared a state of emergency in Mpondoland. Police raided peasants' homes, torched kraals and administered electric shocks to prisoners. Helicopters dropped tear gas on illegal meetings. No residents could enter or leave the district without permission, and migrant workers coming home for the

December holidays found themselves in jail for having entered the area without a permit.[138] The Crown sentenced thirty Mpondoland leaders to death.

The story became specific in the person of Anderson Khumani Ganyile. In January 1960 the Nationalists took control of Fort Hare and expelled a number of politicized students, including Ganyile, a twenty-five-year-old ANC Youth Leaguer and friend of Govan Mbeki. Ganyile returned to Bizana and was detained for four months during the Sharpeville emergency. Upon his release in August 1960, he became one of the leaders directing the Mpondoland revolt and acted as an interpreter for Rowley Arenstein, a lawyer for many accused Mpondos.

Ganyile kept closely in touch with *New Age*. He exchanged telegrams and letters with both Mbeki and M. P. Naicker, and guided Mbeki, Joe Gqabi, and Eli Weinberg around Mpondoland. "Civil War in the Transkei: Murder and Arson as People Fight Bantu Authorities" headlined a 22 September 1960 article written by Mbeki. Weinberg's photographs were masterpieces of photojournalism, with the Mpondos on horseback, sjamboks raised high in salute, etched against the rolling Transkei hills.

On 7 November 1960, while selling copies of *New Age* outside Bizana's magistrate court, Ganyile was arrested.[139] The police deported him via Johannesburg to a detention camp near Mafeking in the Northern Cape. Gqabi followed Ganyile on the Mafeking-bound prison train and, at a whistle-stop in Krugersdorp, managed to interview him.[140]

Although the story might have ended there, in January 1961 Ganyile escaped from the camp and fled into Basutoland. *New Age* celebrated Ganyile's freedom with a photograph of him and John Motloheloa outside a Maseru café.[141] The story unexpectedly continued. The next word from Ganyile was a note scrawled on a scrap of paper that arrived at the Lodgson House in Durban. It said that six South African policemen—crossing an international border in violation of Basutoland's sovereignty—had raided Ganyile's home in Quacha's Nek and smuggled him, his brother, and a friend back into South Africa (the house was only fifty yards from the border.)[142] Ganyile smuggled out the note from solitary confinement in Umtata, the capital city in the Transkei.

His only hope was for *New Age* to publicize the case. Naicker wrote a front-page article on the kidnapping and traveled to Quacha's Nek to see his hut, where he found blood on blankets left behind.[143] Nelson Mandela—in Ethiopia at the time, addressing an international conference—called Ganyile "one of the country's rising freedom stars."[144] The ANC organized a demonstration outside Parliament in Cape Town, and in London the matter was raised in the House of Commons.[145]

Eventually, Pretoria freed Ganyile and allowed him to return to Basutoland. Eric Louw, the minister of foreign affairs, apologized to the British government, and Ganyile sued Pretoria for damages. On 8 February 1962 the weekly ran Ganyile's full-page article "How I Was Kidnapped." "Yes fascism was at the door," he wrote, describing the incident in Quacha's Nek. "The long and the short of it is that they started throwing stones at the door and windows. Bottles and an ax were the only weapons we had to defend ourselves." The whole Ganyile incident exposed the lengths to which Pretoria was willing to go in order to suppress its opponents, as well as *New Age*'s continued ability to rouse a reply.[146]

Ganyile's experience, unfortunately, was not unique for *New Age* staff members.

One simple fact of post-Sharpeville life loomed largest: everyone got arrested. It was almost a joke. In 1961 Walter Sisulu persuaded a young insurance agent named Brian Somana to join *New Age* as a reporter, but he soon missed the quiet life of premiums and deductibles.[147] In his first four months at President Street, Somana was incarcerated four times. While taking photographs of a group of handcuffed Africans at the Johannesburg railway station, the police arrested him under the 1959 Prisons Act forbidding photographs about prisons or prisoners (a law passed in part because of sedulous *New Age* muckraking about prison conditions). Somana was acquitted on that charge, but still fined £4 for abusive language. Weeks later, he again was on the wrong side of the Prisons Act and was again arrested while taking photographs of Indian leader Ahmed Kathrada reporting to a police station while under house arrest. This time the luckless reporter lost the case and was fined £15.

The police arrested *New Age* sellers. In 1961 at Westbury Station, a black railway policeman attacked Andries "General China" Chamile, a star *New Age* seller in Johannesburg. He bashed General China on the head with a baton, dragged him across the railway lines, and then placed him under arrest. General China brought charges and was awarded £60 in damages. Amsden Slomko, an eighty-nine-year-old ANC member, started selling *New Age* at the beginning of 1961; he went to prison four times in the first five months on the job, including one six-week detention. "The police on the Western Rand know me," he said, "and hate me because I sell *New Age*."[148]

Once, Rica Hodgson and Ahmed Kathrada went on a fundraising trip in the Transvaal. Special Branch detectives spotted their Land Rover, pulled them over, and while searching the car, discovered a copy of Ruth First's pamphlet on Bethal in a side pocket. "They thought they had something there," Hodgson remembered. But after a few hours, they let them go because possessing the booklet was not yet against the law.[149]

One afternoon, Walter Sisulu and Michael Harmel walked out of Mercantile House after a meeting at *New Age*. Harmel was carrying a manila folder containing the constitutions of Swaziland and Bechuanaland, which he was using for a *New Age* article. At the corner of Commissioner and President Streets, three Security Branch detectives drove up and pounced on the two men. They body-searched both of them, bullied Harmel and jailed Sisulu on a pass offense for twelve days.[150]

Twelve days became a short detention. In 1962 Mary Butcher Turok was jailed for eighteen months for working for the ANC. At the same time, nineteen-year Commissioner Street assistant Aaron Molete was arrested and sentenced to five years in prison for furthering the aims of the Communist Party. In 1961 Joe Gqabi, working on a story about a pro-government chief in the Eastern Transvaal with Andrew Mlangeni, was arrested and detained for eleven days before being charged; at their trial, Gqabi and Mlangeni were found not guilty of making subversive statements about the chief, but were fined £10 for entering an African trust area illegally. (During the 1961 May stay-away, Gqabi had the bad luck of hitching a ride with an undercover policeman; again he was detained, but this time just for one day.) Leonard Mdingi, on assignment in the Transkei, was detained for three months during the Mpondoland emergency. Ebrahim Ismail Ebrahim was arrested and found guilty of painting slogans on the wall of a Durban bakery. The police detained Alex La Guma in Cape Town during the May stay-away for twelve days. In Port Elizabeth, *New Age* staffers Mountain Ngqungwana and James Kati were arrested and held overnight; Kati had particularly awful stretches: he endured three arrests in one five-day period, and four arrests in another nineteen-day stretch.[151]

In the last issue of 1961, an article appeared in *New Age* with the byline Walter Sisulu, who was then underground. The police arrested Fred Carneson, acting as editor of the weekly, when he refused to answer any questions about the origins of the article. After eight days in jail, Carneson was released on bail. He eventually won the ensuing court case and did not reveal where Sisulu was.[152]

Govan Mbeki overshadowed all others in his tendency to wind up in jail. In 1961 he was arrested in Pretoria's first attempt to try former ANC leaders on charges of furthering the cause of the ANC. The charges, after a trial in Johannesburg, were withdrawn for lack of evidence. In January 1962, while at a friend's home in New Brighton, Mbeki was again arrested. For the following five months—three in solitary confinement—he was held on charges of instructing men in the making of homemade explosives, and for possession of potassium chlorate and permanganate. Mbeki was acquitted after a state witness, who had allegedly been beaten into a confession, withdrew his testimony.[153] (While in jail, Mbeki wrote the bulk of his book on the Mpondoland uprising, *South Africa: The Peasants' Revolt*.)

Afterwards, Mbeki thwarted the police regularly when they tried to arrest him on pass-law offenses; as *New Age* branch manager he signed his own passbook, so his papers were always legally in order.[154] Still, he had no answer but to run when, in October 1962, policemen came to his home in New Brighton to serve a house-arrest order. Mbeki fled out the back door and went into hiding. He took on the code name "Dhlamini" and eventually found his way to MK's headquarters at Lilliesleaf Farm in Rivonia. Mbeki recalled the confusion he caused: "Brian didn't know. I didn't tell him I went underground. He had no idea where I was, but I knew he was angry because so little was coming from Port Elizabeth for *New Age*. And then, once I left, nothing at all."[155]

The Security Branch hammered at the weekly. Detectives raided the newspaper's offices on a weekly basis.[156] They visited Pioneer Press regularly, always in search, as detectives said, "for communist literature." Once, in August 1962, the police raided homes of *New Age* staff members in three cities at the same time. Wolfie Kodesh reported that they spent two hours rummaging through his flat; when they were leaving, they frisked him and emptied his pockets.[157] It was hard to trust newcomers when Special Branch spies abounded. With a puritanically small amount of detail, *New Age* reported on female police spies hired to entrap ANC men—"attractive nice-time girls who attend house-parties in an apparent mood of gaiety."[158] In 1961 Ruth First visited South-West Africa. After four days of unhampered research and interviewing, the Security Branch learned of her presence in Windhoek. "The scrutiny never faltered," she wrote. "The trail to the dry-cleaner and the shoemaker, the skulking next to the telephone booth, both ends of the road and every exit of the hotel patrolled, detectives following me to the airport, to the post office to buy stamps, watching me at breakfast, interviewing people I'd seen."[159] M. P. Naicker endured harassment about his work on the Mpondoland rebellion.[160] In Cape Town, the police arrested

Brian Bunting for trespassing when he went to the exclusive Mount Nelson Hotel to secure an interview with Dag Hammarskjöld, the secretary-general of the United Nations.[161] Bunting awoke one night to find his car, parked in his driveway, burning in a blaze of smoke and flame.[162] A bomb planted in Dennis Brutus's front garden burned much of his house.[163]

Turbulence from the underground ANC also buffeted the newspaper's staff, as Govan Mbeki was not the only staffer who abandoned the weekly. Joe Gqabi crossed into Bechuanaland in March 1962 and, along with Wilton Mkwayi, was a part of the first MK training group.[164] Robert Resha left in June 1961 to become the ANC's ambassador for Africa, stationed in Dar es Salaam.[165] One critical loss that had little to do with underground work was Alex La Guma. In July 1962 Pretoria, incensed by the publication of La Guma's novel *A Walk in the Night*, prohibited him from publishing any writings. On 28 June 1962 "Up My Alley" appeared for the final time. Below the usual headline was stamped a single word: "PROHIBITED."[166]

All remaining staff members operated under some sort of banning orders. Both Dawood and Fatima Seedat had five-year bans that specifically banned them from being with someone else who was banned—so it was, strictly speaking, illegal for the couple to see each other.[167] Most staff members were restricted to certain magistrate districts and forbidden to enter African locations, townships or hostels. In early 1961, the government specifically ordered Kodesh not to enter Alexandra township.[168] Ruth First's prohibitions sounded like a bad joke: "Over the years I had been served with banning orders that prohibited me from leaving Johannesburg . . . from entering African townships . . . from attending meetings, so that others had to take the notes and photographs, from writing anything for publication, so that I had to sit at my desk with a legal opinion that sub-editing someone else's copy might just slip past the ban. Working in the midst of these ministerial bans and under continuous raids and scrutiny was like going to work each day in a mine field."[169]

Minefields traditionally yielded riches, but for the weekly, only suffering was brought to the surface. Circulation, before the emergency at around 28,000, dipped to under 20,000.[170] Advertising revenue was negligible.[171] The Indian traders and shopkeepers were less willing to support the weekly.[172]

Money arrived in sudden bursts. When Bunting was honored with a £150 prize from the International Organisation for Journalists in 1961, he donated the entire sum to *New Age*. Carneson still printed pamphlets, including one by Hilda Bernstein on her trip to China, and hawked Ceylon tea and men's and women's Swiss watches—"Shockproof, Waterproof, Unbreakable Mainspring, 12 months Guarantee." With Sam Kahn's exit, Carneson ran *New Age*'s Christmas Eve Dance at a town hall. He also offered £3 for the best caption for a cartoon of a police constable reporting to his superior.[173]

In 1962 Barrack Street carried a debt of £3,000. In August, Bunting borrowed money and dismissed a number of administrative staff members, a "drastic and dangerous pruning" that left them with "the barest of bare skeletons."[174] Even with the downsizing, the weekly almost closed at the end of the month; Bunting gave notice to the remaining staff and prepared a statement of closure. Adding insult to injury, *Die Vaderland* and the *Cape Argus* both called Barrack Street to ask if the weekly had gone under.[175]

Salvation came from London. In August 1954 Max Joffe and other friends of the South African Left founded the London *New Age* Committee. The LNAC raised hundreds of pounds sterling for the weekly by printing *New Age* Christmas cards and holding parties, including an annual New Year's Eve fundraiser.[176] After the emergency, the committee was the first place South Africans exiled in London turned to, since no other functioning organization existed. Yusuf Dadoo took over the chair of the committee.[177] Two hundred contributors attended a LNAC party where Paul Robeson, the famous African American singer and actor, gave a recital, singing "Joe Hill" and a song of the Warsaw Ghetto; a £200 check and a photograph of Robeson with the inscription "Best Wishes to *New Age*—Paul Robeson" soon arrived at Barrack Street.[178]

In February 1962 the newspaper celebrated its silver jubilee with two dances: one was at Cape Town's Banqueting Hall and the other was at the 4 Aces Club in Fordsburg (the Fischers could no longer host their annual dance because of banning orders, though they did throw one final wild party on the night the Treason Trial concluded in March 1961). Rica Hodgson wrote a letter to friends of the weekly asking for a twenty-fifth-anniversary donation. "It may not be good manners to solicit birthday gifts," she wrote, but "our greatest danger is that we may slip by default." On 22 March *New Age* issued a special twelve-page jubilee edition. Inside, Albert Luthuli said, "I have not always agreed with everything it says, but on questions affecting the non-white peoples in South Africa, *New Age* has been and continues to be the fighting mouthpiece of African aspirations." Bunting devoted two pages to quotations from the early days of the *Guardian*, and one page to birthday greetings from around the world. He stridently confirmed the weekly's goals: "We refuse to accept slavery and death as the price to be paid for apartheid. We demand that the Government abandon policies which lead to an intensification of race hatred and violence. There is room for all in South Africa to live side by side in peace and harmony—but not on the basis of apartheid and the warfare state."

The following week, the newspaper ran a photograph of Ebrahim Ismail Ebrahim cutting a birthday cake in Durban with a grinning Ronnie Kasrils watching.[179]

Less than two months later, it looked like there would be no more birthdays. The new minister of justice, Balthazar Johannes Vorster, stood in Parliament to debate his new Sabotage Bill. Vorster, who had spent almost two years in jail and then a year under house arrest for sabotage against the South African government during the Second World War, furiously waved a copy of the twenty-fifth-anniversary issue of *New Age*.[180] This should be banned, he said: "The *Guardian* was the mouthpiece and propaganda organ of the communists . . . to this day its editor is still an outspoken and active communist. . . . make no secret of the fact that one of the newspapers which ought to be forbidden is this paper, *New Age*, which is the propaganda organ of the Communist Party. . . . It is furthering the aims of communism, and it makes no secret of the fact."[181]

The House roared with approval. Ten days before, Vorster had introduced new legislation that amended Section 6 of the Suppression of Communism Act. It was called the Sabotage Bill, a twenty-one-provision bill that turned South Africa into a police state. It gave the minister the power to ban, house-arrest, and forbid any person from any specific activity. It outlawed strikes, closed the Johannesburg City Hall steps and the Grand Parade to political rallies, and made sabotage a capital offense. Provision 5 was specifically a provision for *New Age*: no new periodical or newspaper could publish without a security deposit of up to £10,000, forfeitable if the newspaper was banned. Vorster slammed shut the loophole that allowed the newspaper to reappear in 1952 and 1954 under a new title.[182]

Two days after Vorster's newspaper-waving speech, a Nationalist MP, Bertie Coetzee, applauded his move to permanently ban the weekly: "I also wish to congratulate the Minister on putting an end to another childishness in this country, and that is that a newspaper like *New Age* can be banned and appear the following day under another name. That is childishness. Surely this country is not a kindergarten. A newspaper which is a danger to the state gets banned by the Minister, and then makes a fool of the state by simply appearing the following day under another name. I wish to congratulate the Minister for the ingenious way in which he has put a stop to this ridiculous situation."[183]

If South Africa was not a kindergarten, Barrack Street was no innocent toddler. Since the Sharpeville emergency, the weekly knew another ban was impending. In October 1960, following the Nationalist victory in the referendum over whether the country should leave the Commonwealth and become an independent republic, Prime Minister Verwoerd said on the radio: "A politically non-conformist press will not be tolerated in the Republic."[184] In early 1961 the police told New Age sellers to stop distributing the newspaper because it had been banned.[185] In August 1961 Eric Louw, the minister of foreign affairs, referred to a story that two reporters and the editor of an Athens newspaper had been jailed for causing, as he said, "alarm and despondency. . . . I wonder if the time has not come for us in this country to follow the example of the Greeks."[186]

Now the wait was over. With four-inch banner headlines, "THIS IS A POLICE STATE," New Age rose to protest its imminent demise.[187] Fred Carneson wrote an open letter to Vorster "to register hereby my formal and emphatic protest." Bunting detailed each provision of the bill and its probable effect on the liberation movement, and in an editorial reiterated the weekly's policies:

New Age insists that it has a right to exist. We have a point of view to put forward which is entitled to be heard.

*We stand for equal rights for all South Africans, an end to apartheid and colour bars, the creation of one integrated South Africa with equal citizenship for all, irrespective of race, creed, or colour.

*We stand for peace and harmony between the nations of the world and the elimination of the last vestiges of colonialism.

*We stand for the right of all peoples to be free from exploitation in any shape or form.

These are the basic principles of decent social living, and we have fought for them in the teeth of Nationalist oppression for all the years of our existence. Now we are to be silenced because the Nats, in their march to the jackboot states, can no longer tolerate any opposition.[188]

With jackboots goose-stepping down Barrack Street, Bunting looked to London for help. On 23 May he typed a letter to Yusuf Dadoo asking for the "maximum possible protest. . . . The essence of the matter, however, is speed. At the moment we can count our future in weeks unless the protest is so overwhelming as to stay the Minister's hand."[189] Dadoo launched a protest campaign in London. As chair of the London *New Age* Committee, he wrote a declaration calling the bill "astonishing," "grim," and "disturbing." Dozens of well-known British writers and politicians signed the declaration, including William Plomer, Basil Davidson, Doris Lessing, Kingsley Amis, Iris Murdoch, Muriel Spark and Robert Bolt.[190] On 7 June 1962 Dadoo sent a copy of the declaration and its signatories to all newspaper editors in the United Kingdom, asking them to write editorials condemning Pretoria.[191]

With the financial crisis of August 1962, the weekly seemed destined to lead itself to the knacker's yard. In September Vorster tightened the noose when he banned the Congress of Democrats. In October he began, starting with Helen Joseph, to house-arrest activists, the same punishment that Vorster himself had endured twenty years before. He placed Rica Hodgson, Sonia Bunting, Alex La Guma, Jack Tarshish, Michael Harmel, Cecil Williams, Rusty Bernstein and Walter Sisulu under twenty-four-hour house arrest for five years. In addition, Vorster forbade those house-arrested to communicate with anyone banned. Since nearly everyone on the *New Age* staff was banned, this meant, as *New Age* wrote, "that inter-office communication will become practically impossible."[192]

To cripple the weekly further, he house-arrested Brian Bunting for thirteen hours a day and forbade him to enter any factory premises—so he could not help Len Lee-Warden put the newspaper to bed at Pioneer. From 6 P.M. to 7 A.M. on weekdays, and from 2 P.M. on Saturday to 7 A.M. Monday, Bunting had to stay in his home above Clifton Beach with his wife, who could not leave at all. Vorster specifically told Bunting that he was not allowed to communicate with Fred Carneson. "Since the two of them work in adjoining offices and are daily in almost constant contact with one another," wrote *New Age* without any understatement, "it will be practically impossible for Mr Bunting to carry out his functions on *New Age*."[193] Of the first twenty people Vorster house-arrested, thirteen were staff members or had direct relationships with *New Age*.[194]

The house arrests represented a new deterioration of civil rights and frightened many South Africans. Alan Paton told the weekly, "These are vicious, barbaric conditions. No one can say now that this is not an imitation of a Nazi country." *New Age* said that "if the paper goes under, the liberation movement will be like a man blinded, sightless in the desert of apartheid."[195]

On Friday, 30 November 1962, nine days after the Paarl riots, Vorster issued a proclamation prohibiting the printing and publication of *New Age*. For the third time in a decade, Pretoria had banned the weekly.

A Cape Town newspaper reporter called Fred Carneson at his home. Moving to a new house that day, he and his wife Sarah were packing boxes. "I got this message at home," Carneson recalled. "I was in the middle of moving from the house where we were staying . . . and we forgot to report to the bloody police. We were both banned, and one part of the banning order was that if you moved you had to advise the police. At that moment they ban the paper, I had to rush into the newspaper office to make all sorts of arrangements, get new things going. . . . We tried to be as legal as we possibly could. And as we stepped out of the door of the office into the street, the bloody police screamed to a halt and arrested my wife and I. Took us to Caledon Square for not reporting."[196] Before getting arrested, Carneson managed to send off telegrams to *New Age* branch offices to stop selling the 29 November edition. For some, the newspaper never even arrived in some places. When Mountain Ngqungwana went to the Port Elizabeth railway station to collect the *New Age* bundles at seven in the morning that Friday, he was told, "The paper is not on the train."[197] That afternoon, detectives raided all four *New Age* offices and homes of staffers, and confiscated all available copies of the newspaper.[198]

Because apartheid was more than ever on other countries' radar screens, protests against the ban popped up everywhere. Not only did he leaders of the Liberal Party, the Progressive Party, SACTU, NIC and the South African Society of Journalists protest, but, the Anti-Apartheid Movement in London objected and on 10 December, Albert Luthuli and Martin Luther King Jr. issued a joint statement that was signed by many prominent Americans.[199] Although the *Rand Daily Mail* did not strongly dissent, a few other South African newspapers supported their fallen colleague. "Besides its ideological alignment which we found distasteful and possibly harmful to the freedom movement in South Africa, *New Age* has over the years been among the staunchest opponents of White Supremacy," Patrick Duncan wrote in *Contact*. "It was a focal point around which a strong body of opposition to apartheid had centred."[200] In Port Elizabeth, the *Evening Post* oddly argued that "the Government's behavior is proving an unearned boon to the communist's cause: from a propaganda point of view, communism in South Africa has 'never had it so good.' The Government is creating the impression among Africans in South Africa and in the rest of the continent that the people chiefly interested in the difficulties created by apartheid are communists."[201] The *Cape Times* editorialized:

The political opposition of *New Age* becomes communism because Mr Vorster chooses to call it communism. He does so without hearing argument, without having to produce evidence, without having to give reasons, subject to no appeal to any impartial authority. How many people outside the ranks of the Nationalist Party will be convinced that Mr Vorster is not simply getting rid of inconvenient political opposition by authoritarian methods which have become so popular in the wilder territories of the new Africa? If this is the reaction, Mr Vorster will have only himself to blame: that is why civilized countries do not close down newspapers until they have evidence acceptable to a court that they are breaking the law.[202]

Reporters crammed into the Barrack Street offices the day of the banning. Carneson told them he was going to sue the government. (As the director of Real Printing and Publishing Company, he did lodge a rather ironic suit against the government, asserting that Vorster had not followed the regulations stipulated in Section 17 of the Suppression of Communism Act—the committee of three, the findings of fact, etc. Dismissing the suit, a magistrate took at face value the minister of justice's assertion that it was contrary to public interest to disclose information on the decision to ban *New Age*.)[203] "I am going to do my best to provide them [*New Age* staffers] with alternative work," Carneson also told reporters. "It is not illegal to produce other publications."[204] But since even Carneson could not pretend that the weekly had £10,000 to register a new newspaper, these sounded like brave but foolish words.

On Thursday, 6 December 1962, six days after the banning of *New Age*, a four-page newspaper called *Spark* came out of Barrack Street. Against all odds, they had done it again. "Communists are the last optimists," Nadine Gordimer wrote, and one more time the people at Barrack Street came out with a new newspaper.[205]

Half a year before, Bunting and Carneson had eyed the Sabotage Bill with trepidation. A proscription surely was in the offing, yet to raise the £10,000 deposit was a nonstarter. They decided to start printing other titles in order to legally have a newspaper ready in case of a ban. Just before the Sabotage Bill became law, Real Printing and Publishing took over two newspapers, *Morning Star* and *Spark*. *Morning Star* had existed in name only, without a single issue published; ten issues of *Spark: The Voice of Oppressed*

Youth had been published by Barney Desai, a coloured activist, in 1952, and four more issues when the ANC had co-opted the fortnightly.[206]

On 25 July 1962 an edition of *Spark* appeared again, and a day later *Morning Star* made its debut. Each ran four pages. Desai registered the newspapers, and then Bunting, as "editor" of the two monthlies, formed a new company, Table View Printing and Publishing, and officially bought *Morning Star* and *Spark*. In August the newspapers appeared again. In accordance with South African law, Bunting published *Morning Star* and *Spark* once a month to maintain their registration status. As Bunting recalled, "we'd shove overmatter, extra bits from *New Age* into them. Anything that was laying around the office. It was not something we'd pay much attention to."[207] Full-page poems, enlarged photographs, long articles on the evils of tobacco and liquor and reprints of newspaper cuttings filled the two monthlies.

Morning Star and *Spark* readers, though, did not care about the haphazard look or unrelated content. There were no readers. Len Lee-Warden printed only a dozen copies of each issue. Bunting sent a copy to the legal deposit libraries that, by South African law, received each registered periodical in the country.[208] No one bought, sold or read the ghost newspapers. The deception was legal, as long as the government did not discover that instead of fifteen thousand copies in circulation, there were just five. In October 1962, playing along with the charade, Bunting lowered the price of both *Spark* and *Morning Star* from three pennies to one penny, "owing to strong pressure from our readers."[209]

If librarians had been watching carefully, on 6 December they would have noticed an explosion in the hitherto sleepy *Spark*.[210] Four pages quadrupled to sixteen. The price shot up from that reader-requested one penny to sixpence. The monthly became a weekly. Nineteen thousand copies were ordered from Pioneer Press, rather than the usual dozen.[211] *New Age* subscribers received the familiar letter: "In order to offset the loss of business caused by the banning of *New Age*, our Company has come to an arrangement with the proprietors of *Spark*. We shall send you this newspaper in the future, subject, naturally, to your explicit or implicit agreement."[212] And with that, the sixth newspaper in the *Cape Guardian* succession appeared in South Africa.

Naturally, *Spark*'s existence was exceptionally tenuous. An infuriated Vorster passed an amendment in December 1962 making it illegal to be in possession of a banned newspaper. As the government had banned only three newspapers, the law pertained only to the *Guardian*, *Advance*, and *New Age*. *Spark* told its readers to destroy all back issues. Friends lit a summer fire in their fireplaces, sent them overseas or buried them. Hilda Bernstein torched her copies in a derelict bathtub in her garden.[213] *Spark* ran a poem by Arthur Nortje called "On Throwing Away a Bundle of Old Newspapers," written on Christmas Day 1962 about the loss of the back issues:

> *These pages mirrored the soul of a nation awakening; they taught us*
> > *to cast out*
> *Hatred of one another, and fear of tyranny.*
> *No wonder then they wish these printed sheets destroyed, expunged*
> *As if they never were.*
> *Yes, paper can be burnt or thrown away. But these records shall not perish*
> *Or be obliterated. They'll live forever in the people's memories, the safe*
> > *Guardian*
> *Of our heritage, as we Advance to a New Age, cherishing the Spark*
> > *of liberation*
> *Struck from the anvil of struggle by the pioneers.*[214]

With almost the entire staff under house arrest, the burden at Barrack Street fell to Fred Carneson. On 3 December 1962 he wrote a letter to Yusuf Dadoo in London, outlining the newspaper's problems:

> The banning of *New Age*, the house-arrest orders on Brian, Sonia and Rica, together with restrictions on others who have helped us in the past, have combined to create a crisis far worse than anything we have ever experienced in the past. . . . We are prepared to face all this and carry on, sailing ever more dangerously close to the wind, for as long as it is humanly possible, exploiting every legal loop-hole that exists. Our plans, however, will all come to naught—and that before the end of the month—unless we receive immediate and substantial financial assistance from our friends overseas. To give you an idea of how serious the situation is, I need only mention that we were ready to announce the closure of *New Age* in the issue of 29 November. Only strenuous efforts on the part of our depleted staff . . . saved *New Age* from the indignity of having to close down before the Nationalists banned it. Our local resources are now exhausted. Even if we had double the personnel now available we would definitely not be able to raise anything like what we need to carry on. Some of our staff have not been paid for October, and it is a battle to find money even for street-sellers' wages.[215]

Carneson asked Dadoo to raise between £10,000 and £15,000, and to send at least £3,000 by the end of December.

Meanwhile, *Spark* soldiered on.[216] Desperate for staff, the newspaper advertised for "young people to act as voluntary trainees—reporters and editorial assistants, for several days a week. You'll be especially useful if you can use a camera and have one; if you can type; if you've done journalism before."[217] No one came forward. The remaining staff juggled their political activity with their reporting. Ruth First worked half days, spending her afternoons at meetings at Rivonia.

Intimidation was commonplace. At eleven in the evening on the last day of the year, the Special Branch crashed into the Buntings' home expecting to find the usual New Year's Eve party—something that now, with the house arrests, would have been illegal. Instead they found Brian and Sonia reading quietly. One detective even looked under the beds of sleeping children—checking, as it were, for Reds under the beds.[218]

A new commander, as of January 1963, reinvigorated the inept Special Branch, and they attacked the newspaper with a fresh vigor. Detectives visited nearly every day. Late in January, the police arrived simultaneously at the Cape Town, Durban, and Port Elizabeth offices, armed with warrants saying they had reason to believe an offense was being committed in the offices.[219]

Spark's content was the same as *New Age*'s. The newspaper reported on ANC and Umkhonto we Sizwe activities. Bunting congratulated Cissie Gool, the "Queen of Politics," on earning her law degree and announced the death of her uncle, Goolam Gool, a founder of the National Liberation League, noting that *Torch*, "a paper of which he was a founder, has maintained an eloquent silence."[220] *Spark* reported that Lovedale was on strike, that the police were still raiding the townships, and that women were still protesting against the passes. "Africa and the World in Pictures" was the title of a New Year's spread of photographs, and "Sten Guns on Sunday Afternoon" described the story of gun-wielding policemen bullying the barbers, buskers and weightlifters at Zoo Lake in Johannesburg.[221] Howard Lawrence wrote a column entitled "Bright Sparks," which followed the same tone and style as La Guma's "Up My Alley." Martin "Chris" Hani wrote an article on the Paarl riots. "My purpose is to help to arrive at a clear analysis of the situation and not to be cynical," he added in a letter to the editor. "We should understand quite clearly that to seek cheap martyrdom at this stage of the struggle is naive and criminal. We must not evade the challenge which faces us." [222]

On 22 February, Vorster delivered the death blow. He issued a proclamation prohibiting all banned persons and those who were former members of now-banned organizations from belonging to a group that prepared, compiled, printed, published, or disseminated any printed matter. Anyone remotely associated with the liberation struggle could now not work for *Spark*. Moreover, he specifically served orders on Ruth First, Brian Bunting, Fred Carneson, Rica Hodgson and Wolfie Kodesh, forbidding them from being on the premises where a publication was prepared, compiled, printed, published or disseminated.[223] For good measure, he also banned First's husband Joe Slovo, Douglas Manqina, Harmel's wife Ray, and Fred Carneson's wife Sarah. These specific orders took effect the first day of April.

"There was nothing we could do," recalled Carneson. "We had struggled so hard and had really done a magical thing bringing out *Spark* after they banned *New Age*, but our luck had dried up."[224] They discussed the idea of making *Spark* a fortnightly or even a monthly, but there was no one left to run the newspaper, as Brian Bunting recalled: "Everyone who could have come forward from our ranks at that stage was incapacitated. It would mean starting with completely new people from scratch. . . . Politically, it would have been a different story. We didn't want to take the chance."[225] To start over was impossible. Len Lee-Warden refused to continue to print *Spark* without experienced editors and managers.[226] Sonia Bunting suggested publishing in Basutoland and smuggling *Spark* back over the border, but this idea was discarded because of logistics and because of taste. As Bunting said, "It would have to be cyclostyled, and we didn't want to cyclostyle the weekly. It wouldn't have the same effectiveness."[227]

Carneson sent a dispirited aerogram to Max Joffe in London. He told him that *Spark* was going to close down at the end of March, and asked him to raise funds to pay the twenty-four remaining staff and administrative workers their March wages and perhaps an extra month's severance salary. Money was also needed to settle the commercial debts of the newspaper, which amounted to over £700:

> Our assets (mostly office furniture of ancient vintage) are a drop in the ocean and our circulation debtors are going to freeze onto their sales monies once they know we have closed down. It will be the devil's own job getting it out of them. So, as I say, and as things stand now, it looks as if we have to throw everyone onto the street as if they were employees found rifling the petty cash! We knew that this might well be the position. The threat of it has been hanging over our heads for years. It was a risk we had

to take and took with full knowledge of what we were doing. Nevertheless, it is sad that it should happen. Some of the staff have served the paper for almost twenty years, which is a very big slice out of a man's working life. And the wages we have paid have never been sufficient to enable anyone to build up a nest-egg out of them! We are in·for a very difficult time. The activists are being put deliberately through the wringer, as an object lesson for those bold enough to think of following in their footsteps.[228]

One week later, the owners of *Spark* issued a two-page letter to subscribers and supporters, informing them of the decision to shut down the newspaper. "We need hardly say," the letter concluded, "that the people's opposition and protest, their fight for a better life, for justice and equality, for the abolition of race discrimination will not cease simply because the Government has succeeded in silencing *Spark*. The struggle is born of the objective conditions in this country, and is not, as the Government alleges, simply due to 'agitation' by subversive elements. The struggle will continue, and so will the agitation, until such time as freedom and democracy have been established in our strife-torn country."[229]

Twenty-six years and 1,328 issues after the first issue of the *Cape Guardian* hit the streets of Cape Town, the final edition of *Spark* appeared on Thursday, 28 March 1963.[230]

Reminiscent of General Douglas MacArthur's famous line on leaving the Philippines in 1942, the front-page, five-column banner headline proclaimed: "WE SAY GOODBYE BUT WE'LL BE BACK." Inside the twelve-page issue were five long biographies of the "five great journalists" who had dominated the newspaper in its final years: Bunting, First, Mbeki, Carneson, and Naicker. Written by Bunting (except his own profile, which Mbeki penned from underground), the five pieces, each accompanied by a photograph, told in loving detail of each journalist's life and work.[231] "Brian actually wanted me to write the final pieces," said Albie Sachs, "but it had quite a large extent to do with the history of the paper and he was the link to the *Guardian*. To a large extent he was the *Guardian*. We forced him to do the writing. . . . and the idea was to go out with a bang, to go out confident and come back one day and look at the issue and say, 'we were successful, we stood firm.'"[232]

Bill Andrews reappeared in a reprint of a message he wrote from jail after the 1922 strike on the Rand. Bunting, echoing the dream of the war years, wrote of the newspaper's goal of returning as a daily. The final list of donations, over £700, was tabulated; £100 was from the London *New Age* Committee.[233]

Two items in the final edition were poignant, considering what was to come. First, a photograph showed Duma Nokwe addressing a Trafalgar Square rally against South Africa, an indication of the shift of focus in the liberation movement to outside the country. Secondly, Barrack Street told readers to "remember the men and women in jail," a place so many activists were soon to be going, some for life, some for death.

Throughout the next three days, the staff wandered in and out of Barrack Street.[234] They slowly emptied the office. They boxed up their framed photographs and personal papers. They arranged for the sale of furniture and equipment, and wholesalers lugged away the old wooden desks and credenzas. They settled accounts and answered telephone calls.

Late on Friday, a cable arrived from Johannesburg.

IMPRESSIVE ISSUE THOUGH SADDEST OCCASION STOP LIVID ABOUT FRONT PAGE PICTURE STOP EVEN CORPSES PRETTIFIED FOR THEIR FUNERALS AND I'M FAR FROM DEAD THOUGH PICTURE MAKES ME LOOK AS THOUGH I SHOULD BE—RUTH.[235]

Sunday was the most dismal day. The new banning orders went into effect the following morning, so this was the last time to even go into Barrack Street. One by one, friends, supporters and staff filtered in and out of the offices. They had tea, and shared long hugs and brief words of encouragement.

Late in the afternoon, Fred Carneson was left alone. He sat in silence, staring at the empty offices and barren walls and the enormity of the years drifting like motes in sunbeams out the window. These rooms had held such passion and hope. So many people had worked here. Now they were gone, scattered, blown to the four corners of the earth. Never again would they be together in this one place.

The autumnal sun dipped out of sight and the room darkened. He locked the door and walked down the three flights of stairs into a quiet Barrack Street and was gone.

Epilogue

Within days of the newspaper's death, the country slipped into hell. A new law, Ninety Days, came into effect: the police could lock up activists for ninety days without charging them with a crime, granting them bail, or even acknowledging they held them—and the ninety days was infinitely renewable.

On a Thursday in mid-July 1963 the police raided Lillesleaf, the headquarters of Umkhonto we Sizwe on a farm in Rivonia. In one fell swoop they cut away almost the entire underground ANC leadership remaining in the country, capturing Govan Mbeki, Walter Sisulu, Rusty Bernstein and six others (Wilton Mkwayi, who was there, again demonstrated his uncanny ability to slip away during a mass arrest, and escaped).

The police hauled Nelson Mandela up from Robben Island and announced they would try him and the Rivonia cohort for sabotage, which was a capital offense. Almost no one believed that Pretoria would not convict the Rivonia trialists and sentence them to death.

A few men and women continued to do political work for the movement, some like Bram Fischer from underground. They printed and distributed handbills and leaflets, tried to establish cells of committed activists, and started delivering money to the families of political prisoners. But eventually the police captured everyone.

By August 1963 the total of prisoners held under Ninety Days reached three hundred. The police held them in solitary confinement. They made them stand for thirty hours. They beat them. They refused to give them books to read. Then the ultimate place of horror: the police started to kill the prisoners.

On 5 September 1963 they murdered Looksmart Solwandle Ngudle. On 19 August the police arrested the long-time *New Age* seller in Cape Town under Ninety Days and drove him up to Pretoria. They interrogated and tortured him. When a Pretoria magistrate visited him, Solwandle complained to him of being assaulted and coughing up blood. Soon after the magistrate reported Solwandle's statement, Solwandle was found dead in his cell, hanging from his shirt. Friends were incredulous. Solwandle was a tall, burly man, and it seemed unlikely that he could have used a thin shirt, as the police declared, to hang himself from his cell door. The police buried his body before his wife heard of his death.

At the inquest that followed, a fellow detainee, Isaac Tlale, who had also been assaulted, testified that the police had administered electric shocks to Solwandle. Despite the evidence, the magistrate ruled that Solwandle had hung himself. Afterwards, the government banned him, making it illegal to quote his statements. The *Star*'s infamous headline read, "DEAD MAN BANNED."[1]

This was no longer a game, no longer serving tea in the 1940s or some cat-and-mouse frivolity in the 1950s. Hints of the new mode of torture and murder had emerged before Solwandle's death: in the third-to-last issue of *Spark*, a report from East London told of an activist named Bongco, whom the police kicked, handcuffed high on a wall, and beat with sjamboks until blood oozed from his ears.[2]

Another early victim of death in detention was Suliman "Babla" Saloojee. A gravel-voiced, witty Indian activist from Fordsburg, Salooje bought *Spark* in April 1963 in hopes of continuing to publish it. He also worked in the ANC underground, shuttling fleeing activists from Johannesburg to the Bechuanaland border (on one trip he drove Julius First—Ruth's elderly father—Maulvi Cachalia, and Ronnie and Eleanor Kasrils.)[3] In September 1963, the police pushed Saloojee, after sixty-five days in solitary confinement, from the seventh floor of the jail on John Vorster Square in Johannesburg. He landed feet-first on a parapet above the street and pitched forward face-first onto the pavement. Taken by ambulance to the hospital, he was dead on arrival. It was just four days after Solwandle had died.[4]

Solwandle and Saloojee became the first two names of a horrifying list: between 1963 and 1990, seventy-three people died in police detention in South Africa.

Dozens of members of the *New Age* community were taken in under Ninety Days, including Eli Weinberg's wife Violet, Wolfie Kodesh, M. P. Naicker, Douglas Manqina and Brian Somana.[5] In August 1963 the police jailed Ruth First under Ninety Days. She remained the next 117 days in solitary confinement, temporarily losing her mind and attempting suicide. Freed, she and her children left South Africa on an exit permit in March 1964 and joined her husband, Joe Slovo, in London. First worked part-time for the ANC, lectured about sociology at Durham University, and wrote a half-dozen books about politics and history, including a searing memoir of her confinement under Ninety Days.[6] In 1978 she became the research director at the Centre of African Studies at Eduardo Mondlane University in Maputo, Mozambique. Four years later First tore open a package sent by the South African police. A bomb exploded, killing her instantly. The bomb was so powerful that it blew a gaping hole in a brick wall and shattered a window, sending an air conditioner flying to the ground two floors below. Ruth First was buried in Maputo's Llanguene Cemetery next to the twelve ANC members gunned down by South African military forces at Matola in 1981.[7] Three thousand people, including government officials from thirty-four countries, attended the funeral. She was fifty-seven.

Mirroring First's fate, Albie Sachs was jailed under Ninety Days; his confinement lasted 168 days. Freed from Cape Town's Caledon Square on an autumn afternoon, Sachs ran six miles to Clifton Beach and dashed into the cold Atlantic Ocean to reward himself for holding out during solitary confinement. He went into exile in 1966, took a Ph.D. in political science at the University of Sussex (Harold Baldry was one of his professors), and wrote a number of books, including two memoirs about his time in jail.[8] In 1977 he returned to Africa and taught law at Mondlane University in Maputo. In April 1988 Sachs opened the door to his car, parked in front of his apartment, and a bomb planted by the South African police exploded. He lost the sight of one eye, and his right arm was blown off right below the shoulder. In 1990 he came back to South Africa, and after the first democratic elections in April 1994 was appointed one of the eleven judges on the Constitutional Court, the highest court in the land.

Pretoria also murdered Joe Gqabi. Captured as an Umkhonto cadre in 1963, Gqabi spent twelve years on Robben Island. After his release he was involved in the 1976 Soweto uprising and was forced into exile. In 1980 the

ANC appointed Gqabi as their representative to newly independent Zimbabwe. In August 1981, while walking down a busy street in Harare, Gqabi was gunned down by South African agents in a passing car and killed.

London was home to a majority of exiled staff members. Brian and Sonia Bunting, under house arrest and unable to find employment, left in July 1963 for London.[9] Brian Bunting authored two major books on South African history, and in the 1980s edited the *African Communist;* Sonia managed the Party's main office. They returned to South Africa in 1991, and in the 1994 election Brian was elected to Parliament, forty-one years after he was kicked out for being a communist. Sonia died in March 2001. Rica Hodgson secretly left South Africa in 1963. She returned in 1991 and became Walter Sisulu's secretary. In 1966, after running the underground ANC in Cape Town almost single-handedly for three years, Fred Carneson was arrested and jailed for six years. On the night of his release in 1972, he and Sarah Carneson left for London; they returned in 1991. Fred Carneson died in September 2000.[10] After her six months in jail, Mary Turok stayed in South Africa until her husband, Ben Turok, finished a three-year jail term. They left in 1966, and after living in Dar es Salaam, moved to London, then Lusaka; in 1991 they returned to South Africa.

A number of staffers lived in Lusaka, Zambia, working at the ANC's African headquarters. Wolfie Kodesh toiled for Umkhonto we Sizwe until getting arrested in May 1963 under Ninety Days. Upon release in July, Kodesh left on an exit permit. He worked in London and then Lusaka for the ANC and returned in 1991; he died in Cape Town in October 2002.[11] Ray Alexander and Jack Simons left in 1965, and after a period in London, moved to Lusaka. Simons taught sociology at the University of Zambia, and together with Alexander wrote a seminal book on South African political history.[12] In 1990 Alexander and Simons were among the first exiles to return to South Africa. Jack Simons died in July 1995.

Like Ruth First and Albie Sachs, Joyce Watson Mohammed ended up in Mozambique. She worked for Arnold's Hampers—which continued after the demise of *Spark* until the end of 1963—until her arrest under Ninety Days. After she was released, she left the country and settled in Maputo, returning in 1992. Mountain Ngqungwana went into exile in 1963. After being captured by Rhodesian troops in May 1968, he was held on death row until Zimbabwean independence in 1980. He returned to South Africa in 1993.

The United States hosted a couple of exiles. Dennis Brutus spent eighteen months on Robben Island after getting shot while fleeing from detention in 1963.[13] He went into exile in 1966 and eventually moved to America. He published poetry and taught at a number of universities. Joining Brutus was Willie Kgositile. He left South Africa in 1975 and lived in Tanzania, Botswana, Zimbabwe, and Zambia before moving to the United States in 1990 to teach creative writing at Wayne State University in Detroit.

Alex La Guma ended up living only ninety miles from the United States. After four years of twenty-four-hour house arrest and two stints in jail under Ninety Days—"His only visitors were the police coming to raid and take him away," wrote Albie Sachs—La Guma left in 1966.[14] After a stint as a writer-in-residence at the University of Dar es Salaam, he moved to Cuba in 1978, becoming the ANC's representative for the Caribbean. He wrote four more novels, all of which were among the 39,000 books banned by Pretoria between 1962 and 1993.[15] In October 1985 he died of a heart attack and was buried in Havana's Christopher Columbus cemetery alongside the family of José Martí.

Returning to South Africa became a vain hope for other staffers. Eli Weinberg was jailed for one year for refusing to testify in the Rivonia Trial and went into exile after being released. He died in July 1981. Michael Harmel went into exile in 1963. He edited the South African Communist Party's main organ, the *African Communist*, and wrote a history of the Party. He died in June 1974 while at a conference in Prague.[16] Alfred Hutchinson died in October 1972 in Nigeria. Vera Poonen died in exile in Canada. Sam Kahn died in August 1987 in an car accident while visiting his son in Israel.[17] M. P. Naicker was detained under Ninety Days and eventually charged with furthering the aims of the ANC. Surprisingly, he managed to secure an acquittal. In 1964 he was detained again, and after his release, left the country. He lived in London and founded and edited the ANC's monthly magazine *Sechaba*. In April 1977, on a plane flying to Berlin, he had a heart attack and died.[18]

Politics extracted its pound of flesh. Robert Resha, a major ANC figure in exile, was the driving force behind the Congress faction that opposed allowing non-Africans the chance to join the ANC. He died of heart failure in December 1973.[19] His fellow ANC dissidents used Resha's funeral as a place to begin a public campaign attacking the influence of communists within the Congress. In October 1975 the ANC expelled eight leaders—dubbed the Makiwane Eight, after their leader, Tennyson Makiwane.[20] T.X. returned to South Africa in February 1979 and found work in Umtata with the collaborationist Transkei government. Makiwane, the grandson of a founder of the ANC, was assassinated in July 1980 in Umtata by a Congress agent.[21]

Jail was home for many staffers. After the Rivonia Trial, Govan Mbeki was imprisoned on Robben Island until November 1987. In 1994 he became chair of the Senate; he died in August 2001.[22] Jack Tarshish worked underground—his code name was "Burnt Blanket"—until he was caught transporting dynamite and given ten years in jail.[23] Wilton Mkwayi managed to stay in hiding until early 1964, when he was arrested and convicted of sabotage in the "Little Rivonia Trial." He was freed in October 1989, after, as he said, "25 years and 15 days."[24]

Ebrahim Ismail Ebrahim suffered greatly for his association with Umkhonto we Sizwe. In August 1963 the police arrested him outside Durban. They took him to a lake, beat him unconscious and almost drowned him.[25] He was the main defendant in the Pietermaritzburg Sabotage Trial and was sentenced to fifteen years on Robben Island. In February 1979 Ebrahim was freed. He spent two and one-half years working for the ANC underground in Durban before fleeing South Africa in December 1980. He moved to Mbabane, Swaziland, to help run MK operations. In December 1986 two South African policeman knocked on Ebrahim's door, tied his hands behind his back with rope, gagged and blindfolded him, placed hand and leg irons on him, and drove him to the frontier with South Africa. Ebrahim was forced through the border fence and driven to Pretoria. For weeks the police tortured Ebrahim: he was put in a soundproof cell and made to endure sensory deprivation, assaulted with electrical shocks, and almost suffocated. Almost two years later, Ebrahim was brought to court and convicted of high treason and terrorism. In 1991 he was released.[26]

Some people refused to leave the country. In July 1964, after working for the underground ANC, Ivan Schermbrucker was arrested. The police continuously interrogated him for twenty-eight hours, beating and punching him. After being convicted in the Little Rivonia Trial, he spent the next six and one-half years in jail at Pretoria Central prison (his wife Lesley was jailed for three years as well). When he was released in March 1972, he stayed in South Africa despite difficult conditions: the government expropriated his house and placed him under twelve-hour house arrest for five years. In July 1981 Schermbrucker died of heart failure.[27] Many old friends heard of Schermbrucker's death at the memorial service in London for Eli Weinberg.[28]

Jackie and Rowley Arenstein continued to work in the struggle, although in the early 1980s they turned their attentions to the Zulu nationalist group Inkatha. Rowley, after enduring the longest continuous ban in South African history (from 1960 to 1986), died in 1996. Ismail Meer lived in Durban and worked outside in Stanger as a lawyer; his wife Fatima wrote a biography of Mandela. Dawood Seedat was again banned in 1964, and died in February 1976. Nondwe Nankhala stayed in Port Elizabeth.

Amy Thornton worked for a variety of grass-roots community organizations in Cape Town. Naomi Shapiro earned a master's degree in history at the University of Cape Town. Harry Snitcher worked as a lawyer. Johnny Morley ran the Xmas Hampers for two more years before police pressure forced him to quit. Len Lee-Warden lived in Clifton and continued to run Pioneer Press, which had expanded its operations to print a range of magazines and journals, including the *South African Medical Journal*. In 1964 he was banned, and confined to the magisterial district of Cape Town for five years. In 1984 he retired from Pioneer, which was soon bought up by the *Cape Times*. At that time he dug up the trunks in his garden and sent the old *Guardian* copies overseas.

By then the weekly was almost forgotten. In the 1980s the editors running the *Weekly Mail*, *New Nation*, and *South*—the new equivalents of the *Guardian*—had never heard of the *Guardian* and did not feel a deep connection to the long lineage of South Africa's resistance press. But older members of the ANC, in exile or in jail on Robben Island, fondly recalled the weekly in discussions.[29] Harry Gwala perhaps said it best: "After 1963 it was gone, but it was never banned in the minds of the people. They couldn't suppress the ideas in the *Guardian*."[30]

Douglas Manqina's experience after the demise of the newspaper was emblematic. The veteran street seller was banned and house-arrested, and in 1963 detained under Ninety Days. The police then charged him with furthering the aims of the ANC. Convicted, Manqina was sent to Robben Island. But in a remarkable turnabout, an appeal of the conviction was successful, and after six months he was freed.

Pretoria deported Manqina to the Transkei district where he was born. His wife, born in Cape Town, could not endure living in the rural Transkei and took their three children back to Cape Town. For a quarter century, Manqina lived with his mother on a remote farm. Each month he received £15 from the International Defense and Aid Fund.

In 1988 he returned to Cape Town, and in 1990 rejoined the Communist Party and the ANC. In an interview just before the 1994 democratic elections, Manqina spoke about the effects of the newspaper: "After I came back from deportation, all those places where I used to sell *New Age*, we now have the strongest ANC branches. We now have many members there. All those places. We have a very big organization now."

Almost whispering, he talked about current politics—the elections, the personalities on the hustings, the rallies, the work still to be done. For Manqina and many other activists, those gossamer days before the 1994 election were the culmination of a lifetime of work. The anticipation was nearly over. They could finally experience the effects of their careers. They had done their part. They had stood up.

A religious man, Manqina used a simple metaphor to describe how he felt. "You see, to me, it appears as the preachers talking to the congregation, as they preach to the people. They say, 'You sow the maize, but it is not for you. That maize must come out from the ground.' We were sowing these people. That seed, we have been sowing it. It came out. *New Age* was the seed that we sowed. Now it has come up and it is very rich."

Acknowledgments

As this history has accompanied me for the past seventeen years, I feel a strange sense of sorrow taking leave of an old and agreeable companion.

From the start, my parents encouraged me to follow this dream wherever it took me. They read through a half-dozen different versions of the manuscript, visited me twice in South Africa, and never lost faith that this would finally appear in print.

My family—sisters, brothers-in-law, nieces, nephews, cousins, aunts, uncles, grandparents, in-laws—were always interested and supportive. In particular, I have been lucky to follow the path blazed by my literary grandfather, Abram T. Collier and for his dedication to our family I dedicate this book to him. My agent, Joseph Regal, lent his professional expertise to the project at crucial moments. Most of all, my wife Rebecca and our sons, Livingston and Collier, made this possible with their love. I am grateful for them and to them every day.

At Dartmouth, I was guided by Greg Finnegan, Gene Garthwaite, Bruce Nelson and Leo Spitzer. Margot de l'Etoile at the John Sloan Dickey Endowment granted me a Richard D. Lombard Public Service Fellowship. In addition, I thank Malcolm Barlow, Steven Fox, Kim Porteus and Arthur D. Serota.

At Oxford, Howard Barrell, John Darwin and Anthony Lemon were most helpful.

Andre Odendaal invited me to work as a Visiting Scholar at the Mayibuye Centre at the University of the Western Cape. He and his staff were especially welcoming and provided an intellectually rich home. Many thanks to Mouravia Dingana, Barry Feinberg, Albert Fritz, Graham Goddard, Anthea Josias, Norman Kaplan, Wendy Manuel, Rachidi Molapo, Gordon Metz, Ciraj Rassool, Karel Roskam and Felicia Siebritz. Pat Fahrenfort admirably transcribed a dozen of my interview tapes. Andre Mohammed, Babalwa Solwandle, Esther Van Driel, Lailah Hisham, and Simphiwe Yako delivered the beautiful photographs inserted in the book, and I thank the Centre for granting me permission to reproduce them.

During my three years in South Africa, I was assisted in a myriad of ways by so many wonderful friends and colleagues: Joe and Cass Abrahams, Kerry Anderson, Ken Beveridge, Colin Bundy, Bill Cote, Appolon Davidson, Josie Egan, Chris and Louis-Marie Guy, the Jesters Club, the Llandudno Squash Club, Louis van Loon, Paul Marsh, John Murray, the Pearson family, the Pennington family, Mark Potterton, Christine Stevens, Andrew and Toinette Shane, Gary and Mandy Fisher, Shane Gibson, Dorothy Woodson, Craig and Alex Tannini, Andy Taylor and Dominic Touwen. Shaun Johnson provided two crucial boxes of research materials from his doctoral thesis, and David Everatt gave me useful advice.

With affection I thank the staff and students at St. Bedes, especially Jim Gole, Bebbington Joseph, Joyce Mafokoane, Phillemon Makwela, Bethuel Mashiane, Phina Mmakola, and Isaac Mohlele. *Ke llalela kua dithabeng.*

Libby and Paddy McCarthy, and Ille and Ola Sall allowed me the undiluted pleasure of a year writing in the hills above Hout Bay. Kristi Jo Miller teamed up with me as we searched for the *Guardian,* and I thank her for such winsome support.

Librarians cordially steered me in the right directions: Jill Gribble, Leonie Twentyman Jones, and Margaret Richardson at Manuscripts and Archives at the University of Cape Town; Michele Pickover at William Cullen Library at the University of the Witwatersrand; the Cape Town Archives Repository on Roeland Street; the National Library of South Africa; the African Studies Library at the University of Cape Town; the Institute for Commonwealth Studies in London; Butler Library at Columbia University; the New York Public Library; and the Library of Congress.

In Great Britain, I was helped by Anthony Berman, Michelle Davies, Shula Marks, Flagg Miller, the Romer Lee family, Anthony Sampson, Ronald Segal, Brian Sparkes and Randolph Vigne.

In the United States, Mohammed Mbodj and Marcia Wright facilitated my work at Columbia. Robert Edgar, Katherine Guckenberger and Denison Lee carefully read the manuscript in draft. Stephen Ellmann and Penny Andrews curated the South African Reading Group in New York, a home for all of us away from South Africa. I also thank Mohamed Adhikari, Elizabeth Grinnell, Robert Frater, Guy Berger, Isa Jacobson, Colby Loud, Douglas Rogers, Sarah Shey, Jane Sismaet and Nelson Tebbe.

Two professors in particular played an enormous and long-standing role in bringing this book to fruition. Les Switzer, the dean of South African media historians, twice read the manuscript, shared research, and provided compelling conversation in Cape Town. Thomas G. Karis, the revered elder statesman of all South African historians, also twice read the manuscript, and commented thoughtfully and extensively. Most of all, Tom affably guided me through the endless thickets of publication. Without his enthusiasm, this book would not have appeared. I thank him. He is the consummate historian.

At Michigan State University Press, I thank Martha A. Bates, Kristine M. Blakeslee, Fred Bohm, Julie L. Loehr, Julie K. Reaume, Ashley Somers, Annette K. Tanner, copyeditor Bonnie Cobb and indexer Sandra Judd. At UNISA Press, I thank Sharon Boshoff, Beth Le Roux, Raymond Suttner, and Abebe Zegeye.

Most of all, I am deeply indebted to the former members of the *Guardian* community who sat for interviews, talked on the telephone, and corresponded. As they told me their stories, they unfailingly showed hospitality, dispensing gallons of tea and sharing meals. Some became friends whom I saw regularly; others opened their archives; almost all passed me along to other people who might help. In particular, Brian Bunting generously assisted me. He twice read through drafts of the manuscript, wrote me long letters, gently offered invaluable criticism and corrections, and acted as reference as I traipsed around the world seeking out former staffers (the first words anyone said when I told them I was working on a book on the *Guardian* were, "Have you talked with Brian?").

Most of the formal interviews were recorded and transcribed, and copies are available at the Mayibuye Centre. Besides talking with the people listed below, I had valuable informal conversations with the following people: Esther Barsil, Breyten Breytenbach, Ethel de Keyser, Flo Duncan, Gerson Ginsburg, Rica Hodgson, Ronnie Kasrils, Phillip Kgosana, Joe Podbrey, Albertina Sisulu, and Ben Turok.

Interviews

- Ray Alexander, *December 1993, March 1994, April 1994, May 1994, and January 1995*
- Rowley Arenstein, *February 1994*
- Jack Barnett, *December 1994*
- Hilda Bernstein, *May 1994*
- Rusty Bernstein, *May 1994*
- Brian Bunting, *November 1993, December 1993, October 1994, and November 1994*
- Sonia Bunting, *December 1993*
- Fred Carneson, *March 1994*
- Sarah Carneson, *March 1994*
- Ebrahim Ismail Ebrahim, *January 1994*
- Sadie Forman, *May 1994*
- Denis Goldberg, *May 1994*
- Adelaide Joseph, *May 1994*
- Paul Joseph, *May 1994*
- Wolfie Kodesh, *December 1993 and March 1994*
- Len Lee-Warden, *December 1993 and October 1994*
- Douglas Manqina, *December 1993*
- Govan Mbeki, *February 1994*
- Ismail Meer, *February 1994*
- Kwedie Mkhlapi, *November 1993*
- Wilton Mkwayi, *January 1994*
- Joyce Mohammed, *January 1994*
- Jill Murray, *January 1994*
- Pauline Podbrey, *December 1993*
- Albie Sachs, *March 1994*
- Jurgen Schadeberg, *July 1994*
- Fatima Seedat, *February 1994*
- Naomi Shapiro, *December 1993*
- Jack Simons, *December 1993 and April 1994*
- Walter Sisulu, *January 1994*
- Harry Snitcher, *January 1995*
- Lesley Schermbrucker Spiller, *January 1994*
- Amy Thornton, *December 1993*
- Mary Butcher Turok, *January 1994*

Telephone Interviews
- Dora Alexander, *November 1994*
- Jackie Arenstein, *March 1994*
- Hymie Bernadt, *March 1994*
- Dennis Brutus, *March 1991*
- Rex Close, *May 1994*
- Nancy Dick, *May 1994*
- Trudy Gelb, *January 1994 and November 1994*
- Harry Gwala, *October 1994 and November 1994*
- Ray Harmel, *May 1994*
- Miriam Hepner, *March 1994*
- Pauline Kahn, *May 1994*
- Willie Kgositile, *December 1994*
- Blanche La Guma, *November 1994*
- Beate Lipman, *October 1994*
- Nondwe Mankahla, *March 1994*
- Sarah Naicker, *May 1994*
- Ralph Mountain Tuli Ngqungwana, *March 1994*
- Hettie September, *March 1994*
- Joe Slovo, *January 1994*
- Errol Shanley, *May 1994*
- Athol Thorne, *December 1993*
- Sheila Weinberg, *October 1994*
- Stanley Uys, *May 1994*

Correspondence
- Benjamin Pogrund, *April 1994*
- Dennis Brutus, *April 1991*
- Brian Bunting, *March 1991 and April 1991*
- Nadine Gordimer, *November 1992, December 1994, and February 1995*
- Doris Lessing, *March 1994*
- Laurens van der Post, *August 1994*
- Arnold Selby, *July 1994 and August 1994*
- Leslie Schermbrucker Spiller, *February 1994*

Notes

PROLOGUE

The epigraph to this book comes from: Thomas Pringle, *Narrative of a Residence in South Africa* (London: Edward Moxon, 1834), 69.

1. *Guardian*, 3 September 1937. I do not offer page numbers for individual *Guardian* editions because each issue was usually eight pages, sometimes just four, and at most sixteen, so the interested researcher can find the relevant material in short order.
2. *Advance*, 1 April 1954.
3. Amy Thornton, a staffer in the late 1950s, recalled Brian Bunting teaching her the basics of journalism: "'In journalism,' he told me, 'the first sentence tells you the story.'"
4. For more on newspapers in South Africa, the essential books are *South Africa's Alternative Press: Voices of Protest and Resistance, 1880s–1960s*, ed. Les Switzer (Cambridge: Cambridge University Press, 1997); and *South Africa's Resistance Press: Alternative Voices in the Last Generation under Apartheid*, eds. Les Switzer and Mohamed Adhikari (Athens, Ohio: Ohio University Press, 2000). See Les Switzer and Donna Switzer, *The Black Press in South Africa and Lesotho* (Boston: G. K. Hall, 1979); and Les Switzer, "Language, Text, Community: A Critical and Historical Perspective on South Africa's Resistance Press," paper given at the Institute of Historical Research and the Department of History of the University of Cape Town, October 1994.

  See also Alex Hepple, *Censorship and Press Control in South Africa* (1960, reprinted 1974); Eric Rosenthal, *160 Years of Cape Town Printing* (Cape Town: Cape Town Association of Printing

House Craftsmen, 1960); Morris Broughton, *Press and Politics of South Africa* (Cape Town: Purnell & Sons, 1961); Rosalynde Ainslie, *The Press in Africa: Communications Past and Present* (London: Victor Gollancz, 1966); Elaine Potter, *The Press as Opposition: The Political Role of South African Newspapers* (Totowa, N.J.: Rowman & Littlefield, 1975); Chenhamo C. Chimutengwende, *South Africa: The Press and the Politics of Liberation* (London: Barbican, 1978); Frank Barton, *The Press in Africa: Persecution and Perseverance* (New York: Africana, 1979); Richard Pollak, *Up Against Apartheid: The Role and the Plight of the Press in South Africa* (Carbondale: Southern Illinois University Press, 1981); William A. Hatchten and C. Anthony Giffard, *The Press and Apartheid: Repression and Propaganda in South Africa* (Madison: University of Wisconsin Press, 1984); John M. Phelan, *Apartheid Media: Disinformation and Dissent in South Africa* (Westport, Conn.: Lawrence Hill, 1987); *The Press in South Africa*, ed. Keyan Tomaselli, Ruth Tomaselli, and Johan Muller (London: James Currey, 1987); William Finnegan, *Dateline Soweto: Travels with Black South African Reporters* (New York: Harper and Row, 1988); *The Alternative Press in South Africa*, ed. Keyan Tomaselli and P. Eric Louw (London: James Currey, 1991); and Gordon S. Jackson, *Breaking Story: The South African Press* (Boulder: Westview, 1993).

Interesting articles are: Frene Ginwala, "The Press in South Africa," *Index on Censorship* 2, no. 3 (Autumn 1973): 27–46; Rene Lefort, "The 'Black' Press in South Africa," *International Social Science Journal* 33, no. 1 (1981): 99–121; Shaun Johnson, "Barometers of the Liberation Movement: A History of South Africa's Alternative Press," *Media Development: Journal of the World Association for Christian Communication* 32, no. 3: 18–21; Les Switzer, "Bantu World and the Origins of a Captive African Commercial Press in South Africa," *Journal of Southern African Studies* 14, no. 3 (April 1988): 351–70; Brian Bunting, "Journalists in the Front Line," *Sechaba* 23, no. 4 (April 1989): 8–15; Peter Orlik, "Under Damocles' Sword: The South African Press," *Journalism Quarterly* (Summer 1989): 347; Les Switzer and Elizabeth Jones, "Other Voices: The Ambiguities of Resistance in South Africa's Resistance Press," *South African Historical Journal* 32 (1995): 66–113.

CHAPTER ONE. A VERY LIVE MENACE:
A CAPE TOWN CHILDHOOD, 1937-1939

1. For more on the Left Book Club, see John Strachey, *The Strangled Cry* (New York: William Sloane, 1962); John Lewis, *The Left Book Club: An Historical Record* (London: Victor Gollancz, 1970); Sheila Hughes, *The Story of a Publishing House: 1928–1978* (London: Victor Gollancz, 1978); Ruth Dudley Edwards, *Victor Gollancz: A Biography* (London: Victor Gollancz, 1987); and Paul Laity, *Left Book Club Anthology* (London: Victor Gollancz, 2001). See also *Guardian*, 7 May 1937 and 13 February 1941.

   John Strachey, Lytton's second cousin and a popular political writer and columnist for the *Daily Worker*, and Harold Laski, a London School of Economics professor, served as selectors with Gollancz. The LBC ended in November 1948 after 260 monthly selections. "The Club was formed to prevent Hitler being allowed to start the Second World War, and to popularise Marxism in Britain," wrote Strachey in a 1954 article on Gollancz. "It succeeded in doing neither."

2. Catherine Burns, "An Historical Study of the Friends of the Soviet Union and the South African Peace Council," BA honours thesis, University of the Witwatersrand, 1987, p. 23. See Max Ozinsky, "For Land and Freedom: The Communist Party of South Africa and the Strategy of United

Fronts in the 1930s," unpublished manuscript, University of the Witwatersrand, Department of Historical Papers, William Cullen Library, 1983, A1736.

3. "A radical group without a paper is a contradiction in terms," wrote Max Schachtman. The subcommittee consisted of Bill Andrews, Ray Alexander, Johnny Gomas, Jimmy Emmerich, Thomas Ngwenya, Harry Snitcher, Sam Kahn, and Jimmy La Guma.

4. Maurice S. Evans, *Black and White in South East Africa: A Study in Sociology* (London, 1911), 296–97.

5. Ray and Jack Simons, *Class and Colour in South Africa, 1850–1950* (London: International Defense and Aid Fund, 1983), described Cape Town as the "hunting ground of tourists, artists and leisurely liberals" (483). Mary Butcher Turok said, "There was the feeling up in Johannesburg that the comrades in Cape Town were simply lollygagging around on the beach. And sometimes we were." See Rica Hodgson in the *Sunday Times* (Johannesburg), 13 November 1993: "Cape Town is too pretty. We used to say that in Cape Town the revolution closed down for the weekend."

6. See Elizabeth Ceiriog Jones, "*Inkululeko*: Organ of the Communist Party of South Africa, 1939–1950," in *South Africa's Alternative Press*, ed. Switzer, 336; and Shaun Johnson, "'Barometers of the Liberation Movement': A History of South Africa's Alternative Press," *Media Development: Journal of the World Association for Christian Communication* 32, no. 3 (1985): 19. The dockworkers refused to load ships from June to August 1935.

7. Bernard Sachs, *South African Personalities and Politics* (Johannesburg: Kayor Publishing, 1959), 118; Joe Slovo, *Slovo: The Unfinished Autobiography* (Johannesburg: Ravan, 1995), 22–23; Simons, *Class and Colour*, 593; Pauline Podbrey, *White Girl in Search of the Party* (Pietermaritzburg: Hadeda, 1993), 48; Brian Bunting, *Moses Kotane: South African Revolutionary* (London: Inkululeko, 1975), 68; and Henry Pike, *A History of Communism in South Africa* (Germiston, SA: Christian Mission International of South Africa, 1985), 207–10. The stock question thrown at communist speakers was, "Would you allow your sister to marry a kaffir?" The stock reply was, "If I had the needle to the kaffir." Issy Wolfson, who had no sister, usually replied: "If you knew her, you'd realise that no self-respecting kaffir would ever marry my sister." Sam Kahn famously twisted the tradition in Parliament by this rejoinder, "What, are you a marriage broker? Have you a client you are seeking to marry?"

8. *Cape Times*, 3 April 1936.

9. *Weekly Mail & Guardian*, 7 January 1994. See Patrick J. Furlong, *Between Crown and Swastika: The Impact of the Radical Right on the Afrikaner Nationalist Movement in the Fascist Era* (Middletown, Conn.: Wesleyan University Press, 1991).

10. Sheridan Johns III, "Protest and Hope: 1882–1934," vol. 1, *From Protest to Challenge: A Documentary History of African Politics in South Africa*, ed. Thomas Karis and Gwendolen M. Carter (Stanford, Calif.: Hoover Institution Press, 1972), 153. A new organization, the All-African Convention, emerged from the protests about the 1936 voter-roll legislation, but the AAC matched its ANC rival for political ineffectiveness.

11. For the definitive history of the early years of the Communist Party, see the work of Sheridan Johns: *Raising the Red Flag: The International Socialist League and the Communist Party of South Africa, 1914–1932* (Cape Town: Mayibuye Centre, 1995); "The Birth of the Communist Party of South Africa," *International Journal of African Historical Studies* 9, no. 3 (1976): 371–400; and "Chasing Votes: The Communist Party and Elections, 1929–1950," paper given at the Africa Seminar, Centre for African Studies, University of Cape Town, August 1994. See also A. Lerumo [Michael Harmel], *Fifty Fighting Years: The South African Communist Party, 1921–*

1971 (London: Inkululeko, 1971); Simons, *Class and Colour*; Mia Roth, "Josie Mpama: The Contribution of a Largely Forgotten Figure in the South Africa Liberation Struggle," *Kleio* 28 (1996): 123; Brian Bunting, ed., *Letters to Rebecca: South African Communist Leader S. P. Bunting to his Wife, 1917–1934* (Cape Town: Mayibuye Centre, 1996).

Helpful examinations of South African politics in the *Guardian* era include: Gwendolen M. Carter, *The Politics of Inequality: South Africa since 1948* (New York: Praeger, 1959) and (ed.) *Five African States: Responses to Diversity* (Ithaca: Cornell University Press, 1963); Edward Feit, *South Africa: The Dynamics of the African National Congress* (London: Oxford University Press, 1962) and *African Opposition in South Africa* (Stanford, Calif.: Hoover, 1967); Edward Roux, *Time Longer than Rope: A History of the Black Man's Struggle for Freedom in South Africa* (Madison: University of Wisconsin Press, 1964) and *S. P. Bunting: A Political Biography* (Bellville, SA: Mayibuye Centre, 1993); Peter Walshe, *The Rise of African Nationalism in South Africa: The African National Congress, 1912–1952* (Johannesburg: AD Donker, 1970); Brian Bunting, *Moses Kotane*; Gail Gerhart, *Black Power in South Africa: The Evolution of an Ideology* (Berkeley: University of California Press, 1978); Tom Lodge, *Black Politics in South Africa since 1945* (London: Longman, 1983); Shula Marks and Stanley Trapido, eds., *The Politics of Race, Class and Nationalism in Twentieth-Century South Africa* (New York: Longman, 1987); Fatima Meer, *Higher than Hope: The Authorized Biography of Nelson Mandela* (London: Penguin, 1988); Steven Mufson, *Fighting Years: Black Resistance and the Struggle for a New South Africa* (Boston: Beacon Press, 1990); Baruch Hirson, *Yours for the Union: Class and Community Struggles in South Africa, 1930-1947* (Johannesburg: Witwatersrand University Press, 1990); Deborah Posel, *The Making of Apartheid, 1948–1961: Conflict and Compromise* (Oxford: Clarendon Press, 1991); Philip Bonner, Peter Delius, and Deborah Posel, eds., *Apartheid's Genesis, 1935–1962* (Johannesburg: University of the Witwatersrand, 1993); Joshua N. Lazerson, *Against the Tide: Whites in the Struggle Against Apartheid* (Boulder, Colo.: Westview, 1994); Paul B. Rich, *State Power and Black Politics in South Africa, 1912–1951* (New York: St. Martins, 1996); Vladimir Shubin, *ANC: A View from Moscow* (Cape Town: Mayibuye Centre, 1999); and Baruch Hirson, *A History of the Left in South Africa: Writings of Baruch Hirson* (London: I. B. Tauris, 2005).

Unpublished manuscripts: Alan K. Brooks, "From Class Struggle to National Liberation: The Communist Party of South Africa, 1940–1950," master's thesis, University of Sussex, 1967; David O'Sullivan, "The Theory and Practice of Communism in South Africa: The Communist Party of South Africa, 1939–1950," BA honours thesis, University of Cape Town, 1984; Jonathan Grossman, "Class Relations and Politics of the Communist Party of South Africa, 1921–1950," Ph.D. thesis, University of Warwick, 1985; Tom Lodge, "Class Conflict, Communal Struggle and Patriotic Unity: The Communist Party of South Africa during the Second World War," African Studies Seminar paper presented at the African Studies Institute, University of the Witwatersrand, October 1985; Joel Bolnick, "Proletarianism, Prejudice, Patriotism and the Party Line: White Radical Socialism in South Africa, 1915–1945," Africa Seminar, Centre for African Studies, University of Cape Town, September 1987; Allison Drew, "United Fronts, Popular Fronts and Non-Collaboration, 1935–1945," Africa Seminar, Centre for African Studies, UCT, August 1989, and "Social Mobilization and Racial Capitalism in South Africa, 1928–1960," Ph.D. dissertation, University of California at Los Angeles, 1991; and David Everatt, "The Politics of Nonracialism: White Opposition to Apartheid, 1945–1960," Lincoln College, Oxford, 1990.

Journal articles: Thomas G. Karis, "Revolution in the Making: Black Politics in South Africa," *Foreign Affairs* (Winter 1983–84); Dennis Davis and Robert Fine, "Political Strategies and the

State: Some Historical Observations," *Journal of Southern African Studies* 12, no. 1 (October 1985): 25–48; Thomas G. Karis, "South African Liberation: The Communist Factor," *Foreign Affairs* (Winter 1986–87); Lulu Callinicos, "The Communist Party during the War Years: The Beginnings of Grass-Roots Politics," *South African Labour Bulletin* 15, no. 3 (September 1990): 101–7: Dominic Fortescue, "The Communist Party of South Africa and the African Working Class in the 1940s," *International Journal of African Historical Studies* 24, no. 3 (1991): 481–512; and David Everatt, "Alliance Politics of a Special Type: The Roots of the ANC/SACP Alliance, 1950–1954," *Journal of Southern African Studies* 18, no. 1 (March 1992): 19–39.

There are a number of good published sources for primary documents: *South African Communists Speak: Documents from the History of the SACP, 1915–1980* (London: Inkululeko, 1981); the seven-volume collection *From Protest to Challenge*, edited by Thomas Karis and Gwendolen M. Carter; two volumes of Allison Drew, *South Africa's Radical Tradition: A Documentary History, 1907–1964* (Cape Town: Mayibuye Centre, 1996 and 1997); and Charles Villa-Vicencio, *The Spirit of Freedom: South African Leaders on Religion and Politics* (Berkeley: University of California, 1996).

12. Julie Frederikse, *The Unbreakable Thread: Non-Racialism in South Africa* (London: Zed Book, 1990), 11. Eddie Roux was also in the group. See also Immanuel Suttner, *Cutting Through the Mountain: Interviews with South African Jewish Activists* (New York: Viking, 1997) and Ray Alexander Simons, *All My Life and All My Strength* (Johannesburg: STE Publishers, 2004), 54.

13. James Zug interview with Ray Alexander, December 1993. To relieve the text of unnecessary endnotes, I do not document quotations when it is clear who gave them and when they derive from interviews I conducted—a list of which appear in the acknowledgments.

14. See, for example, *Cape Times*, 7 July 1934, for a women's-page article, "In Terms of Happiness—Acquiring a New Perspective on Household Equipment."

15. Harold Sandon was the most prominent supporter. Pauline Kahn recalled that Henry Sizerist, a UCT professor of the history of medicine originally from Leipzig, was an active, though quiet, *Guardian* supporter and writer in the early years.

16. James Zug interview with Ray Alexander, March 1994. See also Brian Bunting interview with Ray Alexander, November 1973, Brian Bunting Collection, Mayibuye Centre.

17. James Zug interview with Len Lee-Warden, December 1993; and Jeremy Bernstein interview with Jean Bernadt, December 1988, in "Media Active: The Politics of Progressive Media Production and State Control in South Africa, The Case of the *Guardian*, 1937–1952," honours thesis, University of Cape Town (African Studies), 1988. Trommer later moved to South-West Africa.

18. *Cape Times*, 4 October 1947; and *Guardian*, 9 October 1947.

19. See *An African American in South Africa: The Travel Notes of Ralph J. Bunche, 28 September 1937–1 January 1938*, edited by Robert R. Edgar (Athens: Ohio University Press, 1992), 60. Stewart had recently sold the *Sun*, a newspaper he had founded in 1932 with A. S. Hayes, to Samuel Griffiths. (The *Sun* was later owned by the United Party and died in 1956.) In September 1936 he started a coloured weekly, the *Cape Standard*, which lasted until November 1947.

20. *Guardian*, 18 February 1943.

21. *Weekly Mail & Guardian*, 14 October 1994.

22. James Zug interview with Ray Alexander, April 1994. See *Guardian*, 9 April 1942.

23. *Guardian*, 10 July 1941. James Zug interview with Harry Snitcher, January 1995; and James Zug telephone interview with Dora Alexander, November 1994.

24. *Guardian*, 11 and 18 February 1943.

25. *Guardian*, 2 September 1948.

26. *Guardian*, 19 March 1937 and 7 December 1944. The South African Railways charged exorbitant fees for nonregistered newspapers, and all newspapers sent through the mails and then sold had to be registered.

27. See, for example, *Guardian*, 13 May 1938.

28. Willet's idea, which harkened back to Benjamin Franklin's 1784 humorous suggestion to make all Parisians wake at dawn, was first promulgated in his July 1907 three-penny pamphlet. Although he died in 1915, it was due to his efforts that it became law. In order to save coal, Germany was the first country to adopt daylight saving in April 1916; Great Britain followed suit in May. In March 1918 the United States instituted daylight saving. It was repealed after two years, reinstituted from 1942 to 1945, repealed again, and finally made permanent in 1966. See David Prerau, *Seize the Daylight: The Curious and Contentious Story of Daylight Saving Time* (New York: Thunder's Mouth Press, 2005); and Michael Downing, *Spring Forward: The Annual Madness of Daylight Saving Time* (London: Shoemaker & Hoard, 2005).

29. For biographical information on Radford, see *South African Who's Who*, 34th edition (Johannesburg: Donaldson, 1950), 561; *Cape Times*, 26 August 1973; *Guardian*, 29 July 1943, 21 February 1946, and 2 September 1948; Karis and Carter Microfilm Collection, 9A; *Who Was Who among English and European Authors, 1931–1949*, vol. 3, no. 2 (Detroit: Gale Research, 1978), 1163. For evidence of her not taking a salary, see *Guardian*, 11 September 1939.

30. *Guardian*, 21 February 1946.

31. See Pauline Podbrey, *White Girl*, 107.

32. *Guardian*, 29 July 1943. Appolon Davidson, a Russian historian, has found evidence in the Comintern archives that Stalin used the visit of Betty and George Sacks—not members of the Party—to the Soviet Union in 1935 as an excuse to purge a cadre of supposed Trotskyists.

33. Peter Abrahams, *Tell Freedom: Memories of Africa* (New York: Alfred Knopf, 1954), 350. He would have joined the *Guardian* had Radford offered him a job; see Peter Abrahams, *Return to Goli* (London: Faber & Faber, 1953), 14. Abrahams's association with the *Guardian* did nothing to curry himself favor in the years to come. His novel *Mine Boy* was reviewed by Michael Harmel (*Guardian*, 16 January 1947) who called it "phoney, flat, lifeless."

34. Edgar, 93. Bunche also went to a Khalifa (an Islamic sword ceremony) with George and Betty: "The swords are sharp all right, as we discover when we run our fingers along them. Mrs Sacks cut her finger testing one of them."

35. *Guardian*, 13 May 1943.

36. Dedicated to Radford, the 223-page *Jew Baiting* book outlined the history of anti-Semitism and tackled such diverse issues as historical materialism and Britain's fascist leader Oswald Mosley. "Anti-Semitism," Sacks concluded, "is fundamentally an economic problem." Sacks's book took its title from George Bernard Shaw's *Intelligent Woman's Guide to Socialism*.

37. Sacks lectured at the University of Cape Town from 1934–1961. Brian Bunting, when speaking of Sacks's inability to suffer fools, said, "We used to joke that George was the leading pile surgeon in Cape Town."

38. See *Critic* 5, no. 1 (January–March 1937): 24–25, in which Sacks attacked the *Cape Times* for "sensationalism, emphasis on the trivial and scare headlines," and concluded by seeming to predict the *Guardian*'s future when he wrote, "There does not seem to be room for journals which appeal to a body of opinion interested in more serious subjects than 'South Africa's chances in the Test Match.'"

39. *Guardian*, 6 January 1939, for a two-week holiday; see also the Andrews Collection, box 4, Mayibuye Centre, University of the Western Cape, for a postcard from the Sackses while fishing

in Hermanus, and box 3 for Bill Andrews's diary, 6 December 1946, where Andrews records a story about a fish gnawing at George's finger.

40. Don Pinnock interview with Hilda Bernstein, London, 1988, Mayibuye Centre, University of the Western Cape.

41. *Guardian*, 17 February 1949.

42. See *Guardian*, 19 March 1937: The circulation manager "will dispatch a specimen copy" to interested subscribers.

43. *Guardian*, 24 September 1937; see also 11 June 1937 for Hannah's first column, and 25 July 1946 for another column on food.

44. *Guardian*, 27 February 1941.

45. Much of the information on Andrews comes from his collection at the Mayibuye Centre, UWC. See also *Guardian*, 4 November 1943 and 13 February 1947; Baruch Hirson correspondence with Moore Crossey, May 1991; Podbrey, *White Girl*, 95.

46. *Guardian*, 13 January 1949. In July and August 1937, Andrews wrote about the 1904 railway strike, the 1909 Natal railway strike, the 1897 May Day strike in Johannesburg, the 1908 De Beers lockout, and the 1911 Johannesburg tram-workers' strike.

47. *Guardian*, 17 and 24 December 1937, and 28 January 1938.

48. *Guardian*, 27 February 1947, for mention of Baldry going without a salary.

49. *Guardian*, 8 April 1938.

50. Simons, *Class and Colour*, 528; and *Guardian*, 14 April 1938.

51. *Guardian*, 2 September 1948; and Simons, *Class and Colour*, 583. Unfortunately, no copies of "The Munich Swindle" survived. The same day in London, Victor Gollancz sold two million copies of a one-page leaflet, "The Hitler Menace." See Hodges, *The Story of a Publishing House*, 135.

52. *Guardian*, 21 October 1938. Jack Simons later said, "'The Munich Swindle' did so much to put the paper on the map." Brian Bunting interview with Jack Simons, November 1973, in Brian Bunting Collection, Mayibuye Centre, UWC. Bunting himself wrote that "the reputation of the *Guardian*. . . . was established in its early years by its brilliant exposure of the appeasement policies leading up to the betrayal of Czechoslovakia by the Munich Agreement." Bunting, *Moses Kotane*, 97.

53. *Guardian*, 30 September 1938. Michael Harmel wrote that the *Guardian*'s "broad anti-racist and anti-fascist position in exposing the events of the 1930s came at a time when the English-language press, controlled by big mining and finance houses under pressure from the Hertzog government were virtually silent about Nazi crimes, and the Afrikaans press under editors like Verwoerd increasingly sympathetic"; Lerumo, *Fifty Fighting Years*, 68. See also John Burger [Leo Marquard], *The Black Man's Burden* (Port Washington, N.Y.: Kennikat Press, 1943), 247. Marquard said that "the communist Press is small, struggling and vigorous." Betty Radford had been rumored to be McClausland's mistress before she married Sacks.

54. *Guardian*, 4 February 1938 on Mussolini, and 1 April 1938 on Austria; see also 28 January 1938 for an article about fascism in Britain.

55. *Guardian*, 24 February 1939 about Neville Chamberlain, and 14 April 1939 about Mussolini.

56. *Guardian*, 2 July 1937 for "Topical," and 27 August 1937 for appeal. See also 17 September and 10 October 1937.

57. *Guardian*, 8 July 1938. In that issue was a poem, "Air Raid over Barcelona," by Stanley Richardson.

58. *Guardian*, 4 March 1938. The South African was the *Guardian*'s Johannesburg correspondent,

Charles Fox.

59. *Guardian*, 4, 11, and 18 March 1938; and a letter from the Spanish Consul thanking the newspaper, 8 April.

60. *Guardian*, 17 June 1938.

61. *Guardian*, 28 October 1938. See also 6 May 1938.

62. H. Lindsay Smith, *Behind the Press in South Africa* (Cape Town: Stewart, 1945), 97. A year later, the *Guardian* gained some measure of vindication by printing a Transocean facsimile that confirmed its real status as an official Third Reich news agency; *Guardian*, 23 April 1942.

63. *Guardian*, 13 August 1937.

64. *Guardian*, 30 September 1938.

65. *Guardian*, 9 April 1937 about Greyshirts, and 6 May 1938 about Blackshirts.

66. *Guardian*, 21 January 1938. The *Guardian* regularly printed articles on the woefully ineffective campaigns of anti-fascist organizations See 5 March 1937 and 11 March 1938 about Hilda Watts and Issy Wolfson speaking at a 300-person Johannesburg anti-facism meeting.

67. *Guardian*, 26 February 1937 about Pirow, and 2 and 9 April 1937 about Malan.

68. See Katie Silpert, the secretary of the Cape Town branch of the distributive workers, who wrote on 8 April 1938 and 12 August 1938.

69. *Guardian*, 31 March 1939, for the start of the "Industrial Front" page. See 4 August 1939, when it ran two pages. See 27 October 1939 for the back page changing.

70. *Guardian*, 7 May 1937 for Crateshifter, and 2 April 1937 for Super-Heater. Apparently readers liked Super-Heater's column, for in the 24 December 1937 issue he was called "a popular contributor."

71. See, for example, *Guardian*, 18 February 1938 and 29 October 1937. One advertisement for a Hairdressers' Employees Union's first annual dance, on 5 March 1937, read "Losing your Hair? Athlete's Foot? Run Down? Here's the Cure All."
See 26 February 1937, when Jimmy La Guma, Johnny Gomas, and Eli Weinberg founded the Laundry Employees Union in Cape Town.

72. See *Guardian*, August 1938.

73. *Guardian*, 10 June 1938 on diamond workers, 21 January 1938 on Emmerich, and 27 May 1938 on library opening. International trade-union issues such as unity within the United States trade-union giant the AFL-CIO, and Henry Ford were detailed; see 8 October 1937 and 9 July 1937.

74. *Guardian*, 30 April 1937. They were tramway and omnibus; chemical; stevedoring and dockworkers; distributive; engineers; railway and harbour; laundry, cleaner sand dyers; brewery; garment; butcher, blockmen and ordermen; hotel; furniture;, and typographical workers.

75. *Guardian*, 21 May, 4 June, and 10 October 1937.

76. *Guardian*, 12 November 1937. See also 6 August 1937, when Maitland workers received new clogs and overalls because of the *Guardian*; 30 July 1937, when wages increased for women gut workers; and 18 February 1938, when wages increased for women in the meat industry.

77. *Guardian*, 6 August 1937; 26 November 1937 for headline "Friday Night Shopping Will Go"; 17 December 1937 for more protests; 25 February 1938 for letter to the editor from Jimmy La Guma about the issue; 25 March 1938 for more reporting; and 1 July 1938 for a final victory.

78. *Guardian*, 8 July 1938.

79. *Guardian*, 22 July 1938.

80. *Guardian*, 11 March and 5 August 1938.

81. *Guardian*, 23 April 1937.

82. Andrews Collection, Mayibuye Centre, UWC, box 5; and *Guardian*, 1 July 1938.

83. For many years Kahn and Gool lived together, despite opposition from both families over the scandal the relationship engendered. In early 1943 Kahn moved out of their Gardens flat. When Pauline Podbrey and H. A. Naidoo, another interracial couple, arrived in Cape Town later that year, Gool told Podbrey, "He'll come back to me, but in the meantime you can have a room until you find something permanent." Six months later, in December 1943, Gool threw a party on the day Kahn married another woman. Podbrey, *White Girl*, 100.

84. *Guardian*, 7 May 1937 for the stupidities, and 26 November 1937 for capitalism is unchristian. See 30 September 1938 for a review of a Communist Party leaflet.

85. *Guardian*, 24 June 1938.

86. *Guardian*, 20 October 1937. See 1 December 1939 for a picture of an NLL dance, and 1 April 1938 for a letter to the editor from Jimmy La Guma about the NLL.

87. *Guardian*, 3 September 1937 for Fox, 24 June 1938 on Baldry, and 8 October 1937 about the new membership scheme.

88. *Guardian*, 14 October 1938.

89. *Guardian*, 23 April 1937.

90. *Guardian*, 14 June 1940: "a socialist paper can afford to be consistent in its policy."

91. *Guardian*, 4 June 1937. Examples of the *Guardian*'s letterhead from the 1930s can be found in the Abdurahman Collection, BCZA 83/32, Manuscripts and Archives, University of Cape Town.

92. Brooks, "From Class Struggle," 42.

93. *Guardian*, 4 June 1937.

94. *Guardian*, 3 September 1937. See 19 March 1937 for an attack on *Die Burger*'s "Campaign of distortion—Disrupting the workers."

95. *Guardian*, 16 and 23 April 1937. Later, Burnside was reported to be "looking bronze and well" after a three-month convalescence in England after "a serious breakdown"; 14 January 1938.

96. See *Guardian*, January 1940.

97. *Guardian*, 27 August 1937. See 13 May 1938 for an article about New Zealand, a "Happy Isle" because "Labour Rules There."

98. *Guardian*, 10 September 1937.

99. *Guardian*, 17 December 1937.

100. *Guardian*, 14 January 1938.

101. *Guardian*, 6 and 13 May 1938. There were no official Communist Party candidates in the 1938 election.

102. *Guardian*, 12 August 1938.

103. Afterwards, Snitcher joined the Party and lost a campaign for the Cape Town city council, as well as losing in the 1943 and 1948 general elections. "I think at one time I was the most defeated candidate in South Africa," he wryly said in 1995.

104. *Guardian*, 20 and 27 May 1938.

105. *Guardian*, 22 March 1962.

106. *Guardian*, 30 April 1937.

107. *Guardian*, 9 June 1939 about lipstick, and 6 May 1938 about voting. See 19 May 1939 for an article about women's wages.

108. *Critic* 5, no. 1 (January–March 1937): 22.

109. *Guardian*, 27 May 1938.

110. *Guardian*, 10 February 1939.

111. *Guardian*, 5 August 1938, 23 June 1939, and 2 October 1941.

112. *Guardian*, 26 May 1939.

113. *Guardian*, 6 August 1937.

114. As one historian noted, in the *Guardian*'s coverage of gender issues in the 1930s, "prevailing views on femininity and women's apolitical, domestic nature were tacitly endorsed." Cheryl Walker, *Women and Resistance in South Africa* (London: Onyx Press, 1982), 48. See also Helen Terre Blanche, "Mothers of the Nation: Afriakaans Women's Magazine Advertisements in the 1940s," *Kleio* 28, no. 196: 174–88; "Bottle or Breast-feeding?" *Guardian*, 19 January 1950; and *New Age*, 9 August 1962, for a photograph of a skimpily dressed Marilyn Monroe.

115. *Guardian*, 22 March 1962. Brian Bunting rightly acknowledged this fact: "The political slant of the *Cape Guardian* was progressive but the paper did not concern itself very largely with Non-European affairs."

116. Les Switzer, "*Bantu World* and the Origins of a Captive African Commercial Press in South Africa," *Journal of Southern African Studies* 14, no. 3 (1988): 351.

117. *Guardian*, 24 June 1938.

118. See, for example, the first issue of the *Guardian*, 19 February 1937. An interesting analysis of the *Guardian*'s advertising content can be found in Les Switzer, "Socialism and the Resistance Movement: The Life and Times of the *Guardian*, 1937–1952," in Switzer, *South Africa's Alternative Press*, 287. See also in the same book a discussion of *Inkululeko*'s advertising, which "suggested an intended audience that was poor, urban and African." Jones, "*Inkululeko*," 347–49.

119. *Guardian*, 5 March 1937.

120. Thecla Schreuders, "The Social and Intellectual Life of the Left in Cape Town During the Second World War, As Specifically Reflected in the *Guardian*," in *South African Research Papers*, vol. 5, ed. Helen Bradford and Bill Nasson (Cape Town: University of Cape Town, 1988), 22.

121. *Guardian*, 19 April 1937.

122. *Guardian*, 27 January 1939.

123. *Guardian*, 21 May 1937. See also 14 August 1941 for a Leslie Oney poem, "The Song of the Little Kaffir Boy." See 23 April 1937 and 3 June 1938. See also 20 May 1938 for a back-page piece titled "Coloured Railway Men Scandalously Underpaid"; and 12 May 1939 for a statement by a UCT student leader: "Our mouthpiece, the *Guardian*, should fulfill its function as a searchlight upon social evils wherever they may be." The *South African Worker* in 1938 advocated a dual minimum-daily-wage system: five shillings for Africans and ten shillings for whites.

124. See also *Guardian*, 26 August 1938. Radford attached an editor's note to a letter from Margaret Ballinger, a Native Representative MP: "Mrs Ballinger is well aware that an influential group exists . . . which seeks to improve the economic status of the non-European *at the expense of the European workers.*"

125. "Time to Wake Up, Mister," a sixteen-page illustrated pamphlet, September 1939, no. 605, vol. 7, South Africa, box 34, African Collection, Sterling Library, Yale University.

126. *Guardian*, 4 February 1938. Of course things were much worse in the white commercial press. See *Star* (Johannesburg), 21 February 1937: "Queer Superstitions among Natives."

127. *Inkululeko*, December 1940. Ray Alexander also was quoted in that issue, saying, "There are no other newspapers that speak for the African people, voice their grievances and put forward their demands. I appeal to all trade unionists to introduce *Inkululeko* to their members and thus strengthen the press of the African workers."

128. *Guardian*, 2 September 1948.

129. *Guardian*, 30 April 1937. See R. K. Cope, *Comrade Bill: The Life and Times of W. H. Andrews,*

Workers' Leader (Cape Town: Stewart, 1943), 329: "Its beginnings were modest and amateurish."

130. *Guardian*, 13 May 1938. The article was written by Petronella van Heerden.
131. *Guardian*, 14 April 1938.
132. *Guardian*, 26 February 1948.
133. *Guardian*, 26 January 1940.
134. *Guardian*, 20 August 1937; Radford wrote that "the revenue of the paper is derived exclusively from advertisers." See Switzer, "Socialism and the *Guardian*," in *South Africa's Alternative Press*, 281–88.
135. *Guardian*, 21 May 1937. The list included the Assembly Toilet Saloon in Roeland Street, Baker's Café in Salt River, "Nu" Pharmacy in Claremont, David's Tobacconist in Wynberg, Hurwitz Hairdressing Saloon in Rondebosch, Schumacher's Café on Sir Lowrey's Road, Cramer's News Agency on Longmarket Street, the Rest Tea Room in Mowbray, and Modern Books.
136. *Guardian*, 12 March 1937 about getting friends, December 1938 about apathetic, 19 March 1937 about specimen.
137. Even then, Carneson was an avid supporter of the weekly. He gave £5 each month. See *Guardian*, 20 February 1941 and 12 March 1942. See 11 June 1942 for a letter to the editor.
138. Jeremy Bernstein interview with Jean Bernadt, "Media Active"; and James Zug telephone conversation, March 1994. The Bernadts were long-time supporters of the *Guardian*; Hymie also acted as their lawyer in the 1950s. See *Guardian*, 5 July 1956, for a £100 donation.
139. *Guardian*, 27 May 1938.
140. Sterling Library, Yale, box 24; see *Guardian*, 1 September 1939.
141. It cost two shillings sixpence. One of the few extant copies of "Pins and Needles" is at Sterling Library, Yale. The title was taken from a 1937 Broadway musical that ran for over 1,100 performances. The International Ladies' Garment Workers' Union produced the show, and its workers were the actors. Its hit song was "It's Better with a Union Man."
142. *Guardian*, 27 January 1939.
143. See *Guardian*, 14 January 1938 about nasty thoughts, and 4 June 1937 about bunk and debunk.
144. James Zug interview with Wolfie Kodesh, March 1994, and Brian Bunting, December 1993; James Zug telephone interviews with Pauline Kahn and Errol Shanley, May 1994; and Jeremy Bernstein interview with Jean Bernadt, December 1988. Shanley was the tipster in Durban. Bunting wrote in 1997 that Kahn was not the tipster.
145. *Guardian*, 24 September 1937 about all races, and 11 November 1941 about his £1 salary.
146. *Guardian*, 30 July 1937.
147. One such correspondent was Vivian Philips, author of *Progressive Revelation* and *Modern Knowledge and Old Beliefs*, and "one of the staunchest supporters of the *Guardian*." *Guardian*, 3 September 1937 and 8 July 1938.
148. See *Guardian*, August 1937, for the beginning of Fox's column. Also 14 January and 22 April 1938.
149. See *Guardian*, 18 February, 11 March, and 10 June 1938.
150. *Guardian*, 15 July 1938 for a full-page article by Solly Sachs, and 17 June 1938 for a letter to the editor from him; 17 June 1938 for Burford; and 13 May 1938 for Robertson. Burford was secretly a member of the Party.
151. *Guardian*, 6 August 1937. See George Findlay, *Miscegenation* (Pretoria: Pretoria News and Printing Works, 1936).
152. Bernard Sachs, *South African Personalities and Politics* (Johannesburg: Kayor Publishing, 1959),

116; Rusty Bernstein, *Memory Against Forgetting: Memoirs from a Life in South African Politics, 1938–1964* (London: Viking, 1999), 119–20; and Bernard Sachs, *Multitude of Dreams: A Semi-Autobiographical Study* (Johannesburg: Kayor Publishing, 1949), 144–45.

153. See Edgar, *Ralph Bunche*, 185. "His gestures and manner were as dynamic as those of Groucho Marx. His harangues were punctuated with the same nihilistic thrusts. . . ."; Sachs, *South African Personalities*, 117–18. "He used to snip hair and preach and speak and it was talk all the time, like a gramophone. It would go on and on and on"; David Everatt interview with Issy Heyman, February 1983, Everatt Collection, Mayibuye Centre, UWC. The barbershop was in the Gladstone Hotel, on the corner of Commissioner and Von Weilig.

154. Jeremy Bernstein interview with Jean Bernadt, "Media Active."

155. See Simons, *Class and Colour*, 530.

156. Alan Brooks, "From Class Struggle," 23–25. See Bernstein, *Memory Against Forgetting*, 35–38; and Brian Bunting interview with Ray Alexander, Bunting Collection, UWC. See Francis Beckett, *Enemy Within: The Rise and Fall of the British Communist Party* (London: John Murray, 1995), 90–97.

157. *Guardian*, 22 September 1939.

158. *Freedom*, June 1940. See Doreen Musson, *Johnny Gomas: Voice of the Working Class* (Cape Town: Buchu Books, 1989).

159. *Guardian*, 8 July 1941.

160. Brian Bunting, observing the weekly's oscillation, wrote that the *Guardian* was "now steadily on the right course again." Bunting, *Moses Kotane*, 99. See *1939: The Communist Party and the War*, ed. John Attfield and Stephen Williams (London: Lawrence & Wishart, 1984).

CHAPTER TWO. FORTY THOUSAND NO LESS: THE WAR YEARS, 1939–1945

1. Brooks, "From Class Struggle," 25.

2. See Simons, *Class and Colour*, 484–85; and James Zug interview with Ray Alexander and Jack Simons, December 1993. See also Roux, *Rebel Pity*, 74.

3. See Brian Bunting, "South African Journalists in the Front Line," *Sechaba* 23, no. 4 (April 1989): 15.

4. Reel 8, Simons Collection, Mayibuye Centre, UWC.

5. In 1943 a resolution declared the *Guardian* "essential for the continued development and influence of the Party." In 1948 one of the national conference resolutions discussed the commercial press, saying, "Conference declares that in order to combat this propaganda it is essential to strengthen papers such as the *Guardian* and *Inkululeko* which are devoted to the cause of the workers and democracy. One of the primary duties of every Party organisation and member is to expand the circulation of these papers and to obtain financial support." In 1949 the Party called upon members "to make a special effort to double Party sales" of the *Guardian*. The Party also called for the circulation of *Freedom* and *Inkululeko* to be doubled. See *Freedom* 2, no. 2 (June 1944).

6. Reel 8, Simons Collection, Mayibuye Centre, UWC. There is no record of what Cape Town's poets offered, but no doubt many were challenged by the difficulty of finding another word to rhyme with toilers and spoilers.

7. Don Pinnock interview with Fred Carneson, 1988; and James Zug interview with Fred Carne-

son, March 1994. See also Joe Slovo, *Slovo: The Unfinished Autobiography* (Johannesburg: Ravan Press, 1995), 23.

8. Ginsburg supplemented his income by taking, developing and framing photographs. See People's Pageant Souvenir, December 1941, Abdurahman Collection, BCZA 83/32, UCT; and James Zug telephone conversation with Dora Alexander, November 1994.

9. *Guardian*, 6 April 1944. When Ginsburg got engaged, Radford wrote in "Topical": "There can be few people in Cape Town who do not know Gerson Ginsburg either personally or by sight. He is a Cape Town character—the most indefatigable seller of the *Guardian*." See 1 March 1945. "It was simply a pleasure. I loved doing it. You'd meet the greatest people and you'd see them every week on your route. They'd tell you their problems, what had been happening on their street, to their family, to their friends. You'd take all that back to Betty and there would be a story about it sooner or later." James Zug conversation with Gerson Ginsburg, April 1994.

10. See Albie Sachs, *The Soft Vengeance of a Freedom Fighter* (New York: HarperCollins, 1991), 76. James Zug interview with Wolfie Kodesh, December 1993: "We had no electric lights and we used to bathe in a big tub. We had a paraffin tin filled with water and you pumped up a primus stove to heat the water, put it in a tub, and then my brother and I or my twin and I would sit in the tub, a big tub, and bathe together. For lights we had a sort of pumping affair, you know. The lavatory was outside and next to the lavatory just over the wall was a stable, so we were inundated with bloody rats and mice, you know. We used to have prostitutes, coloured prostitutes right there. We had a little shop in the back and their beat was along that pavement. And in those days the British fleet used to come in a hell of a lot."

11. James Zug interview with Pauline Podbrey, December 1993: "If people didn't know, a lot of Africans would look at us blankly and wonder what white boys and girls were doing there. It was an unusual sight. But, very quickly, the next week we'd come back and we'd be welcomed with a smile. Certainly we never encountered any hostility. We did from the whites on the street corners. There we would be attacked. Oh, yes, abuse us, shout rude words at us—because we were communists and because we were mixing with blacks. There were blacks and whites together. That was a great sin." See Anthony Sampson, *The Treason Cage: The Opposition on Trial in South Africa* (London: Heinemann, 1958), 168–69: "When European Communists went into the locations to hold meetings or to sell copies of the *Guardian*, they went more as missionaries than as colleagues."

12. *Guardian*, 20 January 1944. See Lerumo, *Fifty Fighting Years*, 80. The British Communist Party's membership soared from 15,570 in 1938 to 56,000 in 1942.

13. Dominic Fortescue, "The Communist Party of South Africa and the African Working Class in the 1940s," *International Journal of African Historical Studies* 24, no. 3 (1991): 490.

14. Maurice Nyagumbo, a Rhodesian living in Cape Town during the war, joined with a friend after talking with veteran *Guardian* seller Jean Bernadt: "Although I did not understand a word of what she was saying, I agreed to join the Party, because I was impressed by the behavior of the European girls. . . . We completely lacked political understanding. What appealed to the two of us was the social aspect of the organisation." Maurice Nyagumbo, *With the People: An Autobiography From the Zimbabwean Struggle* (London: Allison and Busby, 1980), 73–76.

15. *Guardian*, 21 April and 7 July 1939, and 26 February 1948. Unexplained spurts of selling occurred sometimes; on 30 June 1939, 753 more copies were sold than the week before.

16. Brian Bunting interview with Jack Simons, November 1973, Brian Bunting Collection, Mayibuye Centre. Snitcher disputed Simons's memory: "As far as I was concerned, there was never, ever—and if there was, it was without my knowledge—an attempt or suggestion that the

Guardian should become an organ of the Party." James Zug interview with Harry Snitcher, January 1995.

Simons also said that Eddie Roux was against the whole idea of the *Guardian*: "He was rather critical of the publication of the *Guardian*. He spoke to me several times about it and thought we were doing the wrong thing by bringing out an English newspaper and neglecting the African people because *Umsebenzi* packed up and he said this was completely wrong. So this discouraged him." Simons added, "The *Guardian* certainly wasn't set up as a formal and official decision of any Party group. It began as a free-lance enterprise."

17. Pinnock, "Raising the Red Flag: The *Guardian*, 1937–1962," a paper presented at "A Century of the Resistance Press in South Africa" at the University of the Western Cape, 6–7 June 1991, p. 14.

18. James Zug interview with Fred Carneson, March 1994: "It didn't have a direct role. From the Party point of view, it was an extremely valuable paper, and it would have been a blow to the whole democratic movement if it went under. So, from that point of view, the Party I think was always concerned with what was happening on the paper and would, when possible and necessary, intervene in that supporting role."

19. The exact date of their joining is not known, but it was before the June 1941 Nazi invasion of the Soviet Union. Discovering the date can be almost impossible, as in the case of Bram Fischer, who also seems to have joined around the same time. Stephen Clingman, *Bram Fischer: Afrikaner Revolutionary* (Cape Town: David Philip, 1998), 147–51. See *Guardian*, 26 June 1941, with a report about George Sacks speaking at a CP rally in the Grand Parade—something a freshly minted member would not probably do; 20 December 1945, with a mention that Radford joined in 1940 and was a member of the Cape Town district committee since 1941; page 12 of the minutes of the Party's 19 April 1941 national conference, where the secretary reports that there is only one Party member on the editorial board of the *Guardian*; and Brooks, "From Class Struggle," 43.

20. Simons, *Class and Colour*, 539.

21. See *Guardian*, 21 May 1942, for an example of a Baldry speech, at the Cape Town Left Club; see *Freedom* 2, no. 6 (December 1944).

22. Abdurahman Collection, BCZA 83/32, Manuscripts and Archives, UCT.

23. Doris Lessing, *In Pursuit of the English: A Documentary* (London: MacGibbon and Kee, 1960), 17–18.

24. In "Let's Talk About Russia," Sacks wrote about the Moscow show trials: "So they began secret negotiations with Hess and other Nazi thugs. So they were discovered, and so they were shot. . . . But in comparison with Tsarist Russia, it was heaven."

25. *Guardian*, 19 July 1943 and 3 June 1943; see 21 October 1944 for article on party politics, and 16 December 1943 on a Cape Town foreshore scheme that led, fifty years later, to the Waterfront complex. Sacks's series on communism ran from 5 August 1943 to 4 January 1944.

26. Nine communists polled 6,800 votes for just over 10 percent of the votes cast in nine constituencies; Simons, *Class and Colour*, 538.

27. *Argus*, 9 December 1981, for his obituary; and *Guardian*, 4 January 1945.

28. Fanny Klenerman Collection, A2031, Department of Historical Papers, William Cullen Library, University of the Witwatersrand, 26 March 1941: "At the discussion with Molteno, Jack and I agreed the local branch should interest itself in legislative attacks on democratic rights, non-European issues, etc.—that while supporting your body in the fight for internees, we should also spread the fight over a wider area of interest."

The internees, most notably Max Gordon, Arnold Latti, E. J. Burford, and the Joffe brothers,

Max and Louis, were detained at Baviaanspoort Segregation Camp. See Simons, *Class and Colour*, 533. Yusuf Dadoo was also jailed for four months because he popularized the slogan "Don't support this war, where the rich get richer and the poor get killed." For more on the internees, see *Guardian*, 3 January, 10 and 17 July 1941, and 27 July 1944; also see 19 August 1943 for mention of the fact that one of the internees, Arnold Latti, had the *Guardian* sent to him every week at Jagersfontein Camp in the Northern Cape.

29. *Guardian*, 20 December 1945; and Jones, "*Inkululeko*," 343.

30. *Guardian*, 9 July 1942. See 13 January 1944 for Radford speaking at the Johannesburg Left Club's symposium.

31. *Guardian*, 14 January 1943 for beginning of the Home Front, and 11 June 1942 for a colleague saying Radford was doing "a stout bit of work." The Springbok Legion's motto was "Do Not Mourn, Mobilise." Ruth First, Vernon Berrange, Bram Fischer and Joe Slovo were also members of the Home Front League. See Barry White, "The Role of the Springbok Legion in the Communist Party of South Africa's Common Front Strategy, 1941–50," *Kleio* 25 (1993): 95–109.

32. *Cape Times*, 7 September 1943. The *Cape Times* reported the morning after the election that "both the communist candidates were successful. Many of their supporters waited for the results, singing party songs and the 'Internationale.'"

33. *Cape Times*, 26 August 1973; and *Guardian*, 9 September 1943. She also joined the markets, public-health, and native-affairs committees; represented the council on the committees of the Woodstock public library and hospital; and started the annual Community Carnival. When Radford died, the *Cape Times* interviewed a colleague on the city council, Gerry Ferry, who was also first elected in 1943. He said Radford was an "extremely pleasant person. However I did not agree with her views, which were very left wing. All the same, she did a lot of good and meant well."

34. *Guardian*, 27 January and 23 March 1944. See 5 March 1945 for four pictures of clubs, and 3 August 1944 on the Claremont club.

35. Reel 8, Simons Collection, Mayibuye Centre, UWC; and *Guardian*, 23 February 1944 and 3 May 1945. Radford angered the more conservative members of the council with her radicalism: in early 1945 she was arrested for organizing and speaking at a city rally without the council's permission, a charge for which eventually she was cleared. *Guardian*, 22 February 1945. See also 29 April 1943 for a letter to the editor from Sam Kahn about absent council members.

36. *Guardian*, 3 February 1944.

37. *Guardian*, 7 December 1944.

38. Bill Andrews diary, box 4, Andrews Collection, Mayibuye Centre, University of the Western Cape. See, for example, Sunday, 26 March 1944: "Spent day with George and Bettie Sacks."

39. *Guardian*, 21 December 1944 and 11 January 1945 for articles, 30 September 1943 for editorial.

40. *Guardian*, 4 March 1943.

41. *Guardian*, 9 December 1943. In court, fighting a 1944 libel case, Betty Radford testified that "many people would attach great importance to what he writes, he is a man with a reputation." *Guardian*, 7 December 1944. Brian Bunting later said: "Bill was a father figure to us all. We would out of duty go see him in Camps Bay. He had had a shaky relationship with my father, felt that he had dropped out. I certainly never brought it up."

42. *Guardian*, 13 December 1945, with a long interview on the forthcoming annual national conference. For a fuller biography, see Bunting, *Moses Kotane*.

43. See *Guardian*, 28 October 1943, for an article on the fishing industry.

44. See *Guardian*, 15 July 1943, for a letter to the editor from Kahn. Snitcher recalled, "Yes, the

Guardian was a large part of our political life in the '40s. We talked about it, we visited the offices, we sold it at meetings, we defended it in court. Not a day went by without the *Guardian*."

45. *Guardian*, 7 October 1943.

46. Dick, secretary of the Textile Workers' Union, recalled, "The *Guardian* was the epicenter of Cape Town politics and we all did what we could." Dick was never a Party member. She also performed a yeoman's task when she catalogued the *Guardian*. See *Guardian*, 27 October 1954, for interview with Dick. See also Podbrey, *White Girl*, 101; *Guardian*, 18 May 1944 for article by Abe W. Jacobs on the coloured community, 5 April 1945 and 11 May 1945 on dried-fruit workers in Worcester, 5 July 1945 for Abe Scholtz on farming issues.

47. "We worked awfully hard for the *Guardian* during the war," Close later said. "Selling, raising funds, writing for it. It was quite a presence." Podbrey, *White Girl*, 110; see *Guardian*, 30 January and 2 October 1941. Close's father was a member of Parliament from 1915 to 1933 and then ambassador to the United States until his death in 1945. See Rex Close, *New Life* (Cape Town: Food and Canning Workers' Union, 1950). Close married Jean Bernadt's sister.

48. Podbrey, *White Girl*, 98.

49. See *Guardian*, 11 December 1941 on Soviet life; 9 September 1943 on the Cape dock strike of 1919; 28 October 1943; 24 February 1944 on Southern Cross magazine; 21 August 1941 for a review. Amy Thornton later said: "We [Modern Youth Society] got a place in Loop Street eventually, and we opened a club. It had one huge wall, and Jack Cope painted a mural. He designed it and we all helped paint it. I'll never forget Jack Simons giving a lecture and explaining a whole thing of economics by using this mural."

50. *Guardian*, 13 February 1941, poem "War Aims"; 21 August 1941 for article; 10 July 1941 for book review.

51. See *Guardian*, 27 March 1941, 12 June 1941, and the final article on 10 July 1941.

52. *Guardian*, 21 September 1944; 15 February 1945 on open letter. See also 9 November 1944; 11 January, 8 February, and 29 November 1945. See Radford's obituary on Cash, 15 June 1950.

53. *Guardian*, 6 February 1941, about Mussie Snitcher. See 28 August 1941 "spend your holiday with *Guardian* friends and sympathisers," and 25 September 1941; 21 May 1942 for vaudeville evening at Hotel Avalon with a "full-length talkie film"; 8 September 1939 for film show, dance, and social "for South Africa's foremost democratic paper"; 24 November 1939 for jumble sale; 1 August 1940 for a bazaar and dance raising £186; 20 February 1941 for a *Guardian* league picnic to Gordon's Bay, which on 27 February 1941 was rightly changed to Hout Bay; 17 July 1941 for card party; 8 January 1942 for New Year's Eve party netting £75; 6 August 1942 for grand dance in Hanover St.; 3 September 1942 for marionette show and dance at Glamorgan in Newlands; 17 December 1942 for Christmas dance at Mount Pleasant, 3s. 6d. donation; 14 January 1943 for *Guardian* birthday dance at Woodstock Town Hall, 3s. 6d. ticket, and see 25 February 1943 on how it raised £138; 22 April 1943 for jumble sale; 18 November 1943 for *Guardian* league news; 5 August 1943 for gramophone recital in Gardens; 16 December 1943 for yet another *Guardian* Christmas ball, this time held in Woodstock, 3s. 6d., and for Southern suburbs dance 21 December and a Christmas Eve party in Organjezicht—obviously quite a busy Christmas season; 29 July 1944 for fete raising £300; 12 October 1944 for freedom fair that netted £500. In the Cape Town league's first year, it held seventeen happenings that netted the *Guardian* a helpful £440. Sometimes the league would hold a collecting blitz and send out its faithful in a one-day, house-to-house assault on Cape Town's moneyed class. See 25 May 1944.

The Schwalbs in Vredehoek held musical evenings, the Goldbergs hosted Shostakovitch recitals, and the Baskins and the Ben Jaffes held dances that went "long past curfew time." See 17 April 1941; 11 March 1943; 8 April 1943 for Baskins raised £25; 16 March 1944.

There appears to have been little difference, besides onomatopoetic, between a jumble and a rumble sale. The bazaars, held every few months at Oddfellows Hall or the Drill Hall in Cape Town, included dozens of cakes, fruit, sandwiches, books, furniture, and clothing stalls, as well as boxing matches, variety shows, music, a children's playground, and an evening dance. See Nyagumbo, *With the People*, 74.

54. *Guardian*, 3 January 1941 for 100 at a Clifton party, 25 February 1943 for the birthday party. Charles Fox, the *Guardian*'s first Johannesburg correspondent, moved during the war to Cape Town and hosted the weekly's annual Christmas dance at his Sea Point home: 21 December 1944, his dances had a 2s. 6d. ticket; 27 December 1945 for a dance raising £54. The dances were not uniformly black-tie, though most guests wore evening clothes. James Zug correspondence with Brian Bunting, October 1998.

55. Jeremey Bernstein interview with Jean Bernadt, "Media Active."

56. Wilfrid H. Harrison, *Memoirs of a Socialist in South Africa, 1903–1947* (Cape Town: Stewart, 1947), 6. See also *Guardian*, 3 January 1941; and Lionel Forman, "Chapters in the History of the March to Freedom," *New Age* pamphlet (1959), 13. Harrison, like most Capetonians, had no time for the Transvaal: "Johannesburg is more a place for hot air than anything of an advanced character in the revolutionary movement" (114).

57. See 8 March 1944 letter from Carina Pearson to Cissie Gool, in Abdurahman Collection, UCT.

58. In March 1994 Wolfie Kodesh and I drove down to Barrack Street to see if the Chames Building still existed. It did, although most of the building's offices were empty, including the old *Guardian* rooms on the third floor. The visit was emotional for Kodesh, for he had not been to Barrack Street in more than thirty years. Louis Lutzno, a tenant on the ground floor since 1953, did not recall the *Guardian*, but did remember from that era of "a constant stream of detectives and policemen going up the stairs."

59. *Guardian*, 5 June 1941, for Radford appealing to readers to supply chairs, tables, desks, and typewriters to furnish the new offices. In May 1958 the weekly paid £54 in rents for all four of its offices, including Barrack Street.

James Zug interview with Albie Sachs, March 1994: "The paper was in Barrack Street and it was impressed upon my memory that progressive organizations were always on the top floor of some old building that you had to walk up all these flights of stairs. So today when I go to Shell House in Johannesburg [the ANC headquarters at the time] and I get into the lift and I get off at the tenth floor, I can't believe it, I still have got the mindset, the psychology of the oppressed. It wasn't like what you see, you know, in your American movies, with paper flying all over the place and editors shouting at everybody. There was a lot of nooks and corners."

60. *Guardian*, 11 September 1941.

61. James Zug correspondence with Doris Lessing, June 1994.

62. Brooks, "From Class Struggle," 38.

63. Simons, *Class and Colour*, 505; see photo of Naidoo in *Guardian*, 24 July 1941. Podbrey, *White Girl*, 90, on H.A.'s mother and leaving school. Naidoo followed his grandmother's example and became a Christian.

64. Simons, *Class and Colour*, 505. Podbrey, *White Girl*, 28.

65. Podbrey described her first meeting with Naidoo: "I shook hands with the handsomest man I'd ever seen. He stood at his table with an easy grace, narrow-hipped, taller than me, dark complexioned with black, wavy hair and smiling eyes set well apart. His chin was as confident as a

man's chin needs to be, without aggression, and his full, shapely mouth suggested kindliness and humour. His shirt was spotless and his well-cut suit contrasted sharply with the faded clothes of those around him but seemed just right on him. . . . Here was a black man who had no need of postures or assertion in his dealings with any group; he could afford to be perfectly at ease across the colour barrier, feeling neither hostile nor inferior. He was relaxed, friendly and fully in control of the meeting and of himself. Little did I guess that evening that this was the man I would one day marry." Podbrey, *White Girl*, 33.

66. See *Guardian*, 12 October 1944 for a guest editorial; 7 September 1942 for a sketch of Zulu Pungula; 13 January 1949; and 23 March 1944. Naidoo had written for a magazine that the nationalist bloc in the Natal Indian Congress (NIC) had produced, so he had some journalism skills.

67. Podbrey, *White Girl*, 93 and 118. James Zug interview with Rowley Arenstein, February 1994: "So they went to Cape Town where they got married. That solved that problem. But it didn't solve the problem of H. A. Naidoo. H. A. Naidoo was a Durban man, he was a leader of the Indian workers. H.A. was never a leader of any other workers." James Zug interview with Ismail Meer, February 1994: "There was an old grandmother who I used to always have tea with and she says, 'Where is H.A.?' So I said, 'He is not going to come here, he is going to be in Cape Town.' And typical Tamil, we say, 'What is this, you people uproot a mango tree and plant it in Cape Town? It can never grow there. Mango trees require tropical climate, requires the base from which it can find its sustenance. H.A. belonged to the sugar fields. He belonged to the workers here. He was not a leader that can muster any force in Cape Town.' And this woman really in a nutshell told us that H.A. should never have gone to Cape Town."

68. Podbrey, *White Girl*, 134.

69. Alan Paton, *Cry, the Beloved Country* (New York: Scribner's, 1951), 10.

70. Lodge, "Class Conflict, Communal Struggle and Patriotic Unity," 2; and Lodge, *Black Politics*, 12. The African urban population in South Africa doubled between 1939 and 1952.

71. Stephen Clingman, *Bram Fischer: Afrikaner Revolutionary* (Cape Town: David Philip, 1998), 133.

72. "This was the most important point: starting in Johannesburg, we decided to make it a Party paper. Every weekend we got the Party to sell the paper. And they did and that's how we actually built it up . . . because by getting all the Party members or most of them to go out on Sundays, first of all, we were organising, we were doing something. We felt we were doing something very useful and very important by selling the *Guardian*. Then you got to know certain people in the area and go and knock on their door and say, 'Look at this and look at that.' You got to know people in the area." James Zug interview with Rowley Arenstein, February 1994.

73. Podbrey, *White Girl*, 50; and James Zug interview with Ismail Meer, February 1994. Joffe's surgery, in the Lewis and Marks Building, was also a meeting place for the Junior Left Book Club; the first political meeting Joe Slovo ever attended was at Joffe's surgery.

74. As Arenstein noted, "If you don't get the news, you can't sell the paper." "I used to go on a Sunday morning to Sophiatown," said Sadie Forman, one of the young YCL comrades whose father was in the Left Book Club, "with Harold Wolpe driving the car. I have an abiding memory of when we finished selling the paper and we'd get back in the car. This was a weekly event. It didn't just happen once. We'd get into the car and Harold would say, 'Am I hungry. Am I hungry.' And then a little while, 'Am I thirsty.' We had regular customers, they knew who we were. We'd go out about four or five of us and were very happy if we could sell like forty copies. When the black comrades came, when Moses Kotane came, that made it much easier."

75. *Guardian*, 24 November 1939.

76. *Guardian*, 7 August 1941. The site is now the Carleton Centre.

77. *Guardian*, 11 June 1942; see article 18 March 1943. The Party's old offices were at the Trades Hall from 1921 until 1927, and then 41a Fox Street until the late 1930s. The *Guardian* advertised for positions in the new Johannesburg office: 23 December 1943 for a circulation manager, 20 July 1944 for a reporter—"this is not a senior post," and for an organizing secretary-fundraiser. A Miss Waterfield was the first official manager. Her office hours (the Capetonians must have grinned) appeared on 28 August 1941: Monday—8–10, 1–2, 3–6; Tuesday—9:30–10:30, 1–2, 3–6; Wednesday—Closed; Thursday—9:30–10:30, 1–2, 3–6; Friday—9:30–10:30, 1–2, 3–6; Saturday—8–4; Sunday—8–12

78. *Guardian*, 20 December 1945.

79. See *Guardian*, 19 October 1944 and 11 October 1945. She became the secretary of the Chemical Workers' Union, a member of the national executive of the South African Trades & Labour Council, and a failed Johannesburg city-council candidate.

80. *Guardian*, 18 June 1942 with a picture of Kaye, the national organizer for a *Guardian* campaign; 8 April 1943 for an article about Kaye's wife donating an oil portrait titled "Shangaan" to be sold for benefit of the *Guardian*. See also 15 March, 12 April, and 3 May 1945. Other contributors included Joe Schields, who wrote numerous trade-union articles, and Gwen Marriner, who was a full-time fundraiser during the war.

81. *Guardian*, 1 October 1942; 25 March, 8 and 29 April, 17 June, and 1 July 1943; 3, 17, and 24 February, and 1 June 1944.

82. *Guardian*, 25 October 1945, for a short biography of Wolfson. He was also secretary for the Tailoring Workers' Industrial Union, a member of the national executive of the SAT&LC, and founder of the Friends of the Spanish Republic. See 22 April and 13 May 1943, and 3 February, 9 March, and 5 October 1944 for articles by him. See 16 October 1941 for Du Plessis, and 25 October 1945 for Watts.

83. James Zug interview with Hilda and Rusty Bernstein, May 1994: "I sold in Braamfontein, which was then a white working-class area, railway workers and so on. Both Hilda and I used to write occasionally, on economic issues from me and articles on the city council from Hilda. Selling was an ordeal, but we felt like we were martyrs to the revolution, that this was good for your soul to do this work you hated doing. It was all for the cause."

   For an extended description and meditation about selling the weekly, see Bernstein, *Memory Against Forgetting*, 45–48: "I like to think that perhaps we did help to change some of their ideas and counter some of their prejudices. Perhaps when the time came for white South Africa to choose between civil war and majority government, our *Guardian* Sundays might have influenced some of their decisions for the better. Perhaps. Whatever the reality, those hours of paper-selling were not totally wasted. We had spread information and ideas which might possibly have helped Braamfontein railwaymen and Mai-Mai beer drinkers to look at their country in a new way, perhaps to start adapting their minds to a new South Africa which was still fifty years away."

84. *Guardian*, 25 October 1945. See *New Age*, 13 August 1959, for an obituary for Arthur Harmel.

85. David Everatt interview with Issy Heyman, May 1987, in Everatt Collection, UWC: "When Michael Harmel came back from England in '39 he impressed us all very much with his theoretical understanding of Marxism...." See *African Communist*, no. 59 (4th quarter 1974).

86. "Michael could be a very tough customer and very awkward, but historically he's a giant," commented Ben Turok. Donald Pinnock interview with Ben Turok, 1988, in Donald Pinnock, "Writing Left: Ruth First and Radical South African Journalism in the 1950s), unpublished man-

uscript, 1993, p. 56. Rowley Arenstein recalled that Harmel "read all night and slept all day. He was so well-versed in theory that he completely dominated the Party." Robert Vincent Lambert, "Political Unionism in South Africa: The South African Congress of Trade Unions, 1955–1965," doctoral dissertation, University of the Witwatersrand, 1988, p. 59.

Nelson Mandela met Harmel in the early 1940s. "I was impressed with the degree, but when I met him, I thought to myself, 'This chap has a M.A. and he is not even wearing a tie.' I just could not reconcile this discrepancy. Later, Michael and I became friends, and I came to admire him greatly, in no small measure because he rejected so many of the rather foolish conventions I once embraced. He was not only a brilliant writer, but was so committed to communism that he lived in a manner no different from an African." Mandela, *Long Walk to Freedom*, 66. Mandela's comment about Harmel's disheveled state was especially amusing because Harmel's wife Ray was a dressmaker and made Winnie Mandela's wedding dress.

87. Harmel wrote for *Inkululeko* and was usually the only non-African to serve on its editorial board. See Jones, "*Inkululeko*," 341–43. See *Guardian*, 10 July and 4 September 1941. See also 1 June 1944, 15 October 1942, and from East London on 24 June 1943.

88. *Guardian*, 6 and 20 February 1941: "details at the People's Bookshop." The Yugoslav Workers' Cultural Club held monthly dances for the *Guardian*. See 5 March 1942: "large numbers of Non-European workers have bought tickets." The leaders of the Johannesburg Guardian league were Dr. J. B. Robertson, chairman of the Johannesburg Left Book Club; Glyn Thomas, the registrar at the University of the Witwatersrand; Colin Legum, editor of the Labour Party journal *Forum*; Ralph Rabb; Jessie Apple; Trudy Gelb; and Molly Fischer, wife of CP leader Bram Fischer. James Zug telephone interview with Trudy Gelb, November 1994. See *Guardian*, 23 April and 14 May 1942, for an article by Glyn Thomas. See 22 October 1942 for list of committees; also 6 August 1942, 25 March, and 29 April 1943. See 25 March 1943 for Apple's obituary.

89. There were branches in Kensington, Doornfontein, Bertrams, Hillbrow, Krugersdorp, Vereinging, Orange Grove, Darnall, and Bellevue. *Guardian*, 16 July, 5 and 19 November, and 10 December 1942; and 9 September 1943. 5 November 1942 reports that Krugersdorp committee has six members; 19 November that Orange Grove, Bertrams, and Vereinging each have ten members. See 8 November 1945 for a picture of Max Cohen: "Star member of the Bertrams league."
For further references to the Johannesburg *Guardian* leagues, see 27 February 1941 dance at garment workers hall; 29 January 1942 dance; 20 February 1942 Rio Cinema for singing and piano; 16 July 1942, two plays in Johannesburg and gramophone evening in Braamfontein; 13 May 1943 People's Choir singing Soviet songs for *Guardian* fund; 20 May 1943 monthly gramophone evening; 16 December 1943 Christmas Eve dance; 26 July 1945 stage and screen show at Lyric Theatre; 22 November 1945 *Guardian* fete at Johannesburg city hall with morning market on President Street, lunch, dancing display, children's tea party, stalls, fishpond and tombola, games, dance at night.

90. *Guardian*, 31 May 1945; see also 11 January 1945. The Kensington league, founded in 1942, was one of the most active, raising £265 in three years; 5 July 1945. The Jewish Workers' Club, a Doornfontein-based organization, also raised enormous sums for the *Guardian*, including £1,000 in 1942. *Guardian*, 20 November 1941, 5 March and 23 April 1942; 8 June 1944 for a *Guardian* fete with fish pond, tombola, and bar, raising £300; 1 April 1943 for a freedom fair; 2 April 1942 for a banquet in Doornfontein for the end of a *Guardian* fundraising campaign. For more on the JWC, see Adler Taffy, "Lithuania's Diaspora: The Johannesburg Jewish Workers' Club, 1928–1948," *Journal of Southern African Studies*, 6, no. 1 (October 1979): 70–92.

91. Clingman, *Bram Fischer*, 224. *Guardian*, 18 February 1943; 20 January and 2 March 1944,

raised £75; 29 March 1945, raised £237; in 1950 the Party raised £250; in 1952, £650. See 11 January 1945 when Bram Fischer stopped by the CapeTown offices, and see 26 July 1945 for a picture of Molly Fischer.

92. *Guardian*, 9 July 1942.

93. *Guardian*, 21 August 1941 and 22 March 1962.The newspaper listed the places whereAfrican sellers worked: on Saturdays at the Jeppe Street post office, the corner of Market and Harrison Streets, and the corner of Market and Rissik Streets; on Sundays at Joubert Park and the corner of Plein and Eloff Streets. *Guardian*, 20 February 1941.Two other sellers wereArthur Demane, a textile worker who sold in Benoni, and Aaron Molete, a consolidated textile mill worker.
In May 1958, for example, the weekly paid £276 in wages to its sellers and £113 in commissions.

94. *Guardian*, 15 May 1941, for first evidence. See 13 November 1947, for it appears that the southern edition extended only as far asWorcester, i.e., every bundle that went by train was northern edition.

95. *Guardian*, 11 September 1941, and 8 January 1942. Stewart continued to print the southern edition. Afrikaanse Pers in Johannesburg first handled the northern edition, and then Unie Volkspers, the United Party printing house, took over.

96. *Guardian*, 5 February 1942.

97. *Guardian*, 27 November 1941.

98. *Guardian*, 12 February 1942.

99. Podbrey, *White Girl*, 79.Alberts's eccentric outfit was caused, perhaps, by the fact that she was a hunchback.

100. Podbrey, *White Girl*, 80; and Ronnie Kasrils, *"Armed and Dangerous": My Undercover Struggle Against Apartheid* (London: Heinemann, 1993), 31 and 27. Kasrils, *Armed and Dangerous*, 27; and James Zug interview with Brian Bunting, November 1994. *Guardian*, 2 October 1941 for an interesting letter to the editor from Johannesburg about increasing sales to Africans; 27 November 1941 in Durban, and 1 July 1943 on the general elections.

101. *Guardian*, 23 January 1941. HughWaterfield, a National Union of DistributiveWorkers leader, sent in news pieces. See *Guardian*, 11 March 1943.

102. *Guardian*, 29 June 1944; see also 27 February 1941 on Indian seamen, and a front page cartoon by W. Storm, 7 September 1944.

103. *Guardian*, 20 December 1945. Her future husband Rowley Arenstein, now working for the Party in Durban, recalled the situation: "Everything was decided together. The Party was discussing how to improve circulation and to improve circulation you had to get news.You've got to have a good reporter. . . . And Jackie became the reporter." Lax, according to her cousin Ronnie Kasrils, "had long black hair, penetrating eyes and an olive complexion." Kasrils, *Armed and Dangerous*, 27.They were first cousins once removed.

104. *Guardian*, 27 February and 24 July 1941; see also 27 August 1942, and 2 August 1945.
For more on the barracks, see 21 May 1942. See also 19 August 1943 for an article by V. Chengiah, the *Guardian* correspondent at the barracks; 30 December 1943 for a DIMES photograph; 28 June 1945 for when Radford visits the barracks. See also *Guardian*, 1 May 1952, and *Advance*, 18 February 1954 and 8 April 1954, for articles by JackieArenstein.

105. *Guardian*, 4 December 1941 for a picture of Shanley; 9 September 1943 for aTamil play benefiting the weekly; 21 September 1944 for the trial, which Dorothy Shanley organized, with Harry Bloom as the judge and Harry Rubin the prosecutor; 17 July 1941 for a *Guardian* musical evening and jumble sale; 22 January 1942 for the *Guardian* league setting a goal of £200 for the year; 29 January and 19 February 1942 for a social raising £13; 29 June 1944 for a winter ball.

See also *New Age*, 13 and 20 June, and 19 December 1957.

106. *Guardian*, 24 July 1941; 19 March 1942 for a jumble sale.

107. I. L. Szucs, "Aspects of Education, Training and Media in Popular Organisations in Durban: 1930–1960." B.A. honours thesis, University of Cape Town, 1985, pp. 47–48 about DIMES selling. See *Guardian*, 6 January and 1 June 1944 for a DIMES youth club with lectures given by Rowley Arenstein and George Poonen; 19 August 1943 about a *Guardian* league being started there. Pauline Kahn recalled, "a lot of Indian women selling the *Guardian* in Durban. They would sit there and call, '*Guardian*, penny, na?' to my mother as we walked down the road."

108. Szucs, "Aspects of Education," 12. See *Guardian*, 22 January 1942.

109. *Guardian*, 16 January and 27 February 1941 about sales, especially on Church Street, and booksellers on Paul Kruger Street; 12 March 1942 with a list of where to get the *Guardian* in Pretoria; and 13 August 1942.

110. *Guardian*, 14 May 1942, for a story and picture about Garment Workers Union member Dorothy Fredericks, who sold four dozen *Guardian*s a week.

111. *Guardian*, 6 February 1941.

112. *Guardian*, 24 September 1942 with a list of league members; 22 October 1942 with a picture of Ethel Woolf and the Radford comment. For the reader's league, see Margaret Ballinger Collection, A410, Department of Historical Papers, William Cullen Library, University of the Witwatersrand. See *Guardian*, 23 April 1942, with a report about the crowd at Findlay's speech.

113. *Guardian*, 10 September 1942, for raising £500, the most of any league.

114. *Guardian*, 22 February 1945. For mention of the Pretoria *Guardian* league: 20 February 1941 when it raised £2 10s.; 21 May 1941 when the Left Book Club changed its name; 12 June 1941 when Findlay spoke at the Left Club; 3 July 1941 when it raised £75 for *Guardian* and *Die Ware Republikein* with jumble sale in Lady Selbourne; 7 August 1941 when it sent £33 in July; 18 September 1941 when the Jewish Workers' Club raised £200 at a meeting with Boshoff and Findlay as speakers; 30 December 1941 for a dance; 8 January 1942 for a picnic with an 8s. 6d. ticket; 29 January 1942 for £15 raised at a Left Club function for the *Guardian* and *Die Ware Republikein*; 12 March 1942 when they performed *Tobacco Road*; 26 March 1942; 21 May 1942 for protesting cable ban; 2 July 1942 for a picture of Joan Findlay and for the Left Club holding dances, film shows, concerts, treasures hunts, and a children's afternoon for the *Guardian*; 17 December 1942 for an appeal from Findlay; 19 August 1943 for a letter to the editor from Joan Findlay.

115. *Guardian*, 31 July 1941 for picture of the Port Elizabeth Left Club at picnic; 25 September 1941 for another picnic photograph, this time at Jeffreys Bay, and mention that the Club has a six musical-evening series; 30 December 1943 for an article on PE slums by Betty Spence, a Wits grad, and also a picture of Henry Wolfson, the twenty-two-year-old secretary of the CP branch in PE; 16 November 1944 with a picture of happy PE sellers; 26 March 1942 about the PE *Guardian* league's Sunday-night lectures at Baboo Bros. Café. For Russell Road offices, see 2 August 1945.

116. Arnold Selby sold copies of the *Guardian* at the local sweets factory, and twenty on a weekly route in town. Coloured readers bought their copies from Chang Foot, a Chinese shopkeeper in the North End.

117. *Guardian*, 28 May 1942; see also 11 June 1942 for Rona Worrall attending a *Guardian*-league social at Maritzburg People's Hall, which had table tennis, cards, and drafts every Monday. See also 15 April 1943.

118. *Guardian*, 14 August 1941 on King William's Town; 15 April 1943 on Harry Du Plessis in Mossel

Bay; 6 June 1944, 12 July 1945, 29 November 1945 on D. M. Rossouw in Worcester. See 29 January 1942 for Queenstown, 1 April 1943 for Uitenhage, and 24 August 1944 with a picture of D. Daniels, a Party member who was organizing sales of the *Guardian* in George; 9 March 1944 for a *Guardian* league in George led by James van Niekerk. See 11 March 1943; 10 December 1942 and 13 April 1944 on Springs Party selling the *Guardian*; 22 April 1943; 4 March 1943; 13 March 1941 for a gramophone evening; 20 May 1943; and 11 October 1945.

119. *Guardian*, 23 October 1941, 14 September 1944, and 8 March 1945 for the ageless Miss Smith. She had been the governess of Bram Fischer's mother, Ella. See Clingman, *Bram Fischer*, 20 and 185.

120. *Guardian*, 30 April 1942.

121. *Guardian*, 4 September 1941; 4 December 1941 for a lecture and recital for the *Guardian*; 16 July 1942; 9 September 1943; 15 April 1943 for a dance at Newby's Cafe.

122. *Guardian*, 20 February 1941; 10 July 1941 with a letter to the editor from England; *Cape Times*, 25 November 1950.

123. *Guardian*, 4 April 1943 for a special Springbok Legion edition.

124. White, "Role of the Springbok Legion," 100. See Michael Fridjhon, "The Torch Commando: A Study in Opposition Politics in White South Africa, 1951–53," B.A. honours thesis, University of the Witwatersrand, 1975, p. 6. The Legion appointed Clapham to organize United Party support for the Legion. He eventually became a UP official.

125. James Zug interview with Wolfie Kodesh, March 1994. See 10 June 1943 for a hint about sending the *Guardian* to soldiers.

Issy Heyman, a South African soldier in the war, recalled how he "used to get the *Guardian* sent in to me and [I] used to go around and sell, distribute the *Guardian*, a dozen or so. We had a lot of young people who joined up and didn't understand what the war was about. We had a number of people who were members of the Ossewa Brandwag." David Everatt interview with Issy Heyman, February 1983, David Everatt Collection, Mayibuye Centre, University of the Western Cape.

Fred Carneson remembered using the *Guardian* to fill out both a Legion and a Communist Party newspaper while in the South African Army Signal Corps: "When I was in Italy, Sarah [Carneson, his wife] used to arrange for the *Guardian* to come through to me. . . . From there the *Guardian* served a very valuable role because it had information that other newspapers just wouldn't touch. It had its call for the second front, its criticism of the British role when they moved into Greece and attacked the democratic movement there, and its coverage of events in the Soviet Union and its support of the Soviet Union. I found that invaluable."

126. *Guardian*, 5 September 1940; 17 April, 1 and 8 May, 3 July, 11 September (circulation at 19,250), and 13 November 1941 (23,000); 12 and 19 February, and 11 June 1942; and 3 January 1946. For other mentions of *Guardian* wartime circulation, see Simons, *Class and Colour*, 537–38; Bunting, "South African Journalists," 11; Smith, *Behind the Press*, 109.

127. Smith, *Behind the Press*, 23.

128. *Guardian*, 28 May 1942 for the start of newsprint restrictions; 11 February 1943 for mention of paper-control regulations that limit the newspaper to eight pages.

129. Smith, *Behind the Press*, 109; *Cape Times*, 24 May 1952, which wrote that the *Guardian*'s quota was doubled. James Zug interview with Ray Alexander, December 1993. People's Pageant Souvenir Programme, back-page advertisement with the *Guardian*'s circulation figures, Abdurahman Papers, BCZA 83/32, Manuscripts and Archives, University of Cape Town. See *Guardian*, 11 June 1942.

130. *Guardian*, 11 June 1942. Most magazines and newspapers lost newsprint quotas. *Soviet Life*, the monthly magazine edited by Hilda Watts Bernstein, was cut in March 1943; *Inkululeko* had to cut circulation from 20,000 to 12,750; see its 27 March 1943 issue. See *Guardian*, 9 March 1944 for "serious curtailment under paper regulations," but 26 February 1948 mentions a rise to limit of wartime paper control.

131. *Guardian*, 22 January 1942. See a Carina Pearson letter to Cissie Gool, 10 April 1941, Abdurahman Collection, BCZA 23/82, Manuscripts and Archives, University of Cape Town: "Owing to a sharp rise in the cost of paper, we regret that this year we are obliged to reduce the normal space of greetings" from three inches to two inches; prices fell to 5s. for two inches.

132. *Guardian*, 17 April 1941 and 11 February 1942. See 26 June 1941 for the northern edition's advertising boom. See also Switzer, "Socialism and the Resistance Movement," in Switzer, *South Africa's Alternative Press*, 287.

133. James Zug interview with Brian Bunting, November 1993, and Fred Carneson, March 1994.

134. Smith, *Behind the Press*, 110; and *Guardian*, 5 November 1942. Barrack Street earned £2 for every thousand copies sold. In other terms, it cost £600 a month to print the newspaper.

135. *Guardian*, 6 February 1941.

136. *Guardian*, 27 November 1941 for Molteno's pamphlet, which cost 8d. per dozen; 7 November 1940 for a supplement about Finland and Socialism. Four thousand extra copies were ordered.

137. *Guardian*, 6 August 1942. For those fascinated by the *Guardian*'s finances, here is a monthly accounting of the monies received, in pounds sterling. *1942*: September–203, October–256, November–324, December–489. *1943*: January–272, February–497, March–273, April–414, May–247, June–318, July–393, August–249, September–311, October–253, November–252, December–280. *1944*: January–423, February–80, March–384, May–135, June–77, July–120, August–166, September–90, October–123, November–213, December–341.

138. *Guardian*, 7 May 1942.

139. *Guardian*, 16 October 1941 for battery, 23 April 1942 for apples; see 25 September 1941 when a Cape Town reader posted a typewriter to the new Johannesburg office.

140. *Guardian*, 11 and 18 June 1942. They sold postcards and autographed photographs of the bust (2s. for a post card, 10s. for photo) as well. See 2 July 1942 for a poem by Kaye on the campaign. Anja Millman was the sculptor of the bust of Lenin.

141. *Guardian*, 25 June 1942.

142. *Guardian*, 30 July 1942.

143. *Guardian*, 3 September 1942. See 11 June 1942 for 33,000 circulation, and 23 July 1942 for 40,000.

144. *Guardian*, 5 November 1942, for Pearson writing, "Being frank is a habit with the *Guardian*."

145. James Zug interview with Brian Bunting, November 1994.

146. *Guardian*, 10 July 1941.

147. *Guardian*, 18 June 1942 for a job with a salary of £13 15s.; 23 December 1943, and 6 and 13 January 1944; 3 May 1945 for a typist in Barrack Street; 31 December 1942 for "do you want an interesting job?" for a shorthand typist and secretary for the editorial department; 5 July 1945 for a clerk—"typewriting essential, shorthand recommended"; 10 January 1946 for a Cape Town job; 28 June 1945 for a journalist for Johannesburg; 12 October 1944 for a staff position; 20 July 1944 for a job that pays SASJ rates, for a job as a reporter in Johannesburg ("this is not a senior post"), and an organising secretary in Johannesburg. See 10 July 1941 when the newspaper lost £68 in June—"our staff is entirely voluntary except for the office boy." See 11 September 1941 for another statement that the editor, circulation manager, ad manager, ac-

countant, and auditor got no salaries; three typists and "Alfred" got wages; and the racing correspondent got £1 a week.

148. *Guardian*, 5 October 1944.

149. *Guardian*, 3 May 1945. It should be noted that despite the financial woes, the *Guardian* had money in the bank at the end of the war; see 7 October 1948.

150. *Guardian*, 10 May 1940; see 23 February 1940 for an interesting editorial on how things could have gone differently in the thirties.

151. *Guardian*, 3 July 1941.

152. *Guardian*, 9 January 1941, for a piece about London's nightlife.

153. *Guardian*, 10 July 1941, for "This Week's War News." See 5 November 1942 for "greet the heroic USSR 1917–42" with yet another photograph of Uncle Joe Stalin; 25 January 1945 for pictures of twelve Soviet generals and the headline "Red Army Has Become the Most Powerful and Steeled of Modern Armies"; 7 January 1943 for the Soviet Information Agency; 27 January 1944 for the Soviet Press Agency; 6 January 1944 for the headline "Soviet Advances Arouse People to Fever Pitch."

154. *Guardian*, 6 November 1941; 15 and 29 January 1942 for the petition, which 4,000 signed; also 27 August 1942 for a petition about the war that was sent to Smuts.

155. *Guardian*, 2 March 1944.

156. *Guardian*, 21 June 1940 for Far East correspondent; 24 February 1939 for North American; 15 August 1940 for Imperial Affairs; 10 October 1940 for Political; 31 July 1941 for Moscow; 20 November 1941 for Diplomatic; 7 September 1944 for Special; and 1 February 1945 for Soviet.

157. *Guardian*, 1 April 1948. See 27 November 1941 for Cook's first byline; 27 March 1941 for a report from his wife Freda Cook, the London correspondent for the *National Herald* in India.

158. *Guardian*, 9 December 1948.

159. Simons, *Class and Colour*, 531.

160. *Guardian*, 17 February 1943; 23 October 1941 from Egypt; 6 November 1941; 18 December 1941; 8 January 1942; 20 April 1942 from Libya; 10 August 1944; 7 May 1942 for when Morley comes home. Morley, before the war, was the assistant secretary for the National Liberation League. Simons, *Class and Colour*, 532.

161. *Guardian*, 21 January 1943 for torrent; 6 August 1942 for affection. George Sacks, her partner on that trip, wrote in his 1943 Communist Party pamphlet that "everything else fades into insignificance besides this job of winning the war." George Sacks, "Communism in South Africa," (Cape Town: Stewart, 1943), 4. A copy of this rare forty-page pamphlet can be found in the Brian Bunting Collection, Mayibuye Centre, University of the Western Cape.

162. *Guardian*, 8 June 1944.

163. *Guardian*, 2 July 1942. See *Inkululeko*, 17 June 1942, for a profile of Edwin Mofutsanyana, who patrolled the streets of Orlando in his air-raid warden's uniform.

164. *Guardian*, 28 August 1941.

165. *Guardian*, 16 April and 2 July 1942 for the newspaper's demand for air-raid shelters; 9 August 1944 for the demand for butter.

166. *Guardian*, 24 August 1944. The first four hundred readers who applied received the free victory-seeds packets.

167. *Guardian*, 21 September 1944, 17 September 1942, and 11 February 1943 on war bonds. Discussion of spies was a regular subject: 19 March 1942, 11 February and 30 September 1943, 9 August and 8 November 1944, and 23 April 1942: "Don't talk about ships or shipping." See also 6 and 27 November 1941, and 6 January 1944 on the Springbok Legion.

168. *Guardian*, 8 January 1942; 24 September and 29 October 1942 for "Fifth Column Front" feature.
169. *Guardian*, 7 October 1943.
170. *Guardian*, 29 July 1943, for a Johannesburg District Committee memorandum. See letters to the editor: 26 March and 17 December 1942 from I. O. Horovitch; 8 January 1942 from David Dryburgh with an obituary; 25 June 1942 from Cissie Gool; 15 July 1943 from Sam Kahn; and 19 August 1943 from Joan Findlay.
171. *Guardian*, 4 January 1945 for a picture of delegates at the Party's national conference; 16 July 1942 for CP News; 9 October 1941 for support of the Six-Point Programme that was calling for the Smuts government to recognize the USSR, end profiteering, raise living standards, stop appeasing South African fascists, protect trade-union rights and bring democracy to South Africa; 30 July 1942; 27 August 1942; 9 December 1943, and 1 June and 31 August 1944 for interviews with H. A. Naidoo and Rex Close about the Party's one-thousand-new-members campaign.
172. *Guardian*, 8 January 1942. *Inkululeko*'s editor, Armstrong Msitshana, declared circulation to be at 18,000. James Zug interview with Rusty Bernstein, May 1994: "It was largely a question of language. You'd offer both newspapers to an African and they would chose what they could read. If they were literate only in Zulu, they'd take *Inkululeko*. The reader decided."
173. *Guardian*, 30 September 1943.
174. *Guardian*, 29 January 1943 for "Trade Union Flashes"; 14 May 1942 for "Trade Union Notebook," written by Sarie Marais. See also April 1943 for articles about shoe repairers on strike; 19 November 1942 for a picture of Ray Alexander in Port Nolloth with a newly organized branch of the Food and Canning Workers' Union; and 17 February 1944 for an article by E. J. Burford on the National Union of Distributive Workers.
175. *Guardian*, 4 November 1943.
176. *Guardian*, 1 May 1941, 30 April and 7 May 1942, and 26 April 1945. In 1945 there were over one hundred, from the major unions like the National Union of Distributive Workers and the Food and Canning Workers' Union, to the decidedly less common groups like the Iron Moulders Association in Port Elizabeth, the Candle and Soap Workers' Union in Johannesburg, and the Brush and Broom Workers' Union in Cape Town. The price was mentioned in a letter from Carina Pearson to Cissie Gool, 10 April 1941, in the Abdurahman Collection, BCZA 82/23, Manuscripts and Archives, University of Cape Town. See also Ivan L. Walker and Ben Weinbren, *2000 Casualties: A History of the Trade Unions and the Labour Movement in the Union of South Africa* (Johannesburg: South African Trade Union Council, 1961).
177. *Guardian*, 4 September 1941 when the strike first began; 15 and 29 January 1942 for the Relief Fund. The *Cape Times* interestingly gave £22 8s. Andrews printed the fund's balance sheet in the weekly in late January 1942, commenting, "In addition to the contributions through trade unions, workers in factories and friends of the workers, particularly through the *Guardian*, have liberally contributed."
178. *Guardian*, 30 September 1943. See 18 October 1945 for the *Guardian* appealing for funds to send Bill Andrews to a London conference. The Party also commissioned a bust of Andrews. See Robert Knox Cope Collection, A953, Department of Historical Papers, William Cullen Library, University of the Witwatersrand. Betty Radford established a fundraising committee to gather the money to pay the four-hundred-pound printing bill from Stewart, the publisher. The committee consisted of David Dryburgh as chair, Charlie Stewart, Cope, Ben Goldberg from the People's Club, and A. W.H. Rose and M. T. King, two union leaders.
Eddie Roux reviewed the book in *Trek* on 22 October 1943.

179. *Guardian*, 8 July 1943.
180. *Guardian*, 13 May 1943.
181. *Guardian*, 3 June 1943.
182. *Guardian*, 24 June 1943.
183. Brian Bunting, "Journalists in the Front Line," 11.
184. Smith, *Behind the Press*, 109.
185. Lodge, *Black Politics*, 28–29. In Cape Town, the Party became extremely active in the coloured community of the Cape—in District Six, Athlone, Retreat, Hout Bay's fishing village, and into the Cape Flats shantytowns of Elsie's River and Windermere; in Johannesburg, Party officials went to coloured areas like Benoni, Indian towns like Fordsburg, and African locations like Sophiatown, Newclare, Martindale, and Alexandra; likewise in Durban, the Party ventured into the non-white areas such as Mayville, Cato Manor, Sydenham, Springfield, Greyville and Clairwood.
186. *Guardian*, 2 December 1943.
187. Guardian, 21 August and 11 September.
188. *Guardian*, 19 June 1941; 30 July 1942 for Rona Worrall writing an article, and three pictures on coloured schoolchildren in Kliptown.
189. *Guardian*, 5 July and 30 August 1945.
190. *Guardian*, 23 October 1941. See also 23 July 1942 for an article on Natal coal miners.
191. *Guardian*, 17 February 1944; 8 February 1945 for two pictures and an article on a Johannesburg shanty town getting soaked; 26 March 1942 for an article and photograph of a Pimville slum; 25 September 1941.
192. *Guardian*, 26 October 1944; 9 August 1945 for three pictures of where Radford and Snitcher visited.
193. *Guardian*, 18 May 1944 for an A. W. Jacobs piece on Windermere; 15 and 29 June 1944 for photographs of a flooded Windermere; 20 July and 17 August 1944.
194. *Guardian*, 3 April 1941. Ray Alexander, Bill Andrews, Donald Molteno, and Cissie Gool commented on the color-bar clause.
195. *Guardian*, 30 March 1944.
196. *Guardian*, 27 March 1941; 24 July 1941 with a picture of Radebe who is going to start a mine union. The article included his address. See 31 July 1941 for an article by Radebe; 28 January 1943 for a piece on the ANC Transvaal's election manifesto: "'Congress has a plan,' says Radebe." See also 26 November 1942 for an article by D. Kosa on African trade unions; and 23 September 1943 and 20 January 1944 with articles by Johnny Gomas on his tin workers' union.
197. *Guardian*, 29 October and 26 November 1942, 7 October 1943, 14 December 1944, and 22 March 1945. See 23 November 1944 for H. M. Basner speaking at a bus boycott meeting where he condemned the ANC and the CP, which "introduced a jarring note." See also Clingman, *Bram Fischer*, 175.
198. *Guardian*, 14 January 1943; the next week's issue contained another picture of a shanty with the caption: "How Workers Live—It's not 'Communist agitation.'"
199. *Guardian*, 3 September 1942 and 21 October 1943.
200. *Guardian*, 24 July 1941, 16 July 1942, 26 March 1942 for discussion on arming blacks to fight the invading Japanese. See Lodge, "Class Conflict," 7–10. The *Guardian* attacked the Army's discriminatory pay scales: a white private was paid 12 shillings, 3 pence a day; a coloured private 7 shillings a day; and an African private 2 shillings, 3 pence.
Hansard, 16 April 1942, col. 6332, for C. R. Swart complaining about Afrikaners getting detained

without trial: "Here I have a little newspaper issued by the communists and I notice the headline is 'Give us Guns, Away with Passes.'" Albert Luthuli, *Let My People Go* (New York: McGraw-Hill, 1962), 176: "Without a pass, an African man is worse than emasculated. Without a pass, we have no right to work, to travel, to walk up a street, even to be alone at home. The only privilege that remains is to go to jail."

201. *Guardian*, 28 August 1941; 9 October 1941 for a piece by him on a kaffir beer committee and a picture of Xuma; 30 December 1943 for mention of an article by him on pass laws in *Freedom*.

202. *Guardian*, 7 October 1943.

203. *Guardian*, 23 December 1943 with a piece by Lucas Phillips on the conference; 21 December 1944 for a page-seven report on the conference, held in Kimberly.

204. *Guardian*, 6 July 1944 and 4 October 1945. See 14 July 1947: 57 percent of Transkei cattle were lost in the 1945 drought. The committee that controlled the fund consisted of Molteno, Andrews, Radford, Dr. Roseberry Bokwe—the only African surgeon in the Union and an ANC executive member—L. E. Hertslet, Mrs. M. Bhola, and Eddie Roux. See Albert Luthuli, *Let My People Go*, 189: "Guardians of great herds of cattle have, with the theft of our land, become keepers of a couple of bony cows."

205. *Guardian*, 8 November 1945 for the article that Radford posted from Middledrift; 6 December 1945 for four pictures of Radford and M. Bhola; 20 December 1945 for Eddie Roux's long article and a report that the fund was at £1,405; 2 February 1947 for a picture of Dr. Bokwe delivering monies from the African Food Fund; and 6 January 1949 for Sam Kahn interviewed after his Xhosaland tour.

The black newspaper *Inkundla* congratulated the weekly on its mission: "The *Guardian*, the Socialist weekly published in Capetown, has opened a fund to relieve famine in the Ciskei and in thanking it for its public-spiritedness in this connection, we wish to urge every African to give as much as they can to relieve suffering in the Transkei." *Inkundla ya Bantu*, October 1945; see 15 February and 20 September 1945. A thorough examination of *Inkundla* can be found in Les Switzer and Ime Ukpanah, "Under Siege: *Inkundla ya Bantu* and the African Nationalists Movement, 1938–1951," in Switzer, *South Africa's Alternative Press*, 215–51.

For more on Bokwe and the history of the Ciskei, see Les Switzer, *Power and Resistance in an African Society: The Ciskei Xhosa and the Making of South Africa* (Madison: University of Wisconsin Press, 1993), 284–312. Bokwe, a brother-in-law of Z. K. Matthews, was treasurer of the Cape ANC until 1954.

206. *Guardian*, 20 February 1941.

207. Hansard, 16 April 1942, col. 6296, and 12 February 1943, col. 1497. In 1944 Prime Minister Smuts instructed government agencies to begin addressing letters to non-whites with a "Dear Sir" or "Dear Madam." Brian Lapping, *Apartheid: A History* (New York: George Braziller, 1989), 79.

208. *Guardian*, 29 October 1942.

209. *Guardian*, 6 and 20 April 1944, the latter with a Party statement. See 5 February 1942 for a piece about Lawrence Nkosi in Orlando.

210. *Guardian*, 19 November 1942. See 3 December 1942, which said that the "root cause is poverty"; 26 July 1945 for a report on a riot in Springs that left six dead and seventeen injured.

211. *Guardian*, 4 September 1941 for a sketch of Maliba and a piece on *Inkululeko*. See 30 October 1941 for a Maliba article: "Starvation—Africans Suffer in Northern Transvaal"; 18 December 1941 for a Moses Kotane article in which he interviews Maliba; 16 July 1942. See Peter Delius, "Sebatakgomo and the Zoutpansberg Balemi Association: The ANC, the Communist Party and

Rural Organization, 1939–55," *Journal of African History* 34 (1993): 293–313. Maliba was killed in a Louis Trichardt police cell in 1967. See also Peter Delius, *A Lion amongst the Cattle: Reconstruction and Resistance in the Northern Transvaal* (Johannesburg: Ravan, 1996), for a history of Sekhukhuneland.

212. *Guardian*, 11 November 1943 on Indian famine; 2 March 1944 with his long obituary of Kasturba Gandhi; 16 March 1944 with his article on an NIC conference.

213. *Guardian*, 21 August 1941; 16 July 1942 for a sketch of Mofutsanyana; 13 August 1942 and 15 April 1943 on the NRC.

214. *Guardian*, 25 November 1943 and 25 May 1944. The ANC's motto in these years was "Right Not Might, Freedom Not Serfdom."

215. *Guardian*, 1 June 1944. A. B. Xuma, Harmel reported, was "always cool, pleasant and restrained." He also praised David Bopape for "his modest and competent presentation of the secretary's report."

216. *Guardian*, 6 April 1944 for a report on Xuma visiting Cape Town; 4 May 1944 for an advertisement for the conference; 16 June 1944 for a report on a Durban anti-pass campaign; 18 May 1944 on the buildup; 7 September 1944 on the anti-pass committee; 19 September 1940 for a letter to the editor advocating a *Guardian* petition protesting pass laws, and 16 December 1943 for the quotation about speeches.

217. *Guardian*, 21 April 1939. See 16 April 1937.

218. *Guardian*, 14 May 1942.

219. *Guardian*, 9 December 1943.

220. *Guardian*, 16, 23, and 30 December 1943. See *South African Worker*, 2 February 1938, for a Party policy accepting a racially discriminatory wage: five shillings for Africans, ten shillings for whites. See also 26 September 1940 for an article about the formation of a separate coloured section with the Garment Workers' Union: "It has been felt that the Coloured workers always remained in the background at general members' meetings, that they hardly ever express their views on questions affecting them, etc."

221. Everatt, "Politics of Nonracialism," 9. Brian Bunting, writing in the 1970s, considered the Communist Party, and by extension the *Guardian*, "a valued part of the grand alliance whose herculean efforts had brought about the defeat" of Nazi Germany. Bunting, *Moses Kotane*, 161. In January 1944, to make the Party more palatable to whites, they deleted from the CPSA constitution a clause that said one of the Party's goals was "the abolition of imperialism and the establishment of an independent republic of the people."

222. See Bunting, *Moses Kotane*, 108, for ban; *Guardian*, 16 November 1944, for *Bantu World*; and Jones, "*Inkululeko*," in Switzer, *South African Alternative Press*, 357.

223. *Guardian*, 23 April and 7 May 1942. Andrews drew the ire of the SABC censor when he touched upon the bogey of race. In the following sentence, the word "colour" got red-penciled by the censor: "May Day is above all an international day, and those who celebrate it have always emphasized the essential brotherhood of the peoples, notwithstanding differences in language, colour, race or culture." See Andrews Collection, Mayibuye Centre, University of the Western Cape.

224. In 1940 major South African newspaper editors signed a voluntary censorship agreement; Betty Radford did not sign the agreement, but agreed to abide by it. *Guardian*, 20 April 1944.

225. *Guardian*, 5 February 1942. Lenton was South Africa's postmaster general and director of signals. See his appointment, 20 November 1939.

226. D. E. McCausland, "An Open Letter," *The Union Review* (August 1946): 1. Cook's cables apparently were a major cause of the announcement. "He [Cook] undertook a regular campaign

of denigration against the British Government and incidentally General Smuts, in which he represented not only their actions but their motives as contemptible. Cook's chief stock-in-trade was a persistent attempt to show that Great Britain and America were endeavouring not to win the War, but to outwit the Russians, and set up Fascist Governments wherever they could." Herbert Morrison, home secretary in Great Britain, banned the *Daily Worker* from January 1941 to August 1942.

227. *Guardian*, 23 April 1942—"Union Censor Bans Our London Cables," screamed the headline. Cook's cables to *Forward* were also banned; see 30 April 1942.

228. *Guardian*, 16 April 1942 for letter to Lenton and Molteno's question in Parliament; 14 May 1942 for the deputation consisting of J. Robertson, Colin Legum, Jack Cope, and Glyn Thomas; 11 June 1942 for a letter from Legum, Robertson, and F.A.W. Lucas to Lenton. See, incidentally, 8 May 1947 for an obituary for Robertson.

229. *Guardian*, 23 April 1942.

230. *Guardian*, 4 February 1943 for a commission of inquiry by the central London branch of NUJ about last April's censoring; 14 May 1942 for NCCL taking up the censoring issue.

231. *Guardian*, 28 May 1942.

232. *Guardian*, 25 February 1943 with the cable being held for 24 hours; 11 March 1943 with the cable being held 12 hours; 21 January 1943 when the British authorities started to delay and censor, as they held up a cable for 24 hours and deleted 42 words. See also 22 October 1942.

233. *Guardian*, 20 January 1944; 2 March 1944.

234. *Guardian*, 15 July 1943. See 8 July 1943 for a cable in which 69 words were deleted; 26 August 1943 for 24 words deleted; 9 September 1943 for a delayed cable; 16 September 1943 for 149 words deleted and delayed 24 hours.

235. *Guardian*, 3 February 1944.

236. *Guardian*, 10 February 1944.

237. *Guardian*, 16 September 1943.

238. *Guardian*, 10 February 1944.

239. *Guardian*, 24 February 1944 for 84 words deleted; 2 March 1944 for 11 words deleted from a 450-word cable; 14 October 1943 for a "Topical" on censorship.

240. Hansard, 1943, col. 455-6.

241. Hansard, 1943, col. 1474. Steyn spoke at MAR meetings on the same platform as Party members.

242. *Guardian*, 25 February 1943.

243. *Guardian*, 1 April 1943. See 30 September 1943 and 6 May 1943 for Louw dropping his claim to £2000.

244. Amy Thornton Collection, Manuscripts and Archives, University of Cape Town, A24.

245. *Guardian*, 30 September 1943. Harry Snitcher was the *Guardian*'s lawyer.

246. *Guardian*, 29 April 1943, for the defense fund.

247. *Guardian*, 7 December 1944.

248. *Guardian*, 8 July 1943.

249. *Guardian*, 7 December 1944.

250. *Guardian*, 22 July 1943.

251. *Guardian*, 2 September 1948. It is not clear whether the South African postal system, not known for its spotless efficiency, was actually delivering the mail at dawn on New Year's Day.

252. *Guardian*, 7 December 1944. The four companies were the Randfontein Estates Gold Mining, Government Gold Mining Areas (Modderfontein), Van Ryn Deep, and East Rand Proprietary

Mines.

253. South African Institute for Race Relations Collection, AD1181, Department of Historical Papers, University of the Witwatersrand. The appeal highlighted some of her worries arising from the suit: "This action raises questions of the utmost importance to the Trade Union movement and to the public generally. Among the issues involved is the question of the protection of witnesses who give evidence before Government Commissions, and the right of trade unions and their offi- cials to present their views before such Commissions without fear of actions for libel. A further issue is the right of a newspaper to comment on such evidence. We claim that this action, if suc- cessful, will not only weaken the powers of the trade unions, but will also strike at the few medi- ums of independent expression of opinion in South Africa and be a blow against such freedom of the Press as we enjoy."

254. *Guardian*, 27 April 1944.

255. *Guardian*, 11 May 1944; 26 June 1944 with the fund at £2,205; 27 July 1944 at £3,129; 31 Au- gust 1944 at £4,232; 28 September 1944 at £4,549; 26 October 1944 at £5,448; and 30 No- vember 1944 at £6,000. See 6 July 1944 when the *Daily Worker* in London responded in "solidarity of the workers' press" and gave £50.

256. *Guardian*, 30 November and 7 December 1944, and 4 April 1945. "We published the report and made editorial comments. We lost that first round. The court came to the conclusion that it was defamatory towards the mine owners. We sat down and talked about the use of fair comment and came to the conclusion that to argue a case on that basis, an appeal would be far too lengthy for Betty. It was quite a severe blow to the *Guardian* at the time. Thereafter Betty would come to me from time to time with articles for me to read in terms of defamation and so forth." James Zug interview with Harry Snitcher, January 1995.

257. *Guardian*, 24 January 1946 and 2 September 1948.

258. Kelsey Stuart, *The Newspaperman's Guide to the Law* (Durban: Butterworths, 1986), 47, on precedent. Radford argued that the *Guardian* was attacking a system, not specific people or companies; the mining companies argued that the *Guardian* was attacking a limited group of people, not a system. See Roux, *Time Longer Than Rope*, 335; *Guardian*, 30 December 1941 about one man being killed, 55 injured in violence at a Randfontein mine; 26 February 1942 for an open letter from Radford to George Head, a columnist at the *Rand Daily Mail* and the *Sunday Times*, who was sacked because he was an executive in the Springbok Legion and Med- ical Aid for Russia.

259. *Guardian*, 19 April 1945 on FDR and Buchenwald; 3 May 1945 on POWs.

260. *Guardian*, 3 May 1945. Messages also came from Harry Pollitt, the British Communist Party chief; Xuma; Andrews; J. B. Marks; and the Party's Central Committee.

CHAPTER THREE. BRASS AND WATER: DEPARTURES, 1945–1950

1. *Guardian*, 7 October 1948. See Ronald Segal, *Into Exile* (London: Jonathan Cape, 1963), 78; the *Guardian* saw its finances "swell to the luxury of a reserve fund."

2. The newspaper returned to a five-column tabloid format in January 1951.

3. *Guardian*, 7 June 1945 and 18 July 1946. It was not until late in 1946, though, that the weekly permanently adopted the seven-column size.

4. *Guardian*, 29 November 1945. See also 20 September 1945. The partnership was organized as

a nonprofit, with 100 A shares sold to the directors—Radford was paid a token £1 share for selling the newspaper—and 4,900 B shares to the public. The company was worth £71; each *Guardian* share was worth, at the time of the banning of the newspaper in May 1952, about three shillings. Pinnock, "Keep the Red Flag Flying," 11. For the co-op, see 20 September 1945. The directors were Bill Andrews as chair, Radford, Yusuf Dadoo, Donald Molteno, and the Rev. Douglas C. Thompson, a Methodist minister and supporter of the South African Left. Thompson was asked to join the Friends of the Soviet Union after a marathon two-hour speech on the history of the USSR at the green-shuttered Pietersburg Town Hall in 1942. When Thompson died, there was an enormous auction of his library on the lawn at Wits.

The *Guardian* board met twice a year and had no formal input into *Guardian* policy. James Zug interview with Brian Bunting, December 1993. Bill Andrews wrote in his diary on 13 June 1946: "4pm *Guardian* office, board meeting canceled. No one at the *Guardian* office knew about board meeting."

5. *Guardian*, 22 August 1946. See 5 September 1946. Betty Radford was particularly emboldened by the strike. Outraged by the violence, and the retreat by former allies, she cabled the British Communist Party's newspaper, the *Daily Worker*, the following message on 16 August 1946: "FOUR DEAD AND MANY HUNDREDS INJURED, MANY SERIOUSLY, IS ROLL TO DATE, RECRUITING FROM GOVERNMENT'S USE POLICE TERROR TO CRUSH STRIKE AFRICAN MINERS." See Peter Lehola, "Communism in South Africa (An Historical Essay)," unpublished and undated manuscript, Dadoo Collection, Mayibuye Centre, University of the Western Cape. Radford was the *Daily Worker*'s representative in Cape Town, and the charges for such cables were collected in London. This cable, witnessed by Marion Florence Knight, an employee of Cable and Wireless Ltd. in Cape Town, was used as evidence in the 1946–48 sedition trial. It is interesting to compare Radford's angry cable to one sent by the national executive of SAT&LC to the World Federation of Trade Unions: "APPEARS NATIVES WERE MISLED BY IRRESPONSIBLE PEOPLE. POLICE METHODS CONTROLLING STRIKE DRASTIC BUT WARRANTED. SUCH ACTION WAS NECESSARY TO MAINTAIN LAW AND ORDER AND PREVENT CHAOS." The 1947 annual conference of the SAT&LC belatedly repudiated the cable by a vote of 69 to 23. Simons, *Class and Colour*, 578.

The strike was so seminal for the *Guardian* that its 1946 Picture of the Year was a compilation of three from the mine strike. See 2 January 1947. See also Nadine Gordimer, *Burger's Daughter* (New York: Viking, 1979), 89–94.

6. *Fighting Talk*, June 1957. The Special Branch was founded in 1935 to investigate illegal diamond buying. These 1946 raids were the first for the branch. As the weekly noted, the raids occurred on the sixteenth anniversary of the Reichstag trial in Nazi Germany.

7. *Star* (Johannesburg), 21 September 1946; *Freedom* 5, no. 6 (November–December 1946); and *Guardian*, 2 January 1947, with a picture of Radford with her lawyer, Mr. Buirski, during the raid.

8. "CID men invaded my room and carried away all my correspondence, private and otherwise. . . . went to office, full of CID men, drove with CID men back to house in Camp's Bay, looked into every cupboard and suitcase, searched for two hours." Andrews diary, box 1, Mayibuye Centre, University of the Western Cape. The diary itself was taken away, only returned a month later. See also *Rand Daily Mail*, 23 September 1946; *Inkululeko*, October 1946; *Inkundla ya Bantu*, September 1946, second fortnight.

9. Radford noted that "the police had no idea what they were looking for" when they left with the boxes of irrelevant materials. *Guardian*, 26 September 1946.

10. *Guardian*, 7 November 1946 and 2 January 1947. The minister of justice and the police "failed to justify their seizure of the documents in question and their refusal to return them." See *Free-*

dom 5, no. 6 (November–December 1946): "The daily press makes no protest against this latest curtailment of the freedom of the press, speech and legitimate criticism of government policy."

11. *Guardian*, 31 July 1947.

12. *Guardian*, 11 December 1947 for testimony written by H. A. Naidoo. See also 30 January 1947 for two-and-a-half pages on trial; 20 February 1947 for two pages on the defense's cross-examination; 31 July 1947 for the defendants committed to trial; and 13 May 1948 for when the "sedition case collapses again." James Zug interview with Harry Snitcher, January 1995. The sedition trial was one major reason why Snitcher, like Radford, dropped out of the Party. Some of the Party's trial advocates were Arthur Williamson, Bram Fischer, George Philby, and Vernon Berrange; the public prosecutor of the case was Percy Yutar, who would reappear for the Treason Trial. There was some controversy concerning the dramatic re-arrest, for the defendants were already out on bail, and Snitcher sued for £10,000 for unlawful arrest. See Simons, *Class and Colour*, 584–88, for a comprehensive account of the sedition trial; and *New Statesman*, 19 December 1947.

13. *Guardian*, 2 September 1948.

14. *Guardian*, 21 February 1946. South African tick-bite fever is caused by buffalo ticks, which live on cattle, when they are infected with *Rickettsia africae*. It is similar to Lyme's disease. Exactly forty-eight years later, I too caught tick-bite fever in the Eastern Cape while researching this book. With Govan Mbeki on the way to a lunch interview, his bodyguard's car stalled. Mbeki—then eighty-three—and I pushed the car up a long hill in the pouring rain. By the end of our lunch, I was swooning wildly with fever. Mbeki showed me the old *Guardian* offices on Adderley Street—gesticulating in the rain at the former police station across the street—and then deposited me at St. George's Hospital.

15. "I remember Betty and George sitting in our living room that evening and crying, crying all night, about losing the baby. I don't think, in many ways, she ever recovered." James Zug interview with Ray Alexander, January 1995.

16. *Guardian*, 14 March 1946.

17. *New Statesman* (London), 19 December 1947, for Radford writing that she "had been ill during most of the period just prior to the miners' strike."

18. The day detectives arrested and hauled Radford to Caledon Square police headquarters, George Sacks became hysterical with grief, according to Sonia Bunting: "Oh Betty, my poor Betty, can't happen. Not to my Betty," he sobbed uncontrollably upon learning of her arrest. Pauline Podbrey agreed, adding, "And he was running around, creating merry-hell."

19. Andrews Collection, box 1, Mayibuye Centre, University of the Western Cape. See *Guardian*, 30 January 1947 and 1 January 1948, for other photographs. Len Lee-Warden filmed a brief moment of the sedition trial in 1946, and it too showed a tired, worn-down Radford. The film, without sound of course, is now in the archives of the Mayibuye Centre.

20. See Andrews Collection, box 4, Mayibuye Centre, University of Western Cape.

21. *Guardian*, 19 June 1947 on nomination, 4 September 1947 on results, which were 1,554 to 1,371. Toby Roy, the businessman, ran on the slogan "Don't Vote for a Goy, Vote for Roy." George Sacks was Jewish, but Radford was not. See 28 August 1947 for a discussion of a rumor about Sim Roytowski, Toby Roy's brother, who told African Clothing Factory workers that they would lose their jobs if they voted for Radford.

22. *Cape Times*, 4 August 1947; Radford's letter to *New Statesman*, 19 December 1947. Brian Bunting interview with James Zug, December 1994. See Andrews diary, box 4, Mayibuye Centre, University of Western Cape, 28 August 1947: "The withdrawal of charges against Betty Sacks has caused some surprise and discussion in Party circles." Other reasons forthcoming

have focused around the possibility that with her illness in the months leading up to the mine strike, she had a reasonable excuse for not being present or active in the CEC.

23. Lodge, *Black Politics*, 20. For a good assessment of the NRC controversy, see Mirjana Roth, "Domination by Consent: Elections under the Representation of Natives Act, 1937–1948," in *Resistance and Ideology in Settler Societies*, ed. Tom Lodge (Johannesburg: Ravan, 1986), 144–67.

24. *Guardian*, 19 June 1947.

25. *Guardian*, 19 June 1947, for both Harmel and Dadoo's letters. Dadoo's was printed on the front page.

26. Andrews diary, 19 June 1947, box 4, Mayibuye Centre, University of Western Cape.

27. *Cape Times*, 17 June 1947.

28. *Cape Times*, 16 June 1947.

29. Brooks, "From Class Struggle," 76. See *Guardian*, 30 September and 4 November 1948, advising readers not to boycott the NRC; and 21 October and 11 November 1948 for commentary from ANC president Xuma about the 1948 general election.

30. *Guardian*, 22 January 1948, for that and a mention about the Milan conference of the Italian CP.

31. *Guardian*, 23 October 1947 for a London letter; 30 October 1947 for a Paris letter; 6 November for an interview with the Czech foreign secretary; 15 January 1948 for a London letter about speaking from the platform at a *Daily Worker* eighteenth-birthday celebration; 22 January 1948 for a front page "Report from Betty Radford." See also 12 August 1948, when she mentions her visit to a concentration camp.

32. *Guardian*, 26 February 1948.

33. *Guardian*, 26 February 1948.

34. *Guardian*, 15 April 1948.

35. *Guardian*, 13 May 1948. Radford was joined in the Cape Town list by Brian Bunting, H. A. Naidoo, and Naomi Shapiro, with Ruth First in Johannesburg and Jackie Lax in Durban.

36. James Zug interview with Brian Bunting, December 1993.

37. *Guardian*, 16 September 1948 for the Roux review, and 2 December 1948 for an obituary for Minnie Bhola, who died in Johannesburg.

38. *Guardian*, 6 January 1949. Radford vacationed for much of the first weeks of the year. See 10 February 1949, which reported she was "spending a few weeks in the country not 100 miles from Cape Town."

39. A year and one-half later, Radford submitted two articles: a caring obituary for Christine Cash, who had died in Texas in February 1950, and a brief piece on the Suppression of Communism Act: "Free expression of opinion is in itself something of a social safety valve to those denied direct representation in the bodies governing the country." See *Guardian*, 15 June 1950 for Cash's obituary, and 11 May 1950 on the Suppression of Communism Act.

40. *Union of South Africa—Report of the Select Committee on the Suppression of Communism Act Enquiry*, April 1952, p. 28; Sam Kahn, in a speech on the Grand Parade on 22 January 1950, after returning home from a holiday overseas, said, "There were some people who during my absence spread the lying rumour that I had run away from the struggle, but you know you can run away from the struggle even here in Cape Town without going thousands of miles overseas, by staying in your home, by cutting yourself off from the working class, and by associating with the policy of the enemy of the people." See also Glenn Frankel, *Rivonia's Children: Three Families and the Cost of Conscience in White South Africa* (New York: Farrar, Straus & Giroux,

1999), 62.

James Zug interview with Mary Butcher, January 1994: ". . . Betty Radford, for example, who was completely cut out once she resigned from the Party. I mean, she was just, you didn't, you never met her, you wouldn't associate with her. You know, she was just beyond the pale."

—"*You never saw her in Cape Town?*"

—"I never saw her, never met her. She was completely ignored. Nobody would talk about her, to her, meet her, anything. I mean, just completely."

James Zug interview with Rusty Bernstein, May 1994: even though the Bernsteins had gone into exile in 1963 and had always lived in or near London, they did not know that Betty and George had actually moved to London as well.

Pauline Podbrey said of Radford: "She was never one hundred percent. You know, she was never as deep as the rest of us. She was always the Lady Bounty, acting the role of very firm, good supporter. She was always not entirely, not one hundred percent. With us, but not of us."

41. See Margaret Ballinger Collection, BC345, A.2.6, UCT. Her diary for 2 April 1960: "Drinks at Sacks. George very flattering over my speech."

42. *Cape Times*, 28 August 1973 and 9 December 1981.

43. *Critic* 5, no. 3 (April–June 1938): 44; see *Guardian*, 22 July 1938, for "Topical" discussion of his article. See Nadine Gordimer, "Visiting George," in the *New Yorker*, 24 and 31 December 2001.

44. Andrews diary, 19 July 1947. Discussing the farewell cocktail party, Andrews writes, "I spoke about our appreciation of their work for ten and eleven years." See also his entry for 25 July 1947: "proceeded to docks to say goodbye to Harold and Carina Baldry and their little girl."

45. Lessing, *In Pursuit of the English*, 17–18; Doris Lessing, *Under My Skin: Volume One of My Autobiography to 1949* (New York: HarperCollins, 1994), 404–11; *Granta*, no. 58 (Summer 1987); and James Zug correspondence with Doris Lessing, October 1994. A Johannesburg publisher had bought her novel with a contract in which there was no advance and he would get 50 percent royalties. Doris Lessing, *Walking in the Shade: Volume Two of My Autobiography, 1949–1962* (New York: HarperCollins, 1997), 3: "I was full of confidence and optimism, though my assets were minimal: rather less than £150; the manuscript of my first novel, *The Grass is Singing*, already bought by a Johannesburg publisher who had not concealed the fact he would take a long time publishing it, because it was so subversive; and a few short stories. I had a couple of trunkfuls of books, for I would not be parted from them, some clothes, some negligible jewelry. I had refused the pitiful sums of money my mother had offered, because she had so little herself, and besides, the whole sum and essence of this journey was that it was away from her, from the family, and from that dreadful provincial country Southern Rhodesia, where, if there was a serious conversation, then it was—always—about The Colour Bar and the inadequacies of the blacks. I was free."

46. *Guardian*, 20 March 1947; ironically, each summer the *Guardian* ran a column for holiday-accommodation seekers dubbed, "Where to Stay."

See *Guardian*, 20 May 1950, for Brian Bunting's review of *The Grass is Singing*. "Disappointing First Novel," read the headline, and Bunting called it "amateurish." See *New Age*, 18 July 1957, for Bunting reviewing *Going Home* and saying she has the "occasional tendency to exaggerate." In *New Age*, 10 and 31 May 1956. Lessing wrote an article about her 1949 visit and earlier visits to Cape Town; it was illustrated with three pen-and-ink sketches and a photograph by Paul Hogarth. Lessing and Hogarth, after visiting Rhodesia, were refused entry into South Africa at Beit Bridge. See also 12 June 1958 for Lessing serving as chair of the South

African Freedom Association.

47. H. C. Baldry's books included *The Unity of Mankind in Greek Thought* (Cambridge University Press, 1965); *Ancient Greek Literature in its Living Context* (London: Thames & Hudson, 1968); *The Greek Tragic Theatre* (London: Chatto & Windus, 1971); and *The Case for the Arts* (London: Secker & Warburg, 1981). See *Independent*, 2 December 1991, for Brian A. Sparkes's obituary of Baldry. James Zug interview with Pauline Podbrey, December 1993: "I bumped into them in London once. I was at an open-air exhibition in Hampstead, which I was running, and they came past. I ran up to them with great warmth, 'Hello, hello, how are you?' They were very cool and very distant. They were clearly not wanting to be involved. It didn't develop into anything. I was rather disappointed with their attitude, but I gathered from them that they had had enough."

48. Molteno Collection, BC579, c5.21; and *Guardian*, 24 January 1946. Brian Bunting said Molteno "was always nervous about being branded a communist." James Zug interview with Brian Bunting, December 1993.

49. *Guardian*, 15 June 1950.

50. *Guardian*, 7 August 1947, with a mention of Walter Storm "replacing Vigilator for a few months" while the Baldrys holidayed in England. See 4 April 1946 at Nuremburg trials, and 24 July 1947 for two long articles from Prague. See also 11 September 1941 for "Walter Storm, the *Guardian*'s Funny Man." In 1947 Bloom wrote to Betty Radford: "And to think that I first learnt journalism on the *Guardian*. I read the first letter you sent me when you got my first story. Your advice is still good." *Guardian*, 7 August 1947.

Pretoria banned Bloom's *Episode* and refused to allow him to travel to London to accept the British Authors' Club prize for best novel in 1956. Alan Doyle [Michael Harmel] reviewed it: "This book is dynamite." *New Age*, 10 May 1956. See also Bruno Mtolo, *The Road to the Left: Umkonto we Sizwe* (Durban: Drakensberg Press, 1966), 11.

Bloom wrote much of his second novel, *Whittaker's Wife* (New York: Simon & Schuster, 1962), while in prison during the state of emergency. He also wrote the libretto for *King Kong: An African Jazz Opera*, performed worldwide in 1961. Bloom went into exile in 1963. He was the father of actor Orlando Bloom, born four years before he died in 1981.

51. James Zug interview with Brian Bunting, December 1993.

52. See Roux, *S. P. Bunting*; and Eddie and Winnie Roux, *Rebel Pity: The Life of Eddie Roux* (London: Rex Collings, 1970), 102. After his expulsion, S.P. Bunting suffered a stroke and had to give up his legal practice. To make ends meet, he became the caretaker of a block of flats in Hillbrow and played the viola in a Johannesburg orchestras. He died in 1936.

53. Roux, *S. P. Bunting*, 42.

54. Roux, *S. P. Bunting*, 43–49. In March 1922, during the Rand Revolt, four Afrikaner workers were arrested on charges of cutting telephone wires and concealing arms. They were interrogated and executed at Rosettenville. A young Arthur Bunting, looking at the bullet marks, was "left with the feeling that the police must have been very poor marksmen."

55. Roux, *S. P. Bunting*, 45. See also, Baruch Hirson, "'Stage' Theory and the South African Left: Bukharin, Bunting and the 'Native Republic Slogan'", *Searchlight South Africa* 1, no. 3 (July 1989): 51–66.

56. *Guardian*, 19 July 1940, for a mention of Bunting's work with NUSAS, a national students' organization.

57. "It was a rather dry dissertation," said Bunting. James Zug interview with Brian Bunting, December 1993. He worked at the newspapers at night and on his thesis during the day. See *Com-*

mission of Enquiry, Suppression of Communism Act, September 1953, 95. He also worked for a year as the registrar for a judge.

58. James Zug interview with Brian Bunting, December 1993, and Sonia Bunting, November 1994. Danie Du Plessis, one of the veteran Party figures in Johannesburg, would not let Sonia join Bunting in Cape Town unless they were married. They hastily eloped in the morning and Bunting left that evening, with Sonia following in a month's time.

59. Apparently, the work was not too taxing. At a Central Executive Committee meeting on 13 August 1946, it was agreed to ask Bunting to write a history of the Party. "I was not so deeply involved in Party political activity as I later became, and it was considered that I might have free time," testified Bunting when asked about this decision.

60. *Guardian*, 2 September 1948 for Bunting's election to the CEC; 8 April 1948 for a list of the Cape Town district committee. In 1946, upon his arrival in Cape Town, Bunting was also made a member of the Propaganda and Organisation Committee.

61. *Guardian*, 17 December 1946 for a Bunting review; 5 June 1947 for a review of a play; 25 September 1947 for an article on international issues; 17 April 1946 for a report on Rebecca Bunting visiting London; 25 September 1947 for an interesting review of Douglas Wolton's *Whither South Africa*—"jumbled . . . great pity, really."

   Bill Andrews, an old friend of Radford's, appeared to be a casualty of Bunting's ascension. In September 1947, Andrews wrote in his diary: "Took article to G. Not suitable says B. Bunting and HA. This is the third rejected short item. Evidently I am not up to Bunting's standard although he asked me for contributions letter." In 1949 Andrews wrote a letter to the editor that Bunting did not run, so Andrews sent it to the *Cape Times*, which published it: "Letter in *CTimes*. The G did not publish it. Evidently the editor does not agree with it and so put censorship on it as he has done before." Andrews diary, 22 September 1947 and 20 September 1949. See *Guardian*, 10 May 1951, for Alan Doyle [Michael Harmel]: "The editor [Bunting] has always allowed the widest latitude to say my say in this column."

62. *Guardian*, 16 September 1948 for an H. J. Simons article on the "Threat to Cape Franchise," and 21 April 1949 for a Ray Alexander article that asked, "Should trade unions take political action?"

63. *New York Times*, 9 November 1946—"3 African Leaders Assail Gen. Smuts"—with an article describing a reception given for Naidoo, Basner, and Dr. Xuma on West 26th Street. Max Yergen and Paul Robeson both were in attendance. Naidoo declared that the policies of discrimination in South Africa, "justified in the name of Christian civilisation, is at once an indication of the degradingly low level to which statesmanship has sunk in South Africa." See *Guardian*, 20 March 1947 for article on the United Nations and the Empire conferences; 30 January 1947 on the money he raised; 27 February 1947 for his standing ovation; 24 October 1946, and 5 and 12 December 1946 for his reports to Barrack Street.

64. *Guardian*, 10 April 1947 for Naidoo's article on the "Crisis in the Empire"; 18 September 1947 on "South Africa and the UNO: The Indian Question"; 29 July 1948 and 12 August 1948—"US on the Road to Fascism" and "Goodbye to Berlin," with its echoes of Christopher Isherwood's book; 2 September 1948—"The Nats are Worried by Africa's Challenge"; and 9 September 1948—"Who Will Save France?"

65. See 18 July 1946, and 21 January 1949. Shapiro, before she married Jack Barnett, lived with Nancy Dick in Newlands. In Johannesburg, Shapiro lived with the Issy Wolfsons in Hillbrow and remembered "working until twelve at night and then I'd take this big envelope to the post box at about two in the morning." Jeremy Bernstein interview with Naomi Shapiro, December

1988, "Media Active": "It wasn't casual at all, it was a very nerve-racking thing. I remember when I was editor I had a pain in my chest for months. I'm sure it was just stress and anxiety." See her articles in 26 August 1948 on meat shortages; 16 September 1948 with pictures of a mine; 14 October 1948 on the Transvaal ANC; and 25 November 1948 at the Transvaal ANC's annual conference in Pretoria. See 18 November 1948 for a listing under of "all political matter" that included Shapiro.

A "gloomy but efficient" German refugee, H. W. Degenhardt took over some of the managerial responsibilities of Carina Pearson. James Zug interview with Brian Bunting, December 1993. Also, a T. Paige did some editorial work in 1949.

66. *New Age*, 3 January 1957. James Zug interview with Jurgen Schadenburg, July 1994. Nxumalo also freelanced for the *Pittsburgh Courier*, one of the major African American newspapers in the United States. See Anthony Sampson, *Drum: A Venture into the New Africa* (London: Collins, 1956), 17–19.

67. "So frequently has this reporter been buttonholed by the regular customers of this column regarding its non-appearance while I was engaged in journalistic activities unconnected with civilized sport. . . ." *Guardian*, 10 March 1949; 3 July 1947 for his first article; 7 August and 4 September 1947, when pictures accompanied his column.

"Henry lived in Orlando and had a courage that not many journalists had," said Jurgen Schadenburg, a colleague of Nxumalo in the 1950s. "He was serious but he knew how to have fun. Perhaps, he drank too much and he certainly wasn't an intellectual, but he was a fine writer." See Sampson, *Drum*, 17. Sampson's book, when Houghton Mifflin published it in the United States, was titled *Drum: The Newspaper That Won the Heart of Africa*. Sampson, the flap copy stated, was a journalist "whose first job after Oxford was three years as the white editor of a Negro paper."

68. *Guardian*, 26 October 1944. See Don Pinnock, "Writing Left: Ruth First and Radical South African Journalism in the 1950s," unpublished manuscript, UWC. Along with her boyfriend Ismail Meer, First founded the Federation of Progressive Students (or Progressive Youth Council) while at Wits. She loathed her city-council job: "I spent my days," she recalled, "checking the figures for the number of play supervisors for white children in white parks, the number of beggars still on the street despite vigorous public relations work by the department to stop the public giving them alms. . . . [It] bored or disgusted me." Don Pinnock, *Ruth First: They Fought for Freedom* (Cape Town: Maskew Miller Longman, 1995), 8; and First, *117 Days*, 117. First also wrote and edited a section on social welfare for a commemorative album for Johannesburg's fiftieth anniversary.

69. First, *117 Days*, 117.

70. Gillian Slovo, *Every Secret Thing: My Family, My Country* (Boston: Little, Brown, 1997), 25 and 37; and Frankel, *Rivonia's Children*, 51.

71. Pinnock, *Ruth First*, 33; and Gillian Slovo, *Ties of Blood* (New York: William Morrow, 1990), 313.
James Zug interview with Sadie Forman, May 1994: "Lionel always saw eye to eye with Ruth. Not always with the others, but certainly with Ruth."

72. James Zug interview with Brian Bunting, December 1993: "Fred [his middle name was Frederick] came in and organized sales of the *Guardian*, something the Party had been doing before. We had to get it on a stronger, more permanent basis. Fred was a tall chap, wore glasses. He had grown up in the Transkei. He was very explosive, dynamic." See Gerard Ludi and Blaar Grobbelaar, *The Amazing Mr. Fischer* (Cape Town: Nasionale Boekhandel, 1966), 74. (Ludi, recruited to be a police spy while at Wits, had infiltrated the Congress movement and MK in the 1960s

and was a key witness at many political trials, including Mandela's and Fischer's.) Dennis Kuny said at Schermbrucker's memorial service: "The qualities which Ivan had were special, varied and endearing and one's lasting impression of him will be of a man who was warm, generous, kind, remarkably well balanced and down to earth, and, above all, human."

73. Ruth First correspondence to Ivan Schermbrucker, August 1981; Lesley Schermbrucker's private collection. "Somehow I thought of him as one of the indomitables, enduring, ever resilient. I was sure we'd make up one day for lost time. . . . he is always there. One of the indestructibles."

"Ivan simply adored the paper," said his wife Lesley Schermbrucker. "It was his lifeblood." The Schermbruckers lived quite close to the Bernsteins in Observatory (Johannesburg), and there was a well-trodden path among the bluegums and grasses between their two gardens. Hilda Bernstein correspondence to Lesley Schermbrucker, November 1981.

74. Yusuf Mohamed Dadoo, *His Speeches, Articles and Correspondence with Mahatma Gandhi, 1939–1983* (Cape Town: Mayibuye Centre, 1991), 42. James Zug interview with Sadie Forman, May 1994: "The person in Johannesburg who did all the hack work was Winnie Kramer. She was very nice, very soft. She was very good in the office, very friendly. There were a lot of people who weren't friendly in those days, I can tell you. But Winnie was."

75. *Guardian*, 16 January 1947. See 4 August 1949 when his column talked about Joe Matthew's piece in *Inkundla* titled "African Nationalism and Communism;" the following two weeks he wrote about a dockers' strike in London and the Ellis Park Test against the All-Blacks, noting how the denizens of the non-European section cheered for New Zealanders.

Issy Wolfson, the veteran communist, continued to write about trade-union issues and posted long pieces from Eastern Europe during a 1949 trip. *Guardian*, 22 September 1949 for "Hungary's New Way"; see also 29 September 1949; 6 and 13 October 1949.

76. Cape Times, 16 June 1947.

77. *Guardian*, 10 April 1947 for the CEC asking all branches to raise money during a month-long *Guardian* fundraising push.

78. *Guardian*, 9 January 1947 for a "stirring" speech by Bill Andrews; 13 January 1949 for a complete list of Party officials, and a photograph; 12 January 1950 with the "determined stand at national conference"; and 30 December 1948 for an advance copy of the Central Committee's report to the annual conference. See 17 July 1947 for an ad about Party meetings on Thursdays at lunch hour in the Grand Parade in Cape Town; and 6 January 1949 for an ad about Party meetings on Thursdays at 5:30 in Durban's Red Square

See also 2 April 1947 and 8 April 1948 for a report on the Cape Town district-committee conference, the latter with a list of officials; 1 May 1947 for the Johannesburg district-committee conference; 10 March 1949 for the Johannesburger's annual report; and 8 January 1948 for "Communist Election Policy Defined."

79. *Guardian*, 1 May and 7 August 1947 for a building workers' strike; 20 November 1947 for a history of the Garment Workers' Union, recounted by Anna Scheepers; 22 January 1948 for a back-page picture of a Food & Canning Workers' Union conference; 2 and 9 September 1948 for articles and pictures about a sweets workers' strike; 4 and 18 November 1948 for more of Issy Wolfson's trade-union column. See 30 January and 25 December 1947 fillers like "Mobilise for Socialism—a job must be done for the workers," and "Build the Worker's Paper and Advance Socialism."

80. *Guardian*, 11 December 1947 for testimony written by H. A. Naidoo. See also 30 January 1947 for two-and-a-half pages on trial; 20 February 1947 for two pages on the defense's cross-examination; 31 July 1947 for the defendants committed to trial; and 13 May 1948 for when the case collapsed.

81. *Guardian*, 20 May 1948 about Carneson's campaign in Athlone; 3 June 1948 about the post-election discussions. In his editorial that week, Jack Simons wrote: "In season and out of season this newspaper has hammered away at one fundamental truth, that a limited democracy is an insecure democracy."

82. *Guardian*, 25 November 1948; 14 October 1948 for an interview with Kahn about election prospects; 27 January 1949 for pictures at a Cape Town rally for Kahn as he entered Parliament, and his maiden speech.

83. *Guardian*, 16 January 1947.

84. *Guardian*, 1 April 1948; see also 20 May 1948 for an editorial on the new state of Israel, saying that the United States "will do all they can to sabotage the new state." 30 September 1948 with Naidoo writing on Berlin; 28 October 1948 on "apartheid in USA," with an article about the University of Oklahoma; 30 December 1949 with an article on Dadoo visiting Sofia, Bulgaria and Kartun, with a long article and four pictures on Mao—"The Giant of the Far East"; 25 August 1949—"The New Miracle of Stalingrad"; and 16 March 1950—"How Russia Solves the Housing Problem."

85. *Guardian*, 1 January 1948.

86. *Guardian*, 6 January 1949. See also 21 March 1938 for a letter from Madame Sun Yat-sen.

87. *Guardian*, 11 December 1947.

88. *Guardian*, 23 January 1947 about Basner, and 6 March and 4 December 1947 for Basner's feelers about a new party. See Miriam Basner, *Am I an African? The Political Memoirs of H. M. Basner* (Johannesburg: University of the Witwatersrand Press, 1993). See 4 November 1948 for a long page-two Basner article that argued, "To get the Nats out we need a liberal party"; "ed note: 'Further contributions on the theme of "how to get rid of the Nats" are invited.'" See 8 January 1948 for Legum's article.

89. *Guardian*, 16 January 1947 on Alexandra slums; 13 February 1947 on District Six; 27 February 1947 for a picture of food rationing in Cape Town; and 13 March 1947 on Benoni.

90. *Guardian*, 30 January 1947.

91. *Guardian*, 20 February 1947.

92. *Guardian*, 13 March 1947.

93. *Guardian*, 13 February 1947 for mention of a European union strike on the mines. See 23 January 1947 for an article about a Food & Canning Workers' Union conference in Cape Town that Betty Radford attended, "bringing fraternal greetings on behalf of the *Guardian*, [emphasizing] that the *Guardian* is a weapon in the fight against racial oppression and the colour bar."

94. Frances Meli, *South Africa Belongs to Us: A History of the African National Congress* (Harare: Zimbabwe Publishing House, 1988), 88.

95. The ANC's offices were next door to Pixley Seme's law practice. See Switzer, *Power and Resistance*, 288.

96. See T.H.R. White, "Z. K. Matthews and the formation of the ANC Youth League at the University College of Fort Hare," *Kleio* 27 (1995): 124–44. Matthews was a liberal rather than a hardcore Africanist, and so conflicts arose between teacher and students. He was even accused of removing copies of *Inkundla ya Bantu* from the library whenever the newspaper attacked the ANC old guard.

97. Meli, *South Africa Belongs to Us*, 108. See also Peter Walshe, *The Rise of African Nationalism in South Africa: The African National Congress, 1912–1952* (Berkeley: University of California Press, 1971), 349–61.

98. See Karis and Carter, *From Protest to Challenge*, 2: 85–86.

99. Meer, *Higher Than Hope*, 32; and Holland, *The Struggle*, 59. Nkomo was chairman of the ANCYL's provisional executive committee; Anton Lembede was the ANCYL's first president. There is some uncertainty as to whether Nkomo was actually a member of the Party.

100. See Karis and Carter, *From Protest to Challenge*, 2: 316.

101. "Basic Policy Document, 1948," issued by the ANCYL national executive committee; Nelson Mandela, *The Struggle Is My Life: His Speeches and Writings, 1944–1990* (Bellville: Mayibuye Centre, 1994), 26–27.

102. Jones, "*Inkululeko*," in Switzer, *South Africa's Alternative Press*, 614.

103. *Guardian*, 20 March 1947 for an interview with Xuma, Lembede, David Bopape, Dan Tloome, Edwin Mofustwana and Yusuf Chachlia on the national-convention idea; 21 August 1947 for an interview with Govan Mbeki on the NRC debate; 23 June 1949 and 28 July 1949 for an interview with Raymond Mhlaba on the Port Elizabeth bus boycott; 25 August 1949 for an article on a YMCA meeting in Durban in which Albert Luthuli is quoted—"raw end of apartheid deal"; 23 February 1950 for a quotation from A.W.G. Champion, "United Against the Common Enemy"; and 2 March 1950 for a little article on the Congress with a quotation from Sisulu.

104. Jeremey Bernstein interview with Naomi Shapiro, December 1988, "Media Active."

105. *Guardian*, 7 August 1947. See 12 June 1947 for a Xuma article on Transvaal squatters; 26 April 1949 for an article on Pungula, the president of a Zulu trade union who was deported from Durban; and 2 June 1949 for an article on a Congress deputation to the commissioner of police in Johannesburg.

106. *Guardian*, 12 June 1947 for a letter to the editor from Govan Mbeki in Idutywa about the NRC boycott; 28 August 1947 for a letter to the editor from L. S. Phillips; 9 October 1947 for a letter to the editor from A. P. Mda, acting president of the ANCYL; 11 December 1947 for an letter to the editor from Albert Kunene; and 7 April 1949 for a letter to the editor by A. S. Damane in Benoni on the Kahn bannings.

107. *Guardian*, 6 February 1947 for a picture of a shantytown rally; 23 January 1947 for a picture of 7,000 squatters marching through Johannesburg on a Saturday afternoon; 10 July 1947 for a report from ANC Cape conference in Craddock, with James Calata speaking on the NRC; 30 October 1947 for the Transvaal ANC conference on the front page; 18 and 25 December 1947 for article Ruth First wrote about the Congress's annual national conference: "New tactics proposed for NRC Boycott: Xuma's Address to African Congress"; 7 July 1949 for an article on the Port Elizabeth branch of the Congress; 15 December 1949 for an article about "Red-Baiting at ANC Conference," 8 December 1949 for an article about the Natal ANC conference; and 2 February 1950 for an article on the Natal ANCYL conference's resolutions.

108. *Guardian*, 16 October 1947 for a Xuma memorandum on South-West Africa; 9 October 1947 for "ANC News," which discussed the Transvaal ANC's conference.

109. *Guardian*, 22 December 1949 and 23 February 1950. See Les Switzer, "Language, Text, Community: A Critical and Historical Perspective on South Africa's Resistance Press," South African and Contemporary History Seminar, Institute of Historical Research and Department of History, University of the Western Cape, October 1994, p. 32.

110. *Guardian*, 22 January 1948 for an article and interview with J. B. Marks; and 25 December 1947 for the last two days' debate on the NRC issue.

111. *Guardian*, 5 February 1948. See 28 April 1949 for an interview with Selope.

112. *Guardian*, 12 January 1950.

113. Carter and Karis, *From Protest to Challenge* 2:398–99.

114. Alan Gregor Cobley, *Class and Consciousness: The Black Petty Bourgeoisie in South Africa,*

1924–1950 (New York: Greenwood Press, 1990), 210. Ramohanoe was soon bounced out of the ANC hierarchy because of his opposition to the Programme of Action. See *Guardian*, 20 April 1950, for a statement by David Bopape: "Now, forced to emerge from his slumbers by the forward march of the masses who seem to be marching too fast for his uncertain attitude, Mr Ramohanoe has had to search for words to cover his failure to keep abreast of the new militant spirit of the people."

One of the "armchair politicians" was Nelson Mandela, whom the *Guardian* quoted as calling cooperation between blacks and whites "a delicate matter." See *Guardian*, 29 July 1948.

115. *Guardian*, 22 April 1948.

116. Nelson Mandela, *Long Walk to Freedom* (Boston: Little, Brown, 1994), 85. In the 1950s there were six African doctors serving a population of over half a million. Xuma also worked at a clinic in Evaton and helped with health services in Alexandra. His full title was Dr. Alfred Bitini Xuma, M.D., B.Sc., L.R.C.P., L.R.C.S., L.R.F.P.&S., D.P.H.

117. *Guardian*, 9 January 1947, for an interview with Xuma on his return from America.

118. *Guardian*, 8 April 1948. See Xuma's interesting response on 22 April.

When train-station apartheid was introduced in Cape Town in early 1949, Xuma gave the *Guardian* a statement that the weekly headed "Africans Angered by Station Ban—Nats Will Reap What They Sow." See 7 July 1949.

119. *Guardian*, 22 January 1947. See also 27 March 1947 for the King visiting Orlando.

120. *Guardian*, 23 March 1950. See also 6 April 1950 for an interview with leaders of the ANCYL; 13 April 1950—"Why Did Xuma Resign?"; 21 September 1950 for Moroka speaking at an NIC conference; 28 June 1951 on Luthuli; and 12 July 1951 on Sisulu.

121. See *Guardian*, 27 February 1947 for two back-page pictures of Sophiatown shanties; 27 March 1947 for an interview with Colin Legum about squatters; 24 April 1947 for an article about Albert Kunene and Alexandra squatters; 8 May 1947 for three pictures of demolished shacks in Tobruck after police raided a shantytown; 15 May 1947 for an article that claimed that there were 70,000 squatters in five Transvaal towns; 10 July 1947 for two pictures of Durban shanties; 31 July 1947 for a report on Moroka Township squatters; 7 August 1947 for two three-column pictures on Moroka; 9 October 1947 for a picture sent in by the Durban SAT&LC of an African scratching around the debris of his house after the railway police burnt it; 29 January and 15 July 1948 for articles on Mooiplatz, a squatter camp seven miles outside Pretoria; 12 February 1948 for an article about 1,000 policeman invading Pimville in a 6 February raid, and for two pictures and an article on Windermere; 26 February 1948 for an article entitled "Life Isn't Easy at Alexandra"; 29 April 1948 for a picture of two women living in a dugout canoe on Green Point commons; 13 May 1948 for an article about Cape squatters, which included an interview with Sam Kahn and two photographs; 23 September 1948 for a photograph of Jabavu Native Township hovels, with blame being directed at the Johannesburg city council; 16 September 1948 for Naomi Shapiro's Chamber of Mines tour of miner's compounds; 24 February 1949 for an interview with Mpanza in Orlando about wanting to buy land; 31 March and 12 May 1949 for two pictures of Cape Town squatters; 9 June 1949 for 100 armed police arresting 191 Africans at the Elsie's River squatter camp; 16 June 1949 for a photograph and article on a Benoni tent town; 28 July 1949—"Durban's Appalling Housing Situation"; 25 August 1949 for a photograph of an African in the rain near some pondokkies; 17 November 1949 for a Ruth First article about Africans killed in police raid at Randfontein—she quotes Xuma at their funerals; 19 January 1950—"Race Terrorism Rising on Rand"; 16 February 1950 for a picture of Sophiatown women, and "More Bloody Clashes on Rand" about dawn raids—275 arrested

Tuesday night in Newclare, riots spread to Sophiatown where barricades went up and shops were burnt; 2 March 1950 for more on the Sophiatown riots.

In a bizarre coda to the squatter camps, see 15 and 22 February 1962 for articles and interviews with Mpanza, who called himself the "black Verwoerd" and supported the National Party. See also Philip Bonner, "The Politics of Black Squatter Movements on the Rand, 1944–1952," *Radical History Review* 46, no. 7 (1990): 89–115. As D. F. Malan put it, "The Negro does not need a home. He can sleep under a tree."

122. *Guardian*, 26 June 1947; 3 July 1947 for two front-page pictures and a page-five story and interview with Schreiner Baduza in Hamaanskraal. Alexandra township was created in 1912 when Africans were first allowed to buy plots there; in the 1950s over 100,000 people lived there, despite the township measuring just one square mile. See Mandela, *Long Walk to Freedom*, 66.

123. Muchaparara Musemwa, "Administering an African Township or a Personal Fiefdom? The Management Style of the Manager of Langa Township, Cape Town, 1938–48," *Kleio* 28 (1996): 137–52. See *Guardian*, 13 March 1947, 27 March 1947, and 15 May 1947 for an account of the trial, with Molteno and Snitcher appearing for the accused and a Mr. Cloete, whom we will see again, on the bench; 25 September 1947; 4 November 1948—"Langa Africans in Horrible Mood"; 3 February 1949—"Langa Upset by Rent Increases"; 28 April 1949 for a picture of Langa woman with kids and an article about school-feeding cuts; and 29 December 1949—"No Christmas Beer for Langa."

124. *Guardian*, 17 April 1947 for a Pretoria bus boycott in Atteridgeville; 30 December 1948 for a Moroka Jabavu bus boycott; 8 September 1949 for a First article on a tram boycott in Newclare and Sophiatown; 13 and 20 October 1949 for photographs of riots associated with the boycott; 17 February 1949—"Orlando Death Trap"—for a First article on Africans forced to walk across railway lines; 5 May 1949 on the Orlando train crash; and 29 July 1948 on Johannesburg's transportation problem.

125. *Guardian*, 17 July 1947 for an article by "Mfundo-Thuto" on African education; 26 February 1947 for the "Nigger" headline; 26 February 1948 on the "Threat to JHB Flower Sellers"; 3 June 1948 for a Shapiro article on Dora Tamana's crèche in the Cape Flats; 24 June 1948 for a Jackie Lax article on a preschool health center (and a somewhat unrelated beer-hall boycott) in Durban; 18 November 1948 on thousands of Africans deported from cities; 17 March 1949 on Helen Joseph planning a community center in Elsie's River; 26 May 1949 for pass-law anger in Johannesburg by Ruth First; 21 June 1949 for an ad for the apolitical black magazine *Zonk*; 28 July 1949 on Alexandra Africans banned from Johannesburg, and a history of Fort Hare under the title "Non-Europeans Prove Their Ability"; 4 August 1949—"My children have had no food for days; Ciskei mother's pitiful cry"; and 8 September 1949: "Apartheid—The Burden of Ill-Health—What Apartheid Means for Non-Europeans."

126. *Guardian*, 6 January 1949 for Marian Anderson and her husband Orpheus Fisher; 21 July 1949 for Seretse. See also 4 and 18 October 1956.

127. *Guardian*, 27 February 1947. Lembede said in the interview, "In the past resolutions by Congress were not implemented; they were even ignored by Congress leaders. This time it is the whole people who are pushing the leaders ahead."

128. *Guardian*, 29 May 1947.

129. *Guardian*, 10 June 1948.

130. *Guardian*, 1 April 1948 for Harrismith—"Why Trouble Is Brewing There—Ruth First Reports on Harrismith"; 17 July 1947 for a farm outside Pietersburg where 979 people were threatened with eviction; 4 September 1947 for two pictures of squatters driven off land in Pietersburg. See

Slovo, *Unfinished Autobiography*, 38–39, for a story of First visiting Badhuza's squatter camp.

131. First and Meer dated seriously for four years in the mid-1940s and almost married. Gillian Slovo, *Every Secret Thing* (Boston: Little, Brown, 1997), 31: "Even today when some people who knew them then talk about Ruth and Ismael [*sic*] Meer, their eyes shimmer with nostalgic regret. It's almost as if this one love affair has been written into the annals of myth." Meer went on to marry his cousin Fatima. Meer's flat at Kholvad House, 27 Market Place, was near Pixley Seme's law offices, where Anton Lembede clerked.

Guardian, 28 August 1947: "On a cold and wintry morning, the *Guardian* reporter was called out to the secondary school in Johannesburg's oldest location, Western Native Township." See 7 October 1948 for a statement by Huddleston.

132. *Guardian*, 11 December 1947. More than 40,000 foreign Africans worked the fields in Bethal.

133. Don Pinnock, "Writing Left: The Journalism of Ruth First and the *Guardian* in the 1950s," in Switzer, *South Africa's Alternative Press*, 314.

134. *Guardian*, 3 July 1947. See 12 October 1944 for an article about Basner, David Bopape, and Selope-Thema organizing farm workers in Bethal; and 1 March 1945 for Christine Cash with open letter to Harry Lawrence about farm labor. See Tom Lodge, introduction to *Am I an African? The Political Memoirs of H. M. Basner* (Johannesburg: Witwatersrand University Press, 1993), xviii.

135. A vivid description of Michael Scott and the Bethal scandal can be found in the writings of Mary Benson, who was his secretary for many years: *A Far Cry* (London: Viking, 1989), 57–93, and *South Africa: The Struggle for a Birthright* (London: Penguin, 1966), 116—this was first published by Faber & Faber in 1963 under the title *The African Patriots: The Story of the African National Congress of South Africa*.

136. *Guardian*, 3 July 1947. Three pounds and one shilling were deducted by the farmer for his pains in transporting the laborer back to the border at the end of six months; for each recruit, the farm had to pay the Boere Arbeidsvereeniging £5. See *De Echo*, 6 and 13 June 1947.

137. Michael Scott, *A Time to Speak* (London: Faber & Faber, 1958), 176. See Freda Troup, *In Face of Fear: Michael Scott's Challenge to South Africa* (London: Faber & Faber, 1950), 135–36 and Anne Yate and Lewis Chester, *The Troublemaker: Michael Scott and His Lonely Struggle Against Injustice* (London: Aurum Press, 2006).

138. *Rand Daily Mail*, 27 June 1947.

139. James Zug interview with Brian Bunting, November 1993; First sent her copy on a Monday morning by air freight, and Bunting's secretary would retrieve it from the airline's offices in Cape Town in the afternoon.

140. Scott, *A Time to Speak*, 180–81.

141. The front page of the *Rand Daily Mail* included a photograph of Hutton and Washbrook opening England's innings against South Africa at Lords.

142. *Rand Daily Mail*, 7 July 1947.

143. *Guardian*, 10 and 17 July 1947.

144. *Rand Daily Mail*, 7 July 1947.

145. *Guardian*, 10 and 24 July, and 20 November 1947. The four Europeans were released on bail of £100 each. See also *Rand Daily Mail*, 16 and 18 July 1947.

146. Benson, *Struggle for Birthright*, 116–17. See also Scott, *A Time to Speak*, 169.

147. Troup, *In Face of Fear*, 135–36. See *Guardian*, 17 July 1947.

148. *Guardian*, 3 July 1947.

149. *Guardian*, 11 September 1947 and 26 January 1950: "A Man Turned Rabbit: The Story of a Life

Ruined by the Pass Laws." See 5 August 1948 for an article by Michael Scott: "No Cure for Crime."

150. *Guardian*, 1 December 1949, 7 August and 11 December 1947. See 2 June 1949: "Early each morning the pick-up vans drive up. They bring the men—and some women—picked up by the police raids the night before. . . . Lining the streets outside this court can be seen cars and lorries with an assortment of platteland number plates. From the maize and potato belts come the farmers looking for cheap labour. In a shed near the court, as they wait, Africans are pressed to accept farm work. The prisoners, none of whom have yet appeared before the court, let alone been found guilty, are told . . . if they accept work the charges against them will be withdrawn."

151. *Guardian*, 2 February 1950. See *Daily Worker*, 1 September 1949.

152. *Guardian*, 25 December 1947.

153. *Guardian*, 4 July 1946 for Dadoo statement; 11 July 1946 for a list of money donated to the Passive Resistance Campaign; 6 November 1947 for a picture of 34 resisters, 24 of whom are women; 19 June 1947 for the one-year anniversary of the PRC; 15 and 22 January 1948 for 15 Indians selected to cross the Transvaal border; 29 January and 5 February 1948 for front-page pictures of their action and the lack of police interference; 12 August 1948 about M. P. Naicker receiving four months in jail for ordering the taxi which transported the Natal PRC group to Newcastle; 12 February 1948 for a lead story on the PRC; 6 October 1949 for an article on the government uprooting Indian families. Ismail Meer recalled that "the *Guardian* was a key part of the passive resistance in the 1940s. It had a dynamic influence in our communities. We began to see it as our paper, as a way to push things along."

"When we were inside jail," said Fatima Seedat, one of the resisters, "the four walls of the jail, then you realize what freedom is. To read of freedom in the paper and to read of freedom in books doesn't teach you. You just read, 'freedom' or 'justice' or whatever. But when you're behind those four gray walls, then you realize what freedom really means to you. You become, you know, more emotional, more determined. Your spirit is engaged."

154. *Guardian*, 2 April 1947.

155. *Guardian*, 18 December 1947.

156. *Guardian*, 20 November 1947.

157. *Guardian*, 27 February 1947 for a letter to the editor from Seedat; 20 November 1947 for G. M. Naicker telling the *Guardian* about the political situation; 20 October 1949 for an interview with Dadoo the day after he returned from India; 15 December 1949 for Doyle calling Dadoo the "storm-bird of the South African revolution."

158. *Guardian*, 10 November 1949.

159. *Guardian*, 20 January 1949 for three pictures (there were seven the next Thursday); 3 March 1949 for "Durban a City of Rumours," with three pictures and an article on Cato Manor; 20 November 1947 on the situation at DIMES; 8 July 1949 for an NIC letter to Malan about the riots. See also *New Age*, 24 November 1960, for a two-page spread on the 100 Years of Indians in South Africa, including seven photographs courtesy of Fatima Meer.

160. *Guardian*, 12 February 1948 on Windermere; 9 August 1945 for Elsie's River; and 26 August 1948 on the bergies. See Gavin Lewis, *Between the Wire and the Wall: A History of South African 'Coloured' Politics* (Cape Town: David Philip, 1987). A *Guardian* fundraising drive one Saturday in Elsie's River, a coloured shantytown, had the slogan "Educate—Organise—Agitate for Socialism." See 12 August 1948; 1 September 1949 for 10 shillings from Mrs. Jimmy La Guma, proceeds from tea made for canvassers; 11 November 1948 for John Aspeling, who sold 240 a week in Worcester and now is ordering 300; 8 January 1948; 1 July 1948 for a jumble sale

in Grassy Park; 30 June 1949 for a letter to the editor from John Motloheloa in Elsie's River.

161. *Guardian*, 23 May 1946 for rice raids; 14 February 1946 for marching on Parliament. See Slovo, *Unfinished Autobiography*, 35.

162. *Guardian*, 11 August 1949 for Morley at a dinner party where he sold twenty-one *Guardians* at one shilling each, twelve times the regular price. See also 16 February 1950 for a letter to the editor. James Zug interview with Amy Thornton, December 1994: "Johnny was marvelous. He was a dapper little chap, my height [rather short], and he always wore khaki—khaki shorts, a khaki shirt, long khaki socks and highly polished shoes. And he was absolutely dedicated to his task."

James Zug interview with Fred Carneson, March 1994: "He was enormously popular in the paper politically. He was never an outstanding political figure, but in actual fact he was quite a charismatic leader. I would say one of the outstanding features of John Morley was his absolute lack of egotism. He was a humble man. He never pushed himself forward. He'd do anything that was asked of him at any time whatsoever. He never thought of himself as a leader of this type or that. He enjoyed enormous love and respect from other people, particularly Africans."

163. *Freedom* (November–December 1946). See also *Guardian*, 2 January and 20 November 1947. Hettie McLeod later recalled: "We worked hard at educating the women, helping them see what was happening." James Zug telephone conversation with Hettie September, December 1993.

164. *Guardian*, 27 June 1946; 2 April 1947 for forty-five queues; 24 July 1947 for Radford speaking at WFC general meeting; 14 July 1949 for the WFC's 1,000 members; 29 January 1948 on food queues in East London organized by the Party. Walker, *Women and Resistance*, 83: The committees were "the beginnings of the growth of political consciousness among previously politically isolated black housewives and women workers." See also *Guardian*, 29 April 1948 about Cape Flats coloured workers backing Carneson; 8 May 1947 for two back-page pictures of a WFC rally in the Grand Parade; and 20 November 1947 for a WFC dance. The motto of the WFC was "Today we fight for food, tomorrow for the vote and then freedom for all."

165. *Guardian*, 4 March 1948, for an article by Marjorie Till about a Saturday afternoon meeting of Cape Town sellers of the weekly with a birthday cake and Mrs. Rose Parkes (see 19 August 1948 about the 65-year-old woman, "one of the best sellers of the *Guardian* and a member of the finance committee of the WFC") and Malotane both selling 288 per week; Mr. Ngwevela, Cedras, Dean, Mrs. Cooper, Kruger, and Mussel all selling over 100 per week; and Mr. Gallant selling 420 per week. See also 26 February 1948 for Till's first article; 8 July 1948 about how Morley opened a savings bank account for them; 30 December 1948 for photographs of 200 children, all *Guardian* sellers, at a party arranged by Morley. One girl, Gagija Edwards, regularly sold twenty-five dozen. See 1 July 1948: "The immediate necessity for calling a local conference to discuss the question of votes for Non-European women was stressed in a resolution."

166. *Guardian*, 27 March 1947 for Colgate; 14 August 1947 for dainty; 30 November 1944 for caresses; 20 May 1947 for a fall jumper; 3 June 1947 for a first-birthday suit by Jessica Brown; 24 June 1947 and 1 July 1947 for more knitting patterns; 9 September 1948 for Bridget's column; 19 January 1950 for "Bringing Up Baby by Mater."

167. *Guardian*, 13 November 1947 for unions, and 11 December 1947 for applicants.

168. *Guardian*, 15 January 1948.

169. *Guardian*, 1 January 1948.

170. *Guardian*, 26 February, and 1 and 15 April 1948. The panel of judges included Gregorie Boonzaier, Cissie Gool, Mrs. H. Southern-Holt, Betty Radford, Johnny Gomas, Marjorie Till and Rita Maas; Sam Kahn acted as master of ceremonies.

171. *Guardian*, 22 April 1948.
172. *Guardian*, 26 February 1948 for her height; 22 April 1948 for her extra jobs.
173. *Guardian*, 29 April 1948. Besides the check, Jacobs earned a studio portrait; the other finalists received a bedside radio, a wrist watch, a length of tweed for a winter costume, bathing costumes, and cosmetic sets, and three *Guardian* readers won free cinema tickets for correctly choosing the three finalists. See 11 December 1947, and 25 March, 1 April, and 6 May 1948.
174. *Guardian*, 30 December 1948 for pictures; 6 May 1948 for Tulip's father. James Zug interview with Brian Bunting, December 1993: "The beauty contest was purely something to boost circulation. We wanted to broaden the appeal of the paper and put in things like Alex's comics and these competitions. But it made no difference to our circulation. People bought the paper for our political stuff. The only thing they wanted was politics."
175. *Selling*, January 1948. Circulation in November 1947 was at 41,000. *Guardian*, 5 February 1948: 46,000; 4 November 1948: 40,000; 24 February 1949: 35,000; 5 February and 4 November 1948; 24 February 1949: 35,000; *Cape Times* 24 May 1952; and 7 April 1949 for the stunning fact that street sales increased by 60 percent over last week, a sales record.
176. *Selling*, May 1948; See *Guardian*, 6 January 1949, for the weekly's rate of two pennies per word.
177. *Guardian*, 5 January 1950. See 6 November 1949: an advertisement for Commando cigarettes read, "How pleasant it is at mid-day to relax and make the most of restful conversation over lunch, and afterwards to enjoy the fine, cool flavour of a Commando cigarette."
178. *Guardian*, 29 January 1948 for needing £600 and a donations list; 15 April 1948 for expenses, apart from those covered by advertising—need £600 a month and getting only £52 2s. in guarantees; 8 July 1948, again needing £600 month; 21 October 1948, now needing £700 a month. The printing bill from a sympathetic Stewart's came to £10,000 per annum.
179. *Guardian*, 26 February 1948 for the gap last month of £600; 7 October 1948 for running at loss of £500–600 a month.
180. 7 October 1948: "Now the reserves built up during the war years are running out," Bunting said. Trevor Huddleston: "Although I do not always find myself in agreement with its policy, I am most grateful for all that it is doing to champion the cause of the under-privileged and oppressed, particularly our Non-European peoples." Lewin said that because of the *Guardian*, blacks "have acquired something of the social significance that rightly belongs to them." The list of figures also included Roseberry Bokwe, Rev. Blaxnall, Michael Scott, Bill Andrews, Pauline Podbrey, and K. Goonam.
181. Ronald Segal, *Into Exile*, 78.
182. Shaun Johnson interview with Fred Carneson, in Shaun Johnson, "Propagandist, Plenipotentiary and Pariah: The Heyday of the *Guardian/New Age* Series, 1946–1960" (unpublished, delightfully titled paper), p. 7.
183. *Selling*, June 1948 for the 100 percent insertion, April 1948 for the only paper, and August 1948 for its estimated sales. "The *Guardian* is exclusively in English. All its Non-European readers (estimated at 85 per cent of total sales) read and understand English! This means no translation worries—no extra production costs."
184. *Guardian*, 27 July 1950.
185. *Guardian*, 3 July 1947 for a children's crossword; 28 August 1947 for a repeat. See 24 April 1951 and 21 January 1954; 4 February 1954—"We'll continue the crossword if we get 50 interested readers."
186. *Guardian*, 10 November 1949.

187. *Guardian*, 4 March 1948; 23 January 1947 the ANC's Wolmaranstad branch; 6 February 1947 the ANC's Cape Town branch giving £2 2s.

188. *Guardian*, 20 January 1949.

189. *Guardian*, 4 August 1949 raised £5 8s. 3d.; 17 November 1949 Jack Simons and H. A. Naidoo at a lecture; 13 October 1949 for used books; 23 December 1948 no calendar this year; 3 July 1947—Cape Town *Guardian* League gramophone evening at home of H. Bernadt; 17 July 1947 *Guardian* Brains Trust Meeting, Main Road Sea Point, with Sam Kahn as the "Question Master"; 4 September 1947 for the Women's Food Committee and the *Guardian* League raising £37 at a dance; 4 March 1948 for a *Guardian* bazaar at the Old Drill Hall—sweets workers, NUDW, Friends of the Soviet Union, the ANC, WFC, and *Guardian* league organizing the koeksisters; 6 May 1948 A. Joffe left £75 in his will for the *Guardian*; 8 July 1948 *Guardian* jumble sale in Grassy Park; 12 August 1948 *Guardian* drive Sunday in Elsie's River; 9 September 1948 *Guardian* league dance, £3—"Make Apartheid Unworkable"; 28 October 1948 *Guardian* Hops at St. Luke Hall, Salt River, £2 6s.; 6 January 1949—Cape Town *Guardian* league raising £110 5s. 3d. at New Year's Eve dance; 10 February 1949 *Guardian* Bop Hop in Salt River postponed; ad for *Guardian* 12th birthday party with map of Claremont—£5; 19 May 1949 jumble sale earning £18; 2 June 1949: "For those who love music come to the home of Mr. and Mrs. Sam Kahn, Claremont £4—for a *Guardian* league musical evening; also rummage sale at Fidelity Hall; 16 June 1949 Kahn giving "impressions of Parliament" in Bride Road, Oranjezicht, canceled until July; 11 August 1949 £100 from Louis Wessman of Johannesburg who died a year ago in Lichtenburg at age 60—"old friend and staunch supporter"; 10 November 1949 jumble sale £11, lecture by Norman Flegg on the "economic problem of South Africa" at Crystal Pool in Kenilworth, and 13 November with Jack Cope on "modernism in art" in Three Anchor Bay, 17 November with Jack Simons on "democracy in South Africa—its institutions" in Vredehoek, and 1 December 1949 with Moses Kotane speaking in Oranjezicht and Ray Alexander speaking in Bantry Bay.

190. A June 1947 campaign set a six-month goal for major South African cities: *Guardian* readers in Cape were to raise £1,250, Johannesburg £1100, Durban £450, Port Elizabeth £200, Pretoria £100, East London and Pietermaritzburg £40. *Guardian*, 12 June 1947 Johannesburg has already sent out an appeal; 17 July 1947 Johannesburg already raised £240, Cape Town at £100; 31 July 1947 Johannesburg raised £375 in June and July; 12 June 1947 for financial needs.

An October 1948 appeal achieved some success, with the weekly finding £365 in guaranteed monthly donations after only five weeks, and £500 by January 1949. But only £400 came in each month "because some of our donors do not make it their business to pay if they are not contacted personally." 4 November 1948 and 6 January 1949.

In June 1949, another national appeal was launched, this time for £1,000 in two weeks and £6,000 by the end of the year. 16 June 1949 for £770 arriving in a fortnight; 7 July 1949 for £19 from jumble sales.

191. The 1945 *Guardian* holiday note cards were designed by Gregoire Boonzaier, Leslie Cope, John Dronsfield, Rhoda Pepys, and Gerard Sekoto.

192. For Johannesburg, see *Guardian*, 13 October 1949 with £585 in jumble sale; 3 July 1947 for Johannesburg *Guardian* League dance raising £160; 24 June 1948 Johannesburg raised £145 in one week, with the Gelbs raising £82 at a card party; 5 February 1948 dance, couple £1 1s., 8:00–1:00 am, dress optional; 22 July 1948, 95 percent of donations from the Transvaal—"why, because our Johannesburg staff and the *Guardian* league are live wires." See also 12 May 1949 Mr. and Mrs. Gelb raising £64 at jumble sales and card evenings; 21 July 1949, £30 jumble sale;

15 September 1949, £36 at rummage sale; 13 October 1949 raised £58 from jumble sale; 27 April 1950 Johannesburg collected £511 in April, £442 in March, for a total of £954, 73 percent of what was raised in last two months. See also 30 March 1950 for the *Guardian* league birthday party in Rosebank that raised £200.

For Fleggs, see 25 December 1947 raised £385; 27 October and 8 December 1949 when it was a masked ball; *New Age*, 12 January 1956 raised £600.

193. For Bram Fischer's annual birthday soiree, see *Guardian*, 18 March 1948 raising £262, and 6 April 1950 raising £250. See Clingman, *Bram Fischer*, 220–21, 224, and 352.

194. Clingman, *Bram Fischer*, 168.

195. Again the weekly sought political heavyweights to give messages of support for the increase. 15 December 1949 and 19 January 1950, with appeals from Moses Kotane, Mick Harmel, George Poonen, Danie Du Plessis and Arthur Damane.

196. James Zug interview with Len Lee-Warden, December 1993. Hendrik Verwoerd, when he started *Die Transvaler* in 1937, had a similar problem, as his new printing press sank in the Atlantic.

197. *Cape Times*, 4 October 1947: "City Printer Found Dead." He was found in his garage "lying on the cement at the back of his car, with his face near the exhaust pipe. Neighbors heard the engine on the car running during the night, but did not attach any significance to the sound." The *Cape Times* added that "Mr. Stewart's company was recently involved in litigation with Senator A.M. Conroy, Minister of Lands." Stewart left his wife and two young children, and the *Guardian* had lost a good friend who was always, as Radford said, "ever ready to lend a helping hand with editorial production."

John H. Merryweather, a linotype operator at Stewart's and longtime supporter of the weekly, also died that year. *Guardian*, 19 January 1947.

198. James Zug interview with Len Lee-Warden, December 1993. See *Guardian*, 8 April 1948. See A. J. Friedgut, "The Non-European Press," in *Handbook on Race Relations in South Africa*, ed. Ellen Hellmann (London: Oxford University Press, 1949), 502. Unie Volkspers printed the UP organ *Die Suiderstem* and small Transvaal newspapers like the *East Rand News* and the *Standerton Advertiser*.

199. *Guardian*, 13 January 1949. He resigned from the *Guardian* board of directors "owing to indisposition."

200. Thirty-two trade unions, dozens of individuals, eight Members of Parliament, and sixteen communist parties from around the world sent birthday greetings. "From the citadel of world reaction which today threatens the rest of the world with atomic devastation," William Foster and Eugene Dennis of the USA CP offered best wishes. Mao Tse-Tung, the newly victorious Chinese leader, sent a treasured telegram, and Jan Smuts, himself turning eighty in a month's time, posted a note to his old rival. The *Guardian* wrote a letter to Andrews saying, "We have been proud of your close connection with this paper and grateful for advice and help we have from you." Andrews Collection, box 3, Mayibuye Centre, University of the Western Cape. Ray Alexander correspondence to Bill Andrews, May 1950, upon reading an article by Andrews in the *Guardian:* "It was the best thing I could have done, to read your article. It is so confident of the future. . . . This morning I advised many others to read your article." See E. S. Sachs, *The Choice Before South Africa* (London: Turnstile Press, 1952), 195: Andrews was "completely free from the spirit of insularity and cold aloofness of the British."

201. "Walked from post office to docks and on to Woodstock, passing on the way the old *City of Lincoln* being dismantled. The docks as quiet as the grave, only one ship in Duncan Dock. Taking

it slowly and was able to do the rather long walk without any protest from heart. But was rather tired at the end." Andrews diary, 26 December 1949. Andrews also felt out of touch with the other comrades. While in Kimberley for a Party conference, he wrote on 15 December 1947: "Feeling that I am no longer suitable company for the younger men."

On the back of his 1912 House of Assembly Standing Orders, he wrote: "After all, it is better in this world of unsatisfying dreams to think we are blessed when we really are not, than to be blessed when we do not think we are."

CHAPTER FOUR. THE CARRY-ON:
BANNINGS, 1948-1954

1. The official name of the party was Nationalist, until it was changed to National in 1951. See Robert Kinlock Massie, *Loosing the Bonds: The United States and South Africa in the Apartheid Years* (New York: Doubleday, 1997), 35.
2. *Guardian*, 2 June 1949; and Simons, *Class and Colour*, 592. On Kahn's first day in Parliament, Jan Smuts told him to be very cautious with the Nationalists, since "these people will put you in jail."
3. Slovo, *Unfinished Autobiography*, 41. Kahn also said in Parliament on 16 June 1949: "I am not hankering after masochistic martyrdom. I do not intend to be driven underground, to bob up here and there like a political submarine."
4. Podbrey, *White Girl*, 134. Sometimes after Kahn's bitter, denunciatory speeches, they would approached him, dig him in the ribs, and joke, "Ag, Sammy, jy's 'n slim john, eh!"
5. *Guardian*, 26 October 1950. See 9 October 1950 for a Kahn column on intolerance and the church instead of on Parliament; 14 December 1950 for a column on Mao.
   James Zug interview with Brian Bunting, December 1993: "Sam was very close. His offices were just around the corner and he would stop on his way to Parliament, his pockets full of speeches, and talk about arch-intrigues in the city council and Parliament. He was hale and charismatic and complex and a good friend. Once he got a Christmas hamper from KWV, that was meant for me. He swallowed the whole lot and didn't tell me. Didn't save anything. We had quite a laugh when I discovered this."
6. *Guardian*, 10 August 1950 for the first column; 16 November 1950 for a Group Areas map of Johannesburg; 12 October 1950 for discussion of the Group Areas Act and Indians (and for Kahn offering a first prize of £1 and two second-place prizes of 10s. 6d., payable in books, for a reader's best list of South African heroes); 27 March 1952 for another Group Areas map; and 7 May 1953 for a map and full-page article on Cape Town Group Areas. See also 6 January 1949 for an interview with Kahn after he went touring in Xhosaland.
7. *Guardian*, 23 March 1950.
8. *Guardian*, 15 February 1949. See 1 September 1949 for Kahn speaking in Durban; 22 September 1949 speaking in Johannesburg, where he was being shadowed by the not-so secret police; 27 October 1949 for a huge picture of the crowd at Fordsburg Red Square; 10 November 1949 for an interview that Dadoo gave to the *Guardian* after he heard news of his banning "told to him by a *Guardian* reporter who read about it in *Die Burger.*" Kahn said in response to the bans, "Where there is an injustice in South Africa, there is my constituency."
9. Benson, *Struggle for a Birthright*, 130; and *Guardian*, 30 March 1950. The Defend Free Speech convention also protested against a threatened pass law for women. The spectacle of the parade

was impressive, but the impact was not too great, as the streets of the city, it being a Sunday, were mostly empty. The 19 March issue contained a revealing two-column, front-page cartoon: it was a supine black man straining against the tethered ropes of "pass laws" and "police raids," and a little white man standing on his chest saying to other little white men attending the ropes, "He's Waking Up, Little Men, What Now?"

10. Lionel Forman and E. S. Sachs, *The South African Treason Trial* (London: John Calder, 1957), 134–35; and *New Age*, 26 April 1962.

11. *Guardian*, 4 May 1950.

12. Mandela, *Long Walk to Freedom*, 101–2.

13. Bloke Modisane, *Blame Me on History* (Johannesburg: AD Donker, 1963), 141–46.

14. Forman and Sachs, *South African Treason Trial*, 135.

15. Simons, *Class and Colour*, 606; and *Guardian*, 8 June 1950. While the bill was in committee, United Party members proposed that communism should be a capital offense. See also the *Economist*, 28 February 1953.

16. *Guardian*, 25 May 1950. Kahn then complained that the fact that he was not on the select committee considering the SCA was "something like Hamlet without the prince."

17. Michael Harmel and Bill Andrews were the only two members to vote against dissolution. Moses Kotane and Isaac Horovitch went to Durban and Johannesburg to explain the decision to the rank and file. Kotane said that "theoretically you can train people to be pilots when there are no aeroplanes. But the realities have to be there." Bunting, *Moses Kotane*, 173. See Clingman, *Bram Fischer*, 187–88.

18. *African Communist*, no. 112 (1st quarter 1988). See also *African Communist*, no. 40 (1st quarter 1970), and no. 46 (3rd quarter 1971).

19. The bill, adopted 23 June 1950, came into force on 17 July.

20. Ronald Segal, *Into Exile*, 90–91. After seeing bloodshed and being threatened by the police during the melee, Segal suddenly glimpsed Amy Thornton across the street. "She was standing on the opposite pavement, looking at the now quiet bodies in the street, and the tears were running down her cheeks. Suddenly she saw me and we stared at each other in dumb desolation."

21. *Guardian*, 29 June 1950. Bunting continued: "We intend also to continue to protest against the Suppression of Communism Act and to use every lawful means to work for its repeal. The basic task before all democrats is to restore to the individual his right to think and speak as he pleases without the restraint of fear. Such a policy, we are convinced, will be supported by the majority of people in South Africa, who want an end to race-hatred and Nationalist tyranny, who long for peace and the opportunity to live out their lives in dignity and freedom. In this conviction we are confident that our readers will continue to give us their moral and material backing, without which our task is impossible."

22. *Union of South Africa—Report of the Select Committee on the Suppression of Communism Act Enquiry* August 1953, 95–96. Bunting testified: "No. The *Guardian* was quite an independent paper. . . . It often did [support the Party] but it was not the official organ of the Party. It had no form of connection with the Party whatsoever. It was an independent company controlled by shareholders and directors in the same way as any other paper. The official paper of the Party was *Inkululeko*. This paper went out of existence at the time of the dissolution of the Party. Amongst the directors of the *Guardian* were persons who were not Communist Party members."

First, *South-West Africa*, 14: "Where flimsy cords of communication between the colours are spun, intimidation severs them instantly."

23. *Guardian*, 31 March 1949. The ban initially fed interest in the newspaper. See 7 April 1949—*Guardian* street sales increased by 60 percent over last week, a "sales record." In a telling move, Sauer authorized the sale of the Ossewabrandung's *Die OB* in September 1948. A railway ban also was levied on *Africa South* in 1957, when publisher Ronnie Segal's application for railway and airport selling got an "unelaborated no." In Parliament, Hymie Davidoff questioned Sauer, and Sauer said *Africa South* "had a bad smell." Segal, *Into Exile*, 144.

   Sauer reappeared on the national scene briefly in April 1960. In the aftermath of the assassination attempt on Verwoerd, he served as acting prime minister and gave a speech at Humansdorp calling for substantive governmental reforms. His call received a good deal of publicity around the world, but was not heeded.

24. Another proscription also occurred in March 1949 when the governor-general of Kenya banned past and future issues of the *Guardian*. Bunting lodged protests with the British prime minister, but received no satisfaction. *Guardian*, 17 March 1949. The ban was announced in Kenya's *Government Gazette*. The governor-general also banned the *Labour Monthly* (London), *New Africa* (New York), *People's Age* (India), and *Blitz*. See Sampson, *Mandela*, 175.

25. *Guardian*, 28 August 1958 and 10 December 1959, for articles by Brian Bunting on Swart. Swart, not a humble man, said in 1953 that "a monument should be erected to me for the way I have vanquished opposition in the last session of Parliament."

26. Hansard, 16 May 1949, col. 5896; Hansard, 17 May 1949, col. 5961; and *Guardian*, 19 and 26 May 1949. Kahn said that the Party "had the most prophylactic effect in South Africa."

   Die Burger wrote perceptively about the banning debate: "It is useless to empower the Minister to suppress Communistic publications. Communism avoids this stamp and sails under a false and innocent flag. . . . We must take steps to prevent a successor."

27. *Cape Argus*, 25 and 30 November 1950—the detectives were "especially interested in overseas news service"; and *Cape Times*, 25 November 1950. See *Guardian* statement to Swart about the raid, November 1951, in Thornton file 24, folder 4, Manuscripts and Archives, University of the Western Cape.

28. *Natal Mercury*, 25 November 1950; see 30 November 1950 for Berrange.

29. Podbrey, *White Girl*, 61; and James Zug interviews with Fatima Seedat and Ismail Meer, February 1994. *New Age*, 7 June 1962, for a picture of Fatima Seedat.

   "I was taken up by his charisma, warmth, gentleness, and friendliness," wrote Paul Joseph, a colleague of Seedat's, in a letter to Fatima. "He was always ready to pass on knowledge and advice, never was conceited, and never arrogant—like some of us."

30. *Cape Argus*, 25 November 1950; and *Natal Mercury*, 25 November 1950.

31. *Cape Argus*, 25 November 1950.

32. *Guardian*, 30 November 1950.

33. Thomas Pringle, *Narrative of a Residence in South Africa* (London: W. Tegg, 1851), 64–67: ". . . although the printing thus cost us more, and was far worse executed." See also Noel Mostert, *Frontiers: The Epic of South Africa's Creation and the Tragedy of the Xhosa People* (London: Jonathan Cape, 1992), 571. John Fairbairn edited his newspaper until 1859 and became an MP in the first Cape Parliament. Pringle left Cape Town in October 1824, became secretary of the Anti-Slavery Society in London, and died in 1834 at the age of forty-five.

34. Hansard, 26 January 1951, col. 232. The question was asked by Mr. Veckermann.

35. *Guardian*, 5 April 1951. See 21 January 1951 for an editorial on a possible ban.

36. Thornton Collection, box 24, folder 4, for a statement submitted to Swart in which Bunting described O'Brien as replying "casually."

37. *Guardian*, 5 April 1951.
38. Hansard, 15 June 1951, col. 9649–50. The committee consisted of chair Claude Cloete, a senior magistrate from Malmesbury who had presided over the 1947 Langa riot case; Tobias Vlok; and Cornelius du Plessis. Each man received £4 4d. per diem, according to a document in the State Library, Department of Finance, Pretoria, CAB, 291082125. See *Guardian*, 15 May and 25 September 1947 about Cloete, and 14 June 1951 on the committee of three.
39. Hansard, 29 January 1952, col. 342.
40. Thornton Collection, box 24, folder 4, UCT; a wealth of material about the 1952 banning of the *Guardian* resides therein.
41. Sonia Bunting had fallen ill while at a youth festival in Berlin, and Brian had flown to bring her home. James Zug interview with Brian Bunting, October 1994.
42. *Guardian*, 2 November 1951. See echoes of this reply in the Rivonia Trial; Clingman, *Bram Fischer*, 308.
43. Hepple, *Press under Apartheid*, 25.
44. In London, Basil Davidson, secretary of the London-based Union of Democratic Control, called for "full ventilation" of the matter in the House of Commons, and the National Council for Civil Liberties wrote of the "growing volume of protest" in Europe. Edmund Morel founded the Union of Democratic Control, along with Charles Trevelyan, in 1914. Morel gained international fame at the turn of the century for instigating protest against King Leopold's colony of the Congo. See Adam Hochschild, *King Leopold's Ghost: A Story of Greed, Terror and Heroism in Colonial Africa* (Boston: Houghton Mifflin, 1998).

    In New York, the United Nations Commission on Human Rights discussed the case. Johnson, "Propagandist," 35; and *Guardian*, 13 December 1951.
45. South African Institute of Race Relations Collection (SAIRR), AD 1181, Wits, for the Civil Rights League file. See *Guardian*, 15 and 22 November 1951. Cope sent delegates to the conference a telegram saying: "CAPE TOWN FREEDOM OF PRESS COMMITTEE SENDS HEARTIEST GREETINGS JOHANNESBURG CONFERENCE STOP WE HAVE ALREADY TREMENDOUS SUCCESS IN AROUSING PUBLIC OPINION AGAINST THREAT TO *GUARDIAN* STOP PEOPLE OF SOUTH AFRICA WILL NOT TOLERATE UNDEMOCRATIC INROAD PRESS LIBERTY." The conference also sent resolutions to Pretoria. Thornton Collection, box 24, folder 2, UCT.

    The Freedom of the Press Committee also issued an open letter that noted, "The *Guardian* has not been accused of breaking the Suppression of Communism Act, or any other law." It was signed, inter alia, by Kahn, Carneson, Jack Simons, Thomas Ngwenya, the Reverend D. C. Thompson, Dadoo, Bram Fischer and Govan Mbeki. The secretary of the committee was A. Newman. See letter from Yusuf Dadoo to D. F. Malan, *Guardian*, 20 February 1952.
46. *Cape Times*, 14 and 22 November 1951. The postcards read: "Your threat to ban the *Guardian* is the worst blow against the Freedom of the Press since Lord Charles Somerset. I protest against this further step toward the elimination of all opposition to your Nationalist Party, and demand the withdrawal of the dictatorial proceedings against the *Guardian*."
47. Five hundred people came to the rally. See Pike, *History of Communism*, 279; Bernstein, "Media Active," 139; and *Guardian*, 24 January 1952.
48. Hansard, 28 January 1952, column 300.
49. SAIRR, AD 1181, Wits.
50. *Guardian*, 18 October 1951. The pipe-lighting motif reminds one of the story told about Joseph Conrad. While sailing on ships as a youth, Conrad read a page of the Bible each night before his watch. Then he tore the page out, lit his pipe with it, and pondered what he had read through

the night.

51. *Star*, 23 May 1952; and *Indian Views*, 28 May 1952.

52. Hansard, 25 February 1952, col. 1692–93.

53. *Guardian*, 29 May 1952. See 29 March 1951: "Workers in the factory . . . on the farm . . . wherever you are—Are YOU doing your bit to assist the *Guardian* in its drive for 5,000 new readers?"

54. *Indian Views*, 28 May 1952.

55. The 19th Article of the United Nations Declaration of Human Rights, adopted in 1948, said, "Everyone has the right to freedom of opinion and expression; this right includes freedom to hold opinions without interference and to seek, receive and impart information and ideas through any media and regardless of frontiers." South Africa did not sign it.

56. *Star*, 23 May 1952; and *Times* (London), 24 May 1952.

57. Brian Bunting, November 1993: "I don't think we had taken any precautions. One didn't know what precautions to take because one didn't know what form the attack would take. I don't think we knew what to expect. We just felt the government had evil intentions towards us. Precisely how they would be manifested, we didn't know."

58. *Cape Times*, 24 May 1952.

59. Carter and Karis, *From Protest to Challenge*, 2:417. See also Martin Nicol, "The Garment Workers' Union of the Cape Peninsula and the Garment Workers' National Unity Movement, 1927–1955," University of Cape Town honours thesis, 1977.

60. *Times* (London), 26 May 1952; and Bernard Sachs, *The Road from Sharpeville* (London: Dennis Dobson, 1961), 141. In the aftermath of the Sachs banning, five white women members of his Garment Workers' Union chained themselves to pillars outside a department store on Eloff Street. They wore placards with slogans like "Set Sachs Free" and "Justice in Chains."

61. *Times* [London], 23 May 1952. On his birthday, Malan described the present situation in South Africa as "graver and bigger than any in our history of crises."

62. *Spark*, 6 June 1952. Paul Joseph, a TIYC leader, called the ban "a mortal blow," and the South African Indian Congress termed it "a most malicious attack."

63. *Star*, 23 May 1952; and *Natal Daily News*, 23 May 1952.

64. *Rand Daily Mail*, 23 May 1952; and *Cape Times*, 24 May 1952—"*Guardian* Ban Seen as Red Herring—Nat. Diversion for Courts Bill." See Bunting, *Rise of South African Reich*, 138, for more on the High Court Bill. S. M. Loubser, a National Party MP, said in debate over the bill: "The United Party comes and whines, 'the constitution.' Anyone would think that the constitution was of greater importance to them than the maintenance of White civilisation in our country."

65. *Natal Witness*, 24 May 1952. They compared the ban to the closing of *La Prensa* in Argentina.

66. *Cape Argus*, 26 May 1952.

67. *Cape Times*, 24 May 1952.

68. *Manchester Guardian*, 24 May 1952. The *Guardian* was the lone English newspaper to support the Afrikaners during the Boer War.

69. *Times* (London), 24 May 1952. The *Times* went on to say, "The *Guardian* is unable to appeal to the courts except on the grounds that the Government acted *mala fide* or *ultra vires*—both pleas which it is impossible to establish."

70. *New York Times*, 24 May 1952.

71. *Times* (London), 26 May 1952. *Die Burger* called the many Swart moves over the long weekend "a blitz campaign."

72. *Wits Student*, 6 June 1952; Dulcie Hartwell spoke at the rally. See also Segal, *Into Exile*, 95.

73. Hansard, 10 June 1952, col. 7620. Barlow ran *Arthur Barlow's Weekly*, a newsletter about politics. See Arthur G. Barlow, *Almost in Confidence* (Cape Town: Juta, 1952).

74. Les Switzer, "The Beginnings of African Protest Journalism at the Cape," in Switzer, *South Africa's Alternative Press*, 66. The ban lasted from August 1901 to October 1902.

75. *Natal Witness*, 26 May 1952. The statement read, "The action of the Government can only be regarded as a temporary success for the extreme anti-democratic forces in South Africa represented by the Nationalists. The *Guardian* will appear again when the right of freedom of the Press, now trampled by Dr Malan's Government, has been reestablished. In suppressing the *Guardian* the Government has called into action methods and devices universally condemned by mankind—the use of force, the avoidance of the courts of law and the exercise of unchecked personal autocracy. The Government can find no offence to charge against the paper, and even the slender reason for the ban contained in the *Government Gazette* are false, since the *Guardian* was never published by or under the direction of the Communist Party. Mr Swart has refused repeated requests to debate this action in Parliament and has denied the *Guardian* an opportunity to present its case before a court or impartial public inquiry. The ban is another long step towards the ultimate goal—the suppression of democracy and the setting up of a Nationalist dictatorship. By this ban and by expelling from office some of the most capable trade union leaders, the Government hopes to cripple the organised working class. A depression is hanging over our heads for which the Government itself is largely responsible, the rise in the cost of living is unchecked and unemployment is growing ominously. In face of these grave events the Government is determined to paralyse the will of the people to resist or voice their protest. Only a Government which is desperate and which has no faith in the public or in the future can rule in such a way."

76. *Cape Times*, 24 May 1952. The board consisted of Dadoo, Mbeki, Bunting, Thompson, and Kahn.

77. The name, the *Clarion*, was not unusual for a newspaper. The National Party produced a coloured newspaper under that title in 1919, using *Die Burger*'s press. The *South African Clarion* rivaled the African Political Organisation's newspaper, the *APO*. See Mohamed Adhikari, "Voice of the Coloured Elite," in Switzer, *South Africa's Alternative Press*, 127–46. See also an old communist song, "Calvary on the Steppe," in Andrews Collection, box 4, UWC: "By friends you were tortured and martyred / for daring to herald the truth / Your message brought hope to the toilers / And kindled the fervour of youth (of youth) / The patient, long suffering masses / Were stirred by your clarion call / Demanding the land for the people / Equality, freedom for all (for all)."

78. *Rand Daily Mail*, 27 May 1952.

79. *Star*, 27 May 1952.

80. *Forward*, 6 June 1952.

81. *Clarion*, 5 June 1952; and Forman and Sachs, *South African Treason Trial*, 139. *Forward*, 6 June 1952: "Two years ago and again last yeyar [*sic*] the Government spent many weeks expressly designing the Anti-Red Act to put the *Guardian* out of action. The only effect seems to hav [*sic*] been to put up its circulation."

82. *Rand Daily Mail*, 27 May 1952.

83. *Rand Daily Mail*, 27 May 1952.

84. James Zug interview with Brian Bunting, November 1993. "Swart smiled and laughed and treated it in a way like a joke." See Bunting, *Moses Kotane*, 185; *Times* (London), 29 May 1952; Eddie and Winnie Roux, *Rebel Pity: The Life of Eddie Roux* (London: Rex Collings, 1970), 200; and John Gunther, *Inside Africa* (New York: Harper and Brothers, 1955), 541. Anthony Samp-

son, *Treason Cage*, said the *Guardian* "went down in a blaze of glory."

85. Cooperative Africana Microform Project (CAMP), MF-2359.

86. *Clarion*, 5 June 1952 for 34,200; 12 June 1952 for 35,500, but need £400 a week to print and only getting £175 from sales and advertisements.

87. *Clarion*, 7 August 1952. See Karis and Carter, *From Protest to Challenge*, 3: 420-21.

88. *People's World*, 2 October 1952.

89. *Clarion*, 14 August 1952. Some of the other suggestions were: *Worker*, *Spark*, *Liberator*, the *Advocate*, *New Dawn*, *Statesman*, *Advance*, *Spokesman*, *People's Voice*, the *Voice*, the *Bulwark*, *Justice*, *Liberty*, the *Champion*, *Vanguard*, the *People*, *Progress* and one particularly inviting name, *Unpopular Opinion*. Bunting rejected many of the names because they were already registered, or they were difficult to pronounce and it "would not be easy for sellers to shout in the streets." Two of the names were later used.

90. *People's World*, 23 October 1952. It was one penny per copy instead of one-fourth a penny.

91. *People's World*, 2 October 1952. He was fined £5.

92. *Rand Daily Mail*, 13 September 1952.

93. Bunting won 4,123 votes, versus A. G. Long's 495, C. C. Johnson's 387, and H. M. Joynt's 58.

94. *Advance*, 4 December 1952. During an interview with Bunting, he proudly brought out the original copy issued that day, as sort of a symbol of a rite-of-passage, "my first banning order."

95. *Advance*, 5 February 1953, for Bunting's maiden speech. James Zug interview with Brian Bunting, December 1993: "I had very little contact with the Nats when I was in Parliament. It wasn't like with Sam. He fraternized with them quite a lot."

96. *Union of South Africa—Report of the Select Committee on the Suppression of Communism Act Enquiry*, September 1953, p. 121. See also Margaret Ballinger, *From Union to Apartheid: A Trek to Isolation* (New York: Praeger, 1969), 394.

97. *Advance*, 1 October 1953.

98. *Advance*, 8 October 1953, for Bunting's final speech in the House. He quoted the Declaration of Independence and said: "It is a recognised principle of history that if a government degenerates into a tyranny under which the liberties of the people are destroyed, they are justified in certain circumstances in using force to overthrow such a government and to bring about a different and better society."

99. *Advance*, 27 May 1954. See *Eastern Province Herald*, 11 February 1994. Alexander's election was of particular note because so few women sat in Parliament. Women were given the vote only in 1930, and just twenty-five women took seats between then and 1994. *Argus*, 5 April 1994. Jack Simons's brother Eric was counsel to the government, and he often advised his brother and sister-in-law, despite their opposing political views.

100. After they returned at the end of 1954, Shapiro, although supportive of the liberation movement, stayed mostly at home to raise her two children. See *Advance*, 12 November 1953, when Walter Sisulu visited them in Israel.

101. See Guardian, 25 January 1951 and 10 April 1952.

102. Podbrey, *White Girl*, 145-48; James Zug interview with Wolfie Kodesh, March 1994; and James Zug interview with Pauline Podbrey, December 1993. See one of the last Naidoo articles, on South-West Africa, *Guardian*, 25 May 1950.

103. James Zug interview with Ray Alexander, May 1994, and telephone interview with Nancy Dick, May 1994. A few weeks after Flegg's death, Bunting wrote a letter to Flegg's mother. It concluded: "Norman was almost everything to the *Guardian*, as you know—a worker, helper and advisor without whose aid we could never have achieved what we have in the fourteen years

of the paper's existence. But more than that, to me and to many others, he was a friend and comrade in the truest sense of the word. I used to go to Norman often for help and advice, and never failed to come away encouraged and strengthened for the fight. Through the whole and trying period of the last couple of years, when many others faltered and fell by the wayside, he remained true to his ideals and in his own quiet, unassuming but always effective way, did everything in his power to fulfill them. Truly his courage and confidence were an example to us all. I know we can say nothing to diminish your sorrow at Norman's death. But, believe me, we share your feelings as if one of our own family had been taken. That is just what he meant to us." Thornton Collection, A24, UCT.

In 1951 the annual Christmas dance was moved to Constantia; see *Guardian*, 29 November 1951. Hilary Flegg ended up living in the Fischer household in Johannesburg in the late 1950s, and during the state of emergency in 1960.

104. James Zug conversation with Ethel de Keyser, April 1994. De Keyser was the younger sister of Tarshish and later leader of the Anti-Apartheid Movement in England.

105. They had met at the People's Bookshop in Johannesburg, where Rubin worked as a clerk.

106. *People's World*, 18 September 1952. Sam Kahn had first edited the newspaper after Bunting's departure, but with his law practice could not devote himself full-time to the job.

107. Johnson, "Propagandist," 44; and James Zug interview with Fred Carneson, March 1994. "He used to battle like anything," remembered Mary Butcher. "He used to get into a terrible stew. He had a terrible temper. He used to rant and rage, but he was always pretty harmless. He was actually a pleasant person to work with." Carneson had some editing experience, having edited two newspapers in the field during the war—an official South African Army newsletter and a Party newsletter. James Zug interview with Albie Sachs, March 1994: "My first essay into journalism came when Fred was editor. I went and reported on a court case where the judge was going through hundreds of Africans on pass offenses. Sam Kahn had decided he was going to defend every single case on an individual basis and the judge was just knocking them through. I wrote a report saying the cases were being processed like in a sausage machine. This is what I felt. Fred said, 'But you can't say that, even if it was true. No, no, no, we're a newspaper. We publish the names and we can get into trouble if we attack the courts and the judges that way. You must indicate it without saying it. Saying one case every two minutes—something like that.'"

108. *Advance*, 8 October 1953.

109. James Zug correspondence with Brian Bunting, April 1991: "Lionel Forman acted as editor for reasons flowing from one of the banning orders against us."

110. *Guardian*, 7 March 1950 for the first issue; 6 May 1952 for a picture of Forman. James Zug interview with Sadie Forman, May 1994: "He was the first student to get his passport taken away. His mother knew Mr. Donges, the Minister of the Interior and persuaded him to give him a passport."

111. Lionel Forman, *A Trumpet from the Housetops: The Selected Writings of Lionel Forman* (Cape Town: Mayibuye Centre, 1992), xiii–xviii. Sadie Forman: "Lionel tried to hide the heart thing. He thought no one noticed."

112. James Zug interview with Sadie Forman, May 1994, and with Brian Bunting, December 1993; and Forman, *Trumpet*, xv–xviii. See *Advance*, 11 March 1954, for a report on the Buntings in Moscow. Sadie Forman: "Sonia Bunting shouted to me as they went past, 'There are sheets for you. There are sheets for you at Wolfie's flat.' We stayed at Wolfie's flat in Sea Point for a few weeks until we found our place in Obs."

113. James Zug interview with Len Lee-Warden, December 1993. Brian Bunting said, "Lionel was a very lively personality, a very capable bloke. He had a good deal of experience, and I felt he had been around for a while and I couldn't rightly give my attention to the paper. For all practical purposes it wasn't even discussed with the Party. Of course, Lionel missed some deadlines too. Jack Cope also was editor for a bit, when we got banned, to make it look real."

114. *Advance*, 11 February 1954, for a clever headline.

115. *Advance*, 11 March 1954, for an article that moved from column 3 to column 5, and the Afrikaans headline.

    Amy Thornton said: "You know, you don't know when you are in a thing, that it's all going to become history. What I do remember was that Brian was an exceptionally neat worker. His desk was hidden under piles of neat paper. . . . When Brian went on leave and Lionel edited the whole paper, there would be a sea of papers on the desk. When it came to Tuesday to give it to the printer, he would pluck these things out. . . . He had a different style. He was just as good. I always marveled at this totally different style and such a good paper came out of it. Lionel, I think, was more of an adventurous person than Brian."

    "You always knew wherever you were in the country when Lionel was editing the paper," said Wolfie Kodesh. "Everything was different."

116. After dissolution, the old Central Committee did hold a few meetings in Cape Town, but no new Party emerged. See Slovo, *Unfinished Autobiography*, 83. For more on the dissolution and reconstitution, see Bernstein, *Memory Against Forgetting*, 120–21.

117. Slovo, *Unfinished Autobiography*, 84. Bunting and Carneson were also members of the Central Committee.

118. Clingman, *Bram Fischer*, 183.

119. James Zug interview with Sadie Forman, May 1994. James Zug conversation with Rica Hodgson, January 1994: "Cape Town is too pretty. We used to say that in Cape Town the revolution would close down for the weekend." Other organizations manifested the inherent bifurcation between Cape Town and Johannesburg. The Liberal Party, for example, was noticeably divided ideologically between the two cities, the Transvaalers more amenable to working with the ANC. The Garment Workers' Union, headed by Solly Sachs, maintained a separate union in each city because of differing attitudes toward racial issues.

120. Switzer, *Power and Resistance*, 414.

121. At the Darragh Hall, Johannesburg, meeting in November 1952 that led to the formation of the COD—one of the first time ANC leaders formally addressed a white meeting—the founding committee created there consisted of Bram Fischer, Eddie Roux, Guy Routh, Jack Hodgson, Cecil Williams, Ruth First, Beate Lipman, Helen Joseph, Trevor Huddleston and Padre du Manoir.

122. Segal, *Into Exile*, 112.

123. David Everatt interview with Ben Turok, Everatt Collection, UWC. Turok was one of the few Capetonians to be an active COD leader nationally. David Everatt interview with Issy Heyman, May 1987: "In Cape Town they organized themselves around the *Guardian* [after 1950]. They spread the message of the *Guardian*. They had *Guardian* committees, and then they sent over people like Wolf Kodesh to reorganize our *Guardian*. We had Ivan Schermbrucker who put all his efforts into the *Guardian*."

    See *Freedom* 7, no. 1 (Summer 1948) for an article written by H. A. Naidoo that succinctly states the Cape Town view: "In my opinion the Party has everything to gain by retaining its independence, by not allowing itself to be so closely identified with the national organisations as to lose its character as a class organisation." See Sophie Mort, "Some Indications of

CPSA/SACP Activity in the Early 50's as Evidenced by 'Leftist' Newspapers of that Period," paper presented at the 18th Annual Congress of the Association for Sociology in Southern Africa, Working Group: State and Politics, held at UWC, July 1987.

124. *Cape Argus*, 30 November 1962. See *Guardian*, 12 June 1947.

125. Shaun Johnson interview with Brian Bunting, January 1984.

126. March 1938—six on Cape Town, three on Johannesburg (seven on overseas news); April 1949—twelve on Cape Town, eight on Johannesburg, and eight on overseas news; September 1956—four on Cape Town, five on Johannesburg, one on overseas news. See also *New Age*, 9 August 1956, "Wake Up Cape Town," an article about contributions. Cape Town is "definitely lagging" and has a "tendency to rest on past laurels."

127. Clingman, *Bram Fischer*, 207; and Turok, *Nothing But the Truth*, 44.

128. James Zug interview with Mary Butcher, January 1994: "I mean, we would meet in cars because it wasn't safe in houses. You'd drive and after a while park somewhere. Then after a while, you'd drive on and park somewhere else. So it was quite hard, paying attention to Albie's lectures."

129. During a private meeting, Brian Bunting asked Ray and Jack to join the underground Communist Party. Jack walked out of the room, and Ray then agreed. When Jack asked Ray why she had not waited to discuss the matter with him, Ray replied that there was no question in her mind. Simons, *All My Strength*, 274. Later Ray commented: "Brian should not have spoken to both of us at the same time. The underground training I received in Riga prior to coming to South Africa was clear that husband and wife must be aware of their membership in an underground organisation. It was not easy for me nor for Jack that I was in and not he." Letter from Ray Simons to Thomas Karis, January 1998.

130. COD members, out of habit and interest, liked to sell in black areas, rather than in white neighborhoods as the COD officially mandated. Congress of Democrats Collection, AD2187, Wits, for a letter from Yetta Berenblatt to Bernard Gottschalk, 2 July 1956 (Berenblatt was the national secretary of the COD, and Gottschalk the Cape Town secretary): "COD members sell *New Age*, some in European areas regularly, although some people have not been weaned away from the Non-European areas. I'll be killed for saying this, because their sales are also important, but we do not as a rule sell them together without our literature. I don't think though that there is any objection to either *New Age* or *Fighting Talk* being sold together with pamphlets. It is only a question of practicality."

See Everatt, "Politics of Nonracialism," 237–39. Only four of the eighty Cape COD members questioned were prepared to do door-to-door work in white areas. Ben Turok told Everatt, "Even the Congress of Democrats, although it constantly reassessed its role and its duty to work among the whites, nevertheless, a tradition had been established—and tradition in politics is a very powerful thing."

131. *South African Communists Speak, 1915–1980*, edited by Brian Bunting (London: Inkululeko, 1981), 217.

132. *Guardian*, 11 January 1951; see Dadoo, 26 April 1951, on the twilight of democracy, and 22 May 1952. *Advance*, 14 May 1953, on the Liberal Party; *New Age*, 24 February 1955, for an interview. See J. B. Marks, *Guardian*, 11 October 1951, on black spots; *New Age*, 16 August 1956, on the ten-year anniversary of the mine strike.

133. See *Guardian*, 11 January 1951, 20 February 1952, and 22 May 1952; and *New Age*, 7 April 1955.

134. James Zug interview with Rusty Bernstein, May 1994. See Moses Kotane, *Clarion*, 19 June 1952; *Advance*, 6 and 13 May 1954, and 10 June 1954. See *New Age*, 16 February 1956 for a

full-page interview about "South African Statesman Overseas"; 29 March 1956 for Kotane quoted as saying "*New Age* has [not] played its proper role in defending the Coloured vote"; 21 June 1956; 18 October 1956 for Kotane opposing cultural and sports boycotts in a full-page article; 8 November 1956; 29 November 1956 for Kotane explaining the difference between the Hungary and Suez invasions; 2 May 1957 for Kotane on the "Great Crisis Ahead"; 9 May 1957; and 24 December 1959 for a guest editorial. See also Michael Harmel, *Clarion*, 26 June 1952, for a letter to the editor about Kotane.

135. Hansard, 21 May 1962, col. 6071. Bunting, *Moses Kotane*, 229–30: "Though the CP was illegal and unable to function openly, everybody knew it was there. . . . Even under conditions of illegality, the Communist Party had at its disposal a machine and cadres to operate it that was more efficient and united than those at the disposal of the ANC."

136. The work of Robert Conquest was controversial, yet his conclusions have been borned out by the opening of Soviet archives. See *The Great Terror: Stalin's Purge of the Thirties* (New York: Macmillan, 1968), *The Harvest of Sorrow: Soviet Collectivization and the Terror-Famine* (New York: Oxford University Press, 1986) and *The Great Terror: A Reassessment* (New York: Oxford University Press, 1990). For a twenty-first-century summation of the Soviet Union's terror, 1917–1953, see Martin Amis, *Koba the Dread: Laughter and the Twenty Million* (New York: Talk Miramax, 2002). See also Simon Sebag Montefiore, *Stalin: The Court of the Red Tsar* (New York: Knopf, 2004) and Robert Service, *Stalin: A Biography* (Cambridge, Mass.: Harvard University Press, 2005).

See *New Age*, 1 November 1962, for an editorial about the Cuban missile crisis: "What needs to be stressed here, however, is the fact that peace was saved last week, as on so many occasions since the end of the last war, by the restraint of the Soviet Union, just as it was imperilled by the provocative unilateral actions of the United States."

137. *Advance*, 11 December 1952 for an open letter about the Rosenbergs penned by Bunting, Kahn, and Alexander; 19 February 1953; and all of June and July 1953. *Guardian*, 15 May 1947 on Tito; 22 December 1949 on Mao; 22 March 1951 on Korea.

138. *Advance*, 12 March 1953. See *Advance*, 3 December 1953, when Stalin was described as "a statesman who devoted the last years of his life above all to the defense of peace."

Stalin's death was a major milestone for many communists. Pauline Podbrey wrote: "Comrade Joseph Stalin was dead. I was thunderstruck. Stalin dead! A world without Stalin! For all my recent doubts and disillusions, Stalin still represented the rock around which our faith clung. . . . Stalin was the Daddy of all my dreams, the point of my ideals for as long as I could remember. In losing him, I'd lost my youth, my childhood. . . . By dying he'd robbed me of a world of dreams. I felt bereft." Podbrey, *White Girl*, 174.

139. Brian Bunting, "Life Is More Joyous," 2 and 15. See *Advance*, 24 June 1954. See also George Sacks, "Let's Talk about Russia," a Friends of the Soviet Union pamphlet, 1942: " . . . and we must never again allow ourselves to be filled with stories about their country which bear no relation to the truth."

"I was assured that there was no anti-Semitism," wrote Sam Kahn after his 1953 journey. Sam Kahn, "South African in the Soviet Union," 4. See *Advance*, 14 October and 25 November 1954, for Ruth First and Albie Sachs's visit.

China endured a similar adulation. Hilda Bernstein, as part of a ten-part series on her 1961 visit to China, said: "No dirt, no smells, no rubbish—no flies: It is like a miracle. . . . I was surprised by the lack of any sign of police, military or similar control." *New Age*, 3 August and 14 September 1961.

See the Summary of the *Report of the Commission for the Socio-Economic Development of the Bantu Areas within the Union of South Africa* (Tomlinson Report), 1955, p. 171: "*Torch* and *Advance* which have a considerable circle of readers, proclaim absolute equality and opposition to so-called Imperialism and Capitalism, while continually keeping countries like Indo-China prominent on the front page."

140. *Advance*, 29 January and 5 February 1953. See Clingman, *Bram Fischer*, 210–11.

141. Turok, *Nothing but the Truth*, 49–50.

142. James Zug interviews with Fred Carneson, March 1994, and Albie Sachs, March 1994. James Zug interview with Brian Bunting, November and December 1993: "As the paper became more consolidated as the sort of organ of the movement as a whole, the whole way in which it went, in all sorts of ways, was determined by collective discussion, by suggestions, by assistance from all sides, by segments of the movement. You'd get reactions from your offices, and they didn't like this or they didn't like that or they wanted this or they wanted that. The job of editor was more of achieving consensus between a lot of pressures. . . . We always did things by consensus. It was a decision of the collective, not really the editorial board as such, but Fred Carneson and Ruth and Ivan, on the telephone."

143. James Zug interview with Mary Butcher Turok, January 1994: "These people were very committed. And maybe they wouldn't have done it if they didn't have this enormous religion, religious conviction for the Soviet Union, for communism, for their beliefs. This is what made them feel absolutely invincible."

144. Sachs also recalled that Cynthia Robinson, a South African woman living in London, would clip articles from the London newspapers and post a packet that supplied a significant part of the international news. See *Life* magazine, 20 April 1953: "For Red Leaders in All Nations: Opportunity and Danger." See also *South African Labour Bulletin*, March 1990, for comments by Ray Alexander.

Nadine Gordimer wrote: "I should say that what I read in *New Age* was analysis of the South African situation along my own convictions, though my literary sensibilities (!) cringed, now and then, at the rhetorical clichés."

145. *Advance*, 18 February 1954, when he told readers that "what goes on in Parliament is no longer very important." See that issue also for the seven rules for using *Advance*.

146. *Advance*, 1 April 1954. Forman goes on to say, "Future historians will find our paper invaluable when they settle down to write the real history of South Africa, the people's history."

147. *Advance*, 22 April 1954. Kenny Jordaan, Thomas Ngwenya, Jack Simons and Forman submitted papers.

148. *New Age*, 5 April 1956. Harmel added that "Stalin rendered services of incalculable value to the cause to which he devoted his life. . . . The Soviet leaders boldly faced the difficult and far from pleasant task of uprooting the myth of the miracle-working hero, which is alien to the spirit of scientific socialism."

149. *New Age*, 1 November 1956. See *New Age*, 19 May 1955, for a long piece by Forman on Vietnam.

150. "It went over very badly. It was a vivid, defining moment in the Party's history," Sadie Forman remembered. "Subsequent to that Lionel had to fight like hell to get his history books published. He had a lot of trouble with Mick Harmel and the Johannesburg lot because they were afraid of what he would say. After 1956, after the 20th Congress, there was a telegram from Joe Slovo to Wolfie saying, 'STOP HIM.'"

151. *New Age*, 22 November 1956; see also 15 November 1956. The *Daily Worker* in London un-

derwent similar convulsions. The editors severely cut or banned completely the dispatches from its Budapest correspondent, Peter Fryer. Nineteen of the thirty-one staff members at the newspaper signed a petition in protest, and a third of the staff soon resigned, including Fryer. See *Weekly Mail & Guardian*, 14 October 1994.

152. This meeting occurred at Jimmy Gibson's chambers on Parliament Street, where a regular group of Liberal Party members like Peter Hjul and Pogrund gathered for lunch.

Forman did not always stick to the facts. Mary Butcher recalled coming back to Barrack Street after attending a Congress meeting on the Grand Parade and reporting in an article that the rally was a certain size; Forman doubled the crowd.

Brian Bunting said, "Lionel was brilliant and loyal, but very impatient. He couldn't abide procrastination and delay. His political views often sped past the contemporary boundaries."

153. James Zug interview with Fred Carneson, March 1994. See Forman, *Trumpet from Housetops*, 156–58; *New Age*, 16 July 1959; and Turok, *Nothing But the Truth*, 50–51.

"Forman kept the poet within himself," Albie Sachs said. WNYC radio interview, 26 October 2000. "Maybe it was best that we never got real."

Bullying colleagues was not unusual. In 1956 Len Lee-Warden read a speech Prime Minister Strijdom gave in London in which he extolled the virtues of apartheid. In consultation with Jack Simons, Lee-Warden wrote a lengthy letter to the *Times* of London. At one point in the letter, he wrote that he had no objection "to peaceful and separate development" if it was as Strydom described it, but, he noted, it was clearly not.

His letter, reprinted in the *Cape Argus*, was at first well-received, and more than thirty people telegrammed congratulations to Lee-Warden. But, due to a long-standing personality conflict with Sam Kahn, it also touched off a political firestorm. An ANC member, Joseph Nkatlo, replied in the *Cape Argus*. Sam Kahn called Lee-Warden and asked him to write a correction to the *Times* and apologize. Lee-Warden refused. He recalled that he had done nothing wrong, that the letter stated his opposition to apartheid. He also appealed to Jack Simons, but Simons said all the responsibility lay with Lee-Warden. Kahn, Brian Bunting, and Ray Alexander wrote a letter to *New Age* attacking Lee-Warden. The Cape Town Congress of Democrats—Lee-Warden was the chair of the Cape Town COD branch—sent a statement to the weekly saying Lee-Warden's views "are his own and do not reflect the policy of this organisation." Lee-Warden in turn replied with a *New Age* letter of his own that was mostly a reprint of the entire *Times* letter, leaving readers "to draw their own conclusions."

The very next week, Kahn, Bunting, and Alexander again jabbed at Lee-Warden for not addressing the issue. A month later, Lee-Warden succumbed and issued a denial of his approval of apartheid, but managed to included a thanks to "the many friends and *New Age* readers who never doubted my intentions."

However, Lee-Warden resigned from the chair of the Cape Town COD. Never again did he play a prominent role in radical politics, although he did stay in Parliament until his seat was abolished in 1960. He and Kahn also remained friendly. See *New Age*, 23 August 1956 for the letter signed by Kahn, Alexander, and Bunting; and 6 and 13 September and 18 October 1956. In one of the interesting codas to the story, Nkatlo switched allegiance to the Liberal Party after it ended its whites-only membership regulation.

154. *Guardian*, 8 March 1951.

155. *Clarion*, 12 June 1952.

156. C. J. Driver, *Patrick Duncan: South African and Pan-African* (London: Heinemann, 1980), 123.

157. *Guardian*, 8 February 1951 for Harold Wolpe founding a *Guardian* league for university stu-

dents in Johannesburg and for him selling 24 dozen papers; 22 February 1952 for the Cape Town *Guardian* league challenging the Johannesburg *Guardian* league to get more readers— they want 5,000 more; 12 April 1951 for a picture of champion *Guardian* sellers in Natal; 10 April 1952 for the annual birthday party raising £650. See also *Advance*, 15 January 1953 for "vacancy filled, thanks to all who applied for post of reporter"; 20 August 1953 for a Cape Town dinner party that raised £42 (a Cape Town dinner party in October 1952 raised £100); 21 January 1954 for the *Advance* reader groups; 1 April 1954 for agents wanted to sell *Advance*.

158. *Advance*, 21 December 1954.

159. *New Age*, 9 June 1955, for a picture of Dhlamini, "*New Age*'s best-known seller in Johannesburg," who had worked for the newspaper since 1954. See 22 September 1960 for Mamuru and Tsehla, and 10 May 1962 for Tshehla.

160. *New Age*, 9 May 1957, for the death of Omar Gallant on 13 April 1957. He was knocked down by a lorry in the street. See *Weekly Mail & Guardian*, 25 March 1994, for a profile of Job Mokgoro, a South African Student Organisation chairman in 1973 and ANC leader who described selling *New Age* as a boy in Kimberley in the 1950s. See *New Age*, 5 April 1956, for obituary for A. Maupa of Galeshewe in Kimberley, who sold twelve dozen a week. Manqina's weekly salary was £2; he earned a threepence commission per newspaper sold after two hundred.

161. Shaun Johnson interview with Brian Bunting, January 1984; and James Zug interview with Wolfie Kodesh, March 1994. See *New Age*, 17 July 1958—"Every crowd to John was a meeting. If he travelled in the train then every person in his carriage heard about the freedom struggle; time and time again he would be locked up at the instance of irate ticket examiners, and each time he would be released by the prison authorities who found him too 'dangerous' an influence amongst the other prisoners, and even amongst the warders!"

162. See *New Age*, 16 October 1958, for his letter to the editor. Manqina also was elected the vice-chair of the Nyanga branch of the ANC Women's League: "Because there was supposed to be one man amongst the women to watch how things were going. . . ." "He would walk for miles," said Amy Thornton. "I remember him with a khaki raincoat, with a little beard and his beautiful dimples."

163. *Advance*, 6 August 1953, for the need of £5,000 by the end of year: last month's budget was £1,300; £900 to print and publish; £500 to sales, subscriptions, and adverts; so a gap of £800. See 21 October 1954 for sales netting £700 and the "sharply declining" advertising revenue brought in £200 a month, donations £1,100 a month; thus they needed £2,000 a month— £1,000 for printing and newsprint, £500 for distribution, and £500 for salaries.

164. *Advance*, 17 September 1953, £2; and 5 November 1953, when Johannesburg got £153 and Cape Town £61.

165. For monthly donations, see 1950: June £297; July £385; August £794; September £792; October £495; November £589; and December £333. 1951 for a new *Guardian* masthead and a twelve-page newspaper in January; February £403, March £611; April £533, eight pages in June. 1953: four pages in March, but eleven advertisements, back to six pages then eight by end of month; August £651, as part of the 5,000 readers campaign. 1954: 29 July need £2,000, debt at £1,000, got £660 the week of 5–12 August; September need more than £1,000, debt at £638, and payment of £900 for shipment of newsprint due at end of month.

166. *Advance*, 26 November 1953.

167. *Advance*, 5 November 1953, when Carneson raised £2,500 in three months but the printer's bills remained outstanding. See *Advance*, 15 April 1954, when Carneson noted that "the size and circulation of a paper like *Advance* is a barometer of the strength of the democratic

movement."

168. James Zug interview with Fred Carneson, March 1994; and Don Pinnock, "Keeping the Red Flag Flying," 11.

169. *Guardian*, 12 October 1950. See Nancy Dick Collection, UWC. The club offered toys, sheets, blankets, jelly, soap, butter, recipes, tea, cocoa, coffee, condensed milk, flour, sugar, peas, fruit, sardines, cream, spaghetti tins, nuts, raisins, chocolate, fish oil, and Christmas stockings.

170. *Guardian*, 10 March and 29 December 1949. See also 14 July 1949 for 1,000. The motto: "Johnny's Xmas Parcels for the Poor People, the best and the cheapest food club"; 29 December 1949, the club had 900 homes and a picture of a woman with 123 customers; 9 March 1950 with slogan "Save throughout the year for your Xmas cheer." *Guardian*, 14 July 1949, for the £750 profit. See Nancy Dick Collection, Mayibuye Centre.

Wolfie Kodesh remembered what happened if a Christmas Club agent was unable to sell all her books: "They used to come in sometimes having not even sold their books. They were as poor as church mice but insisted that since they had those books and it was their newspaper they were going to pay in spite of the fact they hadn't sold. You see, a wonderful spirit. This engendered a terrific closeness and of course it taught them that this is your newspaper. You read it, you'll know what you must do."

171. *Guardian*, 14 February 1952; *Advance*, 18 December 1952 and 1 July 1954.

172. *New Age*, 22 March 1956. His £1 "Sweets Parcel" included figs, prunes, raisins, peaches, toffees, chocolate peanuts; there were two Tiny Tot Toy parcels, boys receiving marbles, a water pistol, knife, and a toy plane, while girls got a skipping rope, a doll, crayons, and a rattle. 2 May 1957.

173. The delivery of her parcels "fell to Fred [Schermbrucker] as he told me 'the reputation of the paper was involved.'" See Arnold Selby, "Autobiography of Arnold Selby," unpublished manuscript in Lionel Forman Collection, Mayibuye Centre, UWC, p. 359. Selby was also at the time of his banning on the executive of the Transvaal Council of Non-European Trade Unions.

174. *Advance*, 16 September 1954, and *New Age*, 29 November 1956, for Arnold's in forty communities. In 1955 Selby delivered over 1,000 parcels, in 1956 over 5,000. In 1958, 8,000 customers participated in the Johannesburg and Cape Town clubs, earning the newspaper £300 a month. *New Age* 1958 budget, Thornton Collection, UCT. Hamper customers were charged ten shillings for a subscription; the 549 subscribers were charged one pound, one shilling.
See Selby's columns on sports in October 1955. See also his unpublished autobiography, Brian Bunting Collection, Mayibuye Centre.

175. Nadine Gordimer wrote: "What comes to mind is the figure of Arnold Selby, doggedly selling it and remembering how he was the phenomenon of a white man living, by choice, in Soweto. What a man, for his time!"

Selby often went into a beer hall or shebeen "for a little snorter and chat," and although he carried a canvas bag bulging with coins, he was never robbed, because "the paper's esteem was its security." Once Ivan Schermbrucker caught two Arnold's Hampers employees stealing: "Ivan chased them down the stairs. No literally, I remember there was a tremendous explosion. I think he just told them, 'That's it' and chased them down the stairs. You see, he was like that. He couldn't conceive of anybody doing anything like that." James Zug interview with Lesley Schermbrucker, January 1994.

Selby left the hamper scheme after an argument with Schermbrucker in the office in 1958: "There was a message that I should phone someone," Selby later wrote. "It was a matter that did not concern me. I considered it a matter that Fred [Schermbrucker] should have handled. I told him so and we had a blow-up. I told him that he could put Arnold's Xmas Hampers where the monkey puts his nuts and walked out. The whole thing was childish and silly especially when Fred and I got along well. Husbands and wives also have moods and blow-ups but that does not mean a broken marriage. Be that as it may, but Arnold's Xmas Hampers carried on and prospered because Arnold's Xmas Hampers was not Arnold Selby it was the Congress movement's paper and it delivered the goods."

Selby set up his own Christmas hamper scheme, but it did not prosper.

176. *New Age*, 10 January 1957, for "Our Benoni representative, Miss Joyce Watson, can be contacted at the African Textile Workers' Union office every Saturday."

177. James Zug interview with Joyce Mohammed, January 1994; and Hilda Bernstein, *The Rift: The Exile Experience of South Africans* (London: Jonathan Cape, 1994), 32–33. She immediately learned about Schermbrucker's temper: "Oh, oh, when I started there, I thought I would never stay because, 'Ahh, what the hell are you doing there, you bloody bastard.' Mary, mother of God, oh. Ivan used to make my nerves, oh, especially. But he was the most wonderful, wonderful, kind-hearted person that you could ever meet."

Sometimes she rode with Selby on his scooter. One day, as they were riding in Jeppe Street with a bundle of ANC leaflets, a white man spit out from the top of a double-decker bus. "That day, Arnold was chasing him and he's swearing. I say, 'Arnold, you can't be arrested, we've got these leaflets.' Ya, Arnold was a terrible person. He would just swear at you anywhere. I was always scared, because he see you and, 'Amandla!, Mayibuye!'"

"I think my happiest days were at *New Age*. It was meeting people, all different people. Oh, I really miss, miss, miss those days. It was my best days, I was just so happy those days."

178. *Clarion*, 29 May 1952.

179. Jeremy Bernstein interview with Len Lee-Warden, December 1988, "Media Active." Bernstein wrote: "The Guardian had established the tradition which ensured the commercial distribution of progressive news. This embodied the news with a certain credibility, while at the same time was able to challenge the dominant discourse."

180. See *Guardian*, 2 August 1951 for "change of printer to Pioneer," and 23 August 1951 for it costing twice as much; see November 1951, when it was printed by Worcester Standard Electric Press, and 3 April 1952. See Segal, *Into Exile*, 145–46.

181. See *Cape Times*, 24 May 1952. See also *Guardian*, 25 May 1950, on *Southern Cross*.

182. See *Advance*, 17 September 1953; *Guardian*, 26 April 1951, cost up £14 a ton. The *New York Times* once lent newsprint to the *Daily Worker* in New York. See Gay Talese, *The Kingdom and the Power* (New York: New American Library, 1969), 92.

183. James Zug interview with Len Lee-Warden, December 1993. In 1957 Pioneer took on the printing contract of *Africa South*.

184. Carter-Karis microfilm, 15B, University of the Western Cape.

185. For information on raid, see *Advance*, 9 September 1954; *Star*, 31 August 1954; *Rand Daily Mail*, 1 and 2 September 1954; *New York Times*, 1 September 1954; and *Cape Times*, 1 September 1954. In Cape Town they raided the homes of Bunting, Carneson, Kahn, Butcher, Shapiro, Ray and Jack Simons, Cope, Morley, Hymie Bernadt, and Lee-Warden; in Johannesburg they raided Schermbrucker, Harmel, Dadoo, Selby, Kotane, Louis Joffe, James Phillips, Forman, Reverend Douglas Thompson and First (who was overseas); and in Durban they raided Seedat and Lax.

186. Thornton Collection, A24, UCT.

187. *Advance*, 9 September 1954, open letter to Swart. *Advance*, 23 September 1954, for a letter to the editor from Chief Luthuli, the president of the ANC. See 16 September for an appeal by Fred Carneson: "There is very little use in talking about defending Press freedom if the free

Press isn't there to defend. The fate of our paper will be decided just as much by the amount of money we have in the bank at the end of the month as by Swart's star-chamber inquisitors."

188. *Advance*, 30 September 1954. The authorizing officer was an S. E. Terblanche.

189. Thornton Collection, A5, UCT.

190. *Star*, 22 October 1954; and *Cape Times*, 23 October 1954: "Bunting will take legal advice as soon as he can establish on what grounds and under what section of the Suppression of Communism Act the Cape Town weekly newspaper has been prohibited."

191. It was 29 October 1954, the same day Ernest Hemingway was awarded the Nobel Prize in Literature.

192. See *Guardian*, 5 January 1950; and *Advance*, 15 July to 12 August 1954.

193. CAMP, *New Age* Series, MP 1223.

194. Carter-Karis microfilm reel 15B.

195. James Zug interview with Fred Carneson, March 1994.

196. Thornton Collection, A24, UCT. Bunting also sent a letter to the United Nations, Division of Human Rights.

197. Thornton Collection, A24, UCT. The Johannesburg branch of the COD released a statement: "This malicious act perpetrated by that group of frightened men in the Government, is in keeping with their many other attempts to silence the voices of the Liberation movement. But neither this act nor their repeated bannings, deportations, proscribings, can still the heart of the people who are determined to stand up for their rights as human beings. Not all their attempts to herd people into ghettoes, deprive them of the right to education, their right to skilled jobs, their right to freedom of movement and speech, can quench the spark that has been lit." *Counter-Attack*, 5 December 1954.

198. *Forward*, 29 October 1954.

199. *Cape Argus*, 18 November 1954; and Thornton Collection, A24, UCT: "In submitting yet a further letter for publication, I hope you won't feel I am presuming on your indulgence, but I do feel there are some fundamental issues involved and that unless the right of the Minister to ban people, papers and parties without check is withdrawn the time is not very far distant when we shall be living in a police state."

CHAPTER FIVE. FLEETING MOMENTS OF HAPPINESS: THE DEMOCRACY DECADE, 1950–1959

1. *New Age*, 28 March 1957.

2. *Guardian*, 4 January 1951. The list of nineteen priorities ran in order of importance: Non-European affairs, South African news, foreign news, political features, trade-union news, education, editorials, readers' views, personal columns, photographs, women's features, cartoons, sports, children's features, and competitions.

3. *Guardian*, 14 February 1952. See 26 July 1951 for a Sam Kahn article on the tercentenary; 20 September 1951 on the boycott; and 7 June 1956 for a Roux article on the Population Registration Act. See also Ciraj Rassool and Leslie Witz, "The 1952 Jan Van Riebeeck Tercentenary Festival: Constructing and Contesting Public National History in South Africa," *Journal of African History* 34 (1993): 447–68.

4. *Guardian*, 20 December 1951 and 3 January 1952; see also 21 June 1951, when the ANC first proposed a civil-disobedience campaign. The six unjust laws were the Suppression of Commu-

nism Act, the Group Areas Act, the Separate Representation of Voters Act, the Bantu Authorities Act, the pass laws, and the Stock Limitation Act.

5. Among the volunteers were thirty-one farm workers from Bethal under Gert Sibande's leadership; Lodge, *Black Politics*, 44. See David Carter, "The Defiance Campaign—A Comparative Analysis of the Organization, Leadership and Participation in the Eastern Cape and the Transvaal," unpublished manuscript, Everatt Collection, UWC. Individual dues for an ANC member were two shillings, sixpence a year.

6. Forman and Sachs, *South African Treason Trial*, 139; *Clarion*, 5 and 12 June 1952, with the circulation figures.

7. Bunting, *Moses Kotane*, 185–86.

8. *People's World*, 18 September and 2 October 1952. Cecil Williams used the *Clarion* to call upon the Torch Commando, a mainly white mass organization that led torchlit marches, to join the ANC and SAIC. *Clarion*, 17 July 1952.

9. *People's World*, 2 October 1952.

10. *Clarion*, 3 July 1952, for a two-page spread of volunteers beaten in jail. Govan Mbeki, *Learning from Robben Island: The Prison Writings of Govan Mbeki* (Cape Town: David Phillip, 1991), 5: "Photographs of group after group of volunteers were a tremendous visual aid that made even illiterate people buy the paper because they could read the message of the struggle from the grim faces of the volunteers and what was then the Congress salute."

11. *Advance*, 6 November 1952.

12. Carter and Karis, *From Protest to Challenge*, 2:426. "Recognising the important role which *Fighting Talk* and *Advance* has played and will play in the democratic movement, the National Council calls on all regions and branches: a) to obtain subscriptions from all members and sympathisers and to assist in their distribution; b) to initiate discussion on *Fighting Talk* and *Advance* with a view to the improvement of their content; c) to stimulate members to contribute articles etc." Resolutions to the National Action Council meeting, 14 February 1954, Everatt Collection, UWC, p. 3.

   On p. 5 of the Draft Plan of Campaign, they wrote: "National Council to consider calling together editors of *Advance* and other pro-Congress papers with proposal for pooling of resources in single national, 3-language edition paper." *New Age* did supply printing blocks and photographs to the *Call*, the leaflet the National Action Council produced after the COP. See reel 8, Simons Collection, UWC.

13. In a scene loaded with symbolism, communists built the lighting, electronics, and staging for the Congress of the People, while the ANC's Women's League prepared the mountains of food. At the end of the first day, the lighting system failed, forcing the three thousand delegates and thousands in the crowd to leave with the aid of only one hurricane lamp for light. See Helen Joseph, *Side by Side*, 46.

14. James Zug interview with Walter Sisulu, January 1994. See *Advance*, 2 January 1953, as NP backbenchers proposed concentration camps for Defiance Campaign participants.
   See 1 April 1954: "From this issue *Advance* will make a start by paying particular care to avoiding the terminology of the oppressor."

15. Lodge, *Black Politics*, 70.

16. James Zug interview with Wolfie Kodesh, March 1994. See "Welcome Freedom Volunteer," a leaflet produced by the ANC as a manual for those mobilizing the masses for the COP. "He must spread amongst the people understanding and knowledge, by distributing to them the Congress leaflet and pamphlets and the publications like *New Age*, *Inyaniao*, *Fighting Talk* and

Liberation which support Congress aims. But to do all this, the volunteer must himself study, learn and discuss."

17. *New Age*, 14 May 1955.
18. *Advance*, 8 April 1954, for an article by Sisulu on raising consciousness; *New Age*, 24 December 1954, on the political achievement of the Congress of the People committees.
19. *New Age*, 19 April 1956.
20. *New Age*, 2 February 1956 about the Evaton boycott, and 5 July 1956 about what happened after the bus company lowered fares to pre-boycott levels; 7 February 1957 for a mass exodus from Alexandra; 14 February 1957 for the funeral of Pretoria women killed at rally, written by Makiwane; 21 and 28 March and 4 April 1957 on the Selby fast. See 28 February, and 7 and 14 March 1957 for front-page bylines on the bus boycott by Michael Harmel.

One of the most stirring images of the Treason Trial was a photograph of James Hadebe, Alfred Hutchinson and Stephen Dhlamini during the Alexandra bus boycott. Under the banner "The Accused Also Walk," the three Trialists were pictured as they walked the nine miles from Alexandra to Johannesburg for their court case. See 17 January 1957.

See also Ruth First, "The Bus Boycott," in *Africa South* 1, no. 4 (July–September 1957): 55–64.
21. *New Age*, 4 July 1957 for telegrams signed by the leaders of the five Congresses to Swart; 6 June 1957 for an ANC memorandum; 4 July 1957 about the annual stay-away.
22. *Guardian*, 6 December 1951. See *New Age*, 15 December 1955, for headline "People's Fight Is Main Bulwark against Fascism" about an ANC executive report soon to be submitted to the annual national conference.
23. *New Age*, 24 December 1959.
24. Mabhida delivered the main eulogy at Ruth First's funeral. It can be found on p. 1 in a pamphlet produced in January 1983, Wolfie Kodesh Collection, UWC.
25. *New Age*, 13 November 1958. See also 28 March 1957 for Z. K. Matthews on the Separate University Bill; 7 June 1956 for Maulvi Chachlia, with a picture and an article about being overseas for a year; 3 January 1957 for Oliver Tambo and Lillian Ngoyi with New Year's messages; 23 February 1956, 3 April 1958, and 1 July 1959 for Tambo, as well as 31 March 1955 and 29 March 1956 for exclusive interviews with Tambo; 26 February 1953 for Albert Luthuli, and 26 April 1954 for a June 26 message; 2 April 1953, 25 February 1954, 7 October 1954, 16 December 1954, 12 April 1956—"In the Transkei, where famine rules, people fear the future," and 27 September 1956 for Walter Sisulu; 3 September 1953 and 22 September 1960 for Nelson Mandela; 7 September 1954, 2 and 23 May 1957, and 14 February 1960 for Helen Joseph; 21 February 1952 for Trevor Huddleston; 4 March 1954 for Molly Fischer; 6 May 1954 and 17 February 1955 for Jack Hodgson; 2 May 1957 for Hilda Bernstein; 30 September 1954 for James Matthews; 8 September 1953, 17 May 1956, and 3 April 1958 for Cecil Williams; 6 January 1956 for J. B. Mafora, president of Orange Free State ANC; 12 July 1956 for the famous photograph of Robert Resha, Helen Joseph, and Leon Levy.
26. See *New Age*, 16 June and 25 August 1955, for Lilian Ngoyi with letters from Europe; 28 June, 8 and 22 November 1956, and 10 October 1957 for Motsami K. Mpho; 2 February and 8 March 1956 for Jonas Kgasane in Bloemfontein, and then Basutoland once he was deported; 9 February 1956 for Bernard Gosschalk; 3 May 1956 for James Hadebe and Florence Mkize; 10 January 1957 for E. Lulamile Vara in Cradock; 12 July 1956 for Zollie Malindi in Cape Town; 12 July 1956 for Mary Moodley; 20 September 1956 and 7 November 1957 for Johnny Gomas; 19 April and 27 September 1956 for Barbara Harmel, the daughter of Michael Harmel; 18 October

1956 for Fezile Mbi; 6 June 1957 for Marabe Miza in Alice; 18 April 1957 for Edmund K. Tollie in Worcester; 17 October 1957 for Henry Naude in Cape Town; 16 May 1957 for Melville Fletcher; 13 June 1957 for Brian Somana; 12 September 1957 for Peter Brown; 29 August 1957 for Moses Mabhida; 19 December 1957 for Chris Hani in Cape Town; 14 November 1957 and 29 September 1960 for Temba Mqota in Kimberley and Port Elizabeth; 7 November 1957 for Billy Mokhonoana in Bloemfontein; 9 February 1956 and 26 June 1958 for Hastings Banda; 19 September 1957 for Ronnie Press; 12 December 1957 for Billy Nair; 6 June 1957 for Henry Dempers; 5 December 1957 for A. M. Mosata; 27 June and 26 September 1957, and 25 February 1960 for Anderson Ganyile in Pondoland; 3 October 1957 for Duma Nokwe; 5 December 1957 for Barney Desai; 17 October 1957 for Alfred Gobs and Joseph Jack; 15 October 1959 for Mandhla Nkosi; 2 February 1961 for George Mbele in Durban; 22 October 1959 for Bertrand Mabe; 19 November 1959 for Joe Morolong in Vryburg; 18 February 1960 for Alfred Kumalo; 26 June 1958 for Bob Hepple; 9 October 1958 for Thomas Nkobi; 4 December 1958 for Joe Matthews; 13 August 1959 for Ben Baartman; 18 December 1958 for Leon Levy; 15 January 1959 for Nancy Dick; 22 January 1959 for Alf Wannenberg; 9 July 1959 for A. W.G. Champion; 17 December 1959 for Thabo Mbeki; 2 February 1961 for George Mbele; 25 May 1961 for Lim Himson; 29 June 1961 for Harry Gwala; 23 November 1961 for Zola Nqini; 23 November 1961 for Joe Louwin; and 15 March 1962 for Alfred Nzo.

See 5 November 1959 for Gatsha Buthelezi's letter in response to an article about his absence from a function in Natal: "As I am merely a servant of the people, I cannot force the issue. . . . I have never opposed the Government either by an act of commission or omission as is averred in this article by your correspondent."

As Douglas Manqina said: "Many whites believed in apartheid in those days, because there were not many Africans who explained things. The white regime gives the whites its explanation and the blacks give their explanation. So people can choose clearly. We were only a few blacks involved in politics in those days, so the story here was that without *New Age*, the story was a one-sided story."

27. Federation of South African Women Collection, AD 1137, Wits, 21 March 1959. See 25 August 1955: "By the way, this week's *New Age* has a lot on us. Next week they will have an article from Dora. I suggest we should keep on having interviews with them alternatively every week, so that they are constantly before our women readers. And we will issue an appeal to our women to read, sell *New Age*."

28. *New Age*, 25 November 1954 and 24 September 1959.

29. Walshe, *Rise of African Nationalism*, 403. See Gary Baines, "The Contradictions of Community Politics: The African Petty Bourgeoisie and the New Brighton Advisory Board, c. 1937–1952," *Journal of African History* 35 (1994): 79–97.

30. Govan Mbeki said: "They watched us every day because we were right there. But we could watch them, and when we saw CID men coming over to visit, we would rush out the back and go away. It was a lot of cat and mouse because we were so close."

See *New Age*, 23 August 1956 for when James Calata stopped by Adderley Street—"stepped hesitantly and almost apologetically into the offices."

31. *New Age*, 31 October 1957. As Bunting wrote in his 1955 memorandum to the Press Commission, "For many years it has been practically impossible to sell in Port Elizabeth. The City Council will only grant a license to sellers approved by the police, and the police have vetoed one name after another submitted by the paper concerned." Thornton Collection, A24, UCT.

Tom Lodge suggested that the Port Elizabeth city council wasn't that conservative in the

1940s: "Because of its housing policies [there were no hostels and single-sex compounds as in most other South African cities] and its reluctance to impose restrictions on the flow of Africans from the surrounding countryside into the city, Port Elizabeth local government had a relatively liberal reputation." Lodge, *Black Politics*, 48–49. In the 1940s New Brighton had no curfew, no pass regulations, and no laws against domestic beer brewing. But the 1948 Nationalist Party victory and the 1952 Defiance Campaign changed that.

32. Lodge, *Black Politics*, 51; see *Advance*, 19 August 1954 for a letter from Tshume about the 1949 boycott; see 12 and 19 September 1957 for Tshume's obituary: "uGlad usishiyile"—Glad has left us. Wilton Mkwayi said: "Tshume was a communist known by everybody, but he would hear different points of view, different people. Before the PAC, we were against communists. They'll say but if all communists were like Tshume, then you'd have no problems to the extent that when they criticised people, they say, 'Well, communists from other areas, places we don't know, that is one thing. But here, we have Tshume. You can go to him and he will advise us. They help, they show us how to do it.'"

33. Carter and Karis, *From Protest to Challenge*, 4:159.

34. The two books were *Transkei in the Making* (Durban: Verulam Press, 1939), and *Let's Do It Together*, ed. Eddie Roux (Johannesburg: Sixpenny Library, 1944).

35. Ruth First, preface to Govan Mbeki, *South Africa: The Peasant's Revolt* (London: Penguin, 1964), 13–14. For more on Mbeki, see Colin Bundy, "Schooled for Life? The Early Years and Education of Govan Mbeki," Africa Seminar, Centre for African Studies, University of Cape Town, March 1994; and Bundy's introduction to Govan Mbeki, *Learning from Robben Island: The Prison Writings of Govan Mbeki* (Cape Town: David Philip, 1991). See also Les Switzer and Ime Ukpanah, "Under Siege: *Inkundla ya Bantu* and the African Nationalist Movement, 1938–1951," in Switzer, *South Africa's Alternative Press*, 217–20; and *Guardian*, 19 April 1945. In 1937 Mbeki was embroiled in a successionist controversy over the headmanship of Mpukane, his ancestral village, and had to decline the position his father had proudly held for many years. Mbeki also was influenced by the American YMCA worker Max Yergan. Nelson Mandela said Mbeki was "serious, thoughtful, and soft-spoken, equally at home in the world of scholarship and the world of political activism." Mandela, *Long Walk to Freedom*, 162.

36. See, for example, *Guardian*, 9 April 1942 on an NRC election; 6 January 1944 for a quotation from a new Mbeki book, *Burden of the Masses*; 12, 19, and 26 April 1945 for a three-part article; 29 November 1945 for a letter to the editor about conditions in the Ciskei and Transkei; 12 June 1947.

37. See *New Age*, 1 September 1955 about Fort Hare; 2 and 16 February 1956 on the Transkei drought, and 1 March 1956 for the Congress statement which "expressed appreciation of the efforts of *New Age*"; 29 March 1956 on "Slum Clearance in PE"; 12 July 1956; 6 September 1956 on the famine: the women were saying, *ikati ilel' eziko*—"the cat is lying on the hearth" (i.e., there is no cooking fire); 8 November 1956 on basket weavers in Port Elizabeth; 7 March 1957; 5 September 1957 on Transkei unrest—"It is not caused by Moscow-trained saboteurs"; 29 January 1959; 16 July 1959 on Kougapoort; and 14 October 1959.

38. James Morris, *South African Winter* (London: Faber & Faber, 1958), 136–38. Morris concluded: "Some people believe Christopher Gell to be a saint." See also Benson, *Struggle for a Birthright*, 202–5; Segal, *Into Exile*, 153; and *New Age*, 12 January 1956, 31 May 1956, 21 June 1956, and 8 November 1956.

39. *Advance*, 17 September 1953. See Holland, *The Struggle*, 91; Lodge, *Black Politics*, 75–76; Mandela, *Long Walk to Freedom*, 126–28; Benson, *Nelson Mandela* (London: Penguin, 1986),

109; and Lazerson, *Against the Tide*, 120–24. The Congress of Democrats wrote lectures for the M-Plan.

40. Mgqungwana's father had been a member of the ANC since 1936. See *New Age*, 12 October and 14 December 1961 for letters to the editor from him; 11 October 1962 when he and James Kati were arrested (Kati's nickname was "Castro"); and *Spark*, 20 December 1962. Mgqung-wana recalled, "It wasn't a properly defined job. There was no job description. I would collect the bundles at the railway every Friday. I would sell it all weekend, take pictures, write articles, translate and type letters that came in written in Xhosa. . . . Our office was disciplined. We called Mbeki 'Tata'—father. There was no doubt he was the boss."

41. Tennyson Makiane, "The Poqo Insurrection," in Lodge, *Resistance and Ideology*, 203: "Then I got to Fort Hare where the Youth League was very well established. And there was the period when the Defiance Campaign was being launched and this attracted tremendous interest among the youth, and we used to go to the neighboring villages and organise people to the Defiance . . . as far as King Williams Town, Adelaide, Beaufort and Port Elizabeth. We used to go to them at night and sometimes over weekends to address meetings of villagers."

42. *Fighting Talk*, March, 1957.

43. *New Age*, 5 April 1956, for Mkwayi quoted at the funeral of John Jebe, an ANC man shot in March 1956 in New Brighton: "All breathed one spirit, a common brotherhood, a common ideal and a common determination to fight for freedom and put an end to the rule of brute force."

44. *New Age*, 7 August 1958 for the report that the figure was 45 percent, and 1 November 1956 for the New Brighton branch raising 33 percent.

45. Benson, *Struggle for a Birthright*, 130. See 2 October 1947, Gerard Sekoto dropped by before moving to Paris.

46. James Zug interview with Rusty and Hilda Bernstein, May 1994.

47. Gillian Slovo, *Ties of Blood*, 186.

48. Govan Mbeki, *Learning from Robben Island*, 7. "One would have imagined that her fork already carried more hay than it could."

49. Bernstein, *Rift*, 452.

50. Hilda Bernstein, foreword to Dorothy Woodson, *Decade of Dissent: An Index to Fighting Talk, 1954–1963* (Madison: University of Wisconsin Press, 1992); and Benson, *Nelson Mandela*, 59. Mandela and Rusty Bernstein were on an active editorial board of *Fighting Talk*. See *Daily Worker* (London), 1 September 1956, for an article by First.

51. See Meer, *Higher Than Hope*, 189. Harry Gwala recalled, "Ruth was always behind me, urging me to write for *Fighting Talk*. She would sit on my neck." First even solicited *Fighting Talk* articles from the minister of defense in Mali, Madiere Keita.

52. James Zug telephone interview with Beate Lipman, November 1994; and Slovo, *Every Secret Thing*. On the walls of her office were two poster-sized photographs of Moses Kotane and Bill Andrews. Nelson Mandela said, "I really respected that lady because of her intelligence and her commitment." Martin Meredith, *Nelson Mandela: A Biography* (London: Hamish Hamilton, 1997), 88.

53. James Zug telephone interview with Beate Lipman, November 1994. Another version of Lipman's story can be found in Frankel, *Rivonia's Children*, 47.

54. *Makhalipile: The Dauntless One*, Trevor Huddleston documentary made by Barry Feinberg, 1989.

55. *Times* (London), 19 August 1982. Slovo was no slouch. He sometimes played squash and once broke Harold Wolpe's front tooth with an overambitious swing. For more, see James Zug,

Squash: A History of the Game (New York: Scribner, 2003).

56. Bernstein, foreword to Woodson, *Decade of Dissent*, iii.

57. In 1951 she discovered that a Johannesburg municipality rent board member had resigned not from ill health, but under protest after the city council doubled rents. *Guardian*, 5 and 19 July and 30 August 1951; and Don Pinnock, *Ruth First*, in They Fought for Freedom series (Cape Town: Maskew Miller Longman, 1995), 27.

58. *Guardian*, 13 March 1952; *New Age*, 5 July 1956 for a report on the police bringing them in by lorries; 2 and 9 August 1956—"Russian leader says police backed his gang"; 6 September 1956 on the Spoilers gang in Alexandra; 28 March 1957 for 700 arrested in a Newclare raid; 1 August 1957 for a Russian-gang killer giving evidence on Evaton bus boycott. See Trevor Huddleston, *Naught for Your Comfort* (Glasgow: Collins, 1956), 76–88; and Lodge, *Black Politics*, 172–78.

59. Turok, *Nothing But the Truth*, 94.

60. Bernstein, *Rift*, 457. In 1957 Edwin Munger went to a small dinner party in Johannesburg that the Slovos attended. He "found them personally charming and acutely perceptive on South African affairs within their ken. Ruth is an attractive woman in her late thirties with creamy skin and jet black hair. She had had trouble that night in finding a baby sitter, and she hoped that the African girl she left in charge had not heard about the recent case of a baby sitter who had learned just the right length of time to put a baby in the gas-filled oven to quiet a screaming child without apparently doing damage. She laughingly related how a reporter came to their house the day they were arrested for treason, and wrote about their highly animated children." Edwin Munger, American Universities Field Staff report, "Notes," p. 36, Everatt Microfilm Collection, UWC.

61. Anthony Sampson, *The Treason Cage: The Opposition on Trial in South Africa* (London: Heinemann, 1958), 168; See Ruth First Memorial Trust, Institute of Commonwealth Studies, 4.1.10, for a 14 October 1957 letter. James Zug interview with Amy Thornton, December 1993: "Ruth was a real star. She was such a person in her own right, it was never in question. I remember speaking at a memorial meeting for her. She never went in for this kind of radical chic kind of dressing, you know, sandals and that. She was always extremely elegant. She didn't think that that in any way detracted, I don't think it even entered her head to think, 'No I am a woman. I am me, I am Ruth First.' And people respected her. I mean she was a real star. Far, far more regarded as a star ever than Joe Slovo."

62. The 480-page manuscript resides in the Reg September Collection, UWC. The novel, *The White People: A South African Novel of and beyond Its Time*, starts: "From the moment I saw them I knew they were spacemen," and ends with author's postscript: "I do not, however, take any responsibility whatever for what you may care to read into my story. That is entirely your own affair." On page 97, Harmel writes about a newspaper interview: "Are we not going to be able to give our own opinions?" asked Jack.

"Of course you must," said Qelvu. "Your opinions are a part of the facts, a part of history. But tell your readers what happened. Let them draw their own conclusions. Isn't that a part of the new world you are building? Making people think for themselves? Making each one responsible for all?"

For more on Central Indian, see *New Age*, 19 January and 19 July 1956; Eli Weinberg, *Portrait of a People: A Personal Photographic Record of the South Africa Liberation Struggle* (London: International Defense and Aid Fund, 1981), 163; and *Unity in Action: A Photographic History of the African National Congress, South Africa 1912–1982* (London: African National Congress, 1982), 62–64. The parents' association of the school had an office in the same Johannesburg building as the ANC.

63. Casey Motsisi wrote that Hutchinson had a "poetic and sometimes turbulent soul." *Casey and Co.: Selected Writings of Casey "Kid" Motsisi*, ed. Mothobi Mutloatse (Johannesburg: Raven, 1983), 129.

64. James Zug telephone interview with Willie Kgositile, December 1994. See also Frederikse, *Unbreakable Thread*, 73. John Nkadimeng: "In fact I found that Ruth used to encourage me a lot. She would say, 'Look, I'm going to talk to you about such-and-such, and I need you to point out some of the problems which you see out of what I'm saying. I will try to be as simple as possible so that you must understand, and if you disagree with me, don't be shy—speak.' She was one of the white people who really made me to feel that she wants me to know as much as she does."

65. Hutchinson's correspondence to First is in the Ruth First Memorial Trust, Institute of Commonwealth Studies, London, 4.1.10. "Incidentally, we did some house-to-house work the other day. The things that the women say about the passes!"

See *Advance*, 15 April 1954, for Hutchinson's first piece; and *New Age*, 6 November 1958 and 5 February 1959, for his departure from South Africa.

66. Switzer, *South Africa's Alternative Press*, 25. See Phyllis Ntantala, *A Life's Mosaic* (Cape Town: Mayibuye Centre, 1992), 69. Makiwane was "an intellectual giant among Africans and one of the best brains that ever came out of Lovedale." His daughter Florence married Professor D. D. Jabavu.

67. Gerhart and Karis, "Political Profiles," in *From Protest to Challenge* 4:70.

68. Morris, *South African Winter*, 164.

69. Huddleston, *Naught for Your Comfort*, 121: "Sometimes looking up at Sophiatown from Western Native Township, across the main road, I have felt I was looking at an Italian village somewhere in Umbria. For you do 'look up' at Sophiatown, and in the evening, across the blue gray haze of smoke from braziers and chimneys against a saffron sky, you see closely-packed, red-roofed little houses. You see, on the farther skyline, the tall and shapely blue-gum trees."

70. *New Age*, 21 June and 23 August 1956.

71. See *New Age*, 31 May 1956 for his first piece, an "exclusive article for *New Age* on township music"; 16 and 30 August 1956 on music; 13 September 1956 on *tsotsis*; 11 October 1956 for an article co-written with Sibande on new investigations about Bethal women; 1 November 1956 on Bethal squatters; 31 January 1957; 9 May 1957 for an article co-written with Hutchinson on Verwoerd deposing a Zeerust chief; 23 May 1957 on jazz; 30 May 1957 for an article on the pass laws; 26 September 1957 on spies at Fort Hare; 9 January 1958 for another article about Zeerust; 30 February 1958 for Makiwane and First covering a Sophiatown women's march; 25 September 1958—"crime reporter"; and 10 October 1958 on his arrest story.

72. *New Age*, 20 September 1956.

73. *New York Times*, 11 February 1955. Resha was the only person arrested when the first Sophiatown families were removed to Meadowlands.

74. Helen Joseph, *Side by Side*, 17; Lodge, *Black Politics*, 165; Mac Fenwick, "'Tough Guy, eh?' The Gangster Figure in *Drum*," *Journal of Southern African Studies* 22, no. 4 (December 1996): 617–32; and *The Drum Decade: Stories from the 1950s*, ed. Michael Chapman (Pietermaritzburg: University of Natal Press, 1989). Resha's address was sometimes given as 41 Birkett Street.

See Don Mattera, *Sophiatown: Coming of Age in South Africa* (Boston: Beacon, 1987). Mattera, a coloured poet who led the Vultures gang in the 1950s, wrote in his memoir that Resha "was like a friend to street kids and gangsters" (130).

75. Maggie Resha, '*Mangoana O Tsoara Thipa Ka Boltaleng: My Life in the Struggle* (Johannesburg: Congress of South African Writers, 1991), 234. See a picture of Maggie Resha, *New Age*, 9 October 1958. James Zug interview with Rusty Bernstein, May 1994: "Robert was a real character. He was one of the Soft-Town boys as they called themselves, a Sophiatown lad. He was a gay character, a gad-about-town. He enjoyed himself, dancing, a womanizer, boxing. He got on well with athletes and quite competent politically, a tendency to go off the handle."

76. *New Age*, 19 April 1956 for his first article, with a picture; 24 May 1956, 5 July 1956, and 26 July 1956; 16 May 1957 for a debate with Lionel Forman on boxing, followed by reply from Arnold Selby on 30 May 1957; 22 January 1959 on the West Rand; 2 July 1959 for a review of a new Fugard play.

77. *New Age*, 1 May 1958; 15 October 1959 on boxing and the Olympics; 3 December 1959 for the birth of a new child to him and his wife Aurelia; 10 December 1959 on housing; 24 March 1960.

78. Weinberg, *Portrait of a People*, 6.

79. *New Age*, 27 January 1955, for the roving quotation and his series on how people live. See *Advance*, 22 July 1954, for an example of his regular advertisement; *New Age*, 12 January 1956 for an advertisement calling himself "The *New Age* Photographer," 17 December 1959 for a review. Weinberg wrote in *Portrait of a People* that working for *New Age* "was a source of great pleasure and inspiration to me, and I am grateful for the opportunities of relief from the routine of commercial photography which *New Age* afforded me." Weinberg had once been briefly married to Ray Alexander.

    According to his daughter Sheila, he "loved photographing for *New Age*. He was so committed and had to find something to do after getting banned from the trade unions. He used to go out on weekends to the townships and locations, while my mother and I went and sold the paper."

80. "Once you carry a pass you are in a way accepting it," Walter Sisulu said. "You are resenting it, but you are accepting because otherwise you can't do your work." See *I Will Go Singing: Walter Sisulu Speaks of His Life and the Struggle for Freedom in South Africa*, ed. George M. Houser and Herbert Stone (Cape Town: Robben Island Museum, 2001), 37.

81. *New Age*, 6 and 19 January 1956. See 22 March 1956 for a *Die Transvaler* reference to "screaming headlines in which gall is spewed against the issue of reference books to women which are appearing in periodicals and newspapers distributed among Natives." See also Pinnock, "Writing Left," 127.

82. *New Age*, 26 January 1956.

83. *New Age*, 29 March and 19 April 1956. The village, according to First, was "swarming with SB detectives."

84. Lodge, *Black Politics*, 143. See *New Age*, 21 June 1956 for two pictures of 200 women marching in Bethlehem and Orlando; 2 August 1956 for 104 arrested in Ermelo; 15 November 1956 for two killed in Lichtenburg protest; 10 May and 14 June 1956 for the Johannesburg march.

85. *New Age*, 19 January 1956. The women also sang, *Li ea chisoa li pasa*—"the passes are being burnt"—and, *Hei, Verwoerd, hei bula teronko / Hei, thina si zo ngena zimankosikaz e / MaZulu, MaXhosa, Sotho, Shangana*—"Hey, Verwoerd, hey! Open up the prison cells. Hey, we are women, we are going to enter. We are Zulu, Xhosa, Sotho, Shangaan." Segal, *Into Exile*, 265; and Mmantho Nkotsoe interview with Mrs S—in *Staffrider* 6. no. 1 (1984): 36.

86. *New Age*, 26 July and 16 August 1956. The women at the Union Building also sang: *Koloi ena, e ya nyanyatha / Koloi ena e ya nyanyatha / Fa a sa sute ya go thula*—"This car is moving very fast, if you don't move out of the way it will knock you down." See Lodge, *Black Politics*, 144–

45; Helen Joseph, *Side by Side*, 1–2.

See also *New Age*, 10 June 1957 on a Zeerust ban on media; 27 June 1957 on Pietersburg women who chased Verwoerd's officials away; 11 July 1957 for a Govan Mbeki article on Queenstown women rejecting passes; 18 July 1957 on 1,000 Standerton women getting arrested—*Ha li tsewe*, "we don't take passes"; 1 August 1957 on 100 Uitenhage women who got arrested; 21 November 1957 for a picture of 120 Uitenhage and Dispatch women released after eight weeks in prison for burning passes; and 26 March 1959 on Port Elizabeth women.

87. James Zug interview with Wolfie Kodesh, March 1994; and Gillian Slovo, *Every Secret Thing*, 45–49. See *New Age*, 10 September 1959, for a letter from Potgieter. See also *The Democratic Journalist* (London), 7 August 1983, for an article by Kodesh about the incident.

88. *New Age*, 18 June and 23 July 1959. "Rumour had it that the Boer who farmed with potatoes had the habit of knocking down his 'lazy' labourers with his tractor. He did not bury them, instead he used them as compost in his potato farm. We were convinced that what we heard was true because even the potatoes themselves were shaped like human beings. In every township, potatoes were boycotted. We argued that eating potatoes was the same as eating human flesh." Mmantho Nkotsoe interview with Mrs S— in *Staffrider* 6, no. 1 (1984): 36. See Mattera, *Sophiatown*, 137–38: "A team of black journalists discovered a prisoner's skull in a potato field."

89. Resha, *My Life in the Struggle*, 44. Albert Luthuli said about the boycott, "I think it caught the imagination of the people because it dragged into the light of day specific and appalling human suffering and misery." Benson, *Nelson Mandela*, 195. Benson, *Struggle for a Birthright*, 210; Helen Joseph, *Side by Side*, 72–73; and Weinberg, *Portrait of a People*, 41.

"I remember that there was a great sense of drama and excitement and pride that it was again an issue that was being taken up nationally and internationally," said Albie Sachs. "It had extensive repercussions. It was a case of political investigative journalism leading to court cases and a resulting attack on the pass laws. It was quite successful as a non-violent means of pressuring the regime."

90. Slovo, *Unfinished Autobiography*, 89.

91. *New Age*, 8 and 22 January and 23 July 1959 for the case of Veldman Mtekeli. He had gotten a letter to Len Lee-Warden, who passed it to *New Age*.

92. *New Age*, 26 March 1959. For other articles about pass laws and forced labor, see *New Age*, 17 May 1956 for an article on the whipping of a 21-year-old in Alexandra; 24 May 1956 on Alexandra raids—"reaping time on the farms"; 31 May 1956 for a "savage beating" of a Newclare man who spent three months on a farm between Witbank and Bethal; 30 August 1956 for "Shanghaied labour is slave labour—Pass Arrests and Farm Labour: Both are sides of the same coin"; 15 November 1956 for a photograph of a 14-year-old who ran away from a Free State farm; 17 January 1957 for when Joseph Molefe was acquitted of perjury—he had told *New Age* about his uncle getting killed at the same Bethal farm last year; 27 June 1957 for the picture of a 16-year-old who was chained to a cow at night; and 8 August 1957. See also 26 January 1961 for a picture of two Africans who came to Barrack Street to complain about treatment on Cape farms.

93. "Dawood was not very serious," Ebrahim Ismail Ebrahim said. "He was quite loose. He would allow anything to come and go."

94. James Zug conversation with Ronnie Kasrils, January 1994. Naicker "commanded a great deal of respect," wrote Kasrils, *Armed and Dangerous*, 31.

95. "MP Naicker came to the Durban office simply because he was active politically." Shaun Johnson interview with Brian Bunting, January 1984.

96. *New Age*, 2 and 9 May 1957. In 1994 I visited Lodgson House. The lime-green walls of the

building were peeling and chipped. I climbed up the narrow staircase to the sixth floor (the elevator with wooden doors was not working). A law firm occupied the newspaper's former offices, and no one there, including Aubrey V. Nyembezi, an attorney there, had ever heard of *New Age* or M. P. Naicker.

97. *New Age*, 5 September 1957: "The building [Lakhani Chambers] is drab and dusty. The upper floors deserted and gloomy."

98. *New Age*, 1 September 1955 for circulation; 28 February 1957 for the NIC promising to raise £1,000 and boost circulation up 5,000; 12 June 1958 when the NIYC planned to sell the newspaper in Clairwood; 3 July 1958—"The appeal has had the effect of starting up a friendly rivalry between the Durban and Johannesburg Indian youth"—the NIYC promised 50 per month, and the TIYC 360 per week; 29 June 1961 for Clairwood branch of NIC selling five dozen weekly. See also "Tribute to MP Naicker," 1977, UWC.

99. *New Age*, 24 May 1956 for Naicker's first article; 26 July 1956; 19 December 1957 at the ANC's annual national conference; 11 February 1959 on a strike wave; 3 September 1959 on beer-hall riots; 5 November 1959 with a picture of Buthelezi. See also William Beinart, "Worker Consciousness, Ethnic Particularism and Nationalism: The Experiences of a South African Migrant, 1930–1969," in Marks and Trapido, *Politics of Race*, 301. Naicker still was involved in organizing sugar workers, even after he joined *New Age*.

See *Spark*, 28 March 1963, for Bunting praising Naicker: "Under his direction the Durban office soon became one of the liveliest centres in the Union. His ability to attract people to him like steel filings to a magnet led to a rapid improvement in sales and finance collecting."

100. Naicker often sent a staff member like Ebrahim Ismail Ebrahim. See Meer, *Higher Than Hope*, 280. E. V. Mohammed, "his self-appointed honorary secretary" and Liberal Party member, brought Luthuli to Stanger. See *New Age*, 15 September 1955, 7 November 1957, 24 April 1958, 12 February 1959, and 17 September 1959 for statements; 23 February 1956 for a statement to *New Age* on the Soviet Consulate affair; 27 June 1957 on June 26th; 7 November 1957 for a statement on ANC election policy; 5 December 1957—"Congress Backs Election Statement"—a joint statement in support of the *New Age* statement; 3 December 1959 for his call for a nationwide observance of Human Rights Day on 10 December.

101. James Zug interview with Ebrahim Ismail Ebrahim, January 1994; and Kasrils, *Armed and Dangerous*, 32. Other sellers in Durban were Michael Mample and A.K.M. Docrat. See *New Age*, 29 March 1962, for Abolani Duma, who was hired as administrative assistant; Duma, an ANC member and MK rural organizer, collected the newspaper bundles at the railway station every Friday.

102. *New Age*, 25 January 1962. See Rudi Boon, *Beyond Fear: Ebrahim Ismael Ebrahim versus the Apartheid State* (Amsterdam: Anti-Apartheid Movement Netherlands, 1989), 13: Seedat transformed the young schoolboy into an "intellectual jack-of-all-trades, always studying and analyzing."

103. Morley also contributed light verse: *New Age*, 14 May 1959 for "Boycott the Bosses"; 16 July 1959 for "Be Wise"; and 18 June 1959 for a letter to the editor.

104. James Zug interview with Sonia Bunting, November 1994. See *New Age*, 10 May 1956 for an obituary Bunting wrote about Babs Meaker; 13 September 1956 for recipes.

105. For Alexander, see *New Age*, 19 July 1956, 7 November 1957, and 4 February 1960. For Kahn, see 1 December 1955 on the Nationalists giving arms to Israel; 29 March 1956 on the Nationalists in Cape Town courting the coloured vote in municipal elections; and 11 September 1958 for a profile of Verwoerd. For Simons, see 12 May 1959.

106. Cope went on to publish a number of well-received novels and short-story collections after *The

Fair House (London: MacGibbon & Kee, 1955), most of which were published by Heinemann in London: *The Golden Oriole* (1958), *The Road to Yesterday* (1959), *The Tame Ox* (1960), *Albino* (1964), *The Man Who Doubted and Other Stories* (1967), *The Dawn Comes Twice* (1969), *The Rain-Maker* (1971), *The Student of Zend* (1972), *Alley Cat and Other Stories* (1973), *Selected Stories* (Cape Town: David Philip, 1976), and *My Son Max* (1977). He wrote a children's book, *Tales of the Trickster Boy* (Cape Town: Tafelberg, 1990), and issued a chapbook of poetry, *Lyrics & Diatribes: Selected Poems by Robert Cope* (Cape Town: AE & JC, 1948), that was hand-bound by his wife Lesley in an edition of one hundred. He also appeared in the leading magazines, such as *London Magazine*, December 1961, and *Paris Review*, Spring 1958. Cope edited a number of books, along with *The Penguin Book of South African Verse* (1968, with Uys Krige), *Seismograph: Best South African Writing from Contrast* (Cape Town: Reijger, 1970— Cope edited the bilingual magazine *Contrast*), and *The Adversary Within: Dissident Writers in Afrikaans* (Cape Town: David Philip, 1982). Cope went into exile in 1980 and died in Hertfordshire, England, in March 1991.

107. *New Age*, 25 November 1954; 21 April, 23 June, 28 July, 4 August, and 29 September 1955; 31 November 1955 on how she spent sixteen hours at a Nationalist Party conference; 19 January, 2 and 16 February, 8 March, and 17 May 1956; and 24 May 1956 on Nyanga. See Naomi Barnett, "The Planned Destruction of District Six in 1940," *Studies in the History of Cape Town*, ed. Elizabeth van Heyningen (Cape Town: University of Cape Town, 1994), 162–83.

For more about SACTU, see *New Age*, 28 April 1955; and Rob Lambert, "Political Unionism in South Africa: The South African Congress of Trade Unions, 1955–65," D.Phil. thesis, University of the Witwatersrand, 1988.

108. *New Age*, 20 September 1956. The opening scene of Alex La Guma's first novel, *A Walk in the Night*, contains a vivid depiction of District Six. See M. Shamil Jeppe, "Aspects of Popular Culture and Class Expression in Inner Cape Town, circa 1939–1959," master's thesis, UCT, 1990. See Brian Bunting's introduction to Alex La Guma, *And a Threefold Cord* (London: Kliptown, 1988), vi: "Nobody who ever passed through District Six could ever forget its winding, crowded streets, its jostling humanity, its smells, its poverty and wretchedness, its vivacity and infinite variety. For all its outward degradation, the pulse of life beat strongly in its veins."

109. *New Age*, 24 May 1956 for his first article, on the tramway union fighting apartheid; 27 September and 4 October 1956 for a two-part series on Roeland Street Jail; 20 September 1956 on gangs in District Six; and 28 November and 12 December 1957 on Windermere removals and the creation of Nyanga.

After dissolution in 1950, La Guma's father, Jimmy, forbade him to stay in politics because he didn't want him to be banned or jailed. Since La Guma still lived at home, he obeyed his father. But once he married in 1954 and moved out, he joined the SACPO.

La Guma's wife Blanche recalled her husband's love for *New Age*. "He went into the office every day to work, to write, to talk, to take photographs. He had a good sense of humor and still took his work seriously. He loved his job at the paper, and I think his happiest days were there." See *New Age*, 2 August 1956 and 20 June 1957, for articles Blanche wrote about being a midwife in Athlone and the nursing community under apartheid.

110. *New Age*, 10 October 1957 and 6 March 1958. See Cecil A. Abrahams, *Alex La Guma* (Boston: Twayne Publishers, 1985), 13: "When *New Age* asked me to take a job, that is when I really started to learn to write. I suppose, inevitably, I sat down and wrote short stories." For other discussions of La Guma and his writing, see Robert Green, "Alex La Guma's *In the Fog of the Season's End*: The Politics of Subversion," *Umoja* 3, no. 2 (Summer 1979): 85–93; Abdul R.

Mohammed, "Alex La Guma: The Literary and Political Functions of Marginality in the Colonial Situation," no. 52, African Studies Center, Boston University, 1982; S. O. Asein, *Alex La Guma: The Man and his Work* (Ibadan: New Horn Press, 1987); Brian Bunting's introduction to Alex La Guma, *And a Threefold Cord* (London: Kliptown Books, 1988); Kathleen M. Baluntansky, *The Novels of Alex La Guma: The Representation of a Political Conflict* (Boulder, Colo.: Three Continents Press, 1989); Cecil Abrahams, ed., *Memories of Home: The Writings of Alex La Guma* (Trenton, N.J.: Africa World Press, 1991); and Balasubramanyam Chandramohan, *A Study in Trans-Ethnicity in Modern South Africa: The Writings of Alex La Guma, 1925–1985* (Lampeter, Wales: Mellon Research University Press, 1992). See *New Age*, 20 September 1956, for "Down My Street" by "Citizen." Another fine example of La Guma's writing is in *New Age*, 20 September 1956, about the dead-end kids of Hanover Street.

See Abrahams, 10: "The owners of *New Age* were liberal-minded, white, English-speaking South Africans who recognized that their paper tended to appeal to a clientele with similar cultural and intellectual background as themselves. To succeed in carrying out the objectives that they had established in their first edition and to increase their readership among the non-white community, the owners of the newspaper sought staff within the black community. Since La Guma was an active participant in the shaping of the Cape colored community, and because he had demonstrated in the *Guardian* his competency as a writer, he was chosen for one of the positions at *New Age*."

111. Switzer, "Bantu World," *Journal of Southern African Studies* 14, no. 3 (April 1988): 366. See *U.S. News and World Report*, 30 January 1959: "But a Communist-line newspaper called *New Age* is sold openly on the streets of Johannesburg and elsewhere in the country. Most of its readers are black Africans."

112. Edwin Munger, American Universities Field Staff report, 8 June 1958, in Everatt Microfilm Collection, UWC, p. 27. See *New Age*, 12 March 1959—"We Uncover an American Snooper"— about Munger's 42-page "smear" of the Congress; and 26 March 1959. In the 1950s, Munger, who had a Ph.D. from the University of Chicago, visited sixty African nations. He later became a professor of geography at California Institute of Technology. See Edwin S. Munger, "New White Politics in South Africa," in *Southern Africa and the United States*, ed. William A. Hance (New York: Columbia University Press, 1968).

113. Rosalynde Ainslie, *The Press in Africa: Communications Past and Present* (London: Victor Gollancz, 1966), 83. Some people could not read the newspaper in public or private. Michael Dingake recalled his reaction when a friend gave him copies of the *Guardian*: "Whether through intuition or from information, I suspected the paper to be a Communist paper propagating Communism. My knowledge of Communism was zero except the injunction of the church: Communism is a Godless creed. Have nothing to do with it! . . . As a result of this indoctrination, I was extremely careful of what I read. Every time, after I had received this paper from my friend, I quickly dumped it into the rubbish bin the moment his back was turned, without even bothering to scan the paper headlines. The mere touching of the paper made me cringe from the sense of betrayal of my Christian principles, a sense of flirtation with the devil. I threw the *Guardian* into the rubbish bin, replaced the lid firmly and washed my hands in the tub." See Shubin, *ANC*, 60.

114. Mandela, *Long Walk to Freedom*, 202. Politically minded Africans in neighboring countries often bought subscriptions. *Sunday Times* (Johannesburg), 25 September 1994, for an obituary by Doc Bikitsha of Thomas Nkobi. While studying in Roma, Lesotho, in the early 1950s, Nkobi got the newspaper by mail.

115. Weinberg, *Portrait of a People*, 160–61. Moretsele was born in 1897 in Sekhukuneland and

thus was the oldest Treason Trialist. See *New Age*, 7 June 1956 for a photograph; 22 September 1960 when Robert Resha visits Retsies; 16 March 1961 for when Moretsele collapsed and died at his café. Retsies was very popular with Africans, especially Pedi, because of the politically vibrant atmosphere and because he served the kind of porridge they cooked in rural areas.

116. Sampson, *Drum*, 21.

117. Sampson, *Treason Cage*, 168–73. "Though the *Guardian* was widely read by Africans, it was essentially a white man's organ, edited and written by Europeans for Africans, not with them, and this laid it open to attacks from the African nationalists."

Johnson, "Propagandist," 44, quoting Anthony Sampson: "It was tremendously important as an information centre . . . like a poster and diary of events. . . . I remember at the huge mass meetings, the paper was tremendously evident. . . . It was very closely linked with political events and very effective."

See Thomas Karis, "South Africa," in Carter, *Five African States*, 554: "*New Age* was undoubtedly a valuable source of information to the government." See also *New Age*, 27 June 1957, when it called itself the "barometer of the liberation movement."

118. "The *Guardian* had acquired the status of unofficial spokesman of the whole Congress movement, and its absence as an organiser and morale-booster would have been a disaster for the Defiance Campaign." Forman and Sachs, *South African Treason Trial*, 139. See also Phelan, *Apartheid Media*, 69.

119. Meli, *South Africa Belongs to Us*, 89. In 1941 Mbeki wrote to Xuma about the "futility of our attempts without a press to prepare the minds of the people for what we plan to do, and to strengthen them once they have undertaken to do a thing." *Inkundla ya Bantu*, February 1941: "He [Xuma] has to draw the professional classes into better understanding of the working classes and their conditions. To do that he will himself have to acquire full knowledge of such conditions, sympathise with them and make the struggle for their general advancement of their lot his goal. [He will need] a newspaper that will further his policy—that is absolutely essential."

120. Les Switzer and Donna Switzer, *The Black Press in South Africa and Lesotho* (Boston: G. K. Hall, 1979), 24.

121. Everatt Microfilm Collection, UWC, p. 5 of draft plan for Congress of the People campaign. See *Advance*, 1 April 1954. Mokxotho Matji, the secretary of the Cape ANC and editor of its newsletter *Inyaniso*, wrote in its first issue: "Although for many years the ANC has realised the need for a vernacular newspaper that could disseminate the truth about our struggles to all the people, it is well-nigh impossible to establish a newspaper from scratch today."

In 1958 ANC president Albert Luthuli, in supporting a *New Age* appeal for donations, said the weekly "does much more organizational work for the ANC than any propaganda material we can muster at present." *New Age*, 26 June 1958.

In 1956, after Bunting denied a request to issue a Xhosa/Zulu supplement to *New Age*, Govan Mbeki and M. P. Naicker teamed up to issue their own cyclostyled newspaper, *Iziwe*, which ran in Zulu and Xhosa for three issues before the Treason Trial began. James Zug interview with Govan Mbeki, February 1994; and *New Age*, 4 December 1958.

122. Shaun Johnson interview with Brian Bunting, January 1984; and James Zug interview with Brian Bunting, November 1993.

123. Pinnock, "Raising the Red Flag," 6. See *Fighting Talk*, September 1958.

124. Delius, "Sebatakgomo and the ZBA," 310. James Zug interview with Paul Joseph, May 1994: "The Party was the movement. It was like the old joke: for meetings, whites were on time, In-

dians were thirty minutes late, Africans an hour late, and coloured never showed up at all."

125. Chenhamo C. Chimutengwende, *South Africa: The Press and the Politics of Liberation* (London: Barbican, 1978), 68: "The ideological development of the African nationalist movement in South Africa was greatly accelerated by" *New Age.*

126. Vigne, *Liberals Against Apartheid*, 143.

127. Bunting Collection, UWC, profile of the *African Communist*, box 26: "The ideological development of the ANC and its allies was reflected in their columns and would not have been possible without them." Bunting said in 1993: "The alliance could not have happened without *New Age.*" The ANC/SACP alliance was partially completed by the Umkhonto we Sizwe merger with the Party in 1961.

128. Julie Frederikse, *The Unbreakable Threat: Non-Racialism in South Africa* (London: Zed Books, 1990), 73.

129. James Zug interview with Brian Bunting, December 1993.

130. *Advance*, 25 March 1954, for some criticism of the National Action Committee. Shaun Johnson interview with Brian Bunting, January 1984: "I think in some respects they could have done better with their own organ, especially in discussing their own internal problems."

131. *New Age*, 10 December 1959.

132. *New Age*, 6 January 1956. Christopher Gell responded to the ban by arguing that "the fact that white South Africans suffer from still greater immaturity in the face of adverse criticism is no reason to condone even a minor encroachment within the jurisdiction of the ANC, in which such high hopes are set."

Much of First's report, partially printed in bold lettering, advised the ANC on proper conference techniques. "The pace-setter for the conference proceedings should be the report of the national executive," First wrote. "The report should not be intended as a surprise address, a Congress secret to be revealed, like the Union budget, only on the day of its presentation. . . . Delegates must adhere to strict rules of debate, must stick to the Conference programme and must agree to limit extraneous issues to the minimum of time and even outlaw them from the floor. Debates must be tackled from a principled point of view, not a personal one."

133. *New Age*, 5 April 1956. See also *Guardian*, 15 December 1949, with an article about early Africanist agitation: "Red-Baiting at ANC Conference."

134. *New Age*, 5 April 1958.

135. *New Age*, 6 November 1958. See 8 and 22 May, and 25 September 1958; and 12 March 1959.

136. Benjamin Pogrund, *How Can Man Die Better: Sobukwe and Apartheid* (London: Peter Halban, 1990), 96–97. Shaun Johnson interview with Matthew Nkoana, September 1984: "The Africanists used *New Age* as evidence of their criticisms of the ANC leadership . . . [who were] influenced by *New Age* against the African nationalist thrust of the movement. [*New Age*] gave a false orientation to the liberation movement, a hostile and negative influence, say counter-revolutionary." Nkoana worked for the *Golden City Post*. See Dan Tloome's article in *Fighting Talk*, September 1958, in which he defends *New Age* against slurs issued by the *Africanist*: "There is no paper in South Africa which is so much loved and respected by the downtrodden and oppressed people as *New Age.*" Robert Resha also attended the 1959 founding conference of the PAC.

137. *Advance*, 25 June 1953 (Bunting spoke of "cleavages and tensions within the European population" to explain the Liberal Party's rhetoric); and *New Age*, 1 December 1955. See *Liberation*, June 1953: Nelson Mandela condemned the LP for its "fine words and promises" that were "essentially reactionary in context"; its leaders were "subordinate henchmen of the ruling circles." See also David Everatt, "'Frankly Frightened': The Liberal Party and the Congress of the

People," unpublished manuscript, Everatt Collection, UWC.

138. *New Age*, 22 November 1956, for an interview with Paton. See *Advance*, 11 and 25 June 1953, and 5 August 1954 when he is accused of "political duplicity"; *New Age*, 5 and 29 September 1957 for Paton on a multiracial conference—"*New Age* has not conquered me and I have not conquered it." See also Alan Paton, *Journey Continued: An Autobiography* (Cape Town: David Phillip, 1988), 68: "Between communists and liberals—even if they cooperated on certain well-defined projects—there was a fundamental incompatibility."
See also *New Age*, 1 and 8 March 1962, when Black Sash refused membership to Sonia Bunting.

139. James Zug interview with Brian Bunting, December 1993; and Shaun Johnson interview with Randolph Vigne, September 1984. Bunting recalled, "We were very different personally. Pat dressed for dinner. He carried a patrician air about it. Our politics were different." One of the roots of the animosity between Duncan and Bunting was an incident in the mid-1950s. Duncan spoke at a COD meeting in Claremont, and in "his totally straight-from-the-shoulder way sort of told them what he thought of the South African Communist Party and all its works, *Das Kapital*. There was a tremendous uproar and a lot of fall-out from that."

140. *Southern African Review of Books* (May–June 1994) for an interesting remembrance by Randolph Vigne. Joining Duncan in his defiance were Manilal Gandhi (son of Mahatma), Bettie du Toit and Freda (Troup) Levson. Vigne, incidentally, was a leading Liberal Party man and the book-review editor for *Contact*. See also the first issue of the *Cape Guardian*, 19 February 1937, for mention of Sir Patrick Duncan, Sr.

141. *New Age*, 1 January 1959.

142. *Contact*, 2 May 1959. See advertisements inserted by the Liberal Party in *New Age*: 6 November 1958 on women and passes; 30 April 1959 for a mass meeting on Grand Parade protesting job reservation; and 16 July 1959 for *Contact*, "South Africa's only non-racial, democratic, illustrated, fortnightly review."

143. Randolph Vigne, *Liberals Against Apartheid: A History of the Liberal Party of South Africa, 1953–1968* (New York: St. Martin's, 1997), 81. The minutes of a 1959 COD executive meeting described an interesting interchange between Duncan and Bunting: "*Contact* refused to take a COD advertisement on the grounds that the COD is a totalitarian organisation. *New Age* took the matter up and on threatening to publish the matter, *Contact* changed its position and agreed to publish the advertisement. . . . It was correct for *New Age* not to have published the report in view of requests from Liberals not to do so. . . . It would be wrong to come out with a strong attack on Duncan, as it would give him an importance that he did not merit as an individual." COD Collection, Wits, AD 2187.

144. Bill Nasson, "The Unity Movement: Its Legacy in Historical Consciousness," *Radical History Review* 46, no. 7 (1990): 189–211; and Neville Alexander, "Non-Collaboration in the Western Cape, 1943–1963," in *The Angry Divide: A Social and Economic History of the Western Cape*, ed. Wilmot G. James and Mary Simon (Cape Town: David Philip, 1989), 180–91.

145. *New Age*, 10 May 1956.

146. Ntantala, *Life's Mosaic*, 153–55. See *New Age*, 8 January 1959.

147. *Torch*, 3 June 1952. For reference, see *Clarion*, 29 May 1952: "Sam Kahn's Last Speech in Parliament: African Voters Lose Their Representatives."

148. *New Age*, 27 June 1957, 11 December 1958, and 20 October 1960.

149. James Zug telephone conversation with Dennis Brutus, March 1991: "Brian was an efficient editor, easy to work with. He kept to the rigid Party line, but made no attempt to impose his views onto me."

150. *New Age*, 26 November and 10 December 1959.

151. *New Age*, 15 October 1959.

152. *New Age*, 29 March 1956, for an exclusive interview with Oliver Tambo.

153. Shaun Johnson interview with Brian Bunting, January 1984.

154. James Zug interview with Jurgen Schadeburg, July 1994: "Of course, *Drum* had a lot of errors as well and was pretty pathetic on a pure journalistic basis. Henry's pieces were an exception."

155. James Zug correspondence with Benjamin Pogrund, April 1994. "At the same time it was years ahead of the rest of the press in its lonely and brave reporting of the real issues of South Africa, that is, the experiences and thinking of the black majority and in calling for change."

   See Irving E. Fang, "A Study of Fourteen African Newspapers," Ph.D. dissertation, UCLA, 1960, p. 24: "The news is heavily slanted and patently propagandistic. As a reader my emotions were stirred up by the indignities the newspaper reported. As a journalist I was left wondering if this or that item was true as reported."

156. *Advance*, 3 September 1953; and *New Age*, 8 February 1962.

157. *New Age*, 8 November 1956. See 16 March 1961, when Ray Alexander examined Bernard Sachs's book on Sharpeville and wrote, "This book tells us nothing." See also a review by Bunting and photograph of Athol Fugard's *Blood Knot*, 15 February 1962.

158. *New Age*, 5 April 1956.

159. *New Age*, 6 November and 11 December 1958.

160. *New Age*, 12 April 1956 for Brutus's "For a Dead African," and 20 December 1956; 2 and 16 October 1958 for Neruda's "Standard Oil," and 27 July 1961; March 1957 for Abraham Bell; 18 October 1962 for John Berger. See *Spark*, 10 January 1963, for Okigbo's "Lustra."

161. *Advance*, 19 November 1953 through October 1954. The novel, according to the National Library of South Africa, was published by Timmins Publishers in Cape Town in 1952.

162. *New Age*, 4 April 1957.

163. *New Age*, 9 June 1955. Harry Gwala, Alfred Hutchinson, Johnny Morley, Alex La Guma, and Richard Moore were some of the winners; Hutchinson won twice, first prize in 1958 and third in 1956. See *New Age*, September–October 1955, for the first year. The stories had to run between two and three thousand words and have a South African background. Stanley Uys and Richard van der Ross were the judges; they received 32 entries. October–December 1956 for the second year; the prize money was £10 for first prize, £7 10s. for second, £5 for third, and £2 for anything *New Age* published. December 1958–January 1959 for the third and final year.

164. *New Age*, 14 August and 4 September 1958.

165. The cartoons started in *New Age*, 5 March 1959. See Alex La Guma, *Liberation Chabalala*, edited by Andre Odendaal and Roger Field (Bellville, South Africa: Mayibuye Books, 1993), 61. James Zug interview with Albie Sachs, March 1994: "It was a very cheeky cartoon, a bit controversial in the office, and we were quite proud of it."

   Blanche La Guma said in March 1988: "You can't go on sort of hammering the serious side because people are human beings before they are politicians or revolutionaries or whatever you like to call them. . . . Something light just sort of lifted it and gave the people a break from reading this heavier stuff." Chandramohan, *Study in Trans-Ethnicity*, 205.

166. *South African Journalist* (July–September 1950). The SASJ was shaken by the affair: "Before the sudden teacup storm in the Society about communism is over . . . we must kick them out. The persistent attempts to secure entry into the Society of two journalists of the *Guardian* in Cape Town proves how right the Minister was. These attempts continue today. They are sinister." James Zug interview with Brian Bunting, December 1993; and telephone interview with Stanley

Uys, May 1994. See *Africa South* (January 1959) for Stanley Uys, "The White Opposition in South Africa." Uys was eventually banned from the House of Assembly's press gallery in 1962; see *New Age*, 15 March 1962. "Uys was a lovely guy. He had a lot of flair. We liked him a lot." James Zug interview with Albie Sachs, March 1994.

Bunting had originally been a member of the SASJ when he worked for the *Rand Daily Mail* and *Sunday Times* in 1940 and 1941. Shaun Johnson interview with Brian Bunting, January 1984. Afrikaans journalists also were not allowed to join the SASJ in the 1940s. When Bunting was banned from newspaper work in 1963, two officials of the Cape Town branch of the SASJ, Ken Owen and Miles Brokensha, sent a protest telegram to Vorster. See Ken Owen, "Media Bosses Who Played the Apartheid Game," *Mail & Guardian*, 18 July 1997.

The Newspaper Press Union, the South African association that organized newsprint deliveries, blackballed the newspaper. As a result, Barrack Street had to import, at great cost, its own newsprint directly from Canada, paying for it in advance and paying import duties.

In 1958 the Commonwealth Press Union, after over a year of dithering, turned down *New Age*'s application for membership. See *Guardian*, 13 March 1947; *New Age*, 19 April 1962; and Thornton Collection, UCT, A24. See also 13 April 1961, when Ruth First, Robert Resha, and Alex La Guma attempted to start a non-racial trade union for journalists called the National Union of South African Journalists.

167. Bunting, *Rise of South African Reich*, 303–4.
168. Brian Bunting Collection, UWC. Bunting wrote, "I would like to emphasize that I am not activated by malice or disrespect towards the Commission in taking this step."
169. Bunting argued: "I stand for the repeal of the Act [Suppression of Communism] and full freedom to propagate communism—I stand for the total repeal of the Act, believing that the South Africa people should have the right to propagate any political creed and work for the establishment of whichever social system they think best." This paragraph was eventually discarded. Thornton Collection, UCT, A24.
170. *Advance*, 6 November 1952. See *Guardian*, 31 March 1941 when they battled *Die Transvaler*; 12 July 1945 for a reprint of a cartoon that ran in a Nationalist Party journal about the *Guardian*. The Afrikaans press extensively campaigned for the government to ban the *Guardian* from the railway bookstalls in the months preceding the March 1940 ban. Bunting, *Rise of South African Reich*, 300: "The man who daily reads the newspapers of his political opponents is bound in the long run to be influenced by what he finds there. Whether he is conscious of it or not, he will be exposing himself."

See a small, three-inch report on the Congress of the People, which focused mostly on the arrests, in the *Cape Times*, 27 June 1955. See Piet Meiring, *Inside Information* (Cape Town: Howard Timmins, 1973). Meiring was an editor at *Die Transvaler*.

See also Albert Luthuli, *Let My People Go*, 142: "The noisy opposition in most of the white Press advertised the Congress and the Charter more effectively than our unaided efforts would have done, so the awakening spread further."

171. *Cape Guardian*, 19 March 1937.
172. Arthur Barlow, *That We May Tread Safely* (Cape Town: Tafelberg-Uitgewers, 1960), 123.
173. Benson, *Struggle for Birthright*, 105. See *Natal Mercury*, 15 February 1918: "It is a grave matter if they [communists] tamper with the 200,000 boys on the Rand. Once they permeate the natives with the pernicious doctrine that they are slaves, and so on, there will be trouble."
174. *Star*, 16 September 1957.
175. Benson, *Far Cry*, 72.

176. *Guardian*, 4 October 1945.

177. *New Age*, 27 December 1956. See 17 October 1957 for when A. P. Cartwright resigned as editor of the *Rand Daily Mail* because of a secret police order concerning the Nationalist cigarette boycott. See *Guardian*, 26 February 1942, for an open letter by Betty Radford about the political harassment of a columnist at the *Rand Daily Mail* and *Sunday Times*.

178. *New Age*, 10 April 1958; and Bunting, "The Story Behind the Non-White Press," 2. His articles that formed the basis of the pamphlet were published in *New Age*, 20 and 27 November and 4 December 1958.

"*New Age* has become the conscience of South Africa," Bunting editorialized on 6 January 1956, after detailing some typical financial hassles on 20 December 1956. Fred Carneson wrote, "We doubt if any other paper in South Africa could have continued to appear under these circumstances."

179. Bunting, *Rise of the South African Reich*, 321. In 1939 Prime Minister Hertzog circulated a draft bill legislating a censorship code. White newspaper editors hastily gathered and devised a code of conduct that they agreed to abide by if Hertzog dropped his bill. The war and Hertzog's removal from office swept the issue away until 1962.

180. *Fighting Talk* 16, no. 6 (July 1962).

181. Bunting, *Rise of the South African Reich*, 322. The code was relatively harmless, subscribing to principles most newspaper editors would naturally agree to, but one clause read: "Comment should take due cognizance of the complex racial problems of South Africa and should take into account the general good and the safety of the country and its peoples."

182. Alan Gregor Cobley, *Class and Consciousness: The Black Petty Bourgeoisie in South Africa, 1924–1950* (New York: Greenwood Press, 1990), 81.

183. See *Guardian*, 7 and 14 June 1945. In 1956 *Bantu World* changed its title to *World*.

184. Sampson, *Drum*, 55: "Henry was the presiding spirit in the *Drum* office. With his gay charm, his massive courage, his fits of wild excess and remorse, he was all African." For more on Nxumalo's investigations, see pp. 37–50 (and *Drum*, March 1952) on Bethal, and pp. 185–97 (and *Drum*, March 1954) on jail.

James Zug interview with Jurgen Schadeburg, July 1994: "Once Henry tried to get arrested by riding in a white compartment and the official, a railway official, saw him and said, 'Aren't you Mr. *Drum*?' And he wouldn't arrest him." For an enlightening perspective on Nxumalo, see Peter Abrahams, *Return to Goli* (London: Faber & Faber, 1953), 119–21 and 139–54. (See *Guardian*, 1 May 1952, for a picture of Abrahams returning to South Africa.)

185. Bunting, "The Story Behind the Non-White Press," 6: "It is only after one has examined the make-up of the so-called Non-European press and realised how little it can really claim to represent or serve the interest of the Non-European people of South Africa that one begins to appreciate the tremendous importance of *New Age*."

186. *New Age*, 29 January 1959, and 5 December 1958. Bunting added: "What ethical standards does the *Post* use, when, after printing a garbled version of what I said, it accuses me of inaccuracy and refuses to print my reply?" See *Liberation* 10, no. 16 (February 1956): *Bantu World* and the *Golden City Post* were "ignorant or malicious scribblers." The *Post* was edited for a time by former *Guardian* columnist Henry Nxumalo. See also Bessie Head, *The Cardinals: With Meditations and Stories* (Cape Town: David Philip, 1993).

187. Bunting, "Story Behind Non-White Press," 3. Carter and Karis, *From Protest to Challenge*, 3:18. See Paton, *Cry, the Beloved Country*, 28. Walter Sisulu wrote a few articles for *Bantu World* in the early 1940s. See Meredith, *Nelson Mandela*, 33. When the ANC launched its cam-

paign for a £1 per day minimum wage, the *World* opposed it and started its own campaign for ten shillings a day. In 1946 *Bantu World*'s circulation, despite the support of its owner, the Argus conglomerate, was 24,000. Les Switzer, "Language, Text, Community: A Critical and Historical Perspective on South Africa's Resistance Press," South African and Contemporary History Seminar, Institute of Historical Research and Department of History, University of the Western Cape, October 1994, p. 10.

188. *New Age*, 12 January 1956. "If Goebbels wished to start up a daily newspaper in South Africa today, *New Age*, for one, would not support his application." *Liberation* 10, no. 16 (February 1956), and *Liberation* 10, no. 19 (June 1956) for an apology given to *Bantu World*. See *New Age*, 6 January 1956, when the weekly printed a letter from a Congress supporter who called the move to exclude *Bantu World* "surprising and regrettable."

189. *New Age*, 6 September 1956. Harmel, writing under the nom de plume Alan Doyle, criticized *Drum*'s tone of "fatuous self-congratulation." See Mac Fenwick, "'Tough Guy, Eh?' The Gangster Figure in *Drum*," *Journal of Southern African Studies* 22, no. 4 (December 1996): 617–32.

190. *Fighting Talk*, June 1955.

191. *New Age*, 19 September 1957. Years later, Brian Bunting explained the hostility towards *Drum*: "I think we were rather contemptuous of all the sort of frivolous, pornographic aspects of *Drum* and *Zonk* and all the rest of it and their social interests. . . . I mean, you did get politics in shebeens, too, but it was almost something artificially encouraged—the sort of atmosphere you know which wouldn't be hostile to us, but not exactly interested. We tended on the whole to feel dismissive of them as any sort of political force." Shaun Johnson interview with Brian Bunting, January 1984.

192. *New Age*, 3 January 1957: his murder "underlined the perilous nature of the teeming African townships." See 10 January 1957 for Phyllis Altman's obituary on Nxumalo, who was working on a book commissioned by Alfred A. Knopf. "It was a mysterious thing," said Schadeburg of Nxumalo's murder. "He officially wasn't working for the paper. He was drinking quite a lot. The story was about a police doctor doing illegal abortions in Sophiatown. Apparently the nurse got wind about Nxumalo, and someone knifed him to death, right around Christmas." Apparently ten years later, before being hanged, a prisoner in Johannesburg confessed to the killing and said he was paid £200. See Anthony Sampson, foreword, "*Drum*: An Index to 'Africa's Leading Magazine,' 1951–1965," ed. Dorothy C. Woodson, African Studies Program, University of Wisconsin, 1988. See also *Drum*, February 1957.

193. James Zug interview with Brian Bunting, November 1994.

194. *Guardian*, 23 March 1944.

During the Treason Trial, the Crown asked Nelson Mandela to explain the Congress movement's relationship to the media:

—What was the best paper from the point of view of your struggle?

—Well, *New Age* did so, but there are other papers, like *Bantu World* at times, although they are hostile papers. . . . It depended on the issue. On the Defiance Campaign, for example, we got a lot of publicity from the English press, from the *Rand Daily Mail*. It gave us a great deal of publicity. In fact, when the Defiance Campaign was on, I don't think you could easily distinguish between the columns of the *Rand Daily Mail* and those of *New Age*. It depended on the issue. But there are issues which the *Mail* and the *Star* wouldn't give publicity to, which the *New Age* gave publicity to them.

See Tom Karis, The *Treason Trial in South Africa: A Guide to the Microfilm Record of the Trial (Stanford, Calif.: Hoover Institution, 1965)*. Mandela gave the testimony on 15 August

1960, so perhaps he was trying to protect *New Age*, which was then banned under the State of Emergency.

195. *New Age*, 26 July 1956—"photo by courtesy of *Evening Post*"; and 14 March 1957 for one from the *Eastern Province Herald*.

196. *New Age*, 18 September 1958.

197. *New Age*, 5 April 1956. Visser was secretly dating an Indian woman, according to Paul Joseph. See 19 April 1956 for a photograph of Solly Jooma.

198. Shaun Johnson interview with Brian Bunting, January 1984. See 18 and 25 September 1958; Len Lee-Warden raised the matter in Parliament.

199. Morris, *South African Winter*, 112.

200. The first time many staffers noticed the surveillance was in 1952, when the Special Branch watched Barrack Street in the days leading up to the *Guardian* banning. See *Cape Times*, 24 May 1952; "Offices Watched for Days, Say Staff" was the headline.

201. See Slovo, *Unfinished Autobiography*, 86, for a story about a Special Branch detective telling Michael Harmel what he was looking for when searching his house: "Politics, man, politics." The police kept on taking copies of one particular book in the Slovo library that First kept buying: Stendhal's *The Red and the Black*.

202. James Zug interview with Brian Bunting, December 1993. In 1955, when the Buntings erected a one-room prefabricated cabin behind their Clifton Beach cottage, the government sent inspectors, who informed the Buntings of missing permits; with the help of Kahn, Bunting was able to avoid a fine. See Cape Archives, Roeland Street, KAB, B4263, 4/2/1/3/2/708.

203. Hilda Bernstein, *The World That Was Ours: The Story of the Rivonia Trial* (London: SA Writers, 1989), 17.

204. *New Age*, 12 March 1959. Tshawe turned out to be an NIYC member who was selling *New Age* at the college.

205. Chris Vermaak, *The Red Trap: Communism and Violence in South Africa* (Johannesburg: APB Publishers, 1966), 78. Vermaak was a chief crime reporter at *Die Vaderland*, an Afrikaans newspaper in Johannesburg, and had close ties to the police. He had to pay £300 damages to the Slovos. See Resha, *My Life in the Struggle*, 189–90; Slovo, *Unfinished Autobiography*, 102–3; and Alfred Hutchinson, *Road to Ghana* (London: Victor Gollancz, 1960), 13–14.

As First so memorably described it on p. 52 in *117 Days*, while in detention in 1963 the police asked her, "Why did you hold mixed parties?"

"To mix."

206. *New Age*, 8 November 1956. See 18 April 1957 for Harmel banned for five years; 24 December 1959 for Amy Rietstein banned from gatherings for five years; 29 October 1956 for Ruth First, banned in 1954 for two years, received a new five-year banning order which was signed 4 July 1956. She was banned from thirty organizations, twenty-four of which she had never been a member. As Len Lee-Warden said, "They could give them [banning orders] out like they could give out flyers."

207. *Advance*, 15 July and 14 October 1954. Apparently Wolfie Kodesh was also arrested at the same party. James Zug correspondence with Brian Bunting, October 1998.

208. Mandela, *Long Walk to Freedom*, 126.

209. Paton, *Journey Continued*, 106–7. Nadine Gordimer wrote about First: "She was so fearless that she made one feel ashamed of hesitations or calculations of risks one would or would not take, oneself."

210. Mandela, *Long Walk to Freedom*, 109. When the police arrived at the scene, they said to Man-

dela, "kaffer, jy sal kak vandag"—Kaffir, you will shit today.

211. *New Age*, 18 April 1957 for Mbeki; 6 November 1958 for Resha; 18 June 1959 for La Guma (once he was with Ronald Segal and Joe Morolong when they were delivering potato-boycott leaflets to Langa); and 30 October 1958 for Tennyson Makiwane.

212. *New Age*, 5 and 26 March 1959, on Garnet Parkin.

213. *New Age*, 16 May and 29 August 1957.

214. James Zug interview with Douglas Manqina, December 1993: "If you cooperate with the police instructions, you won't sell *New Age*. You mustn't cooperate with them, or you won't sell it." See *New Age*, 12 March 1959; 25 September 1958 when Nathaniel Molaoa, an ANC leader, was told not to sell *New Age* in Langa.

215. *New Age*, 29 May 1958 on Joseph; see articles of hers in February and 9 April 1959. For Mosiane, see 14 January 1960; for Ngotyana, see 26 June 1958; and for Molaoa, see 25 September 1958.

216. James Zug interview with Wolfie Kodesh, March 1994; *New Age*, 18 April and 24 October 1957, and 12 June and 17 and 24 July 1958. See 17 December 1959 for a photograph of Motloheloa, Kodesh, Hymie Barsel, Duma Nokwe and Elizabeth Mafekeng in Basutoland.

　　With his usual verve, Motloheloa started selling *New Age* in Maseru. Within a year he had one hundred weekly customers and had organized other sellers who sold ninety a week. See 18 September 1959 and 13 November 1958—"Remarkable how sales of *New Age* have done a Sputnik in Basutoland in the last few months."

217. *New Age*, 13 May 1957. In the first month of operation, 120 ghosts made 2,000 arrests.

218. *New Age*, 23 May 1957. Certificates of Merit apparently were forms given to Africans by the government so that they would not be arrested for a pass offense due to their presence in Johannesburg. The ghost squad handcuffed and threw in jail six other Treason Trialists, a scene that *New Age* caught on film. See *New Age*, 15 August 1957, with front-page photographs of Carneson arguing with the ghosts; Gert Sibande and Isaac Bokala were among those arrested. See also Mbeki, *Learning from Robben Island*, 5.

　　See 5 December 1957 for a picture of the ghost squad in Western Native Townships. The spirit of the ghosts lived on; see 23 March 1961.

219. *New Age*, 31 December 1959. The Windhoek riots occurred on 10 December 1959; twelve Africans were killed and forty wounded.

220. Helen Joseph, *Side by Side*, 43.

221. Weinberg, *Portrait of a People*, 144.

222. *New Age*, 20 August 1959 and 21 January 1960. In 1959 Ronald Segal's car was also blown up; Segal, *Into Exile*, 207–8.

223. *New Age*, 15 May 1958 and 25 May 1961. See Brian Bunting, introduction to *And a Threefold Cord*, iii. James Zug interview with Brian Bunting, December 1993: "We had no clue about it, nobody knew what that was about. Alex was so relaxed, he treated it in an offhand way, but the rest of us were pretty alarmed."

224. Clingman, *Bram Fischer*, 283.

225. *New Age*, 20 March 1958; and Frankel, *Rivonia's Children*, 15 and 52. James Zug interview with Wolfie Kodesh, December 1993: "A lot were in somebody's backyard, and no, I'm sure they're still there, all over Johannesburg, drums in people's yards, full of files and banned literature and accounts."

226. Hilda Bernstein, foreword, "Decade of Discontent: An Index to *Fighting Talk*, 1954–1963," ed. Dorothy C. Woodson, African Studies Program, University of Wisconsin, 1992. "We had to find

'safe' typewriters on which to prepare our contributions because if the homes of the editorial board and the *Guardian* office were raided, as they often were, the typed articles could be traced back to the typewriters of banned people."

227. Rob Bartlema and Johan Kortenray, *Govan Mbeki: An Honorary Doctor Behind Bars* (New York: United Nations Centre Against Apartheid, August 1978) 7.

228. *New Age*, 11 July 1959—Mea Laschinger, a freelance reporter assigned by *New Age* to cover the ANCYL annual national conference, was refused a press card by the police. See also 4 February 1960.

229. Hepple, *Press Under Apartheid*, 47.

230. *New Age*, 2 February 1956.

231. *New Age*, 12 July 1956. See 12 September 1957 for a Makiwane article on spies at Fort Hare.

232. Gordon Winter, *Inside BOSS: South Africa's Secret Police* (London: Penguin, 1981), 65: The police asked General China if he wanted to be an informer. He replied, "I would rather die than betray my people."

233. James Zug interview with Douglas Manqina, December 1993.

234. Ruth First Memorial Trust, Institute for Commonwealth Studies, 4.1.10, for a letter dated 18 March 1959 to Mr. Nkambule: "It was a shock to all of us. . . . It certainly makes you think." First sent Mti to Boksburg to do a story on tenants with rent arrears receiving eviction notices, and to Benoni to do an article on high rents. See *New Age*, 26 February and 12 March 1959. Mti was also sacked from his job as a reporter at *Bantu World*. He threatened *New Age* with legal action. See 24 September 1959, when Mti became a fulltime Security Branch detective.

235. Holland, *Struggle for a Birthright*, 101–2; and Frankel, *Rivonia's Children*, 66.

236. Mandela, *Long Walk to Freedom*, 163.

237. Forman and Sachs, *South African Treason Trial*, 12; Mandela, *Long Walk to Freedom*, 173; and *New Age*, 19 December 1957. See *New Age*, 3 March 1956, for when the weekly anticipated Swart's Treason Trial threat with an editorial on comments in Parliament.

Alex La Guma was taken away while his wife Blanche was still in hospital having given birth to a son, Eugene, a few days before.

James Zug interview with Len Lee-Warden, December 1993: "We were living at Clifton at that stage, and yes, they came at about half past four in the morning with a warrant. I thought they'd come just to search as the usual thing. I said to my wife, 'Go and let them in, make them some coffee and tell them to start searching.' I wanted to go back to sleep. She said, 'No, they want to speak with you.' And so I got up and went in there and they said, 'We've got a warrant for your arrest.' And I remember jokingly saying to my wife, 'I must have forgotten to pay a traffic fine.' And he said with a very stern face, 'No, no, for high treason.'"

238. Actually, only 140 were arrested that first morning. Sixteen more were arrested a week later, including Ruth First, who clearly not that concerned about the mass arrests went to the movies on the evening of 5 December with her husband and the Bernsteins. Clingman, *Bram Fischer*, 235.

See Slovo, *Every Secret Thing*, 41. When newspaper reporters descended on the Slovo home to report on the arrest of three little girls' mother, Shawn Slovo, age six, told them: "Mummy's gone to prison to look after the black people." Bail, when granted, was fixed according to race: £250 for whites, £100 for Indians and coloureds, and £50 for Africans.

239. Mattera, *Sophiatown*, 129: "Perhaps the most shocking arrest. . . ."

240. Karis, *Guide to the Treason Trial*, 63. Govan Mbeki, Fatima Seedat, Eli Weinberg, Arnold Selby, and Ray Alexander were listed as co-conspirators in the final case of thirty accused. See *New*

Age, 17 January 1957 and 6 April 1961, about Accused No. 157. Also, see 19 December 1956 of the Treason Trial for an amendment of the summons to get the official name of Real correct. It appears that Ike Horovitch was included in the Treason Trial solely because he was a director of Real.

"It would be giving away no secrets to say that Sonia's husband Brian, who has been the king-pin of South Africa's left-wing press . . . was a much likelier candidate for the dawn swoop than gentle Sonia." Forman and Sachs, *South African Treason Trial*, 26.

241. Mattera, *Sophiatown*, 128.

242. Slovo, *Unfinished Autobiography*, 100. See Morris, *South African Winter*, 25: "Outside the Town Hall you may often observe a few tattered young liberal zealots, frowsy girls and stark young men, distributing pamphlets of protest and making your flesh creep."

243. *New Age*, 13 October and 12 February 1958.

244. Mandela, *Long Walk to Freedom*, 202. Morris, *South African Winter*, 27: "That little white man with the foxy face is, in everything but name, an out-and-out Communist, and is indeed deep in *New Age*, the irrepressible organ of the neo-Communists."

245. *Sechaba*, May 1987; and James Zug interview with Brian Bunting, November 1994: "It was a difficult situation. It was especially hard those first few months before we sufficiently reorganized ourselves. Basically the entire paper had to be reinvented." See also *New Age*, 21 February 1957 for Bunting also visited Johannesburg, and 15 October 1959 when he opened an NIC conference.

The Treason Trial put a great burden on Bunting. Albie Sachs said: "Fred was arrested and Brian wasn't arrested and he had to carry on. In 1960 when the Emergency started Brian more or less indicated he's not going to go underground. He's not going to carry everything."

246. James Zug interview with Amy Thornton, December 1993. Thornton at that time went by the surname of Rietsteen. See Myrna Blumberg, *White Madam* (London: Victor Gollancz, 1962), 60: "She was short, slim, with a certain organisational bearing. Her face was pretty, with loving, deeply felt, intelligent eyes. She had an unusual amount of guts and generosity, and would frequently break into shouts of good-natured laughter." See *New Age*, 27 July 1961, for Thornton's article on Mary Moodley. See also *New Age*, 5 September 1957, for her first article in the weekly on Eric Chisholm, the director of the South African College of Music: "He was a lecturer in music at the College of Music. He had been to some festival and he'd been to Russia. In those days you'd interview anybody who'd been there. The Iron Curtain was firmly in place. I was told to go out and ask him about his trip to the Soviet Union. So I arrive at this man's house terribly frightened and nervous. The first thing I was confronted by was two dogs, totally terrorized me. He took me into his study and said, 'I want to play something for you. Perhaps you'll recognize it.' I thought, 'Oh, God, this man's a musicologist. I'm not going to recognize it. He'll think I'm dumb and uncultured.' So I look at him and he says, 'Do you know the man?'

I say, 'No.'

He says, 'It's Lenin.'"

247. James Zug interview with Mary Butcher, January 1994: "I remember Albie because he always used to lecture at us, always the great theorist and teacher, and would expound at great lengths on many topics. Even in the Modern Youth Society he was very pedantic. We used to pull his leg. I used to pull his leg. He was always taking himself very seriously."

James Zug interview with Amy Thornton, December 1993: "Albie and I were both in the Modern Youth Society. Albie was very serious, pontificating in those days. What is the word— pompous? He hasn't lost it all yet. But you know, it goes back a long, long time because I've known Albie since he was at school. We were friends, really good friends. Even now, when we see each other, it's a nice, warm feeling that goes back a long way."

James Zug interview with Albie Sachs, March 1994. "I loved it, 'World Stage by Spectator.' It was very enjoyable. I used to take Friday afternoons off from my practice. I had this Jekyll and Hyde existence. I would walk over in my suit to the *New Age* office and work on the international news. I inherited a format from Lionel."

248. James Zug telephone conversation with Athol Thorne, November 1993.

249. James Zug interview with Wolfie Kodesh, March 1994. See *New Age*, 27 June 1957 for a Kodesh article on Elsie's River arrests; and 18 July 1957 on Cape Town unemployment.

250. *New Age*, 26 November 1959 on a raid of an ANC building in Macosa; 11 and 18 February 1960 with Joe Gqabi at an Indian squatter camp in Johannesburg.

251. James Zug interview with Ebrahim Ismail Ebrahim, January 1994. A psychologist named Dr. Danziger looked after things until Mistrey came in; see 28 February 1957 for he sold 750 copies a week.

252. *New Age*, 9 January 1958. See 6 November and 4 December 1958.

253. *New Age*, 3 January 1957.

254. *New Age*, 8 October 1959.

255. *New Age*, 7 March 1957.

256. James Zug interview with Brian Bunting, December 1993. James Zug interview with Sonia Bunting, December 1993: "Fred yelled at them, 'you thieves, you miserable thieves' and chased them out of the building."

James Zug interview with Fred Carneson, March 1994: "The bloody bastards. We found them out and fired them. We laid charges against them and handed the matter over to the police. But, as things were in those days, the matter just got dropped. The police did nothing. And in the end, we went to jail, they didn't. It was an unequivocally nasty business. It was something we could well do without, with the Treason Trial and all the rest, to have this sort of thing happen." Their names, Carneson and Sonia Bunting recalled, were Ismail Mohammed and Cecil ———. See *New Age*, 18 February 1960.

257. *New Age*, 27 June 1957 for 30,000 and want 50,000 readers by Christmas; 26 May 1955 for 25,000; 9 June 1955 for a photograph of a seller who sells 500 a week; 22 May 1958—"weekly sales fluctuate sharply"; 30 August 1956 for circulation up 32 percent; 14 November 1957— "sales steady despite price hike."

Shaun Johnson interview with Brian Bunting, January 1984: "We found by experience that you could try as hard as you like to get readers through other means. Short story competitions, baby competitions, beauty competitions, by various sorts of competitions—nothing made any impact at all except politics."

258. The optician was named De Wet. There were a few other consistent advertisers like the African Housing Insurance, Wolfson, and Jack Tarshish. See *New Age*, 1 August 1957 and 17 July 1958. There was also a somewhat regular advertisement for Aspro, the British-made aspirin: "What? Waste my time 'feeling queer'? NOT ME! When I'm 'away from it all' I make sure I am away from depression, pain, headaches, nerviness and all the rest of it too. No 'feeling queer' when I'm on holiday—time's too precious. And that's why I always have my Aspro on hand."

259. *New Age*, 26 May 1955: *New Age* was "boycotted by big business . . . and advertisers have been completely intimidated by the government." Bunting, "Story Behind the Non-White Press," 7: "Any paper which openly voiced the policies of the liberation movement would also find it extremely hard to attract advertising into its pages, as the experience of *New Age* has

shown." In a 1959 publicity flyer, *New Age* spoke of the problem: "These firms won't advertise in *New Age*, although our paper reaches tens of thousands of readers each week and is an excellent medium for advertising. It's either because they oppose our policy, or because they are afraid of being victimised by the Government."

260. *New Age*, 3 March 1955 about a cigarette boycott; 23 May 1957; 6 June 1957 for the names of firms; 22 August 1957 for the Chapman's advertisement; 23 May 1957 for an Mbeki article on the Cape ANC's boycott; 5 September and 14 November 1957 for the Chapman's advertisement again; and 6 February 1958 about Sadie Forman losing her job. Besides Chapman's, the list included Rembrandts, Senator Coffee, Braganza Tea, Glenryck Canned Fish, Neptune Canned Fish, Laaiplek Farm Feeds, and Protea Canned Fish. See Morris, *South African Winter*, 133–34, for an eyewitness account of the boycott; Forman and Sachs, *South African Treason Trial*, 83; and Segal, *Into Exile*, 225–28. *New Age* published the list of Nationalist products to be boycotted only after Segal quoted the contents of the boycott leaflets in court, so the matter was legally in the public domain.

261. The four weeks after the Treason Trial arrests saw £277, £226, £86, and £179 arrive at Barrack Street, all well below the weekly average of £400.

262. Thornton Collection, UCT, A36: £12,000 arrived in 1857, £8,000 in 1958.

263. *New Age*, 17 July 1958 for loan; 10 January 1957—"the four-pager's no long-term solution to our financial problems" (it cost fifteen shillings a page after four, *Advance*, 11 November 1954); 1 August 1957 for when they need £1,000 for newsprint; 12 February 1959 need £800 to shippers and £2,800 before the end of March; 12 April 1956 for the threat that the newspaper will cease from the end of May because it has no money; 5 and 12 June 1958; 26 May and 6 October 1955; 27 September 1956; 28 February 1957; and 8 September 1960. In April 1958 Bunting announced that unless large sums of money came in during the next month, the weekly would be forced to close. £1,940 came in May, and by August £5,242 had arrived.

264. James Zug correspondence with Brian Bunting, April 1991. In May 1958 the weekly paid out a total of £269 in wages.

265. James Zug interview with Govan Mbeki, February 1994, and Ebrahim Ismail Ebrahim, January 1994; and Slovo, *Unfinished Autobiography*, 88: Ruth First's initial salary in 1946 was £25.

266. *New Age*, 28 March 1957.

267. James Zug interview with Douglas Manqina, December 1993. Selling four hundred newspapers a week, Manqina earned about £6.

268. Rebecca Bunting, Brian's mother, regularly gave large donations to the newspaper; see *New Age*, 3 March 1960. Ben and Mary Turok were also consistent patrons; see 4 February 1960.

269. *Advance*, 1 April and 1 July 1954; *New Age*, 8 March 1955 for SACTU which "organised sales drives and fundraisers"; 26 April and 5 July 1956 for an NIC resolution about the newspaper and the NIC giving £111; 12 July 1956 for the TIC which gave £150 and the Overport Social Club in Durban which gave £16 10s.—they usually gave fifteen shillings a month; 26 July 1956 for the TIYC which gave £60; 2 August 1956 when the TIYC gave £110; 29 November 1956 when the NIC gave £411 for the month.

270. *New Age*, 12 January 1956.

271. In a report prepared by Kodesh and Carneson on Real for the Treason Trial, they wrote that "very little financial assistance has in fact been received from any of the mass organisations themselves." Carter-Karis Microfilm Collection, reel 15B.

272. Congress of Democrats Collection, Wits, 231; *New Age*, 28 March 1957; Carter-Karis Microfilm Collection, reel 4B; 17 May 1956 for the COD gave £46; 2 August 1956 for the Johannesburg

COD raising £127. *Counter-Attack*, 10 January 1955. The Bellevue and Youth Branches donated £65 at a recent joint meeting. The COD once lent "nine chairs, some broken, and one desk" to Commissioner Street. Len Lee-Warden persuaded Cape Town COD members to spend their Sundays selling copies of *New Age* on Clifton and Muizenburg beaches; see 10 January 1957. The COD gave *New Age* guest editorials and often placed large advertisements in the newspaper; see 17 July 1958, and 15 October and 5 November 1959.

273. *New Age*, 26 January 1956 for when the four TIYC taggers were found guilty; 5 July 1956 for the sentence of a £50 fine and £120 to Anglo-American. The ANC in Cape Town sold 1,200 a week, and the ANCYL and NIYC in Durban worked together to sell *New Age* and raise funds. See *New Age*, 23 May 1957 and 17 July 1958.

274. *New Age*, 23 August 1956 for a Joseph review; 2 September 1957 on shantytown in Ferreirastown; 26 September 1957 for an article on the ANC; 3 July 1958 for the old friend.

275. *New Age*, 22 December 1955 and 19 September 1957; 14 November and 12 December 1957 for the £1 calendars; and 12 September 1957 for when they sold old "78" records.

276. *New Age*, 22 December 1955—"Go Gay at Xmas Eve Dance at Kahn's"—it raised £600; 6 January 1956; 29 November 1956—"Rock and Roll at *New Age*'s Xmas Dance"—it raised £500; 3 January 1957; and 27 November 1958—"rock 'n' roll your cares away."

"Ivan was always having jumble sales every month," said Hilda Bernstein. See *New Age*, 28 June 1956 for a Johannesburg bazaar; 21 March 1957 for jumble sales in Grassy Park— "bargains galore in clothing"; 28 March 1957 for a jumble at 102 Aggrey Road in New Brighton—"cricket boots and flannels, frocks, wireless set, odds and eats"; 12 March 1956 for a "Children's party Bring and Buy sale"; 5 April 1956 for a rummage sale on Brede Street in Gardens; 28 June 1956 for jumble wanted and a bring and buy sale of cakes, biscuits, and preserves; 14 March 1957 for jumble sales held every month on the Rand: "Don't Delay—Give Away, Yesterday's Fashion Is Old Today"; and 9 February 1957 planning a May Day party.

277. Supplement to *New Age*, 7 December 1961.

278. *New Age*, 27 June 1957—"agents and full-time sellers urgently needed"; 11 April 1957 for announcement; 2 May 1957 for first issue; 25 April 1957 for subscription; 18 April 1957 for flyer backing higher price.

279. D. C. Thompson Collection, Wits, 1906. The leaders included Luthuli, G. M. Naicker, Piet Beyleveld, Thompson, Sisulu, Dadoo and Kotane.

280. *New Age*, 1 March 1956, for announcement. See 17 November 1955, when Carneson said: "Give till it hurts." The campaign raised £5,234 or 52 percent of the amount, but sales did rise by a third during the period, so they considered the campaign a success. See 20 August 1956.

281. *New Age*, 19 June 1958.

282. *New Age*, 24 July and 17 October 1957, and 4 June 1959.

283. *New Age*, 9 January 1958 for Forman's "Chapters" sold out and second printing; 6 November and 4 December 1958 for his "History"; and 7 July 1958 for a letter to the editor from Michael Harmel that said Forman's treatment of the founding of the ANC "reveals a lack of historical sense and perspective." See 25 August 1955 for First's pamphlet on China, sold-out first edition; and 9 June 1955, a long back-page article on her visit. For "The Law and You," see October 1956, February 1957, July 1957. August 1957 and 22 June 1961 for successive editions; "The Law and You" was printed in Zulu—"Mola O Le Neva"—11 January 1962. See also Mtolo, *Road to Left*, 11.

It was cheap for Pioneer Press to print the pamphlets, since they saved the type from the original articles. The Brian Bunting Collection, Mayibuye Centre, has examples of most of the pamphlets.

284. James Zug interview with Ebrahim Ismail Ebrahim, January 1994. One year it was Schermbrucker who came down; another, it was First. See *New Age*, 17 July 1958—"Several weeks ago when it became apparent that our financial position for July would be in a very precarious position, we sent a team of collectors into Natal."

285. James Zug interview with Ismail Meer, February 1994: "Each year Brian Bunting would come to Durban and we would go to Verulam area. I would go to every shop there. And this is the Indian tradition: 'Oh, I haven't seen you, Ismail. How are you?' and so on. I say, 'Oh, greeting is not going to be sufficient. We want 50 Rand' or whatever it is. And the people just gave. Now this was the tradition of contribution. . . . What was fascinating was all the country shops I took him—everybody paid. Those days £5 was a lot of money. We would raise something like £300 in a matter of half a day in Verulam."

James Zug interview with Brian Bunting, November 1994. "It was more or less automatic after getting the biggest donor. The first one set the standard and the rest followed in line."

286. *New Age*, 23 July 1959. James Zug interview with Ebrahim Ismail Ebrahim, January 1994: "They know that *New Age* was communist, was a leftist paper, but they know at the same time it was an organ that fought against the Group Areas and injustices and other things, apartheid. I mean the paper was campaigning against the Group Areas, so they will support it in that sense, you see. Even if they do not agree with everything the paper says."

287. James Zug interview with Fred Carneson, March 1994. See Dadoo, *His Speeches*. See *New Age*, 12 January 1956, he gave £10, and an article about giving money.

288. James Zug interview with Wolfie Kodesh, March 1994, and conversation with Rica Hodgson, January 1994.

289. Clingman, *Bram Fischer*, 166–67.

290. James Zug interview with Albie Sachs, March 1994. See *Guardian*, 6 May 1952. See also Segal, *Into Exile*, 228—Forman "used occasion of the case [the 1959 permit violation arrests with La Guma] to launch a vigorous onslaught on the whole system of residential segregation. The locations were not concentration camps or leper colonies, he cried. They were simply suburbs in which Africans lived. Why should anyone be prevented from entering them?" Forman lost the case for Segal and La Guma, and they were fined £2.

291. *New Age*, 4 December 1958. See 17 July 1958. Forman's offices were near the South African Library, and he would spend spare hours there working on his doctorate. James Zug interview with Sadie Forman, May 1994: "I once said to him, 'Let's go on holiday.' He said, 'Holiday? Your whole life's a holiday.'"

292. *New Age*, 11 December 1958. See 2 April 1959—"Van Riebeeck Was a Robber." At the Treason Trial, Nelson Mandela said that Forman's articles were "quite inconsistent with the policy of the African National Congress." See #16092 of Mandela's testimony on 15 August 1960.

293. *New Age*, 22 September 1955; 24 May 1956; and 22 October 1959. Despite his illness, Forman was still banned by the government on 6 August 1959.

294. *New Age*, 13 August 1959.

295. James Zug interview with Sadie Forman, May 1994. When Barnard operated on him, he found five leaking valves.

296. *New Age*, 5 November 1959. See *Fighting Talk*, December 1959. Albert Luthuli wrote, "His courageous stand in the freedom struggle will always inspire us." In Basutoland, John Motloheloa wrote, "Will we never see our beloved Lionel again? Is he really gone? One couldn't believe the rumours that went round for four days before we got *New Age*. With Lionel gone, the burden is really going

to be much more heavy in the political field, more especially with you people in the office." Ruth First's tribute read, "His friends knew him as a man of lively and alert mind, serious and taciturn at times, at others puckish and amusing, always considerate, gentle and undemanding."

297. Lionel Forman, *A Trumpet from the Housetops: The Selected Writings of Lionel Forman* (Cape Town: Mayibuye Centre, 1992), 218–22. Jack Simons said: "Lionel's life was like a shining sword pointed straight at the heart of injustice."

298. James Zug interview with Sadie Forman, April 1994, and Brian Bunting, November 1994; *New Age*, 22 October 1959. South Africans usually sang a version of "The Internationale" that began "Arise ye prisoners of starvation. . . ."

The text of the Langa song in English: "Lionel Forman is a small man but in court he is as big as Table Mountain / When Forman passed away / All homes were unhappy when Forman passed away / The white bones of an African are underground where he used to stand / The spirit of Forman still remains in our hearts and so does his good work / The bones of an African are underground where he used to stand / His spirit will live in those who come after and continue."

After Forman died, Sadie Forman spent one year earning an honours degree at UCT under Jack Simons. Between 1964 and 1969, she worked as a proofreader at Pioneer Press. She then went into exile.

CHAPTER SIX. THE BLOODY POLE ON THE HILL: SHARPEVILLE AND BEYOND, 1960–1963

1. See Odendaal and Field, *Liberation Chabalala*, ii.
2. James Zug interview with Sadie Forman, May 1994; Ray Alexander, January 1995; Fred and Sarah Carneson, March 1994; Blanche La Guma, November 1994; and Brian and Sonia Bunting, November 1993. Shaun Johnson interview with Randolph Vigne, September 1984.
   Jack Cope wrote a poem entitled "New Year's Day 1948": "The moon rose late last night, half-turned and sere / shining unseen among the reeling crowd / with linked hands singing out the year. . . ."

   James Zug interview with Mary Turok, January 1994: "I was shocked by all the affairs. People were always going off into dark corners and necking, especially at Christmas time when all the Johannesburgers came down. The world came down and we all let out all the tension. We let our hair down and it often got out of hand." Albie Sachs, *The Soft Vengeance of a Freedom Fighter* (New York: HarperCollins, 1990), 21: "Being in the struggle and willing to give our lives surely does not mean that we must be style-less and dry and without passion for enjoyment."
3. Typical of mining practices in South Africa, 223 of the miners were from Basutoland and 206 were from Mozambique.
4. James Zug correspondence with Benjamin Pogrund, April 1994. See Tom Hopkinson, *In the Fiery Continent* (London: Victor Gollancz, 1962), 242–43. Hopkinson was the editor of *Drum* at the time.
5. *New Age*, 28 January and 4 February 1960, and 5 January 1961. See also *Rand Daily Mail*, 22 January 1960; *Star*, 22 and 23 January 1960.
6. The PAC also called for a minimum wage of £35 a month, adding £5 to the ANC and SACTU's long-standing campaign for £1 a day or £30 a month.
7. Sobukwe, jailed that morning, was not released until nine years later, and then was kept under house arrest until his death in 1978. See Myrna Blumberg, *White Madam* (London: Victor Gol-

lancz, 1962), 23–24.

8. See Ambrose Reeves, *Shooting at Sharpeville: The Agony of South Africa* (Boston: Houghton Mifflin, 1961); Tom Lodge, *Black Politics in South Africa since 1945* (London: Longman, 1983), 201–26, Heidi Holland, *The Struggle: A History of the African National Congress* (New York: George Braziller, 1989), 119–20; and Mary Benson, *The Struggle for a Birthright* (London: Penguin, 1966), 222.

9. Blumberg, *White Madam*, 24. The driver was a coloured *Cape Times* reporter.

10. Fatima Meer, *Higher Than Hope: The Authorized Biography of Nelson Mandela* (London: Penguin, 1988), 147.

11. Lodge, *Black Politics*, 218. One hundred people marched on 23 March, and 4,000 on 25 March. There were only 900 PAC members in Langa at the time.

12. C. J. Driver, *Patrick Duncan: South African and Pan-African* (London: Heinemann, 1980), 173–81; and Lodge, *Black Politics*, 217.

13. Lodge, *Black Politics*, 218–19; and Joseph Lelyveld, *Move Your Shadow: South Africa, Black and White* (New York: Penguin, 1985), 323.

14. *Contact*, 16 April 1960. "Be careful of *New Age*," Kgosana said. "Let us close our ears to what the newspapers say and continue with our dynamic program."

15. *New Age*, 24 March 1960. Bunting might have possibly been envious of Duncan's audience with Harold Macmillan at a garden party, when the prime minister visited Cape Town seven weeks before.

16. Phillip Kgosana, *Lest We Forget* (Johannesburg: Skotaville, 1988), 22: "When Duncan heard the name 'Bunting' he grabbed the receiver from my hand and slammed it down in a wild fury. . . . He was so agitated with my having contacts with communists . . . Bunting roared with laughter when I told him about my debacle with Duncan."

That night Duncan recorded it differently in his diary: "I spoke to him about Bunting. I said the PAC campaign was his campaign, and he must run it the way he wanted, but if he were to work closely with Bunting, he would have to count us out. I reminded him that Sobukwe had split with the ANC over the question of communist domination and told him that the Liberal Party was firmly anti-communist. He was extraordinarily nice about it and thanked me for the advice. "I am still young," he said, "and shall be always grateful to you for advice when you see any way in which you think we are going wrong." Driver, *Patrick Duncan*, 176.

17. Sympathetic shopkeepers, Alex and Blanche La Guma, and the Buntings paid for the food. James Zug interview with Brian Bunting, December 1993, and James Zug conversation with Phillip Kgosana, October 1997. See also Carter and Karis Microfilm Documents, reel 11a, 2DA 17, for Karis notes on interview with Kgosana, p. 5; and Meer, *Higher Than Hope*, 147. Kgosana also gave an interview to the *Argus*; Lelyveld, *Move Your Shadow*, 324.

In 1961, when Brian Bunting wrote a long editorial criticizing Patrick Duncan for his take on the Maritzburg conference, Duncan replied: "We can remember the absurd manner in which *New Age* reported the Cape Town disturbances of 1960 almost without mentioning the Pan Africanist Congress. You criticise us for anti-communism, as if that were something to be ashamed of." Bunting appended an editor's note at the end of Duncan's letter: "All that *New Age* is pleading for is that these prejudices of his should not be allowed to hamper the creation of maximum unity between all sections of anti-Nationalists to defeat apartheid." *New Age*, 9 March 1961.

18. Edward Feit, *Urban Revolt in South Africa, 1960–64* (Evanston, Ill.: Northwestern University Press, 1971), 52; and *New York Times*, 31 March 1960.

19. Lelyveld, *Move Your Shadow*, 315.
20. James Zug interview with Brian Bunting, December 1993. "History was being made. We knew that. We stood on the roof and gasped at the crowd coming down Buitekant. There were so many. We had never seen so many Africans together, all at once. And they were so orderly and quiet. Kgosana was so cool and efficient."

On hearing about the Sharpeville massacre the week before, Ronald Segal had gone to "the hot quiet of Barrack Street to the offices of *New Age*." There, he and staff members joked that "Cape Town would learn the news of successful revolution by telegram from Pretoria." Now the revolution was right outside their offices. Ronald Segal, *Into Exile* (London: Jonathan Cape, 1963), 273.
21. Some onlookers later claimed Duncan pushed his way to the front and advised Kgosana. Descriptions of the Langa March, especially the debate over Patrick Duncan's role, can be found in Lelyveld, *Move Your Shadow*, 315–26—the Colonel was denied promotion to brigadier for negotiating with Kgosana; the *Spectator*, 8 April 1960; *Cape Times*, 31 March 1960; James Zug interview with Kwedie Mhlapi, November 1993; Edward Roux, *Time Longer Than Rope: A History of the Black Man's Struggle for Freedom in South Africa* (Madison: University of Wisconsin Press, 1964), 410; Janet Robertson, *Liberalism in South Africa, 1948–1963* (Oxford: Clarendon, 1971), 216; Anthony Hazlitt Heard, *The Cape of Storms: A Personal History of the Crisis in South Africa* (Fayetteville: University of Arkansas Press, 1990), 96; and *Weekly Mail & Guardian*, 27 March 1997. Interestingly, other demonstrations in South Africa that day were not peaceful. In Worcester, sixty miles from Cape Town, police used tear gas to break up a procession; in Stellenbosch, a police baton charge dispersed marchers, who turned and burned government buildings. *New York Times*, 31 March 1960.
22. Vigne, *Liberals Against Apartheid*, 126.
23. Blumberg, *White Madam*, 33—there were 10,000 marchers in Durban and 3,000 in Johannesburg. See Lodge, *Black Politics*, 223; and *New York Times*, 6–9 April 1960. On 5 April an African policeman was hacked to death and two white policemen were injured in Nyanga.

In an editorial on 6 April the *New York Times* said, "Apartheid is an economic as well as a moral absurdity; in its stubborn attempt to go ahead with it the Verwoerd Government is moving steadily down a dead-end street." With the banning of *New Age*, the *Times* noted on 9 April, "There has been an unusually heavy sale of foreign papers here" in Cape Town.
24. Blumberg, *White Madam*, 35; 234 people were arrested on the morning of 30 March, and over the course of the next week they arrested over two thousand "Section Four" political men and women, as well as 18,000 so-called "idlers" or African men who were considered troublemakers.
25. *New Age*, 8 September 1960; see Thomas Karis and Gail M. Gerhart, *From Protest to Challenge* (Stanford: Hoover Institution, 1977), vol. 3, *Challenge and Violence, 1953–1964*, document 52 ("Congress Fights On" April 1960), 577–79 for list of detainees, which included many *New Age* supporters, sellers, and staff members: Ronnie Press, Trudy Gelb, Hilda and Rusty Bernstein, the Cachalia brothers, Issy Heyman, Jack Simons, Helen Joseph, Paul Joseph, Mary Moodley, Issy Wolfson, Harold Wolpe, Babla Saloojee, Walter Sisulu, Nelson Mandela, Moosie Moola, J. B. Marks, Harry Bloom, Cissie Gool, Jimmy La Guma, Harry Lawrence, Zollie Malindi, Jack Tarshish, Sarah Carneson, Denis Goldberg, Temba Mqota, Raymond Mhlaba, Errol Shanley, Dawood Seedat, Harry Gwala and Z. K. Matthews.
26. *New Age*, 7 April 1960.
27. James Zug interview with Albie Sachs, March 1994.
28. *New Age*, 8 September 1960. "A systematic publishing of matter which is, in my opinion, of a

subversive character," was Erasmus's reason. See *Sunday Times*, 10 April 1960, for a letter from Graham Pringle, a direct descendant of Thomas Pringle.

Contact was not banned, and its circulation jumped to 30,000. See Vigne, *Liberals Against Apartheid*, 127.

29. James Zug telephone interview with Nondwe Mankahla, March 1994: In Port Elizabeth, Nondwe Mankahla, the only staffer left at Adderley Street, confronted the Security Branch detectives when they arrived. They asked her who she was. "I am Nondwe," she said calmly.

"You must close this office," the lead sergeant told her. "Why are you here?"

"To collect letters—" and before she was finished, the detectives were rushing to find any papers of interest.

30. Lee-Warden was able to stash away a few copies, one of which ended up in the hands of Paul and Adelaide Joseph in London. The edition (volume 6, number 25) is not included in microfilmed copies of the newspaper.

31. Mary Benson, *Struggle for a Birthright*, 226; and Kortenray and Bartlema, *Goven Mbeki*, 13.

32. James Zug interview with Douglas Manqina, December 1993.

33. *New Age*, 8 September 1960. Andre Odendaal interview with Blanche La Guma, April 1989, UWC. Blanche La Guma, Sadie Forman, and Hettie September went to Margaret Ballinger to request visiting privileges with the prisoners. The police granted Blanche two half-hour visits a week. Later they halted the visits. "I nearly went mad," Blanche said. "I banged on that bloody door . . . because I demanded a visit." She suspected Alex had been transferred from Roeland Street to Worcester and drove out immediately. "The prison authorities were very surprised to see me for the afternoon visiting hours that day."

34. Lewis Sowden, *The Land of Afternoon: The Story of a White South Africa* (New York: McGraw-Hill, 1968), 214; and Slovo, *Unfinished Autobiography*, 119–43.

35. In 1993 Brian Bunting was amused to return to Roeland Street to do some research at the National Archives, which had been installed in the former jail. While registering, the librarian asked if he had been there before. "Not under these circumstances," he said.

36. James Zug interview with Jack Barnett, December 1993: "Those were the days when the Nats weren't so brutal. Actually, when I look back, that detention was extraordinary. I mean, it was a lot of friends, and we were all together. We weren't in solitary. There was no kind of threat of torture. I was in for nine weeks. We were in Roeland Street and then they took us to Worcester. Brian was one, Johnny Morley, Jack Tarshish, Harry Bloom, I think Jack Simons. In Worcester we were all together, we had a kind of courtyard. In fact, I was actually, two of my staff were detained as well, so we actually ran our practice from there. I had the distinction of being the only architect who practiced from jail." .

37. Dadoo, *His Speeches*, 43.

38. James Zug interview with Amy Thornton, December 1993: "They told me I was being charged with 'sidition.' They spelled it, 'sidition.'" See Blumberg, *White Madam*, 66 and 89. Next to Thornton's neat, long paragraphs on the Freedom Charter was a piece of graffiti written by a previous prisoner—"Sue is a cool-gone cunt." The warder made Thornton scrub off her Freedom Charter, but deemed it appropriate to leave the message about Sue. "This is an Emergency," the warder told Thornton. "Don't you know you can be put against a wall and shot?" Blumberg wrote for the *Daily Herald* in London; her husband Ken MacKenzie worked for *Drum*.

39. Clingman, *Bram Fischer*, 269.

40. Blumberg, *White Madam*, 282–84; and Slovo, *Every Secret Thing*, 51–53. On the morning of the 30th, with her husband Joe Slovo already arrested, First arranged to meet Segal at half past

ten at Magistrate's Court in Johannesburg, where she was offering a test case on a habeas corpus application for Slovo's release. (The wrong *Government Gazette* had been flown to Johannesburg and the emergency had thus not been legally declared.) First never appeared. See Mandela, *Long Walk to Freedom*, 209.

41. Karis and Carter, *From Protest to Challenge*, 3:574. See Turok, *Nothing But the Truth*, 103–18.

42. James Zug interview with Wolfie Kodesh, December 1993: "I had a number of disguises. Oh, Christ, I wore a hat, for instance, a thing I never do. I grew a beard, you know, and wore a tie. I even got a false shoe to make me a bit taller. It wasn't comfortable. I sort of limped, so I chucked it away." See Chris Vermaak, *Bram Fischer: The Man with Two Faces* (Johannesburg: APB Publishers, 1966), 33.

43. James Zug interview with Sonia Bunting, November 1993. She drove up to Johannesburg with Stanley Trapido. After driving halfway through the night, she asked Trapido to drive. He said he did not know how to drive.

"What the hell are you doing then, coming along with me, if you can't drive?" Bunting asked.

"I'm supposed to talk to keep you awake."

44. James Zug telephone interview with Joe Slovo, January 1994. There was a controversy over First's return. According to Ben Turok, the secretariat asked First to come back in June because they needed experienced people like her. She and Jack Hodgson came to Johannesburg from Swaziland. Then First asked to return to Swaziland. "She refused [to stay] on grounds that she had to look after her children. There was a dispute between her and us on this point, and she offered Jack Hodgson instead. We didn't want Jack, we wanted her. I mean, she was a top person, had been on the CC [Communist Party's Central Committee] before. She refused. Anyway, we didn't make an issue of it. She went back at the end, but by then the heat was off." See Turok, *Nothing But the Truth*, 105; and Brian Bunting interview with Ben Turok, November 1973, Brian Bunting Collection, Mayibuye Centre.

First returned to South Africa but lived underground with an assumed name, Ruth Gordon. She boarded with Donald Turgel, an architect, at his home in the northern suburbs of Johannesburg. First began an affair with Turgel, one that lasted until she went into exile in 1964. Her husband, Joe Slovo, returned the favor by fathering a child with Stephanie Kemp while she was married to Albie Sachs. Slovo, *Every Secret Thing*, 49–50, 188–97, and 229–35. See also Slovo, *Ties of Blood*, 312–17.

45. James Zug interview with Amy Thornton, December 1993; and James Zug interview with Brian Bunting, December 1994.

46. *New Age*, 6 October 1960. See Alex Hepple, *The Press under Apartheid* (London: International Defense and Aid Fund, 1974), 37; and Potter, *Press as Opposition*, 118. The magistrate ruled that since the emergency was over, no one could be tried under its regulations. The Crown appealed to the Supreme Court, which referred the case back to a lower court for another hearing. At the second hearing, Real was acquitted on a technicality. Patrick Duncan was also charged with subversion, and 13,000 copies of *Contact* were impounded—he was found guilty and fined £500. John Sutherland, the editor of the *Evening Post*, was charged with contravening the emergency regulations by publishing a report from two Canadian visitors who found South Africa "a country afraid to talk." He was acquitted.

47. *New Age*, 8 September 1960: Bunting referred to how the emergency had thrown the weekly "into complete confusion."

48. *New Age*, 8 September 1960.

49. James Zug interview with Albie Sachs, March 1994.

50. *New Age*, 8 September 1960. Fred Carneson, as so often in these final three years, was officially designated editor. Brian Bunting informed far-flung correspondents that *"New Age* Letter Box Is Now Open Again."

51. *New Age*, 22 September 1960.

52. *New Age*, 6 November 1958 on Hutchinson, and 26 November 1959 on Makiwane. Selby also left, in 1958.

53. *African Communist*, no. 112 (1st quarter 1988). Kahn flew from Accra to London with Adelaide Tambo and her four sons.

54. Dadoo, *His Speeches*, 43.

55. Mandela, *Long Walk to Freedom*, 210–11.

56. *New Age*, 15 September 1960.

57. Ronnie Kasrils, *Armed and Dangerous* (London: Heinemann, 1993), 31.

58. *New Age*, 1 February 1962.

59. *New Age*, 25 January 1962—three Cole photographs on Bantu Education schools; *New Age*, 15 March 1962—on mines and lung disease. Cole was African, but had been able to get himself re-classified as coloured so he could travel freely to work. See Lelyveld, *Move Your Shadow*, 10 and 16. See also Cole's famous collection of photographs, *House of Bondage* ("A South African Ex-poses in His Own Pictures and Words the Bitter Life of His Homeland Today") (New York: Random House, 1967).

60. James Zug correspondence with Dennis Brutus, March 1991. *New Age*, 2 November 1961, and 10 May and 14 and 21 June 1962. See *Fighting Talk*, December 1960. See Colin and Margaret Legum, *The Bitter Choice: Eight South Africans' Resistance to Tyranny* (Cleveland, Ohio: Excalibur World Publishing, 1968). Brutus later recalled, "I did things irregularly. I can't recall, but I did the sports feature every couple of weeks. The news of the fight against apartheid in sport was poorly covered elsewhere. I tried to expose things, what whites didn't know, what the implications of legislation was."

61. *New Age*, 10 August 1961.

62. James Zug conversation with Rica Hodgson, January 1994.

63. For Lipman, see *Fighting Talk* 10, no. 4 (March 1954). *New Age*, 20 April 1961 for an article on SACTU; 4 May 1961 for an article about a clash at Warmbaths, which led to an editorial the following week. James Zug telephone interview with Beate Lipman, October 1994: "It was a very positive, invigorating atmosphere. I was fascinated by sub-editing and typesetting, laying out the newspaper. Through all the intimidation and harassment, I remember we had the strongest urge that we must be seen to publish. We must continue."

For Kgositile, see *New Age*, 13 July 1961, for an article on boxing. James Zug telephone interview with Willie Kgositile, December 1994: "We would meet at the beginning of the week to talk about what was likely to be going on, but Ruth gave us total freedom to take the initiative and find other newsworthy or relevant articles. Eli Weinberg was especially helpful. He trained me and taught me a bit of theory. The paper, especially in those last days, was the movement. The only clear reflection of what Congress was about came out in *New Age.*"

64. Ruth First, *117 Days: An Account of Confinement and Interrogation under the South African Ninety-Day Detention Law* (London: Bloomsbury, 1965), 118.

65. *New Age*, 15 September 1960.

66. *New Age*, 5 July 1962 picture of June 26th celebrations in Dar es Salaam; 26 July 1962 picture of Walter and Albertina Sisulu on their 18th wedding anniversary; and 17 January 1963 article

on opening of ANC centre in Algeria.

67. *New Age*, 24 August 1961. See 11 January and 29 March 1962, the latter an interesting article on why the United Front failed.

68. *New Age*, 27 April 1961. See 23 November 1961 for an article about meeting Jomo Kenyatta.

69. *New Age*, 24 August 1961.

70. *New Age*, 29 September 1960 for an anti-pass leaflet; 23 February 1961; 1 February 1962 on Transkei "independence"; and 24 May 1962.

71. *New Age*, 1 and 8 November 1962—"To date no details on resolutions and conference decisions have reached *New Age*. But reports have filtered in of the vigorous spirit that dominated the proceedings."

72. *New Age*, 1 November 1962; 22 March 1962 for a Nokwe article on Urban Black Councils; 30 March 1961 for a Nokwe interview on the extension of the ban on the ANC.

73. *New Age*, 8 February 1962.

74. *New Age*, 16 November and 14 December 1961.

75. *New Age*, 13 April 1961 message for Africa Day; 12 October 1961; 2 November 1961 for Luthuli's election survey; 21 June 1962 for Luthuli's last statement. He "said it was no coincidence that he had chosen *New Age* to make this statement."

76. *New Age*, 30 March 1961.

77. The law was officially called the General Law Amendment Act, No. 39 of 1961. See *New Age*, 8 June 1961, for an article on solitary confinement for political prisoners.

78. *New Age*, 1 June 1961. For information about the May stay-away, see Benson, *Struggle for a Birthright*, 235–36; Karis and Carter, *From Protest to Challenge*, 3:364; Meer, *Higher Than Hope*, 166.

79. *New Age*, 28 December 1961 for telephone poles, and 16 August 1962 for slogans.

80. *New Age*, 21 December 1961; and *Spark*, 1 January 1963.

81. *New Age*, 21 December 1961 for telephoned near; 8 November 1962 for found its way; 29 September 1960 for an ANC anti-pass leaflet sent to Johannesburg office; 1 February 1962 for by post; 7 June 1962 for slipped under door. See Mtolo, *Road to Left*, 75–76.

82. James Zug interview with Ebrahim Ismail Ebrahim, January 1994. *New Age*, 5 January 1961, sometimes Lodgson House was used as a distribution point. ANC members dropped 20,000 SACOD leaflets about Mpondoland from the top of Lodgson House on Christmas Eve, causing a massive traffic jam.

    James Zug interview with Fatima Seedat, February 1994. Fatima's husband worked underground for a while, and he refused to give her details: "No, I don't know if he was underground—that I don't know.' Because he said to me, 'the less you know the better. Let one man worry. Why must two of us worry?' That part he never used to discuss with me."

83. Mtolo, *Road to Left*, 59–61; and Edward Feit, *Workers without Weapons* (Hamden: Archon, 1975), 168.

84. Indres Naidoo, *Island in Chains: Ten Years on Robben Island*, as told to Albie Sachs (Harmondsworth: Penguin, 1982), 52. See Julie Frederikse, *The Unbreakable Thread: Non-racialism in South Africa* (London: Zed, 1990), 84–85; *New Age*, 31 May 1962, for a picture of Naidoo protesting at a Stravinsky concert.

85. James Zug interview with Douglas Manqina, December 1993: Manqina was not a member of Umkhonto, but he helped recruit Umkhonto soldiers. See *New Age*, 29 November 1962: "I do not think Vorster can suppress communism and he is acting like an old man."

86. "It was an example of too much discipline, unfortunately a too-rare disease." James Zug inter-

view with Govan Mbeki, February 1994. See also Benson, *Far Cry*, 174.

87. Slovo, *Unfinished Autobiography*, 153; Meredith, *Nelson Mandela*, 209; and Mtolo, *Road to Left*, 36. In London, the Hodgsons continued to allow their home to be used as a laboratory. With the help of Ronnie Kasrils, Jack turned the Hodgson bathroom and kitchen into an amateur laboratory as he experimented with propellant powders and homemade rockets. One exploded and burned a mark on the ceiling, which the men hurried to clean before Rica returned home. Kasrils, *Armed and Dangerous*, 107–8.

88. Kasrils, *Armed and Dangerous*, 38: In July 1961 Naicker recruited Kasrils into MK, so he obviously was in a leadership position in Natal.

89. James Zug interview with Ebrahim Ismail Ebrahim, January 1994; Holland, *Struggle*, 142; Mtolo, *Road to Left*, 47–51; and Kasrils, *Armed and Dangerous*, 53–54, for a first-hand description of the attack. See Boon, *Beyond Fear*, 13. Bobby Pillay said Ebrahim was not suited to command a sabotage unit: "In terms of a researcher, Ebrahim was dynamite, but not as a soldier."

90. *New Age*, 27 September 1962, article on the original Pimpernel, Percy Blakeney, an English knight who smuggled reactionary French aristocrats out of France in 1789. Baroness Orczy wrote a 1905 romantic novel based on Blakeney, which in the 1990s was turned into a Broadway musical. Lillian Virginia Mountweazel, the mid-twentieth-century American photographer, once had an exhibit devoted to various Pimpernels. See Bunting Hayden-Whyte, "Esquivalience and Escape: The Pimpernel in History," in the *International Journal of Text* 13, no. 1 (1969): 387–91.

91. Mandela, *Long Walk*, 235–36.

92. See Nelson Mandela, *The Struggle Is My Life: His Speeches and Writing, 1944–1990* (Cape Town: David Phillip, 1994), 156: "I have had to separate myself from my dear wife and children, from my mother and sisters, to live as an outlaw in my own land. I have had to close my business, to abandon my profession, and live in poverty and misery, as many of my people are doing. . . . I shall fight the government side by side with you, inch by inch, and mile by mile, until victory is won. What are you going to do? Will you come along with us, or are you going to co-operate with the government in its efforts to suppress the claims and aspirations of your own people? Or are you going to remain silent and neutral in a matter of life and death to my people, to our people? For my own part I have made my choice. I will not leave South Africa, nor will I surrender. Only through hardship, sacrifice and militant action can freedom be won. The struggle is my life. I will continue fighting for freedom until the end of my days."

93. *New Age*, 13 July 1961. "When *New Age* went to the Mandela home in Westcliff, Orlando, Winnie had just come from a long round of the townships. (She is a social worker.) She laughed when I asked her about her present unsettled life. 'Of course I miss him tremendously,' she said, 'And sometimes Zenani cries for him, but you know we have never had a settled life together. First it was the Treason Trial, and then he was arrested during the Emergency last year. Since we were married in 1958 we have never yet been able to celebrate our anniversary together!'"

94. *New Age* often covered the Basutoland Congress Party. See 7 January 1960 for a report by Joe Gqabi on the BCP's seventh annual national conference; 22 September 1960 for a letter Ntsu Mokhehle wrote to the editor of the Johannesburg *Star* that the *Star* would not print; 5 January 1961 for an article about a plot to murder Mokhehle; and 31 August 1961 for BCP's history.

95. *New Age*, 16 February 1961, long letter to editor from BCP deputy leader O. P. Phoofolo explaining his expulsion and the emergence of a possible rival party.

96. *New Age*, 17 August 1961.

97. *New Age*, 31 August 1961.

98. *New Age*, 7 September 1961. Bunting wrote a letter to Ntsu Mokhehle "assuring him that our columns were open to him if he felt inclined to reply." 14 September 1961, three long letters to the editor.

99. *New Age*, 14 September 1961, reprint of ANC letter to BCP.

100. See *New York Times*, 10 January 1999, for Mokhehle's obituary.

101. Mary Benson, *Nelson Mandela* (London: Penguin, 1986), 99.

102. Mary Benson, *A Far Cry* (London: Viking, 1989), 128; Benson, *Nelson Mandela*, 104; Mandela, *Long Walk to Freedom*, 234–36; and Sampson, *Mandela*, 47–48. Benson remembered entering the flat for the interview: "His welcome was typically exuberant, but when he came to discuss State repression, his demeanor was somber." Benson, *Struggle for a Birthright*, 12.

103. James Zug interview with Wolfie Kodesh, March 1994: "When the emergency ended in 1960, I made up my mind that there were going to be other emergencies in the future, and I was never going to sleep and shiver in the bloody cold. I'd really had enough of that golf course. . . . I learned so much during the emergency that after I leased the flat, I never went into it in the normal course of events, unless I was sure everything was clear, that we weren't being watched. But that, of course, was rare."

104. Lazerson, *Against the Tide*, 156; Mandela, *Long Walk to Freedom*, 241; and Sampson, *Mandela*, 152. The first morning Mandela jogged in the living room, Kodesh was astonished: "I saw him sort of getting up, and he told me he used to run round the townships, you know. I saw him putting on his long johns, vests, and I thought, 'no way, you're not going to run around here. He says, 'who's running, who's going out?' And he was running on the spot. For about two hours. And he said, 'you'll be doing it.' And he got me doing it."

105. Lazerson, *Against the Tide*, 156; Meredith, *Nelson Mandela*, 209; Sampson, *Mandela*, 154. Mandela, *Long Walk to Freedom*, 241: "I fear that I took over his life," Mandela later remembered, "infringing on both his work and pleasure. But he was such an amiable, modest fellow that he never complained."

106. Mandela, *Long Walk to Freedom*, 242; Sampson, *Mandela*, 153; and James Zug interview with Wolfie Kodesh, March 1994. Mandela left the following night.

107. James Zug interview with Wolfie Kodesh, March 1994. Kodesh called himself Keith Shapiro.

108. Meredith, Nelson Mandela, 207.

109. *New Age*, 8 February 1962.

110. Although speculation was rife at the time about who tipped off the police, it is now certain the CIA was involved. See Peter J. Schraeder, *United States Foreign Policy Toward Africa: Incrementalism, Crisis and Change* (New York: Cambridge University Press, 1994), 201–02, 303; Emma Gilbey, *The Lady: The Life and Times of Winnie Mandela* (London: Jonathan Cape, 1993), 305; Benson, *Nelson Mandela*, 107; and Meredith, *Nelson Mandela*, 219–21: Life underground took its toll on Kodesh. When he drove to tell Winnie Mandela of her husband's arrest, she barely recognized him. "He was white as a ghost," she said of Kodesh. "His hair was standing on end. I noticed he hadn't shaved and was wearing a dirty shirt and trousers as if he'd jumped out of bed. You could see something drastic had happened."

    See *New Age*, 14 September 1961, for Michael Harmel reviewing Williams's new play.

111. Sampson, *Mandela*, 174–75, and *New Age*, 25 October 1962, for pictures of Winnie Mandela. First and Harmel were among the visitors Mandela received in prison during the trial. Meer, *Higher Than Hope*, 204.

112. See Carter, *Politics of Inequality*, 42: "While it is always difficult to estimate the effect of a

newspaper which appears under the handicap of potential illegality, the fact that *New Age* openly and vigorously expresses the demand for equality which every Non-European cherishes gives it a power which should not be underestimated."

James Zug conversation with Breyten Breytenback, May 1996: "*New Age* took a heroic stand from the underground in the early 1960s. We all thought of it as vital to the struggle."

113. *New Age*, 26 October 1962 for Parliament bills, and 10 May 1962 for the guest editorial.

114. *New Age*, 9 March 1961; 18 October 1962 Fourie obituary.

115. *New Age*, 23 March 1961.

116. *New Age*, 2 August 1956; see 30 August and 13 September 1956 for a photograph of two Germiston ANC men threatened with banishment.

117. *New Age*, 15 October 1959.

118. *New Age*, 2 and 9 February 1961.

119. *New Age*, 12 July 1962. Helen Joseph, *Side by Side* (London: Zed, 1986), 105–15. The *New York Times* subsequently picked up the story; see Benson, *Struggle for a Birthright*, 271.

120. *Guardian*, 31 March 1939.

121. *Guardian*, 13 September and 18 October 1945; and 20 November 1947 for an article on Angola. *Bantu World*'s column on Africa at the time was entitled "Those Near Us, But Far Away."
   Edwin Munger, "African Notes," 37: "The Slovos share the South African tradition of knowing relatively little about the rest of Africa. When I discussed the general situation in Sao Tome or when a medical researcher described a demographic study in Mozambique, it was clear from the questions that keen interest had to make up for knowledge. Ruth First questioned me on the Mau Mau period in Kenya, and criticised Fenner Brockway for writing without perception of the real situation and not always with the firsthand experience implied."

122. *New Age*, 18 May 1961.

123. *New Age*, 13 July 1961 First in Bechuanaland; 17 August 1961 Gqabi in Swaziland; 7 January 1960 Kodesh in Basutoland.

124. *New Age*, 27 July 1961 for Salisbury; 26 July and 16 August 1962 for Zaza.

125. *New Age*, 23 November 1961 for Tambo; 2 November 1961 for Makiwane.

126. *New Age*, 28 June 1962. Wole Soyinka, a future Nobel Prize laureate, was described as looking "like a dust-coloured Karoo sand-storm."

127. *New Age*, 15 May 1955 for Nkrumah; 7 March 1957; 11 December 1958 for Know Your Continent; 8 January 1959 for Africa on the March; 16 April 1959 for Africa Day; 19 November 1959 for Kenyatta; 19 March 1959 for Banda; 24 December 1959 Bunting; 15 September 1960 massacre in Mozambique; 13 April 1961 for Africa Day; 29 September 1960 for Nigeria; 5 June 1961 for Algeria; 11 January 1962 for Zanzibar; 4 October 1962 for Swapo; *Spark*, 21 March 1963 for Frelimo.

128. *New Age*, 24 August 1961 for Nujomo; 25 October 1962 for Kuanda; 3 May 1962 for Nyerere; and 17 August 1961 for Kenyatta.

129. *New Age*, 5 July 1962.

130. James Zug interview with Albie Sachs, March 1994.

131. *New Age*, 29 November 1962.

132. *New Age*, 16 February 1961. A fine documentary on that story is Raoul Peck's 1991 *Lumumba: Death of a Prophet*.

133. *New Age*, 22 December 1960. See *Contact*, 3 December 1960: "The latest news from the Congo is good. Colonel Mobutu is quietly building up a real Congolese army. . . . When its power is great enough, and the signs are that that day is now near, it will deal with the man who tried to sell

his country to the Russians—Patrice Lumumba."

134. *New Age*, 2, 23, and 30 March 1961. Shaun Johnson interview with Randolph Vigne, September 1984: "The thing that infuriated *New Age* more than anything was Duncan's attitude to Lumumba and the whole Congo. It was a ridiculous blunder. They really got him on that. No, I think I am right about that. I remember taking up with Pat about the Lumumba line. It was totally wrong. Lumumba had an enormous sort of magic."

135. *New Age*, 23 March 1961: "we are nonplussed and saddened"; 30 April 1961 letter to Nasser from Cecil Williams; and 18 May 1961 for a reply from Nasser.

136. Meer, *Higher Than Hope*, 246. Mandela mentioned this story while discussing Mtolo's evidence as part of his statement from the dock at the Rivonia trial.

137. *New Age*, 29 December 1960.

138. Govan Mbeki, *South Africa: The Peasant's Revolt* (London: Penguin, 1964), 121–27. *New Age*, 6 July 1961: the police forced Pondos to drink large amounts of water and then kicked them in the stomach. 10 May 1962: *New Age* was eventually banned in the Transkei.

139. *New Age*, 10 November 1960. See 13 and 20 October 1960.

140. *New Age*, 17 November 1960.

141. *New Age*, 23 February 1961 article by Jones Kgasane. See 26 January 1961 report on Tembuland *New Age* sellers being harassed by the police.

142. *New Age*, 19 October 1961.

143. *New Age*, 5 December 1961. Patrick Duncan accompanied Naicker on this trip.

144. Meer, *Higher Than Hope*, 126. Mandela made the comment in January 1962 in Addis Ababa at the Conference of the Pan-African Freedom Movement of East and Central Africa.

145. *New Age*, 25 January 1962; Fenner Brockway, MP, raised the question in Parliament.

146. See *New Age*, 1 March 1962, for a photograph of Ganyile back at his Basutoland home.

147. *New Age*, 28 June 1962; 9 August 1962 for Somana's abusive language; and 22 November 1962 for Somana and Kathrada. For articles by Somana, see 10 and 31 August and 16 November 1961, and 17 May 1962. See Hepple, *Press under Apartheid*, 42.

148. *New Age*, 27 October and 8 December 1961. See Slovo, *Unfinished Autobiography*, 104. China never missed a day of the Treason Trial. See 8 March 1962 for Grimaas Qinisile; 24 August 1961 and 11 January 1962 for Amsden Slomko; *Spark*, 27 December 1962 for two traffic inspectors who stopped Lydia Tshehle, a Johannesburg seller, and issued her a pink parking ticket for selling without a license. See 6 September 1962 when Perry Verasammy, a seller, and Molete were detained in Sophiatown when Special Branch Detective Dirker stopped their scooter.

149. James Zug conversation with Rica Hodgson, January 1994.

150. Sisulu, *I Will Go Singing*, 131.

151. *New Age*, 18 October 1962.

152. *New Age*, 28 June 1962. Carneson's case was withdrawn after he, with Sisulu's permission, handed in a statement saying he would answer questions. Carneson called the affair "an example of the mechanics of political intimidation which have, unfortunately, become a feature of our life in South Africa."

For more on Mdingi, see 1 February 1962. For more on Turok, see 3 May and 11 October 1962. For more on Sisulu and Harmel, see 26 October 1961, and *Spark*, 7 March 1963, when Sisulu and Harmel were awarded £100 and costs. For more on Gqabi, see *New Age*, 9 February and 27 April 1961, when the case collapsed "like a pack of cards"; and 21 September 1961 for his hitchhiking debacle. For more on Molete, see 31 May 1962 and 24 November 1960 for a letter to the editor from Molete who lived in Moroka—"Make *New Age* their buttered bread." For more on Ebrahim, see 30 August 1962 after he painted "Unite Fight Nazi Bill" around Durban; he was fined R30; 6 July 1961. For La Guma, see 6 July 1961. For Ngqungwana and Kati, see 11 and 18 October 1962, and *Spark*, 20 December 1962: "He rolled up his shirt sleeves and told them he would fight to the death."

153. Harold Strachan and Joseph Jack were also charged in the trial. For an interesting eyewitness account of the trial, see Athol Fugard, *Notebooks, 1960–1977* (New York: Knopf, 1984), 48–51.

154. *New Age*, 22 June 1961; 15 March 1962; Mbeki was arrested at John Soyeye's home and was charged under the Explosives Act after 2 January 1962 explosions near Escom power station and one near Zakele police station; 10 May 1962 acquitted; 11 October 1962 for Mbeki, Ngqung-wana, and Kati who were among twenty Africans arrested and held overnight; 15 May 1962 raid on Port Elizabeth branch offices. James Zug interview with Govan Mbeki, February 1994.

155. James Zug interview with Govan Mbeki, February 1994; Mankhala took over, but didn't write articles. See 3 August 1961 Govan Mbeki, the latter a full-page analysis by Mbeki for the failure of the May stay-away and the "Unholy Alliance" between the PAC and the police.

156. *New Age*, 17 May 1962 Port Elizabeth and Durban offices were raided; in Durban three detectives ended a half-hour search when they found a telegram addressed to Ronnie Kasrils; 19 April 1962 raids after Roeland Street bombs were found (the police also visited the homes of Bunting, Carneson, and La Guma); 23 August 1962 in Port Elizabeth; 20 September 1962 for a lunchtime raid in Barrack Street.

157. *New Age*, 6 September 1962.

158. *New Age*, 29 March 1962.

159. Ruth First, *South-West Africa* (London: Penguin, 1964), 11.

160. *New Age*, 12 January 1961, when two detectives flew to Durban to talk about a 6 December 1960 article titled "Peasants United Against Bantu Authorities." Naicker also received a peculiar phone call from someone pretending to be an African inviting Naicker to a meeting in Bizana.

161. *New Age*, 12 January 1961.

162. *New Age*, 18 and 25 October 1961. James Zug interview with Brian Bunting, December 1993: "One lived in constant tension. You never knew what was going to happen next or who was doing what. We were very much on edge."

163. *Spark*, 27 December 1962.

164. Meer, *Mandela*, 169. See Political Trials Collection, AD1901, Wits, for *State v. Joe Gqabi*. When asked about leaving the country in 1962 without a passport or permit, Gqabi told the court, "I am a journalist photographer by profession. I realised that since *New Age* newspaper was banned, the present paper *Spark* had no future in the country. I thought therefore that if I left the country, I would have better prospects in Dar-es-Salaam."

165. *New Age*, 8 December 1960 Resha article about the lack of advisory-board candidates in Johannesburg; 9 February 1961 Resha articles on the Treason Trial and boxing; 11 May 1961 last Resha article; 29 June 1961 Resha appointed ambassador. If they were not leaving the country, MK soldiers were still ignoring their *New Age* duties. On Boxing Day 1962, Umkhonto hosted its first training camp inside South Africa near Malmesbury in the Western Cape. Albie Sachs, Denis Goldberg, Looksmart Solwandle, and Martin "Chris" Hani were among those instructed in the art of guerrilla warfare. On 29 December, the police raided the camp and took Goldberg and Sachs away for questioning. Lazerson, *Against the Tide*, 231–32; and Holland, *Struggle*, 143–44.

166. *New Age*, 28 June 1962: "As Alex La Guma is banned from attending gatherings we regret that, in terms of the General Laws Amendment Act, we are no longer permitted to publish any of his

writing." A total of 102 people were gagged by the government in August 1962. In *Cape Times*, next to the announcement of the banning of the 102 people was a story on Yves St. Laurent's new collection. See 9 August 1962 for a review of *A Walk in the Night*.

See also Adam Hochschild, *Half the Way Home: A Memoir of Father and Son* (New York: Viking, 1986), 110. As a university student on holiday, Hochschild spent the winter of 1962 in Cape Town working for Patrick Duncan at *Contact*.

While in prison during the state of emergency, La Guma instructed his wife to post the manuscript to Ulli Beier at Mbari Publishers in Ibadan, Nigeria. She did, by registered post. The manuscript was detained at the Cape Town post office for a full year before, by chance, Blanche discovered that the authorities had not actually posted it. She dug out the receipt, retrieved the manuscript, and when Beier passed through Cape Town in 1961, La Guma gave it to him. See Abrahams, *Alex La Guma*, 46; and James Zug telephone interview with Blanche La Guma, November 1994.

167. James Zug interview with Fatima Seedat, February 1994: "If I wanted to speak with Dawood, I must go to the chief magistrate and ask permission. I said, 'bugger that man.' So we stopped that. I even made a baby during that time." The Seedats produced nine children and twenty grandchildren.

168. *New Age*, 12 January 1961. Kodesh said that "it would be a serious hindrance to *New Age* circulation and management in the Transvaal."

169. First, *117 Days*, 118. First was echoing the comment by Horace Flather, the editor of the *Star*, who in 1952 said editing a South African newspaper was "like walking blindfolded through a minefield."

170. James Zug correspondence with Brian Bunting, April 1991. *New Age*, 13 April 1961: "Our circulation is on the up and up."

171. *New Age*, 28 December 1961 for Naaz, a Woodstock restaurant and night club, "the most unique restaurant in South Africa"; 5 April 1962 for "The fabulous Squire 'even-flo' fountain pen"; and 19 April 1962 for an example of professional soccer fixtures run on bottom of back page.

172. *New Age*, 10 November 1960 trip to Natal raised £1,194; 28 September 1961 raised R1,782. August 1961 was a typical month for donations; in four weeks £73, £207, £314, and £13 arrived at Barrack Street. James Zug interview with Brian Bunting, November 1993: once £10,000 arrived from China, without a return address. Bunting never discovered who had sent the *Guardian*'s largest donation ever. See 4 January 1962 and 3 May 1962 for donations.

173. *New Age*, 9 March and 15 June 1961 for Bunting and his IOJ award; 20 July 1961 on Ben Turok; 13 April 1961 Hilda Bernstein in New Delhi; 8 December 1960 watches; 29 September 1960 for advertisements: "We pay a liberal commission"; 4 November 1961 for an all-day fete in Mowbray that raised £300 and had stalls sponsored, inter alia, by the Food and Canning Workers' Union, the Sweets Workers' Trade Union, and the South African Coloured Peoples' Congress; 9 November 1961 for a fete that raised £587; 8 December 1960 for Alf Wylie's band at the Christmas dance.

174. *New Age*, 9 August 1962.

175. *New Age*, 30 August 1962 for notice; 6 September 1962 for both *Die Vaderland* and the *Cape Argus*.

"Politically radical underground newspaper editors operate on the principle that it is impossible to be fiscally sound and editorially free at the same time." Robert J. Glessing, *The Underground Press in America* (Bloomington: Indiana University Press, 1970), 83.

176. *New Age*, 7 June 1956, for the fact that the committee raised £380 in its first two years. See *Guardian* 25 August 1949, money from London party; *New Age*, 2 December 1954, raised £35; 22 December 1955, Christmas cards; 26 January 1956, £40; 31 May 1956, £5 from D. N. Pritt; 19 August 1956, £25; 30 August 1956, £70; 31 January 1957, £65; 4 April 1957, £50; 10 April 1958, £100; 8 January 1959 about Joffe; and 30 July 1959, £100.

177. Essop Pahad, "A People's Leader: A Political Biography of Dr Y.M. Dadoo," unpublished manuscript, Brian Bunting Collection, UWC, p. 207: Rosalind Ainslie, Vella Pillay, Abdul Minty, Kader Asmal, Oliver Tambo, Tennyson Makiwane, Sam Kahn, and Alfred Hutchinson were active members of the committee. See *New Age*, 30 March 1961 Dadoo takes over; 1 December 1960 Alfred Hutchinson and Sam Kahn attended a party raising £125; 30 March 1961, £200; 7 June 1962 Joffe and Dadoo; 1 November 1962, £400; 15 November 1962, £285.

     James Zug interview with Rusty Bernstein, May 1994. "After 1960, when people started going into exile and going to London, they coalesced around the *Guardian* committee. It was the only structure already in place."

178. *New Age*, 30 March 1961. Robeson appeared in the weekly's pages often throughout its history; see *Guardian*, 14 May 1942. The photograph he sent to *New Age* was still proudly displayed on the Bunting's living-room wall thirty years later. 26 October 1961 for Switzerland, where Zeke and Rebecca Mphahlele sent R49.

179. *New Age*, 8 February 1962 for the 25th Anniversary dance—Merry Mac's High-Notes Band was playing and admission was fifty cents; 19 April 1962 for the 4 Aces club in Johannesburg; 8 March 1962 "*New Age* Weekend" announced for the weekend of 24 and 25 March 1962; 29 March 1962 picture of Ebrahim; 5 April 1962 the celebrations raised R1,418.88. The special issue sold 9,000 more copies than normally. Amy Thornton Collection, box 24, Manuscripts and Archives, University of Cape Town, Hodgson letter dated 7 March 1962.

180. *New Age*, 31 May 1962. Vorster, house-arrested in Robertson, had to have a permit to meet his wife when she came down from the Transvaal or when he wanted to go to Cape Town. This experience did not temper his views. In October 1961 he said, "I do not want to belong to this nation of blacks, browns and whites. I want to belong to a white nation."

181. Hansard, 21 May 1962, col. 6070–71; and Hepple, *Press under Apartheid*, 26–27.

182. During the 1824 Somerset Affair, Somerset had insisted George Greig, as printer and publisher of the *South African Commercial Advertiser*, deposit 10,000 rixdollars, lest he publish anything untoward. See Jennifer Crwys-Williams, *South African Dispatches* (Johannesburg: Ashanti, 1989), 15.

183. Hansard, 21 June 1962, col. 6216. *New Age* was noted as "a publication which has not yet been banned."

184. Bunting, *Rise of South African Reich*, 315.

185. *New Age*, 26 January 1961; see 3 April 1958 about a possible attack on *New Age*.

186. Bunting, *Rise of South African Reich*, 316.

187. *New Age*, 17 May 1962.

188. *New Age*, 14 June 1962 for Carneson's letter, and 31 May 1962 for Bunting's editorial. In a letter to subscribers dated 28 May, Bunting wrote, "It is because *New Age* has been the most determined opponent of Apartheid in the ranks of the opposition press that it is to be snuffed out at the pleasure of the Minister of Justice." London *New Age* Committee Collection, Mayibuye Centre archives, University of the Western Cape.

189. London *New Age* Committee Collection, UWC. Bunting continued: "I need hardly emphasise the seriousness of the situation as far as we are concerned. What I am writing to ask now is that

the maximum possible protest should be roused against the proposed banning of *New Age. . . .* It seems to me that this is the sort of issue on which a lot of support could be mobilised abroad, and it would be fine if the Minister could be deluged with protests against his proposal to ban us. . . . An all-out fight is being waged locally. All international support would be welcome."

190. London *New Age* Committee Collection, UWC. Called "A Declaration of Protest against the South African Government's Attacks on the Freedom of Publication and the Press," the letter was also signed by Ronnie Segal, Max Gluckman, John Osborne, Angus Wilson, John Wain, Bishop Ambrose Reeves, six MP's and two CBE's.

191. The *Times* of London declined; the editors of the *Daily Telegraph* and the *Daily Herald* simply signed the declaration; the *Guardian* and the *Observer* published editorials on the issue. See *New Age*, 7 and 28 June 1962. The issue became so internationalized that Vorster received a letter from a man in Gresham, Oregon, about the possible banning of *New Age*.

192. *Spark*, 14 February 1963. In early February 1963, Vorster banned Wolfie Kodesh and M. P. Naicker for five years from gatherings. Each was confined to a magisterial district; directed to report to a police station once a week; forbidden to visit factories, African locations, hostels, and compounds; and forbidden to communicate with any other banned person.

193. *New Age*, 15 November 1962. La Guma was actually house-arrested on 20 December 1962.

194. Bunting, *Rise of the South African Reich*, 219.

195. *New Age*, 18 October 1962; 22 November 1962 for sightless in the desert.

196. Pinnock, "Keeping the Red Flag Flying," 20. See *Evening Post* (Port Elizabeth), 30 November 1962.

197. *Evening Post*, 30 November 1962.

198. *Cape Times*, 1 and 6 December 1962; Hepple, *Press under Apartheid*, 26. In Durban the police came three days in a row; on the third day they drove with M. P. Naicker and Ronnie Kasrils to their homes for further searches.

199. AAM asked supporters to send copies of British newspapers to South African friends "to beat Dr Verwoerd's censorship." London *New Age* Committee collection. See *Spark*, 5 December 1962, for Dadoo in a letter to Vorster calling the ban "arbitrary" and "callous." Peter Brown, the chair of the Liberal Party, issued a statement: "*New Age* has often expressed views with which many of us disagreed, but as a courageous critic of apartheid and as an exposer of the effects of apartheid on those who feel its full weight it was an example to us all." See *Cape Times*, 1 December 1962. *The United Nations and Apartheid, 1948–1994* (New York: United Nations, 1996), 252–53. The statement included a long list of "measures of desperation" besides the banning of the newspaper.

200. *Spark*, 12 December 1962.

201. *Evening Post*, 1 December 1962. The *Times* of London and the *Daily Worker* also reported that angle.

202. *Cape Times*, 3 December 1962.

203. *Spark*, 14 February 1963. See *Cape Times*, 1 December 1962.

204. *Cape Argus*, 30 November 1962.

205. Gordimer, *Burger's Daughter*, 42.

206. Nelson Mandela edited the last issue. See Carter, "Defiance Campaign," 90. *Spark* was the name of Lenin's newspaper—*Iskra*—which he ran in exile at the turn of the century. It was also the name of a duplicated newspaper produced by the South African Trotskyist group The Workers' Party in the late 1930s. There was also a famous quotation attributed to Mao: "A single *Spark* can cause a prairie fire."

207. James Zug interview with Brian Bunting, December 1994; and Shaun Johnson interview with Brian Bunting, January 1984. See *Evening Post*, 5 December 1962.

208. They were the South African Library in Cape Town (until 1954 when the City of Cape Town officially took over that task), the Staats-Bibliotheek der Zuid-Afrikaansche Republiek or State Library in Pretoria, the Bloemfontein Library and the British Museum.

209. *Spark*, 22 October 1962.

210. *Morning Star* continued to come out each month, although it was just two pages long. It even survived the death of *Spark*. Its last issue was 14 May 1963, published by M. I. Cajee of Macosa House, Commissioner Street, Johannesburg.

211. *Evening Post*, 5 December 1962. James Zug interview with Douglas Manqina, December 1993: "I explained to them that, no, the news that we were publishing there, the paper is banned. We publish with this one. It's the same news. They understood that, because most who buy it, they were interested in me and the ANC. They trusted *New Age* because they trust me and the ANC."

212. Letter dated 1 December 1962 in *Spark* microfilm from CAMP. *Spark*, 3 January 1963, the Bishop of Johannesburg wrote back saying he did not want to subscribe to *Spark*. His letter was printed under the headline "Keeping His Copy Book Clean."

213. Bernstein, *World That Was Ours*, 16–17. She did, however, send her *Fighting Talk* copies overseas.

214. *Spark*, 26 December 1962. At least two people were convicted under this law: Reverend A. W. Blaxnall was convicted of having three copies of *New Age* and one of *Fighting Talk* in October 1963; Benjamin Pogrund was given nine-months suspended sentence for possessing copies of the *Guardian*, *New Age*, and *Fighting Talk* in February 1973. Hepple, *Press under Apartheid*, 31–32. See also Benjamin Pogrund, *War of Words: Memoir of a South African Journalist* (New York: Seven Seas, 2001).

215. London *New Age* Committee collection, UWC.

216. James Zug interview with Albie Sachs, March 1994: "It was business as usual in a sense," said Albie Sachs. "We took the banning seriously and re-arranged the editorial board and so forth. But it was the same thing."

217. *Spark*, 14 February 1963.

218. Slovo, *Every Secret Thing*, 54–56. James Zug interview with Sonia Bunting, December 1994: "We lived high on Lion's Head and it was eighty-four steps up the hill. The SB hated to climb up."

219. *Spark*, 7 February 1963. See 7 March 1963, when the police raided all four offices and removed blank *New Age* letterhead stationery.

220. *Spark*, 20 December 1962 for Cissie; 26 January 1963 for *Torch*.

221. *Spark*, 14 March 1963 for Lovedale; 24 January 1963 for township raids; 7 February 1963 for women; 3 January 1963 for New Year's spread; and 14 February 1963 for Zoo Lake.

222. *Spark*, 27 December 1962, and 21 February 1963.

223. *Spark*, 21 March 1963; Hepple, *Press under Apartheid*, 28. The orders on First, Bunting, etc., were issued on 27 February. Vorster might have been motivated by more black-on-white violence. On 2 February 1963 a rabble of Africans used petrol bombs and guns to murder five whites sleeping in caravans near Bashee River Bridge in the Transvaal, and six days later a white debt collector was killed in Langa.

224. James Zug interview with Fred Carneson, March 1994.

225. Don Pinnock interview with Brian Bunting, *Keeping the Red Flag Flying*, 23.

226. First, *117 Days*, 119. James Zug interview with Len Lee-Warden, December 1993.

227. James Zug interviews with Brian and Sonia Bunting, December 1993, and Fred Carneson, March 1994. Carneson even made an exploratory visit to Maseru in 1962 to scout out the possibilities.

   James Zug interview with Jill Murray, January 1994: "I think there was a hell of a lot of tension over people staying and leaving the country. The whites who had worked for the movement had basically been immune from the real force of the Nat government. All of us and them lived very affluent and comfortable lives. I mean, let's call a spade a spade. . . . When the first inkling came that these Nats were really serious and that the fact that you were white didn't mean you were immune came when they went into Ninety Days, when the first people went into Ninety Days. They were tortured and said, 'I'm sorry, but I can't handle this.' Some of the leaving South Africa was a justification. There was a huge tension over that. Nobody will admit it now or very few people because they're all back in South Africa. . . . You have to ask, 'If the paper was doing such a marvellous job, why didn't it function underground?'"

228. 15 March 1963, London *New Age* Committee, UWC. James Zug telephone interview with Eileen Jaffee, May 1994. "There was a small amount of money left over in the bank account in East Finchley, a piffling amount, and a couple of years later Brian asked for it. He was a bit agitated about it."

229. The letter was signed by K. Eagles, a coloured woman on the staff. Other administrative staff at Barrack Street included Joan Adams, a bookkeeper; Gwen Simons, a circulation clerk and Elsie's River comrade; Sonia Dirmeik, a Party member; Ismail Mohammed, a bookkeeper; Ruth Kossew, a seller; Luka Trop, a German refugee whose daughter married Isaac Horovitch; H. Newman, a secretary; and Jellico Ntshona, a circulation clerk.

230. See *Cape Times*, 28 March 1963: "Bannings Cause Newspaper to Shut Down." See also *Sechaba*, May 1987.

231. James Zug interview with Govan Mbeki, February 1994.

232. James Zug interview with Albie Sachs, March 1994: "Fred was very upset because I cut off his head. The photograph in lay-out terms was acceptable and it gave him presence. One of the problems was getting a photograph of Ruth First. We only had one that was years out of date. And she was upset as well."

233. R1,495 was the total.

234. James Zug interviews with Brian Bunting, December 1994, and Fred Carneson, March 1994.

235. Thornton Collection, box 36, UCT.

EPILOGUE

1. First, *117 Days*, 89–102; Bernstein, *World That Was Ours*, 81–82; and "They Were Prepared to Die," ANC document, UWC, February 1967, p. 12. Vernon Berrange represented Solwandle's family at the inquest. Pretoria sent a railway ticket to Solwandle's mother to attend the funeral in Pretoria, but buried the body before she arrived (although they had already waited ten days before burying Solwandle). They also collected his wife, Beauty, and drove her to Pretoria. The ban was served on 19 August, the day he was taken into custody, but only published in the *Government Gazette* on 25 October.

2. *Spark*, 14 March 1963. See also *Cape Argus*, 19 and 22 April and 8 May 1963.

3. Kasrils, *Armed and Dangerous*, 71–74.

4. Vermaak, *Red Trap*, 97–98. First, *117 Days*, 119. The police interrogated First in the same room

from which he was pushed.

5. Gilby, *The Lady*, 69; and Meer, *Higher Than Hope*, 286. While in hiding, Nelson Mandela asked Brian Somana to look after his wife, Winnie. Somana chauffeured Winnie around town and drove her on trips to Cape Town and Swaziland. A small scandal ensued when Somana's wife Miriam cited Winnie as co-respondent in divorce proceedings. In March 1964 Somana was arrested at Winnie's house during a 5 A.M. raid and held under Ninety Days. In January 1965 Somana's younger brother Oscar was charged with arson after a fire was set in Winnie's garage that burned the car of photographer Peter Magubane. Oscar was acquitted because the magistrate thought Winnie had framed him. During the trial, Somana admitted he was in love with Winnie. To cap off this bizarre tale, Gilby quotes the magistrate, R. D. Box, who justified his decision to acquit Oscar Somana by stating, "Transkeian Xhosas were fond of burning their neighbors' properties."

6. *South-West Africa: Travesty of Trust* (Baltimore: Penguin, 1963); *117 Days: An Account of Confinement and Interrogation under the South African Ninety-Day Detention Law* (New York: Stein & Day, 1964); *The Barrel of a Gun: Political Power in Africa and the Coup d'Etat* (London: Allen Lane, 1970); *Portugal's Wars in Africa* (London: IDAF, 1972); *Libya: The Elusive Revolution* (Baltimore: Penguin, 1974); *Olive Schreiner* (with Ann Scott) (New York: Schocken Books, 1980); and *Black Gold: The Mozambican Miner, Proletarian and Peasant* (New York: St. Martin's, 1983).

She also edited a collection of Nelson Mandela's articles, speeches, and statements from the docks, *No Easy Walk to Freedom* (New York: Basic Books, 1965); assisted Oginga Odinga, Kenya's former vice-president, in writing his autobiography, *Not Yet Uhuru* (New York: Hill & Wang, 1967); and helped edit, with Jonathan Steele and Christabel Gurney, *The South African Connection: Western Involvement in Apartheid* (London: Maurice Temple Smith, 1972).

117 Days was turned into a documentary directed by Jack Gold; First played herself, a role that must have brought back painful memories. In it, interrogators asked First why she went to Rivonia to see Mandela. "I went to discuss the government threat to ban our newspaper." These scenes form the core of a 1989 film written by her daughter Shawn Slovo, *A World Apart*.

7. See *New Statesman*, 27 August 1982; *Morning Star*, 24 August 1982; *Manchester Guardian*, 19 and 21 August 1982; Wolfie Kodesh Collection, Mayibuye Centre; and Gavin Williams, "Ruth First: A Socialist and a Scholar," African Studies Center, Boston University, November 1982. The bomb was in a United Nations High Commission for Refugees envelope that had been stolen from UNHCR in Swaziland five years before. The bomb wounded three bystanders—Paulo Jordan, Bridget O'Laughlin and Aquino de Braganca.

Braganca claimed in the Portuguese weekly *Expresso* on 21 August 1982 that the envelope was addressed to him, and that he became aware of something abnormal while trying to open the envelope, letting it fall on the desk, next to which was Ruth First, who died immediately. Braganca, then the director of the Centre, was a close advisor of president Samora Machel and was on the plane with Machel that crashed and killed all aboard in October 1986. See *Mail & Guardian*, 5 August 1994.

See *New York Times*, 27 September 1996, for another mention of the South African police's involvement in her death. Craig Williamson, a South African policeman, admitted to sending the parcel bomb, saying it was meant for Joe Slovo, not First.

In 1992 I visited Mondlane University, but no one there could direct me to the office where she had been killed. Mondlane, ironically, was himself killed by a parcel-post bomb delivered to him in Dar es Salaam in 1969.

See *Weekly Mail & Guardian*, 20 January 1995, for Gillian Slovo's memories of her mother's funeral. First was "sidelined by the movement," according to her husband Joe Slovo, because she had begun to criticize the Soviet Union in the 1970s. *New York Times*, 4 December 1994.

James Zug interview with Joyce Mohammed, January 1994: "[In Maputo] Ruth and I would talk about the old times whenever we got together. We would talk about it. *New Age* was her best. It was her best. The paper and writing, it was her life. That time I'd see her, you know, jumping on the cars, wanting to see what is happening there. She was also small-boned and flexible. One thing is that she was never scared."

Joe Slovo wrote in , "Ruth First Killing Pamphlet," January 1983: "For me there is no measure to gauge her loss. She was a lady of style and elegance both in wit and vanity. She was a comrade whose intolerance of hypocrisy, inefficiency and humbug won her respect even of those who were discomforted by the razor-sharpness of her thrusts. She was a friend and companion with a rich, albeit private, passion."

8. *The Jail Diary of Albie Sachs* (New York: McGraw-Hill, 1966); *Stephanie on Trial* (London: Harvill Press, 1968); *Justice in South Africa* (Berkeley: University of California Press, 1973); *Island in Chains—Prisoner 885/63: Ten Years on Robben Island* (with Indres Naidoo) (Harmondsworth: Penguin, 1982); *Images of a Revolution* (Harare: Zimbabwe Publishing House, 1983); *The Soft Vengeance of a Freedom Fighter* (Cape Town: David Philip, 1990); and *Advancing Human Rights in South Africa* (Cape Town: Oxford University Press, 1992). In 1965 Sachs's girlfriend Stephanie Kemp, a twenty-three-year-old physiotherapist, was the first white women to be assaulted in prison. The police banged her head repeatedly on a concrete floor.

9. *The Rise of the South African Reich* (Harmondsworth: Penguin, 1964); and *Moses Kotane: South African Revolutionary* (London: Inkululeko Publications, 1975).

10. See Nathaniel Weyl, *Traitors' End: The Rise and Fall of the Communist Movement in Southern Africa* (Cape Town: Tafelberg-Uitgewers, 1970). Weyl's book is notoriously hostile, in spite of his Haverford College and Columbia University education. See Albie Sachs, *Stephanie on Trial*, 258. Writing of the years 1963–66: "My eyeballs prickled as I thought of the battering Fred had received, of his loneliness and his consideration for all others. He had fought on when most of us had dropped out and now he alone was to be punished for what we had all done collectively."

11. During Ninety Days, Kodesh was jailed in the same cell where David Platt, the man who had shot Prime Minister Verwoerd in 1960, committed suicide.

12. *Class and Colour in South Africa, 1850–1950* (Harmondsworth: Penguin, 1969); as well as *African Women: Their Legal Status in South Africa* (Evanston: Northwestern University Press, 1968). See also *Struggles in Southern Africa for Survival and Equality* (New York: St. Martin's, 1997); and *Comrade Jack: The Political Lectures and Diary of Jack Simons*, edited by Marion Sparg, Jenny Schreiner, and Gwen Ansell (Doornfontein: STE Publishers, 2001).

13. *New York Times*, 22 September 1963. Brutus was shot in the stomach outside the Anglo-American building as he fled down Main Street in Johannesburg. The man who shot Brutus carried him to the hospital. Brutus's case was especially noteworthy because he held a passport from the Federation of Rhodesia and Nyasaland when arrested. Brutus was seized by Portuguese secret police in Mozambique who turned him over to South Africa. See also *Sports Illustrated*, 26 July 1976.

14. Albie Sachs, *Jail Diary*, 120.

15. His 1962 debut, *A Walk in the Night*, was followed by *And a Three-fold Cord* (Berlin: Seven Seas,

1964); *The Stone Country* (Berlin: Seven Seas, 1967); *The Fog at the Season's End* (London: Heinemann, 1972); and *Time of the Butcherbird* (London: Heinemann, 1979). See also *Quartet: New Voices from South Africa* (New York: Crown, 1963), which included stories by James Matthews, Alf Wannenburgh, and Richard Rive. He edited *Apartheid: A Collection of Writings on South African Racism by South Africans* (London: Lawrence and Wishart, 1972), and wrote a travel book on Russia, *A Soviet Journey* (Moscow: Progress Publishers, 1978). Posthumously, there is *Memories of Home: The Writings of Alex La Guma*, edited by Cecil Abrahams (Trenton: Africa World Press, 1991); and *Jimmy La Guma: A Biography*, edited by Mohamed Adhikari (Cape Town: Friends of the South African Library, 1997). See *African Communist*, no. 104 (1st quarter 1986).

16. *African Communist*, no. 59 (4th quarter 1974).
17. *African Communist*, no. 112 (1st quarter 1988).
18. *African Communist*, no. 70 (3rd quarter 1977).
19. Lodge, *Black Politics*, 301. See Maggie Resha, *My Life in the Struggle*, 239, in which Nelson Mandela wrote Resha a letter from Robben Island, January 1974: "It seems that the old and stable world we once knew so well is beginning to crumble, leaving us with nothing but painful memories."
20. Lodge, *Black Politics*, 303. The group included Albert Luthuli's son-in-law Pascal Ngakane, Makiwane's cousin Ambrose, and Treason Trialist Jonas Matlou. Makiwane had escaped with Hilda Bernstein in 1963 from South Africa.
21. Carter and Karis, *From Protest to Challenge*, 5:44; and *Rand Daily Mail*, 8 July 1980.
22. *Learning from Robben Island: The Prison Writings of Govan Mbeki* (Athens, Ohio: Ohio University Press, 1991); and *The Struggle for Liberation in South Africa: A Short History* (Cape Town: David Philip, 1992). See Adam Hochschild, *The Mirror at Midnight: A South African Journey* (New York: Viking, 1990), 35, for a description of Mbeki in 1988.
23. Ahmed Kathrada, *Letters from Robben Island*, edited by Robert D. Vassen (East Lansing: Michigan State University Press, 1999), 7; and Albie Sachs, *Jail Diary*, 269.
24. See *Star*, 18 December 1964.
25. Kasrils, *Armed and Dangerous*, 68.
26. Boon, *Beyond Fear*.
27. Ivan's nickname in jail was the Old Grey Fox. See Turok, *Nothing But the Truth*, 169. It morphed into Old Griff Ox, which became OGO and then Ogs or Uncle Ogs.

James Zug interview with Lesley Schermbrucker, January 1994. "They blocked everybody who came out of jail. In effect they regarded us as useless because we had gone to jail, that we were now followed, and we were marked. It wasn't true. . . . I think that when the blacks are, you know, when their history is told, when people are talking, they must not forget this part that we played. It was an important part. It was, because our hearts were really in it. We just gave up everything. When we came out of jail, we had nothing, absolutely nothing."

"As long as Ivan was around, they'd have an unfailing and vigorous champion and guardian," wrote Hugh Lewin in 1981 concerning those prison years. "You know, for instance, what Ivan felt about Bram [Fischer]—but I know too what Bram felt about him, how he leant on him and relied on him and was devoted to him. As were we all. Not for any reason of due respect, but for the essential down-to-earth effing and blinding reason that there was nobody who cared more for others, nobody who worried more about how others were feeling and being treated, nobody who was as fearless and staunch in doing everything he could for others, and to hell with the consequences for himself. Come the effing day of reckoning, as he would say, and so on and so forth, Ivan will be remembered as the best."

28. Hilda Bernstein correspondence to Leslie Schermbrucker, November 1981.

29. James Zug interview with Ebrahim Ismail Ebrahim, January 1994: "People were quite proud of *New Age* because it was the one paper that united the whole of the country. It was a common denominator. People even spoke of the *Guardian*. I didn't know the *Guardian*, because it was before my time, but people always spoke fondly of the *Guardian*, selling the *Guardian* and organizing. So you always sort of reminiscence about the old days and talk of the struggle paper *New Age*."

James Zug interview with Wilton Mkwayi, January 1994: "We were talking about *New Age* on the Island, because there was something missing, papers that will analyse the situation. When we saw *New Nation* come up, the *Weekly Mail* coming up, we referred to papers like that."

30. James Zug telephone interview with Harry Gwala, October 1994. See *New York Times*, 21 June 1995, for Gwala's obituary. Gwala said: "The paper was never banned in the minds of the people. They just couldn't suppress the ideas in it."

Arnold Selby wrote: "Whenever the people were in trouble the *Guardian* was there. Whenever the people fought the *Guardian* promoted its case. Let me say the *Guardian* (its spirit still lives) is an integral part of the South African people, rooted in the South African people and born of the South African people."

Ismail Meer said in 1994: "I'm certain that in democratic South Africa the very pages of the *Guardian* will become a very honored, respected record of our history. There was a tremendous need to find common humanity at a time when all sorts of pressures were brought on us to divide us, to segment us, to make us into robots and to emphasize ethnicity as it has never been emphasized elsewhere. The *Guardian* fought that. The *Guardian* fought it only because the people themselves were ready to fight it."

Index

A

Abantu-Batho, 159, 170

Abrahams, Lionel, 121

Abrahams, Peter, 18, 54, 242n.33

Advance: advertising in, 130; banning of, 136–37, 189; circulation of, 130; distribution of, 125; editorial policies of, 297n.142; finances of, 131, 132, 133, 299n.163, 299n.165, 300n.167; founding of, 117–18; function within the South African Communist Party, 125; fundraising for, 130; police raids on, 136, 137; and racial matters, 125; support of Soviet Union, 125–29

Africa South, 191, 288n.23, 301n.183

African Communist, 126, 226, 227

African Mine Workers' Union, 63, 68

African National Congress: and the African Mine Workers' Union, 63; and Anderson Khumani Ganyile, 206–7; banning of, 189, 191; and banning of the *Advance*, 137; and *Bantu World*, 162, 321n.194; and the Basutoland Congress Party, 199; and the Bethal farm workers scandal, 93; Campaign for the Defiance of Unjust Laws, 139–40; and the Communist Party, 87–88, 123, 160–61; and the Congress of the People, 140, 141; and the "Defend Free Speech" convention, 102–3; and distribution of the *Guardian*, 142, 145, 146, 305n.27; early inactivity of, 12, 86; founding of, 12; government in exile, 195; *Guardian* support for, 3, 4, 6, 63, 88, 139, 140, 315n.118; guerilla warfare campaign of, 196; and *Inkundla ya Bantu*, 159; and the M-Plan, 145–46; and the May Day Massacres, 105; and the May Stay-away, 195–96; membership of, 87, 123, 140, 161; and minimum wage, 331n.7; motto of, 265n.14; and the Native Representative Council boycott, 75, 88; and *New Age*, 152, 159, 160, 161–62, 181, 316n.125, 316n.127, 321n.194, 327n.269, 335n.6; newspapers published by, 159, 217; offices of, 276n.95, 312n.97; pass law protests of, 152–53, 186; and the

People's Assembly, 89; potato boycott, 4, 154, 155; revitalization of, 50, 86–87; and the South African Congress of Democrats, 142; and the South African media, 321–22n.194; support for Allies in World War II, 35; and the Suppression of Communism Act, 105

African National Congress Youth League, 50, 87, 89, 103, 105, 143, 159

African Political Organisation, 10, 291n.77

Afrikaanse Pers, 257n.95

Alberts, Vera, xi, 13, 53–54, 227, 257n.99

Alexander, Ray: background of, 152; banning of, 185; and the Cape Town underground, 191; and the Communist Party, 38, 123, 295n.129; and Eli Weinberg, 310n.79; in exile, 226; and factory conditions for women workers, 23; and Food and Canning Workers' Union strike, 61; and *Inkululeko*, 246n.127; and Jack Simons, 19, 295n.129; and labor unions, 13, 24, 45, 63, 152, 202; and Len Lee-Warden, 298n.153; as Member of Parliament, 119, 292n.99; *New Age* writings of, 202; police raids on, 301n.185; role of, at the *Guardian*, xi, 45, 81, 156; and the South African Congress of Democrats, 123; and the Treason Trial, 325n.240

Alexandra bus boycott, 63, 90

Alexandra Township, 90, 279n.122

All-African Convention, 239n.10

Altman, Phyllis, 166

Andrews, Bill: and the African Mine Workers' Union, 68; and Betty Radford, 45, 76; and Brian Bunting, 273n.61; and the Communist Party, 20, 24, 38, 45, 66, 80, 287n.17; death of, 99; eightieth birthday of, 99, 285n.200; and Eric Louw, 67; and the *Guardian*, xi, 20, 45, 239n.3, 268n.4, 283n.180; and the Hunger Relief Fund, 264n.204; imprisonment of, 20; and the International Socialist League, 20, 80; as Member of Parliament, 20, 102; and organized labor, 61; and the Paarl Workers' Relief Fund, 61; police raids on, 73, 268n.8; and racial inequality, 65,

265n.223; retirement of, 99, 285n.199, 286n.201; and the sedition trial, 73, 74; and the South African Labour Party, 20, 26

Anti-Fascist League of South Africa, 11

APO, the, 291n.77

Arenstein, Jacqueline Lax. *See* Lax, Jacqueline

Arenstein, Rowley, 50, 117, 206, 228, 257n.103, 258n.107

Arnold's Xmas Hampers, 133, 226, 300n.173, 300n.174, 300–301n.175

Arthur Barlow's Weekly, 291n.73

Asiatic Land Tenure Act, 94

Asmal, Kader, 343n.177

B

Baldry, Harold: books of, 272n.47; and collective security, 25; and the Communist Party, 24, 43, 78–79; and the *Critic*, 19; death of, 79; and the *Guardian*, xi, 14, 20, 78–79; salary of, 20; and World War II, 36, 58–59, 69. *See also* Vigilator

Ballinger, Margaret, 110, 162, 333n.33

Banda, Hastings, 142, 204

Bantu education boycott, 161

Bantu World: and black Africa, 339n.121; as black newspaper, 82, 88, 170; burning of offices of, 65; changing name of to the *World*, 320n.183; circulation of, 320n.187; hostile relationship with African National Congress, 162, 321n.194,

Barlow, Arthur, 114, 168, 291n.73

Barnard, Christiaan, 184

Barnett, Jack, 119, 190, 274n.65, 333n.36

Barnett, Matthew, 15

Basner, Hyman, 36, 81, 85, 91, 273n.63, 280n.134

Bass, Simon, 33

Basutoland Congress Party, 199, 337n.94

Berenblatt, Yetta, 295n.130

Bernadt, Hymie, 110, 120, 301n.185

Bernadt, Jean, 29, 32, 34, 247n.138, 249n.14

Bernstein, Hilda: burning of *Guardian* back issues, 218; and Communist Party, 123, 127; escape from South Africa, 349n.20;

jailing of, 332n.25; and *Soviet Life,*
260n.130; Special Branch harassment of,
172, 177; trip to China, 211, 296–
97n.139

Bernstein, Rusty: and the *Advance,* 125; and
the African National Congress, 160; and
the Communist Party, 51, 123, 160; in
exile, 271n.40; and *Fighting Talk,*
307n.50; and *Guardian* distribution, 106,
255n.83; and *Guardian* provincialism, 33;
and *Guardian* as the voice of the Communist Party, 51; house arrest of, 214;
jailing of, 223, 332n.25; and *New Age,*
146; police raids on, 177; and the Treason
Trial, 178. *See also* Watts, Hilda

Berrange, Vernon, 108, 251n.31, 269n.12,
346n.1

Bethal, farm worker abuse in, 91–94, 153–54,
281n.150

Black Pimpernel, 198, 200, 337n.90. *See also*
Mandela, Nelson

Black Sash, 317n.138

Bloom, Harry: arrest of, 333n.25; and father
of actor Orlando Bloom, 272n.50; and the
Guardian, 54, 79–80, 258n.105; H.A.
Naidoo replacing, 82; and *New Age* short
story contest, 166; writings of, 272n.50

Bloomberg, Charles, 121

Boere Arbeidsvereeniging, 91, 92, 93,
280n.136

Bokwe, Roseberry, 264n204–5, 283n.180

Boonzaier, Gregoire, 283n.170, 284n.191

Bopape, David, 265n.215, 278n.114,
280n.134

Boshielo, Flag, 161

Braverman, E. R. *See* Alexander, Ray

Brenkman, Balthasar Johannes, 91

British Communist Party, 14, 36, 249n.12

British Empire Service League, 82

Brockway, Fenner, 340n.145

Brooke, Regina, 150

Broughton, Morris, 138

Brown, Peter, 344n.199

Brutus, Dennis, xi, 149, 166, 194, 200, 210,
226–27, 335n.60, 348–49n.13

Building Workers' Industrial Union, the, 69

Bulawayo *Guardian* League, the, 56

Bunche, Ralph, 18, 242n.34

Bunting, Arthur, 80, 272n.54

Bunting, Brian Percy: and *Advance,* 121, 132;
background of, 80–81, 273n.57, 273n.58;
banning of, 118, 173, 220, 292n.94; and
banning of the *Advance,* 136–37, 138,
302n.196; and banning of the *Guardian,*
113, 115, 116, 140, 288n.24, 290n.57;
and banning of *New Age,* 213–14, 343–
44n.188, 344n.189; and Betty Radford,
78; and Bill Andrews, 273n.61; and black
Africa, 203; book reviews of, 166,
271n.46; and the *Clarion,* 115–16, 117;
and commission of inquiry into South
African press, 168; and the Communist
Party, 81, 118, 123, 124, 126, 273n.59,
273n.60, 294n.117, 295n.129; and the
Congress of the People, 141; and the
Defiance Campaign, 140; editorial style
of, 294n.115; in exile, 226; and founding
of *New Age,* 137; and the *Golden City
Post,* 320n.186; and government investigation of the *Guardian,* 107–8, 108–9,
110, 111; and *Guardian* beauty contest,
95, 283n.174; and *Guardian* financing,
97; and *Guardian* political independence,
27, 287–88n.22; and *Guardian* as voice
of the Communist Party, 42, 85; house arrest of, 214; jailing of, 189, 190, 210; and
Langa food donation, 331n.17; and the
Langa March, 332n.20; and Len Lee-Warden, 298n.153; as Member of Parliament,
118–19, 226, 292n.93, 95 and 98; and
Morning Star, 217; and *New Age* editorial
role, 139, 156, 164, 203; and *New Age* Indian fundraising drives, 182, 329n.285;
and *New Age* relationship with the
African National Congress, 159–60; and
New Age short story contest, 166; and
New Year's Eve party, 185; and the Non-
European Unity Movement, 163; and
Norman Flegg, 293n.103; pamphlets of,
182; and Patrick Duncan, 162–63, 187,
205, 317n.139, 317n.143, 331nn.16–17;
and Philip Kgosana, 187–88; and the Pio-

neer Press, 134–35; police raids on, 172, 175, 219, 301n.185, 341n.156; and police raids on the *Advance,* 136; and police raids on the *Guardian,* 107–8, 108–9, 110; and publishing of *New Age* during the Treason Trial, 178, 325n.245; and race matters, 246n.115; and the Real Publishing and Printing Company, 135; role at the *Guardian,* xi, 2, 3, 56, 80, 81, 270n.35; salary of, 181; and the Sharpesville Massacre, 187; and Sonia Bunting, 289n.41; and the South African Congress of Democrats, 123; and the South African media, 169, 170–71; and the South African Society of Journalists, 167, 319n.166; and the Soviet invasion of Hungary, 129; and *Spark,* 217; and the Suppression of Communism Act, 104, 105, 319n.169; travels in Africa, 203; and Xhosa/Zulu *New Age* supplement, 315n.121

Bunting, Margaret, 172

Bunting, Rebecca, 327n.268

Bunting, Sidney Percival, 2, 80, 272n.54

Bunting, Sonia: arrest of, 177, 191–92, 334n.43; and the Black Sash, 317n.138; and the Congress of the People, 141; death of, 226; in exile, 226; house arrest of, 214; and Langa food donation, 331n.17; and Lionel Forman, 294n.112; marriage of, 273n.58; and *New Age,* 156, 166; and New Year's Eve party, 185; and Pauline Podbrey, 120; police raids on, 219; and *Spark,* 220; and the Treason Trial, 325n.240; trip to England, 122

Bunting, Thomas Percival, 80

Burford, E. J., 33, 247n.150, 251n.28

Burnside, Duncan Campbell, 26, 245n.95

bus boycotts, 50, 63, 89–90, 141, 143, 148, 163, 179, 179n.124, 263n.197, 277n.103, 304n.20, 308n.59

Butcher, Mary: and *Advance,* 120; and the African National Congress, 197, 208; and the Communist Party, 127; in exile, 226; and Fred Carneson, 293n.107; and inward focus of South African radicals, 127; jail-

ing of, 208, 226; and Lionel Forman, 298n.152; and *New Age,* 179, 327n.268; and Non-European Unity Movement, 163; police raids on, 301n.185

Buthelezi, Gatsha, 142, 305n.26

C

Cachalia, Maulvi, 104, 224

Calata, James, 305n.30

Cape Argus, 10, 21, 114, 138, 211

Cape Guardian, 14–15, 33, 168

Cape Standard, 241n.19

Cape Times, 10, 75, 112, 114, 134, 168, 215–16

Cape Town: ethnic makeup of, 10; political detachment of, 10, 239n.5, 294n.119; population of, 49

Cape Town *Guardian* League, 46, 52, 77, 252n.53

Carneson, Fred: and *Advance,* 120–21, 164, 297n.142; background of, 32; banning of, 220; and banning of *New Age,* 213, 215, 216; charged with subversion, 192, 334n.46; and the Communist Party, 32, 41, 42, 120, 123, 294n.117; death of, 226; in exile, 226; and financing of the *Guardian* papers, 97, 132, 164, 180–81, 192, 211, 300n.167, 302n.187; and firebombing of *New Age* offices, 180, 326n.256; and the Freedom of the Press Committee, 289n.45; and Govan Mbeki, 144; and the *Guardian,* 39, 42, 120, 247n.137; jailing of, 208, 215, 226; and Len Lee-Warden, 133, 134; and *New Age,* 156, 202, 335n.50; and the Pietermaritzburg *Guardian* League, 55; and police raids, 136, 173, 177, 301n.185, 341n.156; and Ray Alexander, 119; and the Real Publishing and Printing Company, 135; removal from Cape Provincial Council, 113; and the sedition trial, 74; and the South African Congress of Democrats, 123; and the Soviet invasion of Hungary, 129; and *Spark,* 218–19, 346n.226; temper of, 293n.142; and the Treason Trial, 177; underground work of, 191, 197

Carneson, Sarah, 215, 220, 226, 259n.125, 333n.25

Cartwright, A. P., 320n.177

Cash, Christine, xi, 46, 74, 79, 85, 270n.39

Central Indian High School, 149

Chamber of Mines, 69, 278n121

Chamile, Andries "General China," 178, 207, 324n.232, 340n.148

Champion, A. W. G., 97

Chisholm, Eric, 325n.246

Clapham, Vic, 21, 24, 32, 35, 56, 92, 203, 259 n.124

Clarion, 115–17, 140, 291n.77, 292n.86, 303n.8

Cloete, Claude, 289n.38

Close, Rex, 45

Coalbrook mining disaster, 185

Coetzee, Bertie, 212

Cohen, Maurice, 51

Cohen, Selma, 51, 62

Cole, Ernest, 194, 335n.59

Committee for Spanish Relief, 21

Commonwealth Press Union, 319n.166

Communist Party of South Africa: and the African Mine Workers' Union, 63; and the African National Congress, 87–88; and the Alexandra bus boycott, 63; banning of, 3, 4; Central Executive Committee of, 38; and the "Defend Free Speech" convention, 103; dissolution of, 105; founding of, 10, 12, 20; the Guardian as voice of, 38, 42–46, 50–53, 60–61, 84–85, 161, 250n.16; headquarters move to Cape Town, 37–38; Johannesburg branch of, 255n.77; membership of, 37, 41, 54; and the Native Representative Council boycott, 75, 76, 88; 1930s inactivity of, 12; organization of black Africans, 62, 263n.185; and the People's Assembly, 89; police raids on, 72; racial makeup of, 12; racist policies of, 76, 265n.220; role in selling the Guardian, 6, 38–41, 50, 52, 54, 55, 248n.5, 252n.47, 254n.72; and staffing of the Guardian, 13, 42–46, 51– 52, 54, 80, 84; and the Suppression of Communism Act, 105; and World War II,

36. See also South African Communist Party.

Competent Publishing and Printing Company, 117, 178

Congress of Democrats. See South African Congress of Democrats

Congress of the People, 140–41, 159, 303n.13

Congress Speaks, 159

Contact, 163, 215, 317n.140, 317n.142, 333n.28, 340n.133

Contemporary Review, 80

Cook, Eric, 59, 66, 266n.226

Cook, Freda, 261n.157

Cope, Jack: and Advance, 294n.113; background of, 5; death of, 313n.106; and the Freedom of the Press Committee, 111, 289n.45; and the Guardian, xi, 2, 45–46, 263n.178; and Modern Youth Society mural, 252n.49; and New Age, 137, 156, 166; and police raids, 109, 301n.185; writings of, 61, 156, 313n.106

Cope, Leslie, 46, 166, 284n.191

Costello, Will, 26, 64

Criminal Investigation Department. See Security Branch

Critic, 18

D

Dadoo, Yusuf: and Advance, 125; and the African National Congress government in exile, 195; banning of, 102, 286n.8; and banning of New Age, 214; in exile, 191, 193; and the Freedom of the Press Committee, 289n.45; and Guardian board of directors, 268n.4; and Guardian coverage of Indian affairs, 64, 94; jailing of, 251n.28; and Lionel Forman, 128; and the London New Age Committee, 211, 214; and the Native Representative Council boycott, 75; and New Age, 181, 183; and the Passive Resistance Campaign, 94; police raids on, 136, 301n.185

Daily Worker, 14, 127, 266n.226, 298n.151, 301n.182

Damane, Arthur, 285n.195

Davidoff, Hymie, 112, 288n.23

Davidson, Basil, 289n.44
De Braganca, Aquino, 347n.7
De Echo, 91
"Defend Free Speech" Convention, 103, 287n.9
Defiance Campaign, 94, 130, 139–40, 142–44, 155, 158–59, 162–63, 170, 179, 303n.5, 303n.14, 306n.31, 307n.41, 315n.118, 321n.194, 345n.205
De Keyser, Ethel, 293n.104
Demane, Arthur, 257n.93
Democratic and General News Service, 59
Dennis, Eugene, 285n.200
Desai, Barney, 217
De Villiers, Lesley. See Leslie Cope
Dhlamini, David, 131, 299n.159
Diamond, Issy, 34, 248n.153
Dick, Nancy, 45, 119, 252n.46, 274n.65
Die Burger, 25, 112, 114, 135, 168, 288n.26, 291n.71
Die Suiderstem, 285n.198
Die Transvaler, 319n.170
Die Vaderland, 172, 211, 322n.205
Dingake, Michael, 314n.113
District Six, 10, 63, 96, 125, 132, 150, 157, 263n.185, 276n.89, 313n.107–9
Dnibe, Conrad, 133
Dönges, Eben, 102, 108, 293n.110
Doyle, Alan, 84, 272n.50, 273n.61, 281n.157, 321n.188. See also Harmel, Michael
Drum, 151, 158, 170, 171, 309n.74, 318n.154, 321n.189, 321n.191, 330n.4, 334n.38
Dryburgh, David, 263n.178
Duma, Abolani, 312n.101
Duncan, Patrick: and Anderson Khumani Ganyile, 340n.143; and banning of New Age, 215; charged with subversion, 334n.46; and Contact, 162–63, 187; hatred of Communist Party, 163, 187, 205, 317n.139, 331n.17; and Joseph Mobuto, 204–5, 340nn.133–34; and Philip Kgosana, 187, 188, 331n.16, 332n.21; rivalry with Brian Bunting, 162–63, 317n.139, 317n.143, 331nn.16–17
Du Plessis, Danie, 51, 69, 273n.58, 285n.195

Durban Guardian League, 54, 258n.107
Durban riots, 94–95
Du Toit, Bettie, 132, 317n.140

E

East London Guardian League, 55
East Rand News, 285n.197
Ebrahim, Ebrahim Ismail: and Albert Luthuli, 312n.100; and Communist Party, 198; and Dawood Seedat, 311n.93; in exile, 228; jailing of, 208, 228; and New Age, xi, 155, 156, 181, 212; salary of, 181; and Umkhonto we Sizwe, 197, 198, 337n.89
Ehrenburg, Ilya, 59
Emmerich, Jimmy, 23, 24, 26, 27, 239n.3
Erasmus, Francois, 188
Evening Post (Port Elizabeth), 169, 215
Exteen, Joyce Wood, 133

F

Factories Bill, 63
Fairburn, John, 288n.33
Federation of South African Women, 143, 152
Fighting Talk, 81, 147, 149, 303n.12, 307n.50
Findlay, George, 19, 33, 55
Findlay, Jean, 55
First, Julius, 82, 181, 224
First, Ruth: and Advance, 297n.142; and African life, 90–94, 279n.121; and the African National Congress, 87, 197, 316n.132; background of, 82; and banishment camps, 202; banning of, 210, 220, 322n.206; and banning of Bantu World from ANC conference, 161–62, 171; and Bethal farm worker abuse, 91–92, 93, 94, 153–54, 155; and the Communist Party, 82, 123, 251n.31; death of, 225, 347–48n.7; and Drum, 171; elegance of, 82–83, 308nn.60–61; in exile, 191, 192, 225, 334n.40, 334n.44; family of, 308n.60; fearlessness of, 323n.209; and Federation of Progressive Schools, 274n.68; and Fighting Talk, 147, 307n.51; and Govan Mbeki, 144; and Ismail Meer, 280n.131; and Ivan Schermbrucker, 83–84, 275n.73; jailing of, 83, 225; and Lionel Forman,

330n.296; and the May Day free speech rallies, 103; and Nelson Mandela, 200, 339n.111; and *New Age,* 148; and the Newspaper Press Union code of conduct, 169; and Oliver Mti, 177, 324n.234; pamphlets of, 182; and the Pan Africanist Congress, 162; and pass law protests, 152; and police raids, 108, 173, 209, 301n.185, 322n.201; political involvement of, 147–48, 165; and the potato boycott, 4; publications of, 347n.6; and the *Rand Daily Mail,* 168; role at the *Guardian,* xi, 2, 5, 82, 86, 103, 270n.35; salary of, 327n.265; and the South African College of Democrats, 294n.121; and *Spark,* 219; and strain of political involvement, 173–74; travels in Africa, 203, 209; and Treason Trial, 83, 177, 178, 179, 324n.238; and T. X. Makiwane, 151; and young writers, 149, 165, 194, 309n.64

Fischer, Bram: and commission of inquiry into South African press, 168; and the Communist Party, 123, 250n.19, 251n.31; and the Freedom of the Press Committee, 289n.45; and *Guardian* birthday party, 52, 98, 211; and Johannesburg *Guardian* League, 256n.88; and *New Age,* 158, 178, 183; and Sedition Trial, 269n.12; and the South African College of Democrats, 294n.121; and the Treason Trial, 158, 178; underground work of, 223

Fischer, Bram, 52, 98, 123, 158, 160, 168, 176, 178, 183, 211, 223, 250n.19, 251n.31, 257n.91, 259n.119, 269n.12, 275n.72, 285n.193, 289n.45, 293n.103, 294n.121, 349n.27

Fischer, Molly, 52, 98, 149, 211, 256n.88, 257n.91, 304n.25

Flegg, Eric, 14

Flegg, Hilary, 98, 293n.103

Flegg, Norman: death of, 120; and *Guardian* Christmas Eve party, 98, 120; police raids on, 72; role at the *Guardian,* xi, 14, 46, 120, 293n.103

Food and Canning Workers' Union, strike of, 61

Forman, Lionel: and *Advance,* 121–22, 293n.109, 294n.113, 294n.115, 298n.152; arrest of, 177; background of, 121, 293nn.110–11; banning of, 184, 329n.293; and black Africa, 203; and the Communist Party, 121, 128; death of, 183, 184; doctorate of, 329n.291; and ethnicity, 297n.147; and the May Day Massacres, 104; and *New Age,* xi, 156, 166, 183; pamphlets of, 182; police raids on, 301n.185; and residential segregation, 329n.290; and Ruth First, 83, 274n.71; salary of, 181; and the Soviet invasion of Hungary, 129; and the Treason Trial, 179; tributes to, 330nn.296–297

Forman, Sadie, 121, 123, 177, 184, 254–55n.74, 330n.298, 333n.33

Fort Hare, University of, 87, 143, 144–45, 150, 206, 279n.125, 307n.41, 309n.71, 324n.231

Forum, 31

Forward, 33, 115, 138

Foster, William, 285n.200

Fox, Charles, 21, 25, 33, 243n.58, 253n.54

Francis, Joe, 136

Freedom, 38, 43, 120

Freedom Charter, 141, 162, 191, 333n.38

Freedom of the Press Committee, 111–12, 289n.45

Frelimo, 204

Friends of the Soviet Union, 43, 51, 65, 72, 268n.4

Fryer, Peter, 298n.151

G

Gallant, Omar, 131, 299n.160

Gandhi, Mahatma, 94, 170

Gandhi, Manilal, 317n.140

Ganyile, Anderson Khumani, 206–7

Garment Workers' Union, 113, 294n.119

Gelb, Trudy, 98, 256n.88, 332n.25

Gell, Christopher, 145, 306n.38, 316n.132

"General China." *See* Chamile, Andries

General Law Amendment Act, 196, 336n.77, 342n.166

Ghana, 193, 203-4

Gibson, Jimmy, 298n.152
Ginsburg, Gerson, 40, 249nn.8–9
Goldberg, Denis, 39, 253n.53, 333n.25, 341–42n.165
Golden City Post, 144, 170–71, 194, 316n.136, 320n.186
Gollancz, Victor, 9, 18, 25, 35, 238n.1, 243n.51
Gomas, Johnny, 36, 239n.3, 244n.71, 263n.196, 283n.170, 305n.26
Gool, Cissie, 11, 24, 38, 219, 245n.83, 283n.170, 333n.25
Gool, Goolam, 219
Gordimer, Nadine, 166, 297n.144, 323n.209
Gordon, Max, 251n.28
Gordon, Ruth. *See* First, Ruth
Gottschalk, Bernard, 295n.130
Government, Gazette, 113, 137, 189, 291n.75, 334n.40, 347n.1
Gqabi, Joe: and Anderson Khumani Ganyile, 206; and Bethal farm worker abuse, 153–54; and Coalbrook mining disaster, 185–86; in exile, 210, 341n.164; jailing of, 174, 208, 225; murder of, 225–26; and *New Age,* xi, 151–52, 165, 203; travels in Africa, 203; as Umkhonto saboteur, 197
Greig, George, 343n.182
Group Areas Act, 174, 286n.6, 303n.4
Guardian: advertising in, 14, 15, 28–29, 31, 57, 95, 96, 247n.134, 283n.177; African community opinion of, 30, 62; and African life, 90, 278–79n.121, 279nn.122–125; and the African National Congress, 3–4, 6, 63, 88–89, 139, 140, 142–43, 315n.118; African sellers of, 52, 131, 257n.93; and alliance between the Communist Party and the African National Congress, 6; anti-capitalist stance of, 4, 24, 85; banning of, 2, 3–4, 113–14, 140; ban on selling of in Port Elizabeth, 305–6n.31; beauty contest of, 95–96, 283n.170, 283n.173, 283n.174; and Bill Andrews eightieth birthday, 285n.200; birthday party of, 52, 98; branch offices of, 2, 3, 4, 5, 50, 53, 55, 58, 255n.77; and British royal visit, 86; censorship of, 66–67; Christmas Eve dance of, 98; circulation of, 2, 3, 16, 21, 31, 42, 56, 58, 62, 71, 96, 130, 140, 283n.175; and coloured affairs, 95; Communist Party and staffing of, 13, 42–46, 51–52, 54, 80, 84, 294n.123; control of events around it, 4; defamation lawsuits against, 67–69, 267nn.253–258; defense fund of , 68, 69, 267n.255; and dissolution of the Communist Party of South Africa, 105–06; distribution of outside of Communist Party, 23–24, 31–32, 34, 52, 54–55, 95, 106, 131, 142; distribution through Communist Party, 6, 38–39, 50–52, 54–55, 254n.72, 255n.83; early racism of, 6, 64; editorial policies of, 3, 63–64, 105–6, 139, 287n.21; election coverage of, 27, 62, 84; financing of, 2, 97–98, 260n.134, 267n.1, 283n.178, 283n.179; first edition of, 15–16; and Food and Canning Workers' Union strike, 61; format of, 268n.2, 268n.3; founding of, 2, 13–15; fund-raising for, 3, 46, 52, 54, 55, 97–98, 256–57n.90, 257–58n.105, 275n.77, 284n.189, 284n.190, 284–85n.192, 285n.193, 299n.157; government investigation of, 107–13, 322n.200; headquarters of, 2, 14, 30, 47, 253n.59; and housing conditions, 62–63; Hunger Relief Fund, 63, 264n.204, 264n.205; incorporation of, 72, 268n.4; independence from Communist Party, 3, 4, 24, 25; and Indian affairs, 94–95; and *Inkululeko,* 61; and international news, 21, 85; and interracial relationships, 90; investigative reporting of, 23, 62; Kenya banning of, 288n.24; and the labor movement, 3, 14, 15–16, 22–23, 24, 61; leagues of, 46, 52, 54, 55, 56, 77, 98, 130, 252–53n.53, 256n.88, 256n.89, 256–57n.90, 258n.107, 299n.157; and the Left Book Club, 25; May Day editions of, 56, 61, 84; and the May Day free speech rallies, 103; and the mine strike of 1946, 72, 268n.5; mistakes made by, 6–7, 125–30; name change suggestions for, 292n.89; naming of, 14–15, 33; and national liberation

struggle, 86; as national newspaper, 53; and the Native Representative Council boycott, 88–89; and newsprint restrictions, 56–57, 71; nonpolitical content of, 27–28, 32–33, 95–96; northern edition of, 52, 257n.94, 257n.95, 260n.132; as organ of the Communist Party of South Africa, 38, 42–46, 50–53, 60–61, 84–85, 125, 250n.16; and the Pan Africanist Congress, 4, 6; and the Passive Resistance Campaign, 94, 281n.153; police raids on, 2, 72–73, 107–9, 136, 268n.6, 268n.8, 269n.9, 269n.10; political independence of, 24, 27, 42, 106, 287–88n.22; price of, 98; printing of, 133–35; production standards of, 30–31; provincialism of, 33, 34; racial composition of staff of, 5, 28, 82; and race matters, 22, 28–30, 63, 64, 86, 246n.114, 263n.194, 263–64n.200; railway station ban on, 106–7, 288n.23; readership of, 28, 62, 65, 97, 158, 315n.117; and the Sedition Trial, 84; sexism of, 27–28, 95–96, 246n.114; and the South African Labour Party, 3, 26, 65; southern edition of, 52, 257n.94, 257n.95; and the Spanish Civil War, 21–22; and the Springbok Legion, 56; support of the Soviet Union, 7, 128–29; and the Suppression of Communism Act, 104–6, 287n.21; toddler contest of, 97; and the Treason Trial, 2, 3; white reaction to multiracial interests of, 64–65; and the Women's Food Committee, 282n.164; and World War II, 35, 36, 58–59, 60, 69, 71. *See also Advance*, the; *Cape Guardian; Clarion; New Age; People's World; Spark*

Guardian Christmas Club, 132, 300n.169, 300n.170, 300n.172

Guardian [Manchester], 114, 290n.68

Gwala, Harry: arrest of, 332–33n.25; and the Communist Party, 40, 161; and *Fighting Talk*, 307n.51; and the *Guardian*, 40, 160–61, 229, 350n.30; and *New Age* short story competition, 318n.163; and Pietermaritzburg *Guardian* League, 55

H

Hani, Martin "Chris," 142, 219, 341–42n.165

Harmel, Arthur, 51

Harmel, Michael: and the *African Communist*, 227; and African National Congress, 191, 197; background of, 51–52; banning of, 113, 220, 322n.206; and *Bantu World*, 171; and the bus boycott, 304n.26; and the Communist Party, 52, 104, 123, 255–56n.85, 256n.86, 287n.17; and *Comrade Bill*, 61; death of, 227; and *Drum*, 321n.189; in exile, 227; and *Guardian*, xi, 52, 84, 148, 243n.53, 285n.195; house arrest of, 214; and *Inkululeko*, 256n.87; and Johannesburg City Council elections, 101; and Lionel Forman, 297–98n.150; and mine strike of 1946, 72, 87; and Nadine Gordimer, 166; and Native Representative Council boycott, 75; and Nelson Mandela, 201, 339n.111; police raids on, 136, 208, 301n.185, 322n.201; and publishing of *New Age* during the Treason Trial, 179; and Stalin, 129; writings of, 148–49, 182, 308n.62. *See also* Doyle, Alan

Harmel, Ray, 256n.86

Harrison, Wilfred, 26

Hartwell, Dulcie, 291n.72

Head, George, 267n.258

Hendricks, Katie, 166

Hepner, Miriam, 55

Hepple, Alex, 112, 138

Hertzog, J. W., 35, 320n.179

Heyman, Issy, 259n.125, 332n.25

High Court Bill, 114

Hjul, Peter, 298n.152

Hodgson, Jack, 197–98, 200, 294n.121, 334n.44, 337n.87

Hodgson, Rica: banning of, 220; in exile, 226; house arrest of, 214; and *New Age*, xi, 194, 208. 211; and Umkhonto we Sizwe, 198

Hogarth, Paul, 272n.46

Home Front League, 44, 251n.31

Hopkinson, Tom, 330n.4

Horovitch, Isaac, 134, 144, 179, 287n.17, 325n.240, 346n.229

Huddleston, Trevor, 91, 97, 147, 150, 283n.180, 294n.121

Hunger Relief Fund, 63

Hutchinson, Alfred: and the African National Congress, 149; as agitator, 165; and the bus boycott, 304n.26; death of, 227; in exile, 193; and London *New Age* Committee, 343n.177; and *New Age*, xi, 149, 318n.163; personality of, 309n.63; and the Treason Trial, 177, 304n.26

I

Imvo Zabantsundu, 115

Indian Opinion, 170

Industrial and Commercial Union, 12, 63

Inkatha Freedom Party, 228

Inkululeko: as African National Congress organ, 88; banning of, 65; as black newspaper, 146n.127, 246n.118, 250n.87; burning of offices of, 65; circulation of, 262n.172; differences from the Guardian, 50; dissolution of, 44, 287n.22; *Guardian* support for, 61; and newsprint restrictions, 260n.32; as official Communist Party organ, 44, 287n.22

Inkundla ya Bantu, 159, 264n.205

International, 45

"Internationale," 66, 184, 251n.32, 330n.298

International Socialist League, 10, 20, 80

Isaacman, Sonia, 81, 273n.58. *See also* Bunting, Sonia

Isaacson, Lillian, 171

Isigidimi, 150

Iziwe, 315n.121

J

Jabavu, D. D., 309n.66

Jack, Joseph, 341n.153

Jacobs, Abe, 45

Jacobs, Tulip, 96, 283n.173

Jansen, A. J. N., 110–11

Jansen, E. J., 113, 137

Jewish Workers' Club, 65, 66, 256–57n.90

Joffe, Louis, 251n.28, 301n.185

Joffe, Max, 50, 211, 251n.28

Johannesburg, population of, 49

Johannesburg *Guardian* League, 52, 256n.88, 256n.89, 299n.157

Jooma, Solly, 171

Jordaan, Kenny, 297n.147

Jordan, Paulo, 347n.7

Joseph, Helen, 151, 202–3, 214, 279n.125, 294n.121, 332n.25

Joseph, Jenny, 174

Joseph, Paul, 178, 181, 290n.62, 332n.25

Junior Left Book Club, 254n.73

K

Kadalie, Clements, 63

Kahn, Sam: and the *Advance*, 121; and apartheid policies, 102; banning of, 102, 173, 286–87n.8; and banning of the *Guardian*, 107, 113; and British royal visit, 86; as Cape Town city councilman, 44; and Cissie Gool, 245n.83; and the *Clarion*, 116–17; and commission of inquiry into South African press, 168; and the Communist Party, 24, 38, 44; death of, 227; and death of Stalin, 125; in exile, 193, 335n.53; and the Freedom of the Press Committee, 289n.45; and founding of the *Guardian*, 239n.3; and government investigation of the *Guardian*, 108, 112; and *Guardian* horse racing tips, 33, 247n.144; and Len Lee-Warden, 298n.153; and Lionel Forman, 184; and London *New Age* Committee, 343n.177; as Member of Parliament, 84, 102, 105, 113, 286n.3, 286n.4; and *New Age* Christmas Eve dance, 182; pamphlets of, 182; police raids on, 301n.185; and the Real Publishing and Printing Company, 135; role at the *Guardian*, xii, 45, 102, 156, 164, 283n.170; 286n.5, 293n.106; and the South African Congress of Democrats, 123; and the Suppression of Communism Act, 105, 106, 287n.16

Kajee, A. J., 94

Kampala Conference, 203

Kasrils, Eleanor, 224

Kasrils, Ronnie: in exile, 224, 337n.87; and *New Age*, 194, 212; police raids on,

344n.198; and Umkhonto we Sizwe, 197, 198, 337n.87, 337n.88

Kathrada, Ahmed, 207-8

Kati, James, 145, 208, 307n.40, 341n.154

Kaunda, Kenneth, 204

Kaye, Joe, xii, 51, 255n.80

Kaye, Johnny, 20

Kemp, Stephanie, 334n.44, 348n.8

Kensington *Guardian* League, 256n.90

Kenyatta, Jomo, 203–4, 336n.68

Kgosana, Philip, 187–88, 331n.14

Kgositile, Willie, xii, 149, 165, 194, 227, 335n.63

King, Martin Luther, Jr., 215

Klenerman, Fanny, 34, 43–44, 80

Kodesh, Wolfie: banning of, 210, 220, 342n.168, 344n.192; and Bethal farm labor abuse, 153–54; and the Cape Town underground, 191; charged with subversion, 192, 334n.46; and the Communist Party, 40; and the Congress of the People, 141; death of, 226; in exile, 226; and H. A. Naidoo, 119; in hiding, 334n.42, 338n.103; jailing of, 225, 226, 322n.207, 348n.11; and Lionel Forman, 294n.115; and Nelson Mandela, 200, 338n.104, 338n.105, 338n.106; police raids on, 209; and publishing of *New Age* during the Treason Trial, 179; return to *Guardian* headquarters, 253n.59; role at the *Guardian*, xii, 40, 294n.123; travels in Africa, 203; and Umkhonto we Sizwe, 197, 226

Kotane, Moses: and *Advance*, 125; and the African National Congress, 86, 191; and the Communist Party, 40, 45, 86, 125, 287n.17; and the *Guardian*, 30, 37, 45, 285n.195; pamphlets of, 182; police raids on, 301n.185; and the Treason Trial, 178

Kramer, Winnie: in exile, 193; and the *Guardian*, xii, 84, 86, 103, 133, 275n.74; jailing of, 191; and Yusuf Dadoo, 183, 193

Kreel, Sadie. *See* Forman, Sadie

Krige, Uys, 166

Kruger, Paul, 115

Kunene, Abner, 88

L

Labour Party, the. *See* South African Labour Party

La Guma, Alex: banning of, 342n.166; and the Communist Party, 157; death of, 227; in exile, 227; house arrest of, 214, 227, 344n.193; jailing of, 174, 189, 190, 192, 208, 227; and *Little Libby*, 167; and the National Union of South African Journalists, 319n.166; and *New Age*, xii, 2, 5, 157–58, 164, 313n.109, 314n.110, 318n.163; and New Year's Eve party, 185; police harassment of, 175–76, 341n.156; and trade unions, 24; and the Treason Trial, 177, 179, 324n.237; writings of, 349n.15

La Guma, Blanche, 176, 313n.109, 318n.165, 324n.237, 333n.33, 342n.166

La Guma, Jimmy, 97, 157, 239n.3, 313n.109, 333n.25

Langa, riots in, 90, 186

Langa March, 187–88

Lansdown Commission, the, 68

Laski, Harold, 238n.1

Lawrence, Harry, 92, 107, 333n.25

Lawrence, Howard, 171, 193, 219

Lax, Jacqueline: and the Communist Party, 54; and Inkatha, 228; police raids on, 172, 301n.185; role at the *Guardian*, xi, 54, 257n.103, 270n.35; and Ronnie Kasrils, 194; and Rowley Arenstein, 117; and the Treason Trial, 178

Lebova, Phillip, 91

Lee-Warden, Len: and apartheid, 298n.153; banning of, 229; and burial of *Guardian* back issues, 2, 4; as Member of Parliament, 298n.153; and *Morning Star* and *Spark*, 217, 220; and *New Age*, 214, 328n.272, 333n.30; police raids on, 190, 301n.185; and printing of the *Guardian*, xii, 133–35; and the South African College of Democrats, 298n.153; and the Treason Trial, 177, 324n.237

Left Book Club, 9–10, 25, 35, 51, 238n.1

Left Book News, 9

Legum, Colin, 85, 256n.88

Lembede, Anton, 50, 88, 277n.99, 279n.127, 280n.131

Lenton, H. J., 66–67, 255n.225

Lessing, Doris, 43, 48, 79, 214, 271n.45, 272n.46

Letlalo, Thomas, 133

Levson, Freda, 317n.140

Lewin, Julius, 97, 283n.180

Liberal Party, 162, 163, 215, 294n.119, 317n.137

Liberation, 148

Lipman, Beate, xii, 194, 199, 294n.121, 335n.63

Little Rivonia Trial, 228

London *New Age* Committee, 211, 222, 343n.176, 343n.177

Louw, Eric, 67, 207, 213, 266n.243

Ludi, Gerard, 275n.72

Lumumba, Patrice, 204, 340n.133

Luthuli, Albert: and the African National Congress, 186, 195; banning of, 156; and Communist Party, 163; house arrest of, 156, 195; and Lionel Forman, 330n.296; and *New Age*, 156, 163, 195, 211–12, 215, 312n.100, 315n.121; and Nobel Peace Prize, 196; and pass law protests, 186; and the potato boycott, 311n.89; and the Treason Trial, 187

M

M-Plan, 145–46

Mabhida, Moses, 142, 194, 304n.24

Mackenzie, Ken, 334n.38

Madeley, Walter, 26, 61, 66

Mafekeng, Elizabeth, 202

Mahabane, Z. R., 12

Majambozi, Lionel, 87

Makeba, Miriam, 151

Makiwane, Ambrose, 194

Makiwane, Elijah, 150

Makiwane, Florence, 309n.66

Makiwane, Tennyson Xola: and bus boycotts, 141; in exile, 193; intellectual ability of, 309n.66; jailing of, 174; and London *New Age* Committee, 343n.177; murder of, 227; and Nelson Mandela, 201; and *New*

Age, xii, 5, 141, 150–51, 165, 203; police harassment of, 175; and Sophiatown, 150–51; and the Treason Trial, 177, 179

Malan, D. F., 22, 101, 114, 279n.121, 290n.61

Malay Quarter, 10

Maliba, Alpheus W., 64, 265n.211

Malindi, Zollie, 131, 333n.25

Mamuru, Titus, 131

Mandela, Nelson: and the African National Congress, 50, 87, 90, 195, 278n.114; and Anderson Khumani Ganyile, 206; arrest of, 201, 332n.25; and banning, 173; and Brian Somana, 347n.5; and the Communist Party, 87, 160; and the Defiance Campaign, 140; and *Fighting Talk*, 307n.50; and Govan Mbeki, 306n.35; "Letter from the Underground," 199, 337n.92; and the Liberal Party, 317n.137; and the M-Plan, 145; and the May Day Massacres, 103; and the May Stay-Away, 196; and Michael Harmel, 256n.86; and *New Age*, 3, 177, 198–99, 200, 201–2, 205; and Ntsu Mokhehle, 199–200, 338nn.94–100; and Ruth First, 307n.52; and the South African media, 321–22n.194; and the Treason Trial, 178; underground, 3, 198, 199, 200–201, 338n.104, 338n.105, 338n.106. *See also* Black Pimpernel; Motsamayi, David

Mandela, Winnie, 172, 199, 202, 337n.93, 338n.110, 347n.5

Mandela, Zenani, 199, 337n.93

Mandela, Zindiswa, 199

Mankahla, Nondwe, xii, 145, 333n.29, 341n.155

Manqina, Douglas: and the African National Congress, 229, 299n.162; banning of, 220; and the Communist Party, 229; jailing of, 174, 189, 190, 225, 229; and *New Age*, xii, 131, 174, 181, 229–30, 305n.26; salary of, 181, 299n.160, 327n.267; Special Branch harassment of, 174, 177

Marks, J. B., 88, 103, 200, 333n.25

Masekela, Hugh, 151

Masiane, Jack, 131, 174

Matshikiza, Todd, 151

Mattera, Don, 178

Matthews, Z. K., 87, 176n.96, 333n.25

May Day 1950 Massacres, 103–4

May 1961 Stay-away, 195–96

Mbeki, Epainette, 144

Mbeki, Govan: and African National Congress need for a newspaper, 315n.119, 315n.121; and Anderson Khumani Ganyile, 206; death of, 228; in exile, 210; and financing of the *Guardian,* 97; and the Freedom of the Press Committee, 289n.45; and *Inkundla ya Bantu,* 159; jailing of, 174, 189, 190, 208–9, 223, 227–28, 341n.154; and Mpukane headmanship, 306n.35; and *New Age,* xii, 2, 4–5, 144–45, 178, 305n.30; and police spies, 177; salary of, 181; and the Treason Trial, 325n.240; and Umkhonto High Command, 197–98

Mbeki, Thabo, 142, 144

McClausland, K.C., 21, 243n.53

Mda, A. P., 88

Mdingi, Leonard, 194, 208

Medical Aid to Russia, 46, 65

Meer, Fatima, 228

Meer, Ismail: and the Communist Party, 54; and Federation of Progressive Students, 274n.68; and the *Guardian,* 54, 178, 281n.153, 350n.30; and *New Age* Indian fundraising drives, 182; and Passive Resistance Campaign, 281n.153; political activism of, 91; and Ruth First, 91, 274n.68, 280n.131; and the Treason Trial, 178; under apartheid, 228

Merryweather, John H., 285n.197

Meueda Massacre, 204

Mgqungwana, Ralph, xii, 145, 307n.40

Mhalba, Raymond, 333n.25

Millman, Anja, 260n.140

Mistrey, Premchand, xii, 179

Mixed Marriages Act, the, 102

Mkize, I. D., 163

Mkwayi, Wilton: and the African National Congress, 146; escape from police, 223; in exile, 193–94, 210; and Little Rivonia Trial, 228; and *New Age,* xii, 146; and the

Treason Trial, 177, 179, 193–94

Mlangeni, Andrew, 208

Mobuto, Joseph, 204, 340n.133

Modern Youth Society, 120, 179, 252n.49, 326n.247

Modisane, Bloke, 104, 151

Mofutsanyana, Edwin, 37–38, 64, 89, 261n.163

Mohammed, Ismail, 326n.256, 346n.229

Mohammed, Joyce Watson, xii, 133, 301n.177

Mokgoro, Job, 299n.160

Mokhehle, Ntsu, 199–200, 337–38nn.94–100

Molaoa, Nathaniel, 174, 323n.214

Molete, Aaron, 208, 257n.93, 340n.148

Molteno, Donald, 44, 66–67, 79, 264n.204, 268n.4, 272n.48

Moodley, Mary, 133, 332n.25

Moore, Richard, 318n.163

Moretsele, Elias, 158, 315n.115

Morley, Sergeant John: and the *Guardian,* xii, 56, 59–60, 95, 156, 282n.162, 312n.103; and *Guardian* Christmas Club, 132, 156, 182, 229; and the National Liberation League, 261n.160; and *New Age* short story competitions, 318n.163; and New Year's Eve Party, 185; police raids on, 301n.185; and the Springbok Legion, 56; and the Women's Food Committee, 95, 282n.165

Morley-Turner, Lance. *See* Morley, Sergeant John

Morning Star, 216–17, 345n.210

Moroka, James, 103

Morolong, Joe, 323n.211

Motloheloa, John, 131, 174, 199, 206, 299n.161, 323n.216, 330n.296

Motsamayi, David, 201. *See also* Mandela, Nelson

Motsisi, Casey, 151

Mpana, Josie, 37

Mphahlele, Es'kia, 151

Mpondoland Uprising, 205–6

Mqota, Temba, 333n.25

Mti, Oliver, 177, 324n.234

Mtolo, Bruno, 197–98

Mtshali, Esther, 133

Munger, Edwin, 158, 308n.60, 314n.112
"Munich Swindle," 21, 31, 94, 243n.51, 243n.52

N

Naicker, Coetsie, 198
Naicker, G.M., 94
Naicker, M.P.: and the African National Congress underground, 197; and Albert Luthuli, 156; and Anderson Khumani Ganyile, 206, 340n.143; authority of, 312n.94; banning of, 155, 344n.192; and the Communist Party, 155, 198; and the Congress of the People, 155; death of, 227; in exile, 227; and *Iziwe*, 315n.121; jailing of, 189, 225, 227, 281n.153; and the Natal Indian Congress, 155; and *New Age*, xii, 5, 155–56, 182, 312n.95; police harassment of, 209, 341n.160, 344n.198; and trade unions, 312n.99; and the Treason Trial, 177; as Umkhonto saboteur, 197, 198, 337n.88
Naidoo, H.A.: background of, 48, 253n.63, 254nn. 65–66; and the Communist Party, 48; death of, 120; in exile, 119–20; and "Pan-African Review," 203; and Pauline Podbrey, 48–49, 245n.83, 254n.67; and race matters, 273n.63; and Roeland Street Jail, 62, 157; role at the *Guardian*, xii, 48, 82, 270n.35; and the sedition trial, 73, 81–82; and Vera Alberts, 53
Nair, Billy, 198
Nakasa, Nat, 151
Nankhala, Nondwe, 228
Natal Daily News, 114
Natal Indian Congress: and banning of *New Age*, 215; and distribution of *New Age*, 156, 312n.98; police raids on, 72; revitalization of, 94; and Second World War, 35; and the Suppression of Communism Act, 105
Natal Indian Youth Congress, 108
Natal Witness, the, 114
National Action Council, 159
National Council for Civil Liberties, 66, 289n.44

National Liberation League, 24
National Party, 3, 101, 286n.1
National Union of Journalists, 66
National Union of South African Journalists, 319n.166
Native Representative Council, 12, 74–75
Neruda, Pablo, 166
New Africa, 288n.24
New Age: advertising in, 180, 210, 326n.258, 327n.259, 327n.260, 328n.272, 342n.171; and the African National Congress, 152, 159, 161, 194–95, 197, 316n.125, 335n.63; and African nationalist movements, 204–5; and alliance between the Communist Party and the African National Congress, 160, 161, 316n.127; and Anderson Khumani Ganyile, 206; and banishment camps, 202; banning of, 189, 215, 332n.23, 340n.138; and the Basutoland Congress Party, 337n.94; beauty contest of, 167; and black Africa, 203; and the bus boycotts, 141, 304n.26; carry-on readership of, 146; circulation of, 180, 210, 312n.98, 326n.257; and the Congress of the People, 141, 159, 303n.12; correspondents to, 142; distribution of, 145–46, 156, 181, 295n.130, 312n.98, 328n.272, 328n.273; donations to, 180, 196, 210–11, 327n.261, 327n.262, 327n.268, 342n.172; editorial policies of, 212–13, 302n.2; financial troubles of, 180–82, 211, 218; firebombing of offices of, 179–80, 326n.256; as forum for banned ANC leaders, 142–43, 156, 304n.26; founding of, 137, 138; fundraising for, 182–83, 211, 328n.276, 328n.280, 342n.173, 343n.176; as government information source, 158–59, 315n.117; impact outside of South Africa, 205; and the Liberal Party, 162; as link to rural activists, 143; as literary journal, 166; and the M-Plan, 145–46; and Nelson Mandela, 198–99, 200, 201–2; and the Newspaper Press Union, 319n.166; and the Non-European Unity Movement, 163; nonpolitical con-

tent of, 166; offices of, 143, 146–47, 155–56, 194, 312n.96; and other South African media, 168–71, 320n.185, 321n.191; and the Pan Africanist Congress, 162, 316n.136; and pass law protests, 152–53; political independence of, 159, 161; and the potato boycott, 154–55; price of, 182; publishing of during the Treason Trial, 178, 325n.245; return after banning, 192–93; role as reporter vs. role as agitator, 164–66; salaries of staff of, 181, 327n.264; short story competitions of, 318n.163; Special Branch harassment of, 172–77, 209, 341n.156; support of the Soviet Union, 158; and the Treason Trial, 179, 202; and Umkhonto we Sizwe, 196–97; as voice of the liberation movement, 202, 339n.112

Newspaper Press Union, 169, 319n.166, 320n.181

New York Times, 114, 301n.182

Ngakane, Pascal, 349n.20

Ngotyana, Greenwood, 131, 174

Ngoyi, Lilian, 152, 153

Ngqungwana, Mountain, 208, 215, 226, 341n.154

Ngubane, Jordan, 159

Ngwenya, Thomas, 239.3, 289n.45, 297n.147

Ninety Days, 223

Nkadimeng, John, 161

Nkobi, Thomas, 315n.114

Nkomo, Joshua, 204

Nkomo, William, 87, 277n.99

Nkosi, Agnes, 133

Nkrumah, Kwame, 204

Nokwe, Duma, 149, 166, 195, 222

Non-European Unity Movement, 163, 189

Nortje, Arthur, 6, 166, 218

Notlowitz, Rebecca, 80

Ntshona, Jellico, 131, 346n.229

Nujoma, Sam, 204

Nuwe Order, 178

Nxumalo, Henry: background of, 82; and the Communist Party, 85; courage of, 274n.67; and *Drum,* 151, 170, 320n.184; and the *Golden City Post,* 320n.186; mur-

der of, 171, 321n.192; and the *Pittsburgh Courier,* 274n.66; role at the *Guardian,* xii, 82, 102, 165

Nyagumbo, Maurice, 249n.14

Nyerere, Julius, 204

O

O'Brien, William, 107, 110

Okigbo, Christopher, 166

O'Meara, John, 51

Orlando train disaster, 90

Osborne, John, 344n.190

Ossewa Brandwag, 107

Owen, Ken, 319n.166

P

Paarl Workers' Relief Fund, 61, 262n.177

Palestine Post, 134

Pan Africanist Congress, 4, 162, 186, 189, 316n.136, 331n.6

Parkin, Garnet "Hosepipe," 174

Passive Resistance Campaign, 94

pass law protests, 152–53, 186, 310n.84, 310–11n.85, 311n.86

Paton, Alan, 162, 173, 214

Pearson, Carina: and the Communist Party, 24, 43, 78–79; death of, 79; and the *Guardian* leagues, 46; and Harold Baldry, 20; police raids on, 72; resignation from the *Guardian,* 78–79; role at the *Guardian,* xii, 14, 19, 47, 48; salary of, 19; women's columns of, 28

Peet, John, 127

People's Age, 288n.24

People's Assembly, the, 89

People's Charter, 89

People's Weekly, the, 117

People's World, the, 117–18, 127

Pepys, Rhoda, 45, 284n.191

Philby, George, 269n.12

Philips, Vivian, 247n.147

Phillips, James, 301n.185

Pietermaritzburg *Guardian* League, the, 55

Pietermaritzburg Sabotage Trial, 228

Pillay, Vella, 343n.177

"Pins and Needles," 32, 247n.141

Pioneer Press, 134, 136–37, 209, 229, 301n.183

Pirow, Oswald, 22, 178

Platt, David, 348n.11

Podbrey, Pauline: and Betty Radford, 17, 271n.40; and Cissie Gool, 245n.83; and death of Stalin, 296n.138; in exile, 120; and *Guardian* fundraising, 283n.180; and H. A. Naidoo, 48–49, 254nn.65–67; and Vera Alberts, 53

Pogrund, Benjamin, 129, 165, 186, 298n.152, 345n.214

Pollitt, Harry, 77

Poonen, George, 48, 53–54, 258n.107, 285n.195

Port Elizabeth *Guardian* League, the, 55

potato boycott, 154–55, 311n.88–89

Press, Ronnie, 332n.25

Pretoria *Guardian* League, the, 55

Pringle, Thomas, 109, 288n.33

Prisons Act, 207

Progressive Party, 215

Progressive Youth Council, 274n.68

Publications and Entertainments Act, 169

Q

Qinisile, Grimaas, 131

R

Rabb, Ralph, 256n.88

Raddall, Stanley George, 15

Radford, Betty: and Africa, 203; background of, 17–18, 269n.21; as Cape Town city councilwoman, 3, 44, 74, 251n.33, 251n.35; and censorship of the *Guardian*, 66–67, 265n.224; and the Communist Party, 18, 24, 43, 44, 74, 77–78, 84, 269n.12, 271n.40; death of, 78; and gender inequality, 28; and the *Guardian* beauty contest, 96, 283n.170; and the *Guardian* defamation lawsuits, 67–68, 69, 267n.253, 267n.258; and *Guardian* financing, 58, 97; *Guardian* writings of, 16, 17, 23; and Hunger Relief Fund, 264n.204; and K. C. McClausland, 243n.53; loyalty to the Soviet Union, 60;

and the mine strike of 1946, 268n.5; and the Native Representative Council, 75–76; police raids on, 72, 269n.9; politics of, 18; resignation as *Guardian* editor, 73–77; role at the *Guardian*, xii, 13, 16–17, 19, 31, 47–48, 56, 78, 268n.4; salary of, 17; sedition trial of, 71, 73–74, 269n.18, 269n.19, 270n.22; and the South African Labour party, 26; and the Suppression of Communism Act, 104–5

Ramaphukela, Richard, 52

Ramohanoe, C. S., 88–89, 278n.114

Rand Daily Mail, 92, 114–15, 134, 140, 168, 215, 321n.194

Rand Revolt, 20, 72, 272n.54

Real Publishing and Printing Company, 135, 137, 178, 179, 216, 325n.240

Reeves, Ambrose, 344n.190

Resha, Maggie, 151

Resha, Robert: death of, 227; in exile, 210; jailing of, 174; and the National Union of South African Journalists, 319n.166; and *New Age*, xii, 5, 151, 152, 162, 165, 193; and the Pan-Africanist Congress, 162; and the potato boycott, 154; and Sophiatown, 5, 309n.73, 310n.74, 310n.75; and the Treason Trial, 177, 179; as Umkhonto saboteur, 197; vandalization of property of, 176

Retsies, 158, 193, 315n.115

Reuters, 22

Rietstein, Amy. *See* Thornton, Amy

Robertson, J. B., 256n.88

Robertson, T. C., 33

Robeson, Paul, 69, 211, 273n.63

Robinson, Cynthia, 297n.144

Rose, A. W. H., 263n.178

Routh, Guy, 294n.121

Roux, Eddie: and the Communist Party, 48; and Govan Mbeki, 144; and the *Guardian*, 97, 139, 250n.16; and Hunger Relief Fund, 264n.204; and the South African College of Democrats, 294n.121

Rubin, Harry, 258n.105

Rubin, Sarah, 120, 293n.105

Russians gang, 148

S

Sabotage Bill, 212

Sachs, Albie: and African nationalist movements, 204; attempted assassination of, 225; and banning of *New Age*, 192; and Brian Bunting, 164; and the Cape Town underground, 191; and difficulties in getting truthful information on world events, 127; and Fred Carneson, 293n.106; as *Guardian* seller, 39; jailing of, 225; and Lionel Forman, 122; and *New Age*, xii, 2, 106, 179, 189; and *New World,* 326n.247; personality of, 325–26n.247; and potato boycott, 311n.89; salary of, 181; and the Soviet invasion of Hungary, 129; and the Suppression of Communism Act, 106; as Umkhonto saboteur, 197, 341–42n.165

Sachs, Solly, 33, 80–81, 113, 179, 294n.119

Sacks, Betty. *See* Radford, Betty

Sacks, George: background of, 18–19, 242n.37, 269n.21; and the Communist Party, 24, 43, 77–78, 250n.19; and the *Critic,* 18; death of, 78; publications of, 18, 43, 78; role at the *Guardian,* xii, 13, 19, 43, 78; and the sedition trial, 269n.18; and sexist nature of the media, 28; and Second World War, 261n.161

Sadike, James, 153–54

Salisbury *Guardian* League, 56

Saloojee, Suliman "Babla," 224, 332n.25

Sampson, Anthony, 158, 274n.67

Sandon, Harold, 241n.15

Sauer, Paul, 106, 288n.23

"Save the *Guardian*" rally, 112, 289n.47

Schadeburg, Jurgen, 165

Schermbrucker, Ivan: and *Advance*, 297n.142; and the African National Congress underground, 197; and Arnold's Xmas Hampers, 133, 300n.173, 300n.175; background of, 83; and banning of the *Guardian*, 113; death of, 228; and Govan Mbeki, 144; jailing of, 189, 228; and the May Day free speech rallies, 103; and *New Age*, 178–79, 182, 192; and police raids, 136, 301n.185; role at the *Guardian*, xii, 83, 274n.72, 275n.73,

294n.123; and Ruth First, 83–84; temper of, 83, 301n.177

Schermbrucker, Lesley, 228, 275n.73

Scholtz, Abe, 45

Scott, Michael, 91–93, 168, 283n.180

Sechaba, 227

Security Branch, 72–73, 92, 108, 117, 119, 130, 136, 173, 175–77, 184, 188–89, 208–09, 324n.134, 333n.29,

Sedition Trial, 71, 73–74, 76, 82, 84, 99, 268n.5, 269n.12, 269n.19

Seedat, Dawood: banning of, 94, 210, 228, 342n.167; and the Communist Party, 108; death of, 228; and Ebrahim Ismail Ebrahim, 312n.102; and H. A. Naidoo, 119; jailing of, 333n.25; and the Natal Indian Youth Congress, 108; personality of, 288n.29, 311n.93; and police raids, 108, 117, 301n.185; role at the *Guardian*, xii, 94, 108, 155; and the Treason Trial, 178, 325n.240; underground work of, 336n.82

Seedat, Fatima, 210, 281n.153, 336n.82, 342n.167

Segal, Ronald, 97, 191, 287n.20, 288n.23, 323n.222, 332n.20, 344n.190

Sekoto, Gerard, 284n.191, 307n.45

Selby, Arnold, 35; and Arnold's Xmas Hampers, 133, 182, 300n.173, 300n.174, 300–301n.175; and the bus boycotts, 141; in exile, 193; and the *Guardian*, xii, 258n.116, 350n.36; police raids on, 301n.185; temper of, 301n.177; and the Treason Trial, 325n.240

September, Hettie, 333n.33

Seretse Affair, 90

Sergeant John. *See* Morley, Sergeant John

Shanley, Dorothy, 258n.105

Shanley, Errol, 54, 178, 247n.144, 333n.25

Shapiro, Keith, 338n.107. *See also* Kodesh, Wolfie

Shapiro, Naomi: and the *Clarion,* 116; in exile, 119; and the *Guardian*, 82, 88, 111, 113, 270n.35, 274n.65; life at home of, 292n.100; master's degree of, 229; and *New Age*, 156–57; police raids on, 301n.185; and the South African Society of Journalists, 167

Sharpeville Massacre, 186, 318n.187

Shields, Joe, 255n.80

Sibande, Gert, 91–94, 149, 303n.8, 323n.218

Sibongani, John, 52

Simons, Eric, 292n.99

Simons, Gwen, 346n.229

Simons, Jack: and censorship of the *Guardian*, 67; and the Communist Party, 20, 24, 38, 123, 252n.49, 295n.129; and democracy, 276n.81; and ethnicity, 297n.147; in exile, 226; and the Freedom of the Press Committee, 289n.45; and the *Guardian* as voice of the Communist Party, 42, 250n.16; and the *Guardian* as voice of native Africans, 63, 64; jailing of, 332n.25; and Lionel Forman, 330n.297; police raids on, 301n.185; and Ray Alexander, 19; role at the *Guardian*, xii, 19–20, 45, 81, 156; and the sedition trial, 73; and the South African Congress of Democrats, 123; and South African Labour Party Natives Policy, 27

Sisulu, Walter: and the African National Congress, 87, 90, 146, 200; and *Bantu World*, 320n.187; and Brian Somana, 207; and the Congress of the People, 141; and the *Guardian*, 114, 142; house arrest of, 214; jailing of, 208, 223, 332n.25; and the May Day Massacres, 103; and *New Age*, 195; and the pass laws, 310n.80; and Ruth First, 91, 147; and the Treason Trial, 178

Sizerist, Henry, 241n.15

Slomko, Amsden, 207

Slovo, Gillian, 147

Slovo, Joe: athletic ability of, 308n.55; banning of, 220; and the Communist Party, 123, 251n.31; in exile, 225; family of, 147, 348n.7; jailing of, 334n.40; and Lionel Forman, 298n.150; and police raids, 173; and potato boycott, 154; and Umkhonto we Sizwe, 198

Slovo, Shawn, 148, 324n.238

Smith, Nakie, 55, 259n.119

Smuts, Jan Christian: and Bethal farm worker scandal, 92–93; and Bill Andrews,

285n.200; and internment camps, 43; and the Nationalist Party, 286n.2; removal from power, 101; rise to power of, 35

Snitcher, Harry: and the Communist Party, 13, 245n.103, 269n.12; and founding of the *Guardian*, 13, 239n.3; and the *Guardian* defamation lawsuits, 69; and the *Guardian* as voice of the Communist Party, 42, 249–50n.16; as lawyer, xii, 45, 69, 229, 266n.245; and the sedition trial, 73, 269n.12; and the Socialist Party, 24

Snitcher, Mussie, 46

Sobukwe, Robert, 186, 331n.7

Social Democratic Federation, 10, 47

Socialist Party, 26

Solwandle, Beauty, 346n.1

Solwandle, Looksmart, 131, 197, 224, 341n.165

Somana, Brian, xii, 194, 207, 225, 347n.5

Somerset Affair, 109, 343n.182

Sono, Joseph, 131

Sophiatown, 5, 62, 89, 90, 103-4, 147, 148, 150–51, 157, 161, 171, 175, 178, 194, 254n.74, 263n.185, 278n.121, 279n.124, 309n.69, 309n.71, 310n.75, 321n.192, 340n.148

South African Broadcasting Company, 66, 143

South African Coloured People's Organization, 140, 157

South African Commercial Advertiser, 109, 343n.182

South African Communist Party, the: and the African National Congress, 123, 130, 160–61; founding of, 123; role in selling the *Advance*, 125; and the *South African Socialist Review*, 130; and Stalin, 129; underground operations of, 124. *See also* Communist Party of South Africa

South African Congress of Democrats, 123, 140, 162, 181, 214, 294n.121, 295n.130, 302n.197, 328n.272

South African Congress of Trade Unions, 131, 140, 215, 331n.6

South African Indian Congress, 140

South African Journal, 109

South African Labour Party: founding of, 10,

20; and mine strike of 1946, 72; Native Policy of, 3, 18, 26–27

South African Socialist Review, 130

South African Society of Journalists, 167, 169, 215, 319n.166

South African Trades and Labour Council, the, 23, 24, 35, 55, 66, 72, 268n.5

South African Worker (Umsebenzi), 11–12, 37, 48, 50, 246n.123, 250n.16

Southern Cross, 134

South West African People's Organization, the, 120

Soviet Information Agency, 59

Soviet Life, 46, 260n.130

Soviet Press Agency, 59

Soyinka, Wole, 339n.126

Spark: closure of, 220–21; content of, 219; financial difficulties of, 220; founding of, 216–17; fund-raising for, 219–20, 222; police raids on, 219; and the Transvaal Indian Youth Congress, 114, 181

Special Branch: founding of, 268n.6; raids on the *Advance,* 136, 137; raids on the *Guardian,* 72–73, 268n.6, 268n.8, 269nn. 9–10; raids on *New Age,* 172–77, 209; raids on *Spark,* 219

Springbok Legion, 44, 56, 72–73, 147, 251n.31, 259n.124

Standerton Advertiser, 285n.198

Star [Johannesburg], 114–15, 168, 338n.94

Stein, Sylvester, 171

Stewart, Charlie: and the Communist Party, 24; and *Comrade Bill,* 61; death of, 98–99, 285n.197; and the *Guardian,* xii, 14, 16, 24, 30, 257n.95, 263n.178; other newspapers of, 19, 46, 241n.19

Steyn, Colin, 56, 62, 67, 74, 107, 266n.241

Storm, Walter. *See* Bloom, Harry

Strachan, Harold, 341n.153

Strachey, John, 238n.1

Strijdom, J. G., 93

Sun, 241n.19

Sunday Times [Johannesburg], 56, 80, 320n.177

Suppression of Communism Act, 104–5, 107, 287n.15, 287n.19, 303n.4

Sutherland, John, 334n.46

Swart, Charles: background of, 107; and banning of *Advance,* 136–37; and banning of the *Guardian,* 107, 110–13; and the *Clarion,* 116–17, 291–92n.84; lack of humility of, 288n.25; and laws prohibiting Communists from serving in Parliament, 118–19; and the Suppression of Communism Act, 104; and trade unions harboring Communists, 167

T

Table View Printing and Publishing, 217

Tamana, Dora, 279n.125

Tambo, Adelaide, 335n.53

Tambo, Oliver: and the African National Congress, 87, 142, 195; and banning of the *Advance,* 137; and the Congress of Democrats, 142; hometown of, 205; in exile, 190, 191, 195; and Jomo Kenyatta, 203; and London *New Age* Committee, 343n.177

Tarshish, Jack, 120, 214, 228, 293n.104, 333n.25

Terblanche, I. B. S., 188

Terblanche, S. E., 302n.188

Territorial Magazine, 144

Thema, Selope, 89, 170

Themba, Can, 151

Thomas, Glyn, 256n.88

Thompson, Douglas, 178, 268n.4, 289n.45, 301n.185

Thorne, Athol, 179

Thornton, Amy: during apartheid, 229; banning of, 322n.206; and Brian Bunting, 237n.3, 294n.115; and the Communist Party, 124–25; jailing of, 189, 191, 333–34n.38; and Lionel Forman, 294n.115; personality of, 325n.246; role at the *New Age,* xii, 41, 178–79; and violence surrounding Suppression of Communism Act, 287n.20

Till, Marjorie, 283n.170

Times [London], 114, 116, 290n.69, 344n.191

"Time to Wake Up, Mister," 32

Tlale, Isaac, 224

Toiva, Herman Toivo Y., 120
Torch, 163, 170, 189, 219
Torch Commando, 303n.8
Trading and Occupation of Land Restriction
Act, 94
Transocean news agency, 22
Transvaal Indian Congress, 35, 94, 103, 105
Transvaal Indian Youth Congress, 14, 181
Transvaal Peace Council, 113
Trapido, Stanley, 334n.43
Treason Trial, 2–3, 177–79, 187, 202, 304n.26
Treason Trial Defense Fund, 179
Trevelyan, Charles, 289n.44
Trommer, Arthur, 14
Trop, Luka, 346n.229
Tse-Tung, Mao, 285n.200
Tsehla, Hosiah, 131, 193
Tshawe, N. P. D., 172, 322n.204
Tshehle, Lydia, 131, 340n.148
Tshume, Gladstone, xii, 144
Turgel, Donald, 334n.44
Turok, Ben, 124, 148, 191, 226, 294n.123,
295n.130, 327n.268
Turok, Mary Butcher. *See* Butcher, Mary

U

Umkhonto we Sizwe, 3–4, 194, 196–98, 201,
205, 219, 223, 225–26, 228, 316n.127,
337n.85, 341n.165
Umpa, 80
Umsebenzi. See South African Worker
Unie Volkspers, 99, 133, 257n.95, 285n.198
Union of Democratic Control, 289n.44
United Party, 99, 101
Unity Movement. *See* Non-European Unity
Movement, the
University of Cape Town, 14, 18, 19, 20, 41,
44, 45, 114, 120, 121, 178, 183, 187, 229,
241n.15, 246n.123
University of the Witwatersrand, 80, 82, 114,
121, 183, 200, 258n.115, 268n.4,
274n.68, 275n.72,
Uys, Stanley, 167, 171, 200, 318n.163,
319n.166

V

Van der Ross, Richard, 166, 318n.163
Vara, E. Lulamile, 142
Verasammy, Perry, 340n.148
Vermaak, Chris, 322n.205
Verwoerd, Hendrik, 166, 168, 177, 213,
243n.53, 279n.121, 285n.196, 344n.198,
348n.11
Vigilator, 16, 20, 21, 32, 36, 58–59, 62, 79.
See also Baldry, Harold
Vigne, Randolph, 160, 317n.140
Vorster, Balthazar Johannes, 60, 212, 215,
217, 220, 343n.180

W

Wain, John, 344n.190
Wannenburgh, Alf, 193
Waterfield, Hugh, 257n.101
Watson, Joyce, 172, 226
Watts, Hilda, 51, 255n.83. *See also* Bernstein,
Hilda
Weichardt, Louis, 11, 22
Weinberg, Eli: advertising in *New Age,* 180;
and Anderson Khumani Ganyile, 206;
background of, 152; banning of, 152; and
the Congress of the People, 175–76; death
of, 227; in exile, 227; jailing of, 190, 227;
and Ray Alexander, 310n.79; role at *New
Age,* xii, 5, 152, 310n.79, 335n.63; and
the South African Trades and Labour
Council, 24; and the Treason Trial, 179,
325n.240
Weinberg, Violet, 225
Western Areas Campaign, 161
Willett, Marjorie, 28
Willett, William, 17, 242n.28
Williams, Cecil, 56, 166, 189, 201, 205, 214,
294n.121, 303n.8
Williamson, Arthur, 269n.12
Williamson, Craig, 348n.7
Wilson, Angus, 344n.190
Winkhoek riots, 323n.219
Witwatersrand Student, 121
Wolfson, Issy, 51, 255n.82, 275n.75, 332n.25
Wolpe, Harold, 254n.74, 299n.157, 308n.55,
332n.25

Women's Food Committee, 95, 282n.164
Woolf, Ethel, 55
Worcester Standard, 134
Worrall, Rona, xii, 51, 82, 255n.79
Wu's Views, 80

X

Xuma, Alfred Bitini: and the African National
    Congress, 50, 63, 87, 88–90, 159; death
    of, 195; and *Inkundla ya Bantu,* 159; and
    Native Representative Council boycott,
    88; personality of, 265n.215; service as

    doctor, 278n.116
Xuma, Madie Hall, 89

Y

Yergen, Max, 273n.63, 306n.35
Young Communist League, 50, 82, 87, 121
Yutar, Percy, 269n.12

Z

Zanzibar Nationalist Party, 204
Zaza, Victor, 203
Ziervogel, Johannes, 22